SMALL
GROUP
COMMUNICATION

SMALL
GROUP
COMMUNICATION

A
READER

FIFTH
EDITION

Robert S. Cathcart
Queens College of the
City of University of
New York

Larry A. Samovar
San Diego State University

wcb
Wm. C. Brown Publishers
Dubuque, Iowa

Library of Congress Catalog Card Number: 87–71180

ISBN 0–697–0–05187–0

Printed in the United States of America by Wm. C. Brown Publishers
2460 Kerper Boulevard, Dubuque, IA 52001

10 9 8 7 6 5 4 3 2 1

Contents

Preface

Presenting a fifth edition is particularly satisfying. Its existence assures us that the philosophy and orientation infused into the first four editions of *Small Group Communication* are sound. Simply stated, we believe that to be an effective small group participant, one must understand and appreciate the relationship existing between communication and group dynamics. While we may make minor adjustments that reflect developments in the discipline during each edition, all essays, whether carried over from previous editions or presented for the first time, manifest this point of view.

In this edition, as in the last, we emphasize individual skills necessary to effective performance and to the understanding needed of the many forms and functions of small groups in contemporary society. In recent years, research has revealed the importance of project teams, quality circles, and policy committees in the life of an organization, as well as self-help and therapy groups in the lives of individuals. From this awareness has come the realization that the communicative atmosphere and the communicative skills of individual members must be adequate to enable them to deal with the task at hand. Consequently, in this edition we have moved to provide the student with essays that reflect these new trends and offer practical suggestions for becoming skilled in small group communication.

To insure that students have the latest thinking and research findings in the field of small group communication available, we have again asked leading scholars to contribute original essays. In each instance the author, a recognized researcher and teacher in small group communication, has prepared an essay especially for student readers. Thus, the student has twenty important essays not found anywhere else in small group literature available in this one volume. As was the case in earlier revisions, we searched the current literature to find appropriate articles to supplement and update the principles and concepts expressed in those articles retained from previous editions. This edition is meant for the student of group process and group communication, regardless of whether that person is a student of speech communication, business management, health care, human relations, or teacher education.

We again offer a carefully arranged selection of readings designed to provide students an awareness of the latest theoretical and practical advances in the field, as well as an understanding of how this discipline has developed. We give the student and teacher an overview of the field and, at the same time, present recently developed processes and techniques for training in small group communication. It is our belief that this collection will furnish insights into the principles and processes of group communication, together with the motivation to apply them in practice. We hope that this carefully selected and organized collection of readings from many sources will be a desirable adjunct to textbook and classroom instruction.

This collection makes available in one volume representative articles from psychology, sociology, anthropology, philosophy, business and industrial management, and speech communication, all arranged to give readers easy access to the basic principles of small group communication. The editors have avoided advocating any one particular approach to small group processes, preferring to give readers a sampling of the diverse philosophies and concepts that constitute this fascinating area of study. We have brought together writings from theoreticians, from practitioners in the business world, and from those who have developed principles and methods of effective communication, all selected to give students and teachers knowledge of the research and practices continually reshaping our thinking and concepts about small group communication.

This fifth edition represents extensive revision and updating. Almost fifty percent of the selections are new, reflecting our desire to keep abreast of the developing trends in the field. Nine essays are original contributions to this edition and have not appeared elsewhere. These, along with the eleven original contributions retained from earlier editions, make this edition a unique resource for anyone interested in small group communication.

The fifth edition retains the organizational format of the previous one. All readings are grouped within eight chapters. Chapter 1, *Small Groups: Concepts and Characteristics,* presents six essays introducing students to definitions of small groups, descriptions of the place of small groups in our social structure, and explanations of the role of the individual in the group. Chapter 2, *Group Environments: Professional and Personal,* provides seven essays explaining how small groups are used to meet individual and organizational needs. Chapter 3, *Group Decision Making: Form and Structure,* contains six essays covering a range of forms, structures, procedures, and techniques related to decision making. Chapter 4, *Group Communication: Principles and Precepts,* has five articles that examine the nature of the communication process as it is exhibited in small groups. Chapter 5, *Group Messages: Sending and Receiving,* has six essays devoted to the forms and functions of messages in the small group. Chapter 6, *Group Participation: Performance and Practice,* provides five essays addressed to the individual group member offering practical methods of dealing with the obstacles that arise in small group interaction. Chapter 7, *Group Leadership: Approaches and Styles,* contains seven articles that examine a wide variety of concepts, roles, and practices appropriate to an understanding of small group leadership. Chapter 8, *Small Group Evaluation: Process and Participation,* comprises four essays examining the matter of group evaluation, and how it applies to learning group process and to improving individual participation.

Each chapter of the book is introduced with an essay by the editors explaining the background, current theories, and practices relevant to the area covered. These introductions also contain a brief overview of each selection in the chapter. Many of the essays include extensive references that may be used to guide students to other works amplifying the ideas developed in the chapter.

We are extremely pleased to be able to present the nine new essays, written expressly for this revised edition, as well as the eleven original essays from earlier editions. We are deeply indebted to Patricia Hayes Andrews, Wayne A. Beach, Beth Haslett and John R. Ogilvie, Robert L. Husband, Karl J. Krayer, Peter J. Marston and Michael J. Hecht, Marshall Scott Poole, Martin Remland, and Lawrence B. Rosenfeld for their original articles in this new edition. To those who wrote articles for the earlier editions, Janis Andersen, Peter A. Andersen, Ronald L. Applbaum, Judee K. Burgoon, H. Lloyd Goodall, Jr., Dennis Gouran, Stephen W. King, James C. McCroskey and Virginia P. Richmond, Richard E. Porter, Linda L. Putnam, and Susan B. Shimanoff, we again express our appreciation. It gives us great pleasure to introduce these outstanding contributions to the field of small group communication.

The editors acknowledge the assistance of Althea Katz Cohen in helping to assemble this revised edition.

Finally, we acknowledge the contributions of our students and colleagues who helped, both directly and indirectly, to shape this revision. To the many writers and publishers who have made this book possible, we express our gratitude. We now offer a thoroughly revised and updated version we believe will provide both old and new users of this book a better understanding of where we have been and where we are now in the field of small group communication.

Robert S. Cathcart
Larry A. Samovar

1
Small Groups:
Concepts and Characteristics

"Modern life is group life," wrote Eduard C. Lindeman in 1924. He was confirming the twentieth-century view of people as the social interactants shaped by the conditions of group life. Traditionally, in Western culture, persons have been viewed as individuals or single units of society, and only incidentally as members of groups within society: the family, the guild, the community, the class.

It was this traditional view of individuals as a society which produced the classic descriptions of the various forms of political and social organizations: Plato's Republic, Machiavelli's city-state, Hobbe's Leviathan, Rosseau's social contract, and Locke's social compact. All of these formulations were based upon assumptions concerning the inherent nature of the individual and the inflexible structure of society. Groups, the family as an example, were fixed and played little part in theorizing prior to the nineteenth century. This traditional view has gradually given way in the twentieth century to the concept of *groups as society*. Modern sociologists and psychologists, focusing on human's behaviors rather than their inherent nature, have found that the primary or informal groups are the warp and woof of a person's daily life. Such groups shape people's values and attitudes. Small groups are now recognized as the basic mechanisms of socialization. Societies and cultures are seen as a maze of interlocking and overlapping groups in which the individual plays various roles.

The study of the individual and group life has developed at an ever-increasing pace since early in this century when John Dewey, an American philosopher and educator, recognized that the child could not be truly educated apart from the groups which formed the immediate world, and when psychologist Floyd Allport found that experiments with individual behavior were always influenced by the groups of which the subject was a member. The rapid growth of a psychology of groups has developed mainly along two tracks: the political-practical and the theoretical-experimental.

The political-practical stream has focused on the means and methods of improving group processes, operating on the assumption that this would, in turn, improve our democratic society. It has led to a concern for the processes by which democratic decisions are reached—how democratic leadership can be improved, how individual participation can be enhanced, and, overriding all these concerns, the need for improving communication within groups. The practitioners of group process have produced a great array of techniques for understanding and improving groups. They are responsible for the now widely known practices of role-playing, brainstorming, PERT, buzz sessions, T-groups, and sensitivity training.

It is the political-practical approach which produced the group discussion movement in the academic world, the community and the business world. Hundreds of courses and workshops in group communication and group process are held annually, all designed to increase the individual's ability to function more effectively in groups, and in turn, to make groups more effective contributors to our democratic society. Rare is the teacher or business executive who does not use group methods or task committees to enhance learning and decision making.

The principle activating this approach to group study is summed up by Dorwin Cartwright and Alvin Zander in *Group Dynamics:*

> A democratic society derives its strength from the effective functioning of the multitude of groups which it contains. Its most valuable resources are the groups of people found in its homes, communities, schools, churches, business concerns, union halls, and various branches of government. Now, more than ever before, it is recognized that these units must perform their functions well if the larger system is to work.[1]

More recently, group techniques have been applied to the improvement of the individual and *intra*-personal communication. A group, usually unrelated to any specific task, is used as a laboratory for helping the individual explore a self-image and for developing sensitivity to individual feelings. In this way, the study of group process has come full circle. It is used not only to help the group function more effectively as a contributor to our sociopolitical system, but the group becomes a resource and means of enhancing the life of the individual. The whole panoply of human potential group programs from Esalen to EST, from TM to Therapy, reflects this approach to improving individuals through group activities and improving groups through individual growth.

The theoretical-experimental track of group study is inextricably linked to the growth of the social sciences. Its roots lie in the movement which produced the sciences of human behavior: psychology, sociology, and anthropology. It is a part of the tradition which maintains that people's behavior and social relationships can be subjected to the same scientific investigation as is used in studying natural and biological phenomena. The social psychologists of this century brought people into the laboratory and developed the techniques of scientific research and statistical measurement, which eventually led to the experimental study of human groups. The contributors to the theoretical-experimental phase of group study seek a theory of human behavior based upon scientific experimentation. For the most part, they are behavioral scientists who are more concerned with theoretical research than with finding practical answers to the improvement of group functioning.

The scientific study of groups received its greatest impetus in the late 1930s when Kurt Lewin established the Research Center for Group Dynamics, where theoretical problems of group interaction are studied, and when Muzafer Sherif developed ingenious experimental techniques for the investigation of social norms. Thus, an identifiable field of scientific study was established that has come to be known as *group dynamics*. "Group dynamics is [that] field of inquiry dedicated to advancing knowledge about the nature of groups, the laws of their development, and their interrelations with individuals, other groups, and larger institutions."[2]

Not all of the investigations of the group dynamics specialists have been conducted in the artificial atmosphere of the laboratory. W. F. Whyte and Robert Bales, in particular, adapted scientific techniques of observation and measurement to the field, taking their studies into the streets, the classrooms, the boardrooms, etc. There they tested theories of interaction and group process. Whether in the laboratory or in the field, the researcher in group dynamics is concerned with advancing our knowledge about group life.

We are still far from formulating a complete theory of human interaction or group dynamics. However, today the student of group communication has a wide array of theoretical and practical information from which to choose. Experimental research proceeds rapidly, and practitioners are continually evolving techniques for the improvement of group and organizational communication. It is our purpose to bring to you, the student of group process, some of the more significant concepts, principles, and practices that have contributed to our knowledge of groups and organizations, and the part communication plays in them.

Concepts and Characteristics

Chapter 1 focuses on some of the current thought concerning what constitutes a group and what its ongoing characteristics are. The question is asked, "What is a small group?"; the answers given in the essays suggest that there is probably no absolute definition of the small group. Rather, what we *can* do is to develop operational definitions based upon where and how and under what circumstances individuals meet and interact with other individuals, in such a way that a sense of group is created.

For many people the word "group" seems to imply a collection of persons that somehow transcends and supersedes the individuals within the group. This notion of group as supra-entity carries with it the idea that individuals become something less than individual once they affiliate with a group. Although we would agree that each group does take on a certain identity and imposes group norms upon the individual, we believe that members of a group continue to function as individuals, and we must understand what individuals bring to the group. The essays in this chapter all take the position that if we are to understand what constitutes a small group, we must concentrate on the interactions of the individual within that group.

We begin chapter 1 by trying to stake out the territory of small group behavior. We are concerned with what is and is not a group. The first selection, "The Social Group: Definitions" by Charles S. Palazzolo, takes the position that a one-dimension definition of a small group is not adequate, because a group "involves a system of relations in which individuals become meaningful participants in a kind of association which is lasting and which is committed to the achievement of a goal or set of goals." Therefore, it is necessary to operationalize the concept of "what is a group" by analyzing "how groups come about" and "how they operate". He proceeds to describe the bases for group association and the characteristics of groups that make for meaningful relationships, producing a flexible and practical definition of groups.

In the second selection, "Group Processes for Individual Development", Paul G. Friedman takes a somewhat different view of groups. He argues for a definition that includes those groups that provide a means for individual growth and development rather than consensus and task achievement. He explains that these groups foster "individuation", where members are encouraged to attend to, value, express, and regulate their internal states and their behavior. Such groups include classroom discussion groups, community support groups, and personal growth and counseling groups. The author describes the conditions which foster and support individuation-centered groups.

To demonstrate the potential diversity of group experiences, Michael Argyle focuses on "real-life" groups—the family, the work group, groups of friends, committees, and T-groups—in his essay, "Five Kinds of Small Social

Groups". Argyle defines each group, considers similarities and differences, and cites some of the research findings about each.

In the fourth selection, "Group Composition and Group Cohesiveness", Marvin E. Shaw looks at group composition—the relationships among the characteristics of group members. He is "concerned . . . with the effects of each member's characteristics when considered in relation to the character-istics of other group members." Shaw sets forth thirteen hypotheses about group composition and cohesiveness that help define the domain of small groups.

"Group Interaction Via Communication Rules" offers Susan B. Shiman-off's explanation of why all groups require communication rules, and how communication rules govern the various aspects of group interaction. In the article she discusses the following aspects of rule-governed group interaction: 1) types of rules, 2) emergence of rules, 3) functions and outcomes of rules, and 4) factors influencing rule compliance. She concludes with suggestions of how one can identify the rules operative in a group.

"Groups: A Model" is the final piece in chapter 1. It is written by Mike Robinson, taken from his book, simply titled *Groups*. He presents a descrip-tive, schematic model designed to increase our understanding of groups. The model is not a predictive one, but rather a diagnostic model based on how small groups work. His model is derived from the relationships among 1) normative structure—the group's agreed upon values and behaviors, 2) normative strength—the number of members adhering to the group values and behaviors, 3) group size, 4) group activity, and 5) group environment. He draws upon various research and his own observations of groups to illustrate his model.

Notes

1. Dorwin Cartwright and Alvin Zander, *Group Dynamics: Research and Theory*, 2d ed. (New York: Harper and Row, 1962) ix.
2. *Ibid.*, p. 29.

The Social Group: Definitions

Charles S. Palazzolo

Although sociologists who are concerned with the study of the social group have some agreement on certain common elements in their definitions, their interpretations of the group phenomenon have differed greatly. Here are a few of the many definitions which abound in the literature:

1. We mean by a group a number of persons who communicate with one another often over a span of time, and who are few enough so that each person is able to communicate with all the others, not at secondhand, through other people, but face to face (Homans, 1950:1).
2. A group is an identifiable, structured, continuing collectivity of social persons who enact reciprocal roles according to social norms, interests, and values in the pursuit of common goals (Fichter, 1957:110).
3. The following excerpts consider groups as systems of interaction and approach the group in terms of the *range* it encompasses:

   From the standpoint of the extensity of the interaction process, they range from the all-embracing unlimited totalitarian (maximally cumulative) to the slightest, where the interacting relationship is limited to one unimportant 'interest.'

   From the standpoint of duration, from the most durable and continuous to the groups existing only a short moment, sometimes a few seconds.

   From the standpoint of the direction of the interaction, from the maximally and relatively solidary through the mixed groups, to the limited and all-embracingly antagonistic.

   From the standpoint of organization, from the highly organized to the barely organized and unorganized groups (Sorokin, 1970:444).

4. A group, in the social psychological sense, is a plurality of persons who interact with one another in a given context more than they interact with anyone else (Sprott, 1969:9).

There is certainly variety in the above definitions, but among these and most other definitions there is one common factor—the highlight of all social groups—interaction. Marvin Shaw (1976:11) remarks that ". . . interaction is the essential feature that distinguishes a group. . . ." With this understanding of the importance of interaction as a qualifier of group behavior, Shaw (1976:11) defines a group as ". . . two or more persons who are interacting with one another in such a manner that each person influences and is influenced by each other person."

Shaw's definition, at first reading, is simple enough. Once the importance of interaction within the group is established, it must be considered that the process of interaction involves a system of relations in which individuals become meaningful participants in a kind of association which is lasting and which is committed to the achievement of a goal or set of goals.

Common Bases for Group Association

Once there is a basic understanding of what a social group is, a logical question might be: "How do these groups come about?" Groups form in a great variety of circumstances, and for a great variety of reasons. The following is a simple classification scheme suggesting the most common bases for the origin and development of social groups:

1. Physical proximity
2. Familial bonds
3. Common interests
4. Common physical characteristics
5. Positional expectations

(1) *Physical Proximity.* Social groups are real, observable social facts, and the interactions which prevail within them are necessarily limited by the real environment. That is to say, social groups are limited by space and place. This basis for group association is obvious when one realizes that human interaction is a face-to-face phenomenon. It would be extremely difficult, if not impossible, for two friends to meet and maintain a relationship if they were separated by great distances. Members of families live together, collections of families form neighborhoods, and neighborhoods form communities. At each level, physical proximity is an absolute necessity. In fact, when the spatial element is lost or is in the process of being lost, sociologists begin to talk about the disorganization or breakdown of social bonds.

(2) *Familial Bonds.* The basic form of group organization in any society is the human family. The ties which bind family members are those of blood. Group associations based on familial bonds include associations by marriage, by birth, and by adoption. The social groups which are based upon these bonds

are the marital dyad, the nuclear family, and extended families which include a number of nuclear families and other individuals connected by common ancestry.

(3) *Common Interests.* This classification is very likely the most all-inclusive one since it suggests common motivation among group members and an expressed need to cooperate in the pursuit of personal interests. Included here are all those groups within the economic, political, educational, recreational, and religious spheres in which individuals associate because they agree on the most basic values and goals each group specifies. Educationally, for example, individuals associate in order to learn and to prepare themselves for their futures. Within the higher educational institution, faculty groups, student organizations, and clubs are examples of groups based upon common interests.

There is another view of common interests which sociologists have recognized for a long time. The interest is that of companionship. In group terms, Robert MacIver and Charles Page (1949:445) observe that ". . . the interest of companionship is so pervasive that it is in some degree satisfied by every association. . . ."

(4) *Common Physical Characteristics.* Until recently, groups based upon common physical characteristics were more clearly distinguishable than they are today. Changes resulting from both an elimination of patterns of racial segregation and the advent of the Women's Liberation Movement have militated against the easy classification of groups by race and sex. Youth groups, of course, suggest the division of some group associations by age, and, in the sports world, physical ability and talents are characteristics distinguishing sports clubs and organizations.

(5) *Positional Expectations.* There are other groupings which form, usually ones peripheral to specific institutional positions which some individuals occupy. These expectations are often associated with one's job situation. Businessmen, for example, may feel the need to join such groups. To improve business contacts and thereby increase potential profits, businessmen will frequently join local community and political groups, social clubs for purposes of entertaining clients, and even establish friendships for business purposes. The most interesting aspect of these types of group relationships is that there is a certain pressure to join. Failure to do so is often considered a disadvantage to the individual and an indicator of reduced success in the specific position occupied.

The Social Group: Characteristics

Whichever definition one adopts or constructs for social group, it should include interaction. And although interaction is clearly the most important characteristic of groups and group behavior, there are others which help our understanding of the human social group. The remainder of this chapter will deal with four important group characteristics. They are:

1. Interaction
2. Duration
3. Needs and goals
4. Group structure: norms and roles

(1) *Interaction.* Every social group needs participants who will contribute to the development and success of the social group as a whole. Practically speaking, each member should function in an active manner, seeking rewards not only for oneself, but for the entire group. Although it is hoped that each member will behave in a cooperative and useful manner, such is not always the case. Activity among members in the group, be that activity cooperative, competitive, conflict-oriented, or otherwise, is all part of the circumstances surrounding group interaction.

Interaction may be defined as the exchange of meaningful activity between two or more individuals. In simplest diagram form, the interaction between group members can be identified by $A \leftrightarrow B$, where A and B are interdependent group members and where $\leftrightarrow$ is the symbol for the reciprocity (interaction, exchange) between the two. Increasing the size of the group will, of course, increase the number of possible single units of reciprocity. A simple numerical increase in size will result in a proportionately greater increase in the total number of interactions possible between any two members within any group setting. This a very important function of the size of the group and the complexity of the reciprocity within. Table 1 will help make the point clear. The three-person group produces an equal number (three) of two-person interactions but the four-person group (an increase of one person) produces six two-person interactions (an increase of three) and the five-person group (an increase of another person) produces ten two-person interactions (an increase of four).

(2) *Duration.* Many groups endure over long periods of time. One can expect that the long duration of group bonds produces group cohesion and, ultimately, success in achieving group goals. For groups that require long periods of time, this is so. However, the characteristic of group duration is not so much dependent upon long periods of time as it is on the quality of the interaction during the time the group is active. It is reasonable to suggest that depending upon the needs of the group members as individuals and the needs of the group as a whole, *duration* is best interpreted as the amount of time sufficient to allow for the attainment of the desired group goal or goals.

Some groups do not require years to achieve their goals. Ad hoc committees, for example, may require only short periods of time to achieve the

Table 1
Symbolic Representations and Number
of Two-Person Interactions for Groups of *n* Size

Number of Members in Group	Symbolic Representation	Number of Two-Person Interactions
2	A ⟷ B	1
3		3
4		6
5		10

ends for which they were organized. Other types of groups, such as American nuclear families, require the lifetimes of its members to achieve the ends for which they were formed.

There are three effects which result when groups maintain themselves over any given period of time: (1) the group's desired goal may be achieved, (2) the group direction may change and goals other than the expressed or desired ones may be achieved, and (3) the group may actually fail to achieve any goal at all. What is being suggested here is that group activity should be distinguished from actual goal attainment with the qualification that without the expectation of achieving some goal, maintaining a group for any length of time would be extremely difficult, if not impossible.

(3) *Needs and Goals.* A major reason why people form groups is that they have needs which are best realized in concert with others. We all know that certain needs cannot be met alone and that when we cooperate with others in certain ways our needs, particularly our social needs, will be met. It is important to recognize, however, that there is a difference between individual needs and the needs of the group. The distinction, however, is not an easy one.

Individual needs may be defined as forces within the individual, the existence of which is inferred through behavior directed toward the achievement of a goal. Individual needs are presocial or socially derived. Presocial needs refer to the basic survival forces present in the human being. Social needs derive from the experiences individuals have within the social environment from birth. For example, if an individual internalizes the social value placed upon wealth, power, and prestige, it is reasonable to assume that the individual will develop need-dispositions which will orient behavior in the direction of achieving those goals which reflect the values which were internalized.

Group needs, on the other hand, are forces which develop out of group affiliation, and which promote concerted activity directed toward the achievement of a goal acceptable to the group as a whole. All groups, for example, need structure. Groups need some system of norms, statuses, roles, and relationships which is based upon a sense of order and differentiation. Group behavior under any other condition would be chaotic and without goal direction. It might also be argued that all groups need leadership. What is meant here is not only a leader who is elected or appointed but also any individual who emerges from the membership and attains a status above other members. This is the case even between two friends who, under the specific conditions of a given situation, require direction which ordinarily comes from one or the other.

Although the distinction between individual and group needs is an important one, individual and group needs often blend or appear to blend so that it is difficult to distinguish one from the other. Such blends of individual and group needs combine to produce an environment of motivation which is ideal as a basis for achieving individual and group goals.

Since it is often extremely difficult to separate individual and group needs, our discussion is centered around the relationship between the two and the importance of their compatibility. The presence of individual and group needs in any given situation will result in any one of four possibilities: (1) Individual and group needs may be so diverse that they interfere with each other with no positive effects accruing either to individuals within the group or to the group as a whole. (2) Group interaction may result in the realization of goals desired by the group as a whole, while individual needs are not met. (3) Individual needs may be realized by one or more group members to the detriment or destruction of the group. (4) Individual and group needs may blend so completely that the needs realized by the group as a whole are the same needs individuals wish to realize.

It is this last possibility which group analysts consider as the ultimate in group organization and integration. Group integration is facilitated by need compatibility. Such integration will come about if the group as a cooperatively functioning unit can provide: (1) an environment for the mutual satisfaction of needs, (2) an environment in which individual needs, though different from those of the group, become interdependent need components of the group, or (3) an environment in which individual needs develop because of membership within the group, thus suggesting compatibility between individual and group needs. In each of the above instances, the success of the group in finally attaining its goals and the realization of goals which satisfy the needs of the individual will result.

Individual needs are often generalized and lack clarity and substance. A good example of this is the individual's need for companionship. A need such as this becomes more specific and much more clearly defined when the individual becomes an active member of a friendship group or social club. Through participation in the system of interaction within the group, the individual's vague need for companionship is translated into the clear and continuing goal of developing and maintaining a friendship. Table 2 suggests some individual needs which, through group association, are translated into goals.

We are suggesting that human behavior needs direction. Individuals seem to perform best when there is some sense of achievement anticipated for their behavior. This being the case, understanding goals and the direction of people's actions is a necessary part of the analysis of groups. *Goals* can be defined as the ends for which social groups are organized and maintained. These ends form the basis for the satisfaction of individual and group needs.

Goals and goal achievement can be viewed at two levels: the personal level and the group level. Individuals may join social groups in order to achieve goals which are highly personal. Ordinarily, such goal orientation suggests the use of group activity and the interaction within it in a purely utilitarian and self-enhancing way. Using group situations in order to achieve personal goals is not a problem as long as the goals of the individual are consistent with those of the group as a whole. R. B. Cattell's (1951:167) definition of the social group highlights personal goals: "The definition which seems most essential is that a group is a collection of organisms in which the existence of all (in their given relationships) is necessary to the satisfaction of certain individuals' needs in each."

Table 2
Relationship between Needs and Goals and Appropriate Group Choice

Need	Group Choice	Goal
Companionship	Friendship group	Friendship
Love and affection	Marital dyads Family groups	Sexual and emotional support
Achievement	Occupational groups	Recognition and promotion
Knowledge	Educational groups	Diploma, degree, honors
Public recognition	Political groups	Elected or appointed office
Competition	Athletic teams	Winning
Aggression	The military	Defeating the enemy, domination
Altruism	Social service groups Volunteer groups	Well-being of others, helping the under-privileged

The emphasis here should be placed not on the appropriateness of achieving individual or personal goals, but upon the consistency of these with the goals of the group as a whole. This issue is important enough for one author, Clovis Shepherd (1964:122), to remark, "Generally a successful group has clear objectives, not vague ones, and the members of the group have personal objectives which are identical or compatible with the group's objectives." Without such compatibility, the setting of common goals for the development and the maintenance of group cohesion would be meaningless. It should be noted that the degree to which these goals blend and complement each other can be an efficient measure of the success a social group may expect.

Although goals and goal achievement is not the major focus of the interactionist approach, the significance of social group analysis would be diminished without the perspective which an understanding of goals and goal achievement provides.

(4) *Group Structure: Norms and Roles.* All social groups have some kind and some degree of structure. This generalization and its implications are absolutely necessary in order to fully understand the group process.

From the interactionist's viewpoint, the *A* and the *B* of group interaction mentioned earlier are symbols which stand for individuals who behave toward one another and who expect responses in return. Each individual in the group interaction system must have a set of expectations about each other in the social group. For the group process to be a viable one, the position which each individual occupies in relation to each other individual in the group must be fixed. In other words, every social group must have a structure. *Group structure* is defined as a set of fixed positions which individuals occupy in relation to each other and which carry with them well-defined levels of expectations for behavior which each group member can more or less rely upon as a basis for ordering present as well as future behavior.

Alvin Bertrand (1967:142), in discussing the concept of structure, indicates that it ". . . denotes a fixed relationship between the elements or parts which make up a whole." For the social group as well as for other structures, the idea that the parts are fixed and work well only in relation to each other is basic to an understanding of the importance which many sociologists place on the concept of structure.

For the interactionist studying the social group, the structural element is crucial. If interaction is to be studied at all successfully, it must be within the framework of a controlled and organized group setting in which the analyst can observe and interpret the interpersonal components of the interactions within the group setting. This would be impossible without understanding and insight into the structural components of the group itself. Simply put by Robin M. Williams, Jr. (1970:25): ". . . human interactions show structure. . . ." Human beings exhibit, in groups, behavior which is repeated, patterned, and organized around a system of expectations about individual activities within the boundaries of a given group. This is precisely what structure is about—the consistencies in group behavior. Appropriate to the subject is the view offered by Vernon (1965:5): "Sociologists talk about the *structure* of human interaction. In doing so they are emphasizing the uniformities found therein. A study of human interaction is essentially a study of the arrangement or relationship of various units."

Without the fixed and patterned elements in group analysis, it would be extremely difficult to understand anything about the relationships taking place over long periods of time. It would be next to impossible to identify all the forces and group components which identify a particular relationship or set of relationships within a particular social group.

Groups may have either formal or informal structure. The distinction is simple enough and will serve as a worthwhile reference in future discussions about relationships found within various types of groups. *Formal structure* involves clearly defined positions in fixed relationships to other positions. These positions are governed by explicit rules and regulations for individual and interpersonal behavior. *Informal structure* involves less clearly defined positions within groups, and these are usually governed by an informal code of behavior which develops out of previous experiences of the group members with each other. Although the distinction between the two types of structures is not a difficult one, it may be more easily understood through the following example: Family groupings are usually associations bound by ties which stem from the personal needs and interdependencies of their members and which have little need for formal, rigid, written rules and regulations. This type of grouping should be thought of as having an informal structure.

A business office, however, does not require such an informal basis for defining relationships among its workers. Relationships within a business office would dictate, for purposes of efficiency and high productivity, at both the personal and interpersonal levels, a clear and explicit set of rules and regulations. Sometimes, such specific and limiting regulations are found written out in a Book of Rules or Job Description. Such rigid regulation of behavior simply would not do for the day-to-day relationships in a family. The American nuclear family, friendship groups, and informal work groups are all examples of informal group structures; and bureaucracies such as the American military, the federal government, colleges and universities, and prison systems are examples of formal group structures.

One note of caution: There is no reason to assume that members of informal group structures are less aware of the privileges and responsibilities of their positions and that members of formal group structures are ever alert to the requirements of theirs. In each, the controls over both individual and interpersonal behavior are strong, but deviation from those expectations is an individual rather than group decision. On the whole, most people follow most of the rules of their group most of the time.

Joseph Monane's (1967:16–17) insight into the regulation of individual behavior by group structures comes from his understanding of systems analysis: "A component's identity appears strongly dependent upon the social systems to which he belongs. A person's attitudes, for instance, tend to be those of the groups in which he holds membership: his family, his friendships, and his co-workers. This pressure of system upon its components may be called system determinism." What Monane is suggesting is that the individual who identifies strongly with the group in which membership is held accepts the regulations of that group, and, in large measure, behavior is determined by those controls.

In describing formal organizational structures which are systems of low organization, Monane (1967:22) finds a ". . . diversity and a tolerance of diversity, in action and opinion. . . ." and suggests that "Autonomy goes with heterogeneity, and both are especially likely in large rather than small social systems. Meaningful communication and reciprocal impact of components become less as the size of a social system mounts."

Monane (1967:23–24) distinguishes between low and high organizations and his distinction parallels our formal and informal one. He states, "Families throughout the world are usually highly organized social systems." He goes on to say, "Psychological disturbance in one member of a family, for instance, carries a profound impact on other family members and upon the family as a system."

Norms

College students during the late sixties were fond of using the phrase "doing my own thing" with disturbing regularity. The implication was that the individual would or should not be limited by the rules and regulations of the university in which he was matriculating. The following situation involving a student "doing his own thing" will serve to explain student deviation from college norms. One requirement for a small groups course was a term paper due three days before the scheduled final examination date. The assignment was given early in the semester, and there was more than enough time to complete the requirement especially since administrative approval had been given for eliminating the final examination. The day before the term paper was due, a student entered the professor's office and explained that the term paper had not been written and one would not be submitted as required. When asked why, the student replied: "I wouldn't get any pleasure out of doing a paper, and you should respect my right to do my own thing." The professor explained that the student's rights were respected as long as they did not infringe upon the rights of others and hinder the fulfillment of course requirements. The student was told that the "F" grade would result from failure to complete the course requirements. Refusing to accept this decision, the student requested at least the "B" grade, but would not complete the requirement. The student had internalized the individualism of the times thoroughly enough to resist the pressures to conform to the rules established for receiving a passing grade.

In our culture, individuality has been elevated to the status of a highly valued item, as has conformity. There are times, however, when one object of value (individuality) is in direct conflict with the expected behavior (conformity) demanded in certain group situations. The traditional view of group norms and member conformity states that individuals are controlled by the norms and normative expectations to which they have been socialized as a member of the larger society and as a participant in a specific group interaction system. The implication is that individuals conform to norms because they have internalized them and actually believe that conformity to group norms is best for them and for the group as a whole.

Robin M. Williams, Jr. (1970:29–30) presents an interpretation of norms and conformity to norms which suggests that social or group control and the standardization of member behavior "is not achieved by socialization into specific norms . . . but rather is derived from *lack of perceived alternatives.*" Williams explains that individuals often accept the norms imposed upon them simply because they are unaware of other possibilities. This interpretation is interesting but is not substantially different from that of the traditionalist. The lack of perceived alternatives to which Williams refers is, in fact, one effect produced by socialization into a group or social system. Socialization is the process whereby individuals learn how to behave appropriately and how, either explicitly or implicitly, not to behave. Being socialized to accept the normative structure of a given social group includes the rejection of alternatives. Norms are elements which set the limits of acceptable behavior. In this sense, adherence to a normative system requires individuals to eliminate perceived alternatives. It is not the lack of perceived alternatives which necessitates conformity to a set of normative expectations. Socialization to norms places limitations upon the individual's right or wish to select certain courses of action over those which have been approved by the group.

Group norms define the limits within which behavior is deemed acceptable or appropriate. They establish the group basis for controlling behavior, and set the standards by which individual behavior is judged. When individuals enter groups they subject themselves to all the influences which groups exert upon members, and they are expected to conform to the established norms. Group influences also include the means whereby members are pressured to conform to the norms established by the group as a whole. These means by which conforming behavior is exacted from group members are called group or social controls. The basis upon which norms are established and controls are developed exists in the belief that the interests of individual group members and the group as a whole are best served when behavior remains within prescribed limits.

Roles

Within the group system, the structural element which connects group norms to the behavior of the individual group member is the social role. *Roles* are sets of expectations which members in groups share concerning the behavior of each individual who occupies a position within the group structure. When individuals interact with each other over significant periods of time within the same group, a pattern of expectations develops and forms the constellation of expectations which we call roles.

There are a number of reasons why roles are important to groups and group structure. Roles are the bases of interaction. Effective interaction within group settings is based upon the assumption that individuals internalize their roles and perform accordingly. Assuming that all roles are reciprocal and complementary, interaction proceeds without hindrance toward the achievement of group goals. The reciprocal nature of roles is reflected in the degree to which group interaction based upon role expectations coordinates the activities of all members of the group. The reciprocal and complementary qualities of social roles are observable in the most common role relationships found within the complex of group activity. For example, it is impossible to conceive of the role of parent without the role of child or that of husband without the role of wife. Friendship is based upon the assumption that there is another individual who shares the identities and interests common to all friendships. More formal associations also reflect the reciprocal and complementary nature of social roles. The professional roles of doctors and dentists are complemented only by those who perform the roles of their patients; lawyers and clients are complements of each other. The superordination-subordination character common to many role relationships suggests the logical reciprocity and complementarity of the leader-follower relationship. The theme of dominance and submission in role relationships reached a point of clear distinction in the traditional relationship between master and slave.

Roles as Tools of Socialization

Children learn how to behave in a variety of situations and internalize those roles which they will be expected to perform as adults by taking others' roles. Children, by taking the roles of parents, are also internalizing the behavior of those others and, in the process, are able to understand better how they, as children, fit into the relationships which have developed between them and their parents. Roles control and limit the extent to which individuals will deviate from group norms. Roles function as translators of group norms for each individual member of the group and determine the limits within which behavior is approved and rewarded and outside of which behavior is rejected and punished. Since individuals occupy different positions within the group, it is necessary for the group as a whole to make explicit what is expected of each group member.

Roles and Positions

Group structures have been identified as complexes of positions which group members occupy. For each position there should be a clear, precise, and appropriate statement of the expectations which determine the behavior of those individuals who occupy the group positions. In this sense, roles form an overlay which fits the complex of group positions perfectly, at least on paper.

In reality, actual performance usually varies from the stated expectations and is influenced by such individual factors as personality, motivation, ability, and skill. Group structure is an important concept in understanding groups and group organization; roles and the complex of activity and interaction which they promote are the essentials of group behavior. The static quality usually associated with the analysis of structure and position is converted into the dynamics of group interaction by the incorporation of an overstructure of roles which is designed to control the behavior of group members and to order the relationships of those who occupy group positions.

Group Processes for Individual Development

Paul G. Friedman

Research on group interaction has tended to focus on achieving agreement or consensus as a primary group goal. For some groups, however, this is inappropriate—unity is *not* a goal, much less the goal. There are contexts in which groups exist to promote individuals' development. Examples include classroom discussions, community support groups, and personal growth or counseling groups. In each of these cases participants need not reach agreement, nor take joint action, nor prepare a unified public presentation. The groups exist instead as arenas that encourage individuals to meet their own unique needs and goals. The purpose of such gatherings is not to submerge individual differences into a group gestalt, but to use the group's resources to enhance awareness of members' personhood and to encourage expressions of members' unique selves.

This chapter deals with those groups that exist not to reach consensual agreements, but rather to promote the development of each individual member. . . . While consensus is a useful concept and is, in fact, a viable goal in some group situations, it is not a universal description or prescription for group interaction. It has limits, ones this chapter intends to define.

I. Rationale for Individuation in Groups

Groups which nurture individual performance and personal growth fill an essential function. Gordon Allport has affirmed that

> *the outstanding characteristic of man is his individuality.* He is a unique creation of the forces of nature. There was never a person just like him, and there never will be again. Remember the fingerprint, even it is unique. All sciences, including psychology, tend to neglect this paramount fact of individuality. . . . In daily life, on the other hand, we are in no danger of forgetting that individuality is the supreme mark of human nature. All during our waking life, and even in our dreams, we recognize and deal with people as separate, distinct, and unique individuals. . . . In view of the uniqueness of each person's inheritance and environment it could not be otherwise. (p. 4)

Our nation has seen a steady growth toward more interest in and acceptance of individual differences. Large-scale survey studies comparing American attitudes in the 1950s and 1970s indicate that we have become increasingly

From *Emergent Issues In Human Decision Making* by Gerald Phillips and Julia T. Wood (eds.). Copyright 1984 by Southern Illinois University Press. Reprinted by permission. Paul G. Friedman is affiliated with the Department of Communication Studies, University of Kansas.

tolerant of nonconformist views (Nunn et al., 1978). Business organizations have come to realize that their traditional concern with making workers conform to preestablished standards may have negative repercussions (Whyte, 1956). Research on incentive systems reveals that motivation and satisfaction increase when rewards are made contingent on individual performance (Lawler, 1971). Recent "liberation" movements (for example, among women, minorities, the handicapped, and the elderly) attest to a widespread contemporary desire for individuals to resist stereotyping and conformity to normative group expectations. Whether the group context is a business organization, a classroom, a counseling center, or a social gathering among friends, whatever the content of the group discussion, what unifies all group situations to which this chapter applies is their common desideratum—individuation of participants.

An individuated orientation to group interaction has parallels in other disciplines. There are times, in the political arena, when a legislative body seeks to make laws generally applicable to the populace as a whole. In other instances, situations must be adjudicated one case at a time (i.e., individuated), as they are in a court of law. In education, curriculum developers seek to devise courses of study well-suited to all the students at every grade level in their community; teachers, tutors, and parents adapt (or individuate) that curriculum for their particular student(s). Likewise, in social science texts one reads about principles of human behavior that apply to most people most of the time; yet, one also finds value in reading the biography (an individuated study) describing a single person in specific situations. A commercial illustrator might draw a "typical" person for a newspaper advertisement, while an artist would create an "individuated" portrait of a specific individual. Hence, when a group deals with its individual members case-by-case, person-by-person, as unrepeatable, unreplaceable human beings, it is dealing with them in the same way that lawyers, parents, biographers, and artists attend to the foci of their endeavors.

II. Definition

Individuation in a group exists when members are encouraged to attend to, value, express, and regulate their internal states and their behavior. Deindividuation, on the other hand, exists when situational factors in a group discourage members' awareness, affirmation, expression, and regulation of themselves as distinct individuals (see Table 1).

Individuation is task-oriented when other group members inquire about, listen to, support, or provide constructive feedback, or all of these, regarding a task that is an individual's responsibility or a product that he/she has created. Deindividuation regarding tasks occurs when the group tells individuals

Table 1
Group Emphasis

Individuated Emphasis:	*Deindividuated Emphasis:*
Self-Awareness	Attention given to a group as a unified entity
Self-Affirmation	Value comes from group membership
Self-Expression	Joint group messages & activities
Self-Control	Behavior regulated by group norms

what to do, imposes its norms or standards on individuals' work, or subordinates individuals' decision-making power to the group's. The group thereby draws attention, reinforcement power, and control to itself rather than assigning them to individuals. In a deindividuated group each individual's identity and productivity are subsumed by the group; in an individuated group, one's work is self-directed and self-attributed. Individuation can apply to personal development when any (or a combination of) the following goals and processes are encouraged:

Self-Awareness

I can join a group to learn more about myself. When introducing and sharing myself I might articulate what I think and feel more precisely than I had heretofore. By comparing myself to others, I see how I am similar to and different from them. By responding to their questions, I clarify what I believe. By receiving their feedback, I learn how others see me. By responding to the issues they raise, I ponder and react to a greater variety of stimuli than I might on my own. When the group focuses their attention on me, I am encouraged to look inward more deeply and more comprehensively than I usually do when caught up in tasks of everyday life. Hence, a group can serve as a mirror in which I see my reflection more clearly and in more ways than I would otherwise.

Self-Acceptance

I can join a group to enhance my self-esteem. If other group members are involved in dealing with the same issues that I am, I feel less alone, less unique in coping with the difficulties I face. If they give me their attention and listen to me with understanding, I feel that I need not be ashamed about what concerns me. If they consider what I have to say as a worthwhile contribution to their conversation. I grow in perceiving myself as valuable to others. In an accepting group, therefore, I can come to validate my worth as a person.

Self-Expression

I can join a group to enhance my capacity to express my messages fully. In earlier group contexts, I may have learned that self-censorship was essential for social approval. I was influenced to inhibit my feelings, my disagreements, my desires. This pattern of reticence became my characteristic mode of self-presentation. If I now encounter social situations that call for more open or forceful self-expression than those I have dealt with before, I may desire to respond more freely, but still feel uncomfortable when taking an approach that is unfamiliar to me. A group which gives me permission for, and even encourages expression of what I usually repress, can help me to change in more adaptive ways. In a supportive, generally risk-free group environment, I can experiment with greater expressiveness and become more familiar with behaviors that I tended to exclude from my repertoire. I can enlarge the scope and intensity of what I am prepared to share with others, and as a result can come to handle appropriately a greater variety of social situations.

Self-Regulation

I can join a group to gain more control over my own behavior. Previously, I had attributed unwanted habits (or addictions) to circumstances beyond my control. Their detrimental effects have taken a sufficient toll that I now seek to take responsibility for my actions and to redirect them in more self-enhancing directions. If I find myself unable to navigate such a shift on my own, (e.g., to diet, stop drinking, stop gambling, recover from a loss) I might join a group that will assist me in helping myself. The group members will lend me their support, share their own experiences in circumstances similar to mine, help me to plan my change program, and reinforce steps I take toward that end. By viewing me as capable of self-regulation, by modeling that such change is possible, by guiding me through the steps needed to implement my desired transformation, they assist me in reaching my goal.

Within a group there would appear to be inherent tension between the opposing poles of individuation and deindividuation. One way the pendulum could swing is overemphasizing individuation and thereby losing group cohesiveness. Zander (1982) states "A body of people is not a group if the members are primarily interested in individual accomplishments" (p. 2). Excessive individuation exists only if participants see themselves as rivals, as achieving their own goals at the expense of other group members.

This need not be the case; people can have individual accomplishments as a joint concern. They can see themselves as synergistically involved, a condition wherein participants' "selfish" goals are congruent—each person benefits by the others' success.

The opposite extreme is excessive deindividuation. Deindividuation pressures exist whenever a group meets. Groups can whittle away at individual differences until conformity is achieved and a consensus is hammered out. People often seek group identification (deindividuation) to escape individual responsibility (Fromm, 1941).

To prevent deindividuation from dominating, an individuated focus often must be consciously pursued. Certain conditions within the group environment are likely to strengthen and sustain individual-centered group interaction. Occasionally these conditions must be maximized in order to shift the group away from deindividuation.

III. Conditions

If those organizing a group have the intention of creating primarily an individuated group, there are certain conditions they can try to establish to facilitate this orientation. We might view these as characteristics common to an individuated *system* of interaction. No one condition is sufficient to guarantee or to obviate the possibility of an individualized focus. In systemic combination, however, certain conditions are likely to sustain predominantly individuated group interaction.

Size

A *smaller* group is more likely to encourage individuation. Fewer participants allow for more "air time" and initiative by individuals (Latane & Dabbs, 1975). One is less likely to feel impelled to submerge one's own needs or beliefs in a small group than in a large one. Individual differences can be tolerated more when there are fewer individuals present for the group to integrate.

Membership

Individuation is more likely in a *heterogeneous* group. A group of people who are similar in appearance and behavior is likely to think of itself as a collective, as a unified whole. When the group is mixed, persons tend to see themselves and others as unique. In a homogeneous group when participants interact they do not single each other out as individuals (Festinger et al., 1952); perceiving the group as a whole, they speak to the entire group. Heterogeneous groups are more likely to focus on individuals.

Control

When a group is convened, its leader(s) either may take strong control and direct the group's activities or may offer only *loose* control, leaving most decision-making to the group's members. The latter approach increases individuation. When participants learn that they (not the leader) will determine what is to occur in the group, they are encouraged to bring to mind their own goals and behavioral standards. They shift toward looking inward, rather than outward, for direction. They attend more to each other, rather than to the leader, when deciding upon the group's procedures. Hence, their focus becomes individuated.

Activities

The activities performed within a group may be familiar, habitual, and culturally scripted or they may be *novel, requiring conscious intentional choices*. The latter kinds of activities encourage individuation. When people perform preplanned or well-learned acts they frequently are not consciously aware of their own behavior or of themselves as separate persons (Kanfer & Karoly, 1972). When situations require conscious decisions, group participants are more likely to attend to themselves and to other individuals.

Also, simple oral and physical activities sufficient to absorb one's conscious processing capacity tend to be deindividuating. Rapid talking, shouting, and chanting, as well as physical acts such as clapping, dancing, rock throwing, milling, and so on, have been found to reduce or prevent self-awareness (Duvaland Wicklund, 1972). Thus, group participants whose attention is diverted by external, routine activities are less likely to be individuated than those engaged in discussing *complex, cognitively stimulating, multifaceted issues*.

Observation

When people are aware of being *observed by others* or when they *observe themselves*, they become more self-aware. When we know others are looking at us, rather than at an outside object, we become self-conscious (Carver and Scheier, 1978). The same effect occurs when we look at ourselves in a mirror or hear a tape-recording of ourselves. Consequently, when a group's attention is focused on one person at a time or when each person is singled out to be the object of observation and feedback from others, those participants feel more individuated.

Evaluation

When people are impelled to compare their actions to standards, their own or others, they also become self-aware (Diener, 1980). *Self-evaluation* requires that we notice what we do and that we clarify and compare that behavior to what we value or ideally want to do. Evaluation mitigates against immersion in a group's activity. It encourages self-examination and self-checking.

Conformity

A group in which conformity is highly prized—that is, one in which there is strong pressure for uniformity of opinion—may engage in "groupthink" (Janis, 1972) and discourage individuation. A group with *little pressure for conformity,* one that is tolerant of individual differences, can allow for individuals to think, speak, and act independently. Janis maintains that a high level of cohesiveness (members' desire to maintain the group) contributes to groupthink, as does directive or closed leadership. This theory was modified by Flowers (1977), who found the level of cohesiveness in the groups he studied to be unrelated to the degree of individuation (which he defined as openness to alternate information and solutions), but a closed leadership style did increase groupthink.

Uniqueness

One would think that when individuated differences are emphasized, a group would lean toward an individual mode of operation. Indeed, when people are told that they are very similar to others, they tend to act differently from their peers in order to assert their individual distinctiveness. However, when people are told that they are very different from others, they feel uncomfortable and seek to reduce their uniqueness. Snyder and Fromkin (1980) report these findings and posit the theory that people prefer (and will seek to change their behavior to achieve) a *moderate* degree of uniqueness. Consequently, for individuation to prevail in a group over time, *some* bonds of similarity must exist among its members.

In sum, the conditions which (in combination) seem to promote an individuated group are: small size, heterogenous membership, loose control, novel activities, conscious choice making, cognitively complex topics, self-observation, attention focused on individuals by others, self-evaluation, low pressure for conformity, and moderate uniqueness (see Table 2). These need not all exist simultaneously for a group to be individuated. However, when they predominate over their antitheses (characteristics which deindividuate), the group as a "system" reinforces the individual identities of its members. These, therefore, are the conditions which best establish a group designed to serve as a context for individual development.

IV. Effects

When the conditions that optimize individuation exist, certain effects are likely to occur. Group leaders who seek an individualized group orientation must be prepared to deal with these outcomes. Usually, such effects are the intended results of such an emphasis. Some, however, are "side effects" which obstruct what many teachers, counselors, and others desire. The effects of individuation conditions are summarized below.

Self-Focus

Persons in an individuated group are likely to be self-focused. Carver and Scheier (1978) found that subjects asked to provide endings to a number of incomplete sentences—under conditions heightening self-awareness—were much more likely to complete the sentences with some sort of self-reference than those not encouraged to be self-aware. They assumed that these sentence completions reflected a high degree of self-orientation. In another study (Ickes et al., 1978) found that self-aware subjects described themselves in more individuated or unique terms than did non-self-aware subjects (who described themselves in more categorical and abstract terms). Thus encouraging self-awareness seems to bring forth a general state of self-orientation.

Accuracy

People tend to describe themselves more accurately when attention is self-focused, which contrasts with the general finding that self-reports are barely correlated with behavior (Wicker, 1969). Quite often self-descriptions and self-report tests are not terribly valid. Pryor et al. (1977) studied the accuracy of self-reports (regarding subjects' sociability with strangers) under conditions of high and low self-awareness. They compared males' scores on self-report tests of sociability with what they actually did when first meeting an attractive female. There was a much higher correlation between self-report and behavior for those who rated themselves under conditions enhancing individuation.

Attribution

People tend to attribute responsibility to whatever is at the center of their attention. Buss and Scheier (1976) found that subjects asked to ascribe fault for a hypothetical car accident in which they were driving showed consistently more self-blame under conditions of individuation. (This process seemed to

Table 2
Group Characteristics Related to Individuation

Group Conditions	Group Types	
	Individuated	Deindividuated
Size	Small	Large
Membership	Heterogenous	Homogenous
Control	Loose	Tight
Activities	Novel	Routine, familiar, culturally scripted
	Involve choices	Structured
	Complex	Simple
Observation	Of Individuals, Individuals' tasks	Outward, or on group and group tasks
Evaluation	By self	None or by group standards
Conformity	Low	High
Uniqueness	Moderate	Very slight, very high

be independent of the valence of the outcome. The subjects also took credit for winning an imaginary race.) When persons are self-aware, they tend to see themselves as the source or cause of whatever outcome is to be explained.

Exaggeration of Emotional States

When, under conditions of individuation, subjects were encouraged to feel anger, depression, elation, disgust, or sexual thoughts, they reported higher levels of emotional arousal than subjects not in those circumstances (Scheier, 1976). Hence, there is likely to be an increment of emotional intensity for people in an individuated group.

Consistency

When highly self-aware, people are more conscious of "within-self discrepancies."

A discrepancy consists of two points: on the one hand the person's current condition, attainment, or status; on the other hand a goal, rule, or more generally, an 'end point' for behavior. Every one carries around such discrepancies, not always being aware of them. Most of us have histories of untold failures, hypocritical behaviors, or other within-self discrepancies that only seldom if at all come to our conscious attention.

However, if one particular personal discrepancy is highly salient, such as a recent case of cheating a friend out of his money, then self-directed attention will come to focus on that discrepancy, with the following result:

The person will realize the discrepancy—this realization being identical with a condition of self-evaluation. The evaluation of course is an unfavorable one, and continued self-awareness will prompt the person to do something about this uncomfortable state. (Wicklund, 1980, p. 192)

Dealing with Discrepancies

Under conditions of individuation, when people become aware of "within-self discrepancies" they generally deal with them in one of two ways: avoidance or discrepancy reduction.

First, people may attempt to avoid the conditions that lead to continued self-focus. For example, they might divert the attention of the group from themselves, seek to reduce individuation in the group as a whole, or leave the group.

Second, they may try to reduce or eliminate the discrepancy by making an effort to bring their present condition into line with their ideal. "Thus a person whose attention is focused on his lack of productivity can accelerate his efforts, a person whose attention is brought to a hypocrisy can strive to be more consistent in words and deeds, and someone who realizes that he has been too selfish can pursue humane or altruistic acts" (Wicklund, 1980, p. 193).

Self-Protection

When people are self-aware *and* become highly *ego-involved* in their self-presentation, they seem to increase their need for self-protection (or "saving face"). Federoff and Harvey (1976) asked their subjects to help a "phobic" confederate alleviate his fears. They worked with the confederate for a considerable time and then discovered that their efforts had been in vain. When asked to ascribe responsibility for their failure, the subjects under self-aware conditions more often blamed not themselves but the "phobic" person. The only way they were able to resolve the discrepancy between their self-image as capable people and their lack of effectiveness in this instance (they couldn't *do* anything to change the outcome of the interaction) was to resort to self-protection by minimizing their own responsibility for what occurred. This outcome is in contrast to Buss and Scheier's (1976) finding that in a non-ego-involving (hypothetical) situation one's focus of attention (oneself) was the target of attribution.

Consistency with Commitments

People who are self-aware seem to maintain more consistency with their previous commitments, when subjected to group pressure, than those who are in a deindividuated state. McCormick (1979) found that when his subjects' attitudes were based on a recent commitment, self-awareness prompted them to increase their consistency with their commitment, totally independent of the group's attitude. Personal decision seems to carry more weight for a self-aware individual than does group pressure.

Transgressive Behavior

Research has shown that deindividuating factors, such as anonymity and lack of individual responsibility, tend to release transgressive behavior. For example, Diener et al. (1976) used Halloween trick or treaters as subjects. They manipulated the conditions at several homes and measured transgression by whether or not the youngsters took more candy than they were permitted to or stole money. When children were in groups, were anonymous, and were told that another child was responsible, 80 percent transgressed. When children approached the candy bowl alone, were nonanonymous, and no responsibility diffusion took place, only 8 percent transgressed. Individuation, therefore, leads to more normative, prosocial behavior.

Self-Regulation

The self-regulation of behavior involves: (a) monitoring one's own behavior, (b) considering one's behavior in relation to social and personal norms, (c) self-generating reinforcements, and (d) foresight and planning about the outcomes of available alternatives (Kamfer, 1977). The ability to do so requires that a person be in a situation that triggers self-monitoring, consideration of personal standards, having behavioral alternatives, meting out self-reward and punishment, and being able to anticipate the short- and long-range outcomes of one's actions in order to use foresight and planning meaningfully. Clearly, an individuated group allows for more self-regulation than one that is deindividuated. When one conceives of the group as a whole, self-monitoring is difficult. Decisions and novel situations instigate self-monitoring. An outward focus of attention consumes the conscious processing capacity needed to retrieve personal standards from long-term memory in order to compare behavior to them and to plan ahead. With deindividuation the group's responses become more potent than self-generated reinforcements. Thus deindividuation prevents self-regulation (Diener, 1980).

In sum, people in a group characterized by conditions of individuation tend to focus on themselves, see themselves as unique, describe themselves more accurately, attribute causality to self (unless they come to be highly ego-involved regarding their self-presentation), be more aware of "within-self" inconsistencies, seek to reduce such inconsistencies, maintain freely chosen commitments (i.e., resist group pressure), avoid transgressions of social norms, and be more self-regulative (see Table 3). These outcomes are more likely to occur in groups where individuation is emphasized.

Table 3
Effects of Individuation

Outcomes	Group Tendencies	
	Individuated	Deindividuated
Focus	Self	External
Self-concept	Unique	Categorical
Accuracy	High	Low
Attribution	Self	Other
Emotional Arousal	High	Low
When Ego-Involved	More Ego-Protective	Less Ego-Protective
Inconsistencies	More Salient	Less Salient
Dealing with Discrepancies	More eager to Reduce	Less eager to Reduce
Consistency with Commitments	High	Lower
Transgressive Behavior	Low	Higher
Self-Regulation	High	Lower

If we compare these outcomes with what most members and leaders concerned with individual development generally seek through group interaction, these outcomes on the whole are desirable. They would contribute to self-awareness, self-acceptance, self-expression, and self-regulation as described earlier.

• • • • • •

In conclusion, a basic assumption made in this chapter is that a significant distinction to make among group contexts is whether they are intended to seek consensus or to encourage participant individuation. If the latter is preferred, certain antecedents, conditions, and consequences apply. Individuated groups are increasingly emphasized in our post industrial society. Along with the popularity of individuated groups (sometimes called T-groups, sensitivity training, consciousness-raising groups, group therapy, and so on) has come criticism. For the most part, critics have accused such groups of heightening narcissism and vulnerability, as well as deviating from their intended purpose. That is, they claim that instead of liberating their participants for increased self-awareness, affirmation, expression, and control, such groups actually impose on them an alternate set of group norms. These norms can be insidious because they breed insensitivity and embarrassment,and people who deviate from them often are presumed to be wrong, bad, or resistant. As a result deindividuation subtly overtakes and overwhelms the group's original purpose.

The concepts in this chapter are intended to define what characterizes an individuated group, the ways such a group might stray from its primary intention, and if it does, how it might then be redirected toward promoting more constructive individuation. Thus one might pose the questions that follow in regard to a group in which individuation is desired.

1. Is the group relatively small and heterogenous?
2. Are participants oriented at the start and continually encouraged to act and speak with autonomy?
3. Is participation and self-disclosure . . . by everyone encouraged?
4. Do the activities (and/or general discussion) involve novelty, choice-making, and complexity?
5. Does the group focus attention on individuals (and their task performance) and promote self-evaluation?
6. Do participants perceive low pressure for conformity and moderate uniqueness among themselves?
7. Is there freedom and support for experimenting with new behavior? Is feedback provided regarding this "here-and-now" behavior?
8. Is nonpolarization of points of view maintained?
9. Are initiatives helped to be completed and successful?
10. Does the leader show trust in the group process by maintaining loose control?
11. Are interdependence and fundamental similarities among participants emphasized?

If these questions or most of them are answered affirmatively, the group will be a system in which self-awareness, self-affirmation, self-expression, and self-regulation prevail and in which excessive narcissism, vulnerability, and avoidance do not occur. Such conditions and their probable outcomes represent one significant area in which consensus is not a goal of group process. One conclusion to be drawn from this analysis is that teachers, practitioners, and researchers should devote greater attention to the reasons, means, and outcomes of group goals other than consensus.

Five Kinds of Small Social Groups

Michael Argyle

The concentration of research on laboratory groups has diverted attention away from the very varied kinds of interaction taking place in real life groups. We shall describe interaction in the three most important types of group—the family, work-groups, and groups of friends (we shall concentrate on adolescent friendship groups). In addition an account will be given of some other kinds of groups which have been extensively studied—committees, T-groups, and therapy groups. . . .

The Family As a Small Group

There is something like a family in all species of mammals: the mother has to care for the young, and the father often provides food and protection during this period. Only in humans does the father become an enduring member of the family, and only in humans is there a life-long link between children and parents. What is probably the most important kind of small group in human society is often overlooked by small group researchers—and consequently there are important features of the family group which have never been embodied in small group experiments or theorising.

The nuclear family consists of two parents, sons and daughters, and can thus be regarded as a four-role system, divided by generation and sex (Parsons and Bales, 1955). There are also characteristic relations between older and younger brothers, and between older and younger sisters, so that it may be better to see the family as potentially a six-role system, though not all the positions may be filled (Murdock, 1949). The basic features of the relationship between each pair of positions are much the same in all human societies. For example between older and younger brothers there is a 'relationship of play-mates, developing into that of comrades; economic co-operation under leadership of elder; moderate responsibility of elder for instruction and discipline of younger' (Murdock, op. cit.). The family has some of the features of a formal organisation—a set of positions, each associated with a role, including patterns of interaction with occupants of other positions. . . .

Unlike groups of friends, family members have tasks to perform. In primitive societies these are mainly the growing and preparation of food, the rearing and education of children, and maintenance of the house. In modern society

From *Small Groups and Social Interaction,* Volume 1. Edited by H. H. Blumberg, A. P. Hare, V. Kent and M. Davies. © 1983 by John Wiley and Sons, Ltd. Reproduced by permission of John Wiley and Sons, Ltd. Michael Argyle is a lecturer at the University of Oxford.

some of these activities are performed by outside agencies, but there are still the domestic jobs connected with eating, sleeping, and the care of young children. In addition there are leisure activities such as TV, gardening, games, and family outings. Some of these are like activities of friends in that they are performed because of the interaction involved. Interaction in the family is closely connected with these joint activities—eating, watching or playing together. Interaction is also brought about through the members pursuing their private goals under conditions of physical proximity, and where their joint activities have to be more or less closely coordinated—this is an extension of the necessity for meshing. The physical environment and technology have an important effect on family life. Overcrowding of other animals results in aggression, and the murder rate is greater in overcrowded areas (Henry and Short, 1954). The family tasks include looking after one another, in particular caring for the bodily needs of members: in addition to close physical proximity there is also intimacy and interdependence. . . .

What goes on inside the family is private and not readily subject to external control. Models of how families should behave are, however, provided by magazines and TV, and by the previous families of the parents. The actual elements of interaction of which family life consists differ from all other groups, in that greater intimacy, aggression, affection, and emotional violence occurs. Family members see each other undressed, or naked, and there is almost no attempt at self-presentation; they know each other's weaknesses and understand each other extremely well; family life is very much 'off-stage,' in Goffman's terminology (1956). There is physical aggression, mainly of parents towards children, but also between children; there is aggression between parents, but it is mainly verbal. Affection is equally violent and often takes the form of bodily contact, between parents, and between parents and children until they 'get too old for it.' Members of laboratory groups do not usually take their clothes off, laugh uproariously, cry, attack or kiss each other, or crawl all over each other, as members of families commonly do. Interaction in the family is more complex and subtle than most other interaction because of the intense and complex relationships between members, and their long history of previous interaction. Spiegel (1956) describes cases of tense mother-daughter interaction, and suggests that various unconscious fantasies and projections are taking place in addition to what seems to be occurring. This is similar to the interpersonal behavior found in some neurotics. The subtler nonverbal communications may be very important—as in the possible effect of 'double-bind' parents in making children schizophrenic. The dimensions of parent behavior which have the greatest effect on children, however, are probably warmth *v.* rejection, strictness *v.* permissiveness, and type of discipline (Sears, Maccoby and Levin, 1957). . . .

Adolescent Groups

Friendship groups are one of the basic forms of social grouping in animals and men; they are distinguished by the fact that members are brought together primarily through interpersonal motivations and attractions, not through concern with any task. Of all friendship groups, adolescent groups are the most interesting. During adolescence work and family attachments are weak and the strongest attachments are to friends. These groups are formed of young people between the ages of 11–12 up to 21–23, when the members marry and settle down in jobs, and other kinds of group become more important to them.

The motivations of members are partly to engage in various joint activities, but more important are interpersonal needs—sexual, affiliative, and the establishment of identity. It has been suggested that there are certain 'developmental tasks' during this period of life to develop an identity independent of the family, and to establish a changed relation with adults (Erikson, 1956; Muuss, 1962). . . .

The activities of adolescent groups vary with the culture: in the USA groups of boys are concerned with cars, entertainment, sport, and girls (Sherif and Sherif, 1964). There is avoidance of the tasks of home and school. Many group activities are invented, whose chief point is the social interaction involved—such as dancing, listening to records, and drinking coffee. The forms of social interaction involved are rather different from those in other groups—there is more bodily contact, joking, aggressive horseplay, and just being together, less problem-centred discussion. Schmuck and Lohman (1965) observe that 'adolescents in a group often engage in infantile behaviour and pranks, while giggling and laughing hilariously: and are encouraged to feel silly together, and to withhold evaluation from such experiences' (p. 27). They suggest that this behavioural abandon has a regressive element. There is an easy intimacy and social acceptance of those who wear the right uniform. Conversation is mainly about other adolescents, parents, interpersonal feelings and social interaction. These are probably the only natural groups that discuss social interaction (T-groups do it too). Such topics are discussed because adolescents have problems to solve in this area—as well as working out an identity and establishing a changed relationship with adults, they have to acquire the social skills of dealing with the opposite sex, to come to terms with the difficulty of playing different roles on different occasions, and having relationships of different degrees of intimacy with different people (Fleming, 1963).

Adolescent groups are of interest to us because a number of special processes can be seen, which are not present in laboratory groups. (1) There is no specific task, but joint activities are devised which entail the kinds of interaction which meet the needs of members. (2) One of these needs is the establishing of an ego-identity, independent of the family of origin (Erikson,

1956). This explains the emphasis on clothes, the great self-consciousness, and the concern about acceptance by members of these groups. (3) Sexual motivation is a major factor in adolescent groups, and is partly responsible for the intensity of attraction to the groups, and for their pairing structure. (4) There is a group task of acquiring together the social skills of dealing with the opposite sex and dealing with adults.

Work-Groups

In groups of animals the work of gathering food and building homes is often carried out by males. In ants it is a specialised and highly organised group activity. In primitive society this work may be carried out by males or females, and follows a seasonal cycle. In modern communities work outside the home has become a highly specialised activity, mainly performed by adult males, for financial reward, and is done in special social organisations. Work is performed in groups for several reasons—(1) One man alone may not be able to perform the task; in primitive societies this is the case with hunting and building; (2) there can be division of labour, so that different people can use or develop specialised skills; this is a central feature of work in modern communities; (3) people prefer to work together because of their social motivations; (4) another factor is social facilitation; the presence of others is arousing, so more work is done. Even ants work harder when there is more than one of them on the job (Zajonc, 1965).

Work-groups are at the opposite pole from adolescent groups in that their primary concern is with carrying out a task. They are the other main kind of group outside the family in which adults spend most of their time. They are not so well defined as the other two kinds, and often have no clear membership. It is sometimes difficult, in a factory for example, to decide which are the group—all that can be seen are a lot of people, some of whom collaborate over work or interact informally from time to time. Such groups can be defined in terms of the formal organisation—having the same supervisor or being paid jointly, or in terms of informal group-formation—sociometric cliques, or people who think of themselves as a group. Much research in this area has been on groups of manual workers—gangs of men engaged in the maintenance of railway track, men on assembly lines. There has also been research on the more technically skilled men in charge of automated plant, and recently attention has turned to the work of engineers, accountants, scientists and managers. In these latter cases much of the social interaction is between people two at a time, so there is a network rather than a group. They may also meet in committees and similar talking and decision-taking groups, which will be discussed separately in the following section. In this section we are concerned with groups which have a definite task to do, and where the social interaction arises out of the task activity. . . .

What form does interaction take in work-groups? In the first place the task performance may partly consist of interaction. If A passes a brick to B this is both task behaviour and interaction; if A likes B, more bricks will be passed (Van Zelst, 1952). He will pass them with accompanying verbal and non-verbal signals, not strictly necessary for the task, but which sustain the social relationship. If A talks to B, where B is his supervisor, or colleague, it is impossible to disentangle the task and the informal interaction elements of the conversation. Much work in fact consists almost entirely of social interaction—the work of supervisors, interviewers, teachers, and many others. In addition to interaction linked to the task, interaction may take place during coffee breaks, in the lunch hour, after hours, and during unauthorised pauses from work. Non-verbal communication, such as gestures, may occur during the work process. Social interaction of the usual kind is perhaps more limited in work-groups than in groups of other kinds. The relationships established may only operate in the work situation—as when good working relations exist between members of different racial and social class groups. Only part of the personality is involved, but it is an important part, and work-relations can be very important to people. Friendships are made at work, especially between people of equal status in the organization; many of the links joining family members to the outside world are made in the work situation. Relationships at work may also, on occasion, resemble the relaxed informality of the family. This is most common among young people, who know each other very well, and have shared emotional experiences. Life in the services has something of this quality. There is often considerable intensity of feeling in work-groups, because the economic position, the career, the self-image and sometimes the safety of members is at stake. . . .

What special interaction processes are found in work-groups? (1) Interaction arises out of cooperation and communication over task activity, and can be regarded as a secondary or informal system that sustains working relationships and satisfies interpersonal needs. (2) Social relationships at work differ from those in the family or in adolescent groups in that they are based on concern for the task, tend to be less permanent and less intimate, and often do not operate outside the work situation. (3) The boundaries of work-groups are vague, and these groups may in fact consist of networks. (4) In addition to one or more informal leaders, there may be a leader of the opposition.

Committees, Problem-Solving and Creative Groups

This kind of group does its work entirely by talking, and consequently is not found in any species apart from man. Committees are concerned with taking decisions and solving problems; there are other kinds of working group, for example groups of research workers, who are more concerned with the creative solution of problems. There is no sharp division between the two kinds of group.

Committees are small groups of a rather special kind; while their devotion to problem solving and their degree of formality make them different from other groups, these features are found to some extent in most other groups too. . . .

Interaction in committees is unlike interaction in most other groups. It is primarily verbal; furthermore it consists of a number of carefully delivered utterances, in the formal mode of speech. The 12 categories of the Bales system (Bales, 1950) were devised to record interaction in groups of this kind. As well as pure task categories—asking for and giving opinions and suggestions, it includes socioemotional categories—agreeing and disagreeing, showing tension, showing antagonism and solidarity. As with work-groups interpersonal relations are established and maintained during the execution of the task. There is considerable use of non-verbal signals. To speak it may be necessary to catch the chairman's eye, and the regulation of who speaks and for how long is achieved by eye-movements, head-nods and smiles. Comments on what A is saying may be indicated by B's facial and gestural signals; these may be directed to A, or to another listener C. When the non-verbal channel proves inadequate, written messages may be passed along the table. To be an effective committee member requires special skills. These include squaring other people before the meeting, studying the papers before the meeting, and the usual social skills of persuasion and handling groups. There also appear to be skills unique to committees: a member should not seem to be emotionally involved with an issue, but be concerned with what will be acceptable to the others. A chairman should do his [or her] best to come to solutions which are acceptable to all members, rather than coming to majority decisions.

The activities of a committee are problem solving and decision taking. These terms refer to two different elements—arriving at new solutions to problems, and coming to agreements. These are rather different matters which are, however, closely bound up together in committee work. Coming to an agreement has . . . been considered in connection with conformity; each agenda item produces in miniature a norm-formation situation. The item will be more or less closely related to more general norms held by the group, and to issues on which subgroups have their own views. The problem-solving process can be divided into two stages—information exchange and the study of hypotheses. Thibaut and Kelley (1959) discuss the conditions under which information is offered and accepted in groups, and what happens when the information is complementary, conflicting or simply heterogeneous. A number of experiments have been carried out in which the task of the group consists in putting together information related in these ways. In real committees this is certainly part of the story, but information exchange is usually followed by the study of suggestions and is affected by conformity processes. There is a great deal of experimental work in this area, of which one sample will be given. Freedman and Sears (1965), reviewing experiments by themselves and others, show that people do *not* just seek information that supports their existing views, as dissonance theory would seem to predict, but actually want to find out the facts. Thibaut and Kelley (op. cit.) argue that both individuals and groups start to engage in problem-solving activity when they think that they may be able to deal with the external world to better advantage. . . .

T-Groups and Therapy Groups

Finally we turn to a kind of group which did not exist until psychologists invented it. Just as physicists study particles created by special experimental techniques so it is of interest to study the forms social interaction *can* take under quite new conditions. In fact the processes of feedback and analysis of the group found in this setting also take place, although with less intensity, in other groups too. On the other hand these groups are very different from natural groups in a number of ways, so that the findings cannot simply be generalised to other kinds of group. There has been a certain shift of interest away from laboratory groups towards T-groups (cf. Mann *et al.*, 1967), simply because the latter last longer and can be studied in greater detail. Apart from the limited generality of the findings it should be pointed out that most of these studies are essentially clinical investigations of a rather small number of groups (cf. Stock, 1964).

In most T-groups, about 12 trainees meet with a trainer for a number of 2 hour sessions; they may meet once a week, or more frequently for up to two weeks. The Harvard version has 20–30 members. The leader introduces himself, explains that he is there to help the members study the group, and then takes a passive role and leaves the group to get on with this task as best it can. From time to time he will intervene in various ways: (1) he shows how to make constructive and nonevaluative comments on the behaviour of members; (2) he shows how to receive such comments non-defensively, and learn from them; (3) he makes interpretations, i.e., explains what he thinks is happening, interpersonally, in the group; (4) he discusses the relevance and application of the group experiences to behaviour in real-life situations; (5) he tries to teach the members a more cooperative and less authoritarian attitude to people in authority. In addition to the T-group sessions proper there are sometimes lectures, role-playing and other ancillary training experiences (cf. Bradford, Gibb and Benne, 1964).

Therapy groups consist of a psychiatrist and usually 6–9 mental patients. The main differences from T-groups are that: (1) the members are emotionally disturbed and at a lower level of social competence, often suffering from real interpersonal difficulties; (2) the content of conversation is the actual symptoms or difficulties of group members; (3) the therapist creates an atmosphere of acceptance for sexual and aggressive material, but makes sure that the tension level does not get too high; (4) there is a greater gap between leader and group members—the former is not simply a more experienced member of the group; (5) the behaviour of members in the group situation is used to diagnose basic personality disturbances, rather than indicating their level of social competence (Powdermaker and Frank, 1953; Foulkes and Anthony, 1957). . . .

The 'task' of T-groups, like that of committees, consists of conversation, and is difficult to separate from 'interaction.' However, some kinds of conversation are regarded as more relevant to the task—conversation which is concerned with the interaction and relationships of members of the group, and about the symptoms of members of therapy groups. The goal to be attained is insight and understanding of group processes and emotional problems respectively. An important sub-goal is the formation of a sufficiently cohesive group for this understanding to develop in the group setting—i.e., the internal and external goals are closely intertwined (Tuckman, 1965). Unlike committees, however, these groups have no agenda, and proceed in a largely undirected and rambling manner, the leader taking whatever opportunities he can for explaining various phenomena. The content of the conversation is most unusual; language in the natural world is usually about external matters, and other people, rather than about relations between speaker and hearer, or about embarrassing personal matters. This kind of task is emotionally arousing and awkward, and for these reasons is often avoided in periods of 'flight' from the task—by making jokes, talking about other matters, and silence. . . .

The social interaction in T-groups can be thought of as including the task activity. Various classification schemes have been devised to deal with it, which between them provide some account of the forms interaction takes. . . . It should be added that the general atmosphere and flow of interaction are very different in these groups from those in the other groups which we have considered. While committees are formal, and groups of adolescents are relaxed and intimate, T-groups and therapy groups are tense and awkward. Both T-group and therapy group practitioners maintain that some degree of emotionality is necessary for any fundamental changes of behaviour to occur. Interaction sequences are reported in these groups which may be unique to them, for example: (a) an intensification of the process of becoming aware of the self-image from the reactions of others—which are here unusually frank and uninhibited; (b) obtaining insight into oneself through the close observation and study of another person with similar attributes or problems; (c) the 'condenser' phenomenon, in which interaction loosens group resistances, and common emotions, normally repressed, are suddenly released (Foulkes and Anthony, 1957). . . .

References

Bales, R. F. (1950). *Interaction Process Analysis,* Addison-Wesley, Cambridge, Mass.

Bradford, L. P., Gibb, J. R., and Benne, K. D. (1964). *T-group Theory and Laboratory Method,* Wiley, New York.

Erikson, E. H. (1956). 'The problem of ego-identity,' *American Journal of Psychoanalysis,* **4,** 56–121.

Fleming, C. M. (1963). *Adolescence,* Routledge & Kegan Paul, London.

Foulkes, S. H., and Anthony, E. J. (1957). *Group Psychotherapy: The Psychoanalytic Approach,* Penguin, London.

Freedman, J. L., and Sears, D. O. (1965). 'Selective exposure,' in L. Berkowitz (ed.), *Advances in Experimental Social Psychology,* Vol. 2, Academic Press, New York.

Goffman, E. (1956). *The Presentation of Self in Everyday Life,* Edinburgh University Press, Edinburgh.

Henry, A. F., and Short, J. F. (1954). *Suicide and Homicide,* Free Press, Glencoe, Ill.

Mann, R. D., *et al.* (1967). *Interpersonal Styles and Group Development,* Wiley, New York.

Murdock, G. P. (1949). *Social Structure,* Macmillan, New York.

Muuss, R. E. (1962). *Theories of Adolescence,* Random House, New York.

Parsons, T., and Bales, R. F. (1955), *Family, Socialization, and Interaction Process,* Free Press, Glencoe, Ill.

Powdermaker, F. B., and Frank, J. D. (1953). *Group Psychotherapy,* Harvard University Press, Cambridge, MA.

Schmuck, R., and Lohman, A. (1965). Peer relations and personality development. Institute for Social Research, University of Michigan, Ann Arbor, MI. Unpublished manuscript.

Sears, R. R., Maccoby, E. E., and Levin, H. (1957). *Patterns of Child Rearing,* Row, Peterson, New York.

Sherif, M., and Sherif, C. W. (1964). *Reference Groups,* Harper, New York.

Spiegel, J. P. (1956). 'Interpersonal influences within the family,' in B. Schaffner (ed.), *Group Processes,* Josiah Macy Foundation, New York.

Stock, D. (1964). 'A survey of research on T-groups,' in L. P. Bradford, J. R. Gibb, and K. D. Benne (eds.), *T-Group Theory and Laboratory Method,* Wiley, New York.

Thibaut, J. W., and Kelley, H. H. (1959). *The Social Psychology of Groups,* Wiley, New York.

Tuckman, B. W. (1965). 'Developmental sequence in small groups,' *Psychological Bulletin,* **63,** 384–399.

Van Zelst, R. H. (1952). 'Validation of a sociometric regrouping procedure,' *Journal of Abnormal and Social Psychology,* **47,** 299–301.

Zajonc, R. B. (1963). 'Social facilitation,' *Science,* **149,** 269–274.

Group Composition and Group Cohesiveness

Marvin E. Shaw

Groups are composed of individuals, each having his or her own unique characteristics and ways of behaving. Although these idiosyncratic factors influence group interaction independently of the actions of others in the group, the more important effects are those produced by the *relationships* among the characteristics of group members. We will be concerned, then, with the effects of each member's characteristics when considered in relation to the characteristics of other group members. Historically, group composition effects have been studied under at least three different labels: cohesiveness, compatibility, and homogeneity/heterogeneity of group membership.[1] We will try to summarize the findings in each of these areas of research.

Group Cohesiveness

Group cohesiveness refers to the degree to which the group 'hangs together' as a unit. Although cohesiveness has been defined and measured in many different ways, the definition proposed by Festinger is probably the most widely accepted one: group cohesiveness is 'the resultant of all the forces acting on the members to remain in the group' (Festinger, 1950, p. 274). Obviously, many 'forces' may act on an individual to influence him or her to remain in the group, but the force most commonly studied in research is interpersonal attraction. In this sense, cohesiveness may be represented by the number, strengths, and patterns of interpersonal attractions within the group. Research on the consequences of cohesiveness for group process has revealed several important effects. These will be presented and discussed in terms of plausible hypotheses, i.e., hypotheses that appear to be valid in view of the evidence currently available.

Hypothesis 1   *Intragroup communication is more extensive in high-cohesive than in low-cohesive groups*

It is not surprising that persons who like each other engage in more verbal interaction than persons who dislike each other. Research findings are consistent in showing that the amount of interaction is greater in groups composed

From *Small Groups and Social Interaction,* Volume 1. Edited by H. H. Blumberg, A. P. Hare, V. Kent and M. Davies. © 1983 by John Wiley and Sons, Ltd. Reproduced by permission of John Wiley and Sons, Ltd. Marvin E. Shaw is affiliated with the Department of Psychology, University of Florida.

of individuals who are highly attracted to the group than in groups composed of members who are less attracted to or are repelled by the group (Back, 1951; Lott and Lott, 1961).

Hypothesis 2   *Interactions are more positively oriented in high-cohesive than in low-cohesive groups*

Members of highly cohesive groups tend to be friendly and cooperative, and to engage in behaviors that facilitate group integration. Members of low-cohesive groups tend to function as individuals rather than as group members, and when they do enact group-oriented behaviors they tend to be aggressive and uncooperative (Back, 1951; Shaw and Shaw, 1962).

Hypothesis 3   *High-cohesive groups exert greater influence over their members than do low-cohesive groups*

Interpersonal attraction is a source of social power; consequently, members of high-cohesive groups may be expected to have more power over others in the group and therefore more influence over each other. Evidence supporting this expectation derives from several studies which show that: (a) members of high-cohesive groups respond to attempted influence by other group members more than members of low-cohesive groups (Berkowitz, 1954; Schachter *et al.*, 1951); (b) members of high-cohesive dyads change their opinions in the direction of the opinion of others more than do members of low-cohesive dyads (Back, 1951); and (c) members of high-cohesive groups conform to majority judgments more than members of low-cohesive groups (Bovard, 1951; Lott and Lott, 1961; Wyer, 1966). However, one study found that high-cohesive groups conform more than low-cohesive groups only when conformity facilitates group effectiveness (Sakurai, 1975).

Hypothesis 4   *High-cohesive groups are more effective than low-cohesive groups in achieving their respective goals*

The relationship between cohesiveness and group performance has been widely investigated, but the findings have been less than completely consistent. Laboratory studies have typically shown only small increments in favor of high-cohesive groups (Hoogstraten and Vorst, 1978; Schacter *et al.*, 1951) or no difference in the productivity of high- and low-cohesive groups (Berkowitz, 1954), whereas results of field studies generally show that high-cohesive groups are more effective than low-cohesive groups (Goodacre, 1951; Van Zelst, 1952a, b). Still other studies show that cohesiveness may be associated with either high or low productivity, depending on the extent to which group members have adopted high productivity as a goal for the group (Seashore, 1954; Shaw and Shaw, 1962).The best interpretation seems to be that high-cohesive groups are more effective than low-cohesive groups in achieving whatever goals group members have established or accepted for the group.

Hypothesis 5   *Members of high-cohesive groups are usually better satisfied with the group than are members of low-cohesive groups*

Members of high-cohesive groups are motivated to interact with others in the group and to achieve group goals; therefore, their efforts should increase group functioning and high member satisfaction. Research data from both field studies (Gross, 1954; Van Zelst, 1952b) and laboratory experiments (Exline, 1957) support the proposition that members of high-cohesive groups are better satisfied with the group and its products than members of low-cohesive groups.

Group Compatibility

Group compatibility has been analyzed most completely by Schutz (1958). In his words 'compatibility is a property of a relation between two or more persons, between an individual and a role, or between an individual and a task situation that leads to mutual satisfaction of interpersonal needs and harmonious coexistence' (p. 105). Compatibility may be linked to cohesiveness, but not necessarily so. Typically, compatibility is estimated by means of the six interpersonal need scales developed by Schutz. These scales measure the extent to which a person desires to express inclusion, control, and affection needs toward others, and the degree to which the person wants others to express those needs in his or her presence. Two persons are compatible when the expressed behaviors of each are in accord with the wanted behaviors of the other. Theoretically, compatible groups should be more productive and their members better satisfied than incompatible groups. Research data generally support these expectations.

Hypothesis 6   *Compatible groups are more effective in achieving group goals than incompatible groups*

Although there have been some failures to find a significant difference between compatible and incompatible groups, the bulk of the evidence indicates that groups that are compatible with respect to interpersonal needs function more smoothly, devote less of their time to group maintenance, and are therefore more effective than incompatible groups (Reddy and Byrnes, 1972; Sapolsky, 1960; Schutz, 1958).

Hypothesis 7　*Members of compatible groups are better satisfied with the group than members of incompatible groups*

The studies cited to support hypothesis 6 also support hypothesis 7. Other studies indicate that members of incompatible groups experience greater anxiety and more general dissatisfaction with their group than members of compatible groups (Cohen, 1956; Fry, 1965; Smelser, 1961).

Homogeneity/Heterogeneity

Group composition investigated under the heading 'homogeneity/heterogeneity' differ from the types we have considered thus far in that the relation under consideration is similarity/dissimilarity. Again, homogeneity/heterogeneity may be linked to cohesiveness and/or compatibility, but these types of group composition are not necessarily correlated. For instance, persons who are similar with respect to amount of interaction or exchange that each desires are compatible, but persons who are dissimilar with respect to control needs (desires to control others or to be controlled by others) are also compatible.

Obviously, members of a group may be homogeneous or heterogeneous with respect to many different characteristics, and the degree to which group process is affected by this aspect of group composition may depend on the particular characteristic(s) being considered. The effects of homogeneity/heterogeneity have been investigated in at least the following areas: abilities, sex, race, and personality.

Abilities

Interest in ability grouping probably derived initially from educational concerns, revealed most clearly in the long-standing controversy about the merits of homogeneous ability grouping in the classroom. This controversy continues even today, although the evidence seems to support the proposition that students learn more in heterogeneous ability groups (Goldberg *et al.,* 1966). More carefully controlled research on small groups suggests the following hypothesis.

Hypothesis 8　*Other things being equal, groups composed of members having diverse abilities that are relevant to the task perform more effectively than groups composed of members having similar abilities*

Group performance usually calls for diverse activities, each of which requires specific abilities that are more likely to be found in heterogeneous ability groups. Hypothesis 8 is generally supported by research data (Goldman, 1965; Laughlin *et al.,* 1969).

Sex

Stereotypes concerning the characteristics and behavior of men and women suggest that sex composition should be an important determinant of group behavior, and the controversy over the Equal Rights Amendment provided an impetus for research in this area. Several studies support the following hypothesis.

Hypothesis 9   *The interaction styles of men and women are affected differently by the sex composition of the group*

Research data reveal that men are more personally oriented, address individuals more often (as opposed to group), and speak about self more frequently in mixed-sex than in same-sex groups, whereas women become less dominant in mixed-sex groups (Aries, 1976). It has also been found that same-sex and mixed-sex dyads are affected differently by social context (face-to-face v. apart) in bargaining situations (Vallacher *et al.,* 1979). Mixed-sex dyads reached agreement more quickly when they bargained face-to-face than when they bargained apart, whereas same-sex groups were not affected by the social context. Presumably, members of mixed-sex groups are less certain about their partner's expected responses and need cues about the other person that can be derived from face-to-face interaction.

Hypothesis 10   *Mixed-sex groups are more effective than same-sex groups*

Direct evidence for this hypothesis derives from a study by Ruhe (1978). He attributed this difference in effectiveness to differences in the leader's behavior. In the same-sex groups, the amount of disagreement and antagonistic behavior displayed by the leader was inversely related to group effectiveness, whereas no such relationship was observed in the mixed-sex groups. This interpretation appears to be consistent with the finding that leaders of both sexes address more directive behavior toward members of their own sex (Eskilson and Wiley, 1976).

Hypothesis 11   *Group members conform more in mixed-sex than in same-sex groups*

Members of mixed-sex groups appear to be more concerned about interpersonal relations than the task, whereas members of same-sex groups are more concerned about the task. Since conformity usually means decreased accuracy with respect to the task, members of same-sex groups are less likely to conform to group pressure. Research data generally support the hypothesis (Reitan and Shaw, 1964), although there are some inconsistent findings (Tuddenham *et al.,* 1958).

Race

The question of racial composition of groups has become more significant with the advent of desegregation and affirmative action, but there still are relatively few reliable data on its effects. However, the following hypothesis is plausible.

Hypothesis 12   *Racial heterogeneity elicits interpersonal tension which is reflected in the feelings and behaviors of group members*

Research findings indicate that in racially mixed groups blacks talk less than whites, they often are less assertive, reveal a greater expectancy of failure, and are sometimes less efficient than whites (Delbecq and Kaplan, 1968; Katz *et al.,* 1965; Lefcourt and Ladwig, 1965; Ruhe and Allen, 1977; Ruhe and Eatman, 1977). These behaviors may or may not affect group performance.

Personality

Although homogeneity/heterogeneity of group membership with respect to personality characteristics may be expected to have important consequences for group interaction, reliable research is very limited. However, available data support the following hypothesis.

Hypothesis 13   *Groups composed of members who are heterogeneous with respect to personality profiles perform more effectively than groups composed of members who are homogeneous with respect to personality profiles*

Two experiments involving a variety of tasks revealed that heterogeneous groups performed better, both quantitatively and qualitatively, than homogeneous groups, where homogeneity/heterogeneity was based on the Guilford-Zimmerman Temperament Survey (Hoffman, 1959; Hoffman and Maier, 1961).

References

Aries, E. (1976). 'Interaction patterns and themes of male, female, and mixed groups,' *Small Group Behavior,* **7**, 7–18.

Back, K. W. (1951). 'Influence through social communication,' *Journal of Abnormal and Social Psychology,* **46**, 9–23.

Berkowitz, L. (1954). 'Group standards, cohesiveness, and productivity,' *Human Relations,* **7,** 509–519.

Bovard, E. W. (1951). 'Group structure and perception,' *Journal of Abnormal and Social Psychology,* **46,** 398–405.

Cohen, A. R. (1956), 'Experimental effects of ego-defense preference on interpersonal relations', *Journal of Abnormal and Social Psychology,* **52,** 19–27.

Delbecq, A. L., and Kaplan, S. J. (1968). 'The myth of the indigenous community leader within the war on poverty,' *Academy of Management Journal,* **11,** 11–25.

Eskilson, A., and Wiley, M. G. (1976). 'Sex composition and leadership in small groups,' *Sociometry,* **39** 183–194.

Exline, R. V. (1957). 'Group climate as a factor in the relevance and accuracy of social perception,' *Journal of Abnormal and Social Psychology,* **55,** 382–388.

Festinger, L. (1950). 'Informal social communication,' *Psychological Review,* **57,** 271–282.

Fry, C. L. (1965). 'Personality and acquisition factors in the development of coordination strategy,' *Journal of Personality and Social Psychology,* **2,** 403–407.

Goldberg, M. L., Passow, A. H., and Justman, J. (1966). *The Effects of Ability Grouping,* Teachers College Press, New York.

Goldman, M. (1965). 'A comparison of individual and group performance for varying combinations of initial ability,' *Journal of Personality and Social Psychology,* **1,** 210–216.

Goodacre, D. M., III (1951). 'The use of a sociometric test as a predictor of combat unit effectiveness,' *Sociometry,* **14,** 148–152.

Gross, E. (1954). 'Primary functions of the small group,' *American Journal of Sociology,* **60,** 24–30.

Hoffman, L. R. (1959). 'Homogeneity of member personality and its effect on group problem-solving,' *Journal of Abnormal and Social Psychology,* **58,** 27–32.

Hoffman, L. R., and Maier, N. R. F. (1961). 'Quality and acceptance of problem solutions by members of homogeneous and heterogeneous groups,' *Journal of Abnormal and Social Psychology,* **62,** 401–407.

Hoogstraten, J., and Vorst, H. C. M. (1978). 'Group cohesion, task performance, and the experimenter expectancy effect,' *Human Relations,* **31,** 939–956.

Katz, I., Roberts, S. O., and Robinson, J. M. (1965). 'Effects of difficulty, race of administrator, and instructions on Negro digit-symbol performance,' *Journal of Personality and Social Psychology,* **2,** 53–59.

Laughlin, P. R., Branch, L. G., and Johnson, H. H. (1969). 'Individual versus triadic performance on a unidimensional complementary task as a function of initial ability level,' *Journal of Personality and Social Psychology,* **12,** 144–150.

Lefcourt, H. M., and Ladwig, G. W. (1965). 'The effect of reference groups upon Negroes' task persistence in a biracial competitive game,' *Journal of Personality and Social Psychology,* **1,** 668–671.

Lott, A. J., and Lott, B. E. (1961). 'Group cohesiveness, communication level, and conformity,' *Journal of Abnormal and Social Psychology,* **62,** 408–412.

Reddy, W. B., and Byrnes, A. (1972). 'The effects of interpersonal group composition on the problem solving behavior of middle managers,' *Journal of Applied Psychology,* **56,** 516–517.

Reitan, H. T., and Shaw, M. E. (1964). 'Group membership, sex-composition of the group, and conformity behavior,' *Journal of Social Psychology,* **64,** 45–51.

Ruhe, J. A. (1978). 'Effect of leader sex and leader behavior on group problem-solving,' *Proceedings of the American Institute for Decision Sciences, Northeast Division,* May, pp. 123–127.

Ruhe, J. A., and Allen, W. R. (1977). 'Differences and similarities between black and white leaders,' *Proceedings of the American Institute for Decision Sciences, Northeast Division,* April, pp. 30–35.

Ruhe, J. A., and Eatman, J. (1977). 'Effects of racial composition on small work groups,' *Small Group Behavior*, **8**, 479–486.

Sakurai, M. M. (1975). 'Small group cohesiveness and detrimental conformity,' *Sociometry*, **38**, 340–357.

Sapolsky, A. (1960). 'Effect of interpersonal relationships upon verbal conditioning,' *Journal of Abnormal and Social Psychology*, **60**, 241–246.

Schachter, S., Ellertson, N., McBride, D., and Gregory, D. (1951). 'An experimental study of cohesiveness and productivity,' *Human Relations*, **4**, 229–238.

Schutz, W. C. (1958). *FIRO: A three dimensional theory of interpersonal behavior*, Rinehart, New York.

Seashore, S. E. (1954). *Group cohesiveness in the industrial work group*, University of Michigan Press, Ann Arbor.

Shaw, M. E., and Shaw, L. M. (1962). 'Some effects of sociometric group upon learning in a second grade classroom,' *Journal of Social Psychology*, **57**, 453–458.

Smelser, W. T. (1961). 'Dominance as a factor in achievement and perception in cooperative problem solving interactions,' *Journal of Abnormal and Social Psychology*, **62**, 535–542.

Tuddenham, R. D., MacBridge, P., and Zahn, V. (1958). 'The influence of the sex composition of the group upon yielding to a distorted norm,' *Journal of Psychology*, **46**, 243–251.

Vallacher, R. R., Callahan-Levy, C. M., and Messé, L. A. (1979). 'Sex effects of bilateral bargaining as a function of interpersonal context,' *Personality and Social Psychology Bulletin*, **5**, 104–108.

Van Zelst, R. H. (1952a). 'Sociometrically selected work teams increase production,' *Personnel Psychology*, **5**, 175–186.

Van Zelst, R. H. (1952b). 'Validation of a sociometric regrouping procedure,' *Journal of Abnormal and Social Psychology*, **47**, 299–301.

Wyer, R. S., Jr (1966). 'Effects of incentive to perform well, group attraction, and group acceptance on conformity in a judgmental task,' *Journal of Personality and Social Psychology*, **4**, 21–26.

Note

1. A more extensive consideration of group composition effects may be found in M. E. Shaw (1981). *Group Dynamics*, 3rd edn. McGraw-Hill, New York.

Group Interaction Via Communication Rules

Susan B. Shimanoff

And the only way to avoid playing the game is never to belong to a club, class, set, or trade union. As soon as you do, you're accepting someone else's rules, and as soon as you do that, you start looking down on the other chap with different rules. (Bingham, 1978)

They are playing a game. They are playing at not playing a game. If I show them I see they are, I shall break the rules and they will punish me. I must play their game, of not seeing I see the game. (Laing, 1970, p. 1)

Once you know the rules, it's easy to predict opponents' moves, at least easier than when you don't even know you're in a game where explicit rules govern the play. . . .[And] you can't change a game until you can play by the rules that exist. (Harragan, 1977, pp. 35, 383)

Rules indicate what behaviors a group considers appropriate or inappropriate. The above quotations illustrate several important ingredients in the relationship between rules and groups: (1) rules are inherent aspects of group interaction, (2) rules are used to evaluate both members and nonmembers, (3) group members are not always consciously aware of their rules and are often reluctant to acknowledge them, (4) members who know the rules can better predict how others in the group will behave than those members who do not know the rules, and (5) the rules of the group are usually changed through group interaction by members who know how to manipulate the current rules.

Regardless of whether group interactions are predominantly cooperative or competitive, they all require communication rules. Without rules, coordination among individuals in both cooperative and competitive interactions becomes impossible. For example, communication rules restrict who speaks when on what topics. If all members spoke at the same time, members could not understand one another; and if each member independently decided on a different topic to discuss or procedures to follow, decision making would break down.

Rules may be explicit (formally stated) or implicit (unstated, yet known tacitly by group members). Implicit rules are neither written nor openly discussed and yet, even without this explicit acknowledgement, group members conform to these rules. For some members compliance with implicit rules may

Susan B. Shimanoff is affiliated with the Department of Speech Communication, San Francisco State University.

begin by the simple mirroring of what other groups members say and do. Deviations from or questions about typical behaviors in a group may make members consciously aware of previously implicit rules.

Communication rules govern various aspects of group interaction. To illustrate the scope and impact of communication rules in groups, four topics will be discussed: (1) types of rules, (2) emergence of rules, (3) functions and outcomes of rules, and (4) factors influencing rule compliance. These four topics will be followed by suggestions on how to identify rules.

Types of Rules

Rules may apply to any behavior groups wish to encourage or discourage and they may vary from group to group. However, most communication rules can be classified in one of seven categories: (1) who says, (2) what, (3) to whom, (4) when, (5) with what duration and frequency, (6) through what medium, and (7) by what decision-procedure. Examples of each of these types will be given.

Who Says

Groups often assign particular communication roles to individual members. Sometimes the rules regarding these roles are explicit (e.g., the president will open the meeting, the secretary will read the minutes of the previous meeting, the treasurer will report on income and expenditures, and so forth), but at other times, these rules are implicit. Implicit rules most often come to the group's attention when they are broken. For example, a group may come to expect a particular member always to speak first, to exude enthusiasm, or to break the tension by telling a joke. If that member does not perform the expected behavior, then someone in the group may say something like "Pat, why haven't you said anything? We count on you to get us started," or "What do you mean, you're depressed? You can't be depressed. You're our inspiration. If you don't have it together, how can we be expected to succeed?" or "Chris, you're slipping. Where's one of your jokes? We could sure use one now." These remarks indicate that the absence of the expected behavior is a violation of implicit rules requiring certain types of messages from particular group members.

What

Groups regulate what members say and do by sanctioning some messages as appropriate and others as inappropriate. For example, a large faculty organization required all members to state their names and affiliations before speaking. Ostensibly, this rule was meant to acquaint members with one another. Restricting what is said in a group may be used to facilitate the group's goals. For example, in Overeaters Anonymous meetings, members were permitted to talk about food in generic terms (e.g., refined carbohydrates, dessert, snack food), but they were instructed not to talk about specific foods (e.g., pizza, twinkies, fritos). This rule is based on the assumption that talking about specific foods might set up a craving for those foods in a way that general references would not, and that such talk would thus be contrary to the group's goals.

The acceptability of certain types of language may also vary from group to group. For example, in one workshop for worship leaders profanities and obscenities were implicitly prohibited. A member who accidentally broke this rule immediately apologized to the group. In contrast, gang members are expected to surpass the obscenity of the previous speaker; a speaker who utters a weaker one is criticized by the group (Labov, 1972).

The above examples concern verbal communication, but groups may also constrain the nonverbal behavior of its members. For example, some companies have explicit or implicit dress codes. Groups may also vary on how and where members should sit. While in some groups (e.g., "rap" groups) sitting on the floor is the only acceptable location, because sitting in a chair is viewed as being aloof; in other groups (e.g., a board meeting), anyone sitting on the floor would be viewed as peculiar. Rules, then, constrain what group members say and do, and such rules are used to interpret what one's actions mean (e.g., rules determine if sitting in a chair means one is aloof or one is well-mannered).

To Whom

Groups establish patterns for who talks to whom. In some cases, members are expected to address only the person presiding over the meeting; in others, one addresses the entire group; and, in still others, individual speakers may select who the next speaker will be (Sacks, Schegloff, and Jefferson, 1974). Elizabeth Aries (1976) found, for example, that in all the male groups she studied, members spoke to the group as a whole, while speakers in all female groups addressed their remarks to specific persons. Different rules regarding to whom remarks should be addressed may account for the differences between the male and female groups. The all male groups might have had a rule requiring that all remarks be addressed to the group as a whole, on the grounds that such a procedure was more democratic by allowing anyone who wanted to speak to do so. In contrast, the all female groups may have viewed addressing specific individuals as personal and as a way to get everyone to participate, and therefore had a rule encouraging members to call on one another.

Unfortunately, Aries only reported observed regularities. To determine conclusively whether the patterns were prescribed by rules one also needs evidence that the groups considered the observed patterns appropriate, and deviations from them inappropriate (Shimanoff, 1980). Nonetheless, the example illustrates that groups can develop rules regarding to whom remarks should be addressed and that very different rules can be justified as being in the group's best interest.

When

At least two types of rules are related to time constraints in groups: those concerning who speaks when, and those concerning what is said when. Groups structure when a person speaks through explicit or implicit turn-taking rules (rules specifying who speaks after whom). Turn-taking rules may be based on seating arrangements, status, who addresses whom, or who speaks first. These rules may vary across groups or change within one group across tasks.

Groups also structure when certain kinds of remarks are appropriate, with either an explicit or implicit agenda. Adherence to a formal agenda requires that topics be discussed one after the other in the order they appear on the agenda. In other groups the agenda may be implicit. For example, in one Bible study group that utilized visualization different types of communicative behavior were appropriate at different times. Members were expected to remain silent until the visualization exercise was completed, at which time the experience was discussed. During the visualization, questions were asked, but members were expected to reflect quietly on their answers, saving their comments for the discussion phase. At one meeting, a newcomer arrived. No one explained this rule to the newcomer, so that when questions were asked during the visualization phase, she answered them aloud. From her perspective, she was being supportive by facilitating discussion, but the group saw her behavior as rude and disruptive.

This example illustrates several characteristics of the relationship between rules and groups: (1) groups may determine when certain types of talk are appropriate or inappropriate, (2) violating a group's rules will often result in the deviator being evaluated negatively, and (3) the rules of groups vary—in most other groups, failing to respond to a leader's questions would have been perceived as being uncooperative rather than appropriate as it was in the Bible study group.

With What Duration and Frequency

The number of times one speaks and the length of a speaker's utterance may also be governed by group rules. For example, a group may limit its members to only three turns at speaking on any one topic or require a member to wait until all members have had an opportunity to speak before speaking again.

Some groups also structure how long one can speak. This often exists in groups where lengthy debate is expected to occur, but such rules may be used in other groups to limit the amount of time spent on any one task.

In one interpersonal support group, for example, members were limited to a maximum of three minutes of "check-in" time (to indicate how they were and what had happened to them since the group last met). This rule was instituted so that the group could have enough time to discuss its chosen topic for the evening in depth. The group, however, also had a provision for deviating from this rule in a prescribed manner. During one's check-in, one could indicate a need for more time to discuss a personal problem. Such requests were reserved for times when a member was particularly troubled and needed extra support from the group. Since these requests were perceived as consistent with the group's primary goal, they were always honored. This example points out another feature of rules; that is, some rules supersede other rules. In this case, the three minute rule is superseded by a rule to give more time to members who indicate a strong need for additional support.

Through What Medium

Some groups prefer to receive all of the information and arguments on an issue in writing before their deliberation; others prefer that nothing appear in writing until a decision is reached. When a group member deviates from the group's preferences, that member may be ostracized.

In one group, for example, the members felt that all issues should be discussed face-to-face. This rule reflected the group's perception of itself as open, friendly, and flexible. Written messages from members were interpreted as cowardly (afraid to meet one's opponent face-to-face) and hostile (because friendly discussions occur face-to-face). One member refused to follow the group's implicit rule. He viewed written messages as more complete and courteous. He reasoned that with written messages all the issues could be detailed without interruption and members could read them at their leisure rather than be interrupted unexpectedly by a personal visit. He also felt that it was useful to have a permanent record of messages sent and received. Each written document by this member increased the group's hostility toward him. This rule violation along with his deviation from other group rules resulted in his being perceived as belligerent, and the group increasingly ostracized him.

The point here is not that a group's interpretation of written versus oral messages is more correct than a member's. The assigned meaning to the two media by the group and by the member could have been reversed and the outcome would have been the same. The example is meant to illustrate that groups may have implicit rules regarding the medium used and that these rules may be used to govern and evaluate the behavior of group members.

By What Decision-Procedure

One of the most explicit rules used by groups is a formal procedure by which final decisions are made. Rules for decision making range from requiring unanimous to majority agreement to dictatorial rule. Under unanimous agreement, groups must continue to discuss an issue until every member agrees to the decision; under majority agreement, a majority vote determines the outcome; and under dictatorial rule, the leader may consult with other members, but the ultimate decision is made by the leader (e.g., supervisor, coach). Decision procedures that require less agreement than unanimity, but more than majority, are also used by some groups.

Which decision-procedure a group uses can be an important symbol for group members. In one group, members disagreed over whether to require unanimity or to use majority vote to make decisions. The sub-group that favored unanimity thought the majority-vote coalition was more concerned with expediency than the quality of decisions or group cohesion. The majority-vote coalition, on the other hand, thought that the unanimity sub-group was standing in the way of progress and prolonging discussions unnecessarily. Ironically, the group had a history of using a unanimity rule, so that a change to majority rule required unanimous consent, and thus the change never took place.

Summary

The above examples illustrate that groups may develop rules for all facets of communicative behavior within a group. It should be further noted that groups create rules for governing relationships with subcommittees and with persons or institutions outside the group (e.g., clients, other groups, the government). Since the communication rules of one group may be different from those of another group, it is useful to know how specific rules develop or emerge.

Emergence of Rules

Rules may be developed in a variety of ways. Some rules are leader imposed and others are group generated. This section will concentrate on the latter. Some rules are culturally based; that is, they would apply to any group within a particular culture (e.g., rules governing the order of certain utterances, such as, answers should directly follow questions). Other rules are more limited in their scope, in that they apply in only certain social settings (e.g., rules governing classroom as compared to cocktail party interaction), and still other rules are limited to a specific group (e.g., rules governing specific rituals unique to a particular group).

When group members come together for the first time, they bring with them past experiences and expectations regarding cultural and social rules and rules for specific groups they assume may be similar to this new group. It is out of these experiences and expectations as well as the unique interaction of a particular group that a group formulates its rules.

Members may consciously discuss and explicitly delineate its group rules in initial sessions, but, more commonly, the rules evolve over time. Members often assume initially everyone shares their standards of appropriateness (after all, we endow rules with a sense of "rightness"). Many rules develop without the group's conscious awareness. Members begin performing some action in a particular way, establishing a precedent which ultimately becomes a rule to govern future actions. Such rules may be implicit, and group members may become conscious of them only when someone breaks the rules, a newcomer questions the procedure, or members compare procedures in their group to procedures in another group. Therefore, rules are often only explicitly developed when members' expectations are violated.

A violation is likely to prompt a discussion about what behaviors most effectively facilitate group goals. For example, both the rule "don't mention specific foods" and the rule "limit check-in to three minutes" developed as a result of individual and groups needs. In the former case, some members were disturbed by talk about specific foods and because such talk potentially interfered with group goals, it was prohibited. What was an implicit rule for some members became an explicit rule for all members. The time limit on check-in was instituted because members spent so much time on "chit-chat" that intimate disclosures never occurred, and group members considered such disclosures essential to its supportive function. Groups, then, primarily develop rules to maintain and promote the goals of the group and to coordinate group interaction. However, communication rules have many other functions within groups, and rule compliance/noncompliance produces various outcomes.

Functions and Outcomes

In discussing various types of communication rules, several functions of rules were also identified. For example, rules regulate, restrict, and coordinate group interaction and perpetuate group objectives (e.g., turn-taking rules, the Bible's study rule about discussion, or Overeater's Anonymous's rule about reference to specific foods). The rules of a group are also used to attach meaning to symbolic acts within the group (e.g., the meaning of where one sits or the significance of what type of decision procedure is used). Further, groups use meta-rules to arbitrate between competing rules (e.g., for the interpersonal support group, the three minute check-in rule versus the extended support rule).

Group members also rely on rules to justify their own behavior and predict the behavior of other members. If a group member is asked to account for behavior that is consistent with the group's rules that member may use the rules to justify the behavior. For example, when an outsider asked a member of the group that abhorred written arguments, why certain complaints had not been specified in writing, the member explained that for this group written arguments were worse than ineffectual; they were viewed as antagonistic. Since groups enforce rules by negatively sanctioning deviations and deviators, members can use rules to predict how members will behave. For example, if a group values informal persuasion over formal debate, members can predict that members will solicit support and work out compromises prior to formal meetings. Further, members may use this knowledge to their advantage by garnering support for their own positions in informal encounters before attending scheduled meetings, where the decisions that are already made are merely formalized.

Once rules are adopted, they are used to judge behavior and other people. Groups assumed that sane and good members will obey the rules; therefore individuals who deviate from them are thought of as "mad or bad" (Watzlawick, Beavin and Jackson, 1967). Those who violate rules have been judged as less attractive (Berger et. al., 1976; O'Brien, 1978), less likable (Chaiken and Derlega, 1974), less promotable (O'Brien, 1978), less favorable (Bradac, Hosman and Tardy, 1978), and less mentally healthy (Berger, et. al., 1976; Chaikin and Derlega, 1974) than those who comply with the rules. The effects of rule violations are also clear in some of the examples given above (e.g., the woman in the Bible study class or the group member who insisted on using written memos).

Even the victim of a violation can be evaluated negatively because of a rule violation. For example, Geller et al. (1974) investigated the effects of violating the implicit rule that prohibits one from ignoring one's conversational partner. Women who were ignored participated less in conversations and rated themselves and the one ignoring them less favorably than those who were not ignored.

The regulation, interpretation, justification, prediction, and evaluation of behavior are major consequences of communication rules, but rules also indirectly influence other aspects of group interactions. For example, while some rules prescribe specific behaviors for particular roles (e.g., leaders, tension-releasers, arbitrators), other rules may influence indirectly who fulfills what roles in a group.

For instance, turn-taking rules for speaking permit the current speaker to select who will be the next speaker (Sacks, Schegloff and Jefferson, 1974). Therefore, if a coalition decides who they want to emerge as the leader, they can select that person to be the next speaker every time they speak (assuming, that is, the group does not have an equal-time rule). This way, the potential leader has more opportunities to influence the group's decisions in the direction of his or her preference and expertise. Further, the leader can use the speaker-selects-next rule to return the floor to those who agree with his or her position, thus increasing the perceived support for his or her perspective. Finally, the number of messages addressed to and delivered by the potential leader may serve to persuade other members that this person is an expert whose advice should be taken.

Geier (1967) found that potential leaders were eliminated from contention early if they were uninformed or failed to participate. By manipulating turn-taking rules, coalitions can ensure that their choice for leader actively participates in the discussion and that the discussion focuses on a topic on which their choice is well informed.

Rules may also indirectly influence group processes by changing the environment along such dimensions as formal/informal, competitive/cooperative, hierarchical/equalitarian, and so forth. Boukydis (1975), for example, investigated the effects of establishing rules for decreasing interruptions and for increasing listening responses and asking for turns. The introduction of these procedural rules also increased the amount of feelings expressed and the explication of meaning, even though there were no specific rules requiring increases in talk about feelings or meanings. The decrease in interruptions and increase in listener responses may have created an atmosphere in which members felt more at ease when expressing feelings and elaborating assertions.

So far this essay has focused on the benefits of rules to group processes, but some cautions are also in order. Although rules are necessary to coordinate group interactions and can be used to facilitate group processes, an overdependence on rules can be unhealthy. In some groups rules are so restrictive that alternatives are never explored and creativity is discouraged. This may lead to "group think," an unquestioning acceptance of the group's perspective even when such acceptance leads to erroneous and dangerous decisions.

Several researchers have correlated rule rigidity with illness within a group. For example, families with a delinquent, neurotic, or schizophrenic member have a more rigid pattern for who speaks after whom than do normal families (for a summary, see Steier, Staton and Todd, 1982). Because these are correlational studies, it is impossible to determine whether the rigid pattern mirrors the illness in the family or if it is the family's means of coping with the illness. Nonetheless, it would seem advisable for groups to weigh carefully the potential benefits and costs of its rules.

In a healthy group, rules should facilitate group processes without placing unnecessary limits on useful innovations. Further, a group should be willing to reevaluate and change its rules when it is demonstrated that an alternative procedure would be more beneficial. Because rules can significantly affect group processes both positively and negatively, it is essential to understand what factors influence rule compliance within a group.

Rule Compliance

Several factors influence whether group members enforce rules and comply with their prescriptions, including the relative importance of the rule, the degree of deviation, the status of the deviator, the degree of agreement among group members as to the nature of the rule, a group member's knowledge of the rule, and the "clout" stated in the rule.

Generally, group members attach greater importance to rules which are associated with the values and goals of the group (e.g., only a sober alcoholic may lead an Alcoholics Anonymous meeting) than to rules which are tangentially related (e.g., only members sitting in the last two rows may smoke). The more necessary a particular rule is to attaining the goals of a group, the more vigilant its members will be in requiring compliance.

The severity of sanctions imposed by group members is directly related to the relevance or importance of the rule to the group, and the degree of deviation. Sanctions increase as the importance and deviation increase (Mudd, 1968, 1972). Group members may even let a minor rule violation pass, assuming an accounting for the violation will be forthcoming (Hopper, 1981), but once the violation exceeds a "tolerance-threshold" (Boynton, 1979), negative sanctions are sure to follow. Managers indicate that as the seriousness of a deviation increases, so also does the severity of the sanctions (i.e., do nothing, discussion, change job situation, punishment) (Green, Fairhurst, and Liden, n.d.).

The relationship between status and compliance is complex. On the one hand, leaders are expected to comply with group rules, even more than other members; they are supposed to set an example (Stein, 1982). But they are also allowed to deviate from rules with less severe consequences. In reviewing conflicting evidence about whether high status members or low status members received more severe sanctions, Wahrman (1977) concluded that if the deviation is mild, then low status members receive the greater punishment, but if the deviation threatened the group's core values or existence, the high status member would be more severely sanctioned.

Leaders may also be able to deviate from rules without negative consequences, because they have earned "idiosyncrasy credits" for their past behavior (Hollander 1958, 1960, 1961). When leaders violate group rules, they draw upon these credits to compensate for the deviation. Katz's (1982) research supported the idiosyncrasy hypothesis by demonstrating that people are "willing to overlook an individual's deviation if that deviation has been preceded by conformity" (p. 411). Further, a deviation (innovation) by a leader, if it enhances group goals, is more likely to be accepted, even embraced, than a deviation that undermines those goals.

The degree to which members agree on what specific behaviors are prescribed by a rule can also influence compliance and enforcement. As the degree of agreement increases, so will the compliance. However, when members disagree, their behavior may differ from one another substantially. For example, members of one group agreed that they had an "open door" policy and that all members were expected to abide by it, but members disagreed as to what it required. For some, it meant one should be available for consultation whenever one was in the office, while others thought it meant that consultation, even without an appointment, was appropriate during a specified time period. Differences among group members on this issue resulted in variations in the enactment of the open door policy, debates as to what it meant, and a certain amount of resentment on the part of all members, with some feeling their associates were unavailable and others viewing their associates as intrusive. Because group agreement about the rule was low, compliance with it was inconsistent at best. Rules for which there is low agreement are enforced less rigorously than those for which there is high agreement.

Knowledge and attitudes toward particular rules will also affect compliance and enforcement. A newcomer who deviates from a rule because of ignorance is more likely to be pardoned by a group than an established member who is expected to know the rules well. Further, a member who fails to abide by a rule because of a temporary lapse of memory will be forgiven for the transgression more readily than the belligerent deviator, especially if the temporary transgressor apologizes or corrects the error. Finally, members who not only break rules but question their legitimacy may find themselves ostracized by the group, except in a rare case where they are able to persuade the rest of the group that the rules should be changed.

Both greater rule agreement and awareness make explicit rules generally easier to enforce than implicit rules. However, if they are significant to individual members of the group, implicit rules can be enforced with equal strength. For example, in some groups, even though there is not a formally stated seating arrangement, all members honor an implicit arrangement and anyone daring to take the seat of another is duly chastised by group members. The deviator then usually acknowledges the legitimacy of their complaint, apologizes, and moves. In these instances, an implicit rule becomes explicit.

A rule's perceived "clout" can be increased by manipulating what is contained in the statement of the rule, and the greater the perceived clout, the greater the compliance. Specifying (1) who is supposed to enforce a rule, (2) what are the sanctions for following or failing to comply with the rule, and (3) what are the sanctions for the enforcer's behavior, all increase compliance with the rule (Gray and Roberts-Gray, 1979). Because these three features increased compliance, the researchers recommended that a group include them in the rules which are of central importance to the group, and omit them from statements that are intended to be guidelines rather than absolute rules. Such action may increase compliance where it is most desired.

Rule compliance (other than that by pure chance) requires at least tacit knowledge of rules. Because rules may be used to determine what behavior occurs in a group, who fulfills what roles, how one is evaluated, and how a group attains it goals, it is essential that individuals know how to identify the rules of a particular group.

Identification of Rules

The easiest way to identify rules is to ask group members what their rules are. When asked how the group proceeds and whether certain behaviors are considered appropriate or inappropriate, members can often provide insights to a group's rules. Members can be asked to specify what they would be sure to do and not do to achieve an objective. One may also ask members to recount instances where the group was particularly pleased or angered as the result of someone's behavior. These disclosures may be used to infer rules.

Some rules, however, are not part of the conscious awareness of members, and thus they may be unable to articulate them. Further, members sometimes resist admitting that the group restricts its members in particular ways. "Freedom" is such a god term in this culture that people often fail to acknowledge constraints, even valuable ones.

Observing actual behavior provides another approach to rule identification. Because members usually conform to a group's rules, rule-generated behavior reoccurs. Therefore, repetition of a behavior constitutes preliminary evidence that a rule exists. As a starting point, one might use the typology of rule types (i.e., "who says what to whom when with what duration and frequency through what medium and by what decision-procedure") to record reoccurring behaviors in those categories. Further, by comparing this list with similar ones for other groups, one may begin to discover differences between groups in regard to what they consider appropriate, and hence what their rules are.

However, in addition to repetition, one must also observe some evidence that the group approves of certain behavior and disapproves of deviations from it. If a rule prescribes a particular behavior, then deviation from that prescription should result in either a "repair" (e.g., apology or ultimate conformity to the rule) or in a negative sanction of the act and/or actor.

Negative sanctions may take many forms, including (1) ignoring the deviator, (2) sending nonverbal symbols of disapproval, (3) reprimanding the deviator, (4) lowering one's evaluation of the deviator, or (5) ostracizing the deviator. Deviations and their corrections or negative sanctions are particularly useful in identifying rules because they often draw attention to behaviors and subsequently rules, group members take-for-granted.

Deviations help to make implicit rules explicit. The deviations of newcomers, foreigners, children, and others who do not know the rules may be quite helpful in identifying rules. Deviations of newcomers and others who are ignorant of a group's rules will expose patterns which are taken for granted, by demonstrating that alternative behaviors are possible. The reactions of the group to these deviations will help observers determine whether the typical pattern is considered more appropriate than alternatives; that is, prescribed by a rule.

If one thinks a rule exists in a group, but no one deviates from the rule, one can test one's hypothesis by purposely violating it and observing how the violation and the deviator are treated by the group. Purposeful violation of a suspected rule is called "garfinkeling" (Harre and Secord, 1973), after the noted sociologist Harold Garfinkel (1967) of UCLA, who directed his students to violate presumed rules to test their existence and significance. "Garfinkeling" has proven quite useful to researchers in identifying rules. However, group members should keep in mind that if they violate the rules of their group, they probably will be evaluated negatively by the group. In severe cases, this could mean the dissolution of their membership. So "garfinkeling" should be used by group members only with extreme caution. As a method for identifying rules, "garfinkeling" is generally best left to researchers rather than group members and any garfinkeler must evaluate the ethical consequences of rule violations.

Conclusion

In this essay, R. D. Laing's rule—of playing the game of not seeing the game—has been violated; the significance of rules in group interactions has been made explicit. It is hoped, however, that the knowledge gained from this violation compensates for the transgression. Communication rules make it possible for group members to coordinate their interactions and attain their goals. Since the consequences of some rule violations are severe, knowing how to identify rules can be an essential survival skill for group members. Further, before one can successfully manipulate, strengthen, or change a group's rules, one must be aware of the current rules. Armed with the information provided in this essay, it is hoped that group members will enhance group dynamics by the constructive use of communication rules.

References

Aries, E. Interaction patterns and themes of male, female and mixed groups. *Small Group Behavior,* 1976, *7,* 7–18.

Berger, C. R., et al. Interpersonal epistemology and interpersonal communication. In *Explorations in interpersonal communication.* Beverly Hills: Sage, 1976.

Bingham, C. Lucinda, chapter 3 as cited in Elaine Partnow. In *The quotable woman.* Garden City, N.Y.: Anchor Books, 1978, p. 449.

Boukydis, K. N. Expression of negative feelings and explication of meaning as a function of contingent interruptions and contingent listening responses in task-oriented groups. *DAI,* 1976, *36 (12),* 6350–6351B.

Boynton, K. R. Deviation: A communication perspective. *Central States Speech Journal,* 1979, *30,* 83–95.

Bradac, J. J., Hosman, L. A., and Tardy, C. H. Reciprocal disclosures and language intensity: Attributional consequences. *Communication Monographs,* 1978, *45,* 1–17.

Chaikin, A. L., and Derlega, V. J. Liking for the norm-breaker in self-disclosure. *Journal of Personality,* 1974, *42,* 117–129.

Garfinkel, H. *Studies in ethnomethodology.* Englewood Cliffs, N.J.: 1967.

Geier, J. G. A trait approach to the study of leadership in small groups. *Journal of Communication,* 1967, *17,* 316–323.

Geller, D. M., et al. On being ignored: The effects of the violation of implicit rules of social interaction. *Sociometry,* 1974, *37,* 541–556.

Gray, T., and Roberts-Gray, C. Structuring bureaucratic rules to enhance compliance. *Psychological Reports,* 1979, *45,* 579–589.

Green, S. G., G. T. F., and Liden, R. C. Rules and control episodes in the management of ineffective performance. Unpublished paper, n.d.

Harragan, B. L. *Games mother never taught you: Corporate gamesmanship for women.* New York: Warner Books, 1977.

Harré, H. and Secord, P. F. *The explanation of social behaviour.* Totowa, N.J.: Littlefield, Adams, 1973.

Hollander, E. P. Competence and conformity in the acceptance of influence. *Journal of Abnormal and Social Psychology,* 1960, *61,* 365–369.

Hollander, E. P. Conformity, status, and idiosyncrasy credit. *Psychological Review,* 1958, *65,* 117–127.

Hollander, E. P. Some effects of perceived status on responses to innovative behavior. *Journal of Abnormal and Social Psychology,* 1961, *63,* 247–250.

Hopper, R. The taken-for-granted. *Human Communication Research,* 1981, *7,* 195–211.

Katz, G. M. Previous conformity, status and the rejection of the deviant. *Small Group Behavior,* 1982, *13,* 403–414.

Labov, W. Rules for ritual insults. In *Studies in social interaction.* New York: Free Press, 1972. pp. 120–169.

Laing, R. D. *Knots.* New York: Random House, 1970.

Mudd, S. A. Group sanction: Severity as a function of degree of behavior deviation and relevance of norm: Replication and revision of model. *Journal of Psychology,* 1972, *80,* 57–61.

Mudd, S. A. Group sanction: Severity as a function of degree of behavior deviation and relevance of norm. *Journal of Personality and Social Psychology,* 1968, *8,* 258–260.

O'Brien, C. E. A rules-based approach to communication within a formal organization: Theory and case studies. Unpublished manuscript based on her PhD. dissertation at the University of Massachusetts, Amherst, 1978.

Sacks, H., Schegloff, E. A., and Jefferson, G. A simplest systematics for the organization of turn-taking in conversation. *Language,* 1974, *50,* 696–735.

Shimanoff, S. B. *Communication rules: Theory and research.* Beverly Hills, California: Sage, 1980.

Stein, R. T. High status group members as exemplars: A summary of field research on the relationship of status to congruence conformity. *Small Group Behavior,* 1982, *13,* 3–21.

Steir, F., Stanton, M. D., and Todd, T. C. Patterns of turn-taking and alliance formation in family communication. *Journal of Communication,* 1982, *32,* 148–160.

Wahrman, R. Status, deviance, sanctions, and group discussions. *Small Group Behavior,* 1977, *8,* 147–168.

Watzlawick, P., Beavin, J. H., and Jackson, D. J. *Pragmatics of human communication: A study of interaction patterns, pathologies and paradoxes.* New York: W. W. Norton, 1967.

Groups: A Model

Mike Robinson

The groups to which we belong form, in large part, the framework of our lives. As such, they are almost invisible. We think about what goes on—the content—not about the co-ordinates. If we do reflect on groups or relationships *per se,* it is usually because something has gone wrong. . . . I want to look at the form of groups when things are going well as a basis for understanding changes and crises. What is the difference between a viable group— one that is stable or evolves successfully—and a group that disappears? How is it that a group can be 'the same', despite the fact that most of its members have changed? Which variables are important to the functioning of the group— and how are they seen by its members? Which processes are limiting and which can be freely changed? How do these processes relate to each other?

. . . We present a model that defines some limits of group stability; of processes that occur within those limits; and some consequences of going beyond the limits. The general form of the model is descriptive—but it also has a strict form as a computer program that maps our assumptions onto historical data. It should again be emphasized that the *model is not predictive* (for one thing we do not believe there is such an animal), but the model is intended to be a *diagnostic* one. It should inform the understanding without pre-empting change or political choice.

To anticipate the conclusions, the model assumes that group 'identity' is maintained if the group stays about the same size and continues to do the same sorts of things—even despite changes of membership. Such stable groups have two major components: a Normative System and a Size Regulating Subsystem.

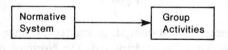

Figure 1.

The Normative System is where the politics (can) appear. It is the method (ritual) by which the group members agree on values and actions. In a general way, the Normative System determines the group activities (Figure 1). But the sorts of activity decided on also determine the size of the group—the approximate number of people needed to carry out the activity (Figure 2).

From Mike Robinson, *Groups.* John Wiley and Sons, Ltd., 1984. Mike Robinson is affiliated with the Social Synthesis Unit, University of London.

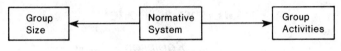

Figure 2.

Then of course the success or otherwise of the activities influences both the size and the normative system. 'Success' can lead to the attraction of new members, 'failure' can lead to losing members. 'Success/failure' in itself, and through membership change, can influence the Normative System (Figure 3).

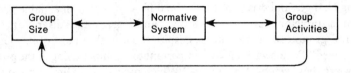

Figure 3.

In fact, it turns out that (quite often) the fluctuations in activity lead to a Size Regulating Subsystem. Role specifications, absenteeism, joining and leaving all combine to form a delicate set of balances which match the group size to its activity—and this in turn maintains the Normative System (Figure 4).

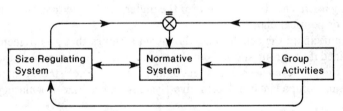

Figure 4.

None of this means that stability is guaranteed. Groups can become 'too big or too small'. Activity can be disrupted. The Normative System can disintegrate into conflict. Warring factions are always an implicit danger. Particular danger points for groups are the 'formation period'—the first few weeks or months in the life of a group. Many (probably most) groups do not survive this. Any moment of sudden growth is equally dangerous, as is a situation where group activity is disrupted for any length of time.

● ● ● ● ● ● ● ●

The Development of a Model: How Do Small Groups Work

'How do small groups work' is a question without a question mark because it is also a statement of assumptions. It excludes a whole number of other ways of looking at groups. It does not raise questions about 'motivation' or about 'attitudes', about 'interpersonal attraction' or about 'leadership qualities'. Nor does it raise questions about typologies of group, about how many there are in each category. It is a question like 'how does a diesel engine work' or 'how does a telephone system work'. It is a question looking for a mechanism. . . .

The assumption above the question is that we are looking for convivial systems—groups where coercion is at a minimum and self activity at a premium. What sort of framework encourages this? That is the political question that is translated into a 'systems' question of how things work. . . . The paradigms were sought out because I liked (some) groups, and wanted to understand them. I wanted them to continue—therefore the natural questions were about existence, about survival, and about viability. . . .

How, then, do small groups work?

The starting point was that groups that exist for significant periods of time have recognizable identities. We refer to them by the same name. The membership may change, but the group does not—or so we assert by our everyday use of language. Our ordinary ideas tell us that *if a group stays about the same size and continues to do the same sorts of things, then, even if there has been a considerable change in the membership, it is the same group.* This commonsense description is not too far from a rudimentary cybernetic analysis. The 'identity' of groups involves—at least—two variables, size and activity, staying at about the same level, or staying within limits. If this is the case, then there should be some reason why size and activity do not change drastically—or at least why this is an unusual event. It should be possible to identify regulatory systems that operate on these variables to keep them within limits. The identification of such systems would be a good start in answering the question about how groups work.

• • • • • • •

Major Variables

Human Social Group

This is of course not a variable in itself but a package of variables. The contents of the package depend on experimental purpose (or whim) rather than on the nature of objects-in-the-world. There have been serious attempts to establish typologies of groups (e.g., Golembiewski, 1962), but these do not seem to have influenced practical research very much. Definitions still range from three strangers behind screens in a social psychology laboratory to fully-fledged subcultures—with little indication of the relationships that might hold between them. The general nature of the sort of group to which our model is intended to apply is as follows.

The groups are 'natural'. They are found in the world rather than in laboratories—the sort of thing that might be mentioned in newspapers rather than created by psychologists. They are 'non-familial'; families may be in groups, but they are so specialized and have so many properties not found in other groups, that they are excluded from the range of this model. They are 'informal'; this means they will not have written constitutions, and the members do not have legal obligations to each other. They do not pay members, nor do they have paid functionaries. Although the model might have implications for work-groups and for organizations with formal structures, these involve many new distinctions and levels of complexity, and in these respects are beyond the scope of the model. They are permeable; members must be able to join or leave at will. They are durable; they should retain an identity over time. This excludes natural 'groupings' such as those studied by Coleman and James (1961) which were casual meetings between people in streets and parks. It also excludes sets of people such as those studied by Newcombe (1961) where there is durable interaction, continuing relations of like and dislike, but where the concept of 'belonging to a group' is missing.

Size

This was defined as the number of people in the group. This commonsense definition later led to problems, and will need refinement.

Although little work had been done on sheer size as an aspect of groups, Shephard (1964) speculates that there is an upper size limit of twenty for information groups, quoting James (1951) and Bales and Borgatta (1955) as evidence. Studies on the psychological or sociological conditions of joining groups—size increase—were also conspicuous by their absence. My initial 'South London' model had nothing to say about this either. Leaving behaviour and absenteeism—size decrease—had fared a little better. Absenteeism had been related to 'span of control' (Acton Soc., 1953), group size (Hewit and Parfitt, 1953), sociometric structure (Moreno, 1953), frustration and work disruption (Herbst, 1962), and participation and responsibility (Stephan and Mishler, 1952). One very early study (Coch and French, 1948) had found an interesting relationship between the size of the standard deviation from the production norm and absenteeism/quitting behaviour. There were also numerous studies that showed size to be inversely related to 'cohesiveness', participation, and satisfaction (e.g., Gibb, 1951; Hare, 1952; Slater, 1958). The common thread underlying these studies was that size was seen as relating, in some way or other, to normative (including emotive) factors.

Activity and Level of Activity

Activity is not itself a group variable. Strictly it is a category referring to a set of group variables. This is because the activities of one group may be totally incommensurable with the activities of another. If we want to compare the activities of a discussion group with a work group on a Ford production line, we have to go to a 'second level' measurement. Since the idea of 'high and low levels of activity' have an intuitive meaning for all groups, this would seem to be justified.

In any specific group, the unit of activity has to be specified—preferably in terms consistent with the subjective perceptions of the group members.

Bales (1953) initiated a distinction between task-orientated and socio-emotional activity in small-group research. Only the former will be considered here: it fits better with the groups own idea of activity, and it simplifies the observational requirements. Activity as productivity has traditionally attracted many measures, and been related to many other variables—especially size, 'cohesiveness', and participation. Productivity is usually an ideologically defined measure, and hence an unreliable index of activity. It also assumes formal organizational structures that may well be missing in informal groups, although the consistent way it has been related—like size—to normative factors should be noted.

Symbolic Conventional Structure

This is best thought of as a set of related symbols, embodying agreements, that define a 'world' and possible actions within that 'world'. Within sociology, it is usually conceptualized in terms of 'norms' and 'roles'—although these terms, like group, tend to be used in many different ways. Attempts at systematization (e.g., Biddle and Thomas, 1969) have not taken any deep roots. Here we will regard the notion of role as a type of norm, following the opinion of Michael Argyle that the two can be collapsed together in small group studies:

> *The shared behaviour* for occupants of a position is sometimes called the *role* for that position, especially when the behaviour is distinct from the behaviour in adjacent positions. This is very similar to the notion of a group norm, and is in fact the same thing if group-membership is classed as a position.

> (Argyle, 1957, p. 175)

Another intuitively close idea is that of 'social script' (Jackson, 1978), but we will adhere to 'norm' as the more widely used concept. This will be broken into two aspects: 'Normative Structure' and 'Normative Strength'.

'Normative Structures'

These are not, of course, fixed. They can be expected to undergo change with time. However, for the purposes of this model, it will be assumed—given the lengths of the observation periods—that in natural groups *significant* changes do *not* take place. A significant change (almost by definition) would transform the group rather than preserve it. An example would be the change from informal to formal structure. This would be an adaptation (amongst other things) to permanently increased size, not a simple mechanism to restore normal size.

A belief can be designated a part of the normative structure if it is believed by a majority of group members to be held by the majority of group members. It should be noted that this allows for false norms. The group may believe a majority holds a certain view when in fact it does not. The totality of these beliefs is the normative structure.

'Normative Strength'

This may be thought of as the power of the normative structure to shape behaviour and action. In terms of the model, it is the ratio of those actually holding a belief to those believed to hold it. Normative strength is represented in the model as a threshold, since its effect is all or nothing. At any point in time an external observer may establish gradual changes in normative strength by interviews. To the group itself, the overthrow of a false norm is instantaneous. At one moment the group believes the majority to hold a given view; suddenly it realises it does not. A new norm is 'revealed'. . . .

Conclusions

From these preliminary studies, it looked as though size, normative strength and structure, and activity were indeed key variables in the maintenance of group 'identity'. Both experimental studies demonstrated the rapid formation of group norms, and of size and activity stabilization around certain levels. . . . It seems reasonable to suppose that in natural groups increasing inactivity will have significant consequences somewhere. High levels of inactivity might be expected to precede people leaving the group—size decay—or a weakening of normative strength, possibly followed by some 'catastrophic' change in the group's functioning. There were also indications that high levels of activity created a 'social visibility' that encouraged new people to join the group. Fluctuations in the activity level—in natural groups—can therefore be expected to have a 'feedback' effect on group size, depending on how 'outsiders' (in the group's 'environment') see the group. Bearing all this

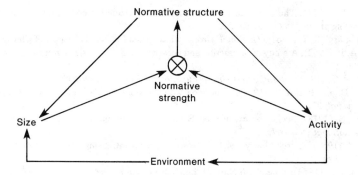

Figure 5. A schematic model of group functioning.

in mind, the schematic model, shown by Figure 5, of group functioning was constructed. This schema represents the following relationships:

1. The normative structure is the most important factor, as it influences both size and activity.
2. Normative strength—the ratio of those actually holding a set of beliefs to those believed to hold them—is represented in the model as a threshold. Its effect on the normative structure is all or nothing. Change in the normative structure, if it takes place at all, is not gradual but 'catastrophic', but is preceded by changes in the normative strength. Normative strength is itself influenced by changes in size and activity levels.
3. Size level does not influence activity level.
4. Level of activity can indirectly influence size level through the environment. High levels of activity may create 'social visibility' and attract new members.

References

Acton Society Trust (1953), *Size and Morale.*

Argyle, M. (1957), *The Scientific Study of Social Behaviour,* London, Methuen.

Argyle, M. (1958), *Religious Behaviour,* London: Routledge, quoted in: Jahoda, M. and Warren, N. (eds.) *Attitudes* Harmondsworth: Penguin.

Bales, R. F. (1953), The equilibrium problem in small groups, *Working Papers in the Theory of Action* (eds. T. Parson, R. F. Bales, and E. A. Shils), Glencoe, Ill., The Free Press, 111–61.

Bales, R. F. and Borgatta, A. F. (1955), Size of group as a factor in the interaction profile, *Small Groups* (eds. A. P. Hare, A. F. Borgatta, and R. F. Bales). New York, Knopf.

Bates, A. P. and Cloyd, J. S. (1956), Towards the development of operations for defining group norms and member roles, *Sociometry,* **19,** 138–151.

Biddle, B. J. and Thomas, E. J. (1969), *Role Theory,* New York, John Wiley & Sons.

Coch, L. and French, J. R. P. (1948), Overcoming resistance to change, *Hum. Rel.* **1,** 512–32.

Coleman, J. S. and James J., (1961), The equilibrium size distribution of freely forming groups, *Sociometry,* **24.**

Gibb, J. R. (1951), The effects of group size and threat reduction on creativity in a problem-solving group, *Amer. Psychol.* **6.**

Golembiewski, R. T. (1962), *The Small Group,* Chicago and London, University of Chicago Press.

Hare, A. P. (1952), A study of interaction and consensus in different sized groups, *Amer. Sociol. Rev.* **17.**

Herbst, P. G. (1962), *Autonomous Group Functioning,* London, Tavistock.

Hewitt, D. and Parfitt, J. (1953), A note on working morale and size of group, *Occupational Psychol.* **27.**

Jackson, S. (1978), Social context of rape: Social scripts and motivation, *Women's Studies International Quarterly,* 1.

James, J. (1951), A preliminary study of the size determinant in small group interaction, *Amer. Soc. Rev.* **16.**

Moreno, J. L. (1953), *Who Shall Survive,* London: Beacon House.

Newcomb, T. (1961), *The Acquaintance Process,* London: Holt, Rinehart and Winston.

Robinson, M. J. (1977), *Thesis,* Brunel University.

Shepherd, C. R. (1964), *Small Groups: Some Sociological Perspectives,* London, Chandler Pub. Co.

Slater, P. E. (1958), Contrasting correlates of group size, *Sociometry,* **21.**

Stephan, F. F. and Mishler, E. G. (1952), The distribution of participation in small groups, *Amer. Sociol. Rev.*

Stephenson, G. M. and Fielding, G. T. (1968), An experimental study of the contagion of leaving behaviour in small gatherings, Dept. Psychology, University of Nottingham (Xerox).

Taylor, I. R. (1971), Soccer consciousness and soccer hooliganism, *Images of Deviance* (ed. S. Cohen), London: Penguin.

Zeeman, E. C. (1976), Catastrophe theory, *Scientific American,* April, 1976.

2
Group Environments: Professional and Personal

Think of all the groups of which you are considered a member. Besides your family group, you may be a member of a church group, a school committee, a sports team, a work group, a study group, etc. It could be a very long list and it is probably an ever changing one. Why participate in so many groups? A simple answer is that small groups are the most effective means of accomplishing a wide range of tasks, goals, and needs, both professional and personal. Most professions, organizations, and institutions utilize small groups to help achieve goals, work out rules, create agreements, and establish policy. Physicians form small group medical teams in order to successfully complete difficult medical procedures like heart transplants. Coaching staffs form ongoing groups to work out game plans and strategies for successful seasons. College professors form committees to plan and revise curricula. Computer programmers are gathered into project teams to work out new software necessary to the functioning of complex organizations and institutions. Communities and institutions form help groups and counseling groups to aid individuals in coping with physical and mental difficulties. Individuals form consciousness-raising and therapy groups to help each other understand and deal with the stress and strain of contemporary life. The list could go on. The essential consideration, however, is to be aware that all professions, organizations, and individuals use and depend upon small groups. In chapter 2 we have gathered seven articles describing the professional and personal uses of small groups, to help in understanding the range, diversity, and uses of such groups.

The first essay, "Understanding the Unique Characteristics of Groups Within Organizations" by Linda L. Putnam, points out that "organizational groups, while similar in some respects to groups in other settings, differ from them in very important ways." She explores some of the unique characteristics of organizational groups—connectivity, hierarchical structure, and multiple-group membership. Throughout, her focus is on communication, both *within* organizations and *between* groups.

David L. Bradford and Leland P. Bradford analyze the pervasive, but often overlooked, *ad hoc* committee—a group which is not part of the formal structure, has a limited life, and comprises a secondary task for most members. In the article "Temporary Committees as Ad Hoc Groups", they "explore the domain of ad hoc groups both from the viewpoint of the person who initiates such a group and of the chairperson who actually leads the committee." They examine the very practical matters that each must be concerned with, and suggest the means for achieving maximum potential in temporary committees.

Kjell Eric Rudestam considers another, sometimes controversial, type of group in his article, "The Experiential Group". He claims there are many kinds of experiential groups, from "organizational development groups" to "personal therapy groups", with a variety of goals, including problem solving, learning interpersonal skills, personal growth, and establishing emotional stability. In a subsection titled "Souls, Goals, and Roles", Rudestam analyzes the many facets of experiential groups, and discusses the positive and negative outcomes associated with them.

David Robinson's "Self-help Groups" looks at one of the most rapidly developing group phenomena of the past twenty-five years. Self-help groups have proliferated so rapidly they are sometimes referred to as "the self-help movement". Acknowledging what is known about long-established self-help groups such as Alcoholics Anonymous, Weight Watchers, and CAR (Cancer Aftercare and Rehabilitation), Robinson explains *why* such groups are needed and *how* the groups do what they actually do. He also reviews the limits of self-help groups, and considers their future.

Edward E. Sampson and Marya Marthas argue in their essay on "The Health Professional and Group Process" that health promotion and maintenance is a function of group process. They point out that personal health is related to the family group, that even the simplest medical interventions involve teams of doctors, nurses, assistants, and that the very system of the delivery of health care is directly dependent on a series of interconnecting groups. For the health professional, as well as the lay person, this essay establishes the role of small groups in a significant area of human interaction.

The newest, and perhaps most intriguing, development of small group dynamics is the formation of human groups by electronic means. An essay by R. Johansen, J. Vallee, and K. Spangler, "Teleconferencing: Electronic Group Meetings", from their book *Electronic Meetings: Technical Alternatives and Social Choices,* explains this latest form of group communication. They describe how physical separation, access to resources, limited communication channels, control of interaction, and dependence on technology all play important roles in determining the dynamics of electronic group meetings. They see teleconferencing not as an entirely new form of communication, but rather a condition which requires new communication choices in order to make its benefits outweigh its drawbacks.

In the final essay in chapter 2, Richard E. Porter suggests we use the small group as a bridge for intercultural communication. In his essay "Intercultural Small Group Communication" he contends that "successful interaction with culturally different people requires that we develop a facility for intercultural communication and learn to use it in a wide variety of communication contexts." He focuses attention on the small group context, showing in which ways small group uses, roles, norms, and values vary from culture to culture—making us aware of how culture-bound we are in our small groups. His goal is to develop awareness to the point at which we can use these insights as ways to better understand and interact more effectively with persons of other cultures.

Understanding the Unique Characteristics of Groups within Organizations

Linda L. Putnam

The advent of quality circles, Theory Z styles of management, project teams, and adhocracies has led to a resurgence of interest in organizational groups. As evidence of this rebirth, both European and American organizations have increased their efforts to "democratize" industry. In 1980 the Scandinavian government passed legislation requiring workers to participate in industrial decision making. In American organizations, management and labor are collaborating to keep companies open, to increase productivity, and to fight tough competition with foreign markets. Their collective efforts extend beyond decision making into the multiple functions that groups perform in modern organizations, functions that range from planning and policy implementation to coordination and conflict management. Even though groups exhibit a number of pathologies that inhibit their overall effectiveness, they bring together individuals with diverse resources to promote rapid communication in a complex structure.

Organizational groups, while similar in some respects to groups in other settings, differ from them in very important ways. Organizations offer more than just a "place" for groups to meet. They constitute a complex structure of groups embedded in other groups. Hence, a project team exists within a research and development group which, in turn, resides within the engineering department. This overlay of groups nested within other groups poses unique problems which affect communication within and between groups. This essay explores three unique characteristics of organizational groups: connectivity, hierarchical structure, and multiple-group membership. More specifically, it examines the way communication between groups impacts upon and is influenced by the interaction within a group.

Connectivity: Communication as Tight and Loose Connections between Groups

Even though organizational groups exist in a web of interrelated units, linkages between groups range from loosely connected threads to tightly coupled bonds. Tight couplings between groups evolve from overlapping tasks, shared goals, a high frequency of communication, and mutual fate control.

Linda L. Putnam is affiliated with the Department of Speech Communication, Purdue University.

Loosely coupled groups share some activities, but they conduct their work independent of the other group. There are three major types of relationships between groups: *dependent, interdependent,* and *autonomous.*[1] A *dependent* group relies on another group for its resources and direction; thus it lacks fate control, in that its destiny lies in the hands of a controlling group. For example, an assembly team frequently depends on another assembly group to complete stages of a product before it can finish its assigned task. Assembly teams also rely on managerial groups for coordination between groups and for directives in assembling the product. In this way, the assembly group exists in a dependent relationship with other assembly units and with authority groups who direct the process.

Interdependent groups share a mutual dependency; both groups rely on one another to accomplish their respective goals. Because they are tightly connected, a change in one group leads to alterations in the other one. For instance, the manufacturing group depends on the supply unit for its resources, but the supply group relies on the manufacturing department to determine what materials need to be ordered. If manufacturing changes the parts in its blueprint, supply must adapt with similar changes in acquisition of materials. In like manner, if the marketplace reveals a shortage of certain raw materials, the manufacturing group must change their design of the product to adapt to this problem. Both groups, then, depend on one another for their respective needs.

In contrast, an *autonomous* group functions without depending on a particular subgroup. The two groups may be linked together through loosely connected exchanges, but they accomplish their task independently of the other group. Departments in a university setting are prime examples of autonomous groups. Even though the English and the Speech-Communication departments may share the same building, the two groups function as semi-autonomous units. Each department runs its own governance system and sets policies independent of the operations of the other. Occasionally, they interact to negotiate space, to exchange students, or to settle disputes over academic jurisdiction but for the most part they function independently. This tradition of operating as autonomous units makes it difficult for members of academic departments to build interdisciplinary programs.

Even though connectivity stems from task function and work-flow interdependence, loosely and tightly-connected relationships are ultimately defined through communication. Overlapping tasks, then, interlink the supply and the assembly departments; but the way they accomplish their work is a communicative problem. In effect, the frequency and type of interaction between them ultimately defines the nature of their relationship and the extent of their dependence on one another. It is possible, then, for autonomous groups to become interdependent if they interact frequently and if they begin to control one another's fate.

In particular, a research and development group often performs tasks independent of other groups. It conducts market research, analyzes the competition, and creates a new product to enhance the company's productivity. If this process is conducted without any input from the engineering manager, the R & D group functions autonomously. But at some point the company has to implement the new product, so that R & D must work closely with engineering and manufacturing groups. This interaction so shapes the relationship between the groups that their newly formed interdependence often leads to changes in the product design. Through communication, then, groups redefine autonomous relationships so that they become interdependent. Moreover, if the engineering group perceives R & D's autonomy as a power play, it may be resentful and cautious in redefining the relationship. It may contend that major coordination problems would not have occurred if R & D had kept it informed. In essence, connectivity between groups is an ever-changing process, not a static quality. It is derived, in part, from the way communication molds intergroup relationships.

As this discussion suggests, building intergroup relationships in organizations becomes a struggle between *differentiation* and *integration*. Organizations form groups through differentiation or division of labor, a process which capitalizes on specialized skills to facilitate efficient task completion. Connectivity is a form of integration—an attempt to link groups together through integrating task functions, developing shared goals, and mediating conflicts. Individuals typically assume this coordination role by bridging the physical and psychological gaps between segmented groups.

Individuals as Linkages between Groups

Individuals who bridge intergroup boundaries are key communicators who perform specialized linkage functions. A *gatekeeper* serves as a member of one group who filters incoming and outgoing information. Secretaries often regulate communication traffic and filter information to management groups. A *liason* bridges communication between two groups but does not belong to either. A staff member in personnel may facilitate hiring between the engineering department and the sales group, but this liason individual is not a member of either group. A *linking pin* belongs to two or more groups and coordinates activities between the two groups. Supervisors typically assume linking pin roles, since they belong to work groups and managerial teams. Members of project teams frequently serve as representatives of their departments as well as participants on the task force. Finally, *boundary spanners* are individuals who link departments and the organization to other organizations. Employees in marketing, public relations, advertising, and supply frequently serve as boundary spanners to connect their departments to the community at large. Boundary spanners, unlike linking pins, translate and interpret equivocal information from external sources; hence, they have strong linkages within the group, within the organization, and outside the organization.

Communication within and outside the group impacts on the emergence of linkage roles and the frequency of contact with external units. High performing teams have more frequent contact with other groups than do low performing units. Research teams rely on several members to perform gatekeeping and boundary spanning functions, while development groups channel their communication through primarily one member.[2] In fifty percent of the cases, this member is the team's supervisor, particularly for the liason functions of the group. Boundary role spanners, however, are frequently professional employees who have a particular technical competence.[3] Liasons tend to perform administrative functions, while boundary spanners specialize in information gathering and decision making. Over forty percent of the employees who are communication stars in their own groups also serve as linkages to other departmental groups, to other departments, and to sources outside the organization.[4]

These specialized linkage roles shape communication within and outside the work group. Blau notes in his study of law enforcement agents that individuals who receive the greatest number of external messages during the day participate more frequently in group discussions by clarifying problems and take the initiative in meetings. Moreover, the internal structure of a group influences the frequency of contacts with other units. Groups with clearly developed roles and centralized decision making engage in more external communication than do groups with role instability and decentralized decision making.

Although forming linkages between groups aids internal communication, individuals who perform these functions often lack formal authority, frequently feel trapped between conflicting demands, and can become scapegoats for organizational ills. They experience considerable role conflict and are rarely rewarded for their contributions as integrators.[5] No doubt some individuals cope with this conflict better than others do. Our inability to understand the way employees manage their linkage roles stems from problems with research in this area. Too much research concentrates on the amount and direction of message exchange between groups and ignores the content, meaning, and quality of interaction. Perhaps researchers as well as practitioners should heed Barnard's advice, "it is not persons, but the services or acts or actions or influences of persons, which should be treated as constituting organizations."[6]

Hierarchical Structure: Communication as a Reflection
of Organizational Level

Differentiation in organizations separates groups into vertical and horizontal levels. Vertical levels signify layers of managerial authority, while horizontal separation forms departmental boundaries. Both levels are represented in an organization's formal chart. Even though the formal structure undergoes frequent changes, its existence impacts on the composition, function, and communicative patterns of organizational groups. Formal meetings, ones officially sanctioned and scheduled by management, differ from spontaneous and informal conferences. Meetings which cross vertical levels of the hierarchy reduce the number of informal sessions between boss and subordinates. In contrast, formal meetings that cross horizontal levels increase the need for coordination through informal contacts across departments.

Group Functions and Types

Organizational structure also impacts on the type and the function of groups. One way to classify organizational groups is to distinguish between *ongoing* and *temporary* units at vertical and horizontal levels. *Ongoing* groups continue to meet even though membership and task function varies. One type of ongoing group, a *standing committee,* meets on a regular basis to perform vital maintenance functions. Executive committees and middle management groups serve these functions at the apex of the vertical hierarchy. Executive committees establish policies and coordinate information generated from middle management, while middle managers execute the decisions made by upper management. Since middle management often feels trapped between the policy makers and the technology of the organization, their communication patterns parallel those of top management and make it difficult for them to function as policy executors rather than policy formulators.[7] A second type of ongoing group, the *specialist team,* consists of members from different horizontal levels who unite to perform a service or to develop a product. For instance, employees from the manufacturing, engineering, and sales departments serve on a company grievance committee. Even though these representatives rotate over a period of time, the committee continues to perform its specialist function.

Temporary groups consist of *ad hoc committees* and *project teams*. After these groups complete their task, they disband. An *ad hoc group* comes together to solve a particular problem. In the university setting, members of different departments may form an ad hoc committee to develop guidelines for an honors program. The Student Senate may appoint an ad hoc committee to plan a homecoming event or to study the problem of inadequate library facilities. Ad hoc committees typically operate outside official channels; hence they can make recommendations, but they lack the formal authority to make decisions. Since service on an ad hoc committee is usually an assignment above and beyond an employee's routine duties, members may lack commitment to the group, unless management sets deadlines for task completion. In a similar manner, *project teams* consist of representatives from different departments, but they function like subcontractors who are working on a highly skilled technical project. Since team members also belong to other project groups, task coordination becomes a problem.[8] Projects that are low in priority tend to drag on indefinitely, but high priority tasks produce action-oriented meetings and increased communication with external sources. In addition to completing the project, internal communication of team members must clarify the urgency of the task, keep members motivated, and reach agreement on the group's jurisdiction.

This discussion of group function and organizational level indicates the need for trade-offs between internal and external communication. At various stages of a group's development, members may devote more time to communication outside the group and less attention to interaction with team members. Other contingencies such as urgency and complexity of the task, and changing environmental conditions motivate members to concentrate on the internal dynamics of their group and to reduce contacts with external groups.[9] In contrast, specialist groups, project teams, and ad hoc committees have greater task uncertainty and higher coordination requirements than do policy-making and standing committees; therefore, group members rely on a higher frequency of information exchange with external groups.

Group Roles and Organizational Levels

Organizational level not only impacts on the functions of groups at work, but it also affects relationships among group members. Individuals bring their organizational titles, prestige, and status into the group setting. The presence of a vice-president or dean, as Janis' seminal work on "groupthink" demonstrates, often inhibits discussion of diverse viewpoints, a process that can lead to ineffective policy decisions.[10] Since executives frequently run group meetings, they represent the interests and values of the organization as a whole; thus they transmit to members, either implicitly or explicitly, their criteria for effective decisions. Open confrontation about these values or even differences of opinion on decision criteria can result in adverse consequences to an "outspoken" employee.

Farris describes an incident that occurs during the board meeting of a subsidiary of a large multinational corporation. The president of the company chairs the eleven-person management committee which is comprised of the executive vice president, other vice presidents, and heads of the major departments. The group is considering whether to renew a current contract or to adopt a new pricing policy. Their decision will be sent to executives of the parent company for final approval. After thirty minutes of discussion, it becomes obvious that the president and the executive vice president differ in their opinions of the new pricing policy. During the meeting a senior vice president speaks out; otherwise group members avoid taking sides with either of the two highest ranking officials of the company. Since no consensus is reached during the first meeting, a second one is scheduled. Prior to this session, four of the committee members informally contact executives of the parent company. Once they learn that the parent company intends to reject the new pricing proposal, group members remain silent and let the president and executive vice president fight it out without input from the committee. As Farris observes, "The small benefits from active participation are strongly outweighed by the high costs of alienating either the president or the executive vice president."[11]

An informal contact system coupled with status differentials between members represents a form of organizational politicking. A political model of group interaction diametrically opposes our logical, rational notions about organizations. It suggests that power relationships between individuals leads to coalition formation, pressures to conform, and bureaucratic wheeling and dealing. Group interaction, then, parallels negotiation whereby representatives from various departments persuade, cajole, and compromise to reach decisions. Groups that adhere to this model may skip key stages of development or may cluster their interaction in the conflict phase. When the group faces a critical decision, communication between members may consist of defining and affirming power relationships and using subtle maneuvers to entice key individuals to adopt pet viewpoints.

An example of this political process occurs when faculty members in a department complete interviews with job applicants and must decide which one will receive the final offer. Several members who favor a particular candidate may form a coalition with other key faculty. These individuals plot strategies to "overwhelm" the opposition and form a power block to gain a competitive edge for their candidate. In a similar manner, a Student Senate committee comprised of representatives from Greek and non-Greek organizations may barter and politic to reach decisions on homecoming activities. The Greeks may form power blocks to override suggestions of the non-Greeks; the non-Greeks may ask for more than their share in the hope that their interests will not be compromised. As these examples suggest, decision making within the political model relies on negotiation rather than group consensus. Trivial issues and routine matters may occupy formal meeting time, while critical policy issues are settled in backroom corridors behind closed doors.

Politics are a fact of organizational life, even though they have a dark and devious side. Researchers have studied this phenomena in the military, university settings, and the British Broadcasting Company.[12] They conclude that it is less than ideal as a model for effective intergroup relations; thus, while we acknowledge its prevalence in organizational life, we do not necessarily endorse it. There are ways to reduce the ill effects of political wheeling and dealing. Pfeffer and Salancik report that political decision making is more commonplace when groups are loosely connected.[13] Since autonomous groups have fewer opportunities to develop effective intergroup relations, they rely on expediency when confronted with coordination problems. Increasing interdependence among subunits, then, may reduce excessive organizational politicking.

The political model, however, induces us to be cautious in accepting group communication at face value. In some cases, organizational groups are primarily symbolic entities, political means of delaying actions on controversial issues. Killing a good proposal by sending it to a committee rings true in a number of organizations. Moreover, certain leadership styles, namely patriarchal leaders, thrive on the "appearance" of participatory decision making. Employees spend endless hours meeting and preparing committee reports, only to find that their manager conveniently ignores their efforts. Political models, then, often provide us with insights about the symbolic meaning of organizational groups.

Multiple Group Membership: Communication as a Reflection of Divided Loyalties

Differentiation into vertical and horizontal levels suggests that individuals function as members of multiple groups. An engineer may serve on several project teams in addition to holding membership on a grievance committee. Managers, especially linking pins, conduct their own staff meetings while serving as members of upper level executive groups. In the university setting, a faculty member's time may be divided into service on an interdisciplinary research team, an ad hoc committee on faculty governance, a standing committee on curriculum matters, and an ongoing group on women's studies. Belonging to several groups integrates various levels of the organization, but it also leads to divided loyalties and dispersed commitments. In effect, we are only "partially included" in any group. If we have only a limited number of work hours per day, the critical test of commitment surfaces when multiple membership creates time pressures, conflicts in values, and overlapping activities. In these circumstances, our allegiance to a primary group may determine how we spend our time.

In general, our strongest commitment goes to our original work group or to our departmental home base; hence project teams and ad hoc groups that cross horizontal boundaries have difficulty building internal allegiances. Moreover, members bring to the group setting divergent interests, disparate values, and specialized jargon that reflects their departmental differences. They sometimes hold stereotypic beliefs about other departments, e.g., "accountants are picky," "computer jocks are anti-social." The challenge for the project team or ad hoc group is to get past these stereotypes and build common norms and procedures which supercede diverse goals.

Service on a college-wide promotion and tenure committee provides an example of this problem. Members from respective departments meet to establish promotion and tenure standards and to agree upon the avenues for enforcing these standards. The department chairs and full professors who serve on this committee have primary allegiances to their respective departments, especially to the administrative, teaching, and research needs within their departments. Moreover, they possess the particular knowledge and skills necessary for evaluating their own faculty members. Yet, they are faced with the realization that crucial decisions about their department's future lie in the hands of a group of faculty who are only loosely associated and who are frequently in pursuit of diverse ends. Even though the committee may continue to function as a loose collection of individuals with weak ties internally and strong ones externally, they must strive to build interdependence by developing common means and by establishing shared goals. Weick convincingly argues that groups coalesce around common *means* for conducting their business; common *ends* evolve after members develop shared means.[14] This practice requires a de-emphasis on technical expertise of members and an emphasis on their interpersonal communication skills, especially conflict management. Group members never abandon their diverse ends; they simply subjugate them for the sake of the group.

Multiple membership also impacts on a project team's development and its relationship to other groups. During the first several meetings, member communication focuses on clarifying group purpose and on ways to negotiate intergroup relations. Similarly, interaction between groups centers on avoiding overlapping functions and establishing jurisdictional boundaries. Group members consult with and refer to external ties more frequently in the early than in the latter stages of their development. After a group establishes a set of common means, internal norms rather than directives from external sources, govern interactions among members. Communication with other units consists of information exchange and verification of group actions. Multiple membership, then, enhances diversity in group composition, but it increases feelings of divided loyalties. In some cases, members serve as representatives of their "home" groups; hence they are reluctant to adopt the norms, procedures, and goals of another group. But frequent meetings aimed at establishing common means and at effective management of tensions aid in building commitment to the internal group.

In summary, since organizations consist of overlapping and interconnected groups, we need to examine the impact of communication between units as well as within groups. This embeddedness requires us to be cautious about generalizing from groups in isolated settings to organizational groups. We need to incorporate assumptions of connectivity, hierarchical structure, and multiple membership into our conceptual schemes of small group communication. In a practical vein, understanding the impact of organizational embeddedness may help us uncover disputes about work standards between groups, accusations of blame and irresponsibility, and accounts for why groups "get stuck" in certain phases of development. Triads and small groups are "eminently sensible as places to understand the major workings of organizations."[15] Organizations that are loosely connected between groups and tightly coupled within subunits tend to persist as stable collectivities.

Notes

1. Karl E. Weick, *The Social Psychology of Organizing,* 2nd edition (Reading, Mass., Addison-Wesley, 1979), p. 72.
2. Michael L. Tushman and Ralph Katz, "External Communication and Project Performance: An Investigation into the Role of Gatekeepers," *Managerial Science* 26 (1980): 1071–1085.
3. See Donald MacDonald, "Communication Roles and Communication Networks in a Formal Organization," *Human Communication Research* 2 (1976): 365–375 and Michael L. Tushman and Thomas J. Scanlan, "Boundary Spanning Individuals: Their Role in Information Transfer and Their Antecedents," *Academy of Management Journal* 24 (1981): 289–305.
4. Tushman and Scanlan, passim.
5. Dennis W. Organ, "Linking Pins Between Organizations and Environment," *Business Horizons* 14 (December, 1971): 73–80.
6. Chester I. Barnard, *The Functions of the Executive* (Cambridge, Mass.: Harvard University Press, 1938), p. 83.
7. Ronald Fry, Irwin Rubin, and Mark Plovnick, "Dynamics of Groups that Execute or Manage Policy," Payne, Roy and Cooper, Cary L. (eds.), *Groups at Work* (New York: John Wiley & Sons, 1981), pp. 41–58.
8. Alan W. Pearson and Hugh P. Gunz, "Project Groups," Payne, Roy and Cooper, Cary L. (eds.), *Groups at Work* (New York: John Wiley & Sons, 1981), pp. 139–164.
9. Michael L. Tushman, "Technical Communication in R & D Laboratories: The Impact of Project Work Characteristics," *Academy of Management Journal* 21 (1978): 624–645.
10. Irving L. Janis, *Victims of Groupthink* (Boston, Mass.: Houghton Mifflin, 1972).
11. George F. Farris, "Groups and the Informal Organization," Payne, Roy and Cooper, Cary L. (eds.), *Groups at Work* (New York: John Wiley & Sons, 1981), pp. 95–117.
12. See Edward Beard, *Developing the ICBM: A Study in Bureaucratic Politics* (New York: Columbia University Press, 1976) and Tom Burns, *The BBC: Public Institution and Private World* (New York: Macmillan, 1977).
13. Jeffery Pfeffer and Gerald R. Salancik, "Organizational Decision Making as a Political Process: The Case of a University Budget," *Administrative Science Quarterly* 19 (1974): 135–151.
14. Weick, passim, pp. 90–92.
15. Ibid., p. 236.

Temporary Committees as Ad Hoc Groups

David L. Bradford and Leland P. Bradford

Committees are a pervasive part of modern organizational life. Staff groups, project teams, standing committees, work groups, task forces, and executive committees are just a few of the forms such groupings take. Some of these are intrinsic parts of the formal system whereas others are as temporary as the subgroup formed at the end of one week's meeting to prepare for the next. But whatever the form or function, as harried managers can attest to, meetings and committees are a constant part of their world. In fact, Mintzberg (1973) in his observational study of chief executives found that over half of their time was spent in scheduled meetings.

This paper cannot do justice to so wide an area. Rather than covering committees in general, we will focus on ad hoc groups. These are groupings not part of the formal structure, that have a limited life, and which comprise a secondary task for the members. Focusing on such groups does not reduce the domain to insignificant proportions because task forces, project teams, and temporary committees are a frequent occurrence in most organizations. This is particularly true of those coping with turbulent environments caused by changes in external conditions, technology, personnel, or organizational goals (Bennis and Slater, 1968).

We are focusing on ad hoc groups for several reasons. First, an adequate literature already exists for established groups; much has been written about team building, developing staff groups, and running meetings (Bradford, 1976; Golembiewski, 1965; Maier, 1963). Secondly, certain unique problems exist for temporary groups that are not as frequent for standing committees. And thirdly, and most importantly, ad hoc groups offer great potential for the practising manager. The manager who knows how and when to use such groups can increase task accomplishment while at the same time developing individuals and changing the organization.

This chapter will explore the domain of ad hoc groups both from the viewpoint of the person who initiates such a group and of the chairperson who actually leads the committee. Our exploration of project teams and temporary committees will discuss what the initiator and the chairperson can do to realize the potential while minimizing the problems of this organizational format.

From *Groups at Work*. Edited by R. Payne and C. Cooper. © 1981 by John Wiley and Sons, Ltd. Reproduced by permission of John Wiley and Sons, Ltd. David L. Bradford is affiliated with the Department of Organizational Behavior at Stanford University. Leland P. Bradford is affiliated with the National Institute of Applied Behavioral Sciences.

Perhaps the major reason why managers consider establishing an ad hoc group is due to new problems that cannot be adequately handled by the existing departments and standing committees. These include changes in the external environment such as breakthroughs in technology, product innovation by a competitor, changes in market conditions, new government regulations, and upturns or downturns in the economy. Or the impetus may be changes needed in the internal environment such as deciding how to decentralize the organization or modifying the compensation system. Finally, task forces may be established in response to anticipated changes in internal or external conditions. For example, a school decides to evaluate its curriculum to see whether or not it has kept abreast of current knowledge and student needs. In all these cases problems arise that may not fall within an existing department's or committee's jurisdiction. Thus, establishing an ad hoc group may be more appropriate than adding still another department.

A second reason for the use of committees is to provide horizontal integration in what is basically a vertical organization. With the traditional notions of division of responsibility and chain of command, the formal system encourages communication flow up and down the organization. Horizontal communication either does not occur or takes place through informal relationships. But as Galbraith (1973) has pointed out, lateral forms of problem solving have to be developed given the massive increase in the amount of information that has to be processed in an organization. Such forms can be parts of the formal systems (as standing committees) but ad hoc groups give the manager much greater flexibility in bringing together just those parts of the organization that are needed for the specific problem at hand.

An ad hoc group is thus a deviation from the existing organizational structure. It is a different response than changing the formal system by reorganization, establishing a new department or division, or setting up a standing committee. But saying that the ad hoc group is a deviation is not saying that it is inappropriate or that it necessarily represents a failure in the existing system. No manager can be effective and totally work within the organization's structure. Likewise, no organization could afford to encumber itself with the great variety of structures to meet all possible problems. Even if one could foresee the future, any attempt to create a structure that can handle all contingencies would produce a system so cumbersome, so rigid, and so resistant to change that it would soon be obsolete. Thus, even if ad hoc groups are a deviation of the formal organization, they are frequently a necessary deviation. But by recognizing that ad hoc groups are separate from the existing system allows us to understand that it is this very separateness which is the source of many of its problems (as well as its strengths).

Thus, the decision to establish an ad hoc group should be made after careful consideration of such costs and benefits. Too frequently, initiators jump to this alternative under the pressure of a crisis without weighing the alternatives. Even if such consideration leads to establishing an ad hoc group, the manager, by being aware that this option is a violation of the existing structure and process, can foresee and prevent many of the problems that might otherwise occur. Such a stance allows the initiator to take full advantage of the opportunities that temporary groups can provide.

Advantages of Ad Hoc Groups

Better Solutions Because the Membership Comes from Different Areas

Some issues can best be solved if members come from different departments, divisions, or regions. Even though an existing department could make a passable stab at the problem, the solution would be decidedly superior if diverse viewpoints were brought together in a task force. For example, organization X has embarked on a new hiring procedure which will require new supervisory skills, a modification of the performance appraisal system, and the establishing of a career development system. Certainly, Personnel could deal with these issues but it might be that the various operating divisions have information based on their experience that would lead to a superior decision.*

A superior decision may arise not because of new information that different departments would bring but because the department normally responsible for resolving that issue is unable to do an adequate job. A fresh look at the problem is needed and assigning the problem to Engineering would produce Engineering's standard response. Or the department is viewed as having a vested interest in a certain outcome thus precluding an objective assessment of the situation. Similarly, the department may be so torn with internal conflict that giving them the task will further polarize the members. But even when such internal difficulties are not present, the initiator may still choose to go the task-force route. The relevant department may not have the time for an in-depth analysis of the situation, or the problem solution is so delicate (e.g., which plants to close down) that the department faced with the decision wants another external group to give it support.

A third reason why involving different departments in the group is beneficial has less to do with the quality of the decision as it does with acceptance

---

*Another advantage of such groups is that it can keep decision making at the appropriate level in the organization. As Jackson and Morgan (1978) point out, there is a tendency for decisions to be pushed up (at least) one level higher than they should be. It is the *superior* of the people who have the relevant information who is the only individual with access to all the information and has the integrative perspective. But a committee (ad hoc or standing) that is composed of members who collectively have the information can together provide the needed integration which keeps the decision making at the desired level.

of the solution. Even if the solution is basically the same as would be produced if sent to Personnel, there will be greater ownership if the areas that have to implement the decision can develop it to meet their specific situations.

The Problem May Be More Quickly Solved

Depending upon how the committee is established, it is possible for quicker problem resolution with an ad hoc committee than with an existing department. The establishment of the committee itself can be a signal that this problem is being given priority consideration. That, plus extra resources and special powers which, when coupled with an energized committee, can produce quick results.

Another reason why ad hoc groups can work more quickly is that they frequently have greater freedom to move across organizational lines (and cut through procedures) to obtain the information they need. This is particularly likely if they have a powerful initiator who provides a strong mandate.

Ad Hoc Committees Frequently Create Less Resistance than Forming a New Steering Committee

A major advantage of a temporary group is that it is temporary! Because such an arrangement does not mean a permanent shift in power within the organization, others are more likely to allow the structure to be temporarily modified and procedures violated than if such an arrangement were to be permanent. The temporary nature of this arrangement also allows the executive to try out an approach without fully committing the organization's resources or his personal credibility to the project. The temporary nature of this arrangement also gives the group greater freedom to use new methods and procedures since it is less restricted by tradition or past practices.

Since it is temporary, the ad hoc committee is not concerned with establishing a permanent power base. Thus, such groups can frequently be more task focused than a new department which often is worried about jurisdictional issues. Ad hoc groups more frequently work *with* others in such a way that *includes* them as contrasted to permanent groups where concerns about boundaries lead them to act *exclusionary* and seek influence *over* others.

Ad Hoc Groups May Be More Economical

When the problem is episodic in nature, it obviously makes no sense to go through the trouble of establishing a permanent committee (e.g., a curriculum review that occurs only every seven years)! But even when the problem is more likely to be ongoing (and/or recurring) forming a task force may be financially preferable since establishing a new department can require extensive overheads. Also, if there are permanent personnel to do the work, work has to be found for such personnel to do! What happens when the group has outlived its usefulness? It is easier to give birth to a standing committee than to kill it off. The statement may be made that 'we will evaluate the usefulness of this program after three years' but such a pronouncement will only guarantee that the department will expend energy to publicize its importance.

Ad Hoc Groups Can Develop Individuals and the Organization

In addition to accomplishing a needed task, a temporary committee can be a way to assess and develop subordinates. Those who have been locked into narrow jobs can develop new skills and learn about other aspects of the organization if assigned to a wide-ranging task force. Young managers who appear to have great potential gain visibility to wider areas in the organization without incurring the risk of a permanent assignment if they do not live up to their promise.

In addition to developing individuals, a temporary committee or task force can develop the organization. Representatives from different departments that have interdependent functions but few previous working relationships can be brought together in the same group. Not only will their different viewpoints lead to a potentially more creative task solution, but relationships can be developed that will prove useful in future interactions.

We have listed five major advantages to using ad hoc groups. But these advantages are not without potential costs. As we will explore in the next section, many of these disadvantages are just the reciprocal of the benefits just discussed!

Potential Problems of Ad Hoc Groups

Weakening the Organizational Structure and Process

The obverse of the temporary group's advantage in cutting across departmental boundaries and violating standard/traditional organizational processes is that such actions can subvert the system. One way that the establishment of an ad hoc group can weaken an organization is by compensating for a flaw rather than correcting it. Is the reason for setting up an ad hoc group the failure of an organizational unit to do its job adequately? Is the formation of a task force to explore new products and new market conditions a sign that strategic planning is lacking in the organization? In such a case, it might be best for the manager to correct the deficiencies in the delinquent department because establishing a temporary committee may just perpetuate an inadequate organizational system by compensating for its deficiencies.

But even when establishing an ad hoc group does not reflect failure in the existing system, it can still weaken the organization. The fact that this group is outside the formal structure may encourage others to violate standard procedures. The task force could make it difficult for established departments to fulfil their normal function in the future. For example, setting up a task force to explore new compensation systems may be interpreted by the rest of the organization as a sign that the Personnel Department is incompetent and should be by-passed when other issues arise.

Leading to a Lower Quality Solution

Bringing together people from different sections of the organization who hold divergent viewpoints does not necessarily lead to a higher quality solution. Interdepartmental rivalries might be so high and the value and attitude gulfs so wide that the diversity cannot be utilized for a creative solution. Instead, a compromise solution evolves and the effort to please everybody satisfies nobody.

Even when the difficulty is not a major conflict between areas or among values, there are other factors that can mitigate against the successful working of ad hoc groups. Given that the committee's assignment is in addition to the members' primary jobs, the latter can take precedence over the former. (This can be the case particularly if there are no clear rewards for serving on the committee—the rewards at performance appraisal time being based on the primary job.) There also may be problems of work overload or demands by each member's superior to give the department's task priority over the committee's.

Personal Needs Rather than Organizational Needs Are Primary

We said that one of the advantages of an ad hoc group is that members could be selected for their competence and the group can be mandated to work just on this assigned task (and not for its own aggrandizement). But what if the initiator had covert, personal reasons for establishing the committee? Feelings, ambitions, fears, worries, likes, and dislikes play a part in all individual behaviour, no matter how 'objective' people believe they are. But what if these motivations play a major part in the formation and composition of the committee? What if the private reason to 'send it to committee' was to block the normal operations of the executive group? What if the task force is a pawn in an ongoing power struggle with another department? What if the selection of the committee chairperson and member serves to pay off old debts, reward friends, or punish enemies? When such covert reasons exist to a significant extent, then the formation of a temporary committee can be at the expense of organizational effectiveness.

Among the numerous hidden motives that could be present in the decision to establish a temporary committee, the following are probably the most general.

(a) *To prevent a larger group from making an immediate decision.* The initiator may feel that the decision the larger group is leaning toward is one that is undesirable because: it may discredit the initiator; it may upset other plans the initiator has in mind; or it may decrease his/her power and prestige. The reasons do not even have to be so Machiavellian. The initiator may feel that the larger group is moving in undue haste, that it has not considered all the relevant information, and is being swept along by the passion of the moment.

There may be many reasons why the initiator is not able to confront directly the larger group. For example, his role may prevent him from expressing his point of view on a divided issue; even if he expressed it, his opinion would not stop the tide; or even if he could decide the issue, such an action would antagonize the losers. Instead, establishing a task force to study the issue gives time to diffuse emotional pressure, disperse the strength of a clique within the larger group, and allow marshalling of counter-forces. The initiator can use delaying tactics to serve personal motives while appearing to use statesman-like caution to arrive at a judicious decision.

(b) *To deflect blame away from oneself.* The task force composed of impartial and valued employees may come up with the same (unpleasant) recommendation that the initiator would have, but now the latter can implement the solution as the committee's idea. Or the problem may be so difficult that no feasible solution exists. The failure of the committee to solve the problem takes some of the onus for previous failure off of the manager.

(c) *To develop alternatives without commitment.* The organization may be at a crucial decision point; which of many paths should top management take? The answer may become clear only after several alternatives have been explored and tentative steps taken. For the executive to make a premature decision raises the possibility of being blamed for the wrong choice. But a temporary committee can serve as a trial balloon and the manager can wait for a recommendation that gains a favorable reception and then accept the credit.

In another situation the task force's report creates conflict and disagreement within the organization. The initiator now steps in, King Solomon-like, and offers the compromise that gains the approval of both camps.

Such personal motivations probably exist in varying degrees in most situations. Some of these reasons might actually be for the betterment of the organization; not all are for personal aggrandizement and empire building. But they have been labelled 'covert' because for any one of a number of reasons, the initiator cannot make them public.

When such covert reasons are a major determinant for establishing a temporary committee, certain problems are likely to arise. If these reasons sabotage a task force's efforts, then frustration and disillusionment can result. Not only will morale and commitment likely decrease for members of that particular group but future groups can be affected as well. The next task-force leader will find it that much more difficult to build commitment and motivation if there is a feeling among members that 'this is all a sham; it does not make any difference what we turn out'.

To Summarize

The judicious use of ad hoc groups can be a powerful management tool. It allows the executive quickly to establish a problem-solving mechanism with hand-picked membership which has authority to cut across organizational boundaries and procedures. Such a tool can explore possibilities without forcing the executive to make a permanent commitment in terms of organizational direction. Finally, it can be used to develop (and assess) potential key subordinates and build important integrative ties across organizational units.

On the other hand, forming a structure outside the formal system, even if it is only temporary, potentially can cause problems. Is the establishment of a task force an indication that the regular department is unwilling to make tough choices? Will dragging out the process, even if a higher quality solution is produced, really warrant the stress produced by the greater time required? Is the temporary group a sign that there are inadequacies in that department which should be corrected? Will the decisions of the temporary committee change the power distribution in the organization (as would be the case when the ad hoc group is deciding on a new organizational structure or new markets to enter), and will other departments see this as a threat to their security and respond with attack rather than with assistance?

These are just some of the dimensions that the initiator(s) should consider. Unfortunately, an exact contingency model cannot be developed which would say 'under these conditions always use (or never use) an ad hoc group'. Each situation is to some extent unique. The most this chapter can do is lay out the general dimensions and leave it to the practising manager to weigh the relevance of each variable in that particular situation. Since any decision always has a cost, the question is whether the benefit of establishing an ad hoc group is worth the cost.

But even when forming an ad hoc group appears to be the appropriate decision, there are steps the initiator (and the chairperson) can take to capitalize on the potential benefits and minimize the costs. The next section will look at the following six key questions that are important for task-group success.

(1) What exactly is the purpose of this group? What should the charge to the committee be?
(2) What criteria should be used for selection of the chairperson and committee members?
(3) What should be the relationship between the initiator and chairperson committee?
(4) How can one build group cohesiveness and member commitment while operating under time limitations?
(5) What ties should the committee form with other parts of the organization?
(6) How should the committee report its conclusions to the initiating group?

Establishing and Managing the Committee

Determining the Purpose

In some cases the charge to the committee may be clear in the minds of the initiator(s). Furthermore, the purpose may be non-political in content so that it can be publicly announced. But in other cases the situation may not be quite as clear. It could be that the decision to form a task force resulted from confusion or disagreement either in the original decision-making group or in the mind of the initiator(s). To further compound this situation, some of the reasons may be of a political or personal nature and cannot be publicly announced.

One of the major dangers in the latter situation is that the charge to the chairperson and committee is given in more definitive terms than is warranted. Thus, the assignment does not reflect the actual confusion, political infighting, or conflicting forces inherent in the problem being tackled. If the committee is not informed of all these factors, members will be misdirected and operate as if there is certainty in that world of ambiguity.

When there are covert reasons behind the formation of the temporary committee, then one of the important criteria for selection of the chairperson is that he/she can be trusted to be privy to these reasons. In the best of all possible worlds these reasons could also be shared with the committee members, but, at least to the extent the chairperson is informed, the greater the chance that wasted effort, error in direction, and frustration will be reduced.

It is inappropriate to lay total responsibility for clarifying the charge on the doorstep of the initiator. As we mentioned, there is a tendency for the initiating persons to express the assignment as more clear-cut than is actually the case. The reciprocal trap is for the chairperson, perhaps wishing to show enthusiasm for the task, to accept such a charge without question. An important initial action by the chairperson is to question the initiator(s) as to the exact reasons for forming the committee. Were there conflicting reasons? Dissention among members of the original decision-making group? Any skeletons the chairperson ought to be aware of? Political interests that the committee's solution should take into account?

The need for a joint clarification of the charge is required, not just at the beginning, but often at different points in the committee's life. As the group gets into the problem, new dimensions may arise. It could be that what the initiator(s) thought was the problem is only a symptom of a more underlying difficulty, or that the general direction the executive preferred is unfeasible. Thus, at these times a re-negotiation of the charge to the committee is necessary. The chairperson and the initiator(s) have to see clarification of the task as an ongoing process. It may be that the greatest benefit the temporary committee can provide is helping the initiator(s) recognize what the core problems are (rather than just going along and coming up with a solution to the initial but irrelevant issue).

Directions to the chairperson and committee include more than *what* has to be done but also *how*. One aspect of the *how* is the final form the committee's work is to take. Is it a report (written or oral), a series of interim presentations, or a prototype or demonstration? Does the initiator want just one outcome, or two or more options from which to select? Another aspect of the *how* is the jurisdiction of the committee. Will members have access to all relevant information? Can they contact and query others in the organization? Or are they only to cogitate in the meeting room dependent solely on their own resources?

Selecting the Chairperson and Committee Members

The choice of committee composition rests on many factors. Some are mundane (such as who is available) and some are more important (such as responding to the political realities of the organization). Obviously, competence should be the central dimension but competence refers to more than just technical ability. There are two other major dimensions of competence: (1) competence in relating to the initiator and other organizational members, and (2) competence in working in a temporary group. The relative importance of these three will be somewhat different depending on whether one is selecting the chairperson or the committee members.

Technical Competence. There is frequently the (erroneous) belief that the chairperson should be the individual with the greatest technical competence. The job of the chairperson is not to come up with the answer, but to *establish conditions where the answer can be developed.* The leader needs only enough technical expertise so that he/she: (1) knows the major blind avenues to avoid and promising routes to follow in order to provide general direction to the committee; (2) knows enough about the subject matter to assess the validity of points being made by the committee; and (3) has enough of a reputation in the technical area to lend credibility to the committee's deliberation and conclusions.

These reasons for technical competence on the part of the chairperson are based not on the notion of knowledge to solve the problem, but knowledge as a *source of power.* If that person is technically unskilled, then others with expertise have an undue amount of influence which can interfere with the chairperson's ability to lead. Thus, the group leader does not have to 'have all the answers' but has to be sufficiently knowledgeable about the topic being considered to know whether or not the committee is finding the answers! Given that the leader has a minimum level of technical ability, then members can be selected to provide the additional expertise.

Relational Competence. Even though the task force is outside the formal organizational structure, it is still part of that larger system. Thus, a crucial role for the chairperson is the external liaison role. As we mentioned, one important aspect of this liaison function is with the initiator. The latter needs to select somebody with whom a good working relationship is possible. The chairperson has to be a person that the initiator can trust (so he/she will not constantly be breathing down the chairperson's neck) and can communicate openly with (including sharing many, if not all, of the covert reasons that the initiator has for establishing the task force).

But such a working relationship can have its own complications. Sometimes the initiator is caught between two opposite pressures. One is to select a person who can be relied upon to 'do the job' (which may mean coming up with a solution the initiator can live with). The other pressure relates to a particular situation in which the committee's assignment demands total independence from the initiator. The latter situation is particularly important in cases where the initiator may receive improper benefits from a certain committee decision (for example, where the group's task is to determine blame for a failure, or to make a decision about the organization's structure, direction or products—all decisions which could favour the initiator). In those situations, independence of the chairperson may be required if the committee's recommendations are to have credibility.

But in both cases the chairperson has to have the relational competence to gain maximum freedom for the committee's activities without jeopardizing the relationship with the powers that be. In the first situation mentioned above where there is no danger of potential conflict of interests the problem facing the task force might be having such close ties that they become a rubber-stamp group. In that case the chairperson has to work to gain independence, whereas in the second situation where independence is built in through the selection of an impartial chairperson, there is frequently the need to build a working relationship with the initiator (so there is sufficient support for the committee's activities).

Picking a chairperson with relational skills carries beyond the ability to have a working relationship with the initiator. The committee will need information and cooperation from the organization. In this case the relational competencies of committee membership often play an important part. Not infrequently, members are selected because of their ties with key organizational members. Although appropriate, this can be a double-edged sword. Such relationships can be invaluable in opening up access to information that is necessary if a successful solution is to be reached and accepted in the organization, but such ties can also allow external members to have undue influence over the committee's deliberations. The problem relates to the flow of influence; is it primarily from the committee member to the key external member or primarily from the latter to the committee member? The former tends to lead to greater task success.

Group Process Competence. The chairperson (and members) need skills in managing the group development and decision-making process. A temporary group with no previous history has unique problems not found in established departments. For example, members come to the committee with a high commitment to the task (since they were probably selected primarily for their interest and expertise) but they also may feel ambivalent about the assignment. This task is in addition to their normal work load; will the group's efforts lead to any beneficial change or personal rewards that compensate for the extra work? Members frequently join a task force as representatives from their own areas. Not only is it likely that they have a particular point of view to champion but they have stereotypes about what the other areas represented on the committee are like. How can these differing viewpoints be expressed and utilized without polarizing the group to the point that a viable solution is blocked?

In addition to such issues which may or may not occur, there are some that can be expected to arise in all temporary groups. From a collection of separate individuals there has to be built: cohesiveness and commitment; norms and procedures; and an openness of communication. Equally important is the ability of members to surface and effectively utilize conflict and disagreement; the pressure to build a cohesive team cannot be at the expense of smothering individual viewpoints and differences. And all of these group-process issues need to be dealt with in a relatively short period of time.

Thus, an important criterion for chairperson and member selection is competence in working together and building a high-performance group. At times it is necessary to sacrifice technical competence or connections with key organizational members for interpersonal and group skills. In most cases it is impossible to maximize all three types of competence so the person selecting the group (the initiator and/or the chairperson) has to make trade-offs in achieving the appropriate combination of these three variables.

Determining the Relationship Between the Committee and Initiator

As mentioned in the previous section, there are some situations in which the chairperson and committee must preserve independence from the initiator (as was the case with the Watergate Investigations *vis-à-vis* the relationship of the Chief Investigator and Nixon). But in most cases the task force is not investigating the initiator but fulfilling a task for that individual. In that situation the initiator and chairperson need to work out the two central issues of support and of control.

Support includes the amount the initiator will back the committee through the use of personal and position power. If there is controversy and conflict, can the committee count on the initiator to provide appropriate defence? If it is necessary to obtain information or cooperation from others in the organization, will the initiator help them achieve it? But support also includes such tangible forms as release time from other activities, a budget, and secretarial assistance. Although these may appear mundane, they can play an important role in facilitating the group's operations (as well as signalling to the committee the importance of their task).

Control refers to the limitations placed on the scope of the committee's activities. This includes not only the content areas that the group can explore but the extent the group has access to other people in the organization. Control is more than a set of restrictions laid down initially, but also refers to the ongoing control the initiator imposes as the task force progresses. Does he/she want to attend all meetings (or to drop in whenever desired)? Does the initiator want frequent interim reports? The amount of latitude the task force is given will be determined by the nature of the task, the perceived competence of the chairperson/members, and the initiator's personal comfort with letting go of control.

Control and support are not opposite ends of the same scale but rather are independent dimensions. That is to say, there can be conditions of high control and high support as well as low control and low support (as well as high on one dimension and low on the other). It is likely that greater control is needed the more important the task and the greater the range of types of outcome. If the task is relatively unimportant then few people will care what the outcome will be. Likewise, if the focus is highly specified and there are few possible outcomes (so that the control emanates from the assignment), then external control is less necessary. High support is needed the more controversial the issue and therefore the greater the chance of opposition and attack.

As with achieving clarity of the committee's charge, working out relationships of support and autonomy must be continuously dealt with over the life of the committee. Even though the chairperson needs initially to negotiate an acceptable amount of backing and freedom (and may not want to accept the committee assignment unless a successful agreement is reached), the amount will vary at different points in time. When first established, the committee may need public support to gain legitimacy and cooperation from other departments but, later on, more freedom is required if the committee is to adequately do its work. But the crucial point is that the chairperson (and initiator) must realize that negotiating issues of support and autonomy is an ongoing process and appropriate for either party to bring up for reconsideration.

● ● ● ● ● ●

Relations with Other Individuals and Departments

One of the issues that the chairperson (and group) will have to struggle with is how isolated they want to be from other people in the organization. On the one hand, close ties may be important to gain information and to make sure there is support for the committee. But such ties can also be a source of pressure. The last thing a committee may need in its attempts to objectively examine the pros and cons of various alternatives is to be harassed by different interest groups. Instead, they may decide to have closed meetings, not issue any progress reports, and not share the content of their deliberations.

But there can be other occasions when such a stance would be counterproductive. It is likely that once into exploring the task, the committee finds that, in order to deliver on their assignment, other aspects of the organization have to be modified (e.g., a new hiring practice to attract better managers will not work until the appraisal and promotion system is overhauled). This may require going back to the original decision-making group to ask for a redefinition of their charge or to go to the relevant department (Personnel in this case) and gain their support. Otherwise, if the committee were to remain isolated and unilaterally take on this added assignment, there might be no support for their final conclusions.

At this stage in the committee's work their activities may well begin to produce reactions from other parts of the organization. The task force is pursuing a line of inquiry that is causing concern in a certain department, or with a powerful member of the executive committee. Group members see that there are certain key individuals or departments whose support they need if the solution is to be accepted and implemented. All of these factors are likely to pull the chairperson away from the task-force meetings and towards spending an increasing amount of time dealing with these other individuals and departments. These activities may involve re-negotiating the original assignment, modifying the relationship of the committee with the initiator, meeting informally with key individuals in the organization, or visiting staff meetings of certain departments to give them a progress report.

Acceptance of the Committee's Solution

Too frequently, the committee sees its end-product as a report (the longer the better) that is delivered cold to the decision-making group. Not only is there the blind hope that the report will be thoroughly read beforehand but also that the logic of the arguments will carry the day. What is ignored is that the decision-making group is back where the task force started in terms of understanding the complexities of the problem. If the distance the committee has travelled is far, the decision-making body may have difficulty understanding the reasoning that led to the final conclusions.

There are various methods the committee can use to report to a larger group. One is bringing the initiator and/or decision-making group along during the committee's deliberations through preliminary reports or briefing sessions. A second method is for the chairperson to meet with each of the members of the decision-making group on a one-to-one basis before the final report is written to see that the conclusions are compatible with what they want. Thirdly, some sub-set of that group could be invited to attend one of the committee's meetings to react to the proposal.

This type of preparatory work by the chairperson before the final presentation should be welcomed by the initiator and decision-making group. If they only see the product at the end, they are faced with the options of either acceptance or rejection and 'sending it back to committee' can be demoralizing for everybody involved. Much more preferable would be discussions during the developmental stage when modifications can be made without such comments being experienced as failure by the committee.

Another aspect of the group's solution is the question of what form should their conclusions take. There is nothing sacrosant about total reliance on written reports. Engineering has the tradition of developing prototypes; 'softer' areas can do the same. For example, if the charge to the task force has been to develop an executive training programme, perhaps one aspect of the 'final report' would be to have the decision-making group personally go through their model programme.

A third aspect has to do with the timing of the presentation or report. Usually that decision is determined by the completion of the committee's work; sometimes it is decided by the running agenda of the decision-making group. But the pressure of other events can increase or decrease the receptiveness of that group to the committee's recommendations.

A fourth aspect has to do with the extent to which the final proposal is, in fact, final. There is a tendency for people to assume that a quality job is defined by having the definitive answer. This leads to conclusions which lock the organization into a course of action far into the future. But the 'final report' of a task force could contain provisions for a period of experimentation and then reassessment. This requires, of course, that the committee has thought through how that assessment is to be done and the dimensions on which the project is to be evaluated.

Conclusion

This chapter has attempted to lay out various issues that need to be considered for the successful operation of a temporary committee. As stated initially, a task force or temporary committee can be a very powerful management tool. It can provide flexibility for the executive to explore new options, bring together disparate areas, and develop and test promising subordinates. When not used excessively, a temporary committee can provide a useful alternative to the formal structure without weakening it. But the power of a temporary committee can be realized only if careful thought is given to the purpose, composition, and charge. Furthermore, the chairperson is not a passive part of this process but can also influence the committee's area of responsibility. Hopefully, by being aware of the various dimensions explored in this chapter, the initiator and the chairperson can structure the process so that the potential of such groups can be fulfilled.

References

Bennis, W. G. and Slater, P. (1968) *The Temporary Society,* New York: Harper & Row.

Bradford, L. P. (1976) *Making Meetings Work,* La Jolla, California: University Associates.

Galbraith, J. (1974) *Designing Complex Organizations,* New York: Harper & Row.

Golembiewski, R. T. (1965) 'Small groups and large organizations', in J. G. March, ed., *Handbook of Organizations,* Chicago: Rand McNally.

Jackson, H. H. and Morgan, C. P. (1978) *Organization Theory: A Macro Perspective for Management,* Eaglewood Cliffs, New Jersey: Prentice-Hall.

Maier, N. R. F. (1973) *Problem-Solving Discussions and Conferences,* New York: McGraw-Hill.

Mintzberg, H. (1963) *The Nature of Managerial Work,* New York: Harper & Row.

Ware, J. (1977) 'Managing a task force', Intercollegiate Case Clearing House (1–478–002).

The Experiential Group

Kjell Eric Rudestam

Experiential groups have been viewed as small, temporary collections of people meeting within a specified time limit, generally using a designated leader, with the general goal of interpersonal inquiry and personal learning, growth, or discovery (Barrett-Lennard, 1975). There is considerable disagreement, however, about what happens in an experiential group. Many would argue that experiential groups are unstructured, here-and-now interactions in which the group members study their own process and share progressively deeper life experiences with one another. This format is certainly common, but some of the groups I will be discussing are very structured (for example, skill-training groups) and some deal with past experiences in addition to here-and-now feelings (for example, psychodrama).

Lakin (1972) has summarized six processes he believes to be common to experiential groups: (1) the facilitation of emotional expressiveness; (2) the generation of feelings of belonging; (3) a commitment to self-disclosure; (4) the sampling of personal behaviors; (5) the making of interpersonal comparisons as sanctioned group behavior; and (6) the sharing of responsibility for leadership and direction with the appointed leader of the group. In our context, these processes are generally applicable with the possible exception of the last one; some experiential groups retain a strong leader who does not democratically share leadership functions with the group members. The experiential group will be considered as a broad concept, reflecting the kinds of groups that are popular today and that were shaped by figures such as Freud, Reich, Moreno, Bion, and Lewin.

Experiential groups may be categorized into four clusters (Cohen & Smith, 1976): groups designed to encourage organizational development or problem solving; groups for learning interpersonal and leadership skills; growth groups; and therapy groups. These four types of groups overlap in practice, so that, for example, many learning groups are also therapeutic in effect. Within each of these clusters, the focus has a broad range: from information- or task-oriented to person- or insight-oriented; from leader-centered to member-centered; from rational thinking to affective spontaneity; from highly structured to unstructured; from short-term to ongoing; from healthy individuals to the severely emotionally ill.

Two of the most critical dimensions relevant to the types of groups described . . . are the extent to which the group leader maintains a dominant role in structuring and directing the group and the extent to which there is a focus on emotional stimulation as opposed to rational thinking. . . . Note that there is considerable diversity with regard to how specific leaders apply the basic concepts and methods of the approach. T-groups and theme-centered groups, in particular, may be either rational or affective in orientation, depending upon the particular task or theme. Encounter groups may be leader- or member-centered, depending upon the particular leader.

Souls, Goals, and Roles

Souls: The Composition of Groups

Depending upon the orientation and function of the group, participants range from relatively well adjusted, emotionally stable college students seeking to know themselves better and grow psychologically to persons in need of help to correct incapacitating emotional or behavioral disorders. Many group leaders screen prospective candidates before admitting them into the group. However, research offers little guidance in gauging who is most apt to be a successful group participant. To generalize from individual studies to all group experiences is especially misleading, because the particular leader or therapist and the type of group are crucial determinants of outcome.

One way of assessing who may benefit most is to study early terminators, or drop-outs, from an ongoing group experience. Individuals may drop out of a group for a variety of reasons, including practical considerations such as a geographical move, time conflicts, or a change of interest. More compelling reasons were cited by Yalom (1966) in his study of nine groups in a university outpatient clinic in which 35 of 97 participants terminated prematurely. One reason given by the drop-outs was external stress—that is, a concern for issues outside the group to the extent that the group itself seemed less compelling or relevant. These external concerns were sometimes seen by the investigator as flight in the face of feeling threatened within the group, or as rationalizations used to avoid fears of aggression, self-disclosure, or intimacy. A second reason was group deviancy: the drop-outs' style of interpersonal behavior was antithetical to the behavior of other participants. These participants showed little psychological sophistication, interpersonal sensitivity, or personal insight. A third category included problems of intimacy manifested in withdrawal, inappropriate self-disclosure, or unrealistic expectations. Ironically, people who fear interpersonal intimacy are in great need of a good group experience. A fourth reason was the fear of emotional contagion: some group

Table 1
Categorization of experiential groups according to executive
function and emotional stimulation

	Leader-centered	Member-centered
Rational	Transactional analysis	T-groups
	Skill-training groups	Theme-centered interaction
Affective	Encounter groups	T-groups
	Gestalt groups	Theme-centered interaction
	Body-therapy groups	
	Psychodrama	Encounter groups
	Dance-therapy groups	
	Art-therapy groups	

members were adversely affected by the problems of others in the group, which too easily spilled over into stimulating upsetting issues of their own.

It is tempting to isolate diagnostic categories or personality attributes that correlate with difficulties such as those mentioned above to select suitable group candidates. In fact, research suggests that diagnosis is not so important (Grunebaum, 1975). In most psychotherapies, including group therapy, the healthiest people make the best clients. Those whose defenses are lowest and are most capable of learning from others tend to be the most successful group participants. Practically speaking, a group of motivated persons with average intelligence should be suitable.

Although a group leader might turn away psychotics, acutely depressed individuals, and homicidal sociopaths as unlikely to profit from a shared group experience, behavior is a better prognostic indicator than is diagnostic category. People who are not appropriate for experiential groups include those who under stress of criticism predictably become either too anxious or too angry to hear what others have to say; those who, when stressed, project such strong feelings onto other group members that they feel victimized; and those who have such low self-esteem that they insatiably seek reassurance (Lakin, 1972).

The implementation of these criteria may have to be adjusted depending upon the type and purpose of the group. Furthermore, people who paralyze group interaction over a long period of time, who can't be reached by other group members because of their own chaotic behavior, who act in destructive, antisocial ways and validly frighten other group members, or who are in such constant anxiety that their behavior makes them a persistent burden to the group would not be good candidates (Leopold, 1957). Although most selection criteria are designed to protect the individual, one must also consider what a significantly disturbed person does to the group process. Those who are overly immature, grossly insensitive to others, or unable to control their impulses are impediments to the flow of the group.

The best diagnostic indicator of successful participation in a group is probably actual behavior in early group sessions. In this regard, a skilled group therapist can use this early group information and lead the group accordingly. Finally, Yalom, Houts, Zimerberg, and Rand (1967) reported that a person's eventual popularity in a group is one of the few predictors of a successful group experience. Those who do become popular, it has been found, are curious about relationships and behavior, and are high in personal self-disclosure and activity in the group.

A group should be large enough to allow opportunity for interaction and small enough for everyone to be involved and feel a part. As groups become larger, there is a tendency for the more dominant and verbal to usurp the group's time and the likelihood that subgroups and cliques will form (Hare, 1976). When a group is too small, it ceases to operate as a group, and the participants find themselves involved in individual counseling or psychotherapy within a group setting. Four members are regarded as constituting the barest minimum for a viable group.

Generally, the depth of therapy decreases as the size of the group increases (Geller, 1951). Thus, psychoanalytic group therapy, in which the therapist probes deeply into an individual's psyche, usually insists on relatively small groups, from about six to ten members. The "rule of eight" (Kellerman, 1979) suggests that eight is a good number for a therapy group—small enough to promote intimacy and allow all participants the opportunity to form direct relationships with all others, and large enough to be dynamic and offer a variety of interactive experiences. The length of each session is a relevant factor as well. It has been suggested that a 90-minute session hypothetically allows each member of an eight-person group (plus a leader) an optimal ten minutes of group time (Foulkes & Anthony, 1957).

In contrast to therapy groups, typical growth groups are somewhat larger and have from eight to fifteen members. Longer sessions, of course, allow for a greater number of participants to speak up and meet their individual needs. At the extreme, group inspirational approaches, team-building or group-orientation techniques can be used with more than 50 persons.

Another issue is whether a group ought to be heterogeneous or homogeneous in make-up. When group practitioners talk about similarities and differences among members they generally refer to demographic variables such as age, sex, and education; identified problems, such as symptoms, diagnoses, and complaints; and personality styles and behavior patterns. The blending of these components of membership will inevitably depend upon the purpose and time frame of the group. Groups that will have a short lifetime or that function to give emotional support to disturbed people tend to seek similarities among the members; groups that will meet for a longer time and that engage in interpersonal insight work may benefit from greater heterogeneity.

There is an inherent trade-off in choosing to emphasize similarities or differences among the participants. Similarity usually leads to a high degree of attraction and support; diversity may offer a better possibility of confrontation and change (Levine, 1979). Most experts favor a relatively heterogeneous mix of complaints and interpersonal styles. Whitaker and Lieberman (1964), for instance, stress striving for heterogeneity among participants with regard to conflict areas and styles of coping. Diversity, which occurs when people with different types of personalities and ways of acting are included in the group, leads to tension and confrontation; working through such issues culminates in optimal learning and growth. An individual with an emotional, expressive style, for example, can benefit from relating to others with more rational, restrained approaches, and vice versa. Kellerman (1979) argues that the ideal group needs to encourage the potential expression of the full range of human emotions, including guilt, depression, hope, sexuality, hate, and anger. Further, in order to achieve the ideal underlying emotional structure, Kellerman recommends striving for heterogeneity in terms of the problems expressed by the members and of the functions the people fill within the group.

The most commonly mentioned rationale for heterogeneity is the desire to create a representative model of society within the group. As Bennis and Shepard (1974) put it, "The more heterogeneous the membership, the more accurately does the group become for each member a microcosm of the rest of his interpersonal experience" (p. 128). However, it is important to keep in mind that group members may require considerable time to grapple with the challenge of encountering very different people who may not immediately fulfill their interpersonal needs. Likewise, the cost of heterogeneity may be too dear if it creates a group isolate. The presence of a solitary individual with an extreme personality characteristic may sap the group's energy away from more useful work. Moreover, token mixes of sex, occupation, or race may be worse than no variety at all. One elderly person in a group of college students can easily get tagged as the "old man"; one Black in a White group may become the target for fantasies and projections of the whole group (Lakin, 1972).

A group with a shorter time frame or a fixed focus, such as helping people overcome agoraphobia, may necessitate a more homogeneous membership. The format of the group is a critical factor. A collection of depressives may work in a programmed, structured format but be deadly dull in an unstructured T-group. The main drawback of homogeneous groups is that they can be self-limiting because of their restricted scope: they may not be challenging enough. On the other hand, Yalom (1975) argues in favor of similarity by stressing that homogeneous groups develop an identity more quickly, are more cohesive, offer more support and less conflict, and have better attendance than heterogeneous groups. Yalom cites research indicating that similarly task-oriented individuals can do very well together in human relationship groups (Greening & Coffey, 1966) and that compatibility in interpersonal styles correlates significantly positively with group cohesiveness. Cohesiveness, as we shall see, is an important determinant of group success. Most group leaders agree, for example, that members ought to be reasonably similar in ego strength, the ability to handle stress. Likewise, Levine (1979), who leans toward diversity in personality types, suggests first organizing groups according to common life problems and ages to encourage cohesion. Real homogeneity, however, is almost impossible to achieve in organizing a group, since people who share common problems and coping styles will still develop conflicts over intimacy, authority, and other relevant group issues.

Goals

In psychology, a small group usually refers to a few people getting together with a specific agenda such as wrestling with a problem, trying to feel better, or having a good time (Phillips & Erickson, 1970). Each person has, during the process, the opportunity to develop a relationship with the other people. Each person can take on behaviors that are either helpful or harmful to the achievement of group goals. Depending upon the type of group, members typically decide upon their own specific goals for the group experience.

When the group function is slanted in a problem-solving direction, the task is of paramount importance and the mental health of the individual is less crucial; when the group is a growth group or a therapy group, the welfare of the individual is preeminent. In growth groups, participants may seek joy and self-fulfillment. In psychotherapy groups, goals are generally concerned with increased self-awareness and self-exploration toward the remediation or prevention of serious emotional problems in an effort to provide psychological and behavioral change and direction. Such groups assume that participants are not functioning well in life and seek to overcome disability and suffering. Often, the initial goals of relief from anxiety or depression convert, as the group progresses, to interpersonal goals of wanting to communicate with others, to be more trusting, honest, and loving toward them (Yalom, 1975). Apparently the goal of building increasingly effective interpersonal interactions comes out of developing recognition of our needs as social beings. In a flexible group, individual goals can be modified and changed during the course of the group experience.

Roles and Norms

The study of social behavior has been defined by Gordon Allport (1968, p. 5) as "an attempt to understand how the *thoughts, feelings* and *behavior* of an individual are influenced by the *actual, imagined* or *implied* presence of others." We are social beings largely as a result of our various affiliations and interactions with groups of relatives, friends, acquaintances, and strangers. The processes that occur in social groups or family units occur in concentrated form in the artificially constructed group. Members enter an unfamiliar group situation with a leader who may or may not give them assistance. As a result of their unique perceptions and past experiences, they arrive with certain expectations of the group and the role they will play. A *role* is the set of behaviors or functions that are seen as appropriate and acted upon within a social context. The need for role flexibility is illustrated by individuals who are expected to assume a role within the group different from that expected of them outside the group. A manager who has defined herself in terms of her abilities to direct and give orders, for example, may be disconcerted to discover that her ability to take charge is not appreciated in the group situation. Moreover, a person who adopts the role of harmonizer by offering sympathy and reassurance in early stages of the group may have difficulty confronting others as it becomes necessary later on in the life of the group.

Various group roles emerge naturally as the group progresses. Most researchers believe that roles are likely to be similar across groups and develop early in the life of a group (see Bales & Slater, 1955). Others maintain that specific roles lie latent within the group until they are elicited by specific group needs during various phases of the group (Stock & Thelen, 1958). Bogdanoff and Elbaum (1978) have concluded that basic roles evolve to help resolve predictable conflict issues faced by the group. For example, a "basic mistruster" may emerge to help group members cope with the issue of how much to self-disclose and how much to conceal from one another.

There is a long list of stereotypic roles used to describe interpersonal behavior in experiential groups. Many carry colorful names, such as self-righteous moralist, help-rejecting complainer, time keeper, and guardian of democracy. A circumplex (Figure 1) helps to organize roles or personality traits by locating them around the circle according to how similar or dissimilar they are from one another.

Factor analysis has been a favorite tool to reduce a large number of roles or group behaviors into a few primary dimensions. Most common, perhaps, are the two dimensions of anger/love and strength/weakness discerned by Leary (1957). Leary based his findings on the theories of Harry Stack Sullivan, observations of psychotherapy and discussion groups, and verbal descriptions and inventories that subjects provided of themselves and other people.

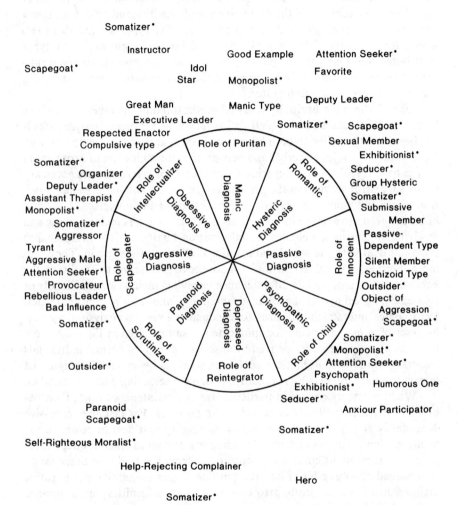

Figure 1. A similarity structure of 50 role types sampled from the group therapy literature and listed outside the circle. These are related to the basic role types expressing emotions and diagnostic dispositions, which are listed inside the circle. Role types listed with an asterisk are duplicated at another point on the circle. (From *Group Psychotherapy and Personality*, by H. Kellerman. Copyright 1979 by Grune and Stratton. Reprinted by permission.)

These descriptions and observations seemed to reflect four kinds of interactive behavior aligned on two bipolar dimensions. One dimension consists of the variable of dominance at one end and the variable of submission at the other end. The other consists of the extreme ends of hostility and affection. Leary constructed a circumplex for describing personality types around these two axes. More recently, Kellerman (1979) has delineated eight basic role types distributed into four pairs of polar opposites: the romantic versus the scrutinizer; the innocent versus the scapegoater; the intellectualizer versus the child; the puritan versus the reintegrator.

One of the most useful systems for understanding member (as well as leader) roles is Robert Bales' (1960, 1970) Interaction Process Analysis, which has been widely applied to both laboratory groups and psychotherapy groups. Observational studies of verbal and nonverbal communication in experiential groups have revealed two categories of functional behaviors that are necessary to the successful survival of the group: *task functions* and *maintenance functions*. Task functions are instrumental, problem-solving processes. They mobilize the group to achieve its defined goals. Task behaviors include giving and receiving suggestions, opinions, or information (Bales, 1970). Maintenance functions deal with the social and emotional climate of the group. They promote interpersonal affiliation and cohesiveness that serve to facilitate the achievement of group goals. Maintenance behaviors include acting friendly or unfriendly, agreeing or disagreeing, dramatizing, and showing tension (Bales, 1970). Bales' interaction categories for conducting a process analysis of a group by describing *how* members communicate are summarized in Figure 2. Note that Bales' categories were derived by observing groups of normal individuals and classifying their interactions act by act, whereas Leary's model originated in part from self-reports by psychiatric patients interacting with one another.

When members engage in particular task or maintenance roles, their behavior can either facilitate or retard group progress. For instance, excessive dependency is a negative task behavior putting a great deal of power in the hands of a few members and often breeding resentment in others. A dependent group member might continually seek advice from the leader or other members instead of stating his or her own position. Excessive tension is a negative maintenance behavior leading to communication difficulties and irrelevant chatter. Within the flow of the group, task and maintenance variables continuously interact. Task decisions will affect members' impressions and feelings about one another; feelings of jealousy or the need to control can block progress on the simplest tasks.

An effective group needs a balance of positive task and maintenance behaviors. When the group is working hard on a task, someone may engage in maintenance behavior to reduce the level of tension; when the group is complacently having a good time, someone else may move to orient the members

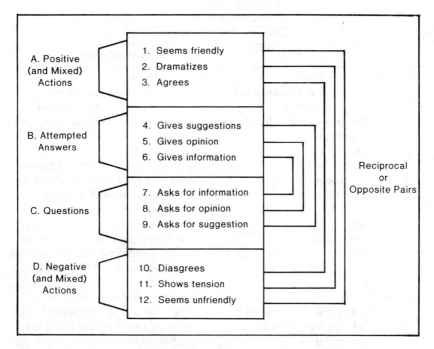

Figure 2. Categories for interaction process analysis. (From *Personality and Interpersonal Behavior,* by Robert Freed Bales. Copyright 1970 by Holt, Rinehart and Winston, Inc. Reprinted by permission of Holt, Rinehart and Winston.)

toward the task. The more flexible members can be in their roles, the more successful the group will be in reaching its ultimate goal.

Typically, some group members will play important task roles while others take charge of keeping interpersonal relationships harmonious. Social/emotional leaders usually end up being the most-liked members of the group. In most experiential groups, of course, the primary focus is social/emotional, so that attention to feelings and attitudes is by definition task-oriented. Table 2 describes a number of task and maintenance roles observable in a group over time. These descriptions, adapted from the early days of T-groups (Benne & Sheats, 1948), can be used to help determine which group functions are being adequately performed and which are being overlooked or inadequately performed.

The flexibility of role behavior will depend upon the group norms. A norm has been defined as "an idea in the minds of the members of a group, an idea that can be put in the form of a statement specifying what the members or other people should do, ought to do, are expected to do, under given circumstances" (Homans, 1950, p. 123). Thus, norms are unwritten rules of behavior

Table 2
Task and maintenance roles

Group task roles	Group maintenance roles
The initiator-contributor: Suggests new ideas or a changed way of viewing the group problem or goal. Suggests ways of handling difficulties and tasks.	*The encourager:* Reinforces and supports the contributions of others. Shows understanding of others' ideas and opinions.
The elaborator: Elaborates and develops more fully the ideas or suggestions initiated by other members.	*The harmonizer:* Mediates the differences between members and diverse points of view. Relieves tension during conflicts.
The coordinator: Pulls together ideas and suggestions or tries to coordinate the activities of various group members.	*The compromiser:* Yields somewhat on his or her own views to accommodate the opinions of others and maintain group harmony.
The orienter: Points the group in the direction of its goals by summarizing what has taken place and identifying departures from the agenda.	*The gate-keeper and expediter:* Keeps lines of communication open by encouraging or facilitating the participation of others or regulating the flow of communication.
The evaluator-critic: Looks critically at group accomplishments and the suggestions of the members by comparing them to some standard of task functioning.	*The standard setter:* Expresses or applies standards for the group in regard to evaluating the quality of the group process.
The energizer: Pushes and stimulates the group to take action, make decisions, or do more.	*The follower:* Passively goes along with the ideas of the group. Serves as an audience in group discussion and decision making.

Adapted from Benne & Sheats, 1948.

that guide member actions and that carry sanctions, in the form of group criticism or rejection, for violation. A sterling example of norms in small groups comes from Sherif and Sherif's (1964) work with adolescent gangs in the southwestern United States. The gangs held powerful shared expectations that members should never criticize another's performance during competitions and that it was okay to foul if one could get away with it during competitions but that it was not okay to foul during practice with other gang members, unless the violator was the gang leader.

Norms, of course, exist in any group. Sometimes the official rules and the informal group norms are discrepant. A problem-solving group, for example, may have an explicit expectation for cooperating in the sharing of ideas, yet operate with considerable backstabbing and competition. Norms help people to resolve questions such as whether and how to express feelings, how involved to become with one another, or whether to respond to someone on the basis of personal qualities or role status. In task groups the entire group can be severely disrupted by members not acting according to the norms. Picture, for instance, a person selling insurance in church.

Each experiential group establishes its own explicit and implicit norms. Typically, the encouragement of emotional expressiveness, warmth, and openness become standards. Norms of behavior should be consistent with the aims of the group. Paramount in importance is that norms for therapeutic communication be established. In most experiential groups, this means that high levels of self-disclosure, the expression of conflict and affection, and the acceptance of one's own feelings are group norms. This includes honest feedback about other members' behavior. The precise style or mode for offering and receiving this feedback may vary, so that in some groups the norms stipulate that suggestions be positive and gentle, while others support raw confrontation. Norms can also change with the life of the group. For example, high disclosure in the beginning may be discomforting to members who are just beginning to feel a part of the group, but as the group progresses, the same behavior may become second nature.

The establishment of helpful communication norms is often hindered by personal needs or concerns. The hidden goals and defenses of participants to protect themselves from anxiety, embarrassment, or potential abuse may run counter to the group's goals. Most group members care about their own images and take on certain role behaviors to insure that this image is preserved. Concern with being accepted as a member of the group may affect one's willingness to take intellectual and emotional risks. The facilitative goals of the group, when successfully implemented and maintained, act in large measure as a basis for furthering effective communication norms.

In experiential groups, it is expected that all members will at some point take on blocking roles that hinder the individual's and the group's progress. This is behavior that perpetuates the individual's hidden goals and maintains the defense and protection of the self either through resistance or manipulation. Such behavior includes withdrawing from the group, criticizing others, interrupting conversations, seeking personal recognition, or interjecting irrelevant ideas. The successful group teaches members to become aware of their blocking behaviors and enlarge their role repertoire. The group attempts to pull the blocked participant out of this nonproductive, static role by using and encouraging more group-oriented behaviors. In interaction-oriented groups, a leader may allow members to use their own caring abilities and instrumental roles to help the problem client.

Even if a leader advises against it, special friendships or subgroups often develop within the group. When these subgroups help attain the goals of the group as a whole, they may be helpful. Two inhibited people may encourage each other by their sensitivity to each other and can, initially, protect each other against pressure to behave in ways they are not yet ready to accept.

Friendships usually develop among people who share common values or experiences. These subgroups may appear more gratifying than the group to the clique and arm them with a sense of security or superiority. Those with a great need for intimacy, dependency, or dominance may be unable to perform their preferred roles with the whole group but be successful within the subgroup. These friendships, when continued outside the group, can inhibit intragroup communication because of mixed loyalties and the hesitancy to betray private knowledge. In the group, the allies tend to agree with each other, send knowing glances in each other's direction, and rally to one another's defense. The honest expression of feelings is stifled, the norms of therapeutic communication are thwarted, and the progress toward growth or change is resisted. Those not included in the subgroup feel part of an "out" group, and the cohesive atmosphere of the membership is undermined.

Conformity to norms is not inevitable in groups, but is tied to certain other group variables. For instance, conformity to group norms has been found to relate to status. Low-status members tend to have low conformity rates and medium-status members tend to have high conformity rates. High-status members tend to conform to group norms as they establish a leadership position and then, once granted leadership status, may deviate on less important norms without receiving negative feedback. (Crosbie, 1975). In other words, participants who are highly regarded in a group earn a certain "idiosyncrasy credit," which enables them to act independently of minor group norms. Of course, some conformity to norms is necessary to maintain order in the group and achieve group goals, since norms serve as guidelines for group interaction. Thus, some groups deliberately build in ways to reward conformity and punish deviance. The structure of the group will also affect a member's loyalty to group norms. For instance, there is more conformity to norms when groups are relatively homogeneous (Crosbie, 1975) than when their composition is heterogeneous.

Members of cohesive, harmonious groups are most apt to have internalized the group's norms. Kurt Lewin (1947) defined cohesion as "the total field of forces which act on members to remain in the group" (p. 30). Cohesion is the key concept of Lewin's group dynamics theory. Basically, the more effective a group is in meeting needs that attract people, the more cohesive it will be. The more cohesive a group is, the more group control there is over the attitudes and actions of its members, the more conformity and commitment to group norms, and the greater acceptance of group values. When a group is cohesive, there is an atmosphere of acceptance, support, and a sense of belonging. Cohesiveness binds members emotionally to the common task and to one another, assures greater stability of the group even in frustrating circumstances, and helps the group develop a shared frame of reference allowing for more tolerance for diverse individual aims (Lakin & Costanzo, 1975).

Certain findings from social psychological research have implications for cohesiveness and experiential groups. In highly cohesive groups, for instance, members communicate more with one another (Shaw, 1976) than in less cohesive groups. They are more open to influence from one another, are more accepting of hostility in the group, place a greater value on the group's goals, are more active in discussion, are less susceptible to disruption if a member leaves the group, remain in the group longer, and experience a greater reduction in anxiety (Goldstein, Heller, & Sechrest, 1966).

No research directly validates the consequences of cohesiveness in psychotherapy groups, but reports from clients and leaders as well as from laboratory work on groups indicate that within such an environment, the mechanism of cohesiveness works like an "adaptive spiral" (Yalom, 1975). By adhering to the norms of a cohesive group, members become more popular, and this helps raise their self-esteem. They are encouraged to use social skills that will further aid them in dealing with interpersonal relationships inside and outside the group. Because they feel pressured to adhere to the norms and are influenced by other members, they listen more attentively, express themselves more openly, explore themselves more deeply, and continue to do so because of reinforcement received in the form of valued peer acceptance. Cohesiveness seems to permit greater expression of hostility and conflict as well. When group members are more attracted to and accepting of one another, they are willing to bear the discomfort of negative emotions and are able to work their conflicts through to a more therapeutic end. The more attracted members are to the group, the more regularly they will attend meetings, the higher the chances they will remain in the group, and the greater their chances for a successful outcome. Since the most unique feature of therapy in a group is the presence and influence of peers, it makes a difference how involved and cohesive these relationships are.

On the negative side, in an overly cohesive group there may be a reluctance among members to think critically and make high-quality decisions. The tightly knit, friendly qualities of the group may induce a naive, overoptimistic decision-making climate, a phenomenon that Janis (1972) has labeled "group-think." Janis believes that groupthink can have devastating effects in problem-solving groups because of the tendency for members to quickly converge on a solution and blithely agree with one another despite the possibly misguided quality of the decision.

Despite these reservations, cohesiveness is generally desirable. How can it be increased? One suggestion for increasing the attractiveness of a group to a potential member is to describe positively what can be anticipated from the experience (Goldstein et al., 1966). Members entering a therapy group with fearful and ambivalent feelings can be helped by a preparation interview in which they learn whether their motivations and expectations are congruent with the realities of the group process outlined by the leader. One approach is to provide a clear description of what "good" participant behaviors are prior to meeting with the group (Bednar, Melnick, & Kaul, 1974). This establishes group norms and behavior patterns early; once established, they are not easily changed (Yalom, 1975). Moreover, getting off to a good start is important, because most drop-outs from group therapy occur in the first few sessions.

Self-Help Groups

David Robinson

Over the past quarter of a century there has been a substantial and rapid growth of self-help groups and organizations which, taken together, now represent a significant feature of contemporary life. This is often referred to as the self-help movement, and some have seen us as moving 'towards a self-help society' (Radford, 1975). Not surprisingly, a good deal of attention has been given to self-help and self-help groups by both professionals and governments as well as by interested laymen and the media. In fact, over the past five years there has hardly been any wide-circulation newspaper or magazine, or any journal of social work, sociology, psychology, psychiatry, nursing or education, which has not carried an article on some aspect of self-help or on the activities of some particular group. Alcoholics Anonymous, of course. has been frequently written about, as have Al-Anon groups, Recovery Inc., Little People groups, Synanon and other drug rehabilitation groups, Gamblers Anonymous, TOPS (Take Off Pounds Sensibly) Inc., and many hundreds more, including the delightful, but as yet unconfirmed, Analysands Anonymous, said to be open to anyone who has been in analysis for twelve years or longer and needs the help of a power greater than his own—or that of his analyst—to terminate the analysis.

As well as the mainstream of self-help groups there are other related developments which are often referred to as part of the self-help movement. Among them are the various volunteer schemes; the 'integrity' groups developed by Mowrer (1971) and other small groups; the growing number of self-treatment groups, self-examination and self-care programmes which aim to lessen dependence on the medical professions and, finally, the 'health by the people' and other self-health projects in the developing world which are, at last, being reported (Newell, 1975). In fact, the rhetoric of self-help is all-pervasive. But what are self-help groups, and how do they work?

Until very recently 'self-help' has received surprisingly little systematic analysis either at a broad general level or at the level of particular groups and activities. In fact, the great bulk of self-help literature, apart from that produced by the groups themselves, has tended to be either rather romantic newspaper reporting or the opinions of conventional helpers, which range from the patronizing and condescending to the snide and openly hostile.

From *Small Groups and Personal Change,* by Peter B. Smith (ed.). Copyright 1980 by Methuen and Company, Ltd. Reprinted by permission. David Robinson is affiliated with the Institute of Psychiatry, London University.

Hurwitz (1970), for example, acknowledged that he may have lost his 'professional objectivity' and be displaying 'non-professional enthusiasm' when, at the end of his much-referred-to article on Peer Self-Help Psychotherapy Groups, he sums up as follows:

> It is important to recognise the PSHPG (peer self-help psychotherapy groups) achieve their goals (of changing people) without the application of specific behaviour modification techniques, without an existential search for identity, without the exploration of human potential, without awareness training to actualize one's potential, without the analysis of the transference neurosis, without psychodrama, without clearing engrams, without creative fighting, without mind expanding drugs, without sensory awakening, without feeling each other up, without taking off one's clothes, and without sexual intercourse between therapists and clients.

Self-help groups achieve their goal, he says, by being:

> fellowships whose members have a common problem. . . . Within such relationships, and in the presence of members who acknowledge the help they receive through fellowship, the peers make it possible and desirable to accept each other's efforts to modify their own and others' behaviour.

In this fellowship lies the essence of *mutual* self-care, which Mowrer (1971) succinctly identified as 'you can't do it alone, but you alone can do it'.

Fortunately, over the past few years there *have* been a number of attempts to analyse the nature of self-help. Writers such as Alfred Katz and Eugene Bender (1976), in particular, and Gerald Caplan and Marie Killilea (1976), have been gathering together the scattered literature in order to discover what self-help is taken to be and to begin to describe what in practice self-help groups do. Killilea (1976), for example, picks out seven characteristics of self-help groups which tend to be stressed. These are:

(1) *Common experience of the members:* the belief that among the primary characteristics of self-help groups is that the care-giver has the same disability as the care-receiver.

(2) *Mutual help and support:* the fact that the individual is a member of a group which meets regularly in order to provide mutual aid.

(3) *The helper principle:* which draws attention to the fact that in a situation in which people help others with a common problem it may be the helper who benefits most from the exchange.

(4) *Differential association:* which emphasizes members' mutual reinforcement of self-concepts of normality and hastens their separation from their previous conception of themselves as deviant.

(5) *Collective willpower and belief:* the tendency of each person to look to others in the group for validation of his feelings and attitudes.

(6) *Importance of information:* the promotion of greater factual under-standing of the problem as opposed to intrapsychic understanding.

(7) *Constructive action toward shared goals:* the notion that groups are action-oriented, their philosophy being that members learn by doing and are changed by doing.

On the basis of the massive literature produced by the groups, they most typ-ically see themselves as 'fellowships'. Great stress is put on the *common* problem, position or circumstances, which are colloquially expressed as 'being in the same boat'. 'Being in the same boat' means, first of all, understanding the problems of others, i.e., 'knowing what it's like'. It is said that only those experiencing the problem can *really* understand. As CARE, the Cancer Af-tercare and Rehabilitation Society, put it:

> The organisation consists in the main of cancer patients—people who know what it is like to have cancer, who know the problems, mental and social, associated with the disease. These people we feel are best fitted to give moral assistance and help to patients and families before and after treat-ment.

It is this understanding based on common experience, say the groups, which produces the necessary common bond of mutual interest and common desire to do something about the problem. And the basic ingredient of this 'doing something' is collectively helping oneself. As SHARE, a self-help group for the disabled, says—to help others is to help yourself, 'SHARE differs from practically all other organizations in the disablement field', they say, 'in that it aims not so much to do things *for* the disabled, as to help them to help themselves.'

In addition to collectively helping oneself, and helping oneself through helping someone else, there is the repeated stress on the importance of 'ex-ample' in the sharing of experiences and coping. A point succinctly expressed again by CARE: 'What better therapy than seeing someone who has had ex-actly what you have got, and who is . . . participating in all the normal ac-tivities of work and social life.' What better therapy indeed! But being in the same boat, sharing experiences and helping yourself by helping others, while excellent statements of what self-help is, give little indication of how self-help groups actually do their work.

What's the Problem?

Before looking at how the groups actually do what they do alone, together, altruistically for themselves, it may be useful to consider why there is any need to do anything at all. In short, what is the problem? Clearly the range of prob-lems, any one of which may be shared in a particular self-help group, is im-mense. They may be physical, practical, mental, emotional, spiritual or social.

In any aspect of physical condition, mental well-being or social position or activity, there will be those who are technically 'abonormal'. There are those with illnesses such as cancer, or disablements such as amputations, colostomy, stammering, skin blemishes or blindness. There are those with abnormal mental attributes such as feelings of chronic depression, guilt or fear. There are those whose interpersonal behaviour is abnormal, such as those who batter children, make love to them, or choose not to have them; and there are those with some social-situational abnormality such as being a single parent, or homeless, or a mental patient, or divorced. Such technical 'abnormalities', however, are not necessarily a major problem. While there may be practical difficulties they may not be insurmountable. As an article in the popular magazine *Honey* (Brown, 1976) explained, under the heading 'Big Problems for Little People':

> The physical limitations of restricted growth are relatively easy to overcome—or at least learn to live with. Clothes can be made to measure and household appliances, and even cars, can be specially adapted to suit the little person's need. Telephone kiosks, door handles and shaver points can, of course, present problems, but Mr. Pocock carries a neat briefcase which opens into two steps for just such eventualities.

Clearly, what turns technical abnormalities into major problems is the way they are interpreted by the people themselves, or by others. To return to the *Honey* article: 'What is distressing for people of restricted growth is the way in which people don't respect the fact that little people have an opinion, a view of life and that they want to contribute.' Despite efforts to discount the attitudes of others, for example by saying 'society doesn't understand', it is easy to see how, for many people, the combination of technical abnormality and social stigma assumes central and overwhelming importance. Listen to how a member of Weight Watchers described it to us (Robinson and Henry, 1977).

> Well, I grew very, very fat over the years and inside me was the slim person that I had always been. But when I was slim I wasn't aware that I was slim. . . . The only thing I wanted was to be slim again. It mattered, it was the only thing that mattered to me. The only thing. It mattered to me passionately. It meant that when I was fat, wherever I went, I was conscious not of being a woman, not of being a nothing, or of being a something, or of being a friend, or of being a stranger. I was conscious only of being a fatty. . . . Day and night for years it got me that bad.

Not surprisingly the end result is to lose all sense of personal value. People describe themselves as feeling guilty and ashamed, feeling inadequate, having no identity, no place in life, distressed, angry, and finally alone, since there may be a gradual slide into secrecy, seclusion and isolation. How, then, does self-help work for people like these with problems of technical abnormality and social stigma?'

How Do Self-Help Groups Work?

At first glance, self-help groups appear to do so many different activities for so many different purposes that any attempt to generalize seems futile. Nevertheless, it is possible to draw out a number of dominant themes and practices which, for the sake of convenience, can be summarized under 'sharing' and 'project work'.

Sharing

Sharing is the sharing of information and common experience. The mechanics of sharing range from formal group meetings where, as in Alcoholics Anonymous, a crucial part is taken up with the telling of life stories, to no less important *in*formal meetings between group members; telephone contact networks, correspondence and newsletters, or tape exchanges and radio contacts when the members are geographically dispersed or prevented by their shared problem from meeting face-to-face. In Touch, for example, a self-help group of parents of mentally handicapped children, has a network of correspondence magazines. In these, parents of children with a similar condition take part in a 'magazine' which consists of letters from each of them. When each mother receives the magazine she reads all the other letters and replaces her own last letter with a new one commenting on the points raised. The magazines circulate continuously and so each member gets up to a dozen letters every few weeks whilst writing only one. Some of them have been in operation for several years.

The degree to which 'sharing' is explicitly recognized as a major feature of self-help activity varies from group to group. But irrespective of this, the crucial question is what does sharing mean? How does it actually feature in the day-to-day working of self-help groups? Needless to say, Alcoholics Anonymous, an archetypal self-help group, has recognized the importance of these questions. *Box 514,* the AA newsletter, put it this way:

> Sharing is truly more than a word. . . . Perhaps we should, from time to time, re-examine what we really mean by sharing—and what it is we are offering to share. What, in other words, is the reality behind the symbolic concept of sharing? What do we really mean, for example, when we say that we share our 'experience, strength and hope'? The problem is not that it is inaccurate to say that we are offering experience, strength and hope—but that the words alone fail to convey the total sense of what we are offering.

The 'symbolic concept' of sharing is *translated into action* in terms of *de*-construction and *re*-construction. De-construction emphasizes the group's attention to specific aspects of their common problems and how these are settled on and then defused, dispersed, and generally coped with. Re-construction emphasizes those activities geared to the production of a new way of everyday life.

Paradoxically, perhaps, the de-construction of the problem initially involves concentrating on it. For a familiar part of the self-help group-work is to help people to settle, from among a whole complex of everyday problems of living, upon one clearly defined problem and agree that it is the 'real' one: admitting that one is 'an alcoholic', for example, or 'a child abuser'. Once 'the'; problem is settled on, admitted, acknowledged or brought out into the open, a second stage of de-construction can begin: the sharing of information about practical solutions to technical difficulties. This may be at the level of physical aids, dietary advice, information about official agencies and rights—in short anything which makes it more possible to handle the technicalities of the shared problem. Clearly, the range of specific practical aids being used in self-help programmes is immense.

The third level of de-construction, the most difficult, aims at destigmatization: dispersing the perceived social discreditability of the members and their shared problems. This position is nicely summarized by the Association of the Childless and Childfree: 'The childless are under the same pressure as the childfree and *their common interest lies in trying to make it quite an unremarkable thing not to have children.*' One way of destigmatizing the problem is by changing members' self-perception, a feat partly achieved by meeting others in the same situation and, therefore, feeling less odd. 'Our self-help groups', said the Director of the National Council for One Parent Families, 'have a double value to lone parents and their children in providing the mutual support that is so helpful to them and also helping the children to have a real social identity by realizing that there are many lone parents and the children are, therefore, not in any way unusual'.

It is common for nearly all groups to direct their destigmatizing efforts towards changing those who are seen as the *cause* of the stigma: 'the general public', or 'society', or just all those who 'do not understand'. The Society of Skin Camouflage says that it 'aims to develop a greater understanding and awareness of our needs and problems in both the public and the medical and allied professions'. In short, then, self-help groups aim to destigmatize the problem by changing both their members *and* outsiders. CHE sums it up this way:

> The Campaign for Homosexual Equality provides a framework within which all women and men—whatever their sexual preference—can work together to end all forms of discrimination against gay people. . . . And while emphasizing the special needs of gay people that must be catered for, we wish to encourage people of different sexualities to integrate freely and to end the gay ghetto situation.

As well as the de-construction and relief of stigmatized problems, self-help groups can also provide recipes for an altered or re-constructed life. At the same time they provide a forum for putting these recipes into action. The 're-structuring of life' may be more or less explicit and more or less detailed; but at whatever level, the enabling and encouraging of a new way of living and a new way of seeing one's self and one's place in the world is a core aspect of self-help activity. In most cases this re-structuring is accomplished through project work.

Projects

It is difficult to generalize about projects, but basically they can be defined as co-operative activities, planned and organized by the members to achieve certain predetermined goals, and more or less explicit depending upon the particular group. But no matter how elaborate or involving a project is, it is essential that it is important to the members. And, clearly, the most important thing to most members is their shared problem and so, naturally, most self-help project work is based on the core task of helping fellow members with their problem.

Indeed, the whole Alcoholics Anonymous programme can be seen as a collection of 'projects' designed to help fellow alcoholics. From merely telling his own drinking story at a group meeting to 'twelfth-stepping' (i.e., sponsoring newcomers), the AA member is actively helping fellow alcoholics. In learning to tell his story appropriately, for example, the newcomer in AA is transforming his past experience into experience of value which can be put to constructive use. His story provides yet another story for the group to draw on and identify with. It is a means of distancing himself from the drinking experience and it is also his personal example to use in the individual work of 'twelfth-stepping' and 'sponsorship'. As time goes on, the problem experience becomes only a part of the member's story. It is added to by reportable stages in the AA group life, and by aspects of life outside the group which are an ever-growing contrast with the 'problem' time before AA (Robinson, 1979).

Time, and in particular the concentration on particular units or periods of time, is a recurrent theme in much self-help activity. Explicit distinctions are often made between time now and time past, while references to origins and 'the first time' are frequently made. Time is often formally structured in 'steps' and tightly maintained by group members and related to time targets which may be formally celebrated as in Gamblers Anonymous's 'Pin Night' or Weight Watchers' measuring of 'Goal Weight'. Time in the future is devalued while learning to live in the present, 'one day at a time', is stressed. Particular problems may be there for *all time* and since relapses can happen at *any time,* self-help commitment must be *full-time.* To ensure that self-help commitment is full-time, it is not enough for project work to be restricted to formal group meetings; it has to carry over into everyday life, and life outside the group. This is a major feature of self-help activity.

Successful self-help groups are much more than huddle-together sessions for people who feel discriminated against or overwhelmed by a common problem or by some aspect of late twentieth-century life. The groups which offer most to their members are those which manage to combine mutual support for those who share a common problem with projects which enable people to build up a new set of relationships. Some women's self-help groups provide a good example of the way in which self-help can be an opportunity for growth rather than just a refuge from an unacceptable world. An important feature of self-health groups is for women to get to know, understand, monitor, respond to, control and appreciate the nature of the functioning of their own bodies. But in the good groups this is only the beginning. The speculum is the instrument for opening up the passage not merely to one's cervix but to a new way of life. Linda Dove (1977), in a familiar declaration, succinctly makes the point: 'Sometimes it seems that doctors and lovers have had more access to our bodies than we have. We must have power over our own bodies to control our lives.' That is the core of the self-help project method; to settle from among all the problems that one faces on a clear, understandable and manageable one, to 'find' that one can manage it and then build a new life as a person who can control one's everyday problems and, thus, one's destiny. The project method, based on a shared appreciation of the need to structure time and transmitted through 'group talk', is then not just a matter of doing but is a matter of being. It is a matter of being in the group but also of being outside the group. Self-help is a way of life. As the founder of the Association for the Childless and Childfree put it:

> just being together improved morale and made us realize that being childless is not just a case for endless feelings of misery and hidden inadequacy but a chance for another kind of future based on finding the best in ourselves and offering it to others in whatever way appropriate.

• • • • • • • •

The Limits of Self-help

Although some people believe that self-help groups are paving the way for a radical change in the way everyday problems are handled, and even providing a blueprint for the construction of a new socio-political order, it does not take long to realize that, for a variety of reasons, most self-help health groups seem neither inclined, nor likely to be able, to accomplish any grand political changes.

One of the major limits to self-help is that most groups tend to operate with the same view of health and illness as conventional helpers. Problems, however they arise, are seen to be the responsibility of the individual. The core aim of both conventional help and most self-help is to do something to, or with, people who 'have' problems, in order that they might be better able to find their way around the world as it is. Those self-help groups which look beyond the immediate concerns of their members do little more than press for some adaptation of the current professional or administrative system. They push for recognition of their problem, or for more humane, accessible or competent professional treatment for it.

Concentration on individuals and their problems is, of course, an essential feature of the self-help process. It is the basis upon which sharing and project work can begin to disperse the problem and construct a more bearable life. But it means, as well, that self-help groups rarely focus their attention on any broader structural features of the shared situation in which they find themselves. The fact that modern industrial production concentrates the workforce, and thus the majority of the population, in dense urban centres where 'homelessness, overcrowding, noise, stress, and loneliness are at their most acute and where the emotional and psychological if not physical health of the population is at its most fragile' (Versluysen, 1977) is never high on the agenda of self-help group meetings. Their attention is much more likely to be given over to making sure that one is serviced properly, rather than to raising the question of whether one needs the service, or of what changes tend to be made in order to make it less likely that the 'problem' which needs servicing will arise at all.

Not only do most groups not look at the broad causes of their problems but they may, by their self-help activities, exacerbate them. The Sidels (1976) use the example of neighbourhood associations to make this point:

> neighbourhood-based mutual aid groups provide an excuse for responsible government authorities to avoid fulfilling their obligations. Suggesting that people attempt, with inadequate resources, to build up their own communities or to provide their own services may divert them from seeking their full share of the resources of the entire society.

Another way in which the activities of self-help groups may exacerbate the very health problem they are trying to alleviate relates to the split between the technical and the caring aspects of professional medicine. Many groups develop in response to the low level of human care in many parts of the medical services. For example, CARE says that medically the patient is checked regularly, but, since 'the shock, worry, and anxiety' goes unheeded this is where the work of CARE starts. In this way, self-help groups are, in many instances, encouraging professionals to avoid the caring aspects of their professional activities and to focus increasingly on its less personally difficult or threatening technological aspects. The activities of articulate middle-class self-help groups may, by taking some of the responsibility for human care away from the professionals, make the medical services even more inhuman and 'technical' for those who are least likely either to cope or complain. On the other hand, reducing professional spheres of activity to the narrow confines of technical expertise could be seen as a step in the right direction by those who want the medical profession's power reduced, by getting them withdrawn from 'community', 'social' and 'caring' commitment to being just one of the many groups of technicians which the lay person calls upon when the need arises.

Clearly everyone involved in self-help groups, however successful they feel they are in alleviating or handling the 'problems' of their members, should ask themselves the following question: 'Is what I am doing likely to increase or decrease the number of people with this problem?' In other words, they must consider the extent to which they collude with the kind of conditions which may have caused, maintained, or accentuated the 'problem' in the first place. That is the core dilemma for everyone who gives 'help', whether they are self-helpers or professionals.

Rather than just tinkering with the existing services, some groups *do* try to wrest control from the professional by disemminating 'technical knowledge' and encouraging the lay person to become their own expert. The separation of the group's experiential knowledge and expertise from the professional's technical knowledge and expertise is an explicit and important political act. Gaining, or regaining, control over aspects of one's own body and life is a clear statement about oneself and one's place in the world. Nevertheless, many self-help groups pre-empt any possibility of building on that base by becoming professionalized clients. Although the self-helpers may gain some control over handling their shared 'problem', the nature of the helping is, often, no different from that given by the professional from whom control has been taken. Rather than offering an alternative to professional services, members seek to 'service' themselves and their fellows as they were once 'serviced' by professional helpers. As Dewar (1976) puts it: "Rather than changing the content of the help, they merely alter *who* does it. Rather than learning about and dealing with the *cause* of the condition in question, they seize control of currently accepted 'cures.'"

One of the consequences of this concentration on who gives expert help, rather than on what is the cause of the problem, is that self-help groups tend to remain separated and isolated from each other. The emphasis on the shared particular problem and how it can best be handled for those in that particular group means that there is little sense of common identity across problems. Not only that, but a familiar feature of the self-help world is the bickering and antagonism between self-help groups which are concerned with similar problems. However, one of the severest limitations of the political impact of self-help comes not from the fact that the self-help world is fragmented, but from the groups' willingness to co-operate with professionals for immediate practical purposes.

Professionals are, and always have been, intimately involved with even those self-help groups which are considered to be most independent and self-sufficient. In their wide-ranging review of self-help organizations, Traunstein and Steinman (1973) found that approximately one in three groups were started in close co-operation with professionals. Nevertheless, the nature of the relationship between self-help groups and professionals varies from group to group. Some groups are clearly proud of having close connections with, and the approval of, the medical and other professions and stress these links in their literature. The U and I Club, while claiming that for many women their self-help procedures have eradicated years of cystitis and thrush, also stress that they 'work within the confines of conventional medicine'. Many other groups see themselves as independent from, but closely related to, the activities of professional services. They 'pick up the pieces' or handle aspects of their members' problems which the professions cannot or choose not to deal with.

This 'separate-but-compatible' view of self-help and the professionals is not shared by all groups. For some, it is precisely because the medical profession could not, or would not, deal appropriately with them or their problems that helping themselves is so important. Most women's self-help groups are not just 'picking up the pieces' or providing peripheral support to the professional services, they are trying to change the nature of the medical enterprise. The core issue is 'control', from learning enough about one's own body and so demystifying the processes of health and illness to working for a radical change in the conventional helping services so that when a particular expertise is needed, it will be geared to the conditions, priorities and expectations of those who receive it.

Not surprisingly, there are many professionals who feel threatened by the growing number of self-help groups. Others, recognizing the value of particular self-help enterprises, have proposed that professionals should become directly involved. Mowrer (1971), for example, suggested that professionals could set up self-help groups and that universities should train and supply persons competent to perform this type of function. Others, not surprisingly, think such enthusiasm should be tempered, since it presents a number of problems which the 'facilitators' ought to be aware of. Will professional involvement, asks Jertson (1975), 'contribute to a loss of that one value uniquely cherished by the self-help group; the perceived ability to help itself?'

The day-to-day relationships between self-help groups, their members and professionals are, however, not laid down in the columns of professional journals. They are worked out in particular situations in accordance with the beliefs, inclinations and priorities of the people involved. It is in these situations that control begins to bite. The most obvious way of preventing a successful group from developing a sufficiently firm power base is, quite simply, to take it over. There is no need to 'facilitate', 'regulate', or 'co-operate', when you can 'incorporate'. As Jack Geiger has crisply described it, 'when the counter-culture develops something of value, the establishment rips it off and sells it back' (Jencks, 1976). The dilemma here is that while it may improve patient care, in the sense of providing a wider service of the kind which the group has shown to be of value, it pre-empts the self-help dimension which underpinned the activity in the first place.

Clearly, as self-help groups continue to thrive and prosper there will be many efforts by both professionals and government departments to control them. Only the most crude professional will say that he wants to control self-help groups because they are taking away his prestige, power or fees. Control will be exercised in relation to the issue of 'quality'; the idea that while many self-help groups are useful, or at least not harmful, there are some whose members are hurt by their participation. It follows from this, runs the argument, that self-help groups must be registered or 'evaluated' in order to protect the general public. Those groups which were thought to be harmful or 'inappropriate' would then be 'disbanded'.

To disagree with this argument is not to say, of course, that every self-help groups improves the health and happiness of all its members. No doubt there are people who are dead now who would still be alive if they had never gone to a self-help group—just as there are people who are dead now who would still be alive if they had never gone into hospital. But the registration of self-help groups is not the answer to the 'quality control' question. The only thing to do as long as groups are operating within the law is to publicize the fact that some groups seem to be harmful in particular ways for certain people.

The most significant developments in relation to self-help health are likely to result not from governmental or professional concessions in the face of current 'economic reality', but from the day-to-day activities of a—hopefully—ever-increasing number of people who are quietly coming together to share and solve their common health problems, rather than put up with the frustrations and humiliations of professional services and large-scale administrative and State structures. That they do not seek dramatic political changes does not necessarily make their actions politically insignificant. In fact, many of them are operating a self-help 'project approach' to political issues. They are making manageable changes together. If such an approach works for 'insoluble problems' like alcoholism, they argue, why not for any other problem as well? Why not indeed, since undermining the foundations is just as effective a way of toppling a fortress as storming the ramparts!

References

Brown, A. (1976) Big problems for little people. *Honey 10:* 21.

Caplan, G. and Killilea, M. (eds) (1976) *Support Systems and Mutual Help: Multidisciplinary Explorations.* New York: Grune and Stratton.

Dewar, T. (1976) Professionalised clients as self-helpers. In *Self-Help and Health: A Report.* New York: New Human Services Institute, pp. 77–83.

Dove, L. (1977) Self-help centres in Los Angeles. *Spare Rib 55:* 26.

Dumont, M. P. (1974) Self-help treatment programs. *American Journal of Psychiatry 131* (6):631–5.

Hurwitz, N. T. (1970) Peer self-help psychotherapy groups and their implications for psychotherapy. *Psychotherapy: Theory, Research and Practice 7* (1): 41–9.

Jencks, S. F. (1976) Problems in participatory health care. In *Self-Help and Health: A Report.* New York: New Human Services Institute, pp. 85–98.

Jertson, J. (1975) Self-help groups. *Social Work 20* (2): 144–5.

Katz, A. H. (1975) Some thoughts on self-help groups and the professional community. Paper to the National Conference on Social Welfare, San Francisco.

Katz, A. H. and Bender, E. I. (eds) (1976) *The Strength in Us: Self-Help Groups in the Modern World.* New York: Franklin Watts.

Killilea, M. (1976) Mutual help organisations: interpretations in the literature. In G. Caplan and M. Killilea (eds) *Support Systems and Mutual Help: Multidisciplinary Explorations.* New York: Grune and Stratton.

Mahler, H. (1977) Problems of medical affluence. *WHO Chronicle 31:* 8–31.

Mowrer, O. H. (1971) Peer groups and medication: the best 'therapy' for professionals and laymen alike. *Psychotherapy: Theory, Research and Practice 8* (1): 44–54.

Newell, K. W. (ed) (1975) *Health by the People.* Geneva: World Health Organization.

Radford, J. (1975) Towards a self-help community. *Talking Point* No. 23. Newcastle-upon-Tyne: Association of Community Workers.

Robinson, D. (1979) *Talking Out of Alcoholism: The Self-Help Process of Alcoholics Anonymous.* London: Croom Helm.

Robinson, D. and Henry, S. (1977) *Self-Help and Health: Mutual Aid for Modern Problems.* London: Martin Robertson.

Sidel, V. W. and Sidel, R. (1976) Beyond coping. *Social Policy 7:* 67–9.

Traunstein, D. M. and Steinman, R. (1973) Voluntary self-help organisation: an exploratory study. *Journal of Voluntary Action Research 2* (4): 230–93.

Vattano, A. J. (1972) Power to the people: self-help groups. *Social Work 17* (4): 7–15.

Versluysen, M. (1977) The politics of self-help. *Undercurrents 19:* 25–7.

The Health Professional and Group Process

Edward E. Sampson and Marya Marthas

Human beings are complicated creatures. We are biological organisms possessing qualities shared with all living systems and with others of our species. We are also psychological beings with distinctly human capabilities for thought, feeling, and reason. But that is not all. To say that we are also social, *group* beings is to recognize the complex web of interconnections that link us with other people. These links help define our *group character* and play a major role in our daily lives as well as our professional practice. It is difficult to imagine an activity in which our group character is not involved. The range within the health professions is broad: from simple conversations with patients and colleagues to meetings, rounds, conferences, training sessions, and so forth.

Nothing mysterious is intended in the reference to a person's group character. The concept directs our attention to two important issues. First, we usually conduct our practice within the actual presence of one or more other persons. And second, in light of this fact, we typically take them into account, adjusting our behavior to theirs, even as they adjust to ours. We and they thereby become participants in a group process. Our group character, therefore, refers to the bonds that connect us with others, a figurative line between persons representing the give-and-take adjustments each makes in the presence of the other.

Direct Connections

At times, these links are direct and relatively obvious:

Nurse Allen is obtaining intake information on her patient. She is preoccupied with asking questions and carefully recording the answers in their proper place on the many forms she must complete. The patient is anxious about this procedure. The more questions Nurse Allen asks, the greater the patient's anxiety becomes: soon, the anxiety interferes with her ability to hear the questions and even to think clearly enough to provide coherent answers. Nurse Allen has many other patients to deal with and so responds with growing annoyance to the patient's halting replies. She becomes more abrupt and demanding. The patient responds with even greater anxiety and difficulty in providing answers.

From Edward E. Sampson and Marya Marthas, *Group Process for the Health Professions,* 2nd ed. New York: John Wiley and Sons, 1981. Copyright John Wiley and Sons, 1981. Reprinted by permission. Edward Sampson and Marya Marthas are affiliated with the Wright Institute in Berkeley, California.

We do not want to belabor the obvious, but only to illustrate the bonds that link Nurse Allen and her patient, which give to each what we have called their group character.

What might appear to be a routine matter, obtaining intake information, involves an interpersonal process. The nurse's behavior is one element in that process; the patient's behavior, the other. Nurse Allen is not simply doing an interview to assess a patient on intake as a technician might assess a blood sample. Rather, she is involved as a participant in a process in which her behavior in conducting the interview affects the patient's response; in turn, the patient's responses affect the nurse's own behavior. Each is involved in adjusting her behavior to the behavior of the other person; this is the link that joins them.

In speaking of Nurse Allen's group character, we call attention to the idea that who she is is affected by who the other person is in the intake interview. Her character is that of someone who is annoyed and impatient. This is not a comment on her personality as much as on her manner of adjusting her behavior to the behavior of her patient. The patient likewise has a group character. Anxiety is not necessarily a quality she possesses separately from her reaction to Nurse Allen and the intake procedure. Each participant not only evokes a particular kind of response from the other but also responds to the other.

Subtle Connections

The links that relate us to others may also be subtle. We may participate in a group process with little awareness of the group character we are portraying.

> The patient and his wife are about to leave the hospital; in her desire to reassure them that all is well, Dr. Welch tells the wife not to worry, that her husband's problem is only minor indigestion, and that nothing is really wrong. The couple begin to argue vehemently as they leave. Dr. Welch turns around and continues with her other work, not realizing that her simple reassurance played a part in their family drama. Her assurance as a medical professional undercut the legitimacy of the husband's illness. Dr. Welch had defined him as not sick, never realizing that he had been using sickness as a way of avoiding responsibilities at home.

We are not suggesting that Dr. Welch should not have offered reassurance; we present this example to illustrate how the health professional may become a part of a group process without much awareness that this has even happened. In this case, Dr. Welch's behavior was less affected by others than it affected them; nevertheless, she became a member of that family's group process, if only for a brief moment. Obviously, knowledge of group process would help her in this type of intervention.

Group Process in Life and in Practice

We have suggested several things regarding group process:

1. A person's life and professional practice involves other people.
2. People's group characters emerge as they interact with others.
3. Rarely if ever does a person practice without taking others into account, just as those others must act in the interpersonal context provided for them.
4. People may be participating in a group process even when they are unaware of that participation and even when "the group" includes only the individual and the patient or the individual and one other person.

This last point separates our approach to group process from some more traditional points of view. The traditional study of groups emphasizes something larger than the two-person (dyadic) transaction that we have used in our opening examples. Group and group process are thereby separated from the dyad and interpersonal process. Many of us have an intuitively larger context or longer-term relationship in mind when we speak of group process. The examples focus on small groups of two or three people; likewise, they examine relatively brief encounters.

Although we partly agree with these intuitive understandings and will even document the many distinctions in process that emerge when we move from the small dyadic encounter to include greater numbers of people . . . , we are also suggesting that some important continuities exist between the study of interpersonal process and group process. The study of group process includes both of these groups as well as those more typically referred to as groups: that is, (1) relationships that have a relatively greater permanence and thus permit the development of relationships and structures, and (2) relationships that include larger numbers of people, encompassing patients as well as other people (e.g., colleagues, community groups, etc.). One point should be evident, we must seek to understand both group and interpersonal process and to develop as keen a sensitivity to our group character as we have of our biologic character.

It will be helpful to our understanding of group process in the health professions if we examine the wide variety of contexts, settings, and groups within which our practice tends to occur. We have outlined in Figure 1 some of the major areas of group participation relevant to the health professional. The point of all of this, quite simply, is to develop and expand group process training among health professionals. Our argument consists of two key ideas: (1) groups are central to human growth and development and play a continuing role in health maintenance or its absence; (2) groups are an important part of our daily practice.

Figure 1. Group practice in life and in practice.

The Role of Group Process in Human Growth and Development

The life history of human beings can be written in terms of the nature and types of groups in which they have been reared and in which they are involved. We are all born helpless and unable to function without support provided by other members of our species. Unlike many animals which achieve independence within a relatively brief period after birth, the human infant must maintain a continued close dependence on others for a substantial period of its life. Even in adulthood, most people need others—the true hermit who can function independently of society is more myth than reality.

Primary Groups. Research suggests some of the serious consequences that face developing children who do not receive enough human interaction and contact. Sociologist C. H. Cooley (1909) early recognized the critical role that these *primary group* contacts played in the emergence of social feelings and civilized persons. For Cooley, a primary group involves close, face-to-face associations of the sort found in the family, in play groups, and in many neighborhood and informal work groups. Such groups are characterized by their sense of "we" and "our" rather than the more individualistic "I" and "mine." These primary groups are the source of the person's emerging human social qualities; and for adults, they remain an important source of support and nurturance.

Although it has become fashionable to speculate on the breakdown of primary groups—e.g., neighborhood and friendship groups—in our modern society, research suggests the continuing importance and role of these groups in the life of the individual. Litwak and Szelenyi, for example (1969), determined where people would turn for help if they had a one-day stomachache, a two-week appendectomy, or a three-month broken leg. Their data suggested the importance of friendship and neighborhood groups for dealing with these and related types of health problems. In other words, even in our often impersonal modern urban society, people in trouble turn to primary groups for help and support.

The role of the primary group, especially the family, in health care has become increasingly relevant in the management of heart and cancer patients. The psychological impact of cancer, for example, has led health professionals to see the need to extend their treatment plans beyond the medical. The initial diagnosis, cancer, sets up a process that has a wide-ranging impact on patients and their families. Often, the initial shock gives way to anger, followed quickly by guilt and blame. The patient is angry but so too is the family, now threatened by the loss of one of its own. Patients and their families often blame themselves for their illness: "Perhaps we should have urged you to seek medical attention earlier; it's our fault." Fear is also a part of this process: "If my father has cancer, will I have an increased chance of getting it myself?"

The process we have briefly outlined is one that implicates the patients and their primary group; the management of the patient, therefore, must take that primary-group network into account as well. When the course of the disease is long-term, as tends to be the case with cancer, the center of treatment should include the family. The health professional must recognize the patient's need for a continuing connection to and support from his or her family at just that time when the family's fears and worries may lead members to withdraw and fail to provide the mutual support and comfort that is so necessary. Our need for our primary-group relationships does not fade once we reach adulthood; the need remains and is implicated in many areas of our lives that fall within the purview of the health professional.

Hospitalization. While much criticism has been leveled at the findings of Spitz regarding what he calls *hospitalism,* his work stands as further testimony to the critical role that early group experiences play in our lives (1945). Spitz observed children in institutions; although they did not lack physical comforts, they lacked the vital social stimulation of other human beings. According to Spitz, these children not only developed lesser intelligence but also were later unresponsive to and disinterested in other persons.

The research of Bowlby, among others, adds further to this picture (1969; 1973). The child who is not provided with a strong mothering relationship tends to have difficulty in forming attachments to other persons. It would seem, then, that one function of our early group experiences is to help us develop intellectually and socially; that is, to help us be capable of later forming those kinds of attachments with others that make the entire fabric of social life and human culture possible. Although he worked with monkeys rather than human children, Harry Harlow (1962) reached a similar conclusion; both parenting and play with peers are essential to adult heterosexual relationships and competency in the tasks of adulthood (e.g., in later being a mother or mothering figure oneself). The peer group forms one of the key primary groups necessary to the development of human beings.

In addition to these effects on the developing child, the reduction of stimulation, including both sensory (e.g., sight, sound, and touch) and social (e.g., interaction and contact with other persons) also has serious consequences for adults. Early research (e.g., Bexton et al., 1954; Scott et al., 1959) has demonstrated a decrement in intellectual functioning and in problem-solving ability when people's normal sensory input is reduced for a period of time. Such people also become more suggestible, open to believing fantastic things (e.g., in ghosts) toward which they otherwise would take a more critical attitude.

Sensory or social isolation, while not usually introduced into adult lives deliberately, nevertheless can result from some medical procedures in which the person is isolated for a period of time—e.g., during radiation therapy.

A similar pattern of *hospitalism* in adults has been described by Sommer and Osmond (1960), among others. It is said to involve such symptoms as the following:

— Deindividuation—a reduced ability to think and act independently; an increased passivity and dependence and loss of a distinct self
— Disculturation—an adoption of institutional attitudes and values and a correspondent loss of earlier attitudes and values
— Isolation and estrangement—a loss of contacts and commitments to things in the outside world
— Stimulus deprivation—a tendency to adapt to a world within the institution, which has a tempo that differs dramatically from that on the outside

These symptoms are said to occur within both patients and staff who must spend a significant amount of time within institutions. The implications of this pattern for both patient care and staff development within institutional settings are clear; use of groups to oppose these symptoms might well become a central aspect of hospital programs.

The Therapeutic Milieu. The concept of the therapeutic community or milieu is a relatively recent one; its origins are primarily in psychiatric settings, but the idea has recently been extended to a consideration of the hospital ward or unit as a therapeutic milieu. Basically, to avoid the effects of hospitalism and sensory-limitation, the health professional, especially the person who has greatest hour-by-hour contact with the patient, must attend carefully to creating a total therapeutic context for patient care. The seemingly little attentions and human concerns shown for patients can and do play an important role in recovery. An attitude of extreme clinical detachment, for example, helps contribute to hospitalism and sensory limitation; the patient's milieu, therefore, becomes one that hinders recovery rather than facilitating it. The quality of the milieu is only as good as the people working in it; they must function as a unit. This requires that they deal with some of their own feelings and concerns and with the host of interpersonal issues that develop within any functioning unit. Knowledge and use of group process is essential at two points: (1) in the development and maintenance of a therapeutic atmosphere for the patients; (2) in the functions of the professional staff and their interpersonal issues as they work toward creating a healthful milieu.

We develop into persons by virtue of having contacts with other persons; we remain persons, relatively intact and functioning, as long as such contacts persist. Without our group memberships and belongingness, therefore, we soon experience various symptoms of deficit. Group processes are critical to all human growth and development and to the maintenance of healthful functioning. We return again to this point in a later part of this opening chapter.

The Role of Group Process in Behavior Maintenance and Change

Social psychologist Kurt Lewin formulated the issue of the role of group process in behavior maintenance and change in his analysis of the way in which people change their attitudes and habits (Lewin, 1947a; 1947b; 1958). Although his initial efforts were concerned with changing eating habits by getting persons during wartime to serve less well-known cuts of meat (e.g., kidneys, brains, etc.), the issue remains the same, whether it is eating behavior, smoking behavior, or other health-related attitudes and actions that we need to understand or to change.

Lewin's analysis can be stated in terms of several key ideas:

1. Individual attitudes and habits do not exist in isolation but rather are related to the attitudes and habits of significant groups to which a person belongs or aspires to belong. The teenager, for example, may take up smoking as a habit because a peer group he or she belongs to or would like to join values smoking.
2. We tend to be rewarded with acceptance and a sense of sharing a common view of things when our behavior generally fits within the norms and guidelines of the groups to which we belong. We meet rejection, hostility, or pressure to change when our behavior strays too much from our groups' standards. A nurse working in a setting in which first names only are used is accepted as long as she or he generally

follows this policy. Pressure to be like the others is brought to bear if this person breaks the implicit group understanding by using the more formal type of address (Dr. Jones).

3. Lewin suggested that since behaviors are frozen within supportive-group settings, to change those behaviors it is necessary to *unfreeze* them from their setting. This means that the individual's support in the group in which the behavior is frozen must be reduced or the group's own standards (i.e., norms, guidelines, and implicit or explicit understandings) for the particular behavior must be altered. For example, the smoking teenager's habit may be frozen in a particular group of friends. That behavior can be changed if the teenager's dependence on the group is lessened or if the entire group's evaluation of smoking is changed.

4. To retain the new behavior the person must be within a group context that will support rather than undermine it. This involves a process that Lewin calls *refreezing*—i.e., locating the new behavior in a supportive group, a group whose standards enforce conformity to the new behavior. These ideas of Lewin have obvious relevance to such treatment programs as Alcoholics Anonymous, to cite one important example. The member of AA both detaches himself from his former "drinking buddies" and simultaneously becomes a member of a group that opposes drinking.

Let us take another example that will help to clarify these points. Suppose that the issue involves helping a person to stop smoking or at minimum to cut down significantly. First, we must recognize that smoking is a habit within a group context. Thus, to change the individual's smoking behavior we must work not only on the person but also on the groups that support that habit. For example, it should be easier to get people to stop smoking if we can bring them and other smokers together in the group to discuss smoking and perhaps collectively agree to reduce it, than by trying to deal with each individual alone. To deal with habits in isolation from the groups to which they are related is not likely to result in change; the person can return to the old ways too easily. Most self-help groups work along these lines. We will examine further facets of the group membership and group process in later chapters. For now, however, it is sufficient for us to recognize that so much of what we do and think has not only developed within group settings but is maintained within those settings. Thus to understand or to change poor health habits or to reinforce positive habits, we must work on the level of the membership group(s) rather than on the individual in isolation. And to work on the level of groups requires that we learn group process skills.

Table 1
Average Change in Aggressiveness

	Tranquilizing Drug	Placebo
High-Conflict Family Setting	−5.67	−6.50
Low-Conflict Family Setting	15.13	5.36

It is not stretching the point to suggest that understanding this key function of group process in the change and maintenance of individual attitudes and behaviors is indispensable to our practice. The promotion and maintenance of health means that the health professional must become sensitive to these processes and capable of working with them effectively.

The Role of Group Process in Health Promotion and Maintenance

The preceding discussion emphasized the important functions that groups play in behavior maintenance and change; and this knowledge is critical in the area of health promotion. Let us take an interesting research study from the psychiatric literature to focus more clearly on this point (Cohen et al., 1958).

The problem of facing Cohen's psychiatric team involved the treatment of a group of aggressive male and female out-patients through the use of tranquilizing drugs. To provide a proper test of the usefulness of the drugs, a drug group was compared with a matched placebo group over a period of some three months. Measures of the patients' aggressive behavior at home were obtained both before and after drug or placebo treatment. Additional measures were obtained of the patient's home environment. Data from the study are reported in Table 1.

The table shows the discrepancies in reported aggressiveness before and after treatment. The negative values indicate that *all* patients showed reductions in their aggressiveness after the three months of treatment. In comparing the data for drug vs. placebo treatment, the most striking finding is that there appears at first to be little apparent difference. A closer examination of the data, however, shows that there is one condition in which the drug produced significantly better results than the placebo; this occurred in the low-conflict family environment. Only when the patient's family setting was low in conflict did the use of a tranquilizing drug prove to be more effective than a placebo. But why?

This research highlights the important function that groups play in health maintenance. The authors suggest several parts to the process. (1) The behavior of those in high-conflict family settings began to change as a function of the drug. (2) These people were in a group in which conflict was the norm, in which aggression and hostility were expected and approved forms of behavior. (3) Any deviation from that normative pattern, as was brought about with the tranquilizing drug, was met with increased pressure to shape up and remain a good group member. (4) In the case of a high-conflict family, being a good group member required being hostile and aggressive. (5) Thus the group process conflicted with the drug treatment program, resulting in an overall ineffectiveness of the drug as compared with the placebo.

Basically, only when the group process reinforces the drug treatment, as in the low-conflict setting, is the treatment program more effective than the placebo. The lesson to be learned is very clear. Anyone involved in the treatment of illness—whether it is psychiatric as in the research example or non-psychiatric—must carefully know how to evaluate the group factor *and* how to intervene in the group process in the service of health. To ignore the group processes that are involved is to engage in what might prove to be questionable patient care.

As we previously noted, heart disease or cancer cases offer us clear instances in which the medical treatment must be expanded to recognize the group factors that can either support or undermine the program. For example, what is the meaning to the family's existing interaction patterns, or to the business associates, of a change in a person's activity after an MI? The health professional must be aware of the role of group processes in such cases, and must also develop skills in working with relevant processes as part of patient care. Acknowledging group effects is the first step; doing something about them is the next.

The importance of group and social processes in the health continuum cannot be overemphasized.

Teleconferencing: Electronic Group Meetings

Robert Johansen, Jacques Vallee and Kathleen Spangler

E. T. Hall offers a valuable insight when he says that "culture is communication and cummunication is culture."[1] When defined as culture—a labyrinthian concept—communication emerges as the complex phenomenon it really is. As culture, communication goes well beyond the exchange of words when people meet in a group. It includes the use of physical space and of time. It also includes other traditional components of culture—play and learning, defense and allocation of resources, assignment and recognition of social roles.

Choices about each of these components of communication are influenced by a variety of rules, assumptions, and perceptions. Many of these guiding assumptions are less than conscious, and most of them are guidelines for meeting *in person*. So when someone chooses to hold an electronic meeting, the old unconscious rules for meetings need revision. And choices about whom to invite, how to establish the agenda, how long and how often to meet all become more prominent. So do choices of leadership styles, protocols for speaking, and procedures for making group decisions.

"Just hooking all these people up electronically" overlooks the importance of these choices. It assumes that "things can't get any worse." But they probably can. And electronic meetings probably can increase the number of ways in which communication can get worse. The potential for easier communication may also be the potential for easier *mis*communication.

Teleconferencing, then, does not eliminate the possibility of ineffective meetings. Instead, it changes the nature of meetings in ways which increase the possibilities for both good and bad outcomes. These changes are linked to the fundamental characteristics of electronic meetings via all three media: physical separation of the participants, access to remote resources, narrow communication channels, potential for control of group interaction, and dependence on technology. Any of the choices about communication in a small group—about leadership and protocols and agenda—should thus be preceded by an examination of the positive and negative implications of these characteristics.

Physical Separation

The most obvious difference between an electronic meeting and face-to-face encounters is the physical separation of participants. An ethereal electronic pulse is the only common "space" for the group. If the participants are far apart, physical separation may also mean a separation in time, as the exchange crosses time zones. This separation redefines communication possibilities in some rather obvious ways: objects cannot be exchanged; the sense of touch disappears. While some participants have their early morning coffee, their cross-country colleagues may be hungry enough to break for lunch. There can be no coffee break chit-chat and no hallway meetings.

But the lack of a shared space also influences communication in more subtle ways. For example, it eliminates the possibilities of using interpersonal distance to communicate.[2] The distance between any two members of a group expresses their feelings toward each other and toward what is being said. It can be supportive or insulting. Communication can proceed without it, but an important cue is lost. Could the miniaturized image of a person on a video screen across the room be interpreted as a detachment from the meeting agenda?

The use of conventional distances to communicate attitudes may be one factor in the *sense of social presence* in a meeting—a sense often found lacking in electronic meetings. Short, Williams, and Christie (1976) suggest, in fact, that the sense of social presence varies from medium to medium.

> Although we would expect it to affect the way individuals perceive their discussions, and their relationships to the persons with whom they are communicating, it is important to emphasize that we are defining Social Presence as a quality of the medium itself. We hypothesize that communications media vary in their degree of Social Presence, and that these variations are important in determining the way individuals interact. We also hypothesize that the users of any given communications medium are in some sense aware of the degree of Social Presence of the medium and tend to avoid using the medium for certain types of interactions; specifically, interactions requiring a higher degree of Social Presence than they perceive the medium to have. Thus, we believe that Social Presence is an important key to understanding person-to-person telecommunications.[3]

This view of social presence may link the concept too rigidly to the characteristics of each teleconferencing medium. It is easy to imagine how different people could perceive varying degress of social presence in the *same* medium. Field tests of computer-based teleconferencing, for instance, have shown that some people see this print-based medium as low in social presence while others have the opposite impression.[4] These varied reactions are clearly linked to the nature of the user groups and their communication needs, as well as the specific characteristics of the medium they are using.

It seems doubtful that social presence is a static variable, attached in simple ways to each teleconference medium. Rather, a sense of social presence can perhaps be cultured by teleconference leaders or encouraged by initial learning sessions. Furthermore, it is not clear that a strong sense of social presence is always best. The use of interpersonal distance, for example, varies from culture to culture. Everyone has probably witnessed a scene in which people from

North and South American cultures negotiated the distance between themselves, with the North American feeling that the Latino was too pushy while the South American tried to understand why the North American was being so "cold" and remote. The different meanings associated with interpersonal distance might just as easily interfere with communication as facilitate it. Also, the separation of participants eliminates the fear of physical violence which, however, subtle, is at least possible in any face-to-face encounter. Could safety from violence encourage "good fights" in electronic meetings?

A related impact of physical separation is that an electronic meeting is, in a sense, out of context. That is, it doesn't take place in a single cultural context or place. Such a displacement may save participants from uncomfortable meetings in unfamiliar surroundings. But it may also disguise important information about both goals and interpersonal needs of the conference participants. In particular, the abstract, electronically created context of a teleconference may obscure differences in perspectives of participants; participants could end up focusing too much attention on words which make little sense without an understanding of the organizational or cultural context of the speaker.

While physical separation is an unmistakable feature of electronic meetings, not everyone in every teleconference will be isolated. In fact, as we have noted, video teleconferences and some audio conferences will be group-to-group meetings. Such meetings combine the dynamics of face-to-face interaction with remote exchanges. Not surprisingly, differences between groups can become exaggerated in these conferences, and personal alliances within each group may be reinforced.

It is tempting to view physical separation as a necessary evil of teleconferencing—as something groups tolerate to gain savings in time and travel. However, this substitution mentality probably discourages creative uses of the unique communications environment of meetings-at-a-distance. Also, the view of electronic meetings as second-best does not acknowledge one very attractive complement to physical separation—namely, access to remote resources.

Access to Remote Resources

Many people, and hence many viewpoints, are routinely excluded from face-to-face meetings for logistical reasons of convenience, cost, and accessibility. Geographic distances remain a major barrier to dialogue on important organizational and societal issues. They limit access to both human and data resources that would otherwise be considered vital to the work of a group. They frequently foster duplication of effort and, in the extreme, parochialism.[5]

Teleconferencing provides an opportunity to organize groups in a non-parochial fashion, to tap resources that may be far away. Decisions about whom to consult or what information to use do not have to be constrained by what is closest. Distant experts can consult with a group more effectively: they can avoid tiring travel which may leave them less "expert"; and they can remain close to their own resources. Similarly, with computer conferencing, a data base on the other side of the world can be searched instantly and the results entered and evaluated immediately in the conference proceedings.

Electronic meetings can facilitate cooperation among geographically separated branches of the same organization—the use of audio conferencing by NASA is an example—or between separate organizations. The U.S. Department of Energy uses computer-based teleconferencing to assist in coordinating the activities of regional laboratories in various parts of the country. This application has also spawned serendipitous interorganizational communication between scientists doing similar work at the Department of Energy and the U.S. Geological Survey. In this case, scientists who happened to be using computer conferencing for other purposes found they had research interests in common with each other and then established a joint conference. Teleconferencing thus seems to expand the opportunities to contact distant colleagues and sometimes even to discover new colleagues.

In spite of these apparent benefits, increased access to resources could actually overwhelm a group. Simple increases in the number of inputs to a group do not always lead to increased effectiveness. Without a social structure to integrate the various views and new sources of information, a group can easily drift into what Doyle and Straus call "The Multi-Headed Animal Syndrome."[6] Many people will be pulling in different directions, all of them feeling that they are acting in the common good but that others are not cooperating. Too much information too fast would only add to this problem, no matter how high the quality of the information.

An overemphasis on the opportunities of *access* could also encourage a too-narrow view of experts and expert information. The expert could become someone "out there" who is available to solve all of the problems if only he or she could be reached. The expert's facts and figures might be viewed as the "truth" when they are only limited truths at best; at worst, they might not even be accurate information.

Teleconferencing probably has the potential to isolate the so-called expert from interaction with the group. Experts play many roles other than that of a data bank. They learn about the important political battles in a group, encouraging objectivity here and taking sides there. They cajole people into new perspectives on their problems. They may even lay groundwork for communicating with other important resources outside the group. But all of these supportive functions require a cultivation of relationships. If experts are simply plugged into a conference to answer questions without knowing their context, is the group likely to be lose some of this support? Will experts lose some of their expertise?

Access will not mean the same thing in an electronic meeting as it does face-to-face. The kind of information which is exchanged and the way it is used will necessarily change. Just as a student having a beer with his professor might learn things he wouldn't learn in the lecture hall, electronic media will set new standards for accomplishing various meeting tasks. At least some of these standards will reflect a third fundamental characteristic of teleconferencing—limited channels for communication.

Limited Communication Channels

Compared to face-to-face, all teleconferencing media offer more restricted channels for the many types of communication which normally occur in small group interaction. These restrictions vary from medium to medium. Audio and computer conferencing, for example, filter out the body language which is preserved (although altered) in a video conference. Computer conferencing further filters voice intonations out of the discussion, but adds a dimension of literacy which is not so apparent in audio, video, or even face-to-face meetings.

In all three media, though, many of the nonverbal messages will be invisible or at least difficult to discern. Communication will be more focused. Differences in cultural background, organizational commitment, and goals and objectives will be less perceptive. These limitations could inhibit group effectiveness in several ways.

First, the narrowness of electronic media might foster a false sense of consensus, encouraging what Irving Janis calls "groupthink."[7] Groupthink is the reverse of the Multi-Headed Animal Syndrome noted above; it is the product of *too much* cohesiveness in a group—cohesiveness which screens out divergent ideas and tends to produce low-quality group decisions. While restricted communication channels may not build cohesiveness *per se,* they may easily limit the perspectives considered in a group by establishing an illusion of consensus. Once established, such an illusion might be aggravated by the isolation of participants from each other. In addition, the type of outside information accepted into the decision-making process could become limited to that which "fits" the available communication channels.

The supression of diverse perspectives does not necessarily produce consensus, however. Stereotyping of participants and polarization of issues are equally probable—and troublesome. Without enough breadth of communication, efforts to explore the underlying sources of differences will probably be frustrated. It is easy to imagine that different organizational perspectives might bring charges of elitism; differences in cultural perspectives might elicit charges of racism. Such charges may eradicate the trust which is vital for any group communication.

Trust is always tentative. But it is particularly so in the intial stages of a meeting before expectations of others are tested in interaction. Much of the communication early in a meeting is, in fact, testing of trust. Laing captures the complexity of this testing process in his description of husband-wife interactions.

> Husband acts on wife so that wife will experience husband's actions in a particular way. But wife has to *act* in such a way before husband can realize that she experiences his act conjunctively or disjunctively to his intention; thus, husband's behavior towards wife affects her experience of him, which, mediated back to him by her behavior towards him, in turn influences his experience of her.[8]

Laing is describing interaction of only two people; as the group grows, the dynamics become even knottier.[9] When such complex dynamics are funneled through the narrow channel of an electronic medium, intentions may not be perceived accurately. The result is likely to be what Laing calls "spirals of misperception"—and mistrust.

These are some of the negatives—false consensus, failure to recognize and reconcile differences in perspectives, and a brittleness of group trust. In favor of limited channels, we need to point out that restricted communication can also help focus a discussion on critical group tasks. In some situations, trust is not really an issue. The group task is well-defined, and the need for divergent perspectives is low. In such situations, a lot of nonverbal messages are extraneous. Electronic meetings might then increase effectiveness by filtering unnecessary and distracting signals.

Electronic meetings could even allow some groups to bypass typical social protocols and become intimate more quickly. In a computer conference, Richard Bach made this observation:

> We are convention bound to comment on the weather, current events, where do you live, what do you do for a living, et cetera. In computer conferencing I can say, and delight in it, "M. Baudot, what for you is real?" In this capacity the system is sort of an intellectual ComputerMate. You can draw preliminary conclusions about a person in minutes that take long times to draft face to face, occluded as face-to-face is with appearance, manner, speech patterns, *und so wieder.*

Though perhaps not typical, Mr. Bach's reaction suggests that the "restrictions" of electronic communication channels need not always be limitations.

The size of communication channels in electronic meetings will undoubtedly elicit varied responses from participants. Some will see these media as terribly limiting, forcing complex communication through simple channels. Others may actually experience a new sense of freedom within the limitations so clearly set by teleconferencing media. Whatever the emotional reaction of participants, however, the narrowness of communication channels will introduce a *potential* for control of group communication in ways which simply could not occur face-to-face.

Control of Group Interaction

While channels of communication in an electronic meeting are more limited than in face-to-face, they are also more easily controlled. Teleconferencing systems often have control panels or consoles. Leaders of video conferences can decide who should be seen on the screen or can switch the view away from the group altogether. In both audio and video conferences, participants in the same room can disconnect their microphones or press "cough buttons" when they want to speak to each other without being heard at the remote site. Volume controls can reduce shouts to whispers. In a computer conference, the organizer of the meeting often has special controls which other participants do not, such as the ability to erase messages, to block all private messages, or to close one conference and open another.

The design of a teleconferencing system will also shape the kind of communication which can occur. A computer conferencing system can be structured to ask direct questions of participants, to specify the form of their response, and to tally the results according to predetermined formulas. A voice-switched audio system technologically prohibits two people from speaking at once. These built-in controls are attempts to eliminate the need for certain social choices, to make communication more orderly and rational, maybe even conflict-free.

On the surface, the orderly nature of electronic meetings suggests that they might promote the carefully deliberated sequential exchanges which typify many formal negotiations. Ironically, this well-ordered, rational consideration of the demands of all parties is often the *least* effective way to reach a solution in which everyone's needs are met. First, the sequential exchange of one demand for another can oversimplify the problem so that many complex differences become collapsed into just a few, highly polarized issues. Furthermore, rigidly controlled interaction inhibits informal interpersonal communication which might focus on areas of consensus and foster some feeling of group trust.

After a detailed review of laboratory experiments in the use of audio and video teleconferencing in conflict situations, Short, Williams, and Christie conclude:

> In contrast to problem-solving discussions, conflict is clearly a major area of sensitivity to medium of communication. Medium can affect the likelihood of reaching agreement, the side which is more successful, the nature of the settlement reached, the evaluation of the other side and the individual opinions after the discussion.[10]

On the positive side, the potential to control group interaction via teleconference, like the limits of electronic channels, can certainly aid in focusing the efforts of a group on the task at hand. More control might also mean more effective procedures for promoting equality of participation, for reducing the importance of personal likes and dislikes in solving a problem, or for ensuring that all important topics are covered within a limited time period. But we suggested at the beginning of this chapter that communication is much more than verbal exchanges on a topic—that it includes more subtle dynamics such as play and developing and defining relationships. If the procedures for group communication are too rigid, if interaction is controlled too much, there could be little room for interpersonal relationships.

Dependence on Technology

A final defining characteristic of teleconferences is their basic dependence on some form of electronic equipment. Whether it uses telephone lines, microwave circuits, computers, or satellites, each form of teleconferencing introduces *some* sort of machine dependence into group communication. This dependence is perhaps the corollary to increased control: if electronic media provide the technology for more orderly meetings, they also render meetings more vulnerable to failures in the technology—and the possibility of complete loss of control.

Machines have been accused of choosing awkward moments at which to fail. And in electronic meetings, there are likely to be many potentially awkward moments. A broken connection during an emotional exchange might be devastating. At best, it would probably slow the whole communication process as group members restart and try to recover their momentum. At worst, a system failure might be interpreted as an intentional act—the slamming of an electronic door. Group trust would likely deteriorate.

Less obvious system failures might produce equally damaging results. For example, spurious numbers or letters in a computer transcript might go undetected, but they could distort an important presentation of data or signal the wrong instructions to some participant. Such occurrences may prove rare; however, it will be difficult to predict when they might occur and what their impact will be.

Most users of electronic media will trust the technology without question—until something goes wrong. Then they will make contingency plans against future malfunctions. These will be useful but probably not infallible. And even if the technology performs flawlessly, users of teleconferencing media may still experience a loss of control in the meeting situation. In a conventional conference room, meeting participants can move chairs around, sit on the floor, or open the window; they can change the meeting environment to make it more hospitable to the task at hand. But the environment in an electronic meeting probably will not be so adaptable. In a video conference room, cameras are set for predetermined chair positions; microphones will place limits on how many people participate in an audio conference. Since electronic technology will be too complex for most people to tamper with, users are likely to accept these constraints as unalterable. In fact, they may be only partially aware of the constraints which teleconferencing imposes upon them.

There is a contradiction in electronic meetings between the apparent increase in control and the possibility of greater loss of control. This contradiction, even if it remains unconscious, will change the dynamics of group communication; group behavior in the meeting will likely reflect some loss of initiative, perhaps even a reduced sense of responsibility for the communication which is taking place.

The Sensitive Zones

The decision to use a teleconferencing system to improve communication sets a dynamic process in motion. It not only introduces new organizational choices for the meeting organizer; it can also change the way people feel about what they are doing. It changes their relationships with other members of the group and the way they perceive themselves as a group. And in the long term, it may change long-standing conventions for communicating in small groups as well as in organizations and even whole societies.

Some areas of small group communication will be particularly sensitive to this change process. The recurring themes in this chapter begin to map these areas: the building and maintenance of group trust is one. The recognition and reconciliation of diverse perspectives, particularly cultural differences, is another sensitive zone. So are group conflict and the use of outside resources, especially outside experts.

• • • • • • • • •

The media do indeed offer real opportunities to improve communication by reducing the barriers of space and time. However, a central theme of this book has been that benefits are easily transformed into liabilities, promises into disappointments, and utopias into dystopias. For every possible improvement suggested by electronic media, it is necessary to add at least a word of caution.

Benefits and Cautions: A Summary

Electronic meetings can be arranged more quickly than face-to-face meetings. People in Toronto, Canada, can meet with people in Atlanta, Georgia, without having to schedule a day for the trip. They can get together when they need to, when a problem first arises, or when an interesting idea first emerges. But . . . quick start-ups may mean some communication failures, too. Planning is as important for electronic meetings as for face-to-face meetings. Often, the barriers of time and space provide an opportunity to think more carefully about the people who should be at the meeting, the resources the group will need, and the tasks that need to be accomplished. With near-instant connections, some of this planning is bound to be neglected. In the extreme, all meetings could develop a crisis atmosphere with crisis approaches to problem-solving.

More people, with more perspectives, can participate in an electronic meeting. And more perspectives can provide more alternatives for untangling a knotty problem. Also, more participation may result in fuller support for the collective decision. At the organizational level, *teleconferencing can open new communication channels,* both within an organization and between different organizations. The warning needed here is that more perspectives may mean more conflict, and protocols have not yet evolved for managing conflict in electronic meetings. Increased communication can actually exaggerate differences in viewpoints, in organizational perspectives, in cultures. Furthermore, the opening of communication channels does not necessarily improve the health of an organization: from the perspective of a division head, new patterns of communication might mean a lower commitment to previous goals and leadership. The new patterns may be an improvement for some members of the division but a threat to the manager.

There are other benefits and other cautions. Just as teleconferencing provides access to more people, it also makes possible easy access *to a wide range of information resources.* The caution: the potential for information overload and for misinformation also increases.

The restricted channels of electronic meetings may encourage *more focus and more objectivity in meetings.* But meetings can become too focused; they may not allow divergent thinking and creativity in solving problems.

Electronic meetings are often more orderly, and the organizer has more control over the interaction. But control may suppress differences of opinion and actually reduce communication.

Finally, the *costs associated with meetings may be reduced by teleconferencing.* However, over the long term, communication costs, as well as travel costs, could actually rise as communication opportunities increase. Direct substitution for travel will be rare.

New Communication Choices

The first decision will probably be the choice among media: Which medium should be used when? Ideally, this choice should be made for each meeting situation. But in reality, the choice may already be made by the time someone begins to plan a meeting. The choice among media will often be made by an entire organization. After all, a video conferencing system is a major investment. So are dedicated audio lines, and the costs of computer terminals can add up. An organization may thus decide to use only one form of teleconferencing. As a result, the choice among media is often a choice between one electronic medium and face-to-face.

Nevertheless, at some point, a group or organization will confront the question of which medium to choose. And several criteria will be improtant in making this decision. Cost will certainly be one of them, but probably not the most important. Increased cost does not necessarily mean better communication. Video, the most expensive of the three media, has both strengths and weaknesses . . . it should never be assumed to be the ideal medium "if only it were affordable."

Portability, Flexibility, and Ease of Use

In fact, other criteria probably will make the real difference in any decision to use one medium or another. Portability is important, particularly if the system is going to be used by many people in different places for different purposes. Flexibility goes hand-in-hand with portability. How quickly can meetings be arranged? How easy is it to vary the number of participants and the number of locations connected? What about flexibility in the use of time? Does everyone have to be present at the same time?

The ability to handle special types of information is another consideration. Computer conferencing, for example, seems uniquely suited to the transfer of technical information. What other types of information might be important for potential electronic meetings? Are there elaborate demonstrations or graphic needs? Do these needs make one medium more attractive than the others?

Each medium also has an inherent "style," which should influence an organizer's choice. . . . Video conferencing can be very glamorous. Audio, on the other hand, is low-key. Computer conferencing may project a kind of accuracy, authority, and scientific quality that will appeal to certain users. While these styles can interfere with communication if they are overemphasized during a meeting, they may be the source of unfortunate mismatches if their importance is underemphasized in the intial choice of which medium to use.

Finally, all of the new media require new skills for effective use. And different people will be willing to learn different skills. Executives who have never typed—and perhaps associate typing with inferior status—may not be the best candidates for a computer conference. Ease of learning the new skills will also differ among users, and these will be important considerations if the system is not to become a white elephant.

Tasks, Groups, and Personal Styles

Once an electronic medium is chosen, either because it seems most appropriate or because it is the *only* option, more important choices must be made. These are decisions about how the medium is to be used. Such decisions can make the difference between genuine communication and a breakdown in communication. The analyses of the scenarios suggest some of the considerations which will be most important in each meeting. They include choices about the identification of tasks and the organization of the group, about personal styles of communicating and technical arrangements.

Many of the evaluations of teleconferencing media have tried to determine which tasks work best in which medium. Generally, these studies have found that all three media work well for tasks such as exchanging information, giving orders or generating ideas. But tasks involving complex interpersonal communication, such as bargaining and negotiation or even getting to know someone, seem to be more difficult for all three media. However, these tasks are also more difficult in face-to-face meetings. Organizers of electronic meetings need not rule out these difficult tasks; instead, they need to look for effective ways of accomplishing them using the various media.

Critical in these decisions will be considerations of order and timing. Which tasks should be addressed first, and how much time should be allotted for them? Also, can some of the complex tasks be accomplished in a series of simpler stages? When is it appropriate to switch to another medium—for example, to use one-to-one telephone calls? Is the meeting organized in such a way that participants can question and redefine the tasks as necessary?

Users will need to make choices about the organization of the group, too. How many people should participate and what roles should be assigned? What will be the protocols for participation? The previous history of the group will influence these choices. Do the participants know each other? If not, what special arrangements might facilitate entry into the first stages of the meeting? The need to communicate will be another criterion in organizing the group. All of the participants may not have the same perception of the need to communicate. How can roles be defined to encourage participation by those who do not seem to need the group as much as the group needs them? In addition, choices about leadership and facilitation will probably be more critical in electronic conferences than in face-to-face meetings. A visible but flexible leader seems to be the most successful model to date.

While decisions about the group may be made by a single organizer of a meeting, each participant will have choices about his or her participation. Most important will be style of self-presentation. . . . Some participants may be more comfortable giving speeches while others will favor intense interactions. These choices will be based on personal skills and qualities as well as intuitive responses to the medium itself. The skilled writer may capitalize on her strength in a computer conference by presenting her views in refined mini-essays. A not-too-self-conscious colleague may respond in messages littered with typing and grammatical errors. These differences in styles may be perfectly acceptable, but they will have to be negotiated in every meeting. If the group cannot agree on a style of self-presentation, there may be no communication.

Even after a medium has been chosen, there will be choices about its technical use. This is the final set of decisions to be made in planning an electronic meeting. How many sites should be connected, and how many people will be at each site? When should the meeting be scheduled, and how long should it last? What additional technical aids, such as tape recorders, slide projectors, or computer data bases, are needed? Perhaps the most important criterion in answering these questions is equality of access. Uneven distribution of participants, inferior equipment, time slots which are easier for some participants than others—all these differences could leave some participants feeling resentful or even prevent their participation altogether.

• • • • • •

The Improvement of Communication

Electronic meetings are alternatives to face-to-face meetings—alternatives designed to improve communication by replacing, enhancing, or extending that which currently occurs. They are responses to two problems of face-to-face meetings. The first is the barrier of geographical distance; the second is the barrier of time. The way in which the technologies of electronic media respond to these problems also produces some secondary benefits, such as increases control over interaction. All of these benefits offer a promise of improved communication. Yet improvements in communication cannot be defined in the abstract. There is no such thing as improved communication *per se;* improvements can be defined only by referring to the specific objectives and values of the participants in the communication situation.

Furthermore, as more people get together without regard for the barriers of time and space, new communication concerns will emerge, and new technologies will attempt to respond to these concerns. These new technologies will further change the definition of "improvement." At the same time, they will likely blur the distinctions we have made in this book among audio, video, and computer-based teleconferencing. Even the distinction between electronic and nonelectronic meetings could become less precise as new combinations of face-to-face and electronic communication are explored. Thus, choices of media for a given communication need will not be simple choices: they will require a careful blending of communication resources and needs.

Communication—electronic or otherwise—is a craft. And as with other crafts, it cannot be taught mechanistically. It must be developed through personal experience. The craft cannot be entirely rational, either. While a systematic evaluation of current and alternative communication patterns will increase the chances of successful meetings, some aspects of communication will resist classification. Differing personal communication styles and unique-to-the-moment group dynamics cannot be calculated in advance. The craft of organizing electronic meetings will depend on intuition in concert with analysis.

Notes

1. Edward T. Hall, *The Silent Language,* New York: Anchor Books, 1973, p. 191.

2. Hall comments on the importance of social distance in group communication by saying that, "Spatial changes give a tone to communication, accent it, and at times even override the spoken word. The flow and shift of distance between people as they interact with each other is part and parcel of the communication process." E. T. Hall, *op. cit.,* p. 180.

3. John Short, Ederyn Williams, and Bruce Christie. *The Social Psychology of Telecommunications,* London, England: John Wiley and Sons, Ltd., 1976.

4. See Jacques Vallee, Robert Johansen, Hubert Lipinski, Kathleen Spangler, and Thaddeus Wilson, *Group Communication through Computers, Volumes 3 and 4,* Institute for the Future, 1976, 1978.

5. In describing alternative modes of organizing an institution, Wilensky points out that "intelligence failures are greatest if location is emphasized" as the basis for organization. He explains that "good intelligence cuts across arbitrary political boundaries" and that specialization by territory "overelaborates administrative apparatus" that makes the transfer of information from one area to another more difficult. See Harold L. Wilensky, *Organizational Intelligence,* New York: Basic Books, 1967, p. 55.

6. Michael Doyle and David Straus, *How to Make Meetings Work,* New York: Wyden Books, 1976, p. 20.

7. Irving Janis, *Victims of Groupthink.* Boston, Massachusetts: Houghton, Mifflin Company, 1972.

8. R. D. Laing, N. Phillipson, and A. R. Lee, *Interpersonal Perception,* New York: Perennial Library, 1966, pp. 34–5.

9. In fact, Laing's metaphor for the entanglement of selves which occurs in groups is simply "knots." R. D. Laing, *Knots,* New York: Pantheon, 1971.

10. John Short, Ederyn Williams, and Bruce Christie, *op. cit.,* p. 109.

Intercultural Small Group Communication

Richard E. Porter

Intercultural communication has become an issue of major concern, inquiry, and study during the past ten years.[1] This concern is prompted by a recognition that people no longer live in relative isolation but find themselves in situations where they are interacting with people from various cultural backgrounds. With rapid increases in transportation and communication capabilities, millions of people now visit many parts of the world or are introduced to a variety of cultures in their own living rooms. At the same time, here at home, racial and ethnic minorities have become both vocal and visible, peacefully, and sometimes violently, demanding their place in the mainstream of American life. Court decisions and legislative actions have forced increased intercultural contact through equal opportunity and affirmative action employment practices; desegregation and integration of public schools; and the establishment of minority quotas for admission to unions, colleges and universities, and graduate and professional schools. In almost every facet of our lives we increasingly are in the presence of and are more aware of others who are culturally different. We must learn to interact successfully with these people if our society is to be one of peace where all people have respect and dignity.

Successful interaction with culturally different people requires that we develop a facility for intercultural communication and learn to use it in a wide variety of communication contexts. One of these contexts, and the one we will examine, is the small group communication setting. Before we consider this, however, brief attention will be given to the basic natures of intercultural communication and to the relationship of culture to communication.

Intercultural Communication

Intercultural communication is defined here as a communication setting in which a source in one culture encodes a message which is to be decoded by a receiver in another culture. In other words, whenever a person who is a member of one culture sends a message—whether it be verbal or nonverbal, spoken or written—to someone who is a member of another culture, both are communicating interculturally.

Today in the United States we find many cultures. Some are based on race: black, Hispanic, Oriental, and the original American—the Indian. Others

Richard E. Porter is affiliated with the Department of Speech Communication, California State University at Long Beach.

are based on ethnic differences: Jew, Italian, German, Pole, Irish, and Greek are but a few of the many ethnic cultures we find in the United States. There are also cultures based on socio-economic differences. The culture of a Rockefeller or a Kennedy is vastly different from that of a third-generation welfare family living in Denver. And, finally, cultures develop around ways of life and value systems. Members of the drug culture share perceptions of the world and values that are vastly different from those shared, for example, by members of the John Birch Society or the Ku Klux Klan. Or, there are followers of Reverend Moon, members of the gay community, or activists in the feminist movement who all have different perceptions and belief-value structures.

If we venture beyond our national boundaries, we find even greater differences in cultures. Religious, philosophical, political, economic, and social role views may differ greatly from our own, as may communities, modes of life, forms of work, degrees of industrialization, and social organization. In these cases, we find people are noticeably different from ourselves in their ways of life, customs, and traditions.

The major communication problem here is one of *cultural variance in social perception,* that is, differences in the ways people develop and attribute meaning to social objects and events. We are all aware that meaning resides in people and that people interpret symbols and messages according to their backgrounds and prior experiences. This problem is minimized when source and receiver are both in the same culture. When source and receiver are from different cultures, however, the problems of understanding and meaning attribution can be magnified many times. Unless interactors are aware of cultural influences on meaning and can act to compensate for this influence, communication attempts may be unsuccessful.

Although problems inherent in intercultural communication may be best solved by becoming what Adler (1976) has described as a multicultural person, this is a long and difficult goal that many cannot attain. Most people, however, can become aware of and sensitize themselves to the effects, which culture imposes on communication, and through this awareness and sensitivity they become better able to communicate interculturally. Some of these effects will be described before we move into our discussion of intercultural small group communication.

Culture and Communication

Analysis of intercultural communication processes has revealed eight sociocultural variables crucial to any intercultural event that are strongly influenced by culture: (1) attitudes, (2) social organization, (3) patterns of thought, (4) roles and role prescriptions, (5) language, (6) nonverbal expressive behavior, (7) use and organization of space, and (8) time conceptualization. As these variables are discussed in detail elsewhere (Porter, 1972; Porter and Samovar, 1976) only those most relevant to small group communication will receive attention here.

Attitudes

"Attitude" symbolizes an internal psychological state of readiness to respond that predisposes us to behave in rather specific and consistent ways when we come in contact with various social objects or events. As Fishbein and Ajzen (1975) point out, attitude formation is a function of our underlying belief and value structures. That is, our predispositions toward social objects and events are a function of the salient beliefs and values we hold. This concept of attitude formation is crucial to intercultural communication because the belief-value structures from which we form our attitudes are culturally determined. What we believe and how we evaluate our beliefs are deeply embedded in everyday experiences of interacting with our environment and culture. The culture in which we establish our beliefs and values in many ways influences (if not dictates) the content and extent of our beliefs as well as the direction and intensity of our values.[2] Our attitudes, then, influence both our overt behaviors and our perceptions. They lead us to interpret events according to our biases and sometimes to see things as we wish or believe them to be rather than as they are.

Four forms of attitudes exert the greatest influence on intercultural communication: *ethnocentrism, world view, absoluteness,* and *stereotypes and prejudices.* Ethnocentrism is a tendency for us to view others, using ourselves as the standard for all judgments; we place ourselves at the center of the universe and rate all others according to their distance from us. We rank one group above another, one element of society above another, one ethnic group, one race above another, and one country above another. We place our own groups, our own country, and our own culture above others; we see ourselves as best.

When ethnocentrism enters our social perceptions, intercultural communication effectiveness is reduced because we lose objectivity toward others. How much ethnocentrism interferes with intercultural communication cannot be predicted, but we do know it is strongest in moral and religious contexts where emotions often promote hostility that prevents effective communication. In the extreme, ethnocentrism robs us of willingness or desire to communicate interculturally.

Our view of the world in which we live is a function of culture. As Americans, we tend to have a man-centered view of the world. We see it as a vast space on which to carry out our desires; we build what we wish, seek to control nature, and when displeased tear it all down and start over again. Urban renewal is but one example of this world view transformed into action. Other cultures see the world differently. Orientals, for instance, are apt to view the human-universe relationship as one of balance in which people share a place between heaven and earth. Each thing a person does exerts some influence on the balance of that relationship. People must act carefully and not upset the balance because the nature of the universe is toward harmony.

World view gives us a perspective from which we shape and form our impressions of social objects and events. As we encounter people with differing world views, our communicative behavior may be hampered because we view events differently. We may use different frames of reference that seem vague or obscure to others, just as theirs may seem to us. Our perceptions become clouded and our attitudes interfere with our ability to communicate effectively with others.

Absoluteness is closely related to and often derived from ethnocentrism and world view. Absoluteness is reflected in culturally derived notions we have of right and wrong, good and bad, beautiful and ugly, true and false, positive and negative, and so on. Absoluteness influences social perception by providing us with a set of basic precepts from which we judge the behavior and beliefs of others. We take these notions to be absolute—to be "truth"—and do not or cannot realize these "absolutes" are not absolute but are subject to cultural variation. An absolute is meaningful to us only in the relative sense of what is accepted or believed within a given culture.

Stereotypes are attitudinal sets from which we assign attributes to another person solely on the basis of a class or category we believe that person belongs to. Stereotypes might lead us to believe, for example, that all Irish are red-headed and quick-tempered; that all Japanese are short and sly; that all Jews are shrewd and grasping; or that blacks are superstitious and that Mexicans are lazy. Although these generalizations are commonly held stereotypes, they are untrue! Prejudices, on the other hand, are attitudinal sets that predispose us to behave in certain ways toward people solely on the basis of their membership in some group. For example, because a person is an Oriental, a homosexual, or a black, we may deny him membership in a country club, force him to live in a ghetto or barrio, or restrict him to low-paying jobs and performance of menial tasks. Stereotypes and prejudices, obviously, are closely interrelated.

Stereotypes and prejudices work in various ways to affect our communication. By predisposing us to behave in specific ways when confronted by a particular stimulus and by causing us to attach generalized attributes to people whom we encounter, we can permit stereotypes and prejudices to interfere with our communicative experiences and to limit their effectiveness. We spend our time looking for whatever reinforces our prejudices and stereotypes and ignore what is contradictory.

Roles and Role Prescriptions

If we encounter members of our cultures and their behavior seems strange to us, it very well could be a matter of different role prescriptions. Roles and role prescriptions vary culturally, and although we might argue the value of a particular role prescription, we must realize—if we are to succeed in our task of communication—that for members of the culture we are communicating with, their behaviors are completely natural, normal, and ethical.

The problem here is one of value. We tend to value prescribed social role behavior, and when role behaviors fail to meet our expectations, conflict can result. In our American culture we sometimes find one segment of society that fulfills a role of social protector. This group has a value system that holds such things as nude sunbathing, homosexual acts, drug use, buying sex, or viewing pornographic materials as absolutely evil and to be prohibited under all circumstances. Yet, those who fulfill roles of nude sunbather, homosexual, drug user, pimp or prostitute, and explicit sex film producer or viewer value these acts differently. Their value systems permit and even approve these acts and hold they are not evil but are the exercise of free choice by mature people in a free society. Values held by various role groups within a culture or between cultures often conflict and can lead to ineffective communication and even violence.

Nonverbal Expression

It is a common experience among people who travel to find that it is difficult to interpret the facial expressions of people of cultures other than their own. This difficulty has frequently been voiced with reference to Oriental people whose modes of expression are found to differ from those of Caucasians (Vinacke, 1949, 407).

The form nonverbal messages take as well as the circumstances for their expression and the amount of expression permitted is culturally determined. Which emotion may be displayed, by whom it may be displayed, the circumstances under which it may be displayed, and the extent of its display are cultural norms that children learn very early. In this regard Klineberg (1954) has noted:

We find that cultures differ widely from one another in the amount of emotional expression which is permitted. We speak, for example, of the imperturbability of the American Indian, the inscrutability of the Oriental, the reserve of the Englishman, and at the other extreme of the expressiveness of the Negro or the Sicilian. Although there is always some exaggeration in such clichés, it is probable that they do correspond to an accepted cultural pattern, at least to some degree (p. 174).

The Japanese smile, for example, is a law of etiquette that has been elaborated and cultured from early times; it not necessarily a spontaneous expression of amusement. This smile is a silent language often inexplicable to Westerners. Japanese children are taught to smile as a social duty so they will appear happy and avoid inflicting sorrow or grief upon their friends.

Cultural variance in nonverbal expression and its potential effect upon social perception and intercultural communication is well expressed by Sitaram (1972):

> What is an effective communication symbol in one culture could be an obscene gesture in another culture. The communication technique that makes a person successful in New York could kill him in New Delhi (p. 19).

An example will serve as a case in point and demonstrate how harmful the use and misinterpretation of nonverbal behavior can be in an intercultural situation. A visiting British professor precipitated a student demonstration and riot at Ain Shams University in Cairo in 1952 when he leaned back in his chair and put his feet upon the desk while talking to his class. What he did not realize is in the Middle East it is extremely insulting to have to sit facing the soles of someone's shoes (Yousef, 1972).

Nonverbal aspects of intercultural communication are probably among the most difficult because of the reliance we place on the interpretation of nonverbal cues in the decoding of verbal cues. We have much to learn about how people from other cultures use nonverbal cues to express themselves. Until we gain this knowledge we will encounter trouble when communicating interculturally.

This discussion of intercultural communication has been extremely brief and has touched only upon the most striking aspects of culture as they influence the communication process. But, we have shown how our culture gives us different backgrounds and experiences not necessarily available to or known by others with whom we may communicate. Our ability to decode and to understand a message requires knowledge of the culture in which it was encoded. Ignorance can result in misinterpreting and misunderstanding, which can cause us to make inappropriate responses.

Intercultural Communication Within Small Groups

Small group communication settings involve intercultural communication when a group is composed of people from differing cultural backgrounds. This quite naturally occurs in international settings when people from various countries and cultures meet to discuss international politics, economics, and business. Or we may find it in domestic areas when civic bodies attempt to solve problems within their communities or when students representing various ethnic and racial backgrounds meet to recommend school policies and actions.

Small group communication is a complex process involving a highly complicated interrelationship of many dynamic elements. The sharing of common goals or purposes, a social organization, the establishment of communication channels, and the sharing of relevant beliefs and values are all recognized necessary ingredients for the emergence of a group and the development of an atmosphere suitable for small group communication. In general, a certain similarity between people is necessary for the creation of this atmosphere and the development of what Fisher (1964) calls "groupness." Successful small group formation and communication is difficult enough a task when group members are culturally similar, but when members are culturally dissimilar, the task may be formidable.

Since intercultural small group communication occurs in both international and domestic dimensions, we will examine each of these situations. Intercultural communication in any context is dependent upon both a desire to communicate interculturally and a recognition of cultural influences on communication processes. Since it is impossible to examine a wide variety of cultures and cultural contexts, we will limit our discussion to examining some of the problems that could arise in intercultural small group communication.

The international dimension of intercultural communication is confused at times by political and ideological issues that inhibit real communicative purposes. Some of these issues include secret agreements, treaties with other countries, hidden agendas, and image maintenance, to name but a few. We will assume a situation in which these influences are absent, an environment in which interested, earnest, and sincere people have gathered to seek consensus and agreement about a political issue, an economic issue, or a business issue. The actual topic does not matter; what is important here is the sociocultural environment in which communication takes place and the way culture influences, guides, and determines communicative behavior. All of the possible problems that could be encountered cannot even be imagined, let alone covered. Considering cultural differences in approaches to small group interaction, however, will give us an insight into difficulties that can arise.

As Americans, we tend to be task oriented, direct, and businesslike, immediately wanting to get at the heart of the matter. We depreciate what we consider to be irrelevant concerns, and urge immediate action to get the job done.

Other cultures are not like us; the small, seemingly trivial matters are very important. Until those matters are resolved, progress toward the task at hand cannot proceed. This was very apparent several years ago at the Paris Peace Conference where there was much controversy over table shape and seating arrangements. We Americans tended to react with a what-difference-does-it-make attitude; we wanted to get down to business, to start negotiating an end to the war. We had difficulty understanding how something as important as ending a war could be bogged down for weeks over something (to us) as silly as the shape of a conference table.

What we did not realize was the importance given to such nonverbal environmental factors as seating arrangement by the Vietnamese. In Oriental cultures social hierarchy is extremely important and before anything as important as peace negotiations can begin, the social hierarchies must be clearly established, understood, and stated in nonverbal terms. This is why table shape was so important. To have a square table would indicate equality of all participants. And, since the government of South Vietnam claimed not to recognize the Viet Cong, to permit them to sit at a square table would imply they were of equal stature—clearly an inconsistency and a detriment to negotiation.

Another problem we may face in intercultural small group communication is the actual communication process itself. This is readily seen if we examine the differences in approach between Americans and Japanese.[3] We Americans want to talk to the top-man, the one in authority who can make tough decisions. We want to get down to business and drive a hard bargain, and we want answers now. We are busy; time is money, and we cannot fool around. The Japanese, however, are quite different in their approach. "If we were to place Japanese concepts of self and group at one end of a continuum it would be possible to produce an almost perfect paradigm by placing American concepts at the other" (Cathcart & Cathcart, 1976, 58). In other words, Japanese concepts of self and group are essentially the opposite of our own. Some distinctions between American and Japanese concepts will be discussed in order to see how different approaches to group interaction influence communication.

Americans tend to view groups as being composed of individuals where the role of the individual is paramount. This concern with the individual is reflected in the American culture through admiration of "rugged individualism" and the desire to interact with the responsible party. The Japanese, on the other hand, have a selfless view of groups. The group is the social entity; individual identity is submerged for group identity.

This distinction between concept of self in relation to groups is important in terms of decision making and the outcomes of intercultural negotiation. The American concept of individual importance leads to a notion of individual responsibility. A single, unique person is ultimately responsible for decisions and their consequences. This individual is also expected to accept blame for decisions that lead to bad consequences. In a sense, we Americans want to know whom to "hang" when things go wrong. The Japanese, however, operate in a group sense rather than an individual sense. Decisions result from group interaction and group consensus; the group, not the individual, is responsible for the consequences of its action, and when something goes wrong the group, not the individual, is held responsible. The extreme of this position is aptly described by Cathcart and Cathcart (1976):

> This embodiment of group can be carried to the point where, in the extreme circumstances, those persons at the top of the group hierarchy feel constrained to answer for the misdeeds of individual group members by committing *hara-kiri* (suicide) in order to erase the blot on the group's honor. This act of *hara-kiri* reflects a total denial of self and a complete loyalty to the group (pp. 59–60).

Contrast this, if you will, in your imagination. Can you imagine the president of a top U.S. corporation committing suicide because a machine shop supervisor made a poor decision that adversely affected profits and angered stockholders?

A further aspect of culture that can have a significant effect on intercultural small group communication is what Hall (1976) has identified as the context dimension. According to this view, cultures vary along a context dimension that ranges from low to high. What this refers to as far as communication is concerned is the amount of shared cultural knowledge and background the communicators possess. Hall (1976) succinctly states:

> Any transaction can be characterized as high-, low-, or middle context. HC transactions feature preprogrammed information that is in the receiver and in the setting, with only minimal information in the transmitted message. LC transactions are the reverse. Most of the information must be in the transmitted message in order to make up for what is missing in context (p. 101).

This notion of context poses problems when interactors are from cultures that differ in context. Oriental cultures tend to be high context while we Americans tend toward low context. When we meet with members of high context cultures, unless we have the requisite contextual preprogramming, we are liable to have difficulty in communication because the high context messages do not contain sufficient information for us to gain true or complete meaning. What is worse, we may interpret a high context message according to our low context dispositions and reach entirely the wrong meaning.

The cultural preprogramming referred to here goes beyond mere information, but involves an entire cultural tradition. It includes the entire nonverbal environment in which a communication takes place. Misunderstanding of the nonverbal context of a high context culture is described by Morsbach (1976):

> An American professor at a Japanese university with an excellent command of Japanese language told me the following:
>
> One day he had attended a faculty meeting where he fully participated in the lengthy discussions, using Japanese throughout. On leaving the meeting, he remarked to a Japanese colleague that, in his opinion, the meeting had finally arrived at a particular conclusion. Had not Professor X spoken in favor? His Japanese colleague agreed. And other professors, too? (going down the list one by one). Again, his Japanese colleague agreed, but finally remarked "All this may be so, but you are still mistaken. The meeting arrived at the opposite conclusion: You have correctly understood all the words spoken, but you didn't understand the silences between them" (p. 258).

In discussing the international dimension of intercultural communication we have reviewed several gross cultural differences that might be found between participants in small group intercultural communication. The point here was to emphasize how culture may affect our participation in small group communication and how it may influence our behaviors and the meanings—both social and literal—we attribute to other people and to their messages. Much of what we have viewed may seem trivial. But, to others these matters are very important. If we are to be successful intercultural communicators, we must realize how seemingly insignificant matters can affect the dynamics of our intercultural groups.

When we shift our interest to the domestic dimension of intercultural communication we are still faced with the problems of cultural differences but in a way that mostly manifests itself in terms of values and expectations. This situation may result when small groups are formed in such a manner as to bring together people of wide diversity within our unifying cultural umbrella. By cultural umbrella, we refer to the fact that although people in a small group situation may represent a variety of cultural backgrounds, they are all mediated to some extent by the overall American culture.

Frequently, culturally diversified groups are found when civic bodies or panels are formed. In this case an often first effort is to empanel as members a priest, a minister, and a rabbi, a black, an Oriental, and a Hispanic as well as women and representatives of other diverse groups within the community such as gays, civil libertarians, youth, welfare recipients, and senior citizens. However admirable this may be in terms of democratic institutions, it can result in artificially created groups whose composition defies the formation of an atmosphere conducive to cohesiveness and member satisfaction which are necessary for the feeling of "groupness" mentioned earlier. This is especially the case when cultural differences represent variability of values, beliefs, and attitudes. Whereas a natural group—one formed through the ongoing process of group dynamics—is composed of members who share similar relevant values, beliefs, and attitudes, artificial groups—those we form by administrative action—may be composed of persons who have dissimilar value systems and who distrust or even dislike the cultural systems of each other. Toleration may be practiced, but it may not overcome differences in basic beliefs and values that influence the outcome of group interaction.

Domestic groups may also be burdened by a variety of expectations. Cultural background as well as intercultural experience lead to the formation of expectations about what a group can or cannot do and what it will or will not do in terms of interaction and task accomplishment. Further, expectational differences may lead to problems of interpersonal trust. In an ideal group situation everyone trusts each other; they do not feel that someone will try to do them harm. But, in many intercultural settings, the situation is different; some people, usually but not always minority members of the community, may sense that others cannot be trusted, that they will ultimately harm or cheat them. An example of how differences in expectations can influence group activity is seen in an exchange between students in an intercultural workshop. A discussion between black and white students about black-white relationships had been going on for about thirty minutes. The general trend of the discussion was that blacks did not trust or believe whites. Finally, a frustrated white student, who could not understand why this attitude prevailed, asked a black woman if he came to her and said that he would like to help blacks achieve equality, how would she respond. She answered by saying, "I wouldn't believe you." When asked to explain why she wouldn't believe him, she outlined the history of the whites' relationship with the American Indian in which promises and treaties were made and later broken when it was to the advantage of the whites. After citing numerous instances of whites having broken promises and treaties and generally mistreating minorities, she queried the white student with, "Why should I believe you?"

One cannot argue that the majority's past behavior toward racial and ethnic minorities has been one that would result in minority distrust of the majority. What must be recognized, however, by both the minorities and the majority is that individuals cannot be judged by the behaviors of the group from which they come. There are very good grounds for blacks and other minorities to distrust some or many whites, but not all of them. Only through mediating individual expectations in intercultural situations can we learn who can and who cannot be trusted. Anyone who hopes to successfully interact in intercultural small groups must be prepared to show, even to prove, their worthiness of trust and belief.

The value systems of people engaged in small group communication at times get in the way of their achieving consensus or agreement on an issue. When group members are from different cultures this often amplifies the problem because of the influence culture has on the development of values. As cultural diversity increases, the chance of value conflict also increases. This aspect is especially a problem in final phases of discussion when decisions about issues are being made. An example of this can be seen in a group discussion class where a group had been formed at the beginning of the semester to discuss the common interest problem of divorce in the United States. For several weeks everything went well. During initial phases of the discussion, agreement was easily reached on the nature of the problem, its extent, its effects, and even its causes. But, when the solution phase of discussion began, difficulty soon developed. One member of the group of Latin origin was a deeply devout Catholic. To him the only possible solution was to make divorce illegal because it was an immoral act that should not be permitted. This was his only solution; he was adamantly opposed to any other possible solution. The result was an initial attempt by other members of the group to communicate with him and attempt to have him modify his position or at least listen to alternatives that could be available to non-Catholics. This effort met with no success, and when it became evident he would not alter his position or even listen to other views, he was banished from the group. He became a mere observer where he had once been an active participant. After a short time, he began to miss the discussions altogether. Here was a case where the prevailing belief-value system of the group was too different from his, and it soon became more rewarding for him not to be a member of the group than to continue his group membership. Consequently, he dropped out of the group.

Granted this example is an extreme event. But it does represent the situation where the value system of an individual derived from his cultural heritage was of sufficient strength to prevent him from interacting with his fellow students and to even consider their positions. We also must realize that although Catholicism transcends culture, it is mediated by various cultures. And, this was one case where the cultural tradition of this man's Latin origin maximized Catholic dogma and made it a very strong part of his value system.

This type of situation can easily crop up when we form groups that represent all views and interests within a community. Perhaps it will not always be so severe as to disrupt the group or lead to its disintegration, but it can lead to problems that must be understood and resolved before a group can form its identity and reach consensus. We must remember that some views just are not compatible with others as some interests are not compatible with others. When we force these views and interests to interact, the outcome may not be what we expect or desire, and frustrate our attempts to obtain representative views in the formulation of community policies.

Here we have emphasized the view that the chief problem in intercultural communication lies in social perception. We have suggested that culture strongly influences social perception which leads to errors in the interpretation of messages. If there is to be successful intercultural communication within small groups in both domestic and international arenas, we must be aware of the cultural factors which affect communication in both our own culture and the cultures of others. We must understand both cultural differences and cultural similarities. Understanding differences can help us recognize problems, and understanding similarities can help us become closer.

Notes

1. See, for example, Samovar and Porter (1972, 1976), Harms (1973), Prosser (1973), Smith (1973), Rich (1974), Brislin, Bochner and Lenner (1975), Condon and Yousef (1975), and Sitaram and Cogdell (1976).
2. A detailed discussion of cultural value systems may be found in Condon and Yousef (1975, 47–121).
3. An excellent discussion of the underlying principles as they reflect Japanese culture may be found in Cathcart and Cathcart (1976), Doi (1976), Morsbach (1976), and Van Zandt (1976).

References

Adler, P. S. "Beyond Cultural Identity: Reflections of Culture and Multicultural Man" in L. Samovar and R. Porter (eds.), *Intercultural Communication: A Reader,* 2d ed. Belmont, California: Wadsworth, 1976.

Brislin, R. W., Bochner, S. and Lonner, W. J. (eds.). *Cross-Cultural Perspectives of Learning,* New York: Halsted Press, John Wiley & Sons, 1975.

Cathcart, D. and Cathcart, R. "Japanese Social Experience and Concepts of Group" in L. Samovar and R. Porter (eds.), *Intercultural Communication: A Reader,* 2d ed. Belmont, California: Wadsworth, 1976.

Condon, J. C. and Yousef, F. *An Introduction to Intercultural Communication.* Indianapolis: Bobbs-Merrill, 1975.

Doi, L. T. "The Japanese Patterns of Communication and the Concept of *Amae*" in L. Samovar and R. Porter (eds.), *Intercultural Communication: A Reader,* 2d ed. Belmont, California: Wadsworth, 1976.

Fishbein, M. and Ajzen, I. *Belief, Attitude, Intention and Behavior: An Introduction to Theory and Research.* Reading, Mass.: Addison-Wesley, 1975.

Fisher, B. A. *Small Group Decision Making: Communication and the Group Process.* New York: McGraw-Hill, 1974.

Hall, E. T. *Beyond Culture.* Garden City, New York: Doubleday, 1976.

Harms, L. S. *Intercultural Communication.* New York: Harper & Row, 1973.

Klineberg, O. *Social Psychology,* rev. ed. New York: Holt, Rinehart & Winston, 1954.

Morsbach, H. "Aspects of Nonverbal Communication in Japan" in L. Samovar and R. Porter (eds.), *Intercultural Communication: A Reader,* 2d ed. Belmont, California: Wadsworth, 1976.

Porter, R. E. "An Overview of Intercultural Communication in L. Samovar and R. Porter (eds.), *Intercultural Communication: A Reader.* Belmont, California: Wadsworth, 1972.

Porter, R. E. and Samovar, L. A. "Communicating Interculturally" in L. Samovar and R. Porter (eds.), *Intercultural Communication: A Reader,* 2d ed. Belmont, California: Wadsworth, 1976.

Prosser, M. H. (ed.). *Intercommunication Among Nations and Peoples.* New York: Harper & Row, 1973.

Rich, A. L. *Interracial Communication.* New York: Harper & Row, 1974.

Samovar, L. A. and Porter, R. E. (eds.). *Intercultural Communication: A Reader.* Belmont, California: Wadsworth, 1972.

Samovar, L. A. and Porter, R. E. (eds.). *Intercultural Communication: A Reader,* 2d ed. Belmont, California: Wadsworth, 1976.

Sitaram, K. S. "What is Intercultural Communication?" in L. Samovar and R. Porter (eds.), *Intercultural Communication: A Reader.* Belmont, California: Wadsworth, 1972.

Sitaram, K. S. and Cogdell, R. T. *Foundations of Intercultural Communication.* Columbus, Ohio: Merrill, 1976.

Smith, A. L. *Transracial Communication.* Englewood Cliffs, New Jersey: Prentice-Hall, 1973.

Van Zandt, H. F. "How to Negotiate in Japan" in L. Samovar and R. Porter (eds.), *Intercultural Communication: A Reader,* 2d ed. Belmont, California: Wadsworth, 1976.

Vinacke, E. W. "The Judgment of Facial Expressions by Three National-Racial Groups in Hawaii: I. Caucasian Faces," *Journal of Personality,* 17, 1949, 407–429.

Yousef, F. "Intercultural Communication: Aspects of Contrastive Social Values Between North Americans and Middle Easterners." Unpublished manuscript. California State University, Long Beach, California, 1972.

Suggested Readings

Altman, Irwin and Taylor, Dalmas, *Social Penetration: The Development of Interpersonal Relationships.* New York: Holt, Rinehart & Winston, 1973.

Austin-Lett, Genelle and Sprague, Jan. *Talk to Yourself: Experiencing Intrapersonal Communication.* Boston: Houghton-Mifflin Company, 1976.

Binder, J. L. "A Method for Small Group Training of Psychiatric Ward Staff," *Psychiatry,* 39 (1976): 365–375.

Blatz, William E. "The Individual and the Group," *The American Journal of Sociology,* 44 (May, 1939), 820–38.

Bradford, Leland R., Gibb, Jack R. and Benne, Kenneth D., eds. *T-Group Theory and Laboratory Method.* New York: John Wiley and Sons, Inc., 1964.

Burton, Arthur, ed. *Encounter: The Theory and Practice of Encounter Groups.* San Francisco: Jossey-Bass, Inc., 1969.

Buss, Allan R. and Poley, Wayne. *Individual Differences: Traits and Factors.* New York: Gardner Press (John Wiley & Sons), 1976.

Condon, John C. and Yousef, Fathi, *An Introduction to Intercultural Communication.* Indianapolis: The Bobbs-Merrill Company, Inc., 1975.

Deutsch, M. And Krauss, R. "Studies of Interpersonal Bargaining," *Journal of Conflict Resolution* 6 (1962): 52–76.

Egan, Gerard, *Interpersonal Living: A Skills/Contract Approach to Human Relations Training in Groups.* Monterey, CA: Brooks/Cole Publishing Company, 1976.

Goffman, Erving. *The Presentation of Self in Everyday Life.* New York: Doubleday & Company, Inc., 1959.

Jacobson, D. *Power and Interpersonal Relations.* Belmont, CA: Wadsworth Publishing Company, Inc., 1972.

Janis, Irving L. "Groupthink," *Psychology Today* 5 (November, 1971), 43–46, 74–76.

Kanter, Rosabeth. *Men and Women of the Corporation.* New York: Basic Books, 1977.

Kephart, William M. *Extraordinary Groups: The Sociology of Unconventional Life Styles.* New York: St. Martin's Press, 1976.

Kiefer, C. W. *Changing Cultures, Changing Times.* San Francisco: Jossey-Bass, Inc., 1974.

McFeat, T. *Small Group Cultures.* New York: Pergamon Press, 1974.

Neer, M. R. "A Speech Communication Perspective of the Small Group," *Communication,* 10 (1981): xi–xx.

Palmer, Stuart. *Deviance and Conformity.* New Haven: College and University Press, 1970.

Porter, L. W., Lawler III, E. E. and Hackman, J. R. *Behavior in Organizations.* New York: McGraw-Hill Book Company, 1974.

Samovar, Larry A. and Porter, Richard E., eds. *Intercultural Communication: A Reader,* 2d ed. Belmont, CA: Wadsworth Publishing Co., 1976.

Shuter, Robert. "Cross-Cultural Small Group Research," *International Journal of Intercultural Relations,* 1 (1977): 90–104.

Smith, B. B. and Farrell, B. A. *Training in Small Groups.* London: Pergamon, 1979.

Young, O. R., ed. *Bargaining: Formal Theories of Negotiation.* Urbana, IL: University of Illinois Press, 1975.

3

Group Decision Making: Form and Structure

Sayings like, "two heads are better than one," express a folk wisdom which reflects accumulated knowledge about human behavior in groups. All of us are aware there are tasks more readily and effectively accomplished when we work through a group, rather than alone. Our society is permeated with work groups wherein individuals join together to accomplish some task. Every organization is made up of one or more small groups, each with an assigned task. All governmental and academic institutions are dependent on departmental groups and committees to make decisions and to formulate policies. In short, we all spend a great deal of our time in work groups and task groups making decisions. It behooves us, therefore, to study the form and structure of group decision making if we are to better understand the dynamics of small group communication.

As pointed out in the introduction to chapter 1, the modern study of small groups has concentrated longer and more extensively on this phenomenon – the decision making small group and how to make it more effective – than any other aspect of small group dynamics. As early as 1910 academicians were applying John Dewey's "reflective thinking" pattern in small groups to improve decision making. In the 1920s there was an upsurge of interest on the part of business and government organizations in the ways of transforming workers into cooperative teams that could resolve complex problems through improved decision-making processes. By the 1930s, almost all colleges and universities in the United States were offering courses in "group discussion" designed to help students learn the art of group problem solving and decision making. Organizations like the National Aerospace Administration (NASA) were utilizing advanced methods of team decision making to ensure the success of space exploration and moon landings in the 1960s and '70s. This is still one of the prime areas of study of small groups today, and there is available a large body of literature for the student of small group communication.

This chapter focuses on task groups and the decision-making process. The seven essays (six written exclusively for this book) concentrate on the problem-solving aspects of group communication. They describe how task groups are organized, the patterns most suited to group problem solving, how groups are structured, and the forms of communication which render decision making more efficient and rewarding. These readings also point out that task functions cannot be separated from interpersonal satisfaction in the small group; it is important to keep in mind that in overcoming task problems, we must deal with interpersonal barriers.

"Structure in Group Decision Making" is the title and the focus of the first essay in this chapter. Ronald L. Applbaum reviews the research that has been done on decision-making structure and analyzes the patterns and sequences that account for the decision-making process in small groups. He finds that all decision-making models have a remarkable number of common elements, which he then summarizes at the conclusion of his article.

Julia T. Wood takes exception to the widely held notion that consensus decision making is the best form of group decision. "Alternative Methods of Group Decision Making" offers two additional methods of group decision making she believes have as much validity as consensus decisions—"negotiation" and "voting". She compares the assumptions and implications among consensus, negotiation, and voting, and concludes that no one of the three is best or ideal in an absolute sense. She believes each of these three methods is a legitimate mode of making decisions in groups.

Rather than describing the structures and forms that lead to successful decision making, in using a unique approach, Dennis S. Gouran explains the influences that are *counteractive* to the group's efforts in reaching a decision. In his essay "Principles of Counteractive Influence in Decision-Making and Problem-Solving Groups", Gouran explicates the behavioral principles at work in groups that inhibit or prolong decision making.

An overview of the formats and procedures available to those involved in decision-making groups is offered in the next essay. "Making Meetings More Successful: Plans, Formats, and Procedures for Group Problem Solving" is the title of David R. Seibold's article, which deals with steps in planning a meeting, possible formats for organizing sessions, and alternative procedures for problem solving. Examples are provided to illustrate these formats and procedures.

"Group Conformity", by Patricia Hayes Andrews, explains that pressure for uniformity and conformity in small groups is a simple fact of group life. She describes and analyzes theories that have been used to account for group conformity, and cites her own research findings. She concludes that individuals need to understand the forces within themselves that make them more or less vulnerable to group influence.

According to Peter J. Marston and Michael L. Hecht, group satisfaction is a socio-emotional outcome in small groups that correlates with group consensus, productivity, performance, effectiveness, and turnover. In their article "Group Satisfaction", they examine some of the most significant factors associated with group satisfaction. They demonstrate, through an analysis of a hypothetical campus group, how group participation, types of messages, feedback, interaction management, status, and motivation are all linked with group satisfaction.

Structure in Group Decision Making

Ronald L. Applbaum

Most studies of decision making are classified into one of three categories: individual, group, or organizational. Researchers working independently, in all three areas, have described the existence of structural patterns during the process of decision making. These structures have usually been conceptualized as phases or stages of decision making.

Despite previous research, as Theodore Mills observed, we tend to underestimate the extent to which group participants follow or create an ordered, often ritualized way of interacting. We fail to perceive these patterns because "we are properly trained to look beyond the surface of overt behavior in order to infer what a man means by what he wants or by what he does, we tend to overlook the design that exists on the surface of interpersonal behavior."[1]

The purpose of this article is twofold: (1) to describe the basic interactive structures that occur during group decision making, and (2) to identify the role of communication in these phase structures.

When examining the literature on group decision making structures, you should proceed with the utmost caution. You should note that researchers and scholars dealing with group structures tend to merge or equate the concepts of group development and decision making. It is, however, not at all clear that every group development model involves decision making processes and vice versa. Although models of individual decision making are often discussed alongside group decision making, research has not shown that the structural properties of group and individual decision making are identical. This article will deal primarily with those "phase theorems" that describe group decision making processes.

Phase Theorems and Decision Making

In this section, I will explore a number of descriptive studies which identify distinct structural phases during the decision making process. I also will describe some of the similarities and dissimilarities between the proposed group structures.

Before proceeding, however, it should be recognized that group phase theorems begin with three assumptions. First, a "natural" process of group decision making exists. That is, groups proceed in the decision making process

Ronald L. Applbaum is Vice President for Academic Affairs, Pan American University.

in a fairly consistent pattern. Second, decision phases are comprised of distinct activities or interactive behaviors. Third, structural phases occur within a specific time frame. And if all three of these assumptions are correct, a basic group phase theorem should be generalizable across a variety of group and organizational contexts. It is also possible that identification of basic phases of the process can have practical application. Such knowledge might provide group participants with the ability to select the skills needed to control or correct on-going decision processes. The effectiveness of group decision making may be more dependent on the *sequence* of behaviors than the types of behaviors occurring during decision making.

Bales and Strodtbeck

Bales and Strodtbeck provided one of the first descriptive studies to support the assumption that decision making groups go through a number of phases as they move toward their goal.[2] Their results were based on observation of laboratory groups dealing with problem solving tasks. Using the twelve category, Interaction Profile Analysis (IPA), they found three distinct phases:

1. Emphasis on problems of orientation
2. Emphasis on problems of evaluation
3. Emphasis on problems of control

Each phase was characterized by a different dominant pattern of group interaction. In phase one, members predominately gave and asked for *orientation*. Members were frequently asking and giving direction, information, utilizing repetition and confirmation. In phase two, members' communicative acts primarily concerned problems of *evaluation*. Members sought and expressed opinion, evaluation, feeling and wishes. In the final phase, problems of *control* were primary. Members asked and gave suggestion, direction, and presented possible ways of action.

A balance between task and social emotional activity occurred over the entire problem solving session. Both positive and negative reactions increased as the group progressed from phase one to phase three. However, the later stages of control phase indicated primarily positive reactions. A. Paul Hare suggested that the positive and negative reactions were related to the socioemotional problems of the group process.

> Since the ratio of negative to positive reactions tends to be higher in response to suggestions than to statements, the decision point is the critical bottleneck in the process. Once the decision point has been passed, the rates of negative reaction usually fall off and the rates of positive reaction rise sharply.[3]

Their model is linear, that is, the group moves directly through the same sequence of phases for each decision. However, Bales and Strodtbeck's research emphasized the cyclical nature of the group process during decision making. A group proceeds through all three phases on each task and recycles back to deal with a new task. While the three phases occur in "normal" group situations, a number of variables may modify the characteristics of the group phases, e.g., status, change, leadership, external authority, type of task, amount of information possessed by members. The communicative behaviors by group members change from meeting to meeting. Generally, positive reactions increase over time, while negative reactions increase initially and then decrease. Groups also have a tendency to swing back and forth between the needs of the task and those of the group members. This phenomenon has been called an equilibrium problem.[4]

Bennis and Shepard

Based on experience with training groups and in educational settings, Bennis and Shepard produced a model of group development consisting of two phases, each with three subphases.[5]

Phase I. Dependence-Power Relations
    Subphase 1. Dependence Submission
              2. Counterdependence
              3. Resolution
Phase II. Interdependence
    Subphase 4. Enchantment
              5. Disenchantment
              6. Consensual Validation

Participants are primarily concerned with their dependence and power relationships in phase one. In the first subphase, the emotional reaction is one of dependence-fight. Participants respond as in an ordinary discussion group and avoid talking about the group task. Aggressive members with experience tend to dominate. In the second subphase, assertive counter-dependent participants are involved in attempts to restructure the group. And, in the final subphase, the group members take over leadership roles and proceed to work intensely on the task. A group emerges from the collectivity of individuals. The second phase is characterized by members dealing with problems of interdependence and personal relationships. The individual emerges from the group. In the fourth subphase, we have a general distribution of participation. The group members joke and laugh. There is a high rate of interaction and participation. The participants are satisfied with the group. In subphase five, the participants become disenchanted with the group and other participants.

Finally subphase six, group members begin to understand and accept each other. The members become more open in their communicative relationships.

Communication in the decision process is affected by the members' orientations toward authority and the intimacy that members bring to the group. Participants are concerned with dependence (how they relate to authority) and interdependence (how they work out the personal relations with their peers). The Bennis and Shepard model like the Bales and Strodtbeck model separates the task and socio-emotional dimensions of the group.

Tuckman

Tuckman developed a phase theory from the published results of studies dealing with group development.[6] The theory was drawn from studies on therapy groups and then applied to training groups, laboratory groups and groups in natural settings. He proposed the existence of four major stages in decision making.

Stage 1. Forming
Stage 2. Storming
Stage 3. Norming
Stage 4. Performing

This model is linear. Like the two previous models, it also makes a distinction between task and socioemotional behavior.

Each stage is divided into dimensions; (1) *group structure* dealing with patterns of interpersonal relations, and (2) *task behavior* concerning the work being done by the group. The characteristics of each dimension change as the group progresses through its developmental phases.

On the task behavior level, the group begins by identifying the task. During the storming stage, members respond emotionally to the task, creating intergroup conflict. The participant may resist attempts toward behavior modification. As task conflicts are resolved, the group moves to the norming stage. The group members discuss their opinions and/or establish criteria for evaluating decision alternatives. The participants are characterized by their openness. And, finally, in the performing stage, we see the emergence of the solution and/or modification of behavior in desired directions.

On the group structure level, the group members first attempt to discover the acceptable interactive behavior. In the storming stage, participants attempt to establish their independence and resist the formation of group structure. As the participants' quest for individuality is repressed, the group begins to develop cohesion. Group feeling increases, and task conflicts are avoided to assure harmony among members. Finally, in the performing stage, members adapt function-oriented roles which support the task structure and exhibit a minimum of social interaction.

Like Bales, Tuckman recognized that a difference could exist between phases during a single meeting and those of longer duration. And, like Bennis and Shepard, he assumed that the primary task was accomplished in the latter stages of the decision making process.

Mintzberg, Raisinghani and Theoret

Based on a field study of 25 decision processes, together with a review of the literature, Mintzberg, Raisinghani and Theoret developed a three-phase multiple sequence model for "unstructured" decision processes.[7]

Phase 1. Identification
  Routine 1. Decision Recognition
  Routine 2. Diagnosis
Phase 2. Development
  Routine 1. Search
  Routine 2. Design
Phase 3. Selection
  Routine 1. Screen
  Routine 2. Evaluation-Choice
  Routine 3. Authorization

The three phases are distinct, but not necessarily sequential phases in the decision process. The *identification phase* consists of two routines: decision *recognition,* in which opportunities, problems and crises are recognized and evoke activity, and *diagnosis,* in which the groups attempt to understand the evoking stimuli and determine any cause-effect relationships. The *development phase* is concerned with activities leading to the development of one or more solutions to a problem. Development is described in two basic routines: search and design. *Search* is evoked to find ready-made solutions: *design* is used to develop custom-made solutions or to modify ready-made ones.

Search is a hierarchical, stepwise procedure. The search begins with the familiar and extends to more remote and less familiar areas as earlier searches fail. If the search does not produce a solution, the group may turn to designing one specifically for that situation. Design is an interactive process.

They factor their decision into a sequence of nested design and search cycles, essentially working their way through a decision tree, with the decisions at each mode more narrow and focused than the last. Failure at any mode can lead to cycling back to an earlier mode. Thus a solution crystallizes, as designers grope along, building their solution brick by brick without really knowing what it will look like until it's completed.[8]

The Selection phase is divided into screen, evaluation-choice, and authorization subphases. It also is a multistage, interactive process involving a progressively deepening investigation of alternatives. Screening reduces the number of alternative solutions; evaluation-choice is used to investigate the remaining solutions and select a course of action. Finally, authorization deals with the ratification of the chosen solution.

One decision process could involve a great number of selection steps, many of these related to the development phase.

Communication occurs throughout the decision process; three specific communication routines are delineated. First, the *exploration* routine involves scanning for information and passive review of unsolicited information. It may be used to identify the decision situation of the problem, build conceptual models, and develop a general data base. Second, the *investigation* routine is for the search and research of specific information. This routine appears during the diagnosis, search and evaluation-choice routines. The third routine is *dissemination*. The greater the number of people involved in the outcome of the decision, the more time decision makers spend disseminating information about its process.

Fisher

The purpose of Fisher's investigation was to discover the structure of the interaction process across time leading to group consensus on decision-making tasks.[9] Ten groups varying in size from four to twelve members were selected for examination. The study did not control or separate the task and social dimensions. Fisher assumed that the observed patterns of interaction would reveal how groups use interaction to achieve consensus on decision proposals. The analysis revealed four separate phases. However, progression through each phase reflects a continuous and gradual change of interaction patterns.

Phase 1. Orientation
Phase 2. Conflict
Phase 3. Emergence
Phase 4. Reinforcement

The first phase of decision-making was called orientation. The members get acquainted, clarify and tentatively express attitudes. Problems of socializing and a socio-emotional climate affect the task interaction patterns in the early phase. Participants seek ideas and directions for proceeding with the task. A degree of ambiguity exists as the initial expression of tentatively favorable attitudes.

The second phase is called the conflict phase. With the emergence of decision proposals, members begin expressing their attitudes, positive and negative, toward specific proposals. With the expression of attitudes comes disagreement among group members and attempts to persuade dissenting members. Coalitions develop from ideational polarization.

The next phase is called emergence. Conflict and argument are reduced during the third phase, but it is in this phase that we have a recurrence of ambiguity. Ambiguity serves as a form of dissent. Fisher suggests the group members proceed to change their attitudes from disfavor to favor on the decision proposals through the mediation of ambiguity. The ideational coalitions dissolve during this phase. The group participants begin to support specific decision proposals, if only in an ambiguous manner.

The final phase has been labeled reinforcement. Decision proposals are reinforced by the comments of participants. Ambiguous dissent is dissipated. This phase is characterized by a spirit of unity. Emerging decisions are reinforced and members show their agreement. Fisher notes that the four phases will not be present in all decision groups. This decision making sequence, like that of the Tuckman, Bennis and Shepard, and Bales and Strodtbeck models, is linear. (See Table 1.)

Table 1
Phase Structure in Decision Making Groups

Bales/ Strodtbeck	Orientation	Evaluation	Control		
Mintzberg, et.al.	Identification	Development	Selection		
Bennis/ Shepard	Dependence	Power Relations	Interdependence-Personal Relations		
	Dependence- Submission	Counter- dependence Resolution	Enchant- ment	Disenchant- ment	Consensual Validation
Tuckman	Forming	Storming		Norming	Performing
Fisher	Orientation	Conflict		Emergence	Reinforce- ment

Phase Theorems: An Analysis

Applicability Problems

In analyzing the different phase theorems, I begin by noting certain methodological differences and assumptions in their development. First, the source of data from which the models are drawn vary considerably. Bales and Strodtbeck used twenty-two problem-solving laboratory groups. Bennis and Shepard's theorem is derived from non-participant reactions and five years of group dynamic classroom observation. Mintzberg, *et.al.*, relied on field study observations of organizations. Fisher utilized non-classroom college groups. Studying groups from such widely different sources or in different contexts is not unusual in small group research. In basic group development research, for example, phase theorems have been developed from as widely divergent sources as neurotic patients, social workers, psychologists, and psychiatrists. While researchers rarely attempt to relate conclusions from such widely divergent sources, our literature indicates no such reservation, and attempts to apply such phase theorems across a wide variety of situations.

The researchers also use different time frames for their analysis and development of theorems. Bales and Strodtbeck observed one meeting sessions. Bennis and Shepard based their findings upon the duration of the training group. Mintzberg, *et.al.*, observed the decision making groups over a three to six month period. And, Fisher used groups that met from twenty-five minutes to thirty hours. Thus, some models describe phases occurring during the course of a single meeting, others over a series of meetings, while some describe the entire history of a group. Time is a crucial dimension in the small group process, yet researchers fail to account adequately for its impact on their theorems.[10]

Validity Problems

Although a number of descriptive phase theorems have been developed over the last three decades, few attempts have been made to establish the validity of the proposed structures or their underlying assumptions. One such attempt by Witte tested whether distinct phases exist and whether they follow a simple sequence as suggested in the literature. The results indicated that decision processes actually consist of a number of different phases. However, the sequence of five phases, problem recognition to gathering of information to development of alternatives to evaluation to alternatives to choice, was not entirely supported. The decision process actually consisted of a plurality of sub-decisions; however, each sub-decision fit the five sequence model.

Witte found that communicative activity dominated every time interval. However, the level of communication activity peaked at the beginning and end of the group decision process, but decreased in the middle periods. He also found that the number of choices peaked at the end of the process. Witte concluded:

> We believe that human beings cannot gather information without in some way simultaneously developing alternatives. They cannot avoid evaluating these alternatives immediately, and in doing this they are forced to a decision. This is a package of operations, and the succession of these packages over time constitutes the total decision-making process.[11]

Although it has been observed that the decision making process can be very cyclical, most models are basically linear. Scheidel and Crowell proposed a spiral or circular model of problem solving emphasizing the communication process in discussion groups.[12] Their model, unlike the previously reported ones, has no specific phases. They describe the "discussion process as one with considerable freedom and flexibility in the movement from contribution to contribution."[13] While order exists in the decision process, the group does not follow a predictable sequence of operations.

Based on a task analysis of group member interactions, they proposed that discussions follow a spiral format, that is, as the group moves toward a solution, it follows a circular course which serves to anchor each new group position.

> Group thought seems to move forward with a "reach-test" type of motion, that is, one participant reaches forth with an inference which seems to be elaborated at length with movements of clarification, substantiation and verbalized acceptance.[14]

They also reported that actual member statements were highly unpredictable, that is, there was a great deal of freedom of choice in group discussion. The generalization of this last finding may be limited. The discussion groups were composed of skilled group participants. Furthermore, the problem given the groups had no correct solution, required a minimum of prior knowledge, if any, and was not subject to external authority or limitations.

Krueger, investigating the communication development of self-analytic groups, found that different groups with similar initial conditions can evolve into different end states. She suggested that earlier phase studies may have investigated structures which were too general and, therefore, not sensitive to actual group differences (Scheidel and Crowell had made the same criticism of the IPA system). The analysis of group communication yielded nonlinear patterns of change in three dimensions of information processing: source of information, time orientation and evaluation of information. Her results provide further support for a nonlinear model. She also observed two occurrences which lead one to question the previous research on phase theorems. First, the groups did not exhibit more "work" in the final stages of the group's life cycie, as had been reported by others. She suggested that models which imposed a structure on the group, rather than allowing the structure to emerge from the data, could have obscured what actually happens at termination of the decision process. And, second, she noted that the development of dimensions occurs at varying rates and patterns. She suggested that including several distinct dimensions or variables in one model may obscure important development differences.[15]

Poole has proposed that group decision making is more idiosyncratic than early phase theorems suggest. Most structural models assume that all groups follow the same sequence of phases. However, he contends that different groups develop different sequences. And a group decision making structure will reflect the internal and external environment of the group. Thus, the decision making sequence will fit the needs of the immediate situation.[16]

Conclusions

Despite a wide disparity in sources of data, time dimensions and measuring devices, the descriptive studies indicate a remarkable number of common elements. All models note the distinctions between socio-emotional and task behaviors. Although the models do not agree on the nature of each phase, several phases include characteristics common to all models. The first stage of decision making in all models is a type of organization: participants become familiar with other group members and the group task. All the models recognize the presence of conflict rising shortly after the orientation phase, and diminishing in the final decision stages. All models have as the last stage the acceptance of the decision. The exact nature of the phases across models is not consistent and therefore phases are difficult to compare or contrast. Table 1 compares the five previously discussed models and the relative structure similarities during the life cycle of the decision making group.

Attempts to apply our limited knowledge of structure to practical use is common in group discussion textbooks. Unfortunately, empirical research regarding the utility of prescribed group structures is limited.

Summary

Despite three decades of descriptive studies in which a number of phase theorems have been proposed in a variety of disciplines, we have barely scratched the surface in attempting to understand how the process of group decision making operates. A major gap in our literature appears in unsatisfactory or inadequate attempts to explain the relationship between decision making and phase structures. We lack a single generalized theory to describe the phasic structures during decision making. All existing models have developed from studies which appear upon close inspection to have some methodological or conceptual flaws. Nevertheless, it is quite obvious that phase structures do exist. These structures are distinguished by clearly defined differences in the communication behavior patterns or group participants. Since communication behavior is to a considerable extent contextually based, we may need to look for different phase structure in different situations; these structures may be consistent across similar contexts.

Notes

1. T. Mills, *The Sociology of Small Groups* (Englewood Cliffs, N.J.: Prentice-Hall, 1976), pp. 61–62.
2. R. F. Bales and F. L. Strodtbeck, "Phases in Group Problem-Solving," *Journal of Abnormal and Social Psychology,* 46 (1951), 485–495.
3. A. P. Hare, *Handbook of Small Group Research,* 2nd ed. (Glencoe, Ill.: Free Press, 1976), pp. 89–90.
4. R. F. Bales, "The Equilibrium Problem in Small Groups," In: T. Parsons, R. F. Bales and E. A. Shils, *Working Papers in the Theory of Action* (Glencoe, Ill.: Free Press, 1953), pp. 111–161.
5. W. G. Bennis and H. A. Shepard, "A Theory of Group Development," *Human Relations,* 9 (1956), 415–437.
6. B. W. Tuckman, "Developmental Sequence in Small Groups," *Psychological Bulletin,* 63 (1965), 384–399.
7. H. Mintzberg, D. Raisinghani and A. Theoret, "The Structure of Unstructured Decision Processes," *Administrative Science Quarterly,* 21 (1976), 246–275.
8. Mintzberg, *et.al.,* 256.
9. B. A. Fisher, "Decision Emergence: Phases in Group Decision-Making," *Speech Monographs,* 37 (1970), 53–66.
10. E. G. Bormann, "The Paradox and Promise of Small Group Research," *Speech Monographs,* 37 (1970), 211–217.
11. E. Witte, "Field Research on Complex Decision-Making Processes—the Phase Theorem," *International Studies of Management and Organization,* 15 (1972), 156–182.
12. T. Scheidel and L. Crowell, "Idea Development in Small Decision Groups," *Quarterly Journal of Speech,* 50 (1964), 140–145.
13. *Ibid.,* 144–145.
14. *Ibid.,* 143.
15. D. Krueger, "A Stochastic Analysis of Communication Development in Self-Analytic Groups," *Human Communication Research,* 5 (1979), 314–324.
16. M. S. Poole, "Decision Development in Small Groups I: A Comparison of Two Models," *Communication Monographs,* 48 (1981), 1–24.

Alternative Methods of Group Decision Making

Julia T. Wood

In the fifty years since discussion gained sway, textbooks have continued to reflect the fundamentally democratic, humanistic assumptions articulated most fully in pioneering works on discussion (Harnack, Fest, & Jones, 1977; Kowitz & Knutson, 1980): Group discussion should be a cooperative enterprise; participation should strive for balance among members; decisions should reflect all members' views and should be supported by all members. While democratic principles pervade multiple aspects of discussion, this is nowhere more evident than in the virtually sacred position awarded to consensus. For five decades consensus has been proclaimed the ideal (often, the only acceptable) method of making decisions in a democratic society (Baird, 1937; Gouran, 1982).

Consistency in thought about discussion seems at odds with radical alterations in the context in which discussion occurs. Perhaps the most notable change in society since the 1930s is that Americans have moved from adherence to relatively monistic values to patronage of pluralistic, frequently incompatible values, leading to divergent assumptions regarding appropriate goals and means for action (Cushman & Thompkins, 1980). If group discussion is to retain its utility as a method of making decisions, then our view and use of the process must be responsive to changes in the sociopolitical milieu that surrounds discussion.

Of the many implications arising from this position, only one will be pursued in this essay: the appropriateness for contemporary discussion of alternative modes of decision making. For each of three methods basic assumptions will be identified and their implications will be traced for individuals' interests, group decisions, and communication within groups.

A Comparison of Assumptions and Implications Among Consensus, Negotiation, and Voting

Although many discussion texts suggest consensus is the only legitimate means of group decision making, at least two other methods merit consideration: negotiation and voting.[1] For each of these it is possible to identify a definition, a set of underlying assumptions, and the implications of these assumptions for group decisions, members' satisfaction, and communicative norms within groups.

From *Emergent Issues in Human Decision Making,* by Gerald Phillips and Julia T. Wood (eds.). Copyright © 1984 by Southern Illinois University Press, Carbondale. Julia T. Wood is affiliated with the Department of Speech Communication, University of North Carolina.

Consensus

Consensus decisions reflect the views of all members and have the acquiescence and, ideally, the support of all members. A consensus decision is one that all members have a part in shaping and that all find at least minimally acceptable as a means of accomplishing some mutual goal.

Inherent in consensus is a set of assumptions about group goals, group processes, and individual and social values. Preference for consensual decision making springs from the twin beliefs that group deliberation should be cooperative and that among reasonable persons agreement is possible. Nestled within these beliefs are the more basic assumptions that group goals are also members' goals and that collective ends should overshadow individual ones. Consensus makes further assumptions about the nature of sound group process: it should be friendly, sufficiently balanced to reflect contributions from all members, and essentially apolitical to ensure that decisions do not reflect pressure exerted by prestigious or powerful members (Tannenbaum, Weschler, & Massarik, 1961; Davis, 1967; Maier, 1978). Regarding individuals, the consensus mode assumes open-mindedness, the absence of unwavering commitments to positions, and roughly equal value of members, that is, each person's ideas are worthy of expression and consideration within the group (Howell & Smith, 1956; Gulley, 1960; Barnlund & Haiman, 1960; Crowell, 1963; Harnack, Fest, & Jones, 1977). In tandem, these qualities constitute individuals with strong team orientations—persons committed to collective goals through collective means. The consensus mode, endorsing as it does shared objectives and balanced participation, is made to order for groups of equals who begin with open minds and monistic values regarding the issues about which they confer.

Consensual decision making regards the function of talk as forging agreements acceptable to all members. In turn, this implies that only certain forms of communication are appropriate (e.g., review, clarification), certain forms are praiseworthy (e.g., support of others' ideas, coordination of views, reconciliation), and certain forms are patently unacceptable (e.g., grandstanding, creating divisions, negativism toward others' ideas) (Likert, 1961; Harnack, Fest, & Jones, 1977).

The assumptive framework of consensus and the constraints it imposes on talk have implications for group decisions and individual attitudes toward those decisions. Because consensus pursues agreement, decisions tend to be moderate, a practical imperative if all members are to go along. At its best, moderation offers a welcome safeguard against potential biases, extremism, and the incomplete knowledge of each individual; at its worst, moderation becomes a euphemism for watered-down decisions that mark the least common denominator among members. Particularly important for continuing groups, however, is the power of consensus to preserve group unity at least in formal ways (i.e., the record, the public decision) and potentially in members' eyes as well. Thus even if a particular decision is in some sense less than ideal, consensus promotes a sense of unity and goodwill that assist the group in approaching future tasks.

Consensus-style discussion influences individuals' attitudes as well as group decisions. This method is reputed to heighten individuals' satisfaction with decisions and—even more so—with the process that so fully incorporated them (Tannenbaum & Kahn, 1958). These outcomes seem probable only in those cases in which a consensual decision genuinely incorporates the values and objectives of individuals who comprise a group. In those circumstances in which a least-common denominator decision is achieved, individuals may experience little satisfaction and substantial frustration with both product and process. Either way, consensus fosters in individuals a commitment to implementation of decisions, partially owing to their investment in creating the decisions and partially owing to the pervading ideal of team spirit (Lewin, 1943; Likert, 1961; Derber, 1963; Ouchi, 1981).

Negotiation

Negotiated decisions, like consensus ones, incorporate the views of various members and obtain at least minimum support from all members. Unlike consensus, however, negotiation is not necessarily built upon shared goals or upon pursuit of a broad agreement endorsed in full by members. Negotiated decisions are typically achieved by individuals with competing goals, each of which is sufficiently accommodated to warrant members' continued investment in a group. Further, with negotiation it is not essential that members like the complete decision; all that matters is that each member find enough of value in that decision to support it. Negotiated decisions, then, are settlements forged through a series of intricate, often tenuous trade-offs among members. While no member may be fully satisfied with the final decision, no member is entirely disgruntled.

The assumptions of negotiation differ markedly from those of consensus. Deliberation is viewed as a means to achieve collective agreements by meeting individuals' objectives. Clearly, this implies that interaction will be more competitive, partisan, and political than is appropriate with consensual process. Negotiation holds no *a priori* assumptions regarding either the balance of participation or the distribution of power; in the given case influence and ascendency evolve and are manifested throughout the process and become integral influences on the nature of that process. Negotiation assumes that individuals have definite preconceived commitments when they enter deliberation. These assumptions regarding group goals, processes, and members render negotiation most appropriate for groups in which members endorse pluralistic values and goals, yet acknowledge their interdependence.

Because it allows members to pursue personal interests while acknowledging those of others, negotiation constrains communication to respect a delicate balance between individualism and interdependence. Thus negotiated decision making tends to promote talk more advocative than that of consensus decision making and less rigid than that of voted decision making. Participants strive to represent their own positions persuasively and yet must bend to other views. Characteristic forms of communication include prioritization of goals, identification of each member's "bottom line," detailed explanations, comparisons among points of view, projection of consequences of alternatives, presentations of revised positions, threats, promises, and inducements designed to convince others of mutual gain from a given option. To the extent that talk addresses the overall group, it tends either to emphasize the fact of interdependence (e.g., to pull in line a member who has become too rigid to bargain) or to argue equity among various members' gains and losses. Within negotiated decision making inappropriate communication is any that fails absolutely to tolerate and adjust to alternative positions, or attempts to maximize one member's gain without adequate acknowledgement of others' goals, or both.

Negotiation has distinct impact on group decisions and members' attitudes. The aim for settlement tends to produce piecemeal decisions, patchwork resolutions that manage—however awkwardly—to meet each participant's minimum requirements. Decisions may also contain intricate, legalistic wording, complex definitions and qualifications, and multiple clauses in order to safeguard members' pluralistic concerns. Like consensus, negotiation tends to produce moderate decisions either because each part is tempered by participants' multiple demands or because the complete decision incorporates alternate types of extremism in a manner that creates an overall balance in tone. Because negotiation proceeds through competitive interaction and does little to build goodwill among members or to establish superordinate goals, this mode of decision making is not productive of group unity or of group continuity. Thus the prognosis for a group's continuation depends not so much on the negotiation method itself as on the perceived equity in particular decisions and especially on the maintenance of conditions that promote members' continued interdependence.

The interaction and decisions characteristic of negotiation theoretically stimulate in individuals a kind of stoic satisfaction that they have gained as much as possible while giving up as little as possible. During the negotiation process this is presaged by members' diminishing expectations regarding the degree to which their preconceived objectives will be met; in turn, this increases the impetus to reinterpret other members' stances and the damage they might do to personal objectives. In its own way negotiation fosters in members a commitment to implementation. If members lack the unity associated with consensus, they nonetheless have a pragmatic cohesion born of necessary interdependence. This is sufficient to ensure each member's stake in effective implementation of group decisions. Thus negotiation engenders a reluctant, yet typically viable cohesion born of practical necessity and maintained by strategic bargaining and carefully balanced trade-offs in gains and losses.

Voting

The voting method of decision making has been much maligned in discussion texts which warn of the dangers of factionalism and narrowly focused resolutions (Barnlund & Haiman, 1960, p. 159; Harnack, Fest, & Jones, 1977, p. 252). Voting is a method that achieves decisions through some predetermined criterion of support (e.g., majority, two thirds). Not all group members will be satisfied with voted decisions, so minority opinions are sometimes included within a group's final report. With voting, unanimous agreement is not required, nor is unanimous acceptance. The primary objective of this method is resolution *per se*.

The voting method carries its own assumptive baggage. Most basic is the assumption that the goal of deliberation is definite disposition of whatever issue(s) confronts a group. Achieving closure on the task supercedes concerns for harmony or equal representation of points of view. By extension, the substance of interaction may include persuasive appeals that run the gamut from locker room trades and threats to more reasoned, artistic attempts at influence, debates complete with rebuttals, and analyses of advantages and disadvantages of competing proposals. The style of interaction often incorporates formal measures such as adherence to stipulations of a group constitution (e.g., quorum, allotments for speaking time), use of a moderator, and an agreed-upon method of registering opinion (e.g., voice vote, roll call, secret ballot). As with negotiation, individual power and participation are not decreed by the method. They may exist before deliberation or may evolve during discussion. Either way, if power is unbalanced, decisions may reflect political allegiances as much as substantive beliefs. There is nothing in the method itself to preclude this possibility.

More than the other two methods considered in this essay, voting assumes there will be winners and losers in a clear-cut, unqualified sense (Barnlund & Haiman, 1960, p. 159). It is further assumed that individuals may have preconceived commitments that may or may not alter as a result of discussion. Group deliberation becomes an arena for partisan appeals and promises, for solicitation of allies, and for calling in of favors to buttress individual positions.

Voting engenders the most potentially divisive and egocentric communication of the three methods examined in this essay. With the fundamental premise that there will be winners and losers, voting allows extreme forms of communication. Members—especially those with high power—may, for example, announce and adhere to dogmatic positions and refuse to entertain alternatives. Further, members' talk may be highly advocative in presenting views persuasively and in attempting to win adherents (allies) either on the basis of demonstrated merits of positions or personal persuasion (bribes, calling-in of favors, threats). Similarly, members' talk may be abusive of alternative positions and those who propose them. The taking of a vote crystallizes lines of allegiance that may engender in members perceptions of factions.

Because voting allows a single point of view to triumph, it permits decisions less moderate than those reached through consensus or negotiation: extreme or narrow resolutions may be approved, and, consequently, diverse perspectives may not be reflected in final resolutions. By implication, decisions resolved via vote may leave in their wake a divided membership consisting of those who carried the day and those who lost the battle. Ironically, this generally acknowledged disadvantage of voting may at times be desirable. For instance, a group may face deadlines for decisions, confront alternatives unalterably defined in mutually exclusive ways, reach a juncture where members are locked rigidly into incompatible, irreconcilable positions. In such cases voting provides an expedient way of limiting conflict. While voting may harden lines within a group, it also permits members to move beyond an impass, possibly to other tasks on which agreement is more feasible.

Because all members' views are not necessarily incorporated in a voted decision, there is a tenuous base of support for implementation (Harnack, Fest, & Jones, 1977, pp. 251–53). In extreme cases, members of the minority may even attempt to sabotage a decision that does not reflect their interests. These implications are particularly pertinent to standing groups that must continue to work together. As a method voting does little to enhance team spirit and may—especially when mismanaged—entrench battle lines that will seriously constrain the efficacy of future group interaction.

If voting has potentially extreme effects on the kinds of decisions reached by groups and on group solidarity, it has similar potential impact on individuals. Participants either win or lose, either find themselves on the team of victors or outside the inner circle. The severity of divisiveness and frustration seems contingent on members' perceptions of group work, the diplomacy characteristic of the deliberative process, the saliency of a particular task, and members' personal commitment to positions. These same factors, combined with members' dependence on a group, influence individuals' support of decisions they did not favor.

The preceding discussion has been descriptive in explicating the nature and implications of three methods of group decision making. Adopting now a more pragmatic thrust, it is possible to identify heuristics to inform choices of decision-making methods. Each of the methods analyzed has unique character and subsequent impact on group communication, decisions, and members' attitudes. Yet there is no basis for absolutist judgments of the worth of any of the methods. Whether a given feature—cohesion, for example—is an asset or a liability, necessary or superfluous, impossible or feasible, depends on basic goals underlying discussion as well as the conditions under which discussion proceeds.

Principles of Counteractive Influence in Decision-Making and Problem-Solving Groups

Dennis S. Gouran

In a 1978 article entitled "Humans Would Do Better Without Groups," Christian J. Buys expresses a sentiment that undoubtedly has been shared at one time or another by virtually everyone who has some experience participating in decision-making and problem-solving groups.[1] Although such a reaction to one's involvement with groups is more likely to be the exception than the rule, in moments of frustration atypical occurrences are the things that tend to stand out. Because they are more memorable, particularly dissatisfying group experiences are the ones to which an individual is likely to refer in envisioning the consequences of future participation.[2]

Despite his seeming exaggeration of the negative qualities of group life, Buys nevertheless has touched on a matter to which nearly all of us can relate. Participation in groups (for purposes of this essay, decision-making and problem-solving groups especially) is frequently a dissatisfying and unproductive experience. Even those who are well schooled in the principles of effective group interaction often feel powerless to contend with problem group discussions that appear to be going nowhere—or at least, not where they are supposed to be going.

Unfortunately, pedagogically oriented literature and formal instruction in the dynamics of group process have inadequately addressed the full range of issues and behavioral competencies of which a practitioner needs to be aware. As a result of this deficiency, most of us are not prepared to contribute to decision-making and problem-solving discussions in ways that maximize the chances for achieving desired group objectives. In the present case, these objectives entail finding the most appropriate answer to a controversial question or the most effective resolution of a problem. Before we can fully appreciate the basis for the preceding criticism, we need to have an understanding of the general classes of influence that determine how well or poorly groups perform.

Sources of Influence in the Performance of Decision-Making and Problem-Solving Groups

Let us begin with a discussion of a metaphor commonly applied to the performance of groups. This metaphor likens groups to vehicles moving along a pathway from a starting point toward some predetermined destination. This likeness is particularly apt in the case of decision-making and problem-solving groups. In the context of the metaphor, movement along the goal-path is controlled by a series of forces or, perhaps more appropriately, influences.[3] The interaction among these influences determines whether or not a group will arrive at its intended destination.

Although there are many ways in which one can classify the influences that affect direction of movement, three designations that appear to be particularly useful are (1) Proactive Influences, (2) Inertial Influences, and (3) Counteractive Influences. Following is a brief examination of the essential properties of each type.

Proactive Influences

Proactive influences represent classes of behavior that, in an obstacle-free environment, would enable the members of a group to move directly toward their goal. The behavior in question is suggested by the nature of the task the group is performing and the inherently logical sequence in which necessary functions ought to be performed, for instance, defining the nature of a problem, determining its causes, establishing the criteria that a solution ideally would meet, identifying possible solutions, assessing alternatives in relation to each criterion, and selecting the solution that best satisfies the agreed upon criteria. Few, if any, task environments are obstacle-free. In most groups, therefore, at some point movement will either be halted or diverted from the goal-path. Whether or not a group successfully resumes movement or returns to the goal-path is a function of the relative strength of the other two categories of influence.

Inertial Influences

In physics, inertia refers to the tendency for an object at rest to remain at rest and for an object in motion to remain in motion. Applied in the context of group life, the concept can refer to either behavior contributing to an inability to progress along the path to a goal or behavior which sustains movement in whatever direction a group is heading.

Inertial forces, it should be clear, may have both facilitative and inhibitory consequences. To the extent that they contribute to movement in a desired direction, they are facilitative. If they help forestall movement or sustain it in a direction away from a group's goal, they are inhibitory.

Counteractive Influences

When a group's inertia is inhibiting movement, counteractive influences may come into play. Broadly defined, there are behaviors directed toward restoration of movement along a group's goal-path.[4] If the amount of counteractive force generated in an influence attempt is insufficient to overcome the group's inertia, movement will either remain in an arrested state or continue in the wrong direction.

An Extended Example

Since the preceding discussion is somewhat abstract, an extended concrete illustration may serve to clarify the concepts just introduced. Consider a group discussing the question, "What should be done to deal with the problem of alcohol abuse among college students?" Preceding any consideration of alternative policy options, logically, would be an effort to determine whether there is a serious enough problem to warrant some kind of action. A first step in this determination might be for the members of the group to achieve agreement on what they mean by alcohol abuse.

Suppose that a participant recognizing the definitional requirement observes, "I think that we need to specify what constitutes alcohol abuse." Another responds that she thinks "alcohol abuse exists whenever a consumer reaches the point that he or she loses self-control." "Could you be more specific?", requests a third party. To this point, the group is under the control of proactive influences. In other words, it is trying to deal with a primary requisite of the discussion task, a definition has been offered, and one member is attempting to elicit a clearer conception of the crucial term in the question being considered.

Now further suppose that someone in the group complains, "We'll never be able to define alcohol abuse. It's all a matter of personal opinion." The first obstacle has been erected in the goal-path. The line of communication initiated by this act, moreover, conceivably could begin to turn the group in a direction other than the one in which the members had intended to move. That is, they might begin quibbling over whether or not terms like *alcohol abuse* are amenable to definition. Were this to happen and were the inertia in that direction to build, the possibility of finding an appropriate answer to the discussion question could well be subverted.

In the situation just described, a member sensitive to the group's departure from its goal-path might try to avert an unnecessary squabble by reframing the issue. For example, "No definition of something as elusive as alcohol abuse, of course, will be completely satisfactory, but surely we can say what we mean by the term in ways to which all of us are able to relate. I believe that most people would agree that the individual who exceeds the legal limit of alcohol consumption and drives an automobile is guilty of abuse. But that is just one type of abuse. Why don't we try to list all of the situations involving the excessive use of alcohol which gave rise to the question in the first place?" An observation of this sort could do much to counteract the digression created by the dissident group member and, thereby, to rechannel the participants' interaction toward their original objective. How likely the chance of such a comment's having the desired effect would depend on how far the group's inertia had carried it from the goal-path.

Deficiencies in Discussion Training

Having examined the influences that affect the achievement of group goals in decision-making and problem-solving discussions, I can more fully develop my earlier criticism of pedagogically oriented literature and instruction. Most discussion training and the materials on which it draws focus on what I have been calling proactive influences. That is, its aim is to acquaint the practitioner with principles of performance which, in an environment free of major obstacles, would be sufficient to assure the achievement of a group's goal(s). Such instruction often derives from rational models of problem-solving and decisional choice. Typically, these models specify (1) the sequence of requirements involved in finding a correct solution to a problem or in making an informed decision and (2) the activities that seemingly best fulfill these requirements.[5]

The crux of my concern is not that the emphasis in discussion instruction is misplaced, but that it does not go far enough. Training based on rational considerations alone does not adequately prepare one to respond intelligently to certain realities of group life that can and do seriously limit the possibilities of achieving desired outcomes. This is not to suggest that those of us involved in offering instruction in decision-making and problem-solving discussions ignore the various and sundry obstacles to effective performance. If our pedagogical practices have been deficient, the problem lies not in a failure to call attention to inhibitory influences. Rather, the difficulty is that we do not provide sufficient bases for knowing how to respond when such influences are operative. In short, we have too little to say about the *art of counteractive influence*.

Exercising Counteractive Influence:
Some Behavioral Principles

Since most of the research which examines obstacles to effective performance in small groups has concentrated on their impact rather than the means of overcoming them, the previously mentioned weaknesses in instruction are quite understandable. As a counterpoint to this argument, one might feel that if we know what negatively influences the performance of decision-making and problem-solving groups, then by implication, we should know how to deal with them. The issue is not that simple, however. Knowing, for example, that an autocratic style of leadership inhibits the objective examination of alternative policy options provides no necessary indications of how one might go about managing the problem.

In spite of the need for considerably more research on the role of counteractive influence and the behavioral principles that enable one to exercise it successfully, present knowledge in a few select areas does allow for the formulation of general guidelines. In the remainder of this essay, therefore, I offer advice concerning how one might counteract the inertial tendencies that come into play when a group specifically confronts obstacles posed by (1) authority relations, (2) pressure for uniformity, (3) status differentiation, (4) disruptive behavior, and (5) incompatibility between individual and collective goals. The problems arising in these five categories by no means exhaust the complete range. Nevertheless, they represent a familiar and recurrent set of difficulties with which participants in decision-making and problem-solving groups often feel ill-prepared to contend.

Overcoming Obstacles Posed by Authority Relations

Among other things, the study of authority relations has revealed how easily people in positions of power can ordinarily elicit compliant responses to their influence attempts. Milgram's controversial research on obedience to authority, for example, rather dramatically underscores this observation.[6] Other research, moreover, has established that because of the relative ease with which authority figures induce compliance, groups may be led to foolish, inappropriate, or otherwise costly decisions.[7]

Apparently, in some circumstances in which authority figures effectively exercise an unhealthy influence, a kind of "pluralistic ignorance" sets in. Although most, if not all, of the other members of the group privately oppose the direction in which the authority figure wishes to move, they remain silent because of the erroneous perception that others are favorably disposed to what the authority figure is doing.[8] In most instances, however, the success of authority influence stems from the perception by less powerful group members that the authority has the right to determine the group's direction or that he or she possesses the resources with which to punish noncompliance.[9]

Not all influence attempts by authority figures have negative consequences, of course. When they do, however, the question that arises from the point of view of the person who recognizes that the authority figure is moving the group away from its goal, is how best to respond. What types of communicative strategies can be employed to redirect the members toward the goalpath? Does one apply some tactic of ingratiation? Will reasoning with the authority figure create a receptivity to redirection? Is a head-on confrontation likely to work?

Many people would follow their intuitive hunches in coping with the sort of situation described above. The danger, however, is that one might do more harm than good. The individual who recognizes the need to counteract the influence of an authority figure requires something more than intuition to guide his or her judgment about how to treat the problem. The question is, can we frame a general principle that will better inform such judgments? I believe that we can.

The knowledge that the power of authority figures is determined by the target of influence suggests that his or her influence can be successfully counteracted.[10] In addition, we know that resistance to an authority figure's influence attempts increases the probability of others' displaying resistance.[11] Finally, we know that reinforcement of one's authority will often result in favorable responses to the source of reinforcement.[12] Guided by these bits of knowledge, we have the basis of a general behavioral principle for dealing with the inhibitory constraints on effective decision-making and problem-solving that authority figures sometimes impose. That principle can be stated in the following manner: *When an authority figure's influence is interfering with a group's progress toward its goal, if possible, try to establish resistance in a way that does not threaten his or her authority.*

To visualize how one might apply the principle of resistance implicit in the work of French, Adams and Romney, and Milgram, consider the following hypothetical situation. A hiring committee in a large business establishment has narrowed its list of job applicants for a position to three and is trying to decide the one to whom the job should be offered. The committee consists of a top level executive, a representative from the middle management level, and a recently appointed junior executive. The objective of the committee members is to select the best qualified applicant; however, in the course of discussion, it soon becomes apparent that the upper level executive, who also happens to be chairing the committee, prefers the least well qualified candidate. The chairperson further makes it clear that concurrence is expected.

One approach that the other committee members might take in dealing with the obstacle created by the chairperson's expressed preference would be simply to voice their disagreement and to make their own preference clear. However, this type of ganging up tactic might only serve to intensify the chair's determination to have his/her way even if that required exercising autocratic rule.[13]

Under the circumstances, the interests of effective decision making would probably be better served were one of the subordinate committee members to ask the chairperson to show how the qualifications of the preferred candidate better satisfy the group's selection criteria than those of the other two choices. The remaining member, then, could reinforce the request. This more subtle form of counteractive influence attempt would redirect the group's attention to substantive concerns. Rather than simply voicing a preference, the chairperson would be obliged to provide the bases for his/her judgment.

From the perspective of theories of social power, the latter approach would be preferable because it would reinforce the superior's authority while simultaneously requiring that he/she focus on the point at issue in a more objective manner. Whether the influence attempt would be successful, of course, is a matter about which one could have no assurance. Still, it represents an intelligent way of avoiding the extremes of acquiescence or of antagonism to the authority figure. In addition, by inducing the authority figure to analyze his/her own judgment, there is a greater likelihood of a change in position. With authority figures, self-reflection tends to be a better stimulus for change than do attempts to impose externally generated influence.

Overcoming Obstacles Posed by Pressure for Uniformity

Pressure for uniformity is a second aspect of group life that sometimes requires the exercise of counteractive influence if a decision-making or problem-solving group is to progress along its goal-path. Deviation from a majority position frequently induces pressure for uniformity, particularly in cohesive groups.[14] Schacter has demonstrated that persistence in one's opposition can lead to rejection.[15] Since one loses all possibility of influencing a group's actions when he or she has been rejected, it is essential to avoid this outcome. Hence, many individuals will respond to pressure by conforming to the majority position.

Although pressure for uniformity and the conformity that it promotes are not intrinsically undesirable, on many occasions they contribute to the ineffective execution of a group's task. When a majority position is in error or is otherwise indefensible, pressure for uniformity constitutes a serious obstacle to those trying to keep the group headed toward its destination. The alternatives of either acquiescing or being rejected, moreover, can leave one with a sense of helplessness. For such individuals a knowledge of communicative strategies that will free them from this dilemma is most desirable.

As in the case of authority relations, previous scholarship has provided some useful leads in devising means of counteracting the inhibitory influence of pressure for uniformity. In a situation very much like the one studied by Schacter, Harnack found that by remaining reasonable and refraining from responding in kind to abusive remarks, not only did opinion deviates continue to be accepted by the majority they opposed, but they actually induced movement toward their own positions.[16] Valentine and Fisher also discovered that different types of deviance have different consequences for a group's performance.[17] The variety of deviant behavior they refer to as "innovative" appears to have constructive effects as opposed to "noninnovative" or simple opposition. The latter forms tend to be personally oriented and conflict producing. Finally, Bradley, Hamon, and Harris uncovered evidence showing that by being well informed, individuals playing a deviant role in decision-making groups were able to maintain their opposition quite effectively in the face of majority pressure. In fact, those who drew upon external sources of information to support their opinions on issues often influenced the thinking of majority group members, many of whom even adopted the deviates' positions as their own in subsequent discussions.[18]

None of these studies is conclusive, but collectively they indicate that one's response to pressure for uniformity need not be reduced to a choice between conformity and rejection. As important, they indicate that one may often be able to devise communicative strategies with which to alter the direction in which a majority is moving.

A common, but understandable, mistake in reacting to group pressure in decision-making and problem-solving discussions is for the target to become defensive.[19] Say, for instance, that the majority in a group, feeling that it has identified the appropriate option to endorse and eager to bring the discussion to a close, is pressuring an individual who is genuinely concerned that the best option has not been put forward. It would not be surprising if the holdout were to become angry and to express that anger. Such defensive communication, however, seldom has any salutary consequences.[20]

Rather than becoming defensive in the face of pressure and hence taking the risk of rejection, the individual in the preceding example would probably be well advised to respond initially with some remark like, "I know that everyone wants to wrap this up. So do I." Continuing, he or she could then point out the reasons for the reluctance to join in the apparent consensus. He or she might even go so far as to acknowledge the appeal of the preferred alternative before explaining the concerns that have led to the expressed opposition. If one wishes his or her ideas to have impact on others, it is necessary that they be in a receptive frame of mind.

The principle that follows from the analysis above and the research on which it is based is that: *When pressure for uniformity is inhibiting the ability of a group to pursue desired objectives, if possible, avoid responding defensively and instead concentrate on developing the substantive bases for opposing the majority position.*

Overcoming Obstacles Posed by Status Differentiation

The differences in status that separate the members of a group into roles of varying importance can lead to a high ranking participant's having influence that is not commensurate with the worth of his or her contributions.[21] When this occurs, the group may be unknowingly led away from its task objective. For this reason, status differentiation is an especially important aspect of group performance, and most of us are not as well prepared to contend with its undesirable consequences.

The greater influence potential of high status group members is usually attributable to others' perceptions that such individuals are more valuable to the group. As a result, those of comparatively lesser rank tend to be deferential in their interactions with persons of high status, to provide inaccurate feedback to them, to devalue their own opinions and judgments, and to be uncritical of the ideas expressed by the more valued members.[22] Even when the members of a group find a person of high status unattractive, they may overlook the offensive aspects of his or her behavior because of that individual's perceived value.[23]

That these aspects of status differentiation can adversely affect a group's ability to pursue its objectives dispassionately has been demonstrated by Torrance. In a study of problem-solving groups, he found that lower status members having a correct solution were prone to endorse the one proposed by the highest ranking member even when it was incorrect.[24]

The privilege that high status affords its possessors to influence the judgment and performance of others is difficult to overcome. As Homans has pointed out, individuals having high status are viewed as controlling scarce psychological and/or material resources. Compliance with their influence attempts is motivated by a desire to share in the benefits these resources may provide.[25] Whether one, in fact, has control of such resources does not matter. In this case, it is the perception that counts. Because of the peculiar nature of high/

low status relationships, questioning or challenging the judgment of a high status group member is not likely to be taken graciously by that individual or others who see compliance as beneficial.

In the circumstances mentioned, how should one react when he or she believes that the influence of a high status member is leading a group in the wrong direction or otherwise inhibiting its movement along the goal-path? Although this question has yet to be answered in any conclusive way, two facts about the maintenance of status offer some potentially valuable insights. First, the status that initial impressions and external factors allow one to have is not permanently assured. In addition, an individual possessing high status, although permitted a certain degree of freedom to violate the norms of a group, cannot engage in such behavior indefinitely. Persistent deviation will eventually result in a loss of status.[26]

The fluidity of status rankings within groups may hold the key to devising strategies for counteracting the influence of high status participants when that influence is functioning in ways inimical to the achievement of desired objectives. It appears that the essential consideration is whether or not one can demonstrate that a high status member's behavior constitutes a serious enough violation of accepted standards of performance to activate change.

By behaving in an ingratiating manner participants in groups will often try to overcome obstacles created by status differentiation and the relatively greater influence potential of higher status members. Sometimes this approach works, but more likely it will only serve to strengthen the influence of those having high status. To the extent that such individuals are interfering with a group's progress toward its goal, feeding their egos may only serve to exacerbate the problem. In addition, as Jones and Wortman suggest, ingratiation often backfires when the motives underlying its uses are transparent.[27]

Tactically more sound than ingratiation are applications of the principle that *in responding to the inhibitory influence of a high status group member, if possible,* one should *make salient the norm(s) which that individual's behavior violates.* Since those possessing high status usually desire to protect it, awareness of the discrepancy can create an internal pressure to begin observing the violated norm(s).

One must be careful in devising strategies based on the principle of calling attention to a high status group member's failure to observe valued performance norms. Often a gentle nudge, such as, "Our usual practice in this situation is to . . . ," or, "Ordinarily, we would . . . ," is sufficient to create an awareness of the problem. More blatant tactics could damage interpersonal relationships and thereby pose additional obstacles with which the group would have to contend.

Overcoming Obstacles Posed by Disruptive Behavior

Disruptive behavior perhaps is the one occurrence with which the average participant in a decision-making or problem-solving group feels least equipped to cope. People are ill at ease when interpersonal flare-ups arise, when a group member becomes deliberately obstructive, or when a participant is being highly defensive about the value of his or her own ideas but completely nonreceptive to those of others. Such disruptions can be generally subsumed under the heading of "affective conflict." This species of conflict, we know from both experience and research, usually has more negative than positive consequences.[28]

Within the last quarter century there has accumulated a rather substantial literature on interpersonal relations; this deals with the avoidance of breakdowns in interpersonal communication.[29] The thrust of this scholarship, however, is aimed at self-improvement through expanded awareness of the sources of behavior, the cultivation of sensitivity toward the needs and values of others, and the management of one's own personal problems. To the extent that a knowledge of what contributes to good interpersonal relationships minimizes the likelihood of one's behaving in a disruptive manner, the literature is valuable.

Unfortunately, the information that has to do with becoming more interpersonally competent does not adequately prepare one for responding to disruptive behavior in groups. The literature provides few insights on which one can draw in dealing with the exigencies created by disruptive acts in small groups. Counteracting the inhibiting influence of disruptiveness requires that one be able to make conflict work in a positive or constructive manner.

A potentially promising principle for responding to disruptive behavior is suggested by the differences between two major classifications of conflict in their impact on the performance of groups. Guetzkow and Gyr discovered that "substantive conflict," that is, disagreements deriving from the issues in a group's agenda, promotes effective interaction and contributes to consensus. "Affective," or personally oriented conflict, on the other hand, militates against consensus and leads to general dissatisfaction among group members.[30] Studies focused on efforts to convert affective conflict into substantive conflict hold some answers to the question of how best to counteract the unwanted influence of disruptive behavior. Several experiments have revealed that such a conversion is possible.[31]

If we take as our general principle the statement that *In responding to a disruptive act, if possible, try immediately to convert it to a constructive contribution,* we can conceive of a variety of specific applications. To illustrate the principle in use, assume that someone in a discussion has reacted to another participant's comment by saying, "That is the most ridiculous thing I have ever heard!" Outbursts such as this usually and understandably induce antagonistic replies. Rather than giving into the impulse to lash out at the offensive participant, however, the injured party in the example could just as easily inquire, "Why do you say that?" This response would place the offender in the position of being invited to become constructive. Accepting the invitation, of course, would entail giving reasons for the previously unflattering characterization of a fellow discussant's ideas. Under these conditions, the atmosphere would begin to calm, and the conflict could move from a personal to a substantive level. As Bell's research has indicated, moreover, substantive comments in a discussion increase the likelihood that similarly oriented contributions will follow.[32] The implication of this finding is that once the disruptive participant began to contribute constructively, the prospects of his/her and others' continuing to do so would be enhanced.

The ability to defuse a potentially explosive interpersonal situation created by disruptive acts sometimes requires a very thick skin, but the outcome can be worth it. If one is unwilling to tolerate some degree of personally antagonistic remarks, he or she may succeed only in contributing to the inertial forces that are moving a group progressively away from its goal. In our illustration, the failure to acknowledge that there could be some substance behind the disruptive group member's abusive comment would preclude the possibility of its being added to the exploration of issues related to the discussion question.

Overcoming Obstacles Posed by Incompatibility between Individual and Collective Goals

The final source of obstacles which this essay treats is the incompatibility between individual and collective goals that all too commonly exists in decision-making and problem-solving groups. When, for whatever reasons, the participants in such groups adopt a competitive orientation, they tend to perform less well than when they share an ostensibly collective goal. This is true even in so-called "mixed-motive" groups in which the interactant's objective is to gain at others' expense.[33]

Morton Deutsch identified the consequences of the compatibility and incompatibility of individual and collective goals early in the history of small group research; such positive and negative consequences have since been rather consistently demonstrated in investigations involving both laboratory and natural groups.[34] The effects of compatibility tend to be positive, whereas those deriving from incompatibility are largely negative.

Incompatibility produces a competitive orientation, at least among some members of a group. This orientation, when it surfaces in the interaction of decision-making and problem-solving groups, has implications for both the task and social dimensions of performance; for instance, productivity is reduced, morale tends to be low, and participants are more likely to attribute responsibility for failure to other group members. Not only is the possibility of achieving a group goal limited when the parties involved interact competitively, but individual goals are frequently achieved.[35] In other words, everyone may be a loser.

Most situations involving decision-making and problem-solving groups call for a cooperative orientation and coordination of effort; competition, therefore, is the unnatural state of affairs. When individuals perceive their personal interests to be at odds with the goal of a group, however, it can be very difficult to prevent the emergence of a competitive climate. Trying to establish an acceptable degree of congruency between individual and group goals appears to be the best remedy to the problem.[36]

Converting a competitively oriented climate into a more cooperatively oriented one is a real test of one's skill in exercising counteractive influence. Direct appeals to become cooperative and to place the interests of the group above those of the individual have little chance of working. Possibly the best way to approach the problem is to break the pattern of communication characteristic of competitively oriented groups. In such groups, this pattern is one of alternation between extolling the virtues of one's own input and pointing to the deficiencies in the input of others. As the pattern in this kind of oneupmanship intensifies, there is a corresponding reduction in the level of objectivity displayed. When this falls below the minimum necessary for exercising sound judgment, finding workable solutions to problems and making intelligent choices become unlikely.

To break the cycle of competition, the operative principle should be to *look for opportunities, if possible, to express honest agreement with other group members even though it may appear that they are unwilling to do the same.* Agreement is reinforcing and increases the probability that the person to whom it is directed will on later occasions reciprocate.[37] Of course, I am not recommending that one agree with others just for the sake of agreeing. The point is that when there are grounds for agreement, one should exploit the opportunity to create a more cooperative group environment. As antagonists begin to point to areas of merit in one another's contributions, they are better able to develop a climate of mutual trust in which the focus of competition shifts from the producers of ideas to the ideas themselves.[38]

Some Final Thoughts

The most neglected aspect of preparing people for participation in decision-making and problem-solving groups has been guidance in how to deal with unforeseen obstacles. I have attempted to address that deficiency by outlining a set of principles on which we can draw in trying to counteract undesirable influences set in motion by authority relations, pressure for uniformity, status differentiation, disruptive behavior, and incompatibility between individual and collective goals.

The principles identified are intentionally general and allow for a variety of specific adaptations. Although a knowledge of these principles does not equip one to deal effectively with every contingency, their application can do much to combat major sources of ineffectiveness in decision-making and problem-solving discussions.[39] To that end, I am hopeful that the ideas I have introduced contribute to the discussion participants feeling more confident of their ability to function constructively in overcoming the perpetual frustrations of group interaction. If enough people become adept in the exercise of counteractive influence, then, who knows, some day we may find an article entitled, "Humans Do Better Because of Groups."

Post Script—1988

Although little has occurred since 1984 to alter the views I expressed in this essay, two books with which I have since become familiar have reinforced the importance of two attributes that underlie much of the advice offered—specifically, the effort to control emotionally damaging responses to others' behavior and the effort to contribute to the development and maintenance of a cooperative climate for group interaction.

Carole Tavris (*Anger: The Misunderstood Emotion*. New York: Simon and Schuster, 1982) reviewed a considerable body of research and theory dealing with anger in human relationships and found that the expression of anger tends not to solve problems, but more often than not either serves to intensify them or to create still others. Members of groups frequently behave in ways that provoke anger, but in most instances, looking for constructive ways of responding will have a much more salutary effect than releasing one's anger. In states of anger, we tend to say unfortunate things that not only impair relationships but result in the emotion, rather than the concern arousing it, becoming a group's object of attention. In the long run, such a condition will have little positive impact on the members' performance.

More recently, Alfie Kohn examined research on the relative merits of cooperation and competition. In a book entitled *No Contest: The Case Against Competition* (Boston: Houghton Mifflin, 1986), he examines the destructive potential of competition in a broad range of human relationships and finds little to commend competitive forms of behavior. A cooperative climate in groups is difficult both to establish and to maintain because ideas are so often in competition and because we have been socialized to believe that competition is desirable. Competition among ideas can and does, therefore, promote competition among people. When this occurs, judgment will suffer, and the likelihood of a group choosing wisely will be substantially reduced. Consequently, it is all the more important that counteractive influence be exercised under conditions in which differences in the merits of ideas lead to participants becoming more concerned with having their views prevail than with making choices that are warranted.

Notes

1. *Personality and Social Psychology Bulletin,* 4 (1978), 123–25.
2. For a carefully constructed analysis of the psychological influences that contribute to the sorts of perceptions discussed here, see Richard Nisbett and Lee Ross, *Human Inference: Strategies and Shortcomings of Social Judgment* (Englewood Cliffs, New Jersey: Prentice-Hall, 1980).
3. In the terminology of Kurt Lewin's group dynamics, a force is "that which causes change." For a more thorough discussion of this concept, see Marvin E. Shaw and Philip R. Costanzo, *Theories of Social Psychology,* 2nd ed. (New York: McGraw-Hill, 1982), pp. 121–26. I prefer the term *influence* even though, as Wheeler notes, the concept does not represent " a logical area that can be adequately defined" (p. vii). Rather, it is a product of implied agreements among scholars that certain processes of interest are its constituents. See Ladd Wheeler, *Interpersonal Influence* (Boston: Allyn and Bacon, 1970).
4. I have discussed the notion of counteractive influence in more detail elsewhere. See Dennis S. Gouran, *Making Decisions in Groups: Choices and Consequences* (Glenview, Illinois: Scott, Foresman, 1982), pp. 149–52.
5. See, for instance, variations of John Dewey's model of reflective thinking in Gouran, *Making Decisions in Groups;* Irving L. Janis, *Groupthink,* 2nd ed. (Boston: Houghton Mifflin, 1982); Irving L. Janis and Leon Mann, *Decision Making* (New York: Free Press, 1977); Gerald M. Phillips, Douglas J. Pederson, and Julia T. Wood, *Group Discussion: A Practical Guide to Participation and Leadership* (Boston: Houghton Mifflin, 1979); and Thomas M. Scheidel and Laura Crowell, *Discussing and Deciding* (New York: Macmillan, 1979).
6. See Stanley Milgram, *Obedience to Authority* (New York: Harper Colophon Books, 1969).
7. See, for example, Janis' discussion of the Bay of Pigs Invasion in *Groupthink,* pp. 14–47. See also Dennis S. Gouran, "The Watergate Coverup: Its Dynamics and Its Implications," *Communication Monographs,* 43 (1976), 176–86.
8. This phenomenon has been discussed in Robert L. Schanck, "A Study of a Community and Its Groups and Institutions Conceived of as Behaviors of Individuals," *Psychological Monographs,* 43 (1932), No. 195. See also Jerry B. Harvey, "The Abilene Paradox: The Management of Agreement," *Organizational Dynamics,* 3 (1974), 63–80.
9. See, for example, Homans' discussion of the reasons for compliance with authority figures in George C. Homans, *Social Behavior: Its Elementary Forms, 2nd ed.* (New York: Harcourt Brace Jovanovich, 1974), pp. 193–224. The concept of behavior control further accounts for compliant behavior. See John W. Thibaut and Harold H. Kelley, *The Social Psychology of Groups* (New York: Wiley, 1959), pp. 100–25, and Harold H. Kelley and John W. Thibaut, *Interpersonal Relations* (New York: Wiley, 1978), pp. 111–207.
10. See John R. P. French, Jr., "A Formal Theory of Social Power," *Psychological Review,* 63 (1956), 181–94, and J. Stacy Adams and Antone K. Romney, "The Determinants of Authority Interactions," in *Decisions, Values, and Groups,* ed. Norman F. Washburn, II (New York: Pergamon Press, 1962), 227–56.

11. Milgram, pp. 113–22.
12. Adams and Romney.
13. Such stiffening of resistance is probable if an authority figure perceives opposition to his or her judgment as a threat to his or her freedom to exercise authority. This type of "boomerang" effect is sometimes referred to as "psychological reactance." For a more complete understanding of the dynamics involved, see Jack W. Brehm, *A Theory of Psychological Reactance* (New York: Academic Press, 1966).
14. See Stanley Schacter, "Deviation, Rejection, and Communication." *Journal of Abnormal and Social Psychology,* 46 (1951), 190–207. See also Janis, *Groupthink,* pp. 2–9.
15. Schacter.
16. R. Victor Harnack, "A Study of the Effect of an Organized Minority Upon a Discussion Group," *Journal of Communication,* 13 (1963), 12–24.
17. Kristin B. Valentine and B. Aubrey Fisher, "An Interaction Analysis of Verbal Innovative Deviance in Small Groups," *Speech Monographs,* 41 (1974), 413–20.
18. Patricia H. Bradley, C. Mac Hamon, and Alan M. Harris, "Dissent in Small Groups," *Journal of Communication,* 26 (Autumn, 1976), 155–59.
19. This type of response is more likely among individuals who judge the appropriateness of their own views on moral grounds. At the other extreme are those who determine how to respond purely on the basis of anticipated costs and rewards associated with compliance and noncompliance. Neither sort of person does much to help overcome obstacles in a group's goalpath. For a more extensive treatment of the styles of conflict management typical of the types of individuals described, one should read Neal Gross, Ward S. Mason, and Alexander W. McEachern, *Explorations in Role Analysis: Studies of the School Superintendency Role* (New York: Wiley, 1957). More likely to be effective is the type of individual Willis and Hollander call "Independent." These individuals tend to be above average in intelligence and knowledge and, hence, are better able than others to articulate the basis of their opposition when they choose to do so. See Richard H. Willis and Edwin P. Hollander, "An Experimental Study of Three Response Modes in Social Influence Situations," *Journal of Abnormal and Social Psychology,* 69 (1964), 150–56.
20. The basis for this assertion may be found in Jack R. Gibb, "Defensive Communications," *ETC.: A Review of General Semantics,* 22 (1965), 221–22.
21. See Paul V. Crosbie, "Status Structure," in *Interaction in Small Groups.* ed. Paul V. Crosbie (New York: Macmillan, 1975), pp. 177–85.
22. Evidence of such characteristics has been reported in the following studies: Harold H. Kelley, "Communication in Experimentally Created Hierarchies," *Human Relations,* 4 (1951), 39–56; William H. Read, "Upward Communication in Industrial Hierarchies," *Human Relations,* 15 (1962), 3–15; Fred L. Strodtbeck, Rita M. James, and Charles Hawkins, "Social Status in Jury Deliberations," *American Sociological Review,* 22 (1957), 713–19; E. Paul Torrance, "Some Consequences of Power Differences on Decision Making in Permanent and Temporary Three-Man Groups," *Research Studies, Washington State College,* 22 (1954), 130–40; J. C. Moore, Jr., "Status and Influence in Small Group Interactions," *Sociometry,* 31 (1968), 47–63.
23. See Alvin Zander, "The Psychology of Removing Group Members and Recruiting New Ones," *Human Relations,* 29 (1976), 969–87.
24. Torrance. See also a study of overestimation of high status group members' performance: Muzafer Sherif, B. Jack White, and O. J. Harvey. "Status in Experimentally Produced Groups," *American Journal of Sociology,* 60 (1955), 370–79.
25. Homans, p. 223.

26. See Crosbie, pp. 182–83 and Eugene Burnstein and Robert B. Zajonc, "Individual Task Performance in a Changing Social Structure," *Sociometry,* 28 (1965), 349–62. Hollander's notions concerning "idiosyncratic credit" are also supportive of this conclusion. See Edwin P. Hollander, "Conformity, Status, and Idiosyncratic Credit," *Psychological Review,* 65 (1958), 117–27.

27. Edward E. Jones and Camille Wortman, *Ingratiation: An Attributional Approach* (Morristown, New Jersey: General Learning Press, 1973).

28. See Harold Guetzkow and John R. Gyr, "An Analysis of Conflict in Decision Making Groups," *Human Relations,* 7 (1954), 367–82; Dale G. Leathers, "The Process of Trust Destroying Behavior in the Small Group," *Speech Monographs,* 37 (1970), 180–87; Thomas J. Knutson, "An Experimental Study of the Effects of Orientation Behavior on Small Group Consensus," *Speech Monographs,* 39 (1972), 159–65; Timothy A. Hill, "An Experimental Study of the Relationship Between Opinionated Leadership and Small Group Consensus," *Communication Monographs,* 43 (1976), 246–57.

29. See, for example, Leland P. Bradford, Jack R. Gibb, and Kenneth D. Benne, eds., *T-Group Theory and Laboratory Method* (New York: Wiley, 1964); Gerard Egan, *Encounter: Group Processes for Interpersonal Growth* (Belmont, California: Brooks/Cole, 1970); Gerald R. Miller and Mark Steinberg, *Between People* (Chicago: Science Research Associates, 1975).

30. Guetzkow and Gyr.

31. See Dennis S. Gouran, "Variables Related to Consensus in Group Discussions of Questions of Policy," *Speech Monographs,* 36 (1969), 387–91; Knutson, "An Experimental Study . . ."; John A. Kline, "Orientation and Group Consensus," *Central States Speech Journal,* 23 (1972), 44–47; Thomas J. Knutson and Albert C. Kowitz, "Effects of Information Type and Levels of Orientation on Consensus Achievement in Substantive and Affective Small Group Conflict," *Central States Speech Journal,* 28 (1977), 54–63.

32. Mae Arnold Bell, "The Effects of Substantive and Affective Conflict in Problem-Solving Discussions," *Speech Monographs,* 41 (1974), 19–23.

33. Walton and McKersie, for instance, discuss the value of "intergrative" bargaining in labor-management contract settlements. This type of bargaining entails emphasizing the gains both parties to a dispute can achieve from an agreement that is less attractive to either side than would ideally be hoped for. See Richard E. Walton and Robert B. McKersie, *A Behavioral Theory of Labor Negotiations* (New York: McGraw-Hill, 1965).

34. "An Experimental Study of the Effects of Cooperation and Competition Upon Group Process," *Human Relations,* 2 (1949), 199–231. For a review of other research, both on laboratory and natural groups, see Marvin E. Shaw, *Group Dynamics: The Psychology of Small Group Behavior,* 3rd ed. (New York: McGraw-Hill, 1980), pp. 378–83.

35. For a convincing demonstration of this sort of outcome, one should read Morton Deutsch and Robert M. Krauss, "The Effect of Threat Upon Interpersonal Bargaining," *Journal of Abnormal and Social Psychology,* 61 (1960), 181–89.

36. This idea is developed in considerable detail in Muzafer Sherif and Carolyn W. Sherif, *Groups in Harmony and Tension* (New York: Harper and Row, 1953).

37. The basis for this assertion has been established in the following sources: Thibaut and Kelley, *The Social Psychology of Groups;* Gay Lumsden, "An Experimental Study of the Effects of Verbal Agreement on Leadership Maintenance in Problem-Solving Discussions," *Central States Speech Journal,* 25 (1974) 270–76; Jon M. Huegli, "An Investigation of Trustworthy Group Representatives' Communication Behavior," Diss. Indiana University, 1971.

38. An excellent discussion of trust-building statements may be found in Leathers.

39. The fact that strategies based on the principles covered will not always prove effective and the fact that those I have tried to discourage sometimes work should not dissuade one from believing that there is a process at work in group interaction. The more attuned one is to the dynamics of that process, the better he or she will be able to function within it.

Making Meetings More Successful: Plans, Formats, and Procedures for Group Problem-Solving*

David R. Seibold

The Chairman of a park beautification committee in an Indiana town stopped short of nothing to keep meetings moving. An argument developed among committee members over whether or not a tree sapling had been planted too near the local war memorial. When the controversy persisted throughout two weeks of meetings, the well-intentioned chairman silenced the group with this announcement: "Ladies and Gentlemen, we've gotten nowhere on this issue. So, this morning I directed the park commission to transplant the tree 10 feet to the north. Now can we address the next item on the agenda?"

At one time or other we may all have wished we could break an unproductive group deadlock by "transplanting the tree"—or personally initiating conclusive action. "Meetings," both small group sessions and larger conferences, have become a major and often frustrating part of our lives. We seem to be attending more meetings than ever before. Our too frequent assessment of these is "What a waste of time; nothing was accomplished."

On the first matter, meetings probably *are* more frequent now. A study sponsored by the 3M Company revealed that the number of meetings and conferences in industry alone nearly doubled during the past ten years and their cost tripled.[1] Estimates suggest that most organizations devote between 7 and 15 percent of their personnel budgets to meetings. One large California-based corporation figures that almost $30 million of its $350 million personnel budget is spent on meetings. At the individual level, middle managers in industry may spend as much as 35 percent of their work week in meetings. That figure can be as high as 50 percent for top management.[2]

This proliferation of meetings is not confined to industry. Doyle and Straus assert that as many as 11 million meetings now take place in America each day.[3] News media reports abound of decisions emanating from civic bodies,

*This essay was prepared for the Michigan State University/Agency for International Development Management-Communication Workshops. Several techniques and examples discussed in the paper are drawn from the author's experiences as a consultant to a project ("A Community Approach to Water Management Planning") undertaken by the University of Illinois Water Resources Center and the Office of Continuing Education and Public Service. The project was supported by the National Science Foundation (OSS 77–21209).

From David R. Seibold, "Making Meetings More Successful: Plans, Formats, and Procedures for Group Problem-Solving," *Journal of Business Communication,* 16, #4 (1979) pp. 3–20. Copyright 1979. With permission of the author and *The Journal of Business Communication.* David R. Seibold is affiliated with the Department of Speech Communication, University of Illinois at Urbana–Champaign.

boards of directors, blue ribbon commissions, juries, legislative subcommittees, school boards, church groups, task forces, councils, local agencies, and bargaining units. If we each attend just four hours of work or civic meetings per week, we will have spent over 9,000 hours in meetings during an average lifetime—more than one year of our life in meetings! Why this extraordinary number of group meetings? Perhaps because, whether in industry, government, legal and civic affairs, or academia, meetings are essential for effective organizational functioning in our increasingly complex and interdependent world. They are a major means by which groups of people—as loosely defined as an *ad hoc* community group concerned with traffic safety near their children's school, or as highly organized as the board of directors for a national electronics corporation—receive or gather information about their environment, arrive at collective orientations toward that information, jointly utilize these interpretations to solve problems, and simultaneously recognize their unity as a purposeful, functioning "group." Meetings may be convened for any or all of these purposes: 1) to inform members; 2) to solicit opinions and request guidance from members; 3) to promote unity and cohesiveness among members; 4) to have members solve problems, make decisions, or recommend policy.

But the second lament is not irremediable; meetings need not be a "waste of time." Careful analysis and proper planning for the meeting, as well as judicious selection from among alternative problem-solving formats and procedures, are preliminary safeguards to the success of any session. This essay treats these aspects as they relate to problem-solving meetings and larger conferences: *planning* for a meeting, possible *formats* for organizing meetings and conferences, and alternative *procedures* for group problem-solving. A concluding example is provided illustrating how these formats and procedures have been combined effectively at town meetings in a rural Illinois community.

Plans

A doctor who sits on contract and review boards for several biomedical agencies and foundations recently told the author that the major factor in the success of review meetings he attended was the care with which the agency's executive secretary and committee chairperson had planned the session. Thoughtful preparation for a meeting is a must, and the chairperson should:

—Determine that a meeting is *necessary*. A TV commentator once characterized a typical government meeting of bureaucrats as "a group of the unwilling, chosen from the unfit, to do the unnecessary." If matters can be handled just as readily by means of personal memoranda, a conference phone call, or individual meetings with selected group members, perhaps a formal face-to-face meeting is unwarranted. On the other hand, the planner must recognize that these alternative communication methods offer problems of their own (e.g., failure to read written messages, members' different interpretations, communication breakdown as contacted individuals pass information to uncontacted members, difficulty in getting feedback, false consensus, etc.).

—Identify the specific *purpose(s)* for the meeting and delineate a range of goals. Is the meeting meant for information dissemination, bolstering morale, problem-solving and decison making, grievance settling, and/or stimulating involvement? What are desirable potential outcomes given each purpose? The chairperson should be prepared to state both purpose(s) and goals in the agenda and in convening the meeting, and even be ready to restate them if members digress too much during the meeting.

—Decide what will be the *composition* of the group for the meeting. If the group is an established one, such as a standing committee, will outsiders be invited to observe and participate? If attendance will not be settled by *de facto* membership, who and how many will be asked to take part in the meeting or conference. How will the participants differ with regard to power; status; experience with the issue under discussion; concern about the problem; interpersonal relationships with other group members; hidden agendas (i.e., personal goals for the session); communication skills in the group? The homogeneity/heterogeneity of the group along each of these dimensions can affect the interpersonal and task dynamics which ensue during the meeting (e.g., conflict, participation, time it takes to solve a problem and number of alternatives considered, quality of the decision, mode of decision making, and members' satisfaction with the group).[4]

—Settle the *logistics* of the meeting. Where and when will the group meet? Determine how long the meeting shall last and abide by the time limit (Samuel Adams reportedly solved the time limit problem by locking fellow Bostonians into a room and threatening continued detention until they resolved their disagreements over whether to form a Congress of Colonists).[5] Seating, audiovisual equipment, room arrangements, refreshments, photocopied materials, visual aids (charts, graphs, diagrams), and demonstrations should also be considered and planned for well beforehand.

—Delineate appropriate group *roles,* assign responsibility, and delegate authority where necessary. Certain members may be asked to act as group recorder, to prepare a special presentation, to introduce an invited expert, to secure room arrangements, or perhaps to lead a portion of the meeting. When possible have these group members report back that they have carried out their responsibility or are prepared to do so during the session.

—*Brief* all members on the general point above by means of an agenda, and identify particular issues germane to individual members (e.g., role responsibilities) in an accompanying memorandum. If members can anticipate the purposes, goals, and issues which form the basis for their meeting, as well as their own responsibilities for its conduct, they may come better prepared and more motivated. The general manager of a hospital supply firm ensures these effects at each meeting by requiring that members come prepared to identify the problem and the group's need to discuss it.

—Try to get your own *"mental picture"* of how the meeting will proceed: opening statements? major themes and issues to be discussed during the meeting? time limitations? format and problem-solving procedures? other problems (e.g., one member dominating discussion time or an unclear presentation by another member)? Then anticipate how to facilitate the good points and how to manage potential problems. The chairperson's job before, during, and after meetings is demanding, a fact that Standard Oil Company recognizes when it suggests that a chairperson must "plan, promote, lead, direct, inform, interpret, encourage, stimulate, referee, judge, moderate, and conciliate."[6]

Formats

One of the major elements in the chairperson's "mental picture" of a meeting is its format, or the general structure for organizing the session and facilitating discussion of the problem. Many alternatives are available, especially for larger conferences.

1. Begin the meeting with a *media presentation* (videotape, film, slides), whose purpose is to provide information to members and stimulate concern about the problem they face, and then initiate collective problem-solving discussion.

2. Start with a *presentation by one person,* such as an invited expert, and follow with problem-solving discussion.

3. Open the session with a *panel discussion* (interrelated, brief, and informal presentations by several persons from within the group and/or invited panelists) or a *symposium* (formal statements by experts), then begin joint group questioning (forum discussion) and problem-solving.

4. Adopt a *format discussion* plan (in which all participants jointly discuss topically or sequentially related issues which have been identified by the chairperson and distributed as questions in outline form), a procedure analogous to following a general agenda at all meetings.

5. Plan for open, *unstructured discussion* at the beginning of the meeting, followed by summarization and further, more focused problem-solving thereafter.

These are preliminary and general superstructures for organizing both large conferences and small group meetings.[7] Each format is sufficiently flexible that several of the problem-solving procedures discussed below can be incorporated into it. Before considering those techniques, however, it is important to recognize that each of the formats above has certain advantages and certain limitations.

For example, the preparation that group members must do to ready themselves for discussion increases from formats 1 through 5. That is, while media presentations, lectures, and symposia are effective means for imparting much of the information necessary for ensuing problem-solving, the success of formats 4 or 5 depends on how much information participants *bring* to the meeting. Too, formats 4 and 5 presuppose that group members have sufficient prior awareness and understanding of the problem, and concomitant motivation, to arrive fully prepared to enter into problem-solving discussion.

On the other hand, participant involvement is highest from the outset in formats 4 and 5, so the chairperson's responsibility for keeping the meeting moving and focused is that much greater than with formats 1, 2, and 3.

In light of these considerations, the first three formats may be especially appropriate for "problem-oriented" group sessions (meetings concerned with acquainting members with the nature and parameters of the problem). Formats 4 and 5 are perhaps better suited for "solution-oriented" sessions in which members' full participation is directed toward solving the problem or making decisions.

Procedures

The final and major part of a chairperson's "mental picture" of a meeting or conference are the potential *problem-solving procedures* which can be suggested to members during the session. These procedures can serve as vehicles for systematizing a group's discussion and decision efforts. Both common experience and research suggest that group members are haphazard and unorganized in their discussion and decision attempts when organizing schemes are not utilized.[8] For example, David Wojick states:

Unstructured discourse involves considerable waste and breeds confusion. We routinely use only about 10 percent of the ideas presented in any group discussion because the logical structure of discourse is too complex. In any series of meetings redundancy may be as high as 60 to 80 percent by the third session. Misunderstandings and conceptual confusion arise . . .[9]

And in decisions that business firms make, write Irving Janis and Leon Mann,

> . . . where the overriding value would seem to be to make the greatest amount of profit, decision makers often do not orient themselves toward finding the course of action that will maximize profits and other tangible net gains. Without careful search and appraisal, corporation executives often make judgments about a multiplicity of conflicting objectives, including "good will," "growth potential," "acceptability within the organization," and other intangible gains that are difficult to measure in any way . . .[10]

Problem-solving procedures help circumvent this inefficiency, delay, confusion, redundancy, and occasional frustration by coordinating members, focusing their attention on common issues, and guiding them through jointly understood aspects of problem diagnosis, solution selection, or implementation.[11] Among the many group and conference procedures which the chairperson may wish to utilize are the following techniques, which have been selected for their focus on means for solving a problem (problem-solving procedures) rather than for selecting among alternative solutions (that is, decision-making strategies such as optimizing, satisfying, incrementalism, mixed scanning, and consensus).[12]

Problem Census

The chairperson systematically polls all members at the meeting about items which should be discussed, or parameters of a problem under consideration, or alternative issues which have not been considered to that point in the deliberation. The purpose is to obtain a "census" from members about issues which should be considered. Results are posted for all to see. They can be used to guide further discussion at the present meeting or to set a future agenda. Whether introductory or interim, this technique also helps draw all members into the discussion.[13]

Rational Reflection

Participants attempt to solve a problem by proceeding through a comprehensive series of predetermined "reflective" phases intended to address specific aspects of a problem in "rational" fashion. Discussion at any time is limited to that phase of the problem. The phases, in order, require discussion of:

1. What *is* the problem? (How can it be stated? What are its relationships to other problems? What are our assumptions about the problem as stated and isolated?).

2. What are the *causes* of the problem and our need to solve it? (Origin and history of the problem? Significance of the present harm? How persistent is the problem?).

3. What are the minimal *criteria* necessary for an adequate solution? (Validity? Feasibility? Desirability?).

4. What are all the *possible solutions* to the problem as analyzed? (What are the data supporting each proposed solution? Have all possible solutions been considered?).

5. What is the *best solution?* (Does it minimize the significance of the problem? Does it alleviate the persistence of the problem? Is it workable? Do the advantages of the solution outweigh disadvantageous consequences?).

6. How shall the chosen solution be *implemented?* If adhered to, these phases can facilitate thorough and efficient small group problem-solving.[14]

Brainstorming

This technique promotes creativity in discussion groups by reducing some of the inhibitory aspects of group problem-solving—especially criticism and evaluation. The sole concern of members while brainstorming should be idea generation, not idea evaluation. Toward this end, the chairperson tells members that criticism of any contribution must be withheld until later. He also suggests that they strive for as many ideas as possible in the time available— the wilder the ideas the better, for it is easier to "tame down" than "think up."

Members should be given some time alone to record their ideas before joint brainstorming is begun. The chairperson should also be prepared to contribute ideas and "prime the pump" when discussion slows, and to have a recorder present to note all contributions. When criticism is genuinely avoided, members usually relax, generate a longer list of contributions than they would otherwise, and often find this portion of the meeting invigorating. Brainstorming can be used to stimulate discussion of any aspect of a problem and it is a particularly good technique for use during phase 3 of the rational reflection procedure above. If employed at the outset of a session, it is usually followed by a period of evaluation of each idea by group members.[15]

Buzz Groups

Participants at the meeting are divided into subgroups and provided a brief period of time to jointly discuss a specific aspect of a problem or solution. Each buzz group may be directed to focus on maximizing the number of ideas generated (like brainstorming), or conversely, on evaluating and discussing an item in more detail than the larger group might devote to it. Each "caucus" then reports back to the larger group.

Like brainstorming, members often get more involved in the problem when this subgroup procedure is used, and a wise chairperson can breathe life into a stagnant meeting by suggesting members break into buzz groups. Buzz groups are also an especially effective means of reducing the anonymity and cumbersomeness of very large meetings, for members can be grouped with four or five persons seated around them. Reports from each of these buzz groups may then indicate on which issues consensus exists and which issues require further discussion by all present.[16]

Nominal Group Technique

This procedure is so called because members are really a group in name only. During most of this procedure members work individually. The chairperson directs each member to create separate lists of the advantages and disadvantages associated with the proposition under discussion (e.g., unionization, shift changes, worker layoffs). After twenty minutes members are sequentially polled and a master list of all nonredundant advantages and disadvantages is posted on a flip-chart or blackboard visible to all.

Then members are directed to work alone again for ten minutes, but this time to rank order all advantages and all disadvantages from highest priority to lowest priority. Members privately submit their priority lists and an "average" master list is compiled while all adjourn temporarily. When the meeting resumes the rank-ordered tabulations provide the basis for collective discussion of the issue.[17] The nominal group procedure thus generates a basis for group discussion which reflects all members' views carefully considered while working alone and expressed without intimidation from more powerful or talkative group members.

Delphi Method

Like the nominal group technique (NGT) discussed above, the Delphi method severely restricts interaction among group members. The procedure is especially useful when the meeting is an *ad hoc* conference of experts. To minimize overcommitment to previously expressed personal views, domination by the most vocal or highest status experts, or the tyranny of majority opinion, the experts' opinions are pooled as the participants work alone and anonymously. The procedure calls for participants to complete an initial questionnaire designed to elicit their expert opinions about some problem, issue, recommendation, or policy. After an intermission, all group members receive a second questionnaire listing others' contributions and are asked to evaluate each idea by several specified criteria. During the following session a third questionnaire reports the second round ratings, a mean rating, and any consensus. Members are asked to revise their earlier ratings in light of the average or consensual view, or to justify their deviant position.

A final questionnaire includes all ratings, the consensus, and remaining minority opinions. Members are given a last chance to revise their original positions.[18] Depending on the nature of the conference, these final data may be forwarded to an independent body of decision makers, or the experts may be directed to initiate face-to-face discussion and strive for a final recommendation. The difficulties associated with gathering experts, administering questionnaires, collating results, writing all opinions, and lack of interaction obviously limit the applicability of this problem-solving procedure. The Delphi method has been employed widely and successfully, however, including recently at an international conference on solutions to world hunger.

Listening Teams

When media presentations, panel discussions, symposia, or guest lectures are used to start a meeting (i.e., before group discussion of the problem takes place), there is always the possibility that information is lost by the time it is needed during the discussion session or sessions which follow. This loss may occur because too much information is presented, the information is too detailed, good information is presented poorly, participants are distracted, or participants only attend to specific aspects of the presentation. Especially when the discussion group is large, much of the preliminary information presented can be retained through the use of "listening teams" according to Potter and Andersen.

Before the presentations, subgroups of audience members are formed and assigned a particular listening task. For example, one group may be asked to listen for causes of the problem, another for solutions suggested, a third to consequences of each solution, and so forth. Each subgroup is then provided time to codify their recollections before the group convenes to jointly discuss the problem. Then, regardless of which problem-solving procedure is utilized by the entire group, these members can serve as resource persons when the aspect of the problem to which they paid special attention is discussed.[19]

Experimental research by Zajonc suggests that persons attend to, comprehend, and recall more of a message when they are cued to the fact that they will be asked to recall and restate it.[20] The same principle may make listening teams an advantageous interface between informational presentations and problem-solving discussions.

Role Playing

In some group meetings the "problem" at issue is a human relations one. A church group meets to consider how to improve family relations among congregants. A work unit is called together to settle grievances with their supervisor. Top management undertakes analysis of their interpersonal relations. Role playing is often a helpful technique for presenting, analyzing, and remedying problematic human and management relations.

In essence, participants are asked to "play" a known or unknown other's role based on their perceptions of how that person does or should act. Members, first, may be supplied a case study similar to their own for warmup purposes. Then they may be asked to jointly construct a case/script which includes all the roles in the problem they are discussing, their interrelationships, and a specific situation. Participants are then asked to act out roles they have been assigned. Discussion among all group members follows, focused on the analysis of the reasons and remedies for the difficulty.

Role playing is used widely for counseling, interviewing, training, and problem-solving. As Ernest Bormann observes, "The drama inherent in role-playing makes it an excellent device to heighten audience interest and involvement. People playing the roles can relax and act out the part, because the group members know that they are not playing themselves."[21] However, role playing is usually directed by a qualified trainer and probably should not be undertaken by the chairperson alone. Good role playing requires motivation on the part of members, careful introduction into the meeting or conference, considerable time, and full discussion afterwards. Bad role playing can damage the momentum of the conference, adversely affect the image that group members have of the role players, and become unwieldy. Qualified role playing trainers increase the probability that the good, not the bad, effects will accrue.[22]

Two-Column Method

The dynamics which accompany controversy about an issue (listening in order to refute rather than to understand; polarization and further entrenchment in one's position; selective search for facts which support one's own view and refute others') mitigate against objective, collective problem-solving. According to Norman R. F. Maier, "the two-column method is designed to deal with controversy constructively and to lead to an appreciation of the fact that each position has merits as well as weaknesses."[23] Like the problem census procedure, the two-column method requires that the chairperson poll all group members and post their reactions in a visible place, as on a blackboard or flipchart. Members express arguments over why position 9x is better than position Y (i.e., favorable and unfavorable points about each), and the chairperson lists all contributions in the appropriate columns.

The chairperson should attempt to elicit as many listings as possible in the shortest time. The discussion turns to consideration of the merits of each column, how to resolve differences, comparison of advantages and disadvantages of both, and so forth. As Maier notes, the controversial dimensions of the issue become objectified during this procedure, and members do not become divided around each position. And once the two lists are completed both sides of the issue can be more realistically and cooperatively appraised.

Risk

After group members have decided upon a solution to the problem discussed, the chairperson may wish to employ the RISK procedure.[24] Participants are asked, one by one, to list what they view as the major "risk" involved with the adoption and implementation of the preferred solution. These "second chance" concerns then receive the attention of the full group. At least, each member's unwarranted fears can be allayed once and for all. At best, risks which appear serious and insurmountable should signal reservations about the solution of choice and the need for further discussion. This technique helps to reduce the chance that members will uncritically adopt a solution or that false consensus about the solution exists.

PERT

Once a group has identified a solution to the problem under discussion, the details of implementing that solution must be discussed. PERT (Program Evaluation Review Technique) is a procedure well suited to systematically reviewing all of the steps needed to carry out a complex plan, in what order the steps should be performed, how long each will take, and what resources and materials are needed. PERT may be performed in a small group meeting as follows:

1. Determine the final step (i.e., how the solution should appear when fully operational).
2. Enumerate any events which must occur before the final goal state is realized.
3. Order these steps chronologically.
4. If necessary, develop a flow diagram of the process and all the steps in it.
5. Generate a list of all the activities, resources, and materials that are needed to accomplish each step.

6. Estimate the time needed to accomplish each step, then add all the estimates to get a total time for implementation of the plan.
7. Compare the total time estimate with deadlines or expectations and correct as necessary (by assigning more persons or less time to a given step).
8. Determine which members shall be responsible for each step.[25]

Example

The following example, based upon a recent series of meetings in a midwestern community, illustrates how different formats and problem-solving procedures discussed above can be mixed effectively. State water resources scientists and representatives of the federal Environmental Protection Agency informed officials of a rural Illinois town that their community faced a series of water problems: inadequacy of supply and reserve during droughts, poor water quality following treatment processes, and a failing distribution system. Improvements were a practical and legal necessity, but the town, which barely had been able to finance the present water system through its meter system, had no funds to make the necessary changes. Community residents were unaware of the scope or severity of the situation. Before improvements could be made they would have to be educated about their water system, informed of the problems with it, persuaded of the need for changes and motivated to finance necessary improvements, and organized for decisions about the best particular solutions to their supply, treatment, and distribution problems.

Following the creation of an advisory board of local leaders, plus public and private water experts, a series of town meetings were held on weeknights during five successive weeks. Each of the meetings was advertised locally, and a core of thirty persons attended all. Under the leadership of a chairperson elected by the advisory board, the participants addressed these issues during successive weeks: overview of the system and the nature of the supply problems and solutions; treatment solutions; distribution solutions; and financial considerations. During the meetings a variety of formats and procedures were utilized.

For example, on the first evening a film was used to educate residents about the elements and processes of a water system. The local water commissioner then lectured on the particulars of that town's system and problems which had been identified in it. A forum discussion followed with questions from the audience. Then, under the guidance of the chairperson, subgroups of citizens were formed to further investigate solutions to the supply, treatment, distribution, and financing problems which had been discussed and agreed upon.

During the following weeks these subgroups played a crucial part as "listening teams" in listening to and questioning invited experts on issues related to each team's specific concerns; as "brainstorming groups" in generating alternative solutions for raising the necessary capital for improvements; as "buzz groups" during deliberations about whether search for a new groundwater supply was preferable to dredging the existing supply lake; and as a "panel" on the evening that each of their topics was discussed.

The chairperson very adeptly used the "two column" method during one session in which participants had become polarized over whether or not to replace existing water pipes with ductible iron or reinforced concrete pipes. On the evening of the final session the chairperson guided the participants to a final decision on raising the necessary funds by means of a "format discussion" plan. Too, after a decision was made to recommend that the city council apply for a federal loan, float a long-term municipal bond, and raise property taxes, the chairperson utilized the "RISK" procedure to allow all participants a final opportunity to express their fears about each of the solutions and how they were to be financed. Finally, a crude form of "PERT" was undertaken in an attempt to see whether the treatment improvements planned could be completed within the time constraints imposed by EPA. The flexibility manifest by the chairperson, the involvement stimulated by participation in the subgroup activities, and the judicious utilization of varied formats and procedures all seemed to keep motivation high and progress smooth in this community's attempts to solve its water problems.

Conclusion

A final caveat is in order. In lieu of a participant-oriented, "group-centered" approach,[26] this essay has emphasized the chairperson's preparation and orchestration in making meetings a success. Too, this essay has focused on "procedures" to the exclusion of "process"—the interactive, dynamic, emergent aspects of task groups' problems-solving, the decision-making.[27] Both these emphases are but one side of the small-group coin. The success of a meeting obviously is not dependent only on a chairperson no matter how skilled he or she may be. As Leland Bradford observes:

> Member interaction and the needs, purposes, and emotional reactions of individuals have a profound effect on the task solution and, therefore, need to be understood and appropriately dealt with. Leadership is not something that just the designated leader does. Leadership happens when any intervention by the leader or a group member moves the group forward toward three goals: the accomplishment of the task, the resolution of internal group problems, and the ability of members to work together effectively as a group.[28]

The designated leader thus shares the leadership role and the responsibility for a successful meeting with all the participants. To suggest an analogy to the systems theory concepts of "inputs," "thruputs," and "outputs," we might say that a successful, productive group meeting of satisfied members ("outputs") can in part be affected by the preparation and judicious choices a chairperson makes concerning purposes, logistics, composition, agendas, formats, and procedures ("inputs"). But the dynamic, mediating effects of "thruputs" variables like group development; the emergence of norms, roles, and power; and the group's socio-emotional climate all interact with the "input" variables to produce final "outputs." The purpose of this essay has been to alert potential chairpersons to specific ways in which meetings can be positively affected by thorough preparation and careful planning. The chairperson's "inputs" should therefore create a structure within which the group *process* can flow more smoothly.[29]

Notes and References

1. Cited in E. F. Wells, "Rules for a Better Meeting," *Mainliner,* May 1978, p. 56.
2. Michael Doyle and David Straus, *How to Make Meetings Work: The New Interaction Method,* New York: Wyden Books, 1976, p. 4.
3. Doyle and Straus, *How To Make Meetings Work,* p. 4.
4. For a review of research on the effects of group member homogeneity/heterogeneity, see Marvin E. Shaw, *Group Dynamics: The Psychology of Small Group Behavior,* 2nd ed. New York: McGraw-Hill, 1976, pp. 219–232.
5. Cited in Wells, "Rules . . .," p. 53.
6. Wells, "Rules . . . ," p. 51.
7. For a more differentiated discussion of formats for discussion groups see Alvin A. Goldberg and Carl E. Larson, *Group Communication: Discussion Processes and Applications,* Englewood Cliff, NJ: Prentice-Hall, 1975, pp. 70–73.
8. See the diverse research evidence provided by A. Paul Hare, *Handbook of Small Group Research,* 2nd ed., New York: Free Press, 1976, pp. 331–356; and Harold H. Kelly and John W. Thibaut, "Group Problem Solving," in Gardner Lindzey and Elliot Aronson (eds.), *The Handbook of Social Psychology,* 2nd ed., IV, Reading, MA: Addison-Wesley, 1969, especially pp. 76–78.
9. David E. Wojick, "Planning for Discourse," *Water Spectrum,* Spring, 1978, pp. 17–23.
10. Irving L. Janis and Leon Mann, *Decision Making: A Psychological Analysis of Conflict, Choice, and Commitment,* New York: Free press, 1977, pp. 24–25. Emphasis supplied.
11. Research supports the importance for good problem-solving of structuring group communication. Larson found that groups following any type of systematic analysis form were more likely to produce adequate judgments about industrial relations problems (i.e., similar to experts' assessments) than groups not provided with a technique for systematizing their discussion. See Carl Larson, "Forms of Analysis and Small Group Problem-Solving," *Speech Monographs,* 36, 1969, 452–455.
12. See John K. Brilhart, *Effective Group Discussion,* 3rd ed., Dubuque, IA: William C. Brown, 1978, pp. 120–121 for elaboration upon the distinction between group problem-solving and decision-making. Also see Amitai Etzioni, *The Active Society: A Theory of Societal and Political Processes,* New York: Free Press, 1968, pp. 249–252 for a useful definition of decision-making and further distinction from more general policy-making.

13. As originally described by Maier, this procedure was called the "Posting Problems" technique; see Norman R. F. Maier, *Problem-Solving Discussions and Conferences: Leadership Methods and Skills,* New York: McGraw-Hill, 1963, pp. 161–171. The procedure has received more widespread recognition as "Problem Census" for the greater descriptive utility of that label.

14. This problem-solving scheme owes its origins to John Dewey, *How We Think,* Boston: Heath, 1910, in which Dewey explicated the steps rational individuals might utilize in solving a problem. James H. McBurney and Kenneth G. Hance, *Discussion in Human Affairs,* New York: Harper and Brothers, 1939, proposed that *groups* could be trained to systematically solve problems through application of Dewey's steps. Since then the "Reflective Thinking" procedure has been described and prescribed in most discussion texts under a variety of labels and minor modifications including "Reflective Pattern," "Truncated Problems," "Single Question Form," "Ideal Question Form," and the "Kepner-Tregoe Approach." I have chosen the label "Rational Reflection" for its fidelity to the reflective nature of these techniques and its generic description of these problem-solving techniques as rationalism. For a comparison of the techniques above see Dean C. Barnlund and Franklyn S. Haiman, *The Dynamics of Discussion,* Boston: Houghton Mifflin, 1960, pp. 91–93; Alvin A. Goldberg and Carl E. Larson, *Group Communication: Discussion Processes and Applications,* pp. 149–151; and Stewart L. Tubbs, *A Systems Approach to Small Group Interaction,* Reading, MA: Addison-Wesley, 1978, pp. 229–233.

15. For a treatment of the origins of brainstorming, the details of its applications, and a review of empirical research on this technique see Fredric M. Jablin and David R. Seibold, "Implications for Problem-Solving Groups of Empirical Research on 'Brainstorming': A Critical Review of the Literature," *Southern Speech Communication Journal,* 43, 1978, 327–356.

16. Buzz groups are general instances of a discussion pattern known as Phillips 66, so called because it was frequently utilized by a conference consultant named *Phillips* to divide large audiences into groups of *six* persons for *six* minutes of discussion time to formulate questions for a panel they had just listened to. These "buzz" periods thus provided a name for any subgroup given brief periods of time. For a description of the original technique see J. Donald Phillips, "Report on Discussion 66," *Adult Education Journal,* 7, 1948, 181–182. For a recent treatment of buzz groups as a conference technique see John K. Brilhart, *Effective Group Discussion,* pp. 218–220.

17. The Nominal Group Technique (NGT) for problem-solving is described more fully in Andre C. Delbecq, Andrew H. Van de Ven, and David Gustafsen, *Group Techniques for Program Planning,* Glenview, IL: Scott, Foresman & Co., 1975, pp. 7–10.

18. See the discussion of the Delphi method and list of references provided by Alvin A. Goldberg and Carl E. Larson, *Group Communication,* pp. 147–148.

19. David Potter and Martin P. Andersen, *Discussion in Small Groups: A Guide to Effective Practice,* 3rd ed. Belmont, CA: Wadsworth, 1976, pp. 177–178.

20. Robert B. Zajonc, "The Process of Cognitive Tuning in Communication," *Journal of Abnormal and Social Psychology,* 61, 1960, 159–167.

21. Ernest G. Bormann, *Discussion and Group Methods: Theory and Practice,* 2nd ed., New York: Harper and Row, 1975, p. 328.

22. Potter and Andersen, *Discussion in Small Groups,* pp. 143–153 provide a good treatment of role playing in discussion groups. Also see A. F. Klein, *How To Use Role Playing Effectively,* New York: Association Press, 1959.

23. Norman R. F. Maier, *Problem-Solving Discussions and Conferences,* p. 179. This comparison of two positions is central to another discussion guide recommended by Martin P. Andersen, "The Agree-Disagree Discussion Guide," *The Speech Teacher,* 8, 1959, 41–48.

24. ———, *Problem-Solving Discussions and Conferences,* pp. 171–177.

25. An excellent treatment of PERT is supplied in Gerald M. Phillips, *Communication and the Small Group,* 2nd ed., Indianapolis: Bobbs-Merrill, 1973, pp. 114–133.

26. Roger A. Kaufman, *Identifying and Solving Problems: A System Approach,* La Jolla, CA: University Associates, 1976.

27. For a discussion of the procedure-versus-process orientation see Dennis J. Gouran, *Discussion: The Process of Group Decision-Making,* New York: Harper & Row, 1974, pp. 23–32.

28. Leland P. Bradford, *Making Meetings Work: A Guide for Leaders and Group Members,* La Jolla, CA: University Associates, 1976, p. 10.

29. For a vivid example of how a manager's planning and choice of problem-solving procedure can complement the dynamics of committee decision-making, see Andre L. Delbecq, "The Management of Decision-Making Within the Firm: Three Strategies for Three Types of Decision-Making," *Academy of Management Journal,* 10, 1967, 329–339.

Group Conformity

Patricia Hayes Andrews

The January, 1986 Challenger tragedy provided a striking reminder of how groups of intelligent people can make flawed, disastrously poor decisions even when equipped with abundant information and sophisticated scientific technology. Historically, other groups of high status, supposedly knowledgeable individuals have made similarly poor decisions resulting in the loss of billions of dollars, important battles, Presidential elections, and hundreds of human lives. Although many scholars and theorists have attempted to explain this phenomenon, no one has done it better or more persuasively than psychologist Irving Janis whose treatise on "groupthink" provides a compelling explanation for such decision-making fiascoes as the Bay of Pigs invasion, the Watergate break-in and attempted cover-up, and the Challenger tragedy.[1]

Groupthink, however, cannot be applied to every group. Janis is largely concerned with decision making by groups who are quite cohesive, have worked together for some time, are deeply embedded in complex organizational structures, and are insulated from the views of others.[2] Undoubtedly, groups fitting this profile are prospective victims of groupthink, defined by Janis as "a deterioration of mental efficiency, reality testing, and moral judgment that results from in-group pressures."[3] However, other groups not meeting the criteria specified above are also capable of making poor decisions.

When groups make bad judgments, select ineffective solutions to problems, or choose seemingly stupid or unethical courses of action, they may do so for a variety of reasons. Sometimes they simply do not have time or take the time to perform effectively. They may not have the assembled expertise needed to do the job well. They may have been assigned the task by a manager who has just learned that participative decision making is a good thing, but does not know how to prepare the group for its newly acquired responsibilities. Perhaps the group is ridden by personality conflict or by ineffectual leadership. Or, and most important to the point being made here, the group may not understand the need for exploring diverse points of view before making a final decision. Yet, most scholars agree that any group's ability to openly examine the diverse, often conflicting, ideas advanced by individual group members is a crucial attribute—one which surely contributes to effective decision making. At the same time they bewail the group's rather pronounced tendency to disregard constructive and critical thinking.

This essay appears here in print for the first time. All Rights Reserved. Permission to reprint must be obtained from the publisher and the author. Patricia Hayes Andrews is Professor of Speech Communication and Associate Dean of Arts and Sciences, Indiana University.

Whenever groups begin to act as if every group member should be alike, and especially think alike, they typically exert pressure for uniformity. How this occurs, why it occurs, and how individuals respond to it have been widely studied. Of particular interest are the factors that help predict the likelihood that a given individual will conform to the expectations, or norms, of the group.

Basic Definitions

Basic to the notion of any group or organization is the idea that individuals alone are often unable to fulfill all of their needs. As groups of men and women coordinate their efforts toward common goals, they may also find that they can accomplish more with relative effectiveness than any one of them could have done alone. Moreover, contemporary managers have grown to believe that their employees feel better and thus perform better when given the opportunity to participate in making decisions that affect their professional lives. In most cases, they are right. Thus, most of us find ourselves involved in a great deal of group activity, often involving problem solving and decision making.

As we interact in groups, we develop norms. Norms are sets of expectations held by group members concerning what kind of behavior or opinion is acceptable or unacceptable, good or bad, right or wrong, appropriate or inappropriate. As new group members we soon learn about what political views are popular, what competitors are respected or feared, and what procedures are considered appropriate for making decisions. We may discover, for instance, that when a certain hour arrives, no one should say anything to prolong the meeting. Or we may learn that this particular group regularly socializes immediately following its Friday meeting.

An individual's compliance with a norm is readily measured by his or her public behavior. Do we join the group for pizza, or do we have other commitments? Do we stifle our criticisms or comments so that the meeting can be dismissed on time? If we do, we are conforming to the group's norms. Most of the time, an individual's act of conformity is assumed to extend to his or her private feelings or beliefs. We go for pizza because we want to. But common personal experience teaches us that this assumption is often false, that we may, some of us often, do things that others want us to do even though we do not want to do them. In the specific context of decision-making groups, we say things we don't completely believe, or we simply refuse to voice our dissent. In these instances, we have complied with group norms publicly, but privately, we continue to feel differently. Thus, an important distinction must be made between public compliance and private acceptance. The need to be liked, to seem congenial, to fit in with the others can be powerful and can cause us to say things we don't believe and act in ways which we later regret. The inability or unwillingness to deviate from group expectations can affect anyone—teenagers, businessmen and women, members of the President's Cabinet, or distinguished scientists.

Whether or not an individual complies with a group's norms may depend, in part, upon whether he is aware of them. Some norms are *explicit,* that is, they are formally stated. They may even be written and passed around. Explicit norms are easily understood because they are overtly expressed. *Implicit* norms, on the other hand, are generally never openly articulated. The new group member may not understand immediately that no one disagrees with the boss or that expressing a preference for Bach over Bon Jovi is a kiss of death. In fact, one of the little games that some groups play is trying to see how quickly a particular individual will figure out the implicit rules of the game.

Most writers discuss conformity in a negative light. It is important to recognize, however, that pressure for uniformity, and the conformity that often follows, is frequently a simple fact of group life. The act of conforming to the prevailing group sentiment is neither good nor bad. Rather, conformity can only be evaluated as a group outcome by examining the process through which it occurs. If a group insists that every group member questions group standards and takes the time to listen to those who represent different points of view, excellent decisions may result. But, if an individual complies with the group for fear of being ignored, ridiculed, or even rejected, then that brand of conformity will likely contribute to loss of self-esteem for the individual and a poor decision for the group.

Understanding Why Groups Exert Pressure

Many explanations have been offered for why groups exert pressure for uniformity. Leon Festinger's *group locomotion hypothesis,* for example, posits that groups have goals and typically attempt to function in ways designed to allow them to achieve these goals.[4] Some goals may even be viewed as instrumental to group survival. A quality control group which cannot improve product quality seems self-defeating. A fund-raising group which cannot generate money will not long exist. Many groups assume that they can only accomplish their goals if each of their members complies with group norms. Based on this belief, the group is motivated to pressure would-be deviates into conformity. This explanation for pressure for uniformity applies most readily to situations involving key norms, or norms directly associated with goal achievement. A top saleswoman may be permitted to wear a punk hairstyle, but if she stops putting in long hours, thus causing the sales team to lose important sales, she will probably be forced to toe the line. Her hairstyle "deviation" is not perceived by the group as impeding their goal accomplishment and so is tolerated. Her slack work habits, however, are a different matter.

Another perspective for considering group pressure also comes from Festinger. According to this scholar's *social comparison theory,* most people do not need to consult the views of others to validate their perceptions of physical reality.[5] A stove is hot; an elephant is huge; a car is red. With matters of opinion and belief, however, an individual often finds comfort in knowing that others share her views. Is the new tax plan good or bad? Should this organization devest in South Africa? Should this curriculum committee add another year of foreign language to students' graduation requirements? These issues are not merely questions of fact. They are all complex, involving attitudes, opinions, and judgment. We can never be certain that our views on these kinds of issues are "right," but in trying to assure ourselves that they are, we often seek to affiliate with those whose views are similar to our own. As we join together in groups, share our ideas and discover that we agree among ourselves, we create a kind of social reality. Social reality is not the same as factual reality, but it does allow us to validate our ideas, and thus, gives us the illusion of having discovered truth. The social validation process works best when group members are uniform in their beliefs. The opinion deviate, then, is pressured into uniformity so that the group's social reality can seem more plausible.

Finally, a number of theorists have advanced *balance theories,* some of which are relevant to understanding the group pressure phenomenon.[6] According to this perspective, any group prefers to exist in a balanced state. Consider the following example where imbalance or inconsistency has become a problem. A group of executives meets regularly to discuss quality problems and to make policy decisions. The group is close-knit, and there is a feeling of shared liking. Suppose further that member A strongly opposes the other four members on an important policy issue. What are the options available to the members of the majority? They may (1) avoid discussing the issue, (2) decide that the issue is not as important as they had originally believed, (3) decide that member A must surely not understand the policy or has been misinformed, or (4) decide that member A is not as likable as they had once believed. The latter two options are particularly pertinent to this discussion of pressure for uniformity. If the third option is pursued and the assumption made that member A needs more information or is misguided, the majority should spend considerable time attempting to inform, elaborate, and persuade. If this approach were to fail, then the fourth option might restore balance or harmony within the group by making possible the rejection of the deviate. Research has shown that both of these options are pursued on occasion, particularly among highly cohesive groups that are dealing with issues they view as important.[7]

Clearly, groups may exert pressure for a variety of reasons, allowing them to better achieve their goals, feel more justified and certain of their views, and exist in a state of harmony and cooperation. Of course, not all groups exert pressure for uniformity; those who do may be more tolerant of deviation on the part of some group members than others. If, for example, the individual deviate possesses extraordinary knowledge, has led the group toward positive results in the past, or possesses high status or power, he or she may be granted certain liberties which would never be permitted the rank-and-file member.[8] Even so, most groups consistently demonstrate a greater concern for maintaining uniformity than for encouraging individuality. While publicly affirming the need for innovation, many decision-making groups, often those embedded in conservative corporate structures, continue to reward those who blend in with and reinforce the views of the majority, or those already in power.[9]

Understanding Why Individuals Conform to Group Pressure

Understanding why groups are motivated to exert pressure is only half of the story. Equally critical is gaining some understanding of why individuals so often conform. Two of the perspectives discussed above provide some explanatory insight. First, from the perspective of Festinger's *group locomotion hypothesis,* the individual who is committed to helping the group achieve its goals and who believes that his or her conformity will facilitate the group's goal achievement will be internally motivated to conform. Some groups demand a unanimous vote before moving forward with any new plan or policy. Under these circumstances, it is clear that one dissenting vote blocks the group's action. Rather than prevent the group from moving forward, the individual may shrug her shoulders and inwardly (or outwardly) say, "I don't want to be the one to hold up the rest of the group." Votes obtained in this manner are clear instances of public compliance.

Also useful in helping us understand the motivation to conform is *balance theory.* This perspective reasons that, like the group, the individual strives for balance or consistency throughout his or her life. If he believes that the group has worthy goals and is comprised of people with good intentions and values, he may find it painful to recognize that his views differ. Rather than reject the group or realign his perceptions of the majority's wisdom, he may elect to go along with the others. In fact, he may try very hard to convince himself that the majority is correct. If successful, this attempt at self-persuasion will restore the individual's personal sense of balance or consistency. If unsuccessful, the individual may conform, but still experience considerable inner tension, or imbalance.

Yet another approach to understanding conformity is Homans' *social exchange view.*[10] According to Homans, conformity is a kind of strategic social act which allows the individual to obtain things she values from the group. The group may provide a satisfying social environment, prestige, or a sense of worth for her. In exchange, she supports the majority, in some cases putting aside her true beliefs. Her self-censorship contributes to the positive social climate, while giving her certain rights and opportunities that she would not otherwise possess. In a real sense, conformity from this perspective becomes a technique of ingratiation.[11]

Research on Conformity

Social influence, and conformity in particular, has been the subject of scholarly investigation for many years. One of the earliest and most extensive conformity studies was conducted by Solomon Asch in the 1950s.[12] Asch confronted naive subjects with the unanimous and clearly erroneous opinions of several of his trained confederates and discovered marked movement in the direction of the majority. The task confronting Asch's subjects was a simple line discrimination exercise in which they were asked to match one of three lines with a comparison line. The correct answers were obvious. Yet, when confronted with the unanimous views of the majority, many of Asch's subjects conformed, announcing responses which clearly contradicted what they saw. In fact, only one fourth of these naive subjects remained completely independent. It is important to recognize that not only were the line discrimination tasks used in this study extremely easy, they were of no intrinsic importance to the subjects. Moreover, the "groups" in this setting were hardly groups in the traditional sense, and the majority made no overt attempts to influence the naive subject's expressed views!

One of Asch's most interesting findings was the striking contrast he found between those individuals who never yielded to the majority's view and those who did so much of the time. Some investigators became intrigued with distinguishing these two basic "types" of individuals and sought to discover the personality characteristics that might be associated with yielding behavior. Crutchfield's research was one of the earliest to unearth a kind of contrasting character profile.[13] According to Crutchfield, the independent person demonstrates great intellectual effectiveness, ego strength, leadership ability, and maturity in social relations. He/she seems to lack inferiority feelings, rigid and excessive self-control, and authoritarian attitudes. Moreover, the independent individual is free from a compulsion to follow rules and is adventurous, assertive, and high in self-esteem. By contrast, Crutchfield argued that the "overconformist" has less ego strength, less ability to tolerate ambiguity, less willingness to accept responsibility, less self-insight and originality, more prejudiced and authoritarian attitudes, and greater emphasis on external and socially approved values.[14]

The quest for personality characteristics that might predict conformity behavior has received less attention in recent years. Most researchers have taken the view that personal attributes are often modified by situational or contextual variables. According to this view, the same individual may be confident and self-assertive in one situation and reticent and uncertain in another.

What are the situational variables that appear most likely to produce conformity behavior? Previous research points to the importance of a unanimous majority.[15] Having even one person (besides the naive subject) disagree with the majority may reduce the conformity rate by as much as thirty percent.[16] Another important situational variable has to do with the task itself. If an individual initially disagrees with the group's judgment on an issue that is unclear, uncertain, ambiguous, or difficult to understand, he is more likely to come around to the majority's point of view than if he is dealing with a straightforward, clear-cut issue. After all the individual reasons, ambiguous matters are open to interpretation—and the group could well be correct.[17] Finally, the extent to which the group is cohesive may have a pronounced impact on the individual's ability to remain independent. Cohesive groups are typically quite close-knit, have been around for some time and may have weathered crises together. Group members usually enjoy each other's company and value their group experience.[18] Highly cohesive groups generally demand, and usually get, great loyalty and conformity from their members.[19]

In spite of the attention that has been devoted to conformity in the past, most scholars and practitioners remain uncomfortable with their understanding of the factors influencing conformity behavior. Perplexing questions remain. Why do some conform in virtually every situation while others almost never yield, regardless of the severity of the pressure? Why are some capable of great independence in certain situations but of equally striking conformity in others?

A Contemporary Examination of Conformity

To attempt to grapple with the questions raised above, I recently undertook a study of conformity behavior.[20] I chose to compare two theoretical perspectives which had not been used in previous research with the hope that they might illuminate the extent to which conformity might be a kind of behavioral predisposition or trait as opposed to a variable response to the discussion of a particular issue in a particular group.

The first theoretical perspective I selected was Sherif and Sherif's *social judgment theory*.[21] To predict the likelihood that an individual will remain uninfluenced by group pressure, this theory contends that one must assess the extent of his or her ego-involvement with the issue or action being considered. The highly ego-involved individual is deeply committed, probably viewing the issue as central to his or her value system. By contrast, the less involved individual is not so committed, viewing the matter as much more peripheral to his or her value core.

The Sherifs' social judgment theory argues that any one of us is likely to demonstrate an entire range of conformity to the group's norms. We might even appear to be both yielding and resistant to group pressures while functioning within the same group. What determines the likelihood of conformity is our degree of ego-involvement as the group moves from one issue to another. If the matter being discussed is of no great consequence to us (e.g., whether to adopt WordStar or WordPerfect as word processing software for the office), we may go right along with the group's preference. If, however, the question before the group pertains to one of our deep and enduring commitments (e.g., whether to support Star Wars), we should be much less likely to conform to others' views. In fact, according to the Sherifs, the highly ego-involved person would virtually never permit himself or herself to be open to group influence, regardless of the intensity of the pressures brought to bear.[22]

This explanation of ego-involvement as the mediator of conformity is very different from that proposed by another researcher, Mark Snyder.[23] Rather than viewing individuals in terms of their commitments to specific issues, Snyder focuses on their sensitivity to social expectations. In particular, he refers to individuals as being either high or low in self-monitoring. Those who are high in self-monitoring are very aware of and concerned with others' expectations for their behavior. They know what others want from them, and if possible, they would like to deliver. What we might expect from an individual who is high in self-monitoring, then, is a good deal of behavioral inconsistency. He or she is likely to conform to the views of others, even though his or her expressed views or actions may vary with movement among different groups with varying norms. By contrast, the non-self-monitoring person is less concerned with the appropriateness of his or her social behavior. This individual should remain relatively autonomous, maintaining consistent positions, regardless of the context in which the discussion occurs.

For my investigation, I placed 96 college students into small groups and asked them to discuss a question of value concerning living together before marriage. Before the discussions, the students were carefully pre-tested so that I knew whether they were either very high or very low in ego-involvement with this particular discussion issue and whether they were high or low in self-monitoring. Each group contained students with diverse points of view and with a variety of ego-involvement and self-monitoring levels. I was interested both in the way that these students communicated with each other and especially in the extent to which they influenced each other.

The results of my investigation provided a good deal of support for social judgment theory. That is, those students who were strongly committed to their views changed their positions far less than those low in ego-involvement. In addition, their communication behavior was influenced considerably by their ego-involvement. Statements made by highly ego-involved students were rated by trained judges as being less reasonable, more dominant, and more emotional than those made by those who were low in ego-involvement.

Although ego-involvement played a critical role in affecting these students' susceptibility to others' arguments and the quality of their communication behavior, their self-monitoring tendencies also proved important. That is, while highly ego-involved discussants refused to alter their expressed views, regardless of their sensitivity to others' expectations and opinions, students who were far less committed (that is, low in ego-involvement) were more likely to change their expressed opinions if they were aware of others' reactions and expectations (i.e., were high in self-monitoring). Self-monitoring also affected the discussants' communication behavior. For instance, students high in self-monitoring typically responded to others' position statements by seeking to find areas of compromise and accommodation, rather than by asserting their own ideas. Moreover, while highly ego-involved students tended to communicate emotionally when advancing their views, those who were high in self-monitoring did so far more than those low in self-monitoring. Apparently, highly ego-involved individuals who are sensitive to social cues are placed in a difficult spot when confronted with a group filled with diversified, often conflicting, points of view. Although in this study these highly ego-involved students did not actually yield, their communication was judged as far more emotional, perhaps suggesting the tension created by the simultaneous and inconsistent desire to stick by their commitments, but to submit to the demands of the consensus-reaching task as well.

Concluding Remarks

More than two decades ago psychologist Marie Jahoda examined historical and empirical instances of conformity behavior in an attempt to discover why some individuals were susceptible to group influence whereas others remained unmoved. She was particularly concerned with inconsistencies in conformity behavior occurring within the same individual. She concluded her examination of conformity with the view that the critical determinant of independence behavior in social influence settings was the individual's "emotional and intellectual investment in the issue."[24] When Sherif and Sherif articulated their social judgment theory, they provided a theoretical framework for assessing Jahoda's argument through an empirical investigation. The results of this study provide support for a social judgment view of conformity.

As was posited early in this piece, individual conformity to group norms is a frequent and often perplexing outcome associated with interacting groups. In many instances, individual movement must occur if group consensus is to be achieved. Yet, that movement can best enhance the quality of the group's decision if it represents the individual's conscious and rational desire to compromise for the benefit of the group. Although "mindless conformity" rarely facilitates any group's goal achievement in the long run, conscious conformity may be helpful, or even essential. Before individual group members can make intelligent choices about maintaining positions of dissent, opening themselves to group influence, or going along for the sake of appearance or civility, they need to understand something of the forces within themselves that might make them more or less vulnerable to group influence. The study reported here represents a step toward gaining that understanding.

NOTES

1. Irving Janis, *Groupthink*, 2nd ed. (Boston: Houghton Mifflin Co., 1982).
2. *Ibid.*, pp. 2–13.
3. *Ibid.*, p. 9.
4. Leon Festinger, "Informal Social Communication," *Psychological Review*, 57 (1950), 271–282.
5. Leon Festinger, "A Theory of Social Comparison Processes," *Human Relations*, 7 (1954), 117–140.
6. See, for example, Fritz Heider, "Attitudes and Cognitive Organization," *Journal of Psychology*, 21 (1946), 107–112; and Charles E. Osgood and Percy H. Tannenbaum, "The Principle of Congruity in the Prediction of Attitude Change," *Psychological Review*, 62 (1955), 42–55.
7. Stanley Schachter, "Deviation, Rejection, and Communication," *Journal of Abnormal and Social Psychology*, 46 (1951), 190–207; and Janis.
8. Leonard Berkowitz and J. R. Macaulay, "Some Effects of Differences in Status Level and Status Stability," *Human Relations*, 14 (1961), 135–148; and Edwin P. Hollander, "Some Effects of Perceived Status on Responses to Innovative Behavior," *Journal of Abnormal and Social Psychology*, 63 (1961), 247–250.
9. J. Patrick Wright, *On a Clear Day You Can See General Motors* (New York: Avon, 1979).
10. George C. Homans, "Social Behavior as Exchange," *American Journal of Sociology*, 63 (1958), 597–606.
11. Edward E. Jones, "Conformity as a Tactic of Ingratiation," *Science*, 149 (1965), 144–150.
12. Solomon E. Asch, "Studies of Independence and Conformity: A Minority of One Against a Unanimous Majority," *Psychological Monographs*, 70 (1956), 1–70.
13. Richard S. Crutchfield, "Conformity and Character," *The American Psychologist*, 10 (1955), 191–198.

14. *Ibid.*, 196.

15. Asch.

16. *Ibid.*

17. Patricia Hayes Bradley, "Socialization in Groups and Organizations: Toward a Concept of Creative Conformity," in Steward Ferguson and Sherry Devereaux Ferguson eds., *Intercom: Readings in Organizational Communication* (Rochelle Park, New Jersey: Hayden Book Co., 1980), 388–402.

18. C. Shepherd, *Small Groups* (Scranton, Pa.: Chandler Co., 1964); and Janis.

19. *Ibid.*

20. Patricia Hayes Andrews, "Ego-Involvement, Self-Monitoring, and Conformity in Small Groups: A Communicative Analysis," *Central States Speech Journal*, 36 (1985), 51–61.

21. Carolyn W. Sherif, Muzafer Sherif, and Roger E. Nebergall, *Attitude and Attitude Change: The Social Judgment-Involvement Approach* (Philadelphia: Saunders, 1965).

22. *Ibid.*, pp. 4–22.

23. Mark Snyder, "Self-Monitoring of Expressive Behavior," *Journal of Personality and Social Psychology*, 30 (1974), 526–537; and Mark Snyder and Thomas C. Monson, "Persons, Situations, and the Control of Social Behavior," *Journal of Personality and Social Psychology*, 32 (1975), 637–644.

24. Marie Jahoda, "Conformity and Independence: A Psychological Analysis," *Human Relations*, 12 (1959), 103.

Group Satisfaction

Peter J. Marston and Michael L. Hecht

If we are to understand fully the processes of human communication and their influence on our personal and social lives, we cannot ignore the importance of satisfaction as both a directing force in our interactions with others and as a primary mode of evaluating our communication and ourselves. In many theories of human behavior, satisfaction is a recurrent concept (Hecht, 1978). According to the principle of hedonism, for example, people are guided by a desire to receive pleasure and to avoid pain. Thus, when we are successful in our quest for pleasure or in our avoidance of pain, we are satisfied. Similarly, exchange theory conceives of human behavior as determined by an individual's comparison of rewards and costs, and so, when rewards exceed costs, we experience satisfaction.

Each of us is familiar with the feeling of satisfaction in communication interactions; perhaps we know it as pride in our performance in a successful job interview, the comfort of handling ourselves well at an important social event, or the warmth of sharing affection with those we love. Though we have an intuitive understanding of satisfaction, it is necessary to provide a more precise definition. Satisfaction is *a holistic, affective response to the success of behaviors that are selected based upon expectations.*

This definition is somewhat complicated. Let us explain in further detail the key concepts involved. First, satisfaction is a *response*. This means that satisfaction is an outcome of behavior. When we experience satisfaction, we are satisfied *with* something—namely, the successfulness of behaviors.

Second, satisfaction is an *affective* response: that is, it involves our emotions. When we experience satisfaction, we are not simply contemplating the success of our behavior, but rather, we are experiencing a *feeling*—one that is associated with various physiological and psychological factors.

Third, satisfaction is a *holistic* affective response that involves an individual's complete emotional state. In itself, satisfaction is not a specific emotion (such as joy or sorrow). Indeed, satisfaction may result from any number of specific emotional states, depending on an individual's experience and expectations. For example, our satisfaction in how we told a particular joke is likely to involve very different emotions than our satisfaction in how we defended our beliefs in a heated debate with our friends or parents.

This essay appears here in print for the first time. All Rights Reserved. Permission to reprint must be obtained from the publisher and the authors. Peter J. Marston is Assistant Professor, Department of Speech Communication, California State University at Northridge. Michael L. Hecht is Associate Professor and Director of the Communication Research Center, Arizona State University.

Fourth, satisfaction is a response to the *success* of behaviors that are selected based upon *expectations*. Satisfaction results whenever [1] we exhibit a behavior based upon an expectation of its appropriateness or effectiveness, and [2] our behavior is successful. Of course, both expectations and criteria for success may vary across individuals; what is satisfying to one person may not be satisfying to another.

To this point, our discussion of satisfaction has focused largely on interpersonal communication. Yet, satisfaction is also an important outcome in small groups. Traditionally, small group texts have analyzed group processes in terms of two general types of outcomes: task outcomes and socio-emotional outcomes. Satisfaction is a socio-emotional outcome, and, as research indicates, is particularly salient in small group contexts (Bostrom, 1970; Dorfman & Stephan, 1984). Further, satisfaction is also correlated with several important task outcomes, such as group consensus, productivity, and—in the business world—performance, effectiveness, and turnover (Hecht & Riley, 1985).

In this article, we will examine some of the most signficant factors associated with group satisfaction, including participation, types of messages, feedback, interaction management, status, and motivation. We are going to approach this subject matter by observing a hypothetical small group through entries in a group communication diary. Following each entry, we will offer an analysis of the relevant variables described by the group members and how these variables are likely to influence satisfaction. And so, the story begins . . .

Near the end of his junior year, Milo Zanelli struck upon a bright idea to make some extra money and to advance his own career as a visual artist. As a student of the University of Washington at Winonah, Milo knew there was a demand for graphics services on campus: for flyers for student organizations, for dorm T-shirts, for publicity for fraternity and sorority functions, and even for diagrams and tables for student papers. He also knew that new computer technology could make the services inexpensive enough for student budgets. Then he met Cindy Alcala, a freshman computer student and casual art enthusiast. All summer they worked on the technical and logistic problems involved in starting up a small business. In the fall, their hopes were realized as "Visual Sensations" opened its office in the Student Union.

It quickly became apparent that Milo and Cindy could not run the shop alone, and so their staff began to grow. Victor Hodgekiss, a senior majoring in organizational communication and Milo's roommate, was the first to be added. Victor handles most of the administrative duties of the business, bookkeeping, billing, payroll, overhead, and so on. Jill Bauman, Milo's girlfriend and fellow graphics major, was also hired to help out with the design responsibilities. Even with both Jill and Milo on staff, "Visual Sensations" often has to farm out design work to other graphics students on a contract basis. Finally, two office workers were hired through an ad in the school paper, Vance Moore and Kelly Dunn. Vance is a freshman studying oral interpretation, and primarily answers the phone and delivers materials to duplicating services and clients. Milo and Victor have given Vance the nickname "Spaceman" because of several embarassing errors early in the semester. Kelly, a sophomore pre-med, also answers the phone, but really spends most of her time in the office studying. However, she is exceptionally intelligent and beautiful, and whenever Cindy or Jill point out her personal use of company time, Milo and Victor are quickly at her defense.

As part of an assignment for one of Victor's organizational communication classes, the Visual Sensations group has agreed to make periodic reports to his professor. Each group member is required to write one such report, concerning either formally planned meetings or informal gatherings of the group. At this point, we will consider each of these reports, the first of which is filed by Victor.

Small Group Journal: Entry #1

[Reported by Victor Hodgekiss]   [October 15]

Today all six of us met to write job descriptions for our positions: responsibilities, duties, all that kind of stuff. This was Milo's idea, and to be honest, I think his newfound interest in the "search for excellence" is annoying the group. I know its annoying me.

The meeting was pretty uncomfortable. Milo directed everything: "you do this, you do that," and so on. And if we talked to each other, Milo would interrupt—like he was a teacher and we could only talk to him. I'm sure he thinks that since the job descriptions were his idea that he should be in charge of everything. But for all the control he had over the group, it didn't really get him what he wanted. It was funny, 'cause when Vance turned in his job description, it said: "Job Title: Office drone; Responsibilities: Submission and humiliation." I don't know if Milo got the point.

Analysis: Group Participation

This entry demonstrates some of the detrimental effects of unequal and unilateral participation in group discussions and reflects the general correlation between participation and satisfaction. It is important to note that there are several different factors involved in group participation, each of which may influence satisfaction. Two such factors are *frequency* and *duration* of participation. Both the number of times an individual contributes to a discussion and the length of these contributions are associated with satisfaction. Typically, group members will be more satisfied if they feel included in a discussion. Both frequency and duration of participation are important in establishing such perceptions. A third factor of participation is *directionality*. Individuals derive satisfaction not only from their own contributions to a discussion, but also from contributions that are directed to them. Again, this is due to a feeling of inclusion that is created when others direct their comments toward us. Thus, bi-directional communication is usually more satisfying than uni-directional communication. A fourth factor of participation is a group member's perceived *freedom* to participate. Even if group members do not contribute to group discussions, they may derive satisfaction from the belief that they are free to do so. Heslin and Dunphy (1964) concluded that actual rates of participation are less important in determining group satisfaction than the perceptions of group members concerning their freedom to interact at a self-determined level.

Unfortunately, Milo was unaware of these various factors. He not only dominated the group's discussion in terms of the frequency and duration of contributions, he also restricted the directionality of communication within the group by requiring that the other group members direct their comments to him. Further, we may interpret Vance's sarcastic job description as an indication that he, at least, did not feel free to participate.

There are a variety of ways in which we may improve participation in the small group, and improve group satisfaction. First, we can control group size. There is little doubt that size is a significant constraint on participation. Research indicates that an ideal size for effective group participation is five members. In larger groups, the time allocated to each group member may be insufficient, whereas in smaller groups, the pressure to participate may be too great (Slater, 1958). Second, we should schedule group meetings that are long enough to allow all members at least some participation. Meetings that are too short may result in both lower rates of participation and decreased perceptions of freedom to participate. Finally, group members who are naturally more talkative or dominating need to defer to other group members from time to time. Although it is impossible (and probably not desirable) to have complete equality in terms of group participation, it is important to recognize the relationship between such participation and group satisfaction.

Small Group Journal: Entry #2

[Reported by Jill Bauman]   [October 23]

Payday! This afternoon most of us came by to get our paychecks from Victor. I guess Kelly and Vance don't need the money since they didn't show up. Usually, everyone can't wait to get out of the office, but today we hung around just to chat about how things were going. Everyone seemed in a pretty good mood in spite of the fact that Victor said our checks wouldn't clear 'til Monday.

We were talking about our plans for the weekend when Milo started complaining about our lack of dedication. He said that we were all lazy and spoiled, and that we should all work harder. Victor kept saying, "Yes, sir, Mr. Mussolini," which Milo found offensive—after all, he *is* Italian! Then Milo said that we should all be careful: he might be moving on to "bigger and better things." I'm his girlfriend and I knew he was just bluffing, but I don't think the others knew what was going on.

After Victor took off, we talked a little about the Pan-Hel dance flyers and came up with some good ideas. Milo may be a bit of an egomaniac when he's talking about the company, but when we're discussing designs, he's really good at organizing suggestions and getting us to focus on the technical problems of getting everything done.

Analysis: Types of Messages

This entry suggests that satisfaction may be affected by the different *types* of messages that group members employ. Although there are many different types of messages, our analysis will focus on three types reflected in Jill's report that are commonly found in small group communication.

First, as we would expect, *negative communication* tends to decrease satisfaction among group members. Jill reports two instances of negative statements: Milo's unsolicited and rather personal criticism that the group is "lazy and spoiled," and Victor's defensive replies of "Yes, sir, Mr. Mussolini." Although it is often necessary for group leaders to criticize other members, when the criticism becomes either hostile or too personal, it is likely to decrease satisfaction. Similarly, humor is an important aspect of a group's social climate—but when humor is cruel or taken with offense, it will decrease satisfaction.

A second type of communication that tends to decrease group satisfaction is *ambiguous communication*. Such communication includes statements with hidden conclusions or statements that are so abstract that it is difficult to determine the speaker's meaning. For example, in Jill's report, Milo issues a vague threat to the other group members that he may be moving on to "bigger and better things." Not only is this statement ambiguous, it also suggests some hidden decision that Milo has made concerning his future with "Visual Sensations." Statements such as this will often lead to confusion, hurt feelings, and equally ambiguous responses from other group members. Each of these effects will tend to decrease satisfaction.

Orienting communication, on the other hand, tends to increase group satisfaction. These messages direct group discussion by clarifying previous statements, asking appropriate questions, introducing new and relevant information, and keeping the discussion focused on the issues at hand (Hirokawa & Pace, 1983). Although Jill does not mention any particular orienting statements, she does comment about Milo's ability to organize group suggestions and to keep the discussion focused. Further, as Jill's report suggests, these types of messages resulted in a more satisfying discussion.

Small Group Journal: Entry #3

[Reported by Milo Zanelli]   [October 27]

Much to my surprise, today's meeting went really well. Once we set up this week's work schedule, I told the group that we had to select a representative for the School of Business campus symposium on entrepreneurism. I committed the group to participate over a month ago, and at the time, I thought I would be able to represent the group. But now something's come up, and we've got to get someone else to do it. I know the group must think I'm a weasel, but things just couldn't be helped.

I told Victor that he had put in a lot of good work in setting up the business end of the company and that the symposium would be a good way for him to get some recognition on campus. He seemed on the verge of saying yes, when Vance—of all people—volunteered. Although I appreciated the offer, there's just no way I could send Vance to represent us. So I told him that he simply hadn't had enough experience with the sort of financial things that were going to be discussed at the symposium. Victor agreed, and said he'd help out. Everyone gave him a big round of applause.

Analysis: Feedback

As noted above, it is often necessary for group leaders to evaluate and perhaps criticize other group members. However, Milo's entry demonstrates how such feedback may be presented without decreasing satisfaction.

In this section, we will discuss three different dimensions of feedback and their influence on group satisfaction. First, feedback may range from *positive* to *negative*. Of course, positive feedback is typically more satisfying than negative feedback (Jacobs, Jacobs, Feldman & Cavior, 1973). For example, when Milo compliments Victor for his efforts in the group, Victor seems to react favorably by giving Milo's request careful consideration (if Victor had been dissatisfied by Milo's comments—if, for example, he had perceived them as manipulative ingratiation—then it is unlikely that Victor would even consider helping out). While this example does not suggest that one should never give negative feedback, it does indicate why positive feedback is generally more effective than negative feedback. Further, a person who is generally positive toward others is more likely to have more negative comments accepted without reducing satisfaction.

Second, feedback may be *person-centered* or *behavior-centered*. If feedback must be negative, then we can best maintain satisfaction by focusing the feedback on behaviors exhibited by individuals rather than on the individuals themselves (Jacobs et al., 1973). When Vance volunteered to represent "Visual Sensations" at the symposium, Milo was put in a position that clearly called for some negative feedback. However, rather than referring to Vance as "Spaceman" or calling him stupid or incompetent, Milo restricts his criticism to Vance's breadth of experience in the company. Thus, Milo reduces the likelihood that he will offend Vance (or the others in the group), and in the process, helps maintain group satisfaction.

Third, feedback may be *performance-descriptive* or *emotion-expressive*. Again, when we must give negative feedback, it is generally best to focus our feedback on describing the group member's performance rather than on expressing our own emotions. For example, had Milo been upset or frustrated by Vance's offer to represent the group, he may have used his feedback to express these emotions by saying, "Listen, Vance—I'm tired of you interrupting the group every time we're on to something important." As we would expect, comments such as these are very likely to reduce satisfaction, and further, are less effective in correcting a group member's performance than more descriptive feedback.

Small Group Journal: Entry #4

[Reported by Kelly Dunn]   [November 5]

Things were a mess at the office today. I was working the phone and writing up a lab report for my Bio class, while Milo, Jill, and Cindy were trying to decide on a format for the Alumni Weekend "memory books." Everything was very disorganized. No one could finish any idea without everyone else jumping in and explaining why the idea was impossible or dumb. I could tell Milo was pretty frustrated because he was stumbling all over his words. I'm just glad I wasn't part of the meeting.

Analysis: Interaction Management

This entry illustrates the importance of successful *interaction management* in establishing group satisfaction (Spitzberg & Hecht, 1984). Interaction management refers to the ability to regulate the flow of communication successfully. This usually requires restricting the number of communicators speaking at any given time and ensuring smooth transitions between speakers. The meeting described in Kelly's report fails on both counts. Group members repeatedly interrupted each other, and apparently, there were often several offenders at the same time.

Turn-taking is a significant factor in determining group satisfaction for two reasons. First, since communicators plan their messages in accordance with their expectations, it is important that there is some predictability in the flow of communication. Individuals want to be secure that once they begin a message, they will be given a reasonable time in which to conclude it. If these expectations are violated (especially repeatedly), then satisfaction is very likely to decrease. Second, communicators seek to avoid interpersonal disputes concerning speaking turns. Accordingly, when turn-taking is irregular and unpredictable, the likelihood of interpersonal conflict increases and group satisfaction will tend to decrease.

There are two commonly observed behaviors that indicate both poor interaction management and decreased satisfaction. One of these—verbal disfluency—is reported above. Like Kelly, we may assume that Milo's stumbling and stuttering is a sign of his frustration and dissatisfaction. Another such indicator is response latency; that is, the amount of time *between* changes in speakers. When a communicator is reluctant to begin an utterance, it often reflects not only his or her confusion with turn-taking in the interaction, but also dissatisfaction with this confusion.

Small Group Journal: Entry #5

[Reported by Vance Moore]   [November 13]

Today we got together to set up a work schedule for the upcoming week. This week's going to be a tough one, too—we've got to get the proofs for the alumni "memory books" done by Monday morning. We were all wondering how many of us would have to work this weekend.

Milo started out by asking for volunteers, but there were no takers. All of us want to go to Pensulia this weekend for the Oregon Tech game. So Milo went around the room, listening to each of our stories. Everyone pleaded with Milo like he was the Sphinx at Thebes.

Finally, Kelly suggested that instead of having one or two of us work all weekend, that *all* of us work through the night on Thursday, and then drive to Pensulia together in Victor's van later Friday night—at that point we could catch up with our other friends. Milo agreed to a vote, and Kelly's suggestion was accepted unanimously.

Analysis: Status

As a general rule, group satisfaction is highest when group members share relatively equal status within the group. Of course, some status differential is inevitable in any small group, but if this differential should become too great, satisfaction is likely to suffer. Using Vance's report as an example, we can see how status can influence satisfaction. On one hand, consider Milo's interrogation of the other group members concerning their plans for the weekend. This pattern of communication reflects a large status differential: the other group members seek approval from Milo, and therefore, allow him to act as a superior. However satisfying this experience might be for Milo, it is probably unsatisfying for the group as a whole. On the other hand, Kelly's suggested solution and Milo's call for a vote seem to diminish this status differential. Not only is Kelly's status increased by the success of her proposal, the status of *all* the group members is enhanced by putting the matter to a vote in which each member's opinion counts.

Small Group Journal: Entry #6

[Reported by Cindy Alcala]   [December 9]

This weekend, I gave an end-of-the-semester party for the rest of the staff and some of our friends. Even though we've still got *a lot* of work to do before break, it seemed a good time to celebrate. It was nice to have a chance to talk to everyone without any deadlines or pressure.

Milo and I were talking about the business and he said I should keep "Visual Sensations" going after he graduates in June. It's great to hear Milo talk about our little corporation and his career as a graphic designer. He just goes on and on about how this has been such a great experience for him and how it's going to get him a good job in an advertising firm. I hope everything works out for Milo—he really deserves it.

I also had an interesting conversation with Kelly. On my way to the bathroom, she cornered me in the hallway and started complaining about her job: the crummy pay, the bizarre hours, Milo's patronizing, and Victor's double entendres. I felt bad that I wasn't a more sympathetic audience, but I really had to get to the bathroom! Anyway, maybe Kelly had just had a bit too much of Vance's famous Bavarian egg nog.

Analysis: Motivation

There are two different types of motivation that are related to satisfaction, each of which is reflected in Cindy's report. First, *long-term motivation* includes one's desire to remain a member of a given group, to contribute to the functions of the group, and to devote personal resources (including time) to the success of the group. Second, *conversational motivation* refers to one's desire to engage in a particular communication interaction. In this section, we will consider both types of motivation and their influence on group satisfaction.

Generally, group members with higher long-term motivation will be more satisfied than group members with lower long-term motivation. The reasons for correlation are apparent when we consider the most common sources of this type of motivation. First, group members may be highly motivated because the group is a significant component of their self-definition or identity. For example, as Cindy reports, "Visual Sensations" is a very important part of Milo's self-image, and accordingly, Milo has perhaps the highest long-term motivation within the group. Second, group members may be highly motivated because there are far more rewards than costs associated with the group. Here we may consider Kelly's situation: her lack of long-term motivation may stem from the fact that, for her, the rewards of being in the group (the "crummy pay") barely exceed the costs (the "bizarre hours" and the difficulty of dealing with Milo and Victor).

Either of these sources of long-term motivation is likely to result in greater satisfaction. Since our self-definition will tend to involve activities and skills that we perform well rather than those we perform poorly, we are more likely to be satisfied with aspects of our lives that are associated with positive skills and activities. Thus, if our membership in a particular group is central to our self-definition, then presumably we are performing successfully and our satisfaction will increase. Similarly, if we perceive our group membership to result in rewards that far outweigh our costs, then it is likely that we are performing successfully in the group and again, our satisfaction will increase.

Conversational motivation is similarly related to satisfaction. The greater our motivation to engage in a given interaction, the more likely we are to be satisfied. Whenever we are more motivated to engage in conversation, we are more likely to exhibit successful behaviors; our attention is focused on the interaction and we are more conscious of the potential and actual outcomes of our behaviors. For example, in the entry above, Cindy has low motivation in her conversation with Kelly. She has been "cornered" in the hallway and she wants to get to the bathroom. Accordingly, she fails to be the supportive listener that would satisfy her expectations and her satisfaction is decreased. In her conversation with Milo, however, Cindy appears to be more highly motivated, and seems to be more satisfied with the interaction.

At the beginning of this chapter, we noted that small group processes are traditionally discussed in terms of two general types of outcomes: task outcomes and socio-emotional outcomes. Further, our present discussion of satisfaction has focused primarily on the socio-emotional aspects of group discussion and membership. It is important, however, to remind ourselves that task and socio-emotional outcomes are interrelated (see Hecht & Riley, 1985). For example, as satisfaction results from the perceived success of behaviors, we should expect task outcomes to be similarly facilitated by the same successful behaviors. Conversely, as task outcomes are completed with greater success, group members should experience increased satisfaction. Indeed, the factors that link socio-emotional outcomes (such as satisfaction) and task outcomes are precisely those that have formed the core of the analysis presented in this article, the nature of participation within the group, the types of messages employed in the group's communication, the feedback that is offered group members, interaction management, and the status and motivation of group members.

Satisfaction, then, is associated with many of the most important processes involved in small group communication. Successful groups (those that use effective procedures to achieve their goals) are satisfied and, in turn, satisfaction provides an emotional foundation for future success. Thus, groups can be more productive by focusing greater attention on the satisfaction of their members.

The principles outlined in this article are gradually becoming recognized by businesses throughout the country. Two new approaches to management that are becoming more prevalent in the private sector are participatory management, and "management by walking around." Both of these approaches provide group members with greater input, participation, and status, and consequently, serve to motivate employees to perform more effectively. Of course, as the readers of this article will observe, the bases of these management techniques are the principles of satisfying group communication. If Milo and Cindy only knew what they were involved in!

References

Bostrom, R. N. (1970). Patterns of communication interaction in small groups. *Speech Monographs* (37), 257–263.

Dorfman, P. W. & W. G. Stephan (1984). The effects of group performance on cognitions, satisfaction and behavior: A process model. *Journal of Management* (10), 173–192.

Hecht, M. L. (1978). Toward a conceptualization of communication satisfaction. *Quarterly Journal of Speech* (64), 47–62.

Hecht, M. L. & P. Riley (1985). A three factor model of group satisfaction and consensus. *Communication Research Reports* (2), 179–187.

Heslin, R. & D. Dunphy (1964). Three dimensions of member satisfaction in small groups. *Human Relations* (17), 99–112.

Hirokawa, R. Y. & R. Pace (1983). A descriptive investigation of the possible communication-based reasons for effective and ineffective group decision making. *Communication Monographs* (50), 363–379.

Jacobs, M., A. Jacobs, G. Feldman, & N. Cavior (1973). Feedback II—the "credibility gap": Delivery of positive and negative and emotional and behavioral feedback in groups. *Journal of Consulting and Clinical Psychology* (4), 215–233.

Slater, P. E. (1958). Contrasting correlates of group size. *Sociometry* (21), 129–139.

Spitzberg, B. H. & M. L. Hecht (1984). A component model of relational competence. *Human Communication Research* (10), 575–599.

4
Group Communication: Principles and Precepts

The need to accentuate the importance of communication seems truly unnecessary to a generation that has participated in what is often referred to as the "communication explosion." From all areas and from every direction we are being confronted with personal examples of how crucial communication is to our existence. Although much of the emphasis is on communication "hardware" – satellites, television, computers, and the like – we need only glance at our daily environments to see the role communication plays in the numerous group situations in which we find ourselves.

It can be generalized that the prevalence of communication in our many group activities can be considered the most significant structural property of a group as well as the most readily observable phenomenon of group life.[1]

If we are going to be able to perform effectively in small groups, we must be able to communicate. Social psychologist Soloman Asch states:

> We have good reason to suppose that conditions from the wider social field reach individuals from their everyday contacts with family, friends, companions. It is in these concrete contacts that communication and discussion takes place and that decisions are reached and pressures exerted to act in given ways.[2]

Just as most organizations are initiated, perpetuated, and held together by communication, so, too, this postulate is true in the life cycle of any group. It is through communication that we form the links that eventually fuse the individuals into what, by definition, can be called a "group." Without this highly complex phenomenon, we would indeed be forced into total seclusion, conscripted into isolation that would set each of us apart from our fellow human beings. In a very real sense it is communication that enables us to tell and to be told; to share our innermost feelings and ideas; to exercise some control over our environments; and to form the countless groups that offer us the support of others, as well as the opportunity to interact and solve problems with those of similar and divergent views.

It should be obvious to this point that there is a crucial link existing between small group behavior and communication. These two activities work in tandem, each influencing the other. In fact, it would be impossible to say which is the cause and which is the consequence, which is the voice and which is the echo. Therefore, to understand both of these processes – group behavior and communication – we must be aware of this interdependence, aware of how these two activities influence each other and, in turn, the way we act when we are members of a group.

It is our contention that your ability to communicate, and to be communicated with, will help determine your success in small groups. If you are going to accomplish your private and public goals through group interaction, you must know something about human communication. It is the purpose of this chapter to add to that understanding. More specifically, the selections in this chapter are intended to explain what communication is, how it works, and its place in small group interaction.

For a long time, due to the ubiquitous nature of human communication, scholars have been faced with the difficult task of trying to decide what *is* and what *is not* communication. Stephen W. King attempts to deal with this very question in an essay that both defines and explains interaction. He defines communication as "a process whereby symbols generated by people are received and responded to by people." He then examines five characteristics that grow out of this definition. In addition, he offers a discussion of some of the common myths most often associated with communication.

While King looked at communication theory in general, our second selection focuses on human communication as it is reflected in a small group setting. In an article called "Elements of Group Communication", Baird and Weinberg examine two categories of communication: verbal and paraverbal. By placing each of these categories in a small group context, the authors are able to analyze the interrelationship existing between communication and the environment in which that communication transpires.

Groups do not consist of mindless individuals all conforming to some preordained path to group consensus. According to Marshall Scott Poole, "Group Communication and the Structuring Process", individuals in groups are continually structuring their groups through their communicative behaviors. He points out that all groups, regardless of how stable they appear, are continuously being produced and reproduced by members' communication interactions. He sets forth a theory of structuration, and explains the internal and external factors which shape this structuring process in small groups.

Our impact on a group is partially determined by *what* and *how* we disclose to the other members of that group. It is this important topic of self-disclosure that is the focus of our next essay. Lawrence B. Rosenfeld explains the role of self-disclosure in human interaction in "Self-Disclosure and Small Group Interaction". He then defines self-disclosure, and considers the reasons both for and against self-disclosure in group settings. His two-part self-disclosure questionnaire will help you assess willingness to self-disclose and willingness to encourage feedback in groups of which you are a member.

As Karl J. Krayer explains, "The maturity of a small group affects the communication which takes place within it. In turn, communication can affect the maturity of a group." His article "Group Maturity" explains the processes which promote group maturity and group immaturity. In addition, he presents his research findings, which establish the important link between group maturity and situational leadership.

Notes

1. Abraham Zaleznik and David Moment, *The Dynamics of Interpersonal Behavior* (New York: John Wiley and Sons, Inc., 1964), p. 71.
2. Soloman E. Asch, *Social Psychology* (New York: Prentice-Hall, Inc., 1952), p. 502.

The Nature of Communication

Stephen W. King

Three weeks into a course entitled "Small Group Communication" an earnest student raised her hand and asked, "Now that we know what a 'small group' is, Professor, what is 'communication'?" Many students snickered, thinking the question tremendously naive and trivial.

However, I was apprehensive. Was this student going to force me to deal with the difficult but essential question of definition? I tried to get out of the tense moment by flippantly saying, "What is *not* communication?"

Undaunted, the student pressed her question, "You didn't answer the question; you merely circumvented it."

Trapped! So I said, "Well, Stevens defined it as 'the discriminatory response of an organism to a stimulus,' Miller and Steinberg asserted that communication 'involves an intentional, transactional, symbolic process,' and Samovar and Mills concluded that communication 'includes all methods of conveying any kind of thought or feeling between persons.' "[1]

Gaining confidence the student looked at me and said, "Professor, that was simply a smorgasbord of definitions offering me a great deal of choice but not much clarification."

I prayed for the bell to ring indicating the end of the period. No bell, so I said, "O.K., Miller and Steinberg's definition is the right one. Now, do you understand?"

"No," said the student, "that's the point. You gave me a definition but I don't understand why that definition captures the essence of 'communication' while the others do not. I guess I want to understand 'communication' not define it."

Of course, she was right. Thus, I begrudgingly began a dialogue aimed at understanding communication, its fundamental nature and conceptual boundaries. I invite you to join us on this expedition in search of understanding.

We can begin our expedition with a brief story:

(1) Professor Samuel Withit left the library one morning and saw one of his students across the quad wave to him. He waved back. (2) A few moments later Professor Withit walked by another of his students who gave a friendly "hello" smile. (3) Professor Withit did not see the student and continued to

Stephen W. King is Dean of the School of Communication, California State University at Chico.

walk to his office without acknowledging the smile. The student, miffed by the rebuff, cut class for the rest of the week. (4) Upon entering the departmental offices, Professor Withit overheard one of his ex-students telling another student, "Professor Withit's class is one of the toughest in this department." (5) Later, Professor Withit dictated a letter to his secretary and requested that the letter be mailed that day. Two days later the letter left the office.

How many of these five incidents would you classify as examples of communication? All five? Two? None of them? Very probably other people would disagree with whatever answer you decided upon. Such difference of opinion is more than just an interesting disagreement; we must ask the question, "Why?" Quite simply, the answer centers on the fact that to decide to call something by a name, in this case "communication," reflects your understanding and, at this point in your study of communication, you *all* probably have different ideas about what is or is not "communication." Let's look at each of these five incidents and try to discover the points at which some of your understandings might differ.

In incident number one (1) no words are exchanged. Because of this, did you exclude this as an example of communication? In incident two (2), a signal—a smile—was sent but not received. Is reception necessary for communication? Professor Withit's behavior in incident number three (3) unintentionally affected his student. Are such accidental effects communication? In incident four (4), Professor Withit was not the intended receiver of the signal sent by one of his ex-students. Did the student communicate anyway? Finally, in incident five (5), the professor's instruction to the secretary was apparently received but not effective. Is the study of communication limited to effective communication?

Possibly your concept of communication allows you to include all the incidents as examples of communication. However, if another person conceived of communication as only those exchanges of ideas through words, incidents one, two, and three would be dropped because words were not uttered. If another individual thought communication dealt only with messages intentionally sent, incidents three and four would not qualify. If success was a prerequisite for yet a third person, incidents two, four, and five would not be included. It is apparent that if we are going to go much further in this study of communication, we must come to a shared understanding of the term.

One way to understand a phenomenon is to identify its parts or components. Accordingly, let's try to decide what the fundamental ingredients of communication are. First, nonverbal communication, which does not rely on words, is a reality. If it were not, why do people get so upset over various hand gestures? Why did Professor Withit's student skip class for a week? Second, to concern ourselves only with successful idea exchange is like calling "teaching" only that which results in the student getting an "A." The result would be that neither education nor communication would ever be improved since no one would have investigated the causes of failure. We must look at both successful and unsuccessful communication. Finally, if we limit ourselves to only those messages intentionally sent, two problems become apparent. First, we have to make some very questionable decisions about what is going on inside a sender's head. Second, and more importantly, we must ignore many messages that do, in fact, have impact, such as Professor Withit's unintentional slight of his student. With these distinctions in mind, let me suggest a description of communication that reflects our understanding of communication to this point: *Communication is a process whereby symbols generated by people are received and responded to by other people.*

Understood in this way we would include all the incidents of Professor Withit's morning except number two (2). In that case the student sent a message, a smile, but it was not received and responded to. Communication was attempted but not achieved. All the other incidents, however, were examples of communication.

Characteristics of Communication

Another way to test the adequacy of our understanding of communication is to see if our concept can accommodate basic truths about communication. Accordingly, let's see if our description of communication fits with five commonly accepted characteristics of communication:

(1) Communication is a process.
(2) Communication is complex.
(3) Communication is symbolic.
(4) Communication is a receiver phenomenon.
(5) Communication is transitory.

Communication is a process. This statement implies that communication "does not have *a* beginning, *an* end, *a* fixed sequence of events. It is not static, at rest. It is moving. The ingredients within a process interact; each affects all of the others."[2] Viewed in this way, communication is both dynamic—that is, constantly changing—and interactive—at least two actively participating individuals are involved. We can separate the ingredients only if we stop the process to look at it. For example, in an argument between an employer and employee many things are happening simultaneously, each one affecting the others—e.g., the employee thinks his boss hates him, the rebuke confirms that impression, the employee's reaction is seen as a challenge to the boss's authority, other employees giggle at the exchange, increasing the employer's determination to reassert authority, etc. To sum up, the idea of process means that many ingredients—variables—are interacting at the same time to produce results.

Communication is complex. The complexity of communication is reflected in two important observations. First, being a process, it is not as direct and one-way as an injection into the arm administered by a physician. Rather, communication proceeds on verbal and nonverbal levels, in both directions.

Second, communication is complex because it involves so many variables, or ingredients. Consider, for example, how many variables are operative during a simple conversation between you and a friend. It is more than just a matter of exchanging ideas with another person; "whenever there is communication there are at least six 'people' involved: the person you think yourself to be; the man your partner thinks you are; the person you believe your partner thinks you are; plus the three equivalent 'persons' at the other end of the circuit."[3] To these six "people," we must add the topic, the communication setting, the goal of communication, and the many other variables that affect any communication event. In addition, everyone has an individual personality, a set of needs, a past history, important personal relationships, and a unique way of seeing the world.

Communication is symbolic. One obvious but important characteristic of communication is that it involves the use of symbols of some kind. Symbols are arbitrary, man-made signs that represent thought. Two important implications of symbol use concern us here. First, a given symbol means something different to everyone. Symbols such as "beauty," "intelligence," and "democracy" illustrate well the many meanings invoked by single symbols. Therefore, communication is not the simple transfer of thought from one person to another. Rather, it is a process in which one individual encodes—translates—his thoughts into a symbol and sends that message via some medium to a receiver. The receiver then translates the message into thought—decodes the symbols. Thought and meaning are not transferred: messages are. Once the student of communication sheds the idea that communication is the transfer of meaning and adopts the view that *communication is an exchange of symbols,* a more realistic conception of the communication process is achieved.

The second important consequence of the fact that communication is symbolic is that not all symbols are words. The peace symbol, "thumbs down," long hair, and sarcastic voice inflection are all symbols that communicate ideas or sets of ideas. Indeed, many researchers contend that more than half of the meaning we gain in face-to-face communication is achieved through these nonverbal cues. The recognition and study of the importance of these nonverbal symbols is a critical aspect of understanding human communication.

Communication is a receiver phenomenon. Remember the second student that Professor Withit met earlier in this essay? That student smiled (an attempt to communicate nonverbally) but the professor did not see the smile. According to the description of communication we developed, the student did not communicate because the professor did not receive and respond to the symbol. This example illustrates an important aspect of communication: "Communication always occurs *in* the receiver."[4] Notice how the concept of communication differs from a concept like "love." It is possible to love someone and not have the person aware of it. Even though the object of one's love is unaware of the existence of the feeling, the feeling nevertheless is real. Communication, on the other hand, requires that the receiver be just that—a receiver. Communication attempts that do not reach the receiver, like the attempts of our hapless smiling student, are merely attempts at communication, not communication.

There is another implication we must keep in mind. If communication occurs within the receiver, the intention of the sender is largely unimportant. For example, whether or not Professor Withit intended to slight his student, he did. Whether or not the student whose discussion Professor Withit overheard intended it, his message was nevertheless picked up. Communication occurred because an individual received and responded to a set of symbols.

Third, if communication is identified by receiver response, we ought to examine the types of responses that occur. Let's again examine the episodes with which this essay began. Clearly, one result of the communication was a change in attitudes: the first student probably likes his professor a little more and the second student a little less, or maybe a lot less. Additionally, the professor probably did not think much of his secretary when he found out that the letter was mailed late. Apparently, then, one general effect of communication is that our attitudes toward people and things change. Another type of response was illustrated by the student who skipped class for a week. Obviously, the student's behavior was changed by the communication. By reading this essay your knowledge of communication will be affected. Clearly, change in knowledge is another general type of response to communication. At this point, we should understand that communication occurs in the receiver and that its potential effects on the receiver are numerous.

Finally, being a receiver phenomenon means that communication occurs when the receiver attaches meaning to others' behavior. As a consequence of the dominant role of the receiver, some researchers have concluded that it is impossible to not communicate. Simply, "one cannot not communicate."[5] All behavior, when perceived by another, has potential message value or communicative significance. That is, people assign meaning to other people's behavior or nonbehavior. For example, Professor Withit's failure to respond to one of his students angered the student. Therefore, if *all* behavior can have message value or meaning, it is impossible to not communicate, since you can't stop behaving. Anything you do or do not do *may* have meaning for one who perceives it. A few examples may illustrate this important characteristic of communication.

If you were to ask your roommate a question, is there anything he/she could do that would not mean something to you? What if he/she ignored your question? What if he/she answered sarcastically? What if he/she responded in a very cheery way? What if he/she left the room? No matter what he/she did, you would interpret the behavior as meaning something to you.

When you sit next to a person in the campus coffee shop and he says "hello," he is obviously communicating. Is not the same person communicating when he just looks at his food and ignores your presence? Of course he is! He is saying, "I'm here to eat and not to carry on idle chatter with a person I don't know." Is there anything that person could do to which you would not attach meaning? Probably not.

The fact that "one cannot *not* communicate" is important. It means that the study of communication must focus on all your behavior and not just on that part of the time when your mouth is open. Furthermore, it increases your responsibility to recognize that what you say and do influences other people.

Communication is transitory. This principle has two parts. First, communication is irreversible. It can only go onward: it cannot back up and try again. This characteristic of communication is best illustrated by the absurdity of the judge's admonition, "The jury will disregard the testimony just given." Impossible! Second, communication is unrepeatable. Even if the message is repeated word for word, the audience has been changed by the first attempt. Therefore, they are different receivers attaching a different meaning to the same message. This principle of communication is well illustrated by the common experience of either telling or hearing a joke the second time; it just is not the same.

So far it works! If we conceive of communication as a "process whereby symbols generated by people are received and responded to by other people" we can account for the observations that communication is a process, is complex, is symbolic, is a receiver phenomenon, and that communication is transitory. Let's test our understanding in yet another way.

Myths of Communication

Another test of the adequacy of our concept of communication is whether it helps us reject myths or misconceptions about communication. Using our description of communication see how it allows us to avoid five of the most common mistaken conclusions about communication.

1.   "I understand communication. I've done it for years." Because of this false assumption, people have communicated poorly for centuries. You have breathed for years, driven cars for years, listened to radios for years, and thought for years, and yet you probably realize that knowing more

about physiology, engineering, electronics, and psychology could improve your own performance. Many successful salespersons do not understand persuasion. Doing something does not necessarily imply that one understands what he or she is doing.

2. "Communication can be improved simply by improving communication skills," This myth is based on two fallacies. First, it assumes that there are "certain unequivocal laws which, if followed, lead to success, and if not, to failure."[6] That simply is not the case. Communication is far too complex a process and our investigation (so far) too unsophisticated for such rules to exist. If such rules were available, they could be printed and distributed at freshman orientation, and all departments of English and Speech Communication could be disbanded.

Second, this myth focuses attention on the speaker, which, according to our description of communication, is stressing the wrong person. Remember, communication is a receiver phenomenon. The study of communication, therefore, should not focus on what the speaker *does to* a receiver (which treats the receiver as a passive, mindless blob), but should focus on what happens within the receiver as the result of the speaker's behavior.

Communication is not necessarily improved merely by improving communication skills. Indeed, communication is improved "first, by the communicator's understanding of the communication process, then by the communicator's attitudes and orientations; and only then by the techniques the communicator employs."[7]

3. "I didn't misunderstand him, he misunderstood me." Because of human nature, we are always convinced that we are right and the other person is wrong. For example, I have heard students say things like, "It was John's fault, his speech was so confusing nobody could have understood it." Then, two minutes later, the same student remarked, "It wasn't my fault, what I said could not have been clearer. John must be stupid." Poor John! He was blamed when he was the sender *and* when he was the receiver. John's problem was that he was the *other* person, and that's who is always at fault.

To understand and to improve communication, you have to be willing to accept the idea that communication is a two-way process with at least two active participants and "fault" must be divided between them.

4. "Most problems, from interpersonal to international, are caused by communication breakdowns. These breakdowns are abnormal and easily correctable." Let's look at the first sentence of this most common of myths. In recent years a number of widely discussed, little understood, and generally ambiguous terms and phrases, such as "communication breakdown," "communication gap," and "credibility gap," have been

introduced into our everyday vocabulary. These terms have become the dumping ground for many phenomena we can't explain in an easier or more direct way. The fact that college administrators and students disagree is not a communication breakdown. The fact that teenagers frequently argue with parents is not a communication gap. The fact that minorities demonstrate for a greater share of the economic "action" in this country is not a communication breakdown. Calling these problems gaps or breakdowns ignores the psychological, economic, political, and physical realities which caused the symptom of poor or infrequent communication.

The second part of this myth is equally erroneous. Ineffective communication is not abnormal. Communication is complex and poorly understood; is it any wonder that without much knowledge or training in communication we are not very good at it? Further, since communication is so complex, can we expect it to be easily corrected when it is found to be inefficient?

5. "All communication is attempting to achieve perfect understanding between participants." This myth is dangerous on two counts. First, it assumes that "perfect understanding" is possible. Second, it denies an important reality: sometimes the goal of communication is to be misunderstood.

To achieve "perfect understanding" through communication limited to a humanly-devised symbol system is impossible. Our symbols frequently do not come close to fitting the ideas that they are supposed to represent; at best, they are approximations. There is always a very real possibility, indeed probability, that the idea you try to communicate will not be the idea your communication partner decodes from the symbols you have chosen to represent the idea. Recognizing that symbols are inexact, we should try to make our communication as deficient as possible. This, rather than "perfection," is a realistic and attainable goal.

Do you always want to be perfectly understood? Probably not. Have you never answered a test question vaguely to avoid demonstrating ignorance? Have you never sidestepped giving an opinion about a friend's new car or clothing? Often we intentionally garble our messages so as to avoid embarrassment or hide our true feelings. The following selection from an Oscar Wilde play illustrates this use of communication well.

THE DUCHESS: "Do, as a concession to my poor wits, Lord Darlington, just explain to me what you really mean."
LORD DARLINGTON: "I think I had better not. Nowadays to be intelligible is to be found out."[8]

What Is Not Communication

One final test of our understanding of communication is whether we can use such understanding to identify what is not communication. That is, we should be able to answer the question, "What isn't communication?"

We have said that communication takes place whenever someone attaches meaning to another's behavior. It is clear that unless one's behavior is perceived by someone, communication has not occurred. That is, what one does or says in isolation is not communication.[9] Furthermore, we must exclude those behaviors which, though perceived, have no meaning or significance for the perceiver. Perceived behavior to which the perceiver does not attach meaning is not communication. Every day we interact with others in ways that result in no significant interpretation or meaning being attached to the perceived behavior. For example, when you jostle your way in or out of a crowded lecture hall, your behavior and that of many others are mutually perceived, but only in the rare circumstances of inordinate rudeness does anyone attach meaning to that type of perceived behavior. Note that this argument retains the focus of our study on the receiver: Does the receiver attach meaning to that which is perceived? Obviously, what is meaningful for one person might be inconsequential for another. For example, you would probably ignore the fact that your friend does not wear a watch, but a psychiatrist may take that to mean something significant about your friend's psyche.

Thus, to answer the original question, behavior that is not perceived by another or to which no significant meaning is attached is not communication. Behavior that is both perceived and meaningful is communication.

You may now argue, "O.K., but earlier you said that communication can't be turned off, and now you say some perceived behavior is not communication. Isn't that contradictory?" Not at all. Not all behavior communicates, but it has the *potential* for communication. The important distinction is that you cannot *avoid* communicating. It is impossible for you to turn communication off as you do a radio. When this point was presented earlier in the essay, I was looking at the sender and forcing him or her to recognize all the ways he or she is constantly giving off communicative behavior. When I say that all behavior need not be communication, I am focusing on the receiver and asking the question—does the receiver actually assign meaning to perceived behavior? Not all behavior actually communicates, but it does have communication potential.

Summary

Are you now ready for a definition? We described communication and then tested our understanding of the thing described in many ways. We found that our understanding of communication helped us identify what is and isn't communication, it assisted in rejecting fallacious myths about communication, and it can accommodate several basic truths about communication. Accordingly, we can now define communication in a way that *reflects* our understanding, rather than merely assert a definition that is separate from our understanding. Simply, we understand communication to be "a process whereby symbols generated by people are received and responded to by other people."

Notes

1. S. S. Stevens, "A Definition of Communication," *Journal of the Acoustical Society of America,* 22 (1950), p. 689; G. Miller and M. Steinberg. *Between People: A New Analysis of Interpersonal Communication.* Chicago: Science Research Associates, 1975, p. 34; L. Samovar and J. Mills, *Oral Communication: Message and Response,* 3rd ed. Dubuque, Iowa: Wm. C. Brown Publishing Co., 1976, p. 4.

2. D. Berlo, *The Process of Communication.* New York: Holt, Rinehart and Winston, 1960, p. 24.

3. D. Barnlund, "Toward a Meaning-Centered Philosophy of Communication," *Journal of Communication,* 2 (1962), p. 40.

4. L. Thayer, *Communication and Communication Systems,* Homewood, Illinois: Richard D. Irwin, Inc., 1968, p. 113.

5. P. Watzlawick, J. Beavin, and D. Jackson. *The Pragmatics of Human Communication.* New York: W. W. Norton, 1967, p. 48.

6. Thayer, p. 8.

7. Thayer, p. 8.

8. O. Wilde, *Lady Windermeir's Fan,* cited by Thayer, p. 306.

9. Of course, communication with ourselves can be considered communication—intrapersonal communication. However, this essay has focused on the social or interpersonal nature of communication.

Elements of Group Communication

John E. Baird, Jr. and Sanford B. Weinberg

In chapter 1 [Baird-Weinberg text], we defined communication as "the process involving the transmission and reception of symbols eliciting meaning in the minds of the participants." We further suggested that those symbols, which can take the form both of words and of nonverbal behaviors, have no meaning of their own—that they serve simply to stimulate meaning in the mind of the receiver. But this suggestion might be a bit misleading, implying that we need not be concerned about words or behaviors because they have no special importance. Quite the reverse. Certain meanings are conjured up by certain words; specific ideas are stimulated by distinct gestures. To understand the meanings which form in the minds of group participants, then, we first must understand the nature of the symbols which elicit those meanings. In this chapter, we will examine the symbols which comprise the communication process.

To facilitate our examination of human messages, we will go beyond the verbal-nonverbal distinction and divide communication into three categories: verbal, paraverbal, and nonverbal. Verbal communication is what you say, paraverbal is how you say it, and nonverbal is what you do while you are saying it. In the following sections of this chapter, we will analyze the verbal and paraverbal elements of human communication, noting their general characteristics and the ways in which they operate in the group setting.

Verbal Communication

The verbal communication channel serves as a good starting point not because it is necessarily the most important element, but because it is the most obvious. When observing a group, we are most likely to notice the spoken and written messages which the members exchange. Nonverbal and paraverbal messages must be carefully focused upon, while the declamations, memos, agendas, and protestations of group members tend to hit the observer squarely between the eyes.

Verbal communication is of two sorts: oral and written. In some formal groups, written communication is dominant. Members exchange and ponder carefully prepared reports, ask a few minor questions, and vote to accept, to

From John E. Baird, Jr., and Sanford B. Weinberg, *Communication: The Essence of Group Synergy* (Dubuque, IA: Wm. C. Brown Publishers, 1977). All Rights Reserved. Reprinted by permission of publisher. John E. Baird, Jr., is affiliated with Baird-DeGroot and Associates in Gurnee, Illinois. Sanford B. Weinberg is affiliated with the Department of Business Administration at St. Joseph's University in Philadelphia, Pennsylvania.

reject, or to modify. Most groups, however, rely much more heavily on oral communication. While there may be a group secretary furiously scribbling notes throughout the meeting, the most important messages are those exchanged orally. Hence the observations we will make in this section will apply to both oral and written communication, but we will be concentrating primarily on the former. But a comment about written communication is in order. Such communication has both advantages and disadvantages. The advantages are that written messages may be carefully prepared, so that they are exact in tone, specific in detail, and presumably exact in wording. In addition, the message has permanence, so that if the receiver forgets what the message said, he can always look it up again. But written messages also have important disadvantages. The most obvious is a loss of immediacy; the sender and receiver do not confront one another. But this leads to a second, more serious disadvantage. A written message is not open to modification through feedback. You cannot correct misunderstandings easily—indeed, you probably will not detect misunderstandings in the first place—and you cannot readily revise the message should misunderstandings occur. A great deal of flexibility is therefore lost, and a high risk of misunderstanding and miscommunication is incurred.

Napoleon is said to have hit upon a solution of sorts. He appointed an idiot to his staff, and had the unfortunate soul read all messages before they were sent to Napoleon's generals. Napoleon reasoned that if a written message was so clear that an idiot could understand it, there was a good chance that his generals would be able to handle it as well. Still, Napoleon met his Waterloo. Our advice, then, is to use oral communication whenever possible, employing direct and immediate feedback to evaluate the receiver's understanding of your message and to clarify that message if further explanation is needed. Your communication practices may not make history, but you will be able to communicate more effectively and, in the process, save wear and tear on corporals, your memorandum writing and sending abilities, and your nerves.

Semantics

Rather basically, verbal communication involves words and phrases. Ideally, member A forms a mental concept, selects the proper word for it, speaks that word, and relaxes. Member B hears the word, translates it, and receives the mental image A intended. Unfortunately, things are rarely so simple.

Take a deep breath. With what did you fill your lungs? air? oxygen? gases? smog? Do you stand on earth? on ground? on dirt? on soil? or in a yard? Do you drive a car? an auto? some wheels? a vehicle?

Perhaps the words in each of these sets are identical to you. But you might note certain minute but meaningful differences. Often, connotative differences have little effect. But an eleven-year-old called a *child* instead of a *kid* or *young person* or a black person called a *Negro* might disagree. The study of words and word meanings is called *semantics,* and it is a complex field overlapping linguistics, philosophy, psychology, and speech.

Some semanticists have been portrayed as eclectics, more concerned with the proper word than with communicative intention. We shall try to avoid a perspective trap here; for the moment we'll accept the hypothesis that words are a method of expressing ideas rather than a tool for forming ideas themselves. And, unlike the semanticist of Ogden Nash's famous poem, we'll try not to get lost debating over whether the approaching lizard is an alligator or a crocodile while the beast is attacking.

Before examining the verbal linguistic code itself, let's take a broad perspective. A few observations ought to be noted. It is helpful that all group members share a common language. Rather basic, you say, but it may be an important problem in international negotiations where certain phrases may not readily translate from one language to another. Until the "universal translator" of Star Trek fame is perfected, we'll have to be sensitive to this problem. *Sympatico,* for example, has no English equivalent. The Russian word for *policeman* is not readily translatable as *cop.* And slang idioms—well, we'll consider that tangle a bit later. Suffice it to say that our initial observation about verbal communication is that, with all the confusion occurring from homonyms, dialects, and connotative differences, a common group language provides the group with at least a fighting chance of success. Perhaps it is for this reason that the Boy Scouts tried desperately to teach Esperanto, an international language, to all boys attending the Internation Jamboree held in Japan.

Another general observation about verbal communication in groups involves the frequency of interaction. Several researchers have reported a strong correlation between leadership and verbal contribution. Apparently, more talkative group members tend to be perceived as group leaders regardless of the worth of their verbal contributions. In one experiment, for example, subjects sat around a table upon which were a series of colored lights. Each subject could see only the set of lights directly in front of him. Participants were instructed to talk whenever their green light was on and to stop talking when their red light was illuminated. The experimenters manipulated the frequency of interaction by changing the duration and pattern of light signals. Even though subjects often could think of nothing valuable to say and spent their green light time repeating nonsense, there was a strong and significant correlation between perceptions of leadership and duration and frequency of the light signals (Hayes and Meltzer 1972). It was possible to make one subject appear as the group leader simply by increasing the talking time of that person.

The phenomenon does have a limit, however. Individuals who dominate conversation to the exclusion of others are considered less benevolent than are relatively quieter group members. This lowering of benevolency ratings produces a reduction in the perceived leadership ratings as well (Smith, Brown, Strong, and Rencher 1975). Talking too much, then, like talking too infrequently, can have a negative effect upon perceptions of leadership contributions. Group members evidently tend to ascribe leadership qualities to individuals who interact frequently but not dominantly.

Rate of speech, vocal inflection, and tone will be discussed later as elements of paraverbal communication. Now, let's look in more detail at the verbal content of the group communication process.

We discover and assign meaning to words through a number of channels: nonverbally, using gestures as clues; paraverbally, relying upon volume, pitch, or inflection; and verbally, attempting to translate the words themselves. While the phrase may be the most meaningful unit for examination, we know that words themselves do have relatively specific meanings. Through the examination of word meanings we can discover information about group communication and group functioning.

S. I. Hayakawa, one of the most famous and persuasive semanticists, has suggested that several problems potentially arise from attempting to ascribe meaning to words (Hayakawa 1949). These problems may produce confusion, false impression, and general misinterpretation of message meaning. For our purposes in examining group communication, we'll concentrate on the three most frequently encountered pitfalls of verbal exchange: the map-territory dilemma, the problem of abstraction, and the purr-snarl controversy.

A map, says Hayakawa, is not a territory. Territory is a concrete thing: we can see it, stand on it, sell it, build a house on it, and pay taxes for it. The map of that territory is merely a summary diagram attempting to represent the major qualities of that land. Do you remember as a child looking for a physical line drawn on the ground when passing from one state into another? Do you expect school buildings to be square with little black flags? While a map denotes (represents) the characteristics of the territory, we sometimes expect the physical land to share some of the connotations (implications) of the map. Here lies the source of some confusion.

Words are simply maps of ideas or physical things. A thing is not its word. But we may expect a *custodial engineer* to be more dignified than a *janitor* and a *multimedia-printed-matter center* to be more than a *library*. We are, in effect, confusing maps and territories. We sometimes expect physical items to share the connotative characteristics of the word describing that item. Is a *memo* more terse than a *message?* Does a committee's *charge* require more dynamic action than a committee's *responsibility?* Does a *board* have more normal tasks than a *group* or *committee?* If you read implications of this sort into the words employed, you may be confusing maps and territories. But what is the danger? Perhaps there is none *if* all of the group members share the same connotations. But because a map is an abbreviated diagram of a territory, the same map may describe closely two similar but distinct pieces of property.

Similarly, the same word with varying connotations may imply very different meanings. Remember that individuals united in a group have some characteristics in common and differ on some other criteria. They have a general unity of purpose, but retain individuality within the group. What if the individual group members have different assumptions which they attach to words? Let's assume, for example, that we're in a group working on the problems of how to help poor children in our community. One member proposes funding a camp for these disadvantaged children. You, perhaps, having worked in a summer camp last year, fully approve of the idea. Another group member is appalled and calls you a Nazi. Why? Perhaps the connotation he attached to the noun *camp* involves the adjective *concentration.* He sees the plan as a method of eliminating the poor kids from the area. A fight is on, and it is likely that neither of you understands why—you don't really disagree about the concept; you simply have different territories associated with the same map.

If this seems contrived, try another example. Discuss the possibility of providing poor people with free birth-control devices. Are you attempting a subtle form of genocide? or providing a vital service that will eventually help people overcome their poverty? or subverting their religion? or commenting on imagined loose morals? or attempting to corrupt the youth? A single map, but widely differing connotative territory.

This problem is closely related to and confounded by yet another verbal difficulty: abstraction. We can, in reality, draw a variety of different maps of the same territory, each varying in exactness of detail and symbolism. A photograph is a map, as is a geological survey map made from the photograph. In the photograph mountains are represented by film images of mountains. On the map, mountains look like curving thin brown lines (contours). From the geological survey map, we could construct a road map which would portray mountains as gray inverted v's $(\hat{\Lambda}\ \hat{\Lambda})$. Or, we could draw a sketch, writing *mountain* in the proper place. Our maps vary in their levels of abstraction, and our verbal interaction varies in much the same way. We can describe a student government election as a *polling,* a *school activity,* or a *youth project.* The ultimate territory is identical, but the maps vary greatly in their specificity. The level of abstraction chosen for a particular message has a significant effect upon the reception of that message. The more concrete a term is, the more likely it is that the individual group members will be able to associate with and understand that term.

For example, we may have some trouble grasping a plan that will "improve the internal decision-making balance capacity of a multinetwork collective organization," but we can more clearly appraise a proposal to "let everyone in the group have a chance to speak." Some organizations and individuals seem to purposely strive for ambiguity and high-level abstraction, perhaps to hide the fact that they are not doing anything important. Generally, the more concrete a message, the more convinced the sender is that the group ought to grasp the full meaning of that message. High-level abstractions diffuse group responsibility, limit concretized understanding, and block full realization of implications. Low levels of abstraction are, in effect, votes of confidence in the group members. You might want to examine your income tax form with that thought in mind.

Some politicians running for office often power their campaigns with abstraction. If asked "Do you favor forced busing?" either yes or no is likely to lose you votes. The response of "I favor an equal opportunity for all Americans" is a safe, spineless out, tempting to many would-be leaders.

The third contribution of Hayakawa we'll consider is the use of purr and snarl words. Often two descriptive terms can be given for the same item or phenomenon. For example, an overweight person can be called *plump* or a *toad*. A smart person might be termed an *egghead* or an *intellectual*. The dictionary tells us these terms are synonyms, but they actually have very different connotative meanings. Hayakawa calls words with a positive connotation "purr" words (as in a loving kitten's calls) and words with a negative connotation "snarl" words (as in a mean cat's growl). For example, what you might call *persuasive* your friend might label *manipulative*. What you think of as *sexy* your parents might consider *lewd*. You have the same territory, but are changing maps to imply different characteristics about that territory.

In a group situation, each member may employ snarl or purr items, each term may elicit a variety of different territories, and each territory might be viewed as one of a number of abstraction levels. In interpersonal communication face-to-face contact allows rapid clarification of a great deal of the resulting confusion. In group communication nonverbal and paraverbal clues aid in interpretation, but some confusion is still likely. In many kinds of groups, the individual members share a common orientation, philosophy, educational level, and background. You and your friends are likely to share a common orientation. Faculty-student committees, while often composed of individuals of varying backgrounds, nonetheless generally contain members used to and trained in dealing with persons of different backgrounds. You, for example, have been trained for at least sixteen years in understanding teachers.

In some groups, however, wide educational and status levels are coupled with the problems of individuals not experienced in communicating with members of differing backgrounds. Perhaps the jury is the prime example of this situation. Since juries are designed to represent a cross section of society, we can expect that some jury members will have difficulty communicating on the same level as their peers. Resulting confusions of map-territories, abstraction levels, and snarl-purr connotations are likely. Perhaps this explains in part the insistence upon complete agreement in most jury decisions.

The verbal code is certainly a major channel of communication in groups and as such is a major source of misunderstanding and misinterpretation. When two people communicate, variations as described by Hayakawa may produce a great deal of confusion. When those problems are multiplied by the five or more group members involved in a discussion, it may be surprising that anything is ever accomplished. Misunderstandings can be minimized, of course, by modifying behavior to avoid the pitfalls just identified. In fact, three relatively simple rules should help greatly:

1. Double check map-territory agreement. Techniques include reliance upon feedback from other group members to make sure that you are all talking about the same thing, careful definition of terms, and identification of important elements through the use of alternate maps (terms) for key concepts. For example, you might begin a discussion by asking each member what the best way to help disadvantaged youngsters might be, and use that description as a concrete territory for the map *camp.* You can alternately reinforce the meaning by calling the experience a *summer play opportunity* (different abstraction level) instead of a *camp.*

2. Move up and down the abstraction level to ensure that all members have an idea of the specific and general implications of the concept. Be as concrete as possible most of the time to avoid ambiguity, but occasionally use an alternate term that clarifies the implications of the idea. Plan an *election,* but remember that it is a *student feedback opportunity.*

3. Strive for neutral terminology. Snarls and purrs both distort meaning and subvert free discussion. If other group members use connotative terms in discussion, ask them to explain what they mean. If you are planning to write a newspaper, don't let the group refer to it as a *rag sheet* or as a *journalistic enterprise* if unrealistic connotations accompany those terms.

These suggestions should help in all communication activities, for they deal with problems that are not unique to group situations. But there is one important communication barrier that does occur only in (or most commonly in) small groups. Before concluding this section on verbal channels of group communication, we'll consider the phenomenon of ingroup speech.

Ingroup Speech

As groups thrive and function and grow, they tend to develop a unique vocabulary to accompany the new syntality. Originally, group members brought to the group a variety of linguistic and verbal patterns. Those terms and phrases with common meaning hopefully became the group staple, forming a specialized vocabulary code for communicating within the group. Eventually, however, some of these terms began to be uniquely abbreviated to save time, or began to take on oncommon specialized meanings, or perhaps began to be used to represent new concepts not easily expressible. Perhaps if the group exists long and functions intensively enough, a special sublanguage of terms evolves. This unique language is understandable only by the other group members. Often, the group members are not even aware they have a special code. Probably, they would have difficulty translating a great deal of it to an outsider.

The code typically speeds and eases communication within the group. It is likely to be rapid, simple, and be common to all the group members. So far, of course, no problems exist. The ingroup speech code is an aid, not a barrier, to communication. Before considering the possible difficulties that might arise, though, let's examine the existence and extent of the ingroup speech phenomenon.

Consider your campus as a defining characteristic of a group. How many specialized slang terms can you find? Some, no doubt, are unprintable. After all, ingroup speech is a rather informal code. But some terms are common to insiders on campuses all over the country. Is your undergraduate library known as the *Ugly?* Are easy courses at your school called *slides, guts, cribs,* or *cake?* Do you try to *ace* exams? Are tests called *hourlies?* We've collected samples of ingroup speech from campuses in several different parts of the country, and these terms seem to be the most common. But would your parents understand if you told them you had "spent the night at the ugly so that you could be sure to ace the hourly in your cake course"?

Slang speech changes rapidly over time and distance. Ask one of your older teachers to define *making out* or *fagging.* Do these meanings conform to your usage? In the Midwest, order a *pop* if you are thirsty—*soda* will get you seltzer water. When you buy something in North Carolina, the salesperson will put it in a *sack;* in Florida you're likely to be asked if you want it wrapped; in New York, a *bag* is used. These kinds of slang differences can be represented in ingroup speech, too. But unique group activities and focuses may have other effects.

Some professions, for example, rely heavily on ingroup terms. The medical profession, for instance, has long been accused of confusing lay persons by employing a highly specialized vocabulary. To your doctor, for example, a *nose job* is *rhinoplasty.* And we've often wondered why psychologists term the inability of an individual to express an idea lying just below the conscious level the *TOT phenomenon*—an acronym for "tip of the tongue."

Ingroup speech, then, has two very definite handicaps: it hinders communications between groups or subgroups, and it slows the integration process when a new member joins a group. Outsiders have difficulty understanding ingroup codes, and hence are clearly identified, perhaps confused, and certainly excluded.

Since the development, use, and problems of ingroup speech are so important to an understanding of the verbal code of group communication, let's examine a few key testable hypotheses concerning the unique vocabulary of slang in group situations.

1. Ingroup speech tends to increase group cohesion. It reinforces the commonalities of group members while identifying and excluding outsiders. Does your group have certain in jokes? As a child, did you ever belong to a group with a secret code word? do you today? The Greek letters of most fraternal organizations stand for some secret motto. Even the name of Phi Beta Kappa, the national honorary scholarship society, is a secret coded message. And, no doubt, somewhere there is someone who cares enough to remember what that message is.

We conducted an informal experiment in which nonfraternity members were invited to fraternity houses for dinner. The use of slang in the fraternity membership was more than double the normal levels with the presence of an outsider. The brothers of that house consciously or subconsciously excluded the visitor and bolstered their cohesion through the use of ingroup speech.

2. Ingroup speech may be used for ease in communication. Some pioneer industries and groups have been forced to invent new terms as they invent new techniques. Hence a stage, motion-picture, or television crewman who moves equipment is called a *grip,* and a computer printout is *debugged* to correct errors.

Ingroup speech may also save time. Hospitals have OB units instead of *obstetrical wards.* Graduate students may be working on an MA or PhD degree. These abbreviations may confuse outsiders, but do ease communication significantly.

3. Ingroup speech seems to proliferate in minority groups. Perhaps in order to maintain identity or prestige, minorities have traditionally developed elaborate ingroup vocabularies. The black culture, for example, has provided a rich and rapidly changing torrent of slang terms. Black English and Yiddish are paralanguages which have emerged from and are maintained in minority groups. Elements of these languages maintain group cohesion and identity.

At the same time, majority groups tend to co-opt slang, perhaps to integrate outsiders or to join desirable subgroups. Do you occasionally use some medical terminology you learned from television to impress your physician? Do you parrot the slang you learned from overhearing another group? Do you find yourself employing minority-group phrases when you talk to members of those groups? It has been suggested that the slang of the youth culture dies as soon as Johnny Carson uses it.

4. Ingroup speech often has a disguised meaning. Words mean the opposite of their usual meaning. To be *bad* is (or was) to be *good*. Some words are developed from other slang. A *deejay* plays records—the name, of course, comes from the slang of the last generation: disc jockey.

This disguised effect may be due in part to the desire to avoid being infiltrated. The more obscure the meaning, the easier it is to isolate outsiders. If the meaning is obvious, most of the exclusionary value is lost.

5. Many terms have forbidden connotations. Perhaps ingroup speech is sometimes a way of talking about the untalkable. Many terms have sexual connotations. But would a foreign-speaking listener realize that the person you called an *ass* does not necessarily share the characteristics of a beast of burden? Perhaps the writing on bathroom walls loses something in the translation.

Of course, if this hypothesis is correct, we ought to see fewer and fewer sexual slang terms as sex increasingly becomes a fit subject of undisguised conversation. No doubt members of some groups, however, will find something else to restrict, for the development of ingroup vocabularies seems to have a universal appeal.

Ingroup speech tends to magnify the commonalities of group members, hence strengthening group cohesion. The increased group efficiency, however, decreases the flexibility of intergroup communication. The result is a strong but communicationally isolated group.

The unusual characteristics of verbal communication shed a great deal of light upon group communication as a whole. We stated earlier that communication was a process of information transference. By now it ought to be obvious that *group* communication, though, serves a dual role. While communication is allowing the group to perform its task as efficiently as possible, that same verbal communication is performing an important maintenance function. By avoiding semantic confusions, we can avoid unnecessary dissention and argumentation within the group that might serve to weaken it. In a further effort to conserve important synergy for task purposes, group communication can increase cohesion through the use of sophisticated slangs. The more tightly knit the group is, the less likely it will develop severe maintenance difficulties. And of course the less energy used for maintenance, the more energy can be devoted to task.

Communication is a tool which allows energy channeled for task accomplishment to serve the dual purpose of maintenance and cohesion building. It is then, the key to efficient synergy utilization. Even while synergy is the essence of groups, communication is the essence of efficient synergy. An examination of nonverbal and paraverbal communication will further illustrate the important linking function communication performs. Through communication, energy need not be divided between the two group functions; it can unite for mutual benefit.

Paraverbal Communication

Group meetings are oral experiences in which a great deal of information is communicated *paraverbally*. As you sit in a group while another member drones on, you presumably are listening to what is being said. You are translating verbal messages, striving to understand the things which the current speaker is trying to say. At the same time, however, you are listening to *how* the speaker is communicating as well as *what* he or she is saying. The way in which a verbal message is delivered is termed *paraverbal communication*. Paraverbal messages are based upon such factors as the speaker's oral style, phraseology, intensity, articulation, and interpretive expression.

Before examining in detail the five most significant variables of paraverbal communication, let's consider for a moment the all-important role that paraverbal messages play in group situations. In a mass lecture, you are not likely to be able to see subtle nonverbal cues (such as gestures) and will probably have to concentrate on paraverbal messages. You will be striving to write down or remember or evaluate what it is the speaker actually says. Of course, some perceptive students concentrate upon the speaker's intensity, thinking that when the professor gets excited a test question is in the air. Most of the audience, though, is probably spending a great deal of their energy on the verbal channel.

Incidentally, television does have a modifying effect upon this generality. When you watch Walter Cronkite you are, in fact, a member of a mass audience. Psychologically, however, you may feel like a participant in an interpersonal conversation and hence devote more of your listening energy to nonverbal and paraverbal channels.

In an interpersonal setting, you can hear the speaker, see the speaker's nonverbal communications, and evaluate paraverbal cues all at the same time. Each channel is generally utilized, and each becomes important.

A group situation magnifies the importance of paraverbal communication in two ways. First, as we just explained, group members come from greatly varying backgrounds but share a common focus. While the focus does much to aid communication, the variety of background may significantly increase ambiguity and confusion. We saw how verbal difficulties may cause distortion and misunderstanding. The other two communication channels, therefore, become increasingly important for interpreting and clarifying verbal messages.

Second, the nonverbal channel may be impeded. While all group members are physically close enough to hear intonations and inflections, they may not be situated properly to observe subtle nonverbal cues. Physical limitations such as rectangular tables, size restrictions, and attention diversions (more than one person speaking, for example) may make it difficult to clearly see what is happening.

Restrictions on verbal communication caused by semantic variations and limitations of the nonverbal channel resulting from observational impediments therefore conspire to increase the significance of the paraverbal communication channel. With this increased importance in mind, let's examine the effects of paraverbal communication in groups.

Although there are many different variables included under the rubric "paraverbal," we will just concentrate on the five that have the greatest significance in group communication. Those factors are *oral style,* the delivery of those words; *intensity,* the emotional impact conveyed by the voice in delivery; *phraseology,* the stringing of words together; and *interpretive expression,* the emphasis or implication of those words and phrases. Before investigating these concepts, however, allow us to make a mild disclaimer. We are well aware that the categories just identified are not distinct. Many situations will overlap the divisions suggested, just as the divisions of verbal, nonverbal and paraverbal sometimes seem to flow together. We suggest, then, that you read the following section not with the intent of being able to cubbyhole interactions, but rather in the hope that these arbitrary and somewhat leaky categories will aid your understanding of the broad process of communication, which transcends all of our attempts to subdivide it.

Oral Style

You have your own unique oral style. Perhaps you are aggressive or assertive. Or you might have a passive, apathetic personality. When you communicate, your choice of words and style of delivery broadcast hints about the person you are. Can you think of someone you instantly disliked as soon as he or she opened a conversation? even before you mentally registered the topic of discussion? Much research is currently being conducted concerning the effect that oral style has on other variables such as trust, willingness to self-disclose, and willingness to assume risk (Norton and Miller 1973). There is apparently a strong link between the paraverbal cues of oral style and interpersonal ties established during the interaction.

If oral style is a valid predictor of relationships between communicators, this aspect of paraverbal communication has important implications for group situations. Consider the possibility that in a small group you form close ties with one person because of his use of inflection, word choice, and speaking pattern. His task-oriented communication can therefore have a significant effect upon maintenance functions within the group. And, of course, the less energy spent on maintenance, the more synergy is available to accomplish that task. Having synergy serve double-duty is the most efficient method of group operation.

Oral style, then, is a potentially invaluable tool for smoothing the wheels of group syntality. A pleasant, amiable style can have considerable impact in arriving at a group decision, while an obnoxious style can add new barriers to consensus.

Articulation

Of course, if people don't understand what it is you are saying, the style with which you say it is of little importance. We saw that speaking in a foreign language is potentially disasterous. Equally serious, and much more common, is speaking with poor articulation.

In normal conversation you receive immediate feedback if the target cannot understand what you are mumbling. In a group setting, however, you are likely to get positive assurance from the members close to you while those on the physical outskirts of the group have difficulty understanding. The point is so obvious that it makes little sense to repeat it: in a group situation, speak up and speak distinctly so that everyone can hear what it is you have to say.

Incidentally, poor articulation can also lead to misunderstanding. How many fights have erupted because of "But I thought you said . . ."? Some research has shown that poor articulation reduces individuals' credibility and persuasiveness (Underwood 1964) as well as waste maintenance synergy. For very real and demonstrable reason, then, it pays to make certain you are communicating whenever you are speaking.

Intensity

The intensity with which a message is delivered may have a significant effect on the importance attached to that message (Mortensen 1972). We tend to pay more attention and to be more impressed by a person who is obviously emotionally involved in his message. Again, the point is important in all communication: utilizing emotionally charged language and intense delivery increase audience interest. In a group setting, a serious payoff is involved. Because groups are ongoing organizations, group members have to make a series of compromises over time. You might have your way on one issue and have to defer to someone else's opinion on a subsequent question. At times, however, you feel so strongly about your position that compromise is impossible. If the group fails to recognize your position, a great deal of synergy can be wasted on simple maintenance functions. If your paraverbal message clearly informs others that you have a strong ethical or moral commitment to your position, or that you have significant ego-involvement in a particular decision, other group members can defer to your position or offer face-saving compromises. If, on the other hand, you purposely feign a high commitment on an insignificant issue, you lose the flexibility to compromise at that time, and force the group to expand synergy unnecessarily. The rule of thumb, then, is this: if your blood is beginning to boil, let others know it. But if the controversy really isn't important, don't paraverbally cry wolf. Remember, the more time the group wastes on disagreement and maintenance, the more difficult it is to arrive at a decisive action.

Phraseology

Sometimes, particularly in more formal group situations, the phrasing of a point or speech may be important. We are not talking here about avoiding obviously biased terminology. Obviously, if you are going to have to work with the group members in the future, name-calling today is likely to backfire tomorrow. But some kinds of phrasing can add significant drama to a statement, emphasizing intensity and suggesting a shift of oral style. For example, consider these three rhetorical devices:

1. Chiasmus: crossing-over or reversing normal word patterns. Isn't "Ask not what you can do . . ." more moving than "Don't ask . . ."?

2. Alliteration: repeating consonant or vowel sound for emphasis. We wonder whether this wording works wonders. If overdone, the effect may be humorous. Properly used, however, the message seems more moving, more meaningful, more motivating, more . . .

3. Parallelism: placing concept in phraseological contrast. Even as synergy is the essence of groups, syntality is the essence of synergy. "We shall pay any price, bear any burden, meet any hardship, support any friend, oppose any foe . . ." (John F. Kennedy, January 20, 1961).

While these stylistic devices can obviously be overdone in a group situation, do not underestimate (underestimate not) their value when you are trying to persuade other group members. Paraverbally they add great impact to your verbal message.

Interpretive Expression

Finally, the interpretive expression of a message can have significant additive meaning. Much of what we said previously applies here, too. One can easily add a note of disbelief, of sarcasm, or of horror to an otherwise innocuous message through paraverbal inflection. How many ways can you interpret the following line?

These statements seem to be reliable.

Is the speaker implying that the statements may seem reliable on the surface, but that they are really distortions? or that other facts seem more reliable? or that previously examined statements are highly questionable? or that

while reliable the statements are incomplete, or inconsequential or not relevant? There may be some confusion in reading the message, but in hearing it
the paraverbal interpretation is likely to remove all doubt.

In a group situation, paraverbal inflection can add greatly to understanding by serving as a readily observable commentary on the message itself.
If the meeting is being transcribed, though, or if you are afraid of being quoted,
better avoid sarcasm. Your "Me, rob a bank? Sure I would!" looks much more
compromising on paper than it might when heard. Although some inflection
may aid in understanding, undue use of sarcasm may boomerang and reduce
effective group communication.

Clearly paraverbal communication is a minor stepchild: it is not intrinsically as important as either verbal or nonverbal channels, while it possesses
overlapping qualities of both. Yet paraverbal communication is a minor stepchild: it is not intrinsically as important as either verbal or nonverbal channels,
while it possesses overlapping qualities of both. Yet paraverbal communication is powerful. As a tool used properly it can add an interpretive dimension
important in face-to-face group settings that is almost impossible in written
communication. Unless you are careful, however, sarcasm, inflection, articulation, intensity, and style can greatly complicate the already complex process
of communication.

References

Hayakawa, S. *Language in Thought and Action.* New York: Harcourt, Brace Jovanovich, 1949.

Hayes, E., and Meltzer, L. "Interpersonal Judgments Based on Talkativeness: Fact or
Artifact?" *Sociometry* 35 (1972): 538–61.

Lott, D., and Sommer, R. "Seating Arrangement and Status," *Journal of Personality
and Social Psychology* 7 (1967): 90–95.

Mortensen, C. *Communication: The Study of Human Interaction.* New York: McGraw-
Hill Book Co., 1972.

Norton, R., and Miller, L. "Oral Style: An Effect of Dyadic Perception." Paper presented at Speech Communication Association Convention, 1973, New York City.

Russo, N. "Connotations of Seating Arrangements," *Cornell Journal of Social Relations* 2 (1967): 37–44.

Smith, B.; Brown, B.; Strong, W.; Rencher, A. "Effects of Speech Rate on Personality
Perception," *Language and Speech* 18 (1975): 145–52.

Sommer, R. *Personal Space: The Behavioral Basis of Design.* Englewood Cliffs, N.J.:
Prentice-Hall, 1969.

Underwood, B. "Articulation and Verbal Learning," *Journal of Verbal Learning Behavior* 3 (1964): 146–49.

Group Communication and the Structuring Process

Marshall Scott Poole

Most social scientific research paints a picture of group members as passive, reactive creatures. Members' behavior is said to be determined by communication networks, group norms, status structures, peer pressure, feedback, and numerous other forces. Members are pictured as though all they do is react to these factors. They are pawns, moved about by forces beyond their control. And the picture of the group as a whole is no less passive. Its effectiveness is explained in terms of the influences of groupthink and other social fallacies, by its level of cohesiveness, its collective motivations, by "necessary" stages of problem-solving, and many other factors. If all an alien from another planet knew about people was what she read in the social scientific journals, she would be highly likely to conclude that they are robots, driven by external and internal forces and with no minds of their own.

We all know that this is not a true picture. Certainly, we are subject to forces beyond our control. Certainly, dynamics like groupthink can take over as though they had a life of their own and lead a group into remarkably bad decisions. But we do have freedom to act as we wish, to make choices that shape our lives. If the group has a norm that we do not agree with, we can choose to break the norm, and we may persist even in the face of severe pressure from other members. If we understand how groupthink works, we can try to prevent it from occurring and, when it does occur, we can inform our group and take measures to counteract its effect. In short, we can control our actions and the actions our groups take. Any social scientific research must take this into account, or it will produce an inaccurate explanation of human behavior.

Now this is not to say that people have total control over their behavior or over how their interactions with others will go. We live in a world not of our own making. Outside forces intrude and shape how we can act. A small architectural firm may suddenly hear that it is in danger of running behind on a project and therefore losing its biggest customer. Group members must drop whatever they are doing and work until this threat to group survival is conquered. Practices and traditions internal to our groups constrain what we

This essay appears here in print for the first time. All Rights Reserved. Permission to reprint must be obtained from the publisher and the author. Marshall Scott Poole is affiliated with the Department of Speech Communication, University of Minnesota.

I would like to acknowledge the contributions of Robert D. McPhee and David R. Seibold to this research. All of us worked together to develop these ideas. I would like to thank Lydia Ford, Lisa O'Dell, and Kimberley Poole for their comments and help in preparing the manuscript.

can do. If a committee has a ten-year tradition of electing a new chair every six months, a new member, no matter how motivated or well-intentioned, is unlikely to be able to convince the group to change the term to two years. The member is better advised to accept the tradition until the group accepts her. Then there is a chance of changing it (unless the new member has come to believe that a six month term really is the best for this group!). We cannot exert absolute control over other group members, and we are affected by their activities. If a member starts to cry for no apparent reason at all, we might feel constrained to disregard other business for a while and comfort him. Interaction is a give and take that no one, no matter how forceful and determined, can control.

So, people can actively control their behavior, but they do so within constraints of external forces, internal group structures, and other members' behavior.

For instance, in a very cohesive secretarial group, which is normally pretty productive, members may decide to take the afternoon off and go on an extended lunch. In this case high cohesiveness does not cause high productivity, it actually works against it. And whether cohesiveness increases or decreases productivity depends on what the group members choose to do. Now, this does not mean that there are no causal forces acting on groups. Productivity will in general be facilitated by higher levels of cohesiveness. But because level of productivity depends on how the members choose to respond to the task, there will be cases where this relationship does not hold.

It is hard to describe and explain the influence of free will on behavior, because there are so many possible ways in which the group could go. Simple cause-effect patterns are no longer possible. To be realistic in our thinking about group behavior forces us to adopt much more complex and less definite explanations. The advantage of this is that our theories of group behavior will be based on much more realistic assumptions than are simple cause-effect theories.

A Theory of Structuration

What would this type of theory be like? It would have to recognize that people in groups actively control their behavior. It would also have to recognize that behavior is shaped and constrained by forces not totally under control of the members. The influence of these forces is channeled by members' choices about how to react to them.

One theory of social behavior that accepts this challenge is the *theory of structuration*. This theory is concerned with how people structure their groups by making active use of social rules and resources. As the word structuration suggests, the process in which members structure groups is ongoing and continuous. It happens throughout the life of the group and is never finished. According to this theory, members are always structuring their groups. They do so with every act. If the structure of the group changes, it is because members have done something that has changed it. If the structure of the group stays the same, it is because members are acting in such a way that the same structure is created and maintained with every act. According to this theory, nothing is ever completely accomplished. The group is never finished or static. Instead, groups are always in the process of creation and re-creation. Nothing ever stops. Even if the group looks very stable and conservative, it is because members are acting in such a way to create the same group structure over and over, creating an appearance of sameness and stability. However, underlying this is a constant process of change.

Definitions

So far we have not defined several terms—structure, rules, and resources. First we will do that and explain a few of the basic assumptions of the theory of structuration. Then we will give an example of structuration in groups. After that we will discuss the theory in more detail.

One of the basic distinctions in the theory of structuration is the distinction between *system* and *structure*. A *system* is an observable pattern of relationships among people. A *structure* is a set of rules and resources used to generate the system. These rules and resources are unobservable and must be deduced from how the system operates. Often people are aware of rules and resources that they use. *Rules* are propositions that indicate how something ought to be done or what is good or bad. For example, a norm is a rule that tells members what the group expects of them, if they are to remain in good standing. Another example is the communication rules that define the meanings of terms and what various behaviors mean. *Resources* are materials, possessions, or attributes that can be used to influence or control the actions of the group or its members. Examples of resources include money, special knowledge in an area important to the group, status outside the group, and formal leadership position.

The final important term *structuration* has a very complex definition, but one which can be understood, if we take it apart. *Structuration* can be defined as the *production and reproduction of the social systems through members' use of rules and resources in interaction.* This is a very complex statement that contains a number of ideas.

First, the notion of structuration implies that the primary constituents of the group system are interaction and relationships among members. The very existence of a group depends on members' interactions. If members stopped interacting and broke off their relationships with one another, the group would cease to exist. This is true even of formal groups, such as organizational work groups, where members are assigned and expected to show up. If members decide to work individually and never meet or interact as a group, there really is no group. It is a group in name only, and members do not identify with the group or feel accountable to each other.

Second, the definition implies that rules and resources (structures) are the "tools" members use to interact. Hence rules and resources are the "tools" that create and maintain the group system. As we noted above, a group system is composed of patterns of relationships and interaction among members. These patterns are created and maintained by members' use of rules and resources. For example, if one norm (rule) is that members of the group must all be good friends, then members will try to get to know each other. They guide their interaction by the rule. In following this rule, members employ various resources—such as their social skills and their status outside the group—to get others to like them. If they are successful at getting to know one another, their interaction will create and maintain a dense communication network. This in turn, will make the group more cohesive. The two properties of the group—high cohesiveness and a dense network—are direct results of members' using rules and resources. The properties will exist only as long as group members continue to apply the rules and resources just mentioned. If members choose not to follow the norm or if they decide to use resources like social skills to control each other rather than to build friendships, the group system will change. The group will have a different character.

So far we have emphasized rules and resources as tools for action. However, they are equally important as tools for interpreting what is occurring in group interaction. For example, consider the group system in the previous paragraph. If a member teases another member for always being late for meetings, the teasing will probably be interpreted as friendly chiding. However, in another group in which there has been considerable tension and in which there is a strong norm favoring punctuality, the same teasing may be construed as a rather "catty" personal attack. Rules are tools for interpreting others' behavior. We think about their behavior in light of related rules. The same is true of resources. If members regularly use their special expert knowledge to influence the group, then making a suggestion is likely to be interpreted as an attempt to be seen as an expert.

A third point is one which makes structurational theory quite different from many other points of view: Structures—rules and resources—are produced and reproduced along with the system. As Anthony Giddens wrote: "Structures are both the medium and the outcome of action." To illustrate what this means, think about rules and resources in groups you have been in. In every group there are somewhat different rules. Even for very common rules, groups develop their own versions and special interpretations. For example, majority voting is often used to make decisions. But this rule differs in different groups. In some groups "majority" really means "the two most important members," while in others it is actually "more than half the members." In some groups a majority vote is interpreted as an expression of democracy; in other groups it is viewed as a power move by which the majority can force the minority to do what it does not want to do. And resources, too, vary from group to group. A college degree is a source of influence in a group of teachers. In a group of steel workers it may actually be a disadvantage.

So each group has, in effect, its own rules and resources. The group's particular structure of rules and resources is created and maintained by members' interaction. For example, a few members might become friends and decide this helped their work. They would then encourage others to build friendships, creating a norm favoring close relationships among group members. As this norm continues to be followed, it becomes a permanent, prominent feature of the group. At some point, however, members may begin to believe that maintaining close friendships saps their energy and prevents the group from functioning as well as it could. If they begin to place less emphasis on building relationships, the norm will become less important. At the extreme, members may stop using the norm altogether, and it will no longer be part of the group's structure. And so it is with every group. The group copies its own versions of some rules and resources and develops others on its own. And, knowingly or unconsciously, it may change or eliminate rules and resources.

Rules and resources do not exist independent of an interaction system. They only continue to exist in a group if members use them. So systems and structures have a reciprocal relationship. Members use rules and resources to create the group system, but rules and resources can only exist by virtue of being used in the system. In producing and reproducing the group system, people are producing and reproducing rules and resources.

As we have noted, a group can change, reinterpret, and even eliminate rules and resources. Sometimes this is done by conscious choices of members. A member might, for example, argue that majority voting procedures are unfair to the minority and convince the group to adopt motions only if all members favor them. But more often structural change comes about without planning or awareness. Members may just gradually drop or reinterpret a norm, without realizing they are doing so. A major interest of research into structuration is how members initiate, maintain, and change rules and resources. We will discuss this in more detail below.

A fourth and final point is needed to qualify what has been said up to here: Members do not totally control the process of structuration. Members' activities are influenced by external forces which limit what they can do. For example, if the group is assigned a very difficult task, members cannot organize their work in any way they please. To be successful, they must structure their work so it is appropriate for the task. The task places limits on their choices. External factors, including the nature of group tasks or goals, the group's general environment (including the larger organization the group is part of), and members' level of competence are limits. Members' actions can "restructure" these external forces. For example, the group may break the difficult task into smaller, easier subtasks. This redefinition changes the task to some extent. But the task still exerts a powerful defining force on group interaction.

Another limitation on members' control over structuration processes is the actions of other members. Interaction, by definition, is beyond the control of any single actor. Members' actions often blend together so that interaction unfolds in unexpected directions. For example, in a conflict one member might make an attempt at reconciliation. If another member attacks the response, it may make the first counter attack, resulting in an escalating conflict no one wanted in the first place. External forces and uncontrollable interaction dynamics can result in *unanticipated consequences* of structuration.

So, according to the theory of structuration, the groups that appear so "real" and stable to us are actually continuously in flux. They are continuously being produced and reproduced by members' interactions. It is the job of researchers to explain how this process of production and reproduction leads to stability or change in groups. An example of structuration processes will serve to illustrate many of the points we have just made.

A Case

The group in question was dedicated to teaching newly-graduated methods of diagnosing psychological ailments. It was composed of three psychiatrists who had M.D. degrees, a psychologist, and two social workers. The group's leader, Jerry, was a "take-charge" person who fully intended to create a democratically-run group, but ended up as the head of a small clique which made decisions in an authoritarian manner.

All of the members of the group were very competent in their areas. When the medical school created the group, the deans hand-picked strong, competent people who had shown exceptional teaching ability. The deans told the group it was free to develop the program as it saw best, provided members could get grants from public and private agencies to support their operations. Jerry had numerous contacts and was able to get a very large grant to support the project for its first two years.

When the group first met to plan the program, it was decided that all decisions would be made "rationally." That is, a decision would be accepted only if *all* members were satisfied it was sound. Jerry was appointed "leader" of the group, but there was an understanding that he would encourage participation and equalize influence over the decision. And Jerry made an active effort to do this. He strongly believed that the best decisions were those with the most member input. He read books on group communication, and did everything he could to facilitate group interaction.

However, there were forces working against democratic control of the group. All members had worked extensively in medical settings and had great respect for people with M.D. degrees. This gave the three members of the group with M.D. degrees more clout than those without them. Further, members knew that continuation of their program depended on garnering funds. This gave Jerry something of an advantage, because he was the primary source of funds for the project.

As a result of these two forces, the psychologist and social workers (the non-M.D.'s) tended to give in to the psychiatrists (the M.D.'s). The non-M.D.'s did not speak as often or as long as the M.D.'s. They were also more tentative than the M.D.'s and let their ideas "die" or be swept aside more easily than did the M.D.'s. These were not large effects, but they did result in a less democratic group than was originally envisioned. And the non-M.D.'s felt they had less influence than the M.D.'s. They were frustrated, and often talked with one another about their lack of influence. In meetings they exchanged meaningful glances that implied "here we go again!", when M.D.'s expressed their opinions.

Jerry noticed that non-M.D.'s contributed less than M.D.'s. He also spoke with one of the social workers, and she expressed her dissatisfaction. He attempted to involve the non-M.D.'s by calling on them, and setting aside special periods for "brainstorming." But this undermined democracy still further, because Jerry was, in effect, directing members to contribute. The non-M.D.'s came to depend on Jerry as an advocate. Ironically, this contributed to his power in the group.

Jerry's manner of running meetings also contributed to the development of a pecking order in the group. He was a rather forceful participant, and talked more than other members. The more a member talks, the more influence he or she has. Jerry also attempted to "help" the group by rephrasing and redefining ideas in order to improve them. Despite his good intentions, Jerry rephrased other members' contributions in line with his own thinking. Without realizing it, he influenced decision-making. And members (especially non-M.D.'s) came to value and count on his rephrasings, reinforcing Jerry's influence. The M.D.'s began to change non-M.D. ideas, to talk longer and more confidently, and to interrupt non-M.D.'s more frequently.

The end result was movement toward a more authoritarian leadership style. The group developed a "pecking order," in which M.D.'s were accorded higher status than non-M.D.'s. The non-M.D.'s lost the confidence necessary for maintaining equal democratic participation. Non-M.D.'s were dissatisfied with the group. Conflict increased and was not handled well, resulting in a tense climate. An outside observer would see a divided group, with clear differentiations in status and power. In spite of its members' best intentions, this group structured an authoritarian climate.

In the psychological training group the following elements can be discerned: The *system* is the pattern of interaction among members, specifically the "pecking order" and communication network. The *structures* in this case are (a) *rules* related to "rational" decision-making, the communication and phrasing of proposals and ideas, and contributions of "superior" members and (b) *resources,* including medical degrees, access to funding, and Jerry's interaction skills. *External forces* that influenced group interaction include the task set for the group by the deans and the need to garner funds to keep the project going.

Structuration processes reinforced and reproduced the rules and resources related to authoritarian group structures. Rules relating to preference for contributions of "superior" members and resources such as medical degrees were supported and validated in the group. At the same time other rules and resources that would support democratic decision-making were not emphasized or reproduced. So, norms like those favoring equal time for each member to talk did not evolve and resources such as the amount of energy and commitment members have were not valued as much as those favoring evolution of status orders.

Structuration led to a group quite different from what members hoped for. Their interaction "got away" from them, producing unintended consequences. In part this was due to the pressure of external forces, particularly the need to get funds to continue the project. This pressure encouraged members to turn to Jerry who could, they thought, "get the job done." The structure also "got away" from members because changes happened very gradually. The shift from a democratic to an authoritarian group did not occur all at once. It emerged slowly, as rules and resources favoring authoritarian operations were used more and more (and therefore reproduced), while rules favoring democracy were used less. And when democratic structures were employed, they were often justified on the grounds that proposals had to be put in "rational" format so that all proposals would be given equal weight. A democratic veneer was put on an autocratic move. The effects of structuration often "sneak up" on groups, because they are so gradual.

Structure Development

Where do structures come from and why do groups choose the structures they do? Occasionally groups create their own rules and resources. For example, some groups develop unique code words for sensitive topics. One group developed a code word for its higher level supervision. Group members called her "Waldo" when outsiders were present, so the outsiders wouldn't know members were talking about her.

But these instances are relatively rare. Usually, groups borrow or adopt rules and resources from other groups or social institutions. Members draw on their own experiences and on what they have learned. They try to do things as they have seen them done in other groups. As a result, we encounter different versions of the same rules and resources in many groups. For example, various interpretations and adaptations of majority voting are found in many groups. The same is true of education as a resource. It is a widely-respected source of influence, although it is interpreted differently and had different weight in various groups. When rules and resources are widely-accepted and used, they become *institutions* in their own right. Majority rule, for example, is often equated with democracy.

So an important part of structuration is the groups' *appropriation* of social institutions for its own uses. Groups fashion themselves after other groups and after their members' ideas about institutions. In doing this the group creates its own version of these institutions. The strength of a social institution—determined by how widespread it is and how much a part of the culture it is—has an important influence on how likely it is to be reproduced. A structure drawn from an institution has a clear reference point, and will be relatively long-lived, even if it is seldom used. Structures created uniquely by the group must be used quite often, or they will die out. The more "institutionalized" the structure is, the less it must be used if it is to survive in the group.

But what are institutions, anyway? Although the majority rule procedure is very common, there is no such thing as a "general" or "abstract" majority rule principle. Majority rule only exists in the groups that use it. The reason majority rule seems to be an abstraction is that it is widely-used and that it is taught and talked about in the abstract. However, this is only an illusion. The majority rule procedure exists only insofar as it is used in our society. And survival of majority rule and other institutions depends on their structuration by groups. If groups (and other social organizations) stopped using majority rule altogether, it would pass out of existence. So groups reproduce social institutions as they produce and reproduce themselves.

Why do groups choose the particular structures they do? There are at least three reasons. In some cases rules and resources are used because the group gives members negative reinforcement if they "deviate." For example, in a group which employed majority rule, a member who attempted to seize control would likely meet with disapproval from the group, and perhaps would be asked to leave. Another reason members use rules and resources is that they are traditions in the group. Often we follow traditions without thinking. They are second nature, used by habit. For example, if a group has always taken a vote to confirm important decisions, members will often continue to do so without really thinking. A final, and probably the most important reason members use rules and resources is because they are useful—they enable members to achieve their goals and build the group. Resources like status, a leadership position, or special knowledge are also useful for members, and so they form an important part of the group system.

Influences on Structuration

What factors influence structuration? Three types of influences on structuration can be identified:

(1) *Member characteristics and orientations.* Members' motivations in the group influence which structures they use and how they use them. Members who are primarily concerned with the group and with getting the job done, will use structures in very different ways than will members whose goal is to realize their own individual interests or to control the group. Group-orientated members will generally use structures in "the spirit" of the rule or resource. Members concerned primarily with themselves or with controlling the group often turn structures in very different directions, as Jerry did in the psychological diagnostic group.

Members' characteristic interaction styles also influence structuration. An autocratic leader will use majority voting procedures very differently than will a democratic leader. Other stylistic differences, such as differences in group conflict management styles, will also influence how structures are used.

Members' degree of knowledge and experience with structures also affect structuration. For example, groups which have had a lot of training in decision-making procedures will incorporate techniques like nominal group procedure into their structures with more success than will less knowledgeable groups.

(2) *External factors.* As mentioned above, forces beyond members' control also influence structuration. Factors such as the nature of group task, the effects of larger organizations on the group, and the talents of personnel assigned to the group limit what the group can do.

(3) *Structural dynamics*. A third influence on structuration are the relationships between different rules and resources. Two main types of relationships can be discerned:

(a) *Mediation* occurs when one structure influences the operation or interpretation of another. In effect, the first structure controls the second. For example, because business is such an important part of American culture, it is common for groups to use an economic cost-return metaphor to guide their behavior. Alternatives are rated with respect to gains or losses they promise, and decisions are made with formal or informal calculations. This even affects how value-related decisions are made. Often groups faced with value choices do not debate ethics or higher ends. Instead they decide which values are important, rate each alternative on the values, and calculate a "utility" score for the alternatives. That alternative with the highest score is chosen. This converts an ethical choice into a "rational" calculation. Economic thinking mediates and controls ethical thinking.

(b) *Contradiction* occurs when two structures, each of which is important to the operation of the group, work against each other. Contradictions in structures create conflicts and dilemmas in groups. Sometimes these take some time to show up, but when they do, they can disrupt the group and often stimulate change. There was a contradiction in the psychological diagnosis group discussed above. Democratic principles were very important to members, and they used these to justify their actions and as behavioral ideals. However, the group operated according to an autocratic structure. The contradiction between democratic values and autocratic operations set up tensions in the group. The members who were left out of decisions resented it, and over time this developed into a major split in the group. Eventually there was a prolonged conflict and the two social workers quit. Contradictions fueled change in the group.

Member characteristics, external forces, and structural dynamics combine to influence how groups structure themselves. To explain structuration it is necessary to account for the influence of these forces on members' actions.

Studying Structuration

Why is it useful to study structuration? There are three reasons to study structuration. First, it gives a more accurate picture of group processes than traditional social scientific theories. The theory of structuration accepts the fact that group members actively control their behavior but it also recognizes limitations and constraints on members' activities. The theory attempts to show how action influences the operation of "deterministic" forces and how external forces constrain action. This can produce important insights into group behavior, as the case of the psychological diagnosis group shows. Many of the points raised there could only have been uncovered through analysis of structuration.

A second advantage of the structurational model is its recognition of the importance of gradual change and unintended consequences of members' behavior. Because of its emphasis on the continuous production and reproduction of social systems and structures, the theory of structuration makes us aware of how small, incremental changes can mount up to a major change in the system. It is well-equipped to study these gradual developments. In addition, the theory explains how structuring processes can lead to outcomes completely different from those intended by the members. These surprises often mark turning points in group development.

Third, and perhaps most important, the theory of structuration suggests ways for members—especially those with little power—to change their groups. The theory points out how members can effect change by altering their behavior in what appear to be small ways. If persisted in, these small changes can alter the group's directions. This strategy is often particularly effective (for members with little or no power) because small moves are less noticeable to powerful members who might squelch attempts at change. In the psychological diagnosis group, the group was temporarily turned in a more democratic direction with this strategy. One of the social workers decided that she would stop allowing Jerry to rephrase her ideas. She insisted that they be stated as she said them. This made Jerry more conscientious of preserving other members' ideas, and for awhile the group operated in a more democratic fashion. Eventually, however, a crisis arose and members (without meaning to) again fell back into their old habits. Jerry was a key figure in handling the crisis, and members continued to turn to him for help after it had passed. As a result, the social worker was unable to sustain her initiative. If changes such as this could have been reproduced, the group could have changed. However, forces operating in the autocratic direction were stronger.

Decision-making methods like Nominal Group Technique, brainstorming, and Reflective Thinking are often employed to structure group interaction and change how groups make decisions. However, their effectiveness depends on how these structures are produced and reproduced in the group. If used as designed, these techniques can equalize power and contribute to more rational decision-making. However, they can also be used to control the group. On one occasion Jerry decided to use brainstorming in the psychological diagnosis group. However, since he ran the session himself, non-M.D.'s were hesitant to contribute and censored their ideas. Although, the group believed, it was increasing participation by using brainstorming, the end result was reproduction of the same autocratic patterns.

The theory of structuration has the potential to help members understand and control the forces that influence group interaction. Its goal is to make people aware of the part they play in the creation and maintenance of structures they would otherwise take for granted.

Bibliography

Joseph P. Folger and Marshall Scott Poole, *Working Through Conflict*. Glenview, Il: Scott, Foresman, 1983.

Anthony Giddens, *New Rules of Sociological Method*. New York: Basic Books, 1976.

Anthony Giddens, *Central Problems in Social Theory*. Berkeley, CA: University of California Press, 1979.

Marshall Scott Poole, David R. Seibold, and Robert D. McPhee, "Group Decision-Making as a Structurational Process," *Quarterly Journal of Speech,* 1985, *71,* 74–102.

Marshall Scott Poole, David R. Seibold, and Robert D. McPhee, "A Structurational Approach to Theory-Building in Decision-Making Research." In R. Y. Hirokawa and M. S. Poole (Eds.) *Communication and Group Decision-Making*. Beverly Hills: Sage, 1986.

Self-Disclosure and Small Group Interaction

Lawrence B. Rosenfeld

To *disclose* is to make known, show, reveal. *Self*-disclosure, then, is the act of making yourself known, of revealing yourself. The risk of letting other people know who you are—*really are*—is often overwhelming, and the rule-of-thumb for interacting is, "be superficial when you talk about yourself." The fears associated with being self-revealing, with being naked and exposed in front of others, may keep you from dropping your masks. Unfortunately, this means a loss of the benefits associated with risking self-disclosure.

The Role of Self-Disclosure in Human Interaction

The important role of self-disclosing communication in your relationships with others may be explained with reference to a model called the *Johari Window,* developed by *Jo*seph Luft and *Har*ry Ingram. Consider, for a moment, that the following box, Figure 1, contains everything there is to know about you, including your likes, dislikes, beliefs, values, experiences, wishes, hopes, desires, and needs.

Are you aware of everything there is to know about yourself? If you are typical, the answer is a resounding "no." You learn new things about yourself almost daily, whether it's a skill you didn't know you could perform, or information you were unaware you knew. So, there are things you know about yourself, and things you don't know about yourself. Figure 1 can be altered to represent this.

Now, other people can be brought into the picture. Just as you are aware of some things about yourself and unaware of others, the same holds true for other people in relationship to you: they are aware of some things, and unaware of others. Figure 1 can be divided to show this.

Finally, if Figures 2 and 3 are superimposed, the result is everything there is to know about you divided into four quadrants: known or unknown by you, and known or unknown by others.

The first quadrant, representing what is known to both you and others, is the *open area* or *arena*. What is interaction like in the arena? Considering that the information in this area—your feelings, ideas, behaviors, and other

This essay appears here in print for the first time. All Rights Reserved. Permission to reprint must be obtained from the publisher and the author. Lawrence B. Rosenfeld is affiliated with the Department of Speech Communication, University of North Carolina at Chapel Hill.

Everything about you

Figure 1.

Known to self	Not known to self

Figure 2.

Known to others
Not known to others

Figure 3.

	Known to self	Not known to self
Known to others	1 OPEN	2 BLIND
Not known to others	3 HIDDEN	4 UNKNOWN

Figure 4.

aspects of who you are—is shared by both you and the other person, interaction is easy, comfortable, and takes little energy. There is mutual understanding and shared information.

The second quadrant, representing what is unknown to you yet known to others, is called the *blind area*. You are blind to some things about yourself of which others are aware. Interaction in this area is not as comfortable as interaction in the arena. Your effectiveness as a communicator may be diminished when the other person knows things about you that you don't know. My favorite example of this occurred in an English class I took as an undergraduate. The professor wore glasses which he constantly took off and put on during his lectures. He may have been unaware of his nervous habit, but we certainly weren't. His effectiveness as a lecturer decreased drastically the day several students started a pool in which we bet on how many times he would remove and replace his glasses during one class period!

The third quadrant, representing what you know about yourself and others don't know, is called the *hidden area*. This is the area which contains all your secrets and takes most of your energy. Keeping things hidden from others requires being on your guard, putting energy into creating and maintaining a facade, a protective front. The result is separateness—you and others are far apart—and inhibited interaction.

The fourth quadrant, the *unknown area,* is sometimes difficult to understand: if you don't know "it" (whatever "it" is) about yourself, and others don't know "it" about you, how do you know "it" exists at all? "It" is known only after "it" moves into one of the other quadrants (and either you know "it," the other knows "it," or you both know "it"). What is important is that whatever "it" is, you can be sure there is information about yourself in the unknown area. Have you ever been surprised that you could do something you didn't know you could do? This often happens when people participate in sports or attempt art projects and find that they have a "natural talent." Your natural talent was in the unknown area until it was realized.

Where does self-disclosure fit into the Johari Window? Self-disclosure, and its companion communication behavior feedback, are two means for increasing the size of the arena, the quadrant where interaction is most comfortable, efficient, and effective.

Feedback, receiving information about yourself from others, decreases your blind area and increases your arena. The other person tells you, "You end almost every sentence with the question, 'You know?'," and this new information about yourself moves from your blind area into the arena.

Self-disclosure decreases your hidden area and increases your arena. You tell the other person one of your secrets, and the information moves from your hidden to your open area. The energy you used to keep the information hidden is released, which might account for why people report feeling "lighter" and as if a "weight was taken off their shoulders."

The effectiveness of feedback and self-disclosure are not as simple as the previous two paragraphs imply. Whether the blind and hidden areas decrease and the arena increases depends on the degree to which you are willing to receive feedback and to disclose, and how large your arena is in the first place.

Consider what you would be like with a very small arena and, consequently, a large blind area (unreceptive to feedback), a large hidden area (unwilling to self-disclose), and a large unknown area. You might appear to be an uncommunicative or secretive person, aloof perhaps, certainly unwilling to take risks, and demonstrating little self-understanding. Interacting with a person with a large arena, your smaller arena would dictate the topics of conversation. For example, if the other person chooses a topic of conversation to which you are blind, a defensive, hostile reaction on your part may result, such as, "I don't end every sentence with 'You know?'!" Similarly, if the other person chooses a topic which is in your hidden area, you are likely to offer a neutral or defensive reaction and switch the conversation to a different topic.

What if you have a small blind area (receptive to feedback) and a large hidden one (unwilling to self-disclose)? You might distrust other people and, therefore, fear exposure. However, because you are willing to listen, you appear very supportive during initial interactions. In the end, however, your lack of disclosure would become an issue (especially if the other person discloses to you), and the other person would most likely view you as detached and distrustful.

In the reverse situation, with a large blind area (unreceptive to feedback) and a small hidden one (willing to disclose), you might appear self-centered and lacking in self-awareness. In the end, your desire to keep center stage by talking about yourself, and your unwillingness to encourage others to share, may cause resentment.

Of course, the perfect mate for the person with small blind and large hidden areas is the person with large blind and small hidden areas. The first person can sit comfortably and listen while the second rattles on and on!

If your arena is large, if you are both receptive to feedback and willing to disclose, you have the best opportunity for a productive relationship. You trust others, so you seek their thoughts and opinions as well as share your own. You may have trouble, however, with initial defensive reactions to your openness. Most people aren't comfortable with openness, at least not at first, since it is uncommon.

A Definition of Self-Disclosure

So far, the words "self-disclosure," "disclosure," "openness," and "revealing" have been used interchangeably. It's time to be specific. In order for your communication act to be considered self-disclosing it must meet the following criteria: (1) it must contain personal information about yourself, (2) this personal information must be verbally communicated, and (3) the target of this verbally communicated information must be another person. This definition excludes confessions (such as when personal information is elicited by force, threat, or drugs), unintentionally revealing behavior (such as Freudian slips and nervous tics), and non-disclosures (such as lying and concealment). Also implicit in this definition is the notion that the information disclosed is generally unavailable from sources other than you.

There are other dimensions of self-disclosure worth considering, although there is no clear agreement on whether any or all of them should be part of the definition.

Honesty

Self-disclosive acts of communication have an honesty dimension. While lying may not qualify as disclosure, there exist degrees of honesty. For example, do you have to reveal *everything* about a secret to be considered honest? Do you have to be absolutely certain that what you say is honest, or can you be "almost" sure? How confident do you have to feel that what you say about yourself is a true reflection of who you are?

Intimacy

Self-disclosive acts of communication vary in the degree to which they are intimate. Is there a point at which the communication is "superficial" and, therefore, not an act of disclosure? And if there is, who determines whether a given act of communication is intimate, the sender or the receiver? You might consider your statement, "I don't like to work in groups because they bring out the competitiveness in me," as highly intimate, but other group members might consider it low in intimacy. Who's right? Who gets to define the level of intimacy of your message?

There is some agreement among people about which topics are more intimate than others. A large number of topics have been categorized according to their level of intimacy. For example, in the general topic area of love and dating, "the age of women/men I like to date" has a low level of intimacy, "the kinds of compliments I give to women/men" has a moderate level, and "bad experiences I have had in love affairs" has a very high level of intimacy.

Besides being a function of the topic, intimacy is also a function of the situation in which the communication takes place. For example, the most intimate disclosures are likely to occur when you and a close friend are alone in a private setting, and least likely to occur when you meet a group of strangers in a public setting. Given this, is it reasonable to consider a topic of moderate intimacy disclosed to strangers in the library as more intimate than the same topic disclosed to a friend in your home?

Intent

Although the definition of self-disclosure includes a consideration of intentionality, it is clear that intentionality comes in degrees, that a message isn't simply intentional or unintentional. You may be fully aware of disclosing some pieces of information, but feel less "in control" talking about other aspects of who you are. You may hear yourself talking and wonder, "Why am I telling all this?" The decision to disclose may have been intentional, but particular aspects of what you disclose may be spontaneous, less intentional. Is it reasonable to consider some aspects of your communication intentional (and acts of self-disclosure) and other aspects unintentional (and not acts of self-disclosure) when they occur together?

Amount and Breadth

Two dimensions that distinguish acts of self-disclosure from each other are amount, the percentage of total time talking that may be considered disclosive, and breadth, the number of topics about which you disclose. Along with intimacy, the second best predictor of someone perceiving you as "highly disclosive" is your overall number of self-descriptive statements per minute of conversation.

Breadth, though not an aspect of a single message, may be used to make judgments about how several disclosive messages relate to each other. Do your self-disclosures concern only one or a few topics when you talk with members of your group (little breadth), or do they cover a large variety of topics (great breadth)? It is common to have different people for different topics of disclosure, for example, one friend with whom to talk about your family, and another with whom to talk about school.

It should be clear from the discussion of self-disclosure so far that this type of communication is rare. Estimates are that only two to five percent of your total communication is self-disclosive. Besides being rare, there are other distinguishing features: it usually occurs in a dyad and infrequently in a group setting (unless the group has openness as one of its goals or is formed with therapeutic aims); it usually occurs in a positive social context characterized by trust; it is usually symmetrical, that is, the intimacy, amount, and breadth of disclosure is often the same for those disclosing; and it usually progresses from less to more intimate, and from highly positive to more negative.

Reasons for Self-Disclosing

There are both personal and relational reasons for self-disclosing. Each reason points to a purpose and benefit of this type of communication.

Catharsis

Sometimes it is necessary to "get something off your chest." The stress caused by lying, maintaining secrets, or not sharing information—whether good and exciting or bad and depressing—can be reduced by sharing openly. You probably have had the experience of "feeling better," less stressed, after sharing information about yourself with a trusted friend.

Self-Clarification

Talking out a problem or an idea with others often helps you clarify your own thoughts and feelings. It is common to discover your own opinion *while sharing it* with others, or learning how intensely you feel about something by listening to your tone of voice. Groups often arrive at better decisions than individuals working alone because of this continual process of self-clarification. Defending your ideas helps clarify them for others and yourself, while providing information that stimulates further discussion.

Self-Validation

If you disclose to someone in the hopes of obtaining agreement for how you see yourself, you are seeking self-validation. The confirmation of *who you are* is rarely sought in a straightforward way, which might be embarrassing, but in an indirect way. For example, the self-disclosure, "I haven't called my parents in a long time. I'm an ungrateful child!," probably is seeking confirmation that you are *not* ungrateful. Feedback such as, "No you're not. You've been very busy lately," is the self-validation you most likely want.

Reciprocity

Known as the "reciprocity effect," self-disclosure has been found to beget self-disclosure. Because of this, you may disclose to another person to encourage her or him to begin sharing.

Disclosure reciprocity is one of the most thoroughly supported findings in self-disclosure research. Why do people respond to your disclosures with disclosures of their own? One explanation is that your disclosures serve as a reward for the other person since they signal that you like and trust her or him. The other person is complimented and communicates, "I like and trust you, too," by disclosing in return.

Another explanation considers that liking is not always a prerequisite for reciprocal disclosure. This explanation argues that underlying the reciprocity norm is the desire to preserve equality in a relationship. Therefore, if you disclose and signal that you are investing yourself in the relationship, the other person discloses to keep the level of investment equal.

A third explanation considers those cases where there is neither trust nor liking, yet reciprocity takes place. Why would someone reciprocate in the absence of both trust and liking? It may be that your disclosures serve as a model or guide for the behavior of the other person. Your behavior defines, perhaps, how the other person should behave, what's expected or appropriate.

Regardless which of these three explanations is best, the point is that your disclosures encourage the other person to disclose, and you can use this fact to get others to talk about themselves.

Impression Formation

By choosing what to disclose you can create a particular impression of who you are. Positive disclosures may reveal your warmth and caring nature, or your willingness to work hard. On the other hand, by selectively revealing your after-school work obligations, you may wish to create the impression that you are busy and cannot be "bothered" in the evening with group meetings.

Relationship Maintenance

Self-disclosure is useful for keeping relationship partners up-to-date with changes occurring in your life. Without this information, those with whom you interact are likely to lose touch with you, fail to see you for the person you are *now*. Relationships may become stale and shallow as old information is used over and over again to make decisions, or conflicts may result. For example, if your "free" weekend to meet with your group suddenly gets taken up with visiting parents, this information must be communicated to group members to maintain a good relationship with them.

Relationship Enhancement

Disclosing to another person tells him or her, "I like you. I trust you. You are important to me." It serves as a compliment because it indicates, "I am willing to take important risks with you." The *act* of disclosing may enhance your relationship as much or more than the actual content of your disclosures! Research with wives and husbands, for example, provides support for this point: both spouses consider mutual disclosure important for their relationship regardless of the significance of the topic.

Disclosures also enhance your relationships when the topics disclosed are new ones, or the information expands what is already known by the other person. Building on your reciprocal disclosures, relational growth is the result of your sharing.

Social Control

Self-disclosure may increase your control over the people with whom you interact. For example, disclosing the information that you plan on being in the library that evening may increase the odds that the group decides to have you gather references for your group's bibliography.

Although most disclosure occurs in one-on-one situations, disclosure in groups is not uncommon. Reasons for disclosing in a group are determined primarily by whether the group is composed of friends or strangers. If the group is composed of friends, relationship maintenance and enhancement, self-clarification, and reciprocity are the three primary reasons for disclosing (in their order of importance). The primary objective for disclosing with friends is to facilitate relational growth, with reciprocity serving as the means to allow this growth to happen. Self-clarification as a goal for self-disclosing with a group of friends indicates that friendships serve personal as well as relational needs: friendships provide the security needed to engage in self-exploration.

The most important reasons for disclosing with groups of strangers are reciprocity and impression formation. You disclose certain aspects of who you are to encourage others to share who they are, all the while creating the impression you think will work best for you in the new situation. Your goal is two-fold: gain information about who these other group members are (to be able to make predictions for their behavior, understand their wants and needs, and make decisions concerning how you might best interact with them), and help them form the best impression of who you are, that is, the impression that best suits your needs.

Reasons for Avoiding Self-Disclosure

Regardless of the benefits of self-disclosure, such as reduced stress, closer relationships, and increased understanding, most people in most situations choose to avoid openness, to defend their dishonesty as a virtue ("The truth would only hurt you! It's for your own good!") and settle for superficial relationships. The risks must be enormous and the fears terrifying for people to live lives summarized by the phrase, "better safe than sorry." What are the common fears?

> I am afraid to be who I am with you . . . I am afraid to be judged by you, I am afraid you will reject me. I am afraid you will say bad things about me. I am afraid you will hurt me. I am afraid, if I really am myself, you won't love me—and I need your love so badly that I will play the roles you expect me to play and be the person that pleases you, even though I lose myself in the process. (Wood, 1976)

> I am afraid to tell you who I am, because, if I tell you who I am, you may not like who I am, and it's all that I have. (Powell, 1968)

Rejection

The primary fear responsible for avoiding openness is the fear of rejection. Emphasized by both Wood and Powell, the fear of rejection taps into the most personal fear someone could have: I am unlovable, undesirable, unworthy of your attention.

If you fear that you might say something that could lead to rejection—whether wittingly or unwittingly, whether you think the disclosure is negative or not—you are apt to remain superficial and quiet, perhaps withdrawn. For example, informing your group that you need more time to complete your work, that you're having trouble understanding the articles you're reading, might strike you as a not-too-negative disclosure, if negative at all. However, group members may react as if what you revealed is very negative, and may go so far as to have you removed from the group, reject you for further interaction.

Projection of a Negative Image

If you are typical, you could communicate things about yourself that might lead to your projection of a negative image, whether it's the childhood pranks that were illegal or the accumulation of D and F grades. This information could reduce others' respect for you and, perhaps, lower your self-esteem. In a society which stresses perfection, any admission of a weakness or a problem is the same as admitting to being less than perfect. And anything less than perfect is not good enough. So, your facade gets thicker, your image more polished, and the person behind the mask rarely is exposed.

Decreased Satisfaction with the Relationship

Satisfaction often is dependent on "going along with the crowd," agreeing with group norms and demands without really being in agreement. You may be familiar with the expression, "You have to go along to get along." Communicating your feelings when they seem to clash with how the group feels may result in a change in your relationship with group members: you may be labeled a "deviant," and members may interact with you in a less satisfying way than before your disclosure. You may become the group's scapegoat or object of ridicule—a very high price to pay for sharing your feelings!

Loss of Control

One of the benefits of self-disclosure is that it may be useful for gaining control of a situation; it can, however, also lead to a loss of control. If you admit to group members that your joke telling is the way you reduce your stress, you have lost the usefulness of this tactic the next time you're anxious. The others will see you as anxious when you tell a joke, and not as funny.

Disclosure Might Hurt the Other Person

Sometimes referred to as the Great Lie Theory, this reason for avoiding disclosure argues that the truth would hurt the other person or have negative consequences for the group. More often than not, the person being protected is the one who chooses not to disclose! The would-be discloser probably fears what others will think of her or him and not what the disclosures reveal.

Lying Is More Advantageous

In a society where it is expected that politicians, used car salespeople, and almost anyone else will lie to look good and achieve their goals, it's hard to see the value in communicating openly. "Lying is the only way to get ahead" appears to be a contemporary motto. Regardless of the drawbacks to lying, such as the increased stress associated with hiding secrets and having to remember who knows what and who is likely to talk to whom, honesty is rarely seen as the best policy.

Self-Disclosing Is a Sign of Emotional Imbalance

The current emphasis on being "cool," detached, objective, and neutral, sets the stage for seeing disclosure as a sign of being "overly emotional" or "unstable." A discloser may be labeled an "exhibitionist" as the reward for risking disclosing important and personal information. The fear of being labeled "crazy" is not limited to men who were taught not to cry or to feel tender emotions, and to adopt as their model the Western hero who speaks few words and keeps everything bottled up inside. The fear is also a real one for women taught not to express their anger or other "masculine" emotions, and to adopt as their model the woman who, like a child, does not speak unless spoken to.

Self-Disclosure Is a Public Commitment

The last fear associated with disclosure considers what happens when you reveal something to another person, i.e., "in public," that makes it clear you should change your behavior or commit yourself to some particular action. Telling someone, "I smoke/drink/eat too much," makes it necessary for you to *do* something about your smoking/drinking/eating.

Assessing Your Willingness to Disclose and Encourage Feedback

Before considering gender differences in self-disclosure and the characteristics of those people to whom you are most likely to disclose, take a moment to assess your own willingness to disclose and to encourage feedback in your group.

Self-Disclosure Questionnaire

The following questionnaire contains two parts, one related to your willingness to disclose, the other related to your receptivity to feedback. Each part contains ten items. Complete all ten; do not leave any out. *Be honest!* Your results are only as useful as you are honest.

Each instrument has four columns, one for each member of your group. If your group has more than five members (you plus four others), add the columns required.

Part I

For each item on the first part indicate how much you are willing to disclose to each group member. Use a scale from 1 to 5. The endpoints of the scale are defined as follows: (1) I would disclose very little, if at all, and only superficial information; and (5) I would disclose a great deal of personal information. Use the points between 1 and 5 to indicate varying degrees of willingness to disclose.

	Member:	*Member:*	*Member:*	*Member:*
1. personal goals				
2. values				
3. strengths				
4. weaknesses				
5. fears				
6. ideas				
7. disagreements				
8. agreements				
9. positive feelings				
10. negative feelings				
TOTALS				

Part II

For each item on the second part indicate how much you are willing to encourage feedback about yourself from each group member. Use a scale from 1 to 5. The endpoints of the scale are defined as follows: (1) I would refuse or resist feedback, and (5) I would encourage a great deal of feedback. Use the points between 1 and 5 to indicate varying degrees of encouragement of feedback.

	Member:	*Member:*	*Member:*	*Member:*
1. personal goals				
2. values				
3. strengths				
4. weaknesses				
5. fears				
6. ideas				
7. disagreements				
8. agreements				
9. positive feelings				
10. negative feelings				
TOTALS				

The possible range for each total score is 10 to 50, with lower scores indicative of an unwillingness to disclose (part 1) or to encourage feedback (part 2), and higher scores indicative of a willingness to disclose and to encourage feedback. Based on responses to the questionnaire from students in several colleges, a cut-off score of 36 separates "high" from "low" scores. Therefore, a total score of 36 and above on part 1, combined with a total score of 36 and above on part 2, indicates a larger than average arena or open area. A total score of 36 and above on part 1, combined with a score below 36 on part 2, indicates an above average willingness to disclose and a below average willingness to encourage feedback. The reverse scoring pattern (below 36 on part 1 and above 36 on part 2) indicates a below average willingness to disclose and an above average willingness to encourage feedback. Finally, scores below

36 on both parts 1 and 2 indicate a smaller than average arena and, consequently, a large unknown area. As scores move further and further away from the cut-off, the descriptions become more and more exaggerated. For example, scores of about 15 on parts 1 and 2 indicate a much smaller arena than scores of about 30, even though both arenas are smaller than average.

An examination of your total scores for each of the other group members should reveal those to whom you are willing (and not willing) to disclose, and those whose feedback you encourage (and discourage). Why are you willing to disclose to some and not others? Why is feedback encouraged from some and not others?

Conditions Affecting Self-Disclosure

To assess your willingness to disclose and to encourage feedback requires an examination of several of your own characteristics as well as those of other members of your group.

Prerequisites for Disclosure

It has already been implied that you are most likely to disclose when your relationship is characterized by trust and liking. There are other conditions which also increase the probability that you'll disclose, such as, perceiving the other person as sincere, warm, and a "good listener." It is also important to perceive the other person as discreet, someone who will treat your disclosures as confidential.

Prerequisites also extend to perceptions of yourself. If you are calm, honest, and feel unprovoked, you are more likely to disclose than under those conditions where you are anxious, feel you need to hide something, or consider yourself pressured into being revealing.

While all these prerequisites are important for both women and men, they are generally more important for women, especially as the topic of conversation becomes more intimate. As the topic becomes less intimate, the prerequisites tend to become less important, and gender differences with respect to the several prerequisites tend to disappear.

Target Gender and Psychological Sex-Type

The other person's gender (anatomical sex, i.e., male or female) and psychological sex-type (i.e., the extent to which she or he exhibits masculine traits, feminine traits, both, or neither) affect your decision to self-disclose. Males prefer female targets; however, the preference is for females with particular psychological sex-types. The most preferred target is an *androgynous female,* that is, a female described as having both masculine and feminine character-istics. Such a person is athletic, independent, forceful, tender, and sensitive. The second most preferred target is a *feminine female,* that is, a female de-scribed as having many feminine and few masculine traits. Such a person is nonathletic, dependent, submissive and, like the androgynous female, tender, gentle, and sensitive. Three targets rejected for self-disclosure are: *masculine males* and *masculine females,* that is, males and females described as domi-nant and insensitive, and *feminine males,* males described as dependent and feminine.

The most preferred target for a female is an *androgynous* person. Whether male or female, such a person is athletic, independent, forceful, tender, and sensitive. The second most preferred target is a *feminine female.* Rejected targets are cross-sexed individuals, that is, *masculine females* and *feminine males.*

Taken together, it appears that the most preferred targets are individuals with both masculine and feminine traits, those described as strong, forceful, and athletic—presumed masculine characteristics—and tender, gentle, and sensitive to others' needs—presumed feminine characteristics. In the absence of a suitable androgynous target, the next most preferred target is a feminine female, a female who does not have the several masculine characteristics, but does have the feminine characteristics of tender, gentle, and sensitive. Clearly rejected are those without feminine characteristics, those described as domi-nant and independent without gentleness or sensitivity, and those who are cross-sexed.

Case Study: Self-Disclosure and Group Cohesion

Self-disclosure in the group setting has been found to relate to a variety of important small group variables, chief among them *cohesion.* Cohesion—the feeling of unity among group members, of being closely knit—is important for a group to be effective and for members to enjoy their experience together. Without cohesion, individual members are unlikely to commit themselves to the group, the task, or each other, and it is common for undesirable tasks (which may include researching articles for the group project or typing the group's bibliography) not to get done.

Prevalent among methods used to generate cohesion are those in which some kind of risk-taking is required, and the most usual form of risk-taking is self-disclosure. Indeed, a great many studies support a positive relationship between self-disclosure and cohesion. Unfortunately, most of these studies consider disclosure in therapy groups and intimate relationships where en-gaging in self-revealing behavior is either required or encouraged. What is the relationship between self-disclosure and cohesion in *classroom groups,* groups that do not have therapy or intimacy as their goal?

To answer this question, members of classroom groups formed to complete a term project were asked to respond to three questionnaires: one measured perceptions of their group's cohesiveness, one measured perceptions of their own disclosure in the group, and one measured perceptions of other group members' disclosures. Analyses focused on possible differences in self-disclosure in groups with high or low cohesion.

The relationship between self-disclosure and cohesion in classroom groups was found to be remarkably different from disclosure in therapy groups and in intimate relationships. In therapy groups and intimate relationships disclosures that are risky—honest, intentional, and often negative—are associated with increased trust, attraction, and cohesion. In the classroom setting, however, *un*intentional and *positive* disclosures (which may not be completely honest) were associated with high cohesion.

An explanation of these results considers group development and group goals in the classroom setting. In early stages of group development disclosures are typically used to establish a topic of common interest, present agreeable personalities, and discuss nonthreatening, noncontroversial issues. Intimate disclosures are inappropriate except in therapy groups where the aim is to develop intimacy quickly. As the classroom group focuses on its educational objectives, personal disclosures unrelated to task matters may be ignored.

The typical academic environment does not require or encourage you to self-disclose at moderate or high levels of intimacy, whether in the classroom interacting with the teacher or in your small group. Also, because intentional disclosure is not required and negative disclosure would be inappropriate, disclosures that do occur are perceived as unintentional and positive. The primary function of these unintentional and positive disclosures appears to be impression formation, which may include "white" lies. The goal of early disclosure is to convince each other that everyone is cooperative and the group will run smoothly—and disclosures that stretch the truth to convey this message are acceptable!

A Final Word

Although revealing personal information has its risks, the potential benefits are at least as great. And without some moderate amount of disclosure, a group may be unable to complete its task: self-disclosure enables members of a group to coordinate their necessary actions and to reduce ambiguity about their intentions and the meaning of their behavior.

Disclosure isn't an all-or-nothing type of communication. The choice of when to disclose, how much to disclose, and what to disclose is yours. You need to consider how important the other group members are to you, whether your disclosures will be treated with respect, whether what you wish to reveal is relevant to the situation, whether you can communicate what you wish to disclose clearly and understandably, and whether the effect of your disclosure will be constructive or destructive.

Self-disclosure is a special kind of sharing, with its own risks and its own rewards. Although it may not be appropriate for every group, for those in which it is, there exists the greatest potential for personal growth and an important experience.

References for Further Study

Chelune, G. J. (1979). Measuring openness in interpersonal communication. In G. J. Chelune (Ed.), *Self-disclosure* (pp. 1–27). San Francisco: Jossey-Bass.

Chelune, G. J. (1981). Toward an empirical definition of self-disclosure: Validation in a single case design. *Western Journal of Speech Communication, 45,* 269–276.

Chelune, G. J., Rosenfeld, L. B., and Waring, E. M. (1986). Spouse disclosure patterns in distressed and nondistressed couples. *American Journal of Family Therapy, 13.4,* 24–32.

Cozby, P. C. (1973). Self-disclosure: A literature review. *Psychological Bulletin, 79,* 73–91.

Derlega, V. J. (Ed.) (1984). *Communication, intimacy, and close relationships.* Orlando, FL: Academic Press.

Derlega, V. J., & Chaikin, A. L. (1975). *What we reveal to others and why.* Englewood Cliffs, NJ: Prentice-Hall.

Derlega, V. J., Durham, B., Gockel, B., & Sholis, D. (1981). Sex-differences in self-disclosure: effects of topic content, friendships, and partner's sex. *Sex Roles, 7,* 433–448.

Drescher, S., Burlingame, G., & Fuhriman, A. (1985). Cohesion: An odyssey in empirical understanding. *Small Group Behavior, 16,* 3–30.

Gilbert, J. R. (1986). *The effects of poetry on cohesiveness and self-disclosure in zero-history classroom groups.* Unpublished master's thesis, University of North Carolina at Chapel Hill.

Goodstein, L. D., & Reinecker, V. M. (1974). Factors affecting self-disclosure: A review of the literature. In B. A. Maher (Ed.), *Progress in experimental personality research VII* (pp. 49–77). New York: Academic Press.

Jourard, S. M. (1971). *The transparent self,* 2nd ed. Princeton, NJ: Van Nostrand.

Kirshner, B., Dies, R., & Brown, R. (1978). Effects of experimental manipulation of self-disclosure on cohesiveness. *Journal of Consulting and Clinical Psychology, 46,* 1171–1177.

Luft, J. (1969). *Of human interaction.* Palo Alto, CA: National Press Books.

Petronio, S., Martin, J., & Littlefield, R. (1984). Prerequisite conditions for self-disclosure: A gender issue. *Communication Monographs, 51,* 268–273.

Powell, J. (1969). *Why am I afraid to tell you who I am?* Niles, IL: Argus Communications.

Rose, G.S., & Bednar, R. L. (1980). Effects of positive and negative self-disclosure and feedback on early group development. *Journal of Counseling Psychology, 27,* 63–70.

Rosenfeld, L. B. (1979). Self-disclosure avoidance: Why am I afraid to tell you who I am? *Communication Monographs, 46,* 63–74.

Rosenfeld, L. B. (1979). Research bibliography (self-disclosure): 1970–1978. In G. J. Chelune (Ed.), *Self-disclosure* (pp. 261–374). San Francisco: Jossey-Bass.

Rosenfeld, L. B., Civikly, J. M., & Herron, J. R. (1979). Anatomical sex, psychological sex, and self-disclosure. In G. J. Chelune (Ed.), *Self-disclosure* (pp. 80–108). San Francisco: Jossey-Bass.

Rosenfeld, L. B., & Kendrick, W. L. (1984). Choosing to be open: An empirical investigation of subjective reasons for self-disclosing. *Western Journal of Speech Communication, 48,* 326–343.

Stokes, J. P., Fuehrer, A., & Childs, L. (1983). Group members' self-disclosures: Relation to perceived cohesion. *Small Group Behavior, 14,* 63–76.

Wheeless, L. R., & Grotz, J. (1976). Conceptualization and measurement of reported self-disclosure. *Human Communication Research, 2,* 338–346.

Wood, J. T. (1976). *What are you afraid of?: A guide to dealing with your fears.* New York: Spectrum Books.

Group Maturity

Karl J. Krayer

Many hypotheses have been advanced concerning factors which make a task oriented group successful. Simply stated, one hypothesis suggests that groups which are well developed as a functional, cohesive unit, matched with a leader appropriate to its development will be more effective than those groups which are less developed and matched with inappropriate leadership. This chapter focuses upon one of the crucial factors which affect this development, group maturity. Situational leadership theory is discussed as a framework in which group maturity is a central concept. The maturity of a small group affects the communication which takes place within it. In turn, communication can affect the maturity of a group.

Historical Assumptions of Group Maturity

The concept of group maturity derives from the assumptions of individual maturity. These assumptions originated in Chris Argyris' perspectives about individuals in organizations. In his work, *Personality and Organization,* Argyris examined the nature of interpersonal relationships in traditional complex organizations and suggested the strategies that an individual uses to achieve success directly conflict with the individual's needs. He argued this conflict inhibits personal growth and effectiveness on the job.

Argyris found that unlike many modern organizations in which the individual worker is considered its most important resource, traditional organizations were far more task-oriented and emphasized productivity, effectiveness and efficiency. An individual was viewed as a constant; a "cog" in a machine which could be replaced at will. Success in traditional organizations, therefore, depended upon the worker's ability to divorce him or herself from all personal goals and feelings and to align with the organization's goals and philosophies.

From Argyris' perspective, interpersonal relationships in traditional organizations are quite strained. In Argyris' words, here is how traditional organizations would view such relationships:

(1) The relevant human relationships are those related to achieving the organizational objectives.

This essay appears here in print for the first time. All rights reserved. Permission to reprint must be obtained from the publisher and the author. Karl J. Krayer (Ph.D., University of Oklahoma, 1981) is a Program Manager in Training Services for the Dr. Pepper and Seven-Up Companies in Dallas, Texas. He has previously served on the faculties of Auburn and Texas Christian University as an Assistant Professor in Speech Communication specializing in Organizational Communication.

(2) Human relations effectiveness increases as behavior is rational, logical, and clearly communicated. Personal attitudes, feelings, and values tend to decrease effectiveness.

(3) Human relations are most effectively influenced through direction, coercions, and controls as well as rewards and penalties that emphasize rational behavior and getting the job done.

In summary, Argyris suggests that traditional organizations place demands on individuals which emphasize productivity and inhibit the development of the individual. In turn, this inhibition requires the individual to assimilate the organization's assumptions and philosophies.

Argyris' perspective suggests that an individual's maturity may be improperly developed in traditional organizations because of the difference between what a mature personality needs and an organization requires. Because individuals in traditional organizations are given limited control over their work environment and because these organizations discourage individual development, workers must be passive, dependent and subordinate in order to survive. The result is immature behavior.

Group Maturity and Situational Leadership Theory

The concept of group maturity was first introduced by Paul Hersey and Ken Blanchard as a component of their situational leadership theory. Their theory is part of the *contingency* school of leadership, which suggests that there is no one best leadership style that is universally applicable to all contexts or situations, but rather, that the effectiveness of a leadership style is dependent upon the circumstances in which it is displayed.

Their perspective suggests that a leader should be matched to a situation. This perspective views a leader as a highly flexible individual, capable of displaying many different behaviors with the competence to know when and where to demonstrate these. In essence, if a leader is mismatched with a certain group, it is his or her responsibility to adapt to the group by adjusting leadership behaviors.

The aspect of a group that the theory calls for the leader to adapt to is the maturity level of the group. The behaviors which must be adapted in a flexible manner are messages concerning the task and personal relationships within the group. In summary, situational leadership theory suggests that an effective group is one which is matched with a leader who has adapted to its maturity level through properly adjusting the emphasis he or she places on task and relationship behaviors.

According to Hersey and Blanchard, group maturity has two components: ability and willingness. Ability refers to knowledge, skill and experience. Compared with more immature groups, groups higher in maturity level can perform tasks without much direction from others in that they are competent in the behaviors necessary to perform effectively. Willingness refers to motivation, confidence and commitment. Unlike groups that are lower in maturity, groups at a higher maturity level have self-confidence, a healthy self-concept and do not need extensive encouragement in order to work on a task.

A mature group, therefore, is able to function independently from its leader, is active, is organized, brings an extensive time perspective to its activities and has an established working history. Conversely, an immature group is dependent upon its leader for proper functioning, is passive, is disorganized, brings a short time perspective to its activities and has an unestablished working history.

Two points are important to stress here. First, group maturity refers to the collectivity as a working unit. The maturity of the individual members of the group is not a significant factor in figuring a group's maturity level. A group may be composed of highly skilled, experienced individuals who have an extended vision for the future, but as a collectivity the group may be quite immature in that it has not gelled as a working unit, relationships among the participants may be undeveloped and highly uncertain and no consensus on procedures for completing a task may be established. Second, while we may discuss the "state" or "level" of a group's maturity (and in fact, must do so) by freezing it at a point in time, group maturity is a continuous variable. As a group continues to work together and develops more of the characteristics which define its maturity, the group should progress from a state of immaturity to a state of maturity. Hence, a group should be viewed as continually developing its maturity as it interacts over time.

Situational leadership theory suggests that a group will be effective to the extent that it is matched with a leader who has adapted to its maturity. The theory includes four leadership styles which differ in the leader's emphasis on task behavior or socio-emotional relationship behavior. Figure 1, which summarizes the four styles, illustrates that as a group matures, leaders need to provide less emphasis on structuring a task or on socio-emotional relationships. As one moves along the curve in the diagram from Quadrant 1 to Quadrant 4, the correct leadership style changes.

Immature groups are located on the right side of the diagram. Two leadership styles are correct matches for immature groups. The appropriate leader for groups of below average maturity (Quadrant I) is a "directing" leader who places high emphasis on the task and low emphasis on relationships. This is an effective style for that maturity level because the leader provides the group with well-developed methods for accomplishing its goals. Subordinates in this

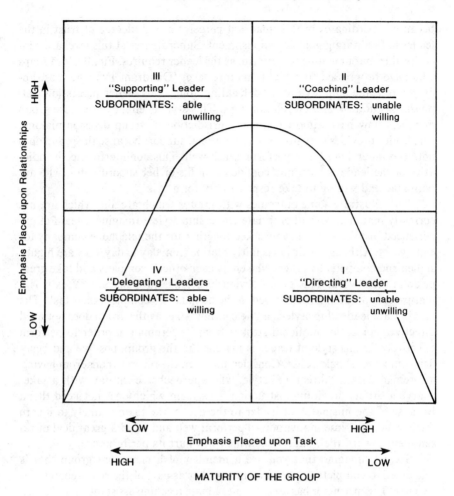

Figure 1.

quadrant are both unable and unwilling to take responsibility for a task. As a group enters a slightly below-average state of maturity (Quadrant II), a "coaching" leader who emphasizes both the task and relationships is needed. This leader satisfies the needs of the group for setting goals and organizing work but also provides a great amount of socio-emotional support. Subordinates in this quadrant are unable but willing to take responsibility for a task.

Mature groups are located on the left side of the diagram. Two leadership styles are appropriate matches for mature groups. For a group of above-average maturity (Quadrant III), a "supporting" leader is the correct match. This leader emphasizes relationships more than the task. This style is effective because subordinates in this quadrant perceive a high degree of trust in the leader in facilitating goal accomplishment. Subordinates at this level are generally able, but unwilling to perform, as the leader requires. Finally, for groups who have progressed to a highly mature level (Quadrant IV), the most appropriate leadership style is a "delegating" one. This leader places low emphasis on the task and on relationships. This style is effective because group members now have almost complete jurisdiction in group decision-making. The leader provides very little socio-emotional support because the group does not need much in order to perform a task well. This noninterference is indicative of the leader's trust and confidence in his or her subordinates, who are both able and willing to take responsibility for a task.

Let's illustrate some outcomes with groups which are and which are not correctly matched with appropriate leadership styles. Imagine a team of experienced installers who have worked together for the telephone company for eight years. Although their job is fairly routine from day to day, they are highly skilled and competent workers who enjoy each other's company and take great pride in their work. This group obviously belongs in Quadrant IV as it is a mature group which is well versed in the demands to complete their task. The appropriate leadership style is a "delegating" one, as the group does not need directives nor socio-emotional strokes from its foreman in order to perform effectively. If this style of leader is matched to the group, positive and beneficial outcomes should result. Consider, however, the repercussions from having a foreman with a "directing" style, who approaches each day with a take-charge attitude, providing instructions to a team which does not need them. Because of the mismatch of leader to the group, the team is likely to ignore the instructions, lose motivation to perform well and build a great deal of resentment toward their supervisor which will hurt its performance.

Second, imagine that you are a member of a classroom group that is scheduled to complete an assignment together as part of the requirements for a course. The instructor has assigned a graduate teaching assistant as the leader for each of the groups. You have never met any of your group members, there is considerable latitude for how your group may proceed on the assignment and there is a perceivable difference in the degree to which the group members appear to be interested in working on the assignment. A "delegating" leader would seal the group's doom as very little work would be accomplished. The group does not have enough information or motivation to perform the assignment well. Obviously, this group is very immature (Quadrant I) and needs a directive style of leader in order to accomplish its task.

In summary, situational leadership theory is built upon a curvilinear relationship among the tasks, relationships and maturity levels of groups. Because a group's outcomes are dependent upon the match of a leader's style to the maturity level of a group, any one of the four leadership styles may produce favorable or unfavorable results, given the appropriateness of the leader's behavior. Any inappropriate match should result in dysfunctional outcomes for the group.

Measuring Group Maturity

Prior to 1984, no rigorous method by which managers or researchers could assess the maturity of a work group was available. While any one of several measurement methods could be used to assess maturity, the style initially selected was a self-report questionnaire, on which participants simply make judgments and provide their reactions or feelings on the various items. After examining the characteristics of maturity as proposed by Argyris and Hersey and Blanchard, Krayer and Fiechtner developed ten scales designed to tap the maturity level of groups. These scales are listed in Table 1. Each of the scales is constructed of bi-polar, opposite characteristics (similar to hot–cold; pretty–ugly; red–green) and are divided by seven spaces. With a certain group in mind, respondents simply examine the two characteristics and decide how close the group is to one of them and rates the group accordingly. For example, when considering whether a group is "guided by leader"—"not dependent on the leader," a member of a group who has been asked to judge its maturity might place an "X" two spaces to the left of "not dependent on the leader," which would indicate a strong tendency, though not complete dependency, for the group to rely on the leader.

Table 1
Characteristics of Mature vs. Immature Groups

Sets clear goals	Fails to set clear goals
*Guided by leader	Not dependent on the leader
Decision-making process shared by all members	Decision-making process not shared by all members
*Very little group interaction	Much group interaction
Has clear purpose or direction	Has no clear purpose or direction
*Irrational, hasty	Acts calmly, rationally
Has flexible methods to solve problems	Has rigid, pre-set ways to solve problems.
*Seem to work as collection of *individuals*	Seem to work as a cohesive *unit*
Has sense of group pride	Lacks sense of group pride
*Very little commitment to group decisions that are reached	Great commitment to group decisions that are reached

*indicates the item is reversed

In its first testing, 100 students at a large midwestern university were given the ten scales and asked to consider "an *established* group which has worked together in an organization for several months and has completed several major projects." From a second instrument using these same ten scales, students were asked to consider "an *unestablished* group which is working together on their first major project."

Advanced statistical tests revealed that four items on the instrument were highly consistent in their ability to discriminate between these two types of referent groups: amount of group interaction (little to high), rational group behavior (irrational to rational), cohesiveness (collection of individuals to unit) and decision commitment (little to high). Using these four items will provide a rigorous and statistically consistent instrument for the measurement of small group maturity.

A second test on these ten scales was performed using members of actual established and unestablished groups as respondents in order to see whether the instrument could effectively discriminate between mature and immature groups. The scales were administered to 80 students who were members of groups constructed for the purpose of the project from basic speech communication courses and 79 students who were members of teams which had interacted for three months as a part of a senior-level management course.

The statistical procedures used in this test apply the ten scales in an attempt to classify members of the mature and immature groups. The results indicated that the items correctly placed 87.5 percent of the members of the immature groups (70 of 80) and 91.1 percent of the members of the mature groups (72 of 79). Overall, the ten maturity scales correctly placed 89.3 percent of all group members.

Similar results were achieved in a later attempt to classify members of twenty-eight mature and twenty-eight immature groups. The findings indicated that the ten scales were powerful discriminators between the mature and immature groups. Of the members of immature groups, 80.3% were correctly placed while 82.3% of the members of mature groups were correctly placed. These two tests demonstrated the reliability and validity of the instrument which was later used to uncover further knowledge about group maturity and situational leadership theory.

Tests of Maturity and Situational Leadership Theory

Study One: Should Groups Progress in Their Maturity?

Despite the efforts listed above to develop an instrument to measure group maturity, some question still remains of the worth of cultivating the maturity of groups. One of the key components of Hersey and Blanchard's situational leadership theory is that leaders not only act as responders, adapting his or her style to a group's maturity, but the leader can also act as an agent of change, altering his or her style to stimulate group maturation. This intervention takes a considerable amount of effort by a leader. If there is no significant advantage for a group to progress from an immature to a mature state, then such efforts on the part of leaders are unwarranted. The advantages of this progression could be three-fold: (1) do mature groups behave in ways differently than immature groups? (2) do members of mature groups affectively react to each other (i.e., liking, satisfaction) differently than members of immature groups? and (3) do mature groups perform better on tasks as a collectivity better than immature groups?

A study by Krayer investigated these questions by studying classroom groups of students who were working together as part of the requirements for a course. He argued that mature groups should *behave* differently than immature groups in that the self-direction and purposiveness which a mature group brings to its task should result in the group holding more meetings as a unit voluntarily. Second, mature groups should also produce *affective* reactions differently than immature groups. Because mature groups have a more established work history than immature groups, their members are more familiar with each other. Having established particular regularities of working habits with each other, as well as potential friendships, participants in mature groups should be more favorably disposed toward each other than participants in immature groups. As a result, when compared with immature groups, participants in mature groups should express more satisfaction with the group, a greater desire to work with the group again in the future and a greater desire to socialize with the group members. Finally, mature groups should differ from immature groups in their *performance* outcomes. The clarity in purpose and direction, together with the presence of more rational sorts of interaction, should result in mature groups being awarded higher grades on project evaluations than immature groups.

The results of the study indicated strong advantages to holding membership in mature groups. Mature groups held significantly more meetings on their own time, outside of regular class sessions, than immature groups. Interestingly, there was no difference in the number of meetings held during class meetings, indicating that mature and immature groups met relatively the same amount under non-voluntary conditions. Members of mature groups reported significantly more satisfaction with their groups, significantly more desire to work with their group again in the future and significantly more willingness to socialize with the group than immature groups. Mature groups also scored significantly higher on their semester projects than did the immature groups.

The study uncovered several important factors which are associated with membership in mature groups. First, the need for groups to develop independence from a leader, to act in a calm and rational manner, to allow for a high degree of interaction among group members, and to set clear and realistic goals was found to be strongly associated with behavioral, affective and performance measures. Second, the results indicate a considerable rationale for leaders to intervene in moving a group toward greater states of maturation. As discussed previously when describing situational leadership theory, this requires flexible behavior on the part of a leader. The leader must be willing to take a risk and delegate some responsibility to the members he or she works with. Because the group members may be asked to complete a task which they have never tried before, a leader cannot expect an outstanding performance on the initial attempt. The group members cannot learn a new task all at once and for the leader to expect them to do so only sets them up for failure and punishment. In order to properly intervene, a leader should provide direction and structure, gradually reduce the amount of direction and supervision, and after adequate performance follows, increase socio-emotional support.

Take for example, a simple task such as "constructing visual aids for a group presentation on a project to the class." The leader should first provide some direction and structure, such as establishing a deadline or a ceiling on the cost of materials. Second, the leader should delegate some responsibility through his or her task behavior by turning over the direction and supervision of the project to some group members. If the response is favorable, then the leader should positively reinforce the behavior by increasing the socio-emotional support.

Third, the results from this study indicate that there are some positive reasons for instructors to organize courses in ways which utilize intact groups or teams. Student groups which are allowed to work over the course of a term have a great opportunity to develop maturity in that they complete activities, assignments and examinations as intact units as well as build friendships. Groups which matured in this way were shown in this study to produce highly favorable results when compared with groups which remained at lower levels of maturity. The end result is a class in which students enjoy working with their peers, voluntarily choose to meet and complete assignments on which they perform well.

Study Two: Does Matching Leaders to Group Maturity Make a Difference?

A central tenet of Hersey and Blanchard's situational leadership theory is that groups which are correctly matched with leaders who adapt to their level of maturity will perform better than groups which are incorrectly matched. A study by Fiechtner and Krayer tested this assumption by studying student groups who were asked to complete a task during a regular class session.

Fifty-six groups comprised of four to seven students each participated in the study. Twenty-eight of the groups were immature groups which were assembled for the sole purpose of participating in the study. Fourteen of these groups were correctly matched with "directing" or "coaching" leaders while the other fourteen were incorrectly matched with "supporting" or "delegating" leaders. The other twenty-eight groups were mature and were formed at the beginning of the semester. At the time of this study, they had completed at least five major projects for the class. Fourteen of the mature groups were correctly matched with "supporting" or "delegating" leaders while the other fourteen were incorrectly matched with "directing" or "coaching" leaders.

The results indicated that in all cases, members of correctly matched groups were significantly more satisfied than members of incorrectly matched groups. However, mixed results were found for the effectiveness and efficiency measures. Correctly matching groups with leaders appropriate to their maturity levels did not consistently result in lower group error scores and faster solving of tasks when compared with incorrectly matched groups.

It is interesting to speculate about why the theory worked consistently only with satisfaction. One possible explanation may be based upon an examination of what situational leadership theory represents. Situational leadership theory is based upon maturity, a mentally-based concept, derived from questionnaire, self-report data. Similarly, satisfaction is a mentalistic concept, which is also based upon perceptions. Conversely, performance measures such as effectiveness and efficiency, are tangible concepts which are measured non-perceptually. Because situational leadership theory is based on maturity, a perceptual, mentally-based concept, the theory should relate better with perceptual outcomes (satisfaction) than with non-perceptual outcomes (effectiveness and efficiency). The assumption that matching leaders to appropriate levels of group maturity will result in better outcomes appears to lack validity with tangible, more behaviorally-oriented concepts.

What Does the Future Hold?

Despite the historical roots of group maturity and recent attempts to measure and test the concept, a great deal of work remains to be done. One of the most important studies to be conducted concerns the ways in which the interaction patterns, or actual communication, vary among groups of different maturity levels. The research reviewed in this chapter documents well the notion that the style of leadership present in the group is a major factor which influences a group's interaction. From this, the frequency with which group members interact with each other, the kinds of content they discuss (such as "seeking information," "harmonizing," etc.) and the division of their input into "task" and "maintenance" areas should be described for various groups of these four maturity levels. Given some of the findings described in this chapter, it would seem appropriate to provide one set of descriptions for groups which are matched with the appropriate style of leadership while a second set of descriptions should be made for groups which are incorrectly matched.

Yet another area for investigation revolves around the existence and effect of counteractive influences on a group's maturity, such as those discussed by Gouran. Counteractive influences refer to behavior which alters the direction of a group. For instance, a group which is operating under "groupthink" principles should undertake certain counteractive behaviors which will allow for the critical appraisal of its ideas. Or, a group which has a high degree of disruptive behavior, such as unproductive conflict, should produce counteractive behaviors in order that the conflict can be used productively. Similarly, research in this area should attempt to discover whether there are certain communication behaviors which, when present in a group, impede a group's progress in maturing at the correct pace. Groups which are both correctly and incorrectly matched should be investigated separately.

Group maturity is a concept which is very important in describing the development of a task-oriented unit. While there is still a considerable amount of work to be done, preliminary investigations suggest that where possible, groups should indeed strive to achieve characteristics of maturity as a collective unit. Further, leaders of groups should strive to identify and adapt to a group's level of maturity as an asset toward achieving optimal performance. Instructors, leaders of groups, or others who may be responsible for them, should not ignore the consequences which result for a functioning group when it fails to develop from a state of immaturity or is improperly matched with a leader who fails to adapt to its level of maturity.

References

Argyris, C. (1962). *Interpersonal competence and organizational effectiveness.* Homewood, Ill.: Dorsey Press.

Argyris, C. (1962). *Personality and organization: The conflict between system and the individual.* New York: Harper and Row.

Carew, D. K., Parisi-Carew, E., & Blanchard, K. H. (1986). Group development and situational leadership: A model for managing groups. *Training and Development Journal, 40,* 46–50.

Fiechtner, S. B., & Krayer, K. J. (1984). An empirical test of Hersey and Blanchard's life cycle theory. Paper presented to the Speech Communication Association, Chicago, Illinois.

Hersey, P., & Blanchard, K. H. (1982). *Management of organizational behavior: Utilizing human resources* (4th ed.). Englewood Cliffs, New Jersey: Prentice-Hall.

Kast, F. E., & Rosenzweig, J. F. (1978). *Experimental exercises and cases in management.* New York: McGraw-Hill.

Krayer, K. J. (in press). Exploring group maturity in the classroom: Some differences in behavioral, affective and performance outcomes between mature and immature groups. *Small Group Behavior.*

Krayer, K. J., & Fiechtner, S. B. (1984). Measuring group maturity: The development of a process-oriented variable for small group communication research. *Southern Speech Communication Journal, 50,* 78–92.

5

Group Messages:
Sending and Receiving

The last chapter offered readings introducing you to some basic principles of human communication. The assumption is that participation in a group experience, regardless of the group's purpose, is a communication activity. Chapter 4 sought to highlight the link existing between communication and groups. While still pursuing the general theme of communication, the current chapter looks at the way the *individual* communicates within the group. More specifically, it examines how members of the group send and receive messages, how they express their ideas verbally and nonverbally, and how those ideas are received. It's this exchange of individual messages that actually makes a group of individuals function *as a group*. Message exchange offers the group the means to solve problems and to work out interpersonal relationships. By understanding something about messages and how they are received, you can better understand your own actions in the group, as well as the actions of others.

To underscore the importance of messages in the group setting we have selected six essays that stress verbal and nonverbal messages, listening, and ways of responding to messages (feedback).

In its most elementary form, group discussion involves people talking to one another. An intriguing question asks what these words look like. That is to say, how is conversation employed by members of a group as they carry out their private and shared purposes? The topic of verbal messages, and how they are related to group communication, is the subject of the first essay in this chapter. In a selection titled "Talking in Groups: Understanding Conversational Structure", Wayne A. Beach examines some of the ways in which conversations are used as the major vehicle for accomplishing group business. He looks at conversations that display support, keep the group moving, and regulate topic selection. In each of these instances, we can see how verbal messages are altered by the group experience.

In recent years teachers and students of human communication have become aware of the fact that we communicate with more than words. Many of our actions are nonverbal, yet people attach meaning to them and make them part of the communication experience. In an essay by Peter A. Andersen, the issue of nonverbal communication is examined within the context of the small group. The importance of this examination becomes apparent when we realize that nonverbal cues, if interpreted correctly, can provide a means for successful group interaction. In addition, many of our feelings and attitudes are projected to other group members by our nonverbal behavior. Being able to understand our own behavior, as well as the behavior of others, will greatly facilitate the group process. As a means of contributing to that understanding, Anderson investigates the influence and impact of the following nonverbal cues on the individual and the group: physical appearance, oculesics (eye contact), kinesics (facial expressions, gestures, body synchrony, regulation, quasi-courtship), vocalics (human voice), chronemics (time), haptics (touch), proxemics (territoriality, personal space, density and crowding, setting and furniture arrangement).

Judee K. Burgoon offers yet another perspective on nonverbal communication within the small group. Because of its importance to successful communication, she concentrates on *spatial relationships*—specifically, *informal space* (how we orient toward and distance ourselves from other members of the group), and *fixed feature* and *semi-fixed feature space* (the ways in which architecture, interior design, furniture arrangement, and the like influence spacing behavior). Burgoon is concerned with how these two relationships and the potential messages they contain relate to comfort, status and leadership, interaction patterns, relational communication, and spatial deviancy.

Students of communication have long agreed that communication is a two-way process, with speaker and listener sharing equal roles in this transaction. Although this axiom is widely accepted in the writings of communication, the literature reveals an uneven distribution in favor of the speaker. One possible reason for this unevenness might be that people have long believed *receiving* a message was the same as *listening* to a message, and therefore, listening was a rather simple process. They equated reception with comprehension. Our position is that reception and comprehension are *not* the same; rather, reception is only the first phase of the listening cycle. We maintain that in order to understand how listening operates, you must examine a host of interrelated variables.

Some of these variables are treated in the essay by Jane Whitney Gibson and Richard M. Hodgetts. They look upon the psychological environment (mental variables internal to the speaker and listener) and the physical environment (the setting in which the speaker and listener find themselves) as parts of the listening environment. They also examine the topic of "active listening"—listening that includes empathic and supportive behaviors. Their analysis offers a brief description of active listening and some specific guidelines for improving listening.

We have included a second selection on listening because so much of your time in small groups finds you in the role of listener rather than speaker. Recently, many organizations have become aware of this obvious conclusion. They have also come to realize that while we spend a great deal of time listening, we don't do it very well. The Sperry Corporation is one such organization. It started a major training program in listening, and concurrently presented a corporate advertising theme that stated "We understand how important it is to listen." The popularity and success of the Sperry program is worthy of your consideration. In a brief essay called "Your Listening Profile", Sperry offers an outline of its training course, some facts about listening, several ways to test your listening profile, and ten "keys" to effective listening.

This chapter concludes with an essay discussing a type of message exchange that includes verbal and nonverbal messages, in addition to listening—feedback. Feedback is an essential part of any communication experience. It represents the messages people send each other regarding what is happening at the moment. Both communicators give feedback as they respond to each other's behavior. This important form of communication is explored by Beth Haslett and John R. Ogilvie in a selection titled "Feedback Processes in Task Groups". While they look at feedback in general, their main focus is on feedback that operates within the group. They discuss dimensions of feedback, feedback and group performance, and feedback as a communication process. Also, they examine some factors influencing feedback. Source, message, and recipient characteristics are treated in this section. In conclusion, they present commentary on how to give feedback. As you would suspect, feedback is crucial to the group's success. It is the way individual participants are able to keep their peers informed as to what they think and feel about what is transpiring.

Talking in Groups:
Understanding Conversational Structure

Wayne A. Beach

And the loosest message is that the world you live in is much more finely organized than you would imagine. [The point is to become] armed with some materials that would permit you to wander around noticing things that you might not have noticed, and find them ghastly. (Sacks, 1970)

It should come as no surprise to suggest that how one looks at small groups strongly influences what one finds as interesting and meaningful within group communication. What is somewhat alarming, however, is the fact that the ordinary, routine stuff of everyday communication—naturally occurring talk— is so rarely examined as a topic in its own right. Throughout the history of group research, it is indeed the exception—rather than the rule itself—to train students in the gathering and analysis of their own audio and/or video recordings of actual groups. The overriding goal of working directly with conversational recordings is to describe and explain how groups rely on talk to organize diverse *settings* (e.g., business, government, medical, legal, school, home, recreational), in and through the accomplishment of particular *activities* (e.g., planning sessions, committee meetings, diagnostic and therapeutic encounters, bargaining and negotiating discussions, recess at an elementary school, family dinners, community support groups). More specifically, questions are raised regarding what *methods* group members use to get practical activities done—collaboratively, interactionally—in the process of *doing* planning, diagnosing, bargaining, recessing, dining, supporting, and the like. In short, the more closely group conversations are examined, the more likely is the possibility of discovering how members themselves orient to—and actually structure—those activities of which they are an integral part.

These concerns with *conversation analysis* may be traced back to some preliminary obervations by Harvey Sacks:

Our aim is to get into a position to transform, in an almost literal, physical sense, our view of "what happened," from a matter of a particular interaction done by particular people, to a matter of interactions as products of a machinery. We are trying to find the machinery. In order to do so we have to get access to its products. At this point, it is conversation that provides us such access.[1]

Adapted from Nadler (1979). This original essay appears here in print for the first time. All Rights Reserved. Permission to reprint must be obtained from the publisher and the author. Wayne A. Beach is affiliated with the Department of Speech Communication, San Diego State University.

The gross aim of the work I am doing is to see how finely the details of actual, naturally occurring conversation can be subjected to analysis that will yield the technology of conversation. The idea is to take singular sequences of conversation and tear them apart in such a way as to find rules, techniques, procedures, methods . . . that can be used to generate the orderly features we find in the conversations we examine.[2]

When conversation is viewed as the major vehicle for getting group interactions done (verbally and nonverbally), it soon becomes clear that a host of group concepts and variables—leadership, conflict, primary and secondary "tensions", cohesiveness, conformity, deviance, dominance, submission, decision-making "phases"—are *themselves* conversational accomplishments. To the extent these and related phenomena exist and influence group behavior, they reflect social products of talk's machinery.

The task remains, however, to *locate the action in the interaction,* i.e., to turn directly to group conversations and begin to describe and explain how talk is used to get activities done. To facilitate these understandings, this chapter examines portions of a transcript generated from audio-recordings of a high-technology focus group meeting.[3] An understanding of these transcribed segments will be facilitated by first reading through the transcribing conventions (i.e., notation symbols) in Appendix A. These conventions or symbols are employed to "map" the details of naturally occurring talk onto written text, so as to precisely capture the sounds, timing, and locations of utterances-in-sequence.[4] Exactly why such attention should be given to the details of transcribing talk will hopefully become apparent in the following analysis as we attempt to, following Sacks, "take singular sequences of conversation and tear them apart". Before doing so, however, it may prove useful to offer some suggestions as to how you might gather and begin to analyze group conversations.

Gathering and Transcribing Group Conversations

For the moment, suffice it to say that all you need to do to begin an analysis of *how groups accomplish their interactions* is: 1) Gain access to a setting within which groups routinely interact; 2) Audio and/or video-record the group in a manner that a) is not secretive (and therefore possibly unethical) but rather is predicated on permission granted by group members, b) insures the group that transcribing will be anonymous while also adhering to other possible constraints understandably imposed by the group (e.g., a request that you not make the recording publicly available to whomever asks for a copy), c) informs the group of your reason(s) for collecting such data (e.g., for a class research project), and d) retains clear, crisp audio-quality for purposes of transcribing and repeated listening; 3) Begin listening to your recording(s). Set your "counter" at zero so as to be able to mark (and eventually locate) any interesting segments (from two utterances to several minutes) you may wish to examine in more depth; 4) Start with a straightforward segment. When one or more segments is located, begin transcribing. Attempt to capture basic words and speaker designations first, and then go back and layer in specific conversational details. Remember: Repeated listenings lead to increasingly detailed transcripts, *and* increasingly insightful analyses of not only what's going on in the talk but also how that "something" is getting interactionally organized by the group as a whole.

Now that you have a basic sense of the research steps involved in studying group conversations, the next move is to begin to notice certain features of talk within your data. As an illustration, let's begin with the *turn-taking sequence* appearing below.

Turn-Taking in an Introduction Sequence

Consider the following sequence that appeared near the beginning of a group focus meeting:

(1) INDAX: 87–107 (00:22:25)

87	Jan:	O:k. .hh > So I just started to introduce myself. I'm
88		( ) < (.) > How about if you just go
89		around and and *may*be first names (can be) emphasized
90		cuz we'll never remember last names so (.) *I'm* Jan
91		(.) Ok?=
92	Joyce:	=I'm Joyce.
93	Jan:	Joyce?=
94	Joyce:	=Um hum.=
95	Jan:	=Ok.
96	Betty J:	I'm Bet.ty?
97	Betty:	I'm Betty also.Hehheh heh!

              [

| 98 | Jan: | Oh::hhh! Ok. |

             [

| 99 | Betty J: | Betty *Jane*! Betty Jane. |

| 100 | Jan: | Betty Jane an nd |

       [

| 101 | Betty: | Just Bett y. |

        [

| 102 | Jan: | Betty, Ok? |

103	Al:	I'm Al:ll
104	John:	I'm Joh:n.
105	Barbara:	*Bar*bara?
106	Bill:	Bill.
107	Julie:	Julie.

How is this introduction sequence structurally organized? What are the components inherent in the talk, and how are they interrelated? What "work" is getting done by group members as they orient to the task-at-hand?

A useful point of departure stems from Sacks, Schegloff, and Jefferson's pioneering work on conversational *turn-taking*.[5] Throughout the above sequence, attention might initially be drawn to certain basic features: Group members take turns talking (i.e., speaker change recurs); Overwhelmingly, one person speaks at a time; When two or more group members overlap and/or speak simultaneously, attempts are made to repair the conversation in such a way that one person (and one only) retains the floor. (Of course, when groups sub-divide into separate conversations simultaneous talk occurs. However, these sub-conversations are themselves regulated by turn-taking constraints.); As transitions are made from turn to turn, it is common to have little or minimal gap or overlap; Speakers may select themselves to speak, or by selected by another to take the floor (e.g., when one group member asks a question to another); Turn order and size are not necessarily fixed in advance, nor is the length of a conversation or what group members "say". (Of course, the introduction sequence above possesses several redundant features, as with turns 103–107. But also notice that options exist when introducing oneself, such as Betty Jane's elaboration of her name in turn 99.); Talk may be continuous or discontinuous (as well as speed up and slow down); and more.

These features by no means reflect an exhaustive account of turn-taking components yet they do apply directly to how group members introduce themselves to one another. More importantly, however, these features reappear in most (if not all) conversational involvements. The power of this statement is evident in its generalizability: If you cannot find a group conversation that fails to adhere to these turn-taking regularities, then these features are inherent in *all* group accomplishments. Consequently, a strong foundation is constructed upon which additional explanations of group interactions might be built.

Having now become "armed" with these initial insights about conversational turn-taking, return to segment (1) and attempt to answer the following questions: Is there a predominant "leader" in this sequence? If so, what actions constitute leader-like behavior? (Remember: It is often wise to begin small and work up to more general observations. For example, how might you account for Jan's "Ok" in turns 87, 91, 95, 98, and 102?); What evidence can be provided that group members recognize this sequence as "doing introductions"? How does this introduction sequence differ from typical greetings and introductions among two or three persons?; How would you describe what's going on in turns 96–102? Is there a "trouble" here that is "repaired" by group members?

When examining portions of a transcript, it is often helpful to work with others and contrast alternative explanations of utterances-in-sequence. As disagreements arise, always move back to the text as a means of seeking evidence for claims; it is better to struggle with "what is" rather than remain abstract and hypothetical by playing the game of "what if".

How Does Group "Facilitation" Get Done?

It is obvious in segment (1) that Jan was using several methods to facilitate and thus lead group interaction. Not only does she "set up" the introduction sequence in turns 87–91, but she also displays attention through her clarification in turn 93, and acknowledged support in turns 95, 98, and 102. A perusal of the larger transcript does indeed reveal that Jan uses a variety of methods to: 1) Create an environment conducive to open, supportive discussion; 2) Summarize and regulate topical talk; and 3) Also encourage group members to structure discussions quite on their own. But what do these *methods* look like in actual fragments of group conversation?

1) *Displaying Support.* In segment (2) below, Jan initially queries Julie about her use of "the games". Julie then proceeds to provide a rather lengthy response, a series of utterances prompted by Jan's continual *backchanneling:*

(2)	INDAX:	284–315	(00:57:34)

284	Jan:	You you shook your head now. I forgot your name too
285		(what is it)
286	Julie:	Oh: *Ju*lie.=
287	Jan:	=Julie you shook your *head* and nodded when somebody
288		said something to you about the the .hhh games or
289		whatever do you remember what that ( ).
290	Julie:	Uhh. ( )=
291	Jan:	=Whadda you ah whadda you *use* it for.
292	Julie:	Uhh (0.5) well: basically when (0.5) you said about
293		the gam e
		[
294	Jan:	Uh huh.=
295	Julie:	=uh is it more fun than the com*pu*ter. it has replaced

296		out Atari system.
297	Jane:	Ah hah!
298	Julie:	We have stopped buying the .hhh ya know little games
299		and we are no: longer even (.) in fact the A*t*ari
300		hasn't been hooked up? so.
301	Jan:	*Wow:?*
302	Julie:	Since you went *really* big with the games for a while
303		(they were being sold) but uh .hhh and in that respect
304		it's financially *cheap*er for us as a family.
305	Jan:	Su:re.
306	Julie:	It cuts down on the *stor*age (.) it cuts down on having
307		ah the Atari system in use and tying up that TV when
308		somebody *else* is playing in

[

309	Jan:	*In:*:ter esting. Ok?
310	Julie	in there uh the ga:::mes
311		are a major (1.5) you know (.) *part* of the time
312		we've used Indax and I (.) have kids in all ages and
313		they're all just ((Julie continues her "story" and Jan
314		continues to acknowledge and support Julie's
315		"telling" for another minute))

As Julie describes her experiences with "the games", Jan continually backchannels by showing support and interest in turns 294, 297, 301, 305, and 309. What's interesting here is the *timing and placement* of Jan's utterances, for it is clearly the case that Julie does not relinquish the floor, nor does Jan choose to use the floor for more than providing ongoing reinforcement. Moreover, Julie felt comfortable to continue her "story" and thus provide useful information to the organizers of the focus group meeting.

One implication arising from this sequence, however, is as follows: Does continual reinforcement by a "facilitator" prompt tellings that are too lengthy and detailed? If so, how then does the facilitator attempt to "close down" another's telling without appearing rude and possibly causing embarrassment for the teller? Might Jan's "Ok" in turn 309 be an initial attempt to close down one person's telling so as to move onto other speakers and topics? We could only answer these questions by turning directly to the transcript—for within the structural organization of the talk resides not only members' recognitions of "troubles", but also the methods giving rise to (and employed to remedy) situations-at-hand.

2)   *Regulating Topical Talk.* Exactly how "topics" get initiated, developed, and changed is one of the most difficult yet intriguing set of conversational phenomena. The efficient organization of group discussions, however, is due to a large extent upon how attention is drawn to (and away from) particular issues. Throughout the INDAX transcript, Jan facilitates by regulating topical talk with a variety of interactional methods, several of which appear below:

(3)   357   Jan: Oh::k. (.) How about the rest of you. (0.8) do

       358   you use it in your house?

       359   Betty: Yes. ((continues))

(4)   370   Jan: =Ya know I I hear something you sp- both of you

       371   just said in that > and let me see if I'm reading

       372   it right. < .hhh I hear you guys saying that

       373   you're sorta ple::sed by that. Do you *like* this

       374   better than A*t*ari for your kids.

                                                    [

       375   Betty: *Much*...... more creative I

       376   think.

       377   Jan: And more challenging?

       378   Betty: And as she indicated ((continues))

(5)   712   Jan: Whu-what do you mean by that when you say=

       713   Al: =My kids have an Apple ((continues))

(6) 729 Jan: Does that make you *feel* good?=

    730 Betty J: =*Oh:* ya?
                     [

    731 Barbara: Sure sure it makes you feel ((continues))

(7) 792 Jan: Ok .hhh um: real let's talk about if there are

    793   some other issues of consent. We talked a little

    794   bit about *privacy.* .hh *Lots* of people in the kind

    795   of technology w:horld are talking about *eye*

    796   strain. .hh Is this

    797 Betty: *Yes.*

    798 Jan: is this *hard* to work with for a while (with) more

    799   straining?

    800 Betty: Yes some of the background ((continues))

(8) 976 Jan: Uh: ka. .hhh Well you said there's lotta ways you

    977   could go with it. If you could just have *one*

    978   thing (0.5) that this system could do (1.0) what

    979   would that one thing be. Why do you think the

    980   *best* thing that *this* system does that .hh you

981   know isn't done as well by some other system.

982   What's the *best* aspect of Indax. (1.0) Let's

983   just kinda go around the table.

984   Group: ((Several group members proceed to offer

985   opinions, beginning with Barbara, Betty J., and

986   Julie))

When examining segments (3)–(8), it must be remembered that Jan's task was to elicit information from group members regarding a wide variety of attitudes, experiences, and problems with INDAX. How does she facilitate the gathering of such information? In segments (3), (6), and (9) it is evident that she typically uses focused, directive questions to stimulate topics. In (4) and (7) she integrates and summarizes *prior* topics so as to not only justify her move to another topic, but also to show the relevance of one topic to another. And in (8) Jan directs focus on "the best aspect of Indax" in a way that invites multiple speakers to offer their opinions (and they did).

Effective facilitation—and leadership in general—requires numerous interactional skills. These skills are apparent in the sequential organization of group talk as a facilitator moves in, out, and around topics. Knowing when to "sit back" and allow members to freely interact, however, is similarly an important method.

3)   *Refraining from Direct Facilitation.* Once a group discussion gains momentum, conversation can generate a life of its own reflective of how members engage one another in certain activities. Jan's facilitative presence is obvious in many of the segments presented above, yet there are also many segments where Jan assumes a minimal role and group members simply "take the ball and run with it". In this sense, members are their own facilitators at times as they extend topics, brainstorm possibilities, or engage in argument. The final segment illustrates only a portion of a more extended argument between two group members— a segment wherein Jan is noticeable in her backchanneling only:

(9)   INDEX   618–638   (00:28:18)

618   Joyce: Well I finished the *sur*veys. but I had a lot of uhm

619   (1.0) frus*tra*tion on some of those games that I did

620   especially the business? game.
                                    [

621   Jan: Uh hum.

622   Joyce: It was so::: inept it was so totally nonrelated to

623   *real*- I'm a small business person and a so totally

624   nonrelated to wh-to the *real:* business. I mean in

625   in *fact* .hh I was a little bit frustrated becuz it

626   (1.0) according to *that:?* (0.5) game. it tells you how

627   to *cheat?*

628   John: Ya. W*ell::* see now just becuz you're *hon*est doesn't

629   mean that the other companies are. Now that's a

630   that's a
                                    [

631   Joyce: I know bu t-
                                                    [

632   John: that's almost word fer word how

633   General *Mo*tors got started.
                                                              [

634   Joyce: Bu t-

635   John: And in fact I've
                                                                    worked

636   for a company like that and I'm unemployed now
                         cuz-
                                                          [

637   Joyce: But *then* is *then* and this is

638   *now*::! What I'm saying is it doesn't relate to now?=

639   John: =Ya it *does* I'm out of work be*cuz* of it!=

640   Joyce: =Ya but ((argument continues))

Here it is seen that valuable information is being disclosed as John and Joyce interrelate their professional experiences with the Index "games". The background knowledge group members bring *to* their Index experiences, and how such knowledge influences likes and dislikes with Index services, is central to the purpose of such a focus group meeting. Thus, the argument emerged in such a way that two contrasting perspectives were being worked out—in and through talk. Much could be said here about the organization of argument sequences—a phenomenon you may locate and wish to analyze in your own recordings—but a more basic point concerns how facilitation can promote non-facilitated sequences in the group. At what point might this argument have gotten too emotional and "out of hand", and how might Jan have handled such an occurrence? Once again, the answers reside in the methods members themselves enacted in this everyday life setting.

Conclusion

This chapter began with an observation that how one *looks* at groups will determine what one *finds* in the study of group interaction. Having briefly introduced a way of looking at talking in groups, it is hoped that you now have a greater appreciation of the need to examine talk on its own merits, as well as an enhanced understanding of the intricate details of group interaction awaiting your discovery. A move toward talk sequences is itself a commitment to the naturalistic "order of things" in groups as members collaboratively achieve "social order". Accounting for *how* this work gets accomplished—such as facilitation—may require tedious effort, but the ultimate reward is the ability to provide grounded *evidence* of the conceptual and theoretical claims you are making about group communication. Within this evidence resides the key to fruitful and heuristic explanations of group conduct.

Notes

1. Harvey Sacks, Unpublished Lecture Notes, University of California–Irvine, (Lecture 1, Winter, 1970). See also Harvey Sacks, "Notes on Methodology", in *Structures of Social Action: Studies in Conversation Analysis,* J. Maxwell Atkinson and John Heritage (Eds.), (Cambridge: Cambridge University Press, 1984, pp. 21–27).
2. Harvey Sacks, Unpublished Lecture Notes, University of California–Irvine, (Lecture 1, Spring, 1970). See also Harvey Sacks, "On Doing Being Ordinary", in Atkinson and Heritage, pp. 413–429).
3. This focus group meeting was organized by the Communications Research Center at San Diego State University. Its basic purpose was to assess consumer/user reactions to services made possible via a TV-mainframe computer hook-up in homes (e.g., games, community announcements and information bulletins, book reviews, etc.). Eight consumers/users participated in this meeting, along with several faculty members engaged in this research project. Meetings were audio-recorded with full knowledge and consent by group members. The INDAX transcript referenced throughout this chapter was generated from a thirty-five minute portion of these meetings, resulting in a fifty-three page transcript.
4. A useful methodological introduction to "conversation analysis" is offered by Robert Hopper, Susan Koch, and Jennifer Mandelbaum, "Conversation Analysis Methods", in *Contemporary Issues in Language and Discourse Processes,* Donald G. Ellis and William A. Donahue (Eds.), Hillsdale, New Jersey: Lawrence Erlbaum Associates, 1986, pp. 169–186.
5. See Harvey Sacks, Emmanuel Schegloff, and Gail Jefferson, "A Simplest Systematics for the Organization for Conversation," *Language,* 53, 361–382.

Appendix A

The transcription notation system employed for the segments is an adaptation of Gail Jefferson's work in conversation analysis (see Atkinson and Heritage, 1984, pp. ix–xvi). The symbols may be described as follows:

Colon(s). An extended sound or syllable is noted by a colon (:). A single colon indicates a short prolongation (e.g., "Uh:h"). Longer sound extensions are indicated by more than one colon (e.g., "de::scribe");

Underlining. Vocalic emphasis of syllables, words, or phrases (e.g., "att*ack*ed you was the *eyes*");

Single Parentheses Enclosing Numbers or Periods Within an Utterance. Speakers often pause during an utterance. If the pause is too short to be timed it is indicated by enclosing a period within parentheses (e.g., "is the *only* thing that (.) made you believe that (.) the photograph"). Intervals of longer duration are indicated by seconds and tenths of seconds (e.g., "Um:m (1.2) on that occasion (0.4) preliminary hearing (0.2)");

Single Parentheses Enclosing Numbers Between an Utterance. Intervals between same or different speaker's utterances are so noted:

W: Yes.

   (2.6)

p: Uh:h (1.6) did you

Single Parentheses Enclosing Utterances or Blank Spaces. Indicates transcriptionist doubt as to words or sounds transcribed as best possible (e.g., "cuz I (left early)."), or when undecipherable and/or when names of interactants are anonymous (e.g., "start work or do ya (   )?").

Double Parentheses Enclosing Words. Are employed when providing details of the scene (e.g., "((angered)) When you see somebody").

Periods. A falling vocal tone is indicated by a period. Such tones do not necessarily occur at the end of a sentence, though they may (e.g., "I'm not sure.")

Question Marks. Indicate a rising inflection, not necessarily a question (e.g., "you saw the suspect's footwear?")

Asterisk. A passage of talk noticeably softer and/or quieter than surrounding talk (e.g., "*Yes.")

Equal Signs. Suggest latching of adjacent utterances, with no interval and no overlap between utterances:

D: *three* o'clock?=

W: =*Some*time

Single Brackets. When overlapping utterances do not start simultaneously, the point at which an ongoing utterance is joined by another is marked with a single left-hand bracket:

P: after they occurred (0.4) or wo rse.

                                  [

W: Worse.

Exclamation Points. An animated, though not necessarily exclamatory, tone (e.g., "don't you think you'd recognize 'em!!!").

Hyphens. Indicate a halting, abrupt cut off of a word or sound (e.g., "wi- dirty bu- shoes on").

Less Than/Greater Than Signs. When portions of an utterance are delivered at a pace quicker than surrounding talk, they are so marked:

J: both of you just said in that > and let me see if I'm reading it right. < .hhh

Nonverbal Communication in the Small Group

Peter A. Andersen

Each day we communicate in numerous small groups otherwise known as families, parties, car pools, seminars, meetings, work groups, assembly lines, writing projects, dinner engagements, camping trips, and "bull sessions." Many researchers have estimated that nonverbal or nonlinguistic communication has more impact on listeners than does verbal communication. Nonverbal communication can send messages even when no verbal messages are being exchanged. A silent smile, wink, or touch can often convey far more than a whole string of statements. Nonverbal communication can also have a significant effect on what we say. A facial expression or tone of voice may provide emphasis for what is said. Nonverbal communication sometimes contradicts and undercuts what we say. At these times the nonverbal messages are usually believed instead of the verbal messages. Nonverbal communication is a ubiquitous phenomena; nonverbal messages are being sent whenever a receiver is aware of another's presence. Moreover, every verbal message is constantly modified by our nonverbal behavior. In this article the various codes of nonverbal communication are discussed in a small group context. Groups are rich sources of nonverbal behavior. In a group, so many messages are sent and received nonverbally that the best thing to do is to analyze each piece separately before reassembling the nonverbal puzzle.

These codes or channels of nonverbal communication are qualitatively different from verbal communication in a variety of ways. Verbal communication is single-channelled, precise, digital, linguistic, discrete, and governed primarily by left hemispheric brain processes. Nonverbal communication is multichannelled, subtle, analogic, nonlinguistic, continuous, and governed primarily by right hemispheric brain processes (Andersen, Garrison, & Andersen, 1979). The concern for nonverbal communication comes from a realization that verbal and linguistic models provide an incomplete and inaccurate description of the communication process. This article is an attempt to show that behavior and meaning in small group interaction is to a large extent dependent on nonverbal and nonlinguistic experiences.

By analyzing seven codes of nonverbal communication discussed in this essay some important group functions will be examined. Within this essay the following questions regarding nonverbal behavior in the small group will be addressed: What determines and facilitates group leadership? How much of the group's total interaction time should each member use? How can a person hold the floor while being interrupted? How can one group member appropriately reply to another over-talkative group member? What are the good "vibes" or feelings that characterize the communication in some groups? How is interpersonal attraction and warmth communicated in small groups? What effect do various types of communication anxiety have on small group communication? Is a crowded group environment most desirable? How do group members manipulate each other's behavior? What intercultural differences can lead to problems in a small group? How can you be more effective as a small group communicator? Hopefully these questions have whetted your appetite for learning how to be more nonverbally effective in your small group interactions.

Physical Appearance

Long before nonverbal communication is initiated, persons in a small group begin to make judgments about others based on physical appearance. Obviously, information regarding your sex, race, and occupation are transmitted to others by your appearance. But more than that is communicated. Rightly or wrongly, others infer from your appearance attributes such as: your income, your relative status, your political attitudes and affiliation, your recreation likes and dislikes, and whether or not you are a friendly person. These judgments are not always correct; nonetheless, all of us form powerful initial impressions based solely on physical appearance.

Since appearance is so important, you might think that everyone dresses to communicate. Not so. People often dress to please themselves, to maintain a certain self-image, or to keep up with fashion. Instead, effective small group members should view clothes and hair styles as an important silent statement made to the group. Dress that is appropriate is perhaps most important. Wearing jeans and a t-shirt to a corporate board meeting would lead to ineffectiveness and probably ridicule on the part of other group members. Likewise, wearing a business suit to a pool party would be perceived as inappropriate, if not weird, behavior. Dress and hair style can be used to effectively manipulate the perceptions of others.

Similarly, your physical appearance has an effect on your own self-perception and behavior. Think back to a group situation where you felt really good about the way you looked. Were you more outgoing, flirtatious, confident, happy, or relaxed? Most people report one or more of these feelings when they are well-dressed. Inappropriate dress can lead to insecurity and may result in reactions of hostility, withdrawal, or aggression toward other small group members (Barker, *et al.,* 1979, p. 184).

The shape of your body is related to the attitudes others hold toward you and also to your own attitudes about yourself. Sheldon (1940) classified people into three basic body-types: Endomorphs, rounded, heavy people; Mesomorphs, angular, athletic people; and Ectomorphs, linear, thin people. Of course an infinite range or combination of these body types is possible, so that most people don't fit neatly into one category.

Considerable discrimination occurs against the endomorph in American culture. They are often perceived as happy, lazy, sloppy, slow, jolly, stupid, and socially undesirable (Andersen & Singleton, 1978; Spiegel & Machotka, 1974). Mesomorphs are usually perceived positively in a group and are often chosen as leaders. Nonetheless, some people equate muscles with stupidity and treat mesomorphs in accord with the "dumb jock" stereotype. Ectomorphs are perceived as frail, sickly and nervous, but studious and intelligent as well. Recent research has found that female ectomorphs are more shy and fearful about communication than other people (Andersen & Singleton, 1978) and may try to avoid communication entirely. While a stereotype based on physical appearance may have some validity, the intelligent small group member should view stereotypes as weak and tentative data. Waiting to observe numerous nonverbal and verbal contributions of a group member before making an evaluation is much more advisable.

Oculesics

Vision is one of the two primary ways in which human beings receive verbal and nonverbal messages (the other primary channel is sound). The study of how the eyes *send* messages is called oculesics, the most important form of which is eye contact or gazing. In general American culture eye contact is an invitation to communicate. When you look at another person you signal your interest to him or her, and the fact that you want to communciate. Avoidance of eye contact is common in public places or among strangers because we usually do not want to encourage communication in these circumstances.

In a small group, eye contact invites interaction, particularly when it involves the group leader. Returning the leader's gaze signals readiness to respond whereas averting the leader's gaze shows desire to avoid interaction (Barker, *et al.*, 1979, pp. 187–188). Mehrabian (1981, p. 38) maintained that conversation is likely to occur in a group only if members select seats where eye contact can be comfortably initiated. An arrangement where each group member can establish eye contact with every other group member will maximize group interaction. Indeed, Mehrabian (1981) suggested using zig-zag counters in bars and restaurants to facilitate interaction. Sitting directly across from a stranger is too forward, but sitting at a long counter or bar prevents eye contact and frustrates communication.

Group leaders need to be particularly attuned to the importance of eye contact. Silverstein and Stang (1976) found that group members with visual centrality spoke most often. A number of studies reported by Mehrabian (1981, p. 68) found that leaders or persons of high status assume central positions in a group where they can easily monitor others. Although more will be said about seating positions later in this article a group member must have visual access to the other members if he/she is to assume a leadership role.

Aversion of eye contact in a group often leads to negative evaluations on the part of other group members. They may perceive the lack of eye contact as disinterest or apathy, as rude or inappropriate, as shy or nervous behavior, or, worst of all, as dishonest or deceitful. These attributions may not be correct; however, communication of erroneous information can destroy a group member's image with other members and even damage the process and productivity of the group. Good small group listening behavior requires considerable visual attention to the speaker. However, group members should also be aware that these norms are valid for white North Americans and that people from other parts of the world have different oculesic norms. Many blacks in America treat eye contact as a putdown. People from Latin America, particularly children, often look down as a sign of respect. Applying our stereotypes of white Americans to other racial and ethnic groups can lead to serious misunderstandings (Scheflen, 1972, p. 96).

Another oculesic behavior that affects interpersonal relationships is pupil dilation. A number of studies have found that the pupils of a person's eyes dilate when that person is experiencing positive affect for or attraction to another person (Hess, 1965, 1975). More surprisingly, individuals with dilated pupils are perceived as more attractive by others (Andersen, Todd-Mancillas, & DiClemente, 1980; Hess, 1975). People report that persons with dilated pupils are more good looking, friendly, warm and pleasant, but rarely identify pupil dilation as the factor responsible for the increased attraction (Hess & Goodwin, 1973; Stass & Willis, 1967). Pupil dilation is one of the ways affect and attraction are communicated at the intuitive level, with little or no conscious awareness on the part of the receiver. In groups, such nonverbal cues may increase or decrease the interpersonal attraction of group members without any apparent reason. Evidently, pupil dilation increases our perceived social and physical attraction, but has no apparent effect on task attraction (Andersen, et al., 1980). Thus, while low level intuitive cues are important in interpersonal and affective relationships among group members, the task-attraction and ability of group members to work together seem not to be affected.

Kinesics

Kinesics is the study of communication through body movement. From subtle facial expressions to the larger movements of gestures and posture, kinesic cues are always available for small group members to perceive and evaluate.

Facial Expressions

Perhaps the part of the body richest in kinesic cues is the face. It is the face that conveys emotional states and evaluations better than any other communication channel. Ekman and his associates have established that basic facial expressions are universal and carry the same fundamental meaning throughout the world (Ekman & Friesen, 1975; Ekman, Friesen, & Ellsworth, 1972). Intercultural communication in groups is made possible by reading other group members' facial expressions even when verbal communication is limited or nonexistent. You can't read other group members like a book, though, despite such claims in the popular media. Most people are conscious of the meanings their face conveys to others. As a result, many of us mask or conceal our facial expressions with public faces having little to do with our internal feelings or emotions. White Anglo-Saxon protestant (WASP) culture, the predominant culture in the United States, and male WASPS in particular, frequently mask and internalize their facial expressions. Interestingly, internalizers (who display little emotion in their face) have larger psychological responses such as sweat and increased heart rate (Buck, Miller, & Caul, 1974).

Gestures

Many types of kinesic gestures have been studied by nonverbal researchers. Next time you observe a small group look for gestures which accompany speech called *illustrators*. These gestures are tied to the rhythm of speech and can aid group members in following the flow of speech. Comadena and Andersen (1978) found that very relaxed speakers used more illustrators than others, probably because they were not constrained by fear of speaking. Highly nervous speakers also used more gestures than moderately relaxed speakers, probably in an effort to overcome their anxiety. Self-touching behaviors called *adaptors* are also signs of nervousness or discomfort (Ekman & Friesen, 1969). Sensitive group members can tune in to the feelings of others by observing these kinesic cues. Some gestures have explicit meanings such as the OK sign and are called *emblems*. These gestures can complement or emphasize verbal statements and can be used as verbal substitutes in a noisy environment.

Postures, when walking or sitting, communicate much about a person's moods and emotions. Barker, et al. (1979) maintained that as group members enter the room one can determine if they are happy, sad, afraid, or determined. Similarly, LaFrance and Mayo (1978) reported several studies which show that wider, more open body postures result in more credibility and persuasive power (pp. 110–111). If you assume a narrow posture (legs and arms held close together), you reduce your status and persuasiveness in a group. Not coincidentally, males generally use much wider postures and have typically exercised much more power in groups than have females.

Body Synchrony

One of the most interesting aspects of kinesic behavior in groups is the fact that interactions mirror or imitate each other's kinesic behavior. This phenomena, also called postural echoes, body synchrony or body congruence, seem to occur when group members are tuned in to one another and literally on the same "wavelength." Morris (1977) contended being out of synchrony leads to the "bad vibes" or vibrations referred to in American slang. Scheflen (1972) provided a number of examples of parallel group postures for arm positions, self-touching behaviors, and leg positions (pp. 54, 73). Teachers often observe simultaneous movements or congruent body postures which indicate that the class is tuned in to one another and to the teacher. Likewise, the initiator of a simultaneous movement is often a leader (Thompson, 1973).

Thompson also maintains that in small groups of three people, two will often sit parallel. Morris (1977) argued that two subgroups maintaining different postural echoes are often "taking sides" in a controversy. This may be perceived as a coalition or clique. Cohen (1977) found that movement profiles could be established for entire groups. Likewise it was found that some individuals had a similar or synchronous movement profile with the entire group that could be an indicator of group leadership. Burgoon and Saine (1976) reported several studies which found that people are more likely to mirror the posture and gestures of persons with high status and power. Analyzing the degree of kinesic synchrony can tell an observer much about the workings and structure of a group.

Work groups are very reliant on all aspects of nonverbal communication, particularly kinesic cues. Argyle (1975) maintained that the smooth flow of words is accomplished through nonverbal communication. Some of the forms of kinesic communication used for work purposes include: the rate of coordinated movements; helping; guiding through bodily contact; gesture language where noise or distance reduce the effectiveness of talk; kinesic comments on performance, including raised eyebrows, head or arm gestures, and facial expressions, and directions communicated by body movements or pointing.

Not being tuned in to the kinesic communication of one's work groups, from drafting tables and writing projects to construction crews, reduces work productivity and increases interpersonal friction.

Regulation

Kinesic communication is also used in groups to control and regulate interpersonal communication behavior. In conversations, speaker turns are negotiated kinesically. Speakers in a group frequently signal the end of their turn through a group of kinesic cues which serve to yield the floor to others. Duncan (1972) has shown that termination and relaxation of hand movements (illustrators) serve as a turn-yielding cue. Likewise, Scheflen (1972, p. 50) maintained that at the end of a point, speakers generally change head and eye positions and shift their posture. Similarly, when a receiver leans forward or uses gestures prior to speaking, it signals the speaker that the receiver wants a turn to speak. These are called turn-acquiring cues. Finally, speakers can suppress others' turns by using many different nonverbal cues. Scheflen (1979) discussed group therapy sessions where members of the group use movements of the body and legs to "box in" another group member and prevent her from participating. In ordinary social groups dominant persons often use gestures and forward leans to maintain the floor and prevent interruptions by other group members (Scheflen, 1972, p. 98). In large part, it is kinesic behavior that establishes who talks when and for how long.

Listener's kinesic movements also can determine who makes decisions and who leads the group as well as who talks the most. Scheflen (1972, p. 67) showed that listeners often turn their bodies toward someone they want to hear. Often listeners will turn toward and look at the leader, thereby eliciting a response. Even the very act of being allowed to participate in a group is dependent on kinesic cues. When outsiders approach a conversational group they seldom move right into the group. Instead, they wait a short distance from the group until group members turn toward them and gesture them in (La France & Mayo, 1978, pp. 128–129).

Vocalics

Vocalics is the study of the nonverbal elements of the human voice. This includes vocal qualities of speech such as pitch, rhythm, tempo resonance and control; vocal characteristics such as laughing, crying, sighing, yawning, coughing, inhaling or exhaling; vocal segregates such as "uh-huh," "uhn-ah," "ah," and "um" (Trager, 1958), as well as singing (Andersen, Andersen & Garrison, 1978).

The most important function of vocalics is the modification of verbal messages. One evening the author and several of his friends found over twenty-five ways to say the word "yes." There were positive and negative yeses; happy and sad ones; seductive and repugnant yeses; confused and assured ones. Indeed, the meaning of a spoken utterance has less to do with the word one selects than the way it is spoken. Receivers are inclined to believe the vocal meaning when verbal and vocal messages contradict each other. In a small group it is not sufficient to say the right thing but to say it in the correct way.

One common problem with interpersonal communication in the small group is misunderstanding sarcasm. During a group's attempt to put together a major group-written project, one member hands an illegible half-page outline to the group leader. The leader looks at the outline and responds, "this is just great," in a sarcastic tone of voice. The group member smiles and feels satisfaction at the "obvious" delight shown by his group leader. Later the group member is shocked because the other group members think the work is inadequate. Children and people with poor listening and/or intellectual skills often misunderstand sarcasm. A recent study by Andersen, Andersen, Wendt and Murphy (1981) revealed that only 14% of kindergarteners and 25–30% of children in primary grades understand sarcasm. Not until the senior year of high school are two-thirds of the students able to understand sarcastic messages.

Vocalic cues often take place in the backchannel as listener responses. The backchannel includes all verbal and nonverbal cues sent by a receiver back to a speaker. In this way a speaker knows a receiver is listening and understanding. Receivers frequently backchannel with vocal utterances such as "mm-hmm," "mmmm," or "uh-huh." White Americans do not utilize the backchannel as much as blacks, Chicanos, or Southern Europeans. This sometimes leads to the impression by people from these groups that white Americans are not listening or are not "tuned-in" to the conversation. Similarly, white Americans often think blacks and Chicanos are rude and interrupting. These intercultural differences in backchannel behavior should be recognized by group members to prevent intercultural misunderstandings.

Chronemics

The way we use and structure time and the meanings we attach to time use is the study of chronemics. In the United States, time is thought of as a commodity. The way we talk about time is indicative of our attitudes toward it. We think we can "save" time much as we save money. We speak of "wasting" time which usually means we would rather be doing something other than what we are doing presently. We talk about "spending" time as though it has a dollar value attached to it. Of course, we cannot really save or waste time. Time moves irreversibly on. But the rhetoric we use divulges our underlying attitudes about time. Though people in some European countries such as Germany and Switzerland are even more time-conscious than Americans, most of the world's people do not share the time-commodity orientations of Americans. Since our own cultural time orientation is something we take for granted, it is particularly important to understand the time orientations of other peoples. In the third world, people have little understanding of formal schedules, what is meant by being in a hurry, or how to formally structure time. On a trip to some rural islands in the Bahamas the author found that life stops when it rains. The ground crew would not unload the airplane and gas station attendants would not pump gas until the rain stopped. The American college students who were visiting the island on their short one-week spring break were outraged. Their anger was useless for they were up against a cultural custom of Caribbean people. It is very important to remember when working in a group of people from different cultures that the beat of their life is to a totally different drummer. In such a group, you would be safe to assume that all your assumptions about time are false.

In a fast-paced, time-conscious culture like America, being late is not viewed with much tolerance. Late people are thought of as inconsiderate, selfish, undisciplined, and incompetent. A work group will almost certainly start without you if you are more than ten minutes late. Arrivals delayed by more than five minutes are usually accompanied by verbal excuses such as, "my car wouldn't start," or "my child was ill." University professors have undoubtedly heard every excuse for being late ever invented.

People also vary greatly in body speed. Individuals who move very slowly are labeled *hypokinetic,* and those who move rapidly are termed *hyperkinetic* (Barker, et al., 1979). There are a number of factors that produce slow or fast body speeds. Metabolic differences are certainly important. Hyperkinetic people are more likely to be found in the north rather than rural areas. Barker, et al. (1979) outline the problem when these different individuals work with one another:

> Hypokinetic group members and hyperkinetic group members potentially are annoying to each other. For example, you may have wondered how a particular person could talk so fast (or so slowly). However both a rapidly moving group member and a more slowly moving group member may be frustrated if they must work on a task together. . . . In extreme cases the two individuals cannot work together. Therefore, you should keep individual differences in movements in mind as group members are assigned to different tasks (p. 192).

Similarly, some people have much longer response latency, the time it takes to respond to another person's statement or question. Group members should be aware that rapid or slow responses are not necessarily signs of rudeness or stupidity but often are characteristics of the individual's family or culture.

Finally, can an individual talk too much or too little in a group? Harper, Wiens, and Matarazzo (1978) summarized this research and maintained that the answer is yes. In three-person groups, people who talked 50% of the time were judged most favorably on leadership qualities, whereas those who talked 33% of the time were liked most by other group members. Evidently overly talkative and dominant group members are perceived as rude and selfish. However, being slightly more talkative and dominant is perceived as highly credible and indicative of leadership qualities. Sharing talk-time will result in the best affective and interpersonal outcomes. Talking little is evaluated negatively and reflective of low investment in or commitment to the group.

Haptics

The study of communication via interpersonal touch is called haptics. Perhaps no form of communication is so intimate as is tactile contact. Touch has the power to repel, disgust, insult, threaten, console, reassure, love, and arouse. Of course, many variables determine how touch is perceived, the most important of which is the relational history of the interactants. Among close friends, even after long periods of separation, touch is acceptable and expected. Among enemies or strangers touch is considered rude, inappropriate and threatening.

Touch in a small group may establish greater teamwork, solidarity, or sharing. In some northern European countries at Christmas, families join hands and dance around the Christmas tree. The handholding symbolizes the togetherness of family during this important holiday. A few years ago the defensive unit of the Denver Broncos began holding hands in the huddle. Initially, announcers snickered and suggested that really tough men would never hold hands. The snickers disappeared as the "Orange Crush" defensive unit became one of the most successful and closest knit units in football. Touch became the symbol of the solidarity of the defensive unit that made many tackles as a group.

An important variable that affects how much individuals will touch and how favorable they will perceive touch is touch avoidance. Touch avoidance is a trait-like characteristic and individuals can be placed on a continuum ranging from touch approachers to touch avoiders (Andersen & Leibowitz, 1978). Research on touch avoidance shows it is unrelated to verbal approach/avoidance measures such as communication apprehension or self-disclosure. Similarly, no strong relationships between touch avoidance and self-esteem were observed (Andersen & Leibowitz, 1978). The best predictors of touch avoidance were cultural role variables. Females, middle-aged, and protestants were most likely to avoid opposite sex touch. Whereas males, middle-aged, and protestants were most likely to avoid same-sex touch. In a small group it is important to realize that some persons enjoy or even expect touch. However, others may avoid touch even after developing close relationships with group members.

The type of touch is also crucial in determining what touch communicates. Pats are friendly, and strokes are sensual and/or sexual. Likewise, certain parts of the body are rarely touched except in very intimate relationships. However, the shoulders, back, arms and hands are highly accessible and seldom create a negative reaction except in the most touch-avoidant individuals.

Touch can be used supportively and affirmatively in a group, or as an aggressive and offensive tool. Appropriate forms of touch for most individuals communicate solidarity and affection. Barker, et al. (1979) maintained that a major function of touch in small groups is reassurance and consolation. They contend touch is also used in small groups to communicate encouragement, happiness, or emotional support. Conversely, touch can be used to intimidate. Pushing, shoving, finger pointing (whether touch actually occurs or not), and grabbing not only communicate negative affect but are often a prelude to physical violence. A rude turn-taking cue often observed in highly verbal groups is to use a hand on another group member's shoulder to either gain or maintain the floor. This is a "subtle" form of pushing the other person out of the conversation and will almost always lead to bad feelings.

Proxemics

The ways in which we communicate through the use of interpersonal space and distance is called proxemics. More small group research has been done on proxemic communication than on any other topic of nonverbal communication behavior. Certainly, the issues of territorialty, personal space and density, seating arrangements, and barriers to communication can facilitate or destroy the effectiveness of small groups. (Eds. note: After reading this brief summary on proxemics be sure to read the essay by Judee Burgoon in this volume.)

Territoriality

If someone sat in "your" desk chair or parked in "your" driveway, you would probably be upset and at least want to know why someone is in "your" territory. These reactions are quite natural in almost all human societies as well as in animal species. The need to designate and protect your own space is a basic need of all people. In fact, the writers of the Bill of Rights recognized this need and required that people, their places of residence, and their papers and effects be free from unreasonable searches even by government and police officials.

Indeed, to maintain our territory we often resort to verbal labels such as office signs, "keep off the grass" signs and "do not disturb" signs. Moreover, we usually designate personal or group territory with markers such as blankets or coats that reserve space at a football game, or books and purses that save seats in class. In several unreported experiments the author has noted that a full soda pop cup will generally reserve a university cafeteria seat for over an hour. On the other hand, a half-full cup rarely lasts ten minutes, probably because it is not perceived as a marker but only as someone's garbage. A series of studies reported by Harper, Wiens, and Matarazzo (1978, p. 285) found: (1) male markers were more effective than female markers, though both worked to some extent; (2) females were equally likely as were males to invade marked space; (3) markers were less effective in reserving space in prime areas for social interaction; (4) verbal comments were made frequently by neighbors in defense of marked space.

Tenure, even in the absence of markers, tends to claim and reserve space. Students who sit at the same high school or college cafeteria table each day regard it as theirs by the tenure they exercise. They may even attempt to oust another group of students who have inadvertently occupied "their" territory. Indeed, in someone's home territory, such as their house or office, territorial rights include choice of seats (as in Archie Bunker's famous chair), higher status, and greater freedom of movement with the territory.

Personal Space

Wherever we go, whatever we do, we are surrounded by a personal space bubble. This bubble is neither visible nor physical, but psychological and interpersonal. Most people stay outside our bubble, which is reserved for those we trust and like. People in various cultures have different sized bubbles. For North Americans who have large personal space bubbles, Hall (1968) maintained there are four distinct zones of interaction.

The first of these zones is called *intimate distance* which extends from bodily contact to a distance of about eighteen inches. The only people who enter this zone are persons with whom we share an intimate relationship such as close friends, lovers, and some family members. Small children, who have yet to learn American proxemic norms, are most free to penetrate our intimate space. Rarely will groups of people interact in one another's intimate space zones. It is probable that at such close distances group members will feel inhibited from interacting and will make an attempt to restore their personal space bubble by moving back even if that means leaving the group.

Personal distance extends from one-and-one-half to about four feet and is our typical zone of interaction with friends and acquaintances. This distance (not coincidently, at about an arm's length) makes touch more difficult and defines this interpersonal distance as non-intimate. Most groups interact at this close, yet safe, distance. Invasions of space by strangers or new acquaintances will often result in group members restoring their interpersonal bubble by turning away, moving back, or breaking off eye contact.

The final two interaction distances are *social-consulting space,* which extends from 4 to 8 feet, and *public space,* which is any distance over 8 feet. Social space requires that we recognize another person's presence, whereas public space does not. Social space is the distance we sit or stand from strangers, very new acquaintances and some businesspeople. Public distance is reserved for mass lectures, speeches, and for public figures. Groups should be careful not to maintain distances at the far range of social consulting space or they literally lose contact with one another and often break into interacting subgroups.

How well a group cooperates is often a function of their interaction distance. Mehrabian (1981) argued that when professionals interact with clients or patients at large distances or behind physical barriers the establishment of interpersonal trust and rapport is made difficult (p. 37). Patterson (1978), in his summary of proxemic research, reports that groups making collective decisions sat closer together and in more circular arrangements than the same groups when they made individual decisions. Sommer (1965) found that cooperating groups, working together on a common project, preferred close, face-to-face distances. Indeed, Stacks and Burgoon (1979) found that individuals in a group were more persuasive and credible at 18 inches than at 36 or 54 inches, indicating greater communication effects at the close end of the personal distance zone. In general, groups perform better, more persuasively, and more cooperatively at close, face-to-face distances.

Density and Crowding

When a group is confined to a small amount of space it has a greater density than the same group in a large space. Group density can be objectively measured by the number of square feet or square meters per interactant. Crowding, on the other hand, is a perception of each group member. Some individuals may feel crowded at one density level while others feel little crowding in the same circumstances.

Generally, high density group environments are perceived as more crowded and less satisfactory by group members. Aiello (1976) examined four-person groups of fourth, eighth, and eleventh grade students in a small (4 ft. $\times$ 2½ ft.) room versus a large room (10 ft. $\times$ 12 ft.). At all three grade levels students characterized the smaller room as more crowded and less comfortable than the larger room. Moreover, measures of physiological stress and psychological discomfort were greater in the smaller room than the larger room.

In studies of adults, similar results are reported. Aiello, Epstein, and Karlin (1975) studied identical dormitory rooms containing either two or three residents. Subjects living in the triple rooms felt more crowded and less satisfied than those in double rooms. Moreover, during the semester physiological tests of stress (urine cortisol) showed increased stress for the tripled students and decreased stress for the doubled ones. However, results did not show a decrease in work productivity in more socially dense environments. Research summarized by Insel and Lindgren (1978) showed that male work groups in high density conditions rated their space as more crowded and less satisfactory than those in low density conditions. Nonetheless, there were no differences in work productivity between these two groups (pp. 18–19). Other studies summarized by Insel and Lindgren (1978, p. 58) demonstrate that group members may get used to high density environments over time through the process of adaptation. When invasion of privacy and crowding occur repeatedly over time, people may not only accept these conditions but come to enjoy higher group density.

Finally, it is evident that sex differences do exist in reactions to group density. Barker, et al. (1979) observed that in America females generally sit closer together in groups than do males. Patterson and Schaeffer (1978) found that all male groups sat farthest apart, mixed groups at intermediate distances, and all female groups sat closest together. The authors argue that, in part, these findings are explained by the fact that women are more likely to develop warm, dependent, close, affiliative relationships than are males. Insel and Lindren (1978) found that men who carried on group discussions in larger rooms were more psychologically comfortable and rated each other higher on traits such as likability, unselfishness, and calmness. On the other hand, women reported more positive feelings toward themselves and others when they carried on group discussions in the more congested, smaller room (p. 44). In their study of residential density, Aiello, et al. (1975) found that in dense rooms males withdrew from communication, whereas females increased their level of interaction. Certainly, dense environments have more negative effects on males than on females.

Small Group Ecology

The study of seating positions and furniture arrangement in groups is called small group ecology (Sommer, 1965). In general, arrangements that bring people closer together, permit them to face one another, and engage in eye contact stimulate the highest levels of group interaction. Knapp (1978, pp. 133–135), in his summary of seating behavior, maintained that for casual conversation groups people in both the U.S. and Britain prefer adjacent seats at round tables and either face to face or at a 90° angle at a rectangular table. In cooperative groups, working on a common task, individuals prefer adjacent seats or face-to-face positions. When students were given an opportunity to assemble chairs in a classroom to facilitate interaction, they chose a U-shape arrangement (Heston & Garner, 1972). In this way students could establish eye contact with one another and with their teacher. In traditional straight-row classrooms Rosenfeld and Civikly (1976) reported a series of studies that show the students in the front and center of the classroom participate more. Likewise, in seminar rooms participation was greatest by those sitting opposite the instructor. These studies also indicate that those seminar students who sit directly beside the instructor, and thus out of eye contact, participated the least. Mehrabian (1981, p. 119) reported several studies showing that sofas minimize interaction for groups of people. The conversational effective capacity of a sofa, whatever its length, is two people.

Environments that make communication difficult and keep people apart have been called *sociofugal*. Environments that bring people together and stimulate interaction are labeled *sociopetal* (Sommer, 1967). In a summary of sociofugal and sociopetal room arrangements Leathers (1976, pp. 54–55) suggested that barriers (such as desks or tables) between interactants impede the quantity and quality of communication. Mehrabian (1976, pp. 258–259) reported a series of interesting experiments in bars which indicates the straight-line bar is a sociofugal environment, except for the corners where patrons can face one another. Circular or zig-zag bars provide better body orientation, facilitate eye contact, and result in much more group communication.

A whole host of studies have examined the locations selected by leaders, dominant individuals, and extroverts in small groups and are summarized by Knapp (1978, pp. 132–133) and LaFrance and Mayo (1978, pp. 100–101). These studies show that leaders usually select the head of the table, though socioemotional leaders often select the middle of the table. Similarly, people in these "high interaction" locations talk more. Leaders probably select these positions because they can see and be seen by other group members. This enables them to interact with, monitor, and influence other persons in the group. Being at the head of the table also positions leaders far enough away from the group to indicate status yet close enough to maximize interaction.

High status may be a barrier to close interpersonal relations. While status carries with it power and persuasive influence, several studies reported by Mehrabian (1981) and Thompson (1973, p. 38) found that group members tend to avoid seats directly beside group leaders, classroom teachers, or other high status individuals. These seats may be intimidating to subordinates in a group and are poor for interacting because they remove much eye contact with the leader.

Many small group members, teachers, and group leaders fail to stimulate interaction and lead groups effectively due to their insensitivity to proxemic communication. Familiarity with some of the principles discussed here can help individuals communicate more successfully in small groups.

Conclusion

The purpose of this essay was to increase your awareness of how some important types of nonverbal communication function in small group interaction. This article has focused not only on zero-history groups of college sophomores but also on real groups encountered in daily life such as families, seminars, and work groups. Being tuned in to the nonverbal behavior of others in the small group will reveal meaning in interpersonal communication that you may be surprised to find. Recent research has shown that nonverbal behavior is sufficiently complex that few of us process most of the nonverbal messages available to us in everyday life. Moreover, knowledge of nonverbal communication can increase your awareness of your own nonverbal behavior. Many students of nonverbal communication begin to examine critically and to change their own behavior as well. Critics of these suggested changes in nonverbal behavior argue that manipulating one's own behavior leads to insincere and aritificial communication. Of course, this is no more true than increasing vocabulary. Some people discover how to communicate effectively in the nonverbal domain through observation, modelling, reinforcement, or trial and error. Others fail to acquire sufficient nonverbal skill. I am struck by how many people I encounter who desire warmth, want leadership, need friends and want to communicate, yet fail in their interpersonal encounters to achieve what they desire. Although it is difficult to feign real warmth or turn a follower into a leader, it is not so difficult to teach people to communicate what they already feel. This brief exploration of the realm of nonverbal communication in the small group is an attempt to provide that knowledge.

References

Aiello, J. R. "Effects of episodic crowding: a developmental perspective." Paper presented at the Eastern Psychological Association Convention, New York, April, 1976.

Aiello, J. R., Epstein, Y. M., & Karlin, R. A. "Field experimental research on human crowding." Paper presented at the Eastern Psychological Association Convention, New York, 1975.

Andersen, P. A., Andersen, J. F., and Garrison, J. P., "Singing apprehension and talking apprehension: the development of two constructs." *Sign Language Studies,* 1978, *19,* 155–189.

Andersen, P. A., Andersen, J. F., Wendt, N. J., and Murphy, M. A. "The development of nonverbal communication behavior in school children grades K–12." Paper presented at the annual convention of the International Communication Association, Minneapolis, Minnesota, May, 1981.

Andersen, P. A., Garrison, J. P., and Andersen, J. F. "Implications of a neurophysiological approach for the study of nonverbal communication." *Human Communication Research,* 1979, *6,* 74–89.

Andersen, P. A. and Leibowitz, K. "The development and nature of the construct touch avoidance." *Environmental Psychology and Nonverbal Behavior,* 1978, *3,* 89–106.

Andersen, P. A. and Singleton, G. W. "The relationship between body type and communication avoidance." Paper presented at the Eastern Communication Association Convention, Boston, March, 1978.

Andersen, P. A., Todd-Mancillas, W. R., and DiClemente, L. "The effects of pupil dilation on physical, social, and task attraction." *Australian Scan: Journal of Human Communication,* 1980, *7 & 8,* 89–95.

Argyle, M. "Non-verbal communication in human social interaction." In R. A. Hinde (Ed.) *Nonverbal Communication.* Cambridge, England: Cambridge University Press, 1975.

Barker, L. L., Cegala, D. J., Kibler, R. J., and Wahlers, K. J. *Groups in Process: An Introduction to Small Group Communication.* Englewood Cliffs, N.J.: Prentice-Hall, 1979.

Buck, R. W., Miller, R. E., and Caul, W. F. "Sex, personality, and physiological variables in the communication of affect via facial expression." *Journal of Personality and Social Psychology,* 1974, *30,* 587–596.

Burgoon, J. K. & Saine, T. *The Unspoken Dialogue: An Introduction to Nonverbal Communication.* Boston: Houghton Mifflin Company, 1978.

Cohen, L. R. "Small group leadership and the parakinesic level of body movement behavior: a systems view." Paper presented at the annual convention of the Eastern Communication Association, New York, March, 1977.

Comadena, M. E. and Andersen, P. A. "Kinesic correlates of communication apprehension: a study of hand movements." Paper presented at the annual convention of the International Communication Association, Chicago, April, 1978.

Duncan, S., Jr. "Some signals and rules for taking speaking turns in conversations." *Journal of Personality and Social Psychology,* 1972, *23,* 283–292.

Ekman, P. and Friesen, W. V. "The repertoire of nonverbal behavior: categories, origins, usage and coding." *Semiotica,* 1969, *1,* 49–98.

Ekman, P. and Friesen, W. V. *Unmasking the Face.* Englewood Cliffs, N.J.: Prentice-Hall, 1975.

Ekman, P., Friesen, W. V. and Allsworth, P. C. *Emotion in the Human Race.* New York: Pergamon Press, 1972.

Hall, E. T. Proxemics. *Current Anthropology,* 1968, *9,* 83–108.

Harper, R. G., Wiens, A. N., and Matarazzo, J. D. *Nonverbal Communication: The State of the Art.* New York: John Wiley & Sons, 1978.

Hess, E. H. Attitude and pupil size. *Scientific American,* 1965, *212,* 46–54.

Hess, E. H. The role of pupil size in communication. *Scientific American,* 1975, *233,* 110–119.

Hess, E. H. & Goodwin, E. "The present state of pupillometrics." In M. P. Janisse (Ed.) *Pupillary Dynamics and Behavior.* New York: Plenum Press, 1973, pp. 209–248.

Heston, J. K. & Garner. P. "A study of personal spacing and desk arrangement in a learning environment." Paper presented at the International Communication Association Convention, Atlanta, Georgia, April, 1972.

Insel, P. M. & Lindgen, A. C. *Too Close for Comfort: The Psychology of Crowding.* Englewood Cliffs, N.J.: Prentice-Hall, 1978.

Knapp, M. L. *Nonverbal Communication in Human Interaction.* New York: Holt, Rinehart, and Winston, 1978.

LaFrance, M. & Mayo, C. *Moving Bodies: Nonverbal Communication in Social Relationships.* Monterey, CA: Brooks/Cole Publishing, 1978.

Leathers, D. G. *Nonverbal Communication Systems.* Boston: Allyn and Bacon, 1976.

Mehrabian, A. *Public Places and Private Spaces: The Psychology of Work, Play, and Living Environments.* New York: Basic Books Inc., 1976.

Mehrabian, A. *Silent Messages.* Belmont, CA: Wadsworth Publishing, 1981.

Morris, C. *Manwatching: A Field Guide to Human Behavior.* New York: Harry Abrams Inc., 1977.

Patterson, M. L. "The role of space in social interaction." In A. W. Siegman & S. Feldstein, *Nonverbal Behavior and Communication.* Hillsdale, NJ: Lawrence Erlbaum Associates, 1978.

Patterson, M. L. & Schaeffer, R. E. "Effects of size and sex composition on interaction distance, participation and satisfaction in small groups." *Small Group Behavior,* 1977, *8,* 433–442.

Rosenfeld, L. B. & Civikly, J. M. *With Words Unspoken: The Nonverbal Experience.* New York: Holt, Rinehart and Winston, 1976.

Scheflen, A. E. *Body Language and the Social Order: Communication as Behavioral Control.* Englewood Cliffs, NJ: Prentice-Hall, 1972.

Sheldon, W. N. *The Varieties of Human Physique.* New York: Harper and Row, 1940.

Silverstein, C. H. & Stang, D. J. "Seating position and interaction in triads: a field study." *Sociometry,* 1976, *39,* 166–170.

Sommer, R. "Further studies of small group ecology." *Sociometry,* 1965, *28,* 337–348.

Sommer, R. Sociofugal space. *American Journal of Sociology,* 1967, *72,* 654–660.

Spiegel, J. & Machotka, P. *Messages of the Body.* New York: The Free Press, 1974.

Stacks, D. W. & Burgoon, J. K. "The persuasive effects of violating spacial distance expectations in small groups." Paper presented at the Southern Speech Communication Association Convention, Biloxi, MS, April, 1979.

Stass, J. W. & Willis, F. N. "Eye contact, pupil dilation, and personal preference." *Psychonomic Science,* 1967, *7,* 375–376.

Thompson, J. J. *Beyond Words: Nonverbal Communication in the Classroom.* New York: Citation Press, 1973.

Trager, G. L. Paralanguage: a first approximation. *Studies in Linguistics,* 1958, *13,* 1–12.

Spatial Relationships in Small Groups

Judee K. Burgoon

An old German fable has it that one fall night, the porcupines came together in the forest for a little socializing. Finding the night air to be quite cold, they tried to move close together for warmth but found they kept pricking each other with their quills. So they moved farther apart but once again became cold. They continued moving back and forth until they finally arrived at a distance which afforded them both warmth and comfort. Henceforth, that distance became known as good manners.

Like the porcupines, we humans also seek optimal spacing arrangements when in groups. Our *proxemic* patterns—the ways in which we perceive, utilize and arrange our spatial environment— seem to be governed by two competing needs. One is the *need for affiliation.* We are social creatures who desire to associate with other people and to form bonds of attachment with them. Close proximity both signals that desire and permits those social bonds to develop.

The other requirement is a *need for privacy.* There are times when we wish to distance ourselves from the group, to achieve greater physical security, to escape stimulation and stress, to gain a greater sense of personal control, or to permit greater psychological freedom and self-reflection. Greater distance provides a form of insulation, a cushion against intrusions from others.

These two conflicting needs sometimes lead us to approach the group and sometimes to avoid it. Typically, group spacing behavior reflects an equilibrium state in which these approach-avoidance tendencies are brought into balance within individual members and among members of the group. Because our proxemic patterns relate to some of our most fundamental human needs, proxemic behaviors, and especially deviations from the equilibrium or expected spatial arrangement, can convey some very powerful albeit subtle messages.

The Organization of Space

There are two perspectives from which group spacing behavior can be examined. One is to consider the nature of the people involved and the purposes of the interaction factors which dictate how individuals choose to distance themselves from one another. This aspect of spacing is what the

Judee K. Burgoon is affiliated with the Department of Speech Communication, Arizona State University.

anthropologist Edward Hall has called *informal space*.[1] The second is to consider what constraints on spacing are imposed by the environment, or the arrangement of what Hall calls *fixed feature* and *semi-fixed feature space*.[2] At any point in time, the proxemic patterns of a group will be influenced by both considerations.

Informal Space

This facet of proxemic behavior concerns how we orient toward and distance ourselves from other members of the group. Whether that group be our family, a circle of friends at a social gathering, a committee working on a task, or a department within an organization, we will have characteristic distances that we adopt and characteristic means of insuring that those distances are maintained. These spacing patterns usually operate outside our conscious awareness but are of great importance. As Hall has said,

> ". . . informal spatial patterns have distinct bounds, and such deep, if unvoiced, significance that they form an essential part of the culture. To misunderstand this significance may invite disaster."[3]

There are three levels at which informal space can be analyzed. One is *territoriality*. A territory is a fixed, geographically identifiable space to which an individual or group has laid claim. An obvious example is one's home or neighborhood. These often have *territorial markers* such as fences, signs, or locks that clearly signal boundaries and degree of accessibility to "outsiders."

But there are also other kinds of territories to which we lay claim, ones for which the right of possession may be more ambiguous. Have you ever noticed that in a classroom, many people gravitate to the same seat time after time? They come to feel it is "their" seat. If someone else then sits in it, they feel their territory has been violated. At public beaches, we claim a space for ourselves and attempt to ward off intrusions by spreading out towels and other personal possessions as territorial markers, even though the space actually belongs not to us but the public at large.

This territorial urge seems to be deep-seated and possibly innate. By demarcating a tangible geographic area under our personal control we apparently gain a greater sense of security and autonomy. In times past, the ability to secure and defend a territory undoubtedly had survival value. Today, one's physical survival may not be at stake (street gangs defending their turf being one exception), but the ability to maintain a territory provides greater protection and privacy for the individual and for the group. Consequently, when our territory is violated, even when the violation seems unintended or inconsequential, we react strongly. Archie Bunker's vitriolic reactions to people sitting in "his" chair are a prime example. Because territorial invasions provoke such strong emotional reactions and may lead to physical aggression, it is important to understand how individuals within groups express their territorial proclivities and how groups in turn operate on these territorial imperatives.

The instincts that give rise to territorial behavior also shape a second level of informal spacing behavior that has been identified: *personal space*. In contrast to the visible and fixed nature of territory, personal space is an invisible, flexible and portable "bubble" of space that surrounds us. It expands and contracts according to our needs and the situation. It may be very large when we are interacting with a hostile stranger, and may temporarily disappear entirely in an intimate situation. As with territorial invasions, personal space invasions arouse and distress us. We will therefore want to consider how groups can recognize these distress signals and can arrange themselves in ways to minimize such stress.

Our personal space needs in turn determine the third level of informal spacing: *conversational distance*. This is the distance at which we normally conduct face-to-face interactions. This may coincide with or exceed the personal space needs of the individual participants. It permits a measure of spatial insulation and comfort, and is largely governed by cultural norms. Hall attempted to identify four categories of interpersonal distance that correspond to different sensory experiences and different interaction purposes. His widely accepted categories are as follows:

1. *Intimate distance* (0–18 inches)—a distance reserved for physical contact or intimate encounters and entailing high sensory involvement.
2. *Personal distance* (1½–4 feet)—a distance used for close interpersonal relationships or more private discussion topics; it entails a high degree of kinesthetic involvement but doesn't have the same impact on cutaneous, visual, olfactory, auditory and thermal receptors as does intimate distance.
3. *Social distance* (4–12 feet)—a range of distances used for informal social activity, business consultations, and other relatively impersonal encounters; this distance category is outside the range of touch and involves less sensory impact.
4. *Public distance* (12 feet and beyond)—a distance reserved for highly formal encounters, for platform presentations, and for interactions with public figures; this distance minimizes kinesthetic involvement and requires a louder speaking voice than normal.[4]

While these distance categories have proven useful in elevating awareness that people adjust distances according to the intimacy level of their interpersonal relationships and conversational topics, some social science research (to be discussed shortly) indicates that these categories fail to capture the complexity of the norms governing spacing behavior. For example, gender, age, degree of acquaintance, social status and personality, among other factors, will all dictate the normative distance for a given interaction.[5] If groups are to maximize their effectiveness, they must recognize how these various factors influence the behaviors and desires of individual members.

Fixed Feature and Semi-fixed Feature Space

This facet of proxemic behavior encompasses the ways in which architecture, interior design, furniture arrangement, and the like influence spacing behavior. Fixed feature space, as the name implies, concerns the spacing patterns resulting from permanent structures such as walls, doorways, and the configuration or use of those spaces. For example, in this culture we divide homes into a number of smaller compartments, some of which become individual bedrooms, some of which are designated for private and personal hygiene activities (bathrooms) and some of which are available for mulitiple functions (e.g., family rooms).

Fixed features of the environment may dictate what proxemic patterns people establish among themselves. The volume of space available is one major influence. Take the case of a committee assembling to plan campaign strategy. If they meet in a large hall, they may adopt rather close seating positions in the center of the room, but distribute themselves evenly within the space. This permits an audible conversation while giving everyone a "share" of the space around the perimeter of the group. If instead the committee meets in a small conference room, members may distribute themselves unevenly and closer to the walls to maximize their spatial freedom.

The normal functions of the environment may also constrain behavior. If the committee meets in the family room of someone's home, the informality associated with the room may encourage more informal seating arrangements. On the other hand, if the committee is forced to meet in the sanctuary of a church, the normal reverent behavior elicited in this environment, coupled with the large volume of space, may cause people to cluster close together so that they can speak in hushed tones.

Semi-fixed feature space refers to the proxemic arrangements resulting from movable environmental structures such as partitions and furniture. As with fixed feature space, the configuration of these elements at a given point in time will affect how people distance themselves from one another. A formal conference table, for example, specifies one kind of spacing pattern; sofas in a lounge necessitate another.

Environmental psychologists have identified two different arrangements of semi-fixed feature space that produce very different kinds of interaction. One is a *sociopetal* arrangement. This pattern, as exemplified in Figure 1, brings people together. Well-designed restaurants, bars, or living rooms use a

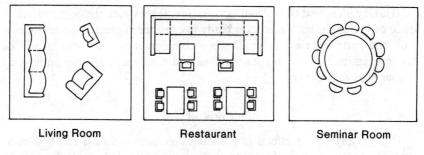

Living Room   Restaurant   Seminar Room

Some Sociopetal Arrangements

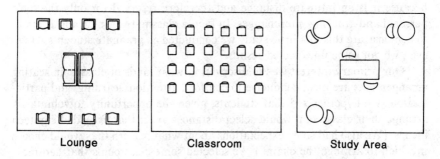

Lounge   Classroom   Study Area

Some Sociofugal Arrangements

Figure 1.

sociopetal spatial pattern to facilitate interaction among people. By contrast, *sociofugal* patterns turn people away from one another and discourage interaction. These types of arrangements, as illustrated in Figure 1, are commonly found in public places such as hotel lobbies or airports, where social interaction and loitering are intentionally discouraged. Psychologist Robert Sommer also found this pattern in state institutions such as hospitals. Often chairs lined the walls of lounges so as to ease the work of custodians and orderlies. Sommer found that by simply rearranging the chairs to create a sociopetal space, previously depressed and noncommunicative patients showed significant improvement in their mental health and their ability to relate to others.[6] His observations confirmed the profound effects that environmentally imposed spacing can have on our emotional states, our behavior, and our relationships with other people.

Having identified the various perspectives from which the organization of space can be analyzed, we are now ready to consider in greater specificity how proxemic patterns relate to small group communication. Of interest will be how proxemics regulate our interactions and what messages are implied by various spatial behaviors.

Comfort

Underlying all the effects of proxemics on human behavior is how comfortable people are with the amount of space provided them. If we were to trust Hall's distance categories as a guide, we would asume that anything closer than eighteen inches would typically be an uncomfortable interaction distance because it is an intimate distance and therefore reserved for only the most personal and arousing interchanges. In fact, a classmate of mine and I set out to demonstrate this in a little study we conducted as graduate students. However, we got some unexpected results.[7]

Our primary interest was in discovering what kinds of classroom seating arrangements are most conducive to comfort, attention, learning, and participation. We hypothesized that students, given the opportunity to voluntarily arrange their classroom, would select distances apart that exceeded eighteen inches. (We also had some expectations about what pattern they would choose in which to arrange the chairs.) We selected some classrooms that had movable chairs and prior to the students arriving for class, pushed all the chairs into a jumble in the center of the room. After the students had arrived and created their own arrangement, we entered the room, measured the distance between chairs, recorded the arrangement, and gave students a grid on which to record their preferred classroom arrangement.

The unexpected result from the study was that students voluntarily placed themselves an average of seventeen inches apart. This was greater than the average distance of thirteen inches that we found in comparable, undisturbed classrooms but still less than we had anticipated. We concluded that people are able to tolerate relatively close distances without becoming uncomfortable, and in fact may prefer some degree of closeness. The results also made us aware that the four distance categories alone do not give us enough information; a number of other factors need to be taken into account in ascertaining at what distances people are most likely to be comfortable.

Research suggests that there are three kinds of considerations that will determine what the normative, and presumably most comfortable, distance is for a given interaction. These considerations include the nature of the people in the group, the nature of the interaction itself, and the environmental constraints. Regarding people characteristics, the following have all been identified as important:[8]

1. *Gender:* Females sit and stand closer to other females than do males interacting with one another. The research is mixed on whether opposite-sex pairs adopt closer distances than female-female pairs. Specifically, in a group setting females tolerate crowding far better than males and may respond in a more intimate, pleasant way to close proximity, while males may respond with aggressive, unpleasant reactions.

2. *Cultural background:* Some cultures interact at closer distances than others. Those who are accustomed to close proximity during face-to-face encounters are called contact cultures. Those that display more distant interaction patterns are called noncontact cultures. The United States in general is considered a noncontact culture, although many subcultural groups (such as those from southern Europe, the Middle East or Central America) would qualify as contact groups.

3. *Race:* The research here is very mixed but there is some evidence that black males in the U.S. adopt the greatest distances and black females adopt the closest, compared to white males and females. Blacks also appear to have a more fluid approach to distancing, as compared to the more static (fixed) pattern exhibited by whites.

4. *Age:* People maintain closer distances with people who are the same age than with those who are younger or older than they are, even if the older person is a parent.

5. *Status:* Like age, the greater the differential between interactants, the greater the distance.

6. *Degree of acquaintance:* Not surprisingly, people adopt the closest distances with close friends, adopt intermediate distances with acquaintances and maintain the greatest distance from strangers.

7. *Personality:* Different personality types have characteristic distances they adopt from others. For example, introverts and highly anxious individuals require more space than their extroverted or less anxious counterparts. Some research with violent prisoners has documented that they require as much as twice the space that nonviolent prisoners need, suggesting that the discomfort they experience in close proximity to others may be a factor in their aggressive tendencies.

Other people factors no doubt also play a role. In addition, the nature of the interaction itself influences how comfortable people are likely to feel. For example, if the group is gathering for a social purpose, people will expect and be comfortable at closer distances. If the purpose is a formal meeting or a task-oriented discussion, they may be more comfortable at greater distances.

The environment plays a role by setting limits on the options available to people. In a living room situation, if people have a choice they will usually opt for across seating. This is particularly true if the available side-by-side seating is one to three feet. However, if the across seating exceeds three and a half feet, and especially if it is farther away than an alternative side-by-side seat which is at a reasonable distance, people will choose to sit alongside another. This implies that the "arc for comfortable conversation" is about a five and a half foot distance nose-to-nose.

If the available seating arrangement forces people into close proximity, such as in an auditorium, a classroom, or a small meeting room, people may adapt temporarily, recognizing that the proximity between themselves and their neighbors has been imposed upon them rather than being a matter of choice. One way that people adapt is to develop a *nonperson orientation*. This means essentially acting as if the other person were not present or were merely an object. This is exactly how people adjust to being confined in an elevator with a group of strangers. They look straight ahead, avoiding contact with the other riders, and pretending that they are unbothered by the closeness of the others.

Collectively, all research on proxemic norms indicates that the process of arriving at a comfortable distance is a rather complex one. It is governed by a large number of factors that must all be brought into balance. This becomes particularly complicated in a group situation, where there is a mix of individual characteristics and preferences that must be accommodated. Fortunately, the research also reveals that we humans are adaptable creatures who can tolerate deviations from our preferred spacing for short periods of time.

Nevertheless, we have strong physiological reactions to inappropriate spacing, and over a period of time will display evidence of our discomfort. Studies have shown that, compared to being in close physical proximity to a paper figure or an object (such as a hatrack), people manifest much greater physical arousal (as measured by galvanic skin response) when their personal space is invaded by another person.[9] Other reactions to spatial invasions that have been documented include: 1) displaying anxiety through such behaviors as restless leg and foot movements, fidgeting with objects, scratching the head, and touching oneself; 2) sometimes staring hostilely at the intruder but more often avoiding eye contact; 3) erecting barriers with personal possessions such as books or coats; 4) erecting "body blocks"—shading the eyes or putting arms and elbows between oneself and the intruder; 5) increasing distance by leaning away, moving farther apart, or reorienting the body away from the intruder; and 6) if the invasion is prolonged, taking flight (i.e., actually leaving the situation altogether). It is interesting to note that people rarely respond to an invasion or experience of crowding verbally. Rather, they rely on nonverbal signals to reveal their discomfort and to ward off a continued intrusion.

If it can be assumed that discomfort reduces a group member's satisfaction and the quality of his or her contributions to group process, then groups would be wise to watch for these symptoms of spatial inadequacy and attempt to compensate for them. As a minimum, it might mean making adjustments between members within a location. As a maximum, it might mean finding a different location in which to interact.

Status and Leadership

As noted earlier, status confers the privilege of greater spatial insularity. Politicians, celebrities and corporate presidents are always accorded greater distances from those of lesser status. The story is told that when John F. Kennedy became President, friends with whom he had formerly socialized suddenly began observing an invisible threshold some thirty feet from him they would not cross until he first breached the distance. It served as eloquent recognition of the significant change in status he had achieved.

People in positions of status and power enjoy other proxemic privileges. They are permitted to initiate whatever seating arrangement or distance is going to be observed, they are free to violate spatial norms, they have access to more and better territory and they are accorded more privacy.[10]

In the context of small group communication, individuals of power and status often emerge as the group leader. Or the person designated as leader takes on status and power by virtue of his/her position. Therefore, these proxemic power relations should have analogues in the group setting. They do.

For one, the high status individual and/or group leader typically occupies the best position in the group. Selecting the best position, in turn, confers status on its occupant and the expectation that the individual will demonstrate leadership. Research has shown that leaders, high status members, and dominant individuals gravitate toward the end positions of a rectangular table; i.e., they take the head of the table. Or they choose to sit opposite the most other people. In unacquainted groups, the people who select these positions will more often be perceived as the leader, and people placed in these positions will be induced to become more dominant in the ensuing interactions.[11]

For those wishing to have influence in a group, the implications are clear: Choose a spot that places you at the symbolic head of the group or across from the most other people. If your goal is to elicit more leadership from a particular member, place them in those positions. And if your goal is merely to identify who in a group is most likely serving as its leader, look for the individual around whom the spatial arrangement revolves, who is accorded more space, and who occupies a central position within the group.

Interaction Patterns

Just as group proxemics affect leadership emergence and vice versa, so do proxemic patterns influence the ways in which the group communicates. Proximity in itself encourages interaction. The act of bringing people together usually impels them to speak to one another. Even a group of strangers will often strike up a conversation if placed in close proximity long enough. In a classroom, unacquainted individuals seated next to one another will often develop a friendship before the term is over. There is even a high rate of marriages among people who live within six blocks of each other!

So physical closeness alone is a powerful force determining to whom we will talk. The "who" and "how" of small group communication also depend on the existing furniture arrangement and the purposes of interaction.

One type of group context that has been frequently studied is the classroom. It will be recalled that in my study with Pat Garner, we observed what spatial arrangements students adopted and asked them what arrangement they would prefer so as to maximize participation, learning, and attention. Overwhelmingly, students expressed a preference for a U-shaped or circular arrangement and tended to approximate such an arrangement when they placed their own chairs in the room. This preference seems to be based on two considerations: the proximity and visual access to one another and to the instructor which this arrangement affords to students.

Other classroom research supports the importance of the twin elements of proximity and eye contact. Classrooms with straight row seating tend to produce the greatest interaction from the front and center seats, creating almost a "triangle of participation." It should be obvious that such seats, by virtue of their spatial and visual access to the instructor, make it easier to see the teacher and gain his/her attention. Similarly, classrooms with laboratory seating (i.e., everyone seated around small lab tables) produce the greatest amount of total participation, presumably because students are close to one another and can maintain a high degree of eye contact with one another. Proximity alone, however, apparently is not sufficient to induce equal participation. In seminar seating arrangements (i.e., everyone seated around one large table), the most participation comes from those opposite the instructor and the least comes from those seated at the instructor's side. So long as the instructor takes an active role in leading the group, most interaction comes from those who can maintain eye contact with the instructor.[12]

In small group discussions, the same principle holds: whoever is in the most central position or has visual access to the most other people is likely to participate the most. This conclusion must be tempered somewhat by the nature of the interaction and the presence or absence of a strong leader. There is some evidence that task discussions produce more "across" interaction, while social discussions produce more "alongside" interaction. However, the presence of a directive leader may also encourage more conversation among people seated next to one another.[13]

The nature of the task also affects people's preferences for a seating arrangement. A number of studies have demonstrated that people prefer corner-to-corner or side-by-side seating for cooperative and conversational activities. They prefer opposite seating for competitive activities. One even seems to provide some degree of distance yet permits surveillance of one's opponent. When people are engaged in co-action, i.e., they are engaged in simultaneous, non-interacting activities, they prefer greater separation and less opportunity for direct eye contact.[14] These preferences suggest that when planning seating arrangements for group activities, one could facilitate cooperative and social interchange by placing people close together but with some ability to make eye contact with one another (as in a circular or "catty-corner" arrangement). If the activities require competition, somewhat greater distance is desirable, with a concomitant increase in the ability to make direct eye contact with one's competitors.

Relational Communication

An aspect of proxemic behavior that is gaining recognition is the relational messages which are conveyed by distance and seating selection. Relational messages are statements that help define the nature of a relationship: whether people like each other, how involved they are in the relationship, who is controlling the relationship, and so forth. Usually such messages are expressed nonverbally. And one of the chief nonverbal channels through which they are communicated is proxemics.

One of the more obvious relational messages signalled proxemically is liking and attraction. Musical lyrics speak of being "close to you," of "getting together," and "the nearness of you." We show our attraction and favorable regard for others by moving closer to them physically and we show our dislike by distancing ourselves. If people choose to sit near us in a group meeting, we take that as a sign of their affection or positive regard for us. Conversely, if they elect to sit at the opposite end of the room, we may interpret that as a message that we are being rejected.

In a similar vein, we interpret distance as a message of involvement. If someone sits very close, orients himself/herself so as to face us directly and/or leans forward, we take that as an indication that this person is very interested in what we have to say, that he or she is involved in our relationship. Certainly that kind of closeness insures high sensory involvement. If, on the other hand, someone takes a more distal position, orients himself/herself more indirectly (that is, faces away to some degree), or leans away from us, we are likely to read detachment into such behavior. We think that the individual is disinterested in us personally, in our conversation, or in our total relationship. Or the person may simply be expressing a desire for greater privacy.

Another kind of message we may read into a person's distancing behavior is how aroused and uncomfortable or relaxed and composed that person is in our presence. Because people in a rage or a high state of emotional arousal often move extremely close to others, sometimes even putting their nose in someone else's face, we tend to equate extreme proximity with more arousal and less self-control. By contrast, someone who is very relaxed may lean sideways or backward (if in a chair), thereby increasing the distance to some degree. This creates some difficulty for us in the interpretation of proxemic relational messages because we could interpret backward leaning as having either the negative connotations of disinterest and disregard or the positive connotation of relaxation. We could likewise construe close proximity as a sign of affection and attraction, or as a sign of hostile emotional activation. In other words, the meaning of the proxemic message may be ambiguous by itself. In practice, we rely on other nonverbal cues and the verbal content to decide which interpretation to select.

One final set of meanings associated with spatial behavior further compounds our interpretation task; these concern dominance and control. We have already noted that high status individuals and group leaders maintain greater distances between themselves and others, and in group meetings tend to occupy the most central, controlling position. The selection of distance or seating position by such individuals not only is instrumental in their gaining control of the group, it also conveys the relational message that they are dominant. By contrast, those adopting subordinate or submissive roles wait for more dominant individuals to dictate the pattern to be observed and may find their personal space violated by the more powerful individuals.

The knowledge that proxemic choices carry relational meaning can be used to advantage. If you wish to make a group member feel better liked and accepted, you can place him or her in closer proximity to others. If you instead want to communicate rejection and exclusion, you can symbolically convey that message by placing the person at the periphery of the group. If you wish to elicit greater participation on someone's part, you can convey your own interest in what this person has to say by moving closer, facing him or her more directly, and leaning forward. Finally, you can assert power and dominance by violating another's territory or distancing yourself (both of which are ploys that have been recommended for people seriously engaged in power games). If you wish to communicate submissiveness or deference, you may do so by waiting for another's proxemic initiative and then conforming to the pattern that person establishes.[15]

Effects of Spatial Deviancy

Some of the recommendations in the last section may have struck you as unorthodox, because most writers in the area of nonverbal communication tell you to conform to the norms if you want to be successful. At least that is the dictum in most popular literature. For some time I have felt that conformity to the norms may not always be the best strategy. Therefore, my colleagues, students and I undertook a series of experiments to test this thesis.

The initial research began with the premise that deviations from the normative, or expected, distance may have positive or negative communication consequences, depending on who engages in the distance violation. After some false starts, my cohorts and I arrived at the following predictions: People who are "rewarding," that is, who are high status, attractive, givers of positive feedback, controllers of tangible rewards or favorably regarded for some other reason, have the freedom to violate distancing expectations with impunity. In small group language, they have idosyncratic credits; they are allowed to be deviants at no or little cost. Moreover, when they engage in a violation, they arouse the "victim," making him or her more attentive to the relationship between violator and victim. In the process of searching out explanations for the arousal, they become more conscious of the violator's rewarding characteristics and therefore choose to select positive connotations for the violator's proxemic behavior. The final result is that the violator gains even better communication outcomes than if he or she had conformed to the norm.

In the case of a less rewarding person, for example, someone who is unattractive, who is unpleasant to be around, who is always criticizing, or who is of low status, exactly the opposite predictions are made. Violations of the expected distance—moving closer or farther away—has negative consequences, because the aroused victim is more sensitized to the violator's negative characteristics and ascribes more unfavorable meanings on the violator's proxemic behavior. For example, a "close" violation is seen as pushy or threatening; a "far" violation is seen as dislike or disinterest. People who enter a situation with few rewards to offer the recipients, then, are better off conforming to the norms.

A series of experiments has largely supported these predictions. What is of special interest here is one study we conducted using small groups. We wanted to see whether violations would still be effective for a "high reward" person when in the presence of another rewarding individual who did not deviate. We wanted to see how it would affect ability to influence others and how it would affect the individual's credibility and attraction. At the same time, we were interested in whether the negative consequences for a "low reward" person would become even worse if that individual engaged in deviant behavior in the presence of another nonrewarding individual who did not deviate.

In brief, this is how we designed the experiment: we told subjects that they were going to participate in a small group activity intended to test the effects of different sizes of juries on decision-making. They were told they had been assigned to a three-person group. Unknown to them, the other two members of the group were our confederates who were dressed to be physically attractive and given more prestigious background in their introductions (high reward condition) or were made to look unattractive and given less prestigious background (low reward). One confederate presented defense arguments from an actual murder trial and one presented prosecution arguments. The subject was asked to serve as an undecided member. In the process of presenting their arguments, the confederates either maintained their initial distance (normative condition) or one of them engaged in a violation, moving 18 inches closer (close violation) or 18 inches farther (far violation) than the initial distance.

The results were intriguing and have real implications for actual group processes. In the high reward discussions, the deviating confederate was more persuasive and rated as more attractive, competent and of good character when he or she engaged in a distance violation, particularly a far violation. This was true both when compared to his or her own results in the normative condition and when compared to the other, nondeviating confederate. In other words, deviant behavior improved the person's influence and interpersonal evaluations relative to conforming to the norm *and* relative to another rewarding group member. In the low reward discussions, distance violations lowered the confederate's perceived persuasiveness and caused him or her to lose ground on persuasiveness, sociability and attraction, as compared to the other nondeviating confederate. In other words, the nonrewarding person's deviant behavior tended to confer greater credibility and persuasiveness on his or her opponent. These results thus strongly suggest that deviant proxemic behavior may have pay-off for people who are well regarded by the rest of the group. For those who are less well regarded, the main beneficiaries of their deviant behavior are their opponents.[16]

Summary

It should be clear from this brief review that proxemic patterns play a subtle but powerful role in human interactions. People's proxemic behavior reflects competing needs between desires for affiliation and desires for privacy. Usually, the distance or seating position they adopt will indicate at what distance they feel comfortable in that context with those participants. The voluntarily selected or environmentally imposed spatial relationships may signal or influence who exercises leadership, may affect who talks to whom on what kind of topics, and may convey messages about the interpersonal relationships among group members. Finally, contrary to popular opinion, spatial deviancy may sometimes prove profitable in gaining greater control over the group and/ or improving others' evaluations of one's credibility and attractiveness.

Notes

1. Edward T. Hall, "The Anthropology of Space: An Organizing Model," in H. M. Proshansky, W. H. Ittelson and L. G. Rivlin (Eds.), *Environmental Psychology: Man and His Physical Setting* (New York: Holt, Rinehart & Winston, 1970), pp. 16–27.
2. Ibid.
3. Ibid, p. 20.
4. Edward T. Hall, *The Silent Language* (Garden City, NY: Doubleday, 1959).
5. Judee K. Burgoon and Stephen B. Jones, "Toward a Theory of Personal Space Expectations and their Violations," *Human Communication Research,* (1976), 131–146.
6. Robert Sommer, *Personal Space: The Behavioral Basis of Design* (Englewood Cliffs, NJ: Prentice-Hall, 1969).
7. Judee K. Heston and Patrick Garner, "A Study of Personal Spacing and Desk Arrangement in the Learning Environment," Paper presented to the International Communication Association convention, Atlanta, April 1972.
8. For a review of research on norms, see Burgoon and Jones, *op. cit.,* and Judee K. Burgoon and Thomas Saine, *The Unspoken Dialogue: An Introduction to Nonverbal Communication* (Boston: Houghton Mifflin, 1978), p. 93–96.
9. *Ibid.* Also see Judee K. Heston, "Effects of Anomia and Personal Space Invasion on Anxiety, Nonperson Orientation and Source Credibility," *Central States Speech Journal,* 25 (1974), 19–27.
10. For a comprehensive summary of proxemic correlates of status and power, see Nancy M. Henley, *Body Politics* (Englewood Cliffs, NJ: Prentice-Hall, 1977).
11. For some of the classic research in this area, see A. Paul Hare and Robert F. Bales, "Seating Pattern and Small Group Interaction," *Sociometry,* 26 (1963), 480–486; L. T. Howells and S. W. Becker, "Seating Arrangement and Leadership Emergence," *Journal of Abnormal and Social Psychology,* 64 (1962), 148–150; D. F. Lott and Robert Sommer, Seating Arrangements and Status," *Journal of Personality and Social Psychology,* 7 (1967), 90–95; F. L. Strodtbeck and L. H. Hook, "The Social Dimensions of a Twelve Man Jury Table," *Sociometry,* 24 (1961), 397–415; Robert Sommer, "Leadership and Group Geography," *Sociometry,* 24 (1961), 499–510; Charles D. Ward, "Seating Arrangement and Leadership Emergence in Small Discussion Groups," *Journal of Social Psychology,* 74 (1968), 83–90. See also Marvin E. Shaw, *Group Dynamics: The Psychology of Small Group Behavior* (New York: McGraw-Hill, 1971), pp. 117–154.
12. For a review of this literature, see Heston and Garner; Sommer, 1969.
13. Some of the original research in this area includes Hare and Bales; G. Hearn, "Leadership and the Spatial Factor in Small Groups," *Journal of Abnormal and Social Psychology,* 54 (1957), 269–272; Bernard Steinzor, "The Spatial Factor in Face to Face Discussion Groups," *Journal of Abnormal and Social Psychology,* 45 (1950), 552–555; Strodtbeck and Hook.
14. M. Cook, "Experiments on Orientation and Proxemics," *Human Relations,* 23 (1970), 61–76; Gary A. Norum, Nancy Jo Russo and Robert Sommer, "Seating Patterns and Group Task," *Psychology of the Schools,* 4 (1967), 276–280; Robert Sommer, "Studies of Small Group Ecology," in R. S. Cathcart and L. A. Samovar (Eds.), *Small Group Communication: A Reader, 2nd Ed.* (Dubuque, IA: William C. Brown, 1974), pp. 283–293.

15. For reviews of relevant literature and a report of one experiment on relational communication, see Judee K. Burgoon, "Privacy and Communication," in M. Burgoon (Ed.), *Communication Yearbook 6* (Beverly Hills, CA: Sage Publications, 1982), pp. 206–249; Judee K. Burgoon, David B. Buller, Jerold L. Hale and Mark deTurck, "Relational Messages Associated with Immediacy Behaviors," paper presented to the International Communication Association convention, Boston, May 1982.

16. For the details of this particular study, see Judee K. Burgoon, Don W. Stacks and Steven A. Burch, "The Role of Interpersonal Rewards and Violations of Distancing Expectations in Achieving Influence in Small Groups," *Communication, Journal of the Association of the Pacific,* 11 (1982), 114–128. For a review of research on proxemic violations of expectations, see Judee K. Burgoon, "Nonverbal Violations of Expectations," in J. Wiemann and R. Harrison (Eds.), *Nonverbal Interaction* (Vol. 11, Sage Annual Reviews of Communication) (Beverly Hills, CA: Sage, 1983, forthcoming).

The Listening Environment

Jane Whitney Gibson and Richard M. Hodgetts

The Listening Environment

Listening can take place in virtually any kind of environment from a quiet office to a noisy street corner. This environment can be broken into two sub-environments: the psychological and the physical. The psychological environment is that which exists within the people who are listening. The physical environment is that which exists around the listeners. Of the two, the psychological environment is the more important. Regardless of how much noise there is in the external environment or what kinds of time demands the listener is under, if the latter wants to hear, then listening is going to occur. It may not be 100 percent effective, but it will take place. Conversely, if an individual does not want to listen, regardless of the surroundings, listening will not occur. Psychological environmental factors determine whether listening will occur; physical environmental factors help influence the degree of listening efficiency that results. The following examines both of these environments.

Psychological Environment

The psychological environment consists of the mental variables internal to the speaker and the listener. Four of the most important are codes, value systems, education, and psychological set.

Codes. In Chapter 1 we noted that the encoding and decoding processes are central to the transfer of meaning. As we then explained, codes of past experience are unique compilations of everything the speaker or listener has gone through. It includes memories, values, and beliefs. The resultant attitude with which the listener and/or speaker approaches the communication determines, to a large extent, how successful it will be. For example, a manager, who has had an accumulated negative experience with union representatives, will often approach a conference with the shop steward with preconceived ideas and mindblocks. Effective listening can still occur but *only* if the manager recognizes the mindset and works hard to be open-minded.

Value Systems. The operating value systems of the speaker and the listener help determine what is said and what is heard. These systems are a result of the early life experiences of the individuals. To a large degree, each of us is what we were at the age of twenty. In fact, of this period the first ten years are the most significant. For example, people now in their fifties were developing their value systems during the 1930s when the Great Depression was in full swing. As a result, for many members of this group, job security and the importance of hard work are key values. Many children of the 1950s, on the other hand, grew up in a period of affluence and abundance. For many of them, an entirely different attitude exists about work. How does this affect listening? Consider the following.

Foreman (age 55) to employee (age 22):	We've got to get this shipment out tonight or we'll lose this account. We're all going to have to pitch in and work until midnight.
Employee:	You've got to be kidding—count me out! I've got tickets to the soccer game.

How can an understanding of values have helped this encounter? Consider the following.

Foreman:	I know you've got better things to do but we're in a real bind. If you can help me out tonight and stay until this order is out, I'll owe you one.
Employee (Scenario One):	I know you're really desperate, but I've promised to take my kid brother to this soccer game. Let me see if I can get Joe to stay back and help you out.
Employee (Scenario Two):	I know how important this is to you, so I'll give you a hand. Maybe Joe will buy my soccer tickets.

Taking time to recognize the other person's values can greatly help in the listening and communication processes—but it cannot be one-sided!

Education. Education level has a major impact on the listening experience. While formal education in no way implies formal training in listening, the educated person has a better chance to listen effectively to another educated person because they "speak the same language." Two high school dropouts speaking "street language" will likewise be more able to listen effectively to each other. As with values and age, *similarity* in educational background is the key to more effective listening. Lacking this, the communicators must recognize the differences and compensate for them.

Psychological Set. The psychological makeup of the listener and speaker also impact on the results. Is one or the other defensive in some way? Aggressive? Hostile? Is he or she repressing part of the conversation or projecting onto the listener?

Physical Environment

The physical environment includes the setting in which the speaker and listener find themselves. Five of the most important physical environmental elements are physical acuity, age, place, time, and noise. The first two are internal to the person and virtually beyond the control of the listener. The last three are external to the person and can be manipulated to create a more effective listening environment.

Physical Acuity. Hearing ability and speech ability are major factors in listening effectiveness. This is easily seen if you try to speak to a deaf person who does not read lips. Hearing and speaking ability are fundamental skills that become critical whenever they are not well developed.

Age. Age is a correlate to the value issue discussed earlier under the psychological environment. Similarities and differences intrude upon the listening environment. Children are taught to "listen to your parents," which actually means doing as you are told, not listening for meaning. Adults, in turn, sometimes fail to listen to their children and miss the opportunity for understanding and mutual growth. Between these two groups are teenagers who often fail to listen to adults because they believe the latter have nothing worthwhile to say. We are much more likely to really listen to someone near our own age—someone we suspect will say something of interest to *us*.

Place. While we spend a great deal of our communication time listening, there are times when the place is neither appropriate nor optimally effective. While the corporate cafeteria may be all right for casual banter, serious listening can usually be enhanced by a move to a more private, comfortable spot.

Time. How often have you had someone say to you, "Let's talk about that later," or "I'd like to resolve this issue before Wednesday," or "Give me your analysis, in a five-minute summary, right now." Statements such as these are time-related. The big problem, of course, is that you may find that when you do get to talk, the other person is not ready to listen.

Noise. Noise is a very common environmental variable. Typical examples include the ringing of a telephone, the clacking of a typewriter, and the loud conversation of those seated nearby. Noise often impedes the listening process. When there is a great deal of it in the immediate environment, listening becomes very difficult and often impossible. On the other hand, some kinds of noise can enhance communication. Soft music is an example. Many firms pipe in music so that the employees can work in an environment more conducive to productivity.

Finally, noise made by the speaker personally will affect the listening process. Voice intonation, pauses, and the rapping of one's hand on the table all influence the listener's interpretation of what is *really* being said. So does lack of noise. Consider the manager who tells the subordinates "I just don't understand how you could have made a mistake like this," and then says nothing. Is the individual waiting for the subordinate to respond? Maybe not. The manager may be using silence to add weight to his statement. These pauses help accentuate the message and give it more importance than would otherwise be the case.

Active Listening: The Key to Effectiveness

Effective listening involves more than just paying attention. It also includes active, empathetic, and supportive behaviors that tell the speaker, "I understand, please go on." This mode of response is called active listening.

Of course, not all speakers are active listeners. Many fall into one of the other four response modes. The following is a brief description of all five, beginning with the directing orientation.

1. Directing: The "directing listener" leads the speaker by guiding the limits and direction of the conversation. Consider an employee telling the supervisor of his inability to get along with a co-worker. The directing supervisor would make a reply such as, "If I were you, I'd just ignore him" or "Don't worry about it—everybody thinks he's a pain in the neck."
2. Judgmental: The "judgmental" listener introduces personal value judgments into the conversation. The listener tends to offer advice or make statements regarding right or wrong behavior. In responding to the employee plight described above, the judgmental listener might say, "You'll just have to learn to get along with your co-workers" or "You're absolutely right, Tom is impossible to get along with."
3. Probing: The "probing" listener asks a lot of questions in an attempt to get to the heart of the matter. This individual tends to lead the conversation and satisfy his or her personal needs rather than those of the speaker. A probing listener might answer the above employee as follows: "Exactly what has this person done to you so that you can't get along?" or "When did all this start?" or even "What do you want me to do about it?"

4. Smoothing: The "smoothing" listener tends to pat the speaker on the head and make light of his or her problems. The underlying belief here is that conflict is bad and should be avoided at all costs. The smoothing listener would tell the employee in our example "You and Tom just had a bad day; don't worry—tomorrow it will all be forgotten."

5. Empathetic/Active: The "empathetic/active" listener tries to create an encouraging atmosphere for the speaker to use in expressing and solving the problem. Active listeners tend to feed back to the speaker *neutral summaries* of what they have heard in order to (a) establish that understanding has occurred and (b) allow the speaker to continue. The active listener might respond to the employee in our example as follows: "It seems you are troubled by the fact that you and Tom can't seem to get along."

Here is another example of the five listening responses mentioned above. Read it carefully so as to develop a working knowledge of the five response pattern modes.

Employee: I know I'm late again this morning, and I really tried to get here on time. But something always seems to happen to delay me in the morning.

Manager Responses:

Directing: "Just get up a half an hour earlier and you'll have plenty of time to cope with anything unexpected."

Judgmental: "Being late so often really looks bad for you. You'd better find a way to get here on time."

Probing: "Well, what happened this morning to make you late?"

Smoothing: "We're all late sometimes no matter how good our intentions are."

Active Listening: "You sound frustrated that you were late again this morning."

Table 1 provides a detailed summary of these response patterns. Read the figure carefully and note how the listener acts and the speaker reacts in each of these modes.

Table 1
Listening response pattern identification

Pattern	Listener's focus	Response mode	Responds to	Listener's attitude and posture	Speaker's reaction
Directing	Listener's own ideas	Limited to the listener's way of looking at the problem	Speaker's content	Superior attitude	Speaker's focus is lost as the listener pursues his or her own track.
Judgmental	Listener's own ideas	Gives the verdict of what to do or not do	Speaker's content	Superior attitude	Speaker may feel defensive, resentful and/or misunderstood
Probing	Speaker's ideas or listener's ideas	Directing and/or leading by asking questions	Speaker's content	Impatient; wants to get to the point	Must focus on listener's questions even if they go away from the central problem
Smoothing	Speaker's feelings	Ignores the problem; feels it is not important	Speaker's content and emotion	Healing and encouraging	Compromising at best; frustrating at worst
Active/ empathetic	Speaker's ideas and feelings	Encouraging and accepting behavior	Speaker's emotion	Attentive, forward leaning, good eye contact	Must look more closely at own problem; free to continue talking

The Nature of Active Listening

According to Fisher, there are four components underlying active listening behavior: empathy, acceptance, congruence, and concreteness. *Empathy* is the quality of trying to understand the speaker from his or her own viewpoint rather than from any external criterion, such as the listener's past experience or personal preference. *Acceptance* is the quality of deep concern for the other person's welfare along with a respect for the other's individuality and worth as a person. *Congruence* is the quality of openness, frankness, and genuineness on the part of the listener, which tends to encourage the same pattern in the speaker. *Concreteness* is the quality of focusing on specifics and avoiding vagueness by helping the speaker concentrate on real problems and avoid generalities such as "they say" or "everyone knows." Active listeners develop and nurture these four components.

Active listening offers a number of important benefits to managers who want to increase their effectiveness. In particular the process

1. Encourages the individual to speak his or her mind fully.
2. Provides the speaker with a sounding board in solving problems.
3. Offers a motivational benefit to the speaker, who feels important in the eyes of the listener.
4. Encourages the speaker to think through his or her problem thoroughly and not be quickly diverted.
5. Encourages the speaker to become more open and less defensive in communication, thus fostering emotional maturity.
6. Makes the speaker feel his or her ideas are worthwhile and can be helpful in stimulating creative thinking.
7. Makes the speaker listen to his or her own ideas more carefully.
8. Provides the listener with a wealth of information on facts, attitudes, and emotions that were previously unexpressed.
9. Provides a growth experience for both the speaker and the listener.

Becoming an Active Listener

Now that you know that active listening is a worthwhile tool, what habits or techniques do you need to develop to build your base skills?

1. Listen for total meaning. This means being receptive to both the message and the accompanying emotional content.
2. Respond to feelings. Remember that the emotional content often is far more important than the verbal message.
3. Note all cues. Keep in mind that the entire nonverbal behavior of the speaker must be observed in order to get the total picture.

Robert Bolton, an expert in human relations skills, has suggested a series of useful guidelines for building active-listening skills. His recommendations include the following:

1. Do not fake understanding. Admit when you lose track of what the speaker is saying and ask him or her to explain further.
2. Do not tell the speaker you know how he or she feels. This is often seen as patronizing and phony.
3. Vary your responses. There is no single "right" response to every communication situation. Depending on the environment, paraphrase, remain silent, or give an encouraging word such as uh-huh, to let the speaker know you are paying attention.
4. Focus on feelings. Do not ignore the emotional content of the message; be aware of the speaker's attitudes, values, and opinions.
5. Choose the most accurate-feeling word. Try to be specific in identifying the emotion, and the degree of that emotion, appropriate to the situation. Degrees of the word "sad," for example, can be expressed as "very sad," "distraught," "despairing," and "heartbroken."
6. Develop a vocal empathy. No matter how empathetic your words, if your voice is cold and clinical, the speaker will not feel comfortable. As much as your words, have your tone of voice and its rate, rhythm, and volume reflect the speaker's emotional state.
7. Strive for concreteness and relevance. Help the speaker come to the point rather than continue in generalities by making your responses specific and, if necessary, asking clarifying questions such as "How did you feel when that happened?"
8. Provide nondogmatic but firm responses. State these responses in such a way that the speaker feels comfortable in disagreeing with your paraphrasing.
9. Reflect the speaker's resources. Often, the speaker will become so involved with his or her problem that the individual focuses on negative points and neglects strengths. The active listener will highlight these strengths when he or she hears them and thus provide a bit of encouragement to the speaker.
10. Reflect the feelings that are implicit in questions. When a speaker asks you directly what you would do in his position, it becomes difficult not to give advice. A truly skilled active listener, however, can reflect the feeling of the direct question back at the speaker. For example,

Employee: Jones is sure messing up my production quota—what would you do with him?"

Manager: This really has you troubled, hasn't it?

11. Accept the fact that many interactions will be inconclusive. Few listening incidents will come to closure. The active listener often must settle for the knowledge that he or she has left the speaker with a sounder basis for further thought.

Your Listening Profile

Sperry Corporation

Toward Better Listening

Thank you for your interest in listening. If listening is ever to receive the attention it deserves . . . in schools, homes, businesses . . . it will come about because concerned people like you have made themselves heard in the silence that surrounds the subject.

At Sperry, we've emphasized good listening for many years. Research shows that it's been important to our success and is one of our greatest strengths in the marketplace. We're proud of that—but we aren't satisfied that we're listening, understanding and responding as well as we can.

That's why Sperry's corporate advertising theme, **we understand how important it is to listen,** is more than a slogan. It expresses a basic management philosophy and is fundamental to the way we do business. We're dedicated to listening effectively and responding in the right way to the people who have direct interest in the products and performance of the company.

Long before the advertising program was conceived, Sperry had stressed the importance of listening and responding in its personnel development courses, management conferences, small group meetings, roundtable discussions and other continuing programs.

But because the training covered other aspects of communications as well, it was felt that more concentrated attention should be devoted specifically to the development of listening skills.

Additional training was prepared by Sperry's own senior management development specialists, and listening classes are being conducted for our personnel.

They are tailored to the special needs of our managers who supervise the work of others, our marketing executives and other employees as well.

The Sperry instructors who conduct the classes received orientation to make them more familiar with the subject matter and how to teach it effectively.

The training in listening has four objectives:

- To build an awareness of the importance to business of listening.
- To increase understanding of the nature of listening and its impact on the total communications process.

From Sperry Corporation Listening Program material by Dr. Lyman K. Steil, Communication Development, Inc., for Sperry Corporation, Copyright 1979. Reprinted by permission of Dr. Steil and Sperry Corporation.

- To diagnose listening abilities and practices.
- To develop skills and techniques to improve listening effectiveness.

Group participation is emphasized, rather than lectures by the instructor. Also employed are film, videotape, audiotape, individual self-evaluation, testing of abilities, analysis of listening case situations and role playing in small groups.

Attendance at each session ranges from 16 to 24. That assures a good level of interchange during the group participation exercises without making the size of the class unwieldy.

The training covers understanding the listening concept and its various elements. It concentrates on specific on-the-job applications showing how Sperry employees in various real-life situations can do a better job of responding—the end product of the listening process.

Real listening occurs in four stages—sensing (hearing the message), understanding (interpreting it), evaluating (appraising it) and responding (doing something with it).

Intelligent, sincere response is central to the Sperry philosophy, and is, in fact, the ultimate point of the training.

We believe the training we are doing in this field is appropriate for Sperry and the employees who receive it. Other institutions have different environments, requiring different approaches. So we do not provide training aids or other materials used in our own internal programs to outside organizations or individuals.

However, many books, articles, films and other materials are available on various aspects of listening. Current books on the subject are listed elsewhere in this pamphlet. We at Sperry really believe **we understand how important it is to listen.** And we encourage those interested in developing their own programs on better listening to do so, using these and other sources.

Facts about Listening

1. **First of all, you should know what we mean by "listening."**
   It's more than just hearing. That's only the first part of listening . . . the physical part when your ears *sense* sound waves. There are three other parts equally important. There's the *interpretation* of what was heard that leads to understanding, or misunderstanding. Then comes the *evaluation* stage when you weigh the information and decide how you'll use it. Finally, based on what you heard and how you evaluated it, you *react*. That's listening.

2. **Before we can become good listeners, it helps to know why people talk to each other.**

   There are four basic types of verbal communication. There's the "getting-to-know-you" or the "building of relationships" kind of talk which is called *phatic* communication. Next, there's *cathartic* communication which allows the release of pent-up emotion and often amounts to one person spilling his or her troubles on concerned, caring ears. Then there's *informative* communication in which ideas, data or information is shared. Last of all is *persuasive* communication where the purpose is to reinforce or change attitudes or to produce action.

3. **Listening is our primary communication activity.**

   Studies show that we spend about 80% of our waking hours communicating. And, according to research, at least 45% of that time is spent listening. In schools, students spend 60%–70% of their classroom time engaged in listening. And in business, listening has often been cited as being the most critical managerial skill.

4. **Our listening habits are not the result of training but rather the result of the lack of it.**

   The following chart shows the order in which the four basic communication skills are learned, the degree to which they are used and the extent to which they are taught. Listening is the communication skill used most but taught least.

	Listening	Speaking	Reading	Writing
Learned	1st	2nd	3rd	4th
Used	Most (45%)	Next Most (30%)	Next Least (16%)	Least (9%)
Taught	Least	Next Least	Next Most	Most

5. **Most individuals are inefficient listeners.**

   Tests have shown that immediately after listening to a 10-minute oral presentation, the average listener has heard, understood, properly evaluated and retained approximately half of what was said. And within 48 hours, that drops off another 50% to a final 25% level of effectiveness. In other words, we quite often comprehend and retain only one-quarter of what is said.

6. **Inefficient and ineffective listening is extraordinarily costly.**

   With more than 100 million workers in America, a simple ten dollar listening mistake by each of them would cost a billion dollars. Letters have to be retyped; appointments rescheduled; shipments reshipped. And when people in large corporations fail to listen to one another, the results are even costlier. Ideas get distorted by as much as 80% as they travel through the chain of command. Employees feel more and more distant, and ultimately alienated, from top management.

7. Good listening can be taught.

In the few schools where listening programs have been adopted, listening comprehension among students has as much as doubled in just a few months.

How Well Do You Listen?
(A Personal Profile)

Here are three tests in which we'll ask you to rate yourself as a listener. There are no correct or incorrect answers. Your responses, however, will extend your understanding of yourself as a listener. And highlight areas in which improvement might be welcome . . . to you and to those around you. When you've completed the tests, please turn to page 381 to see how your scores compare with those of thousands of others who've taken the same tests before you.

Quiz 1

A. Circle the term that best describes you as a listener.

Superior	Excellent	Above Average	Average
Below Average	Poor	Terrible	

B. On a scale of 0–100 (100 = highest), how would you rate yourself as a listener?

_____

(0–100)

Quiz 2

How do you think the following people would rate you as a listener? (0–100)

Your Best Friend _____

Your Boss _____

Business Colleague _____

A Job Subordinate _____

Your Spouse _____

Quiz 3

As a listener, how often do you find yourself engaging in these 10 bad listening habits? First, check the appropriate columns. Then tabulate your score using the key below.

Listening Habit	Frequency					Score
	Almost Always	**Usually**	**Some-times**	**Sel-dom**	**Almost Never**	
1. Calling the subject uninteresting						
2. Criticizing the speaker's delivery or mannerisms						
3. Getting *over*-stimulated by something the speaker says						
4. Listening primarily for facts						
5. Trying to outline everything						
6. Faking attention to the speaker						
7. Allowing interfering distractions						
8. Avoiding difficult material						
9. Letting emotion-laden words arouse personal antagonism						
10. Wasting the advantage of thought speed (daydreaming)						

TOTAL SCORE

Key

For every "Almost Always" checked, give yourself a score of **2**
For every "Usually" checked, give yourself a score of **4**
For every "Sometimes" checked, give yourself a score of **6**
For every "Seldom" checked, give yourself a score of **8**
For every "Almost Never" checked, give yourself a score of **10**

Profile Analysis

This is how other people have responded to the same questions that you've just answered.

Quiz 1

A. 85% of all listeners questioned rated themselves as *Average* or less. Fewer than 5% rate themselves as *Superior* or *Excellent*.

B. On the 0–100 scale, the extreme range is 10–90; the general range is 35–85; and the *average* rating is 55.

Quiz 2

When comparing the listening self-ratings and projected ratings of others, most respondents believe that their best friend would rate them highest as a listener. And that rating would be higher than the one they gave themselves in Quiz #1 . . . where the average was 55.

How come? We can only guess that best friend status is such an intimate, special kind of relationship that you can't imagine it ever happening unless you *were* a good listener. If you weren't, you and he or she wouldn't be best friends to begin with.

Going down the list, people who take this test usually think their bosses would rate them higher than they rated themselves. Now part of that is probably wishful thinking. And part of it is true. We *do* tend to listen to our bosses better . . . whether it's out of respect or fear or whatever doesn't matter.

The grades for colleague and job subordinate work out to be just about the same as the listener rated himself . . . that 55 figure again.

But when you get to spouse . . . husband or wife . . . something really dramatic happens. The score here is significantly lower than the 55 average that previous profile-takers gave themselves. And what's interesting is that the figure goes steadily downhill. While newlyweds tend to rate their spouse at the same high level as their best friend, as the marriage goes on . . . and on . . . the rating falls. So in a household where the couple has been married 50 years, there could be a lot of talk. But maybe nobody is *really* listening.

Quiz 3

The average score is a 62 . . . 7 points higher than the 55 that the average test-taker gave himself in Quiz #1. Which suggests that when listening is broken down into specific areas of competence, we rate ourselves better than we do when listening is considered only as a generality.

Of course, the best way to discover how well you listen is to ask the people to whom you listen most frequently. Your spouse, boss, best friend, etc. They'll give you an earful.

10 Keys to Effective Listening

These keys are a positive guideline to better listening. In fact, they're at the heart of developing better listening habits that could last a lifetime.

10 Keys to Effective Listening	The Bad Listener	The Good Listener
1. Find areas of interest	Tunes out dry subjects	Opportunitizes; asks "what's in it for me?"
2. Judge content, not delivery	Tunes out if delivery is poor	Judges content, skips over delivery errors
3. Hold your fire	Tends to enter into argument	Doesn't judge until comprehension complete
4. Listen for ideas	Listens for facts	Listens for central themes
5. Be flexible	Takes intensive notes using only one system	Takes fewer notes. Uses 4–5 different systems, depending on speaker
6. Work at listening	Shows no energy output Fakes attention	Works hard, exhibits active body state
7. Resist distractions	Is easily distracted	Fights or avoids distractions, tolerates bad habits, knows how to concentrate
8. Exercise your mind	Resists difficult expository material; seeks light, recreational material	Uses heavier material as exercise for the mind
9. Keep your mind open	Reacts to emotional words	Interprets color words; does not get hung up on them
10. Capitalize on fact *thought* is faster than *speech*	Tends to daydream with slow speakers	Challenges, anticipates, mentally summarizes, weighs the evidence, listens between the lines to tone of voice

"Listening" Reading List

Banville, Thomas G. *How to Listen—How to Be Heard*, LC 77–17961. 1978. (ISBN 0–77229–332–X). Nelson-Hall.

Barbara, Dominick A. *Art of Listening*. (Illus.). 1974. (ISBN 0–398–00086-7). C. C. Thomas.

Carin. *Creative Questioning & Sensitivity: Listening Techniques.* 2nd ed. 1978 text ed. (ISBN 0–675–08421–0), media (ISBN 0–675–08485–7). Merrill.

Cassie, Dhyan. *Auditory Training Handbook for Good Listeners,* LC 75–26439. 1976 pap. text ed. (1762). Interstate.

Crum, J. K. *Art of Inner Listening.* 1975. pap. (ISBN 0–89129–092–3, PV092). Pillar Bks.

DeMare, George. *Communicating At The Top.* 1979. John Wiley & Sons. Price Waterhouse & Co.

Duker, Sam. *Listening Bibliography.* 2nd ed. LC 68–12630. 1968. (ISBN 0–8108–0085–3). Scarecrow Press.

———. *Listening: Readings.* 1966. LC 68–22752. Scarecrow Press.

———. *Listening: Readings. Vo. 2.* 1971. (ISBN 0–8108–0364–X). Scarecrow Press.

———. *Teaching Listening in the Elementary School: Readings.* 1971. Scarecrow Press.

Ernst, Franklin H., Jr. *Outline of the Activity of Listening. 3rd ed.* 1973. softbound (ISBN 0–916944–09–3). Addresso' set.

———. *Who's Listening—Handbook of the Listening Activity.* LC 73–84380. 1973. (ISBN 0–916944–15–8). Addresso' set.

Erway, Ella, A. *Listening: A Programmed Approach.* 2nd ed. 1979.

Faber, Carl A. *On Listening.* 1976. (ISBN 0–918026–02–4).

Friedman, Paul. *Listening Processes: Attention, Understanding, Evaluation.* 1978. National Education Association.

Geeting, Baxter and Corinne Geeting. *How to Listen Assertively.* (Illus.). 1978. (ISBN 0–671–18365–6). Monarch.

Girzaitis, Loretta. *Listening: A Response Ability.* LC 72–77722. (Illus.). 1972. pap. (ISBN 0–88489–047–3). St. Marys.

Goldstein, H. *Reading & Listening Comprehension at Various Controlled Rates.* (Columbia University Teachers College. Contributions to Education: No. 821), Repr. of 1940 ed. (ISBN 0–404–55821–6). AMS PR.

Hirsch, Robert O. *Listening: A Way To Process Information Aurally.* Gorsuch Scarisbrick, Pub.

Johnson, Ida Mae. *Developing the Listening Skills.* 1974. (ISBN 0–914296–18–3). Activity Rec.

Keller, Paul W., Charles T. Brown. *Monologue to Dialogue.* 1973. Prentice-Hall.

Koile, Earl. *Listening As a Way of Becoming.* LC 76–48520. 1977. (ISBN 0–87680–510–1). Word Bks.

Kratoville, Betty L. *Listen, My Children and You Shall Hear. Bk. 1.* LC 68–29770. 1968. pap. (1044); pkg. of 20 extra grading sheets (1045). Interstate.

Langs, Robert. *The Listening Process.* 1978. (ISBN 0–87668–341–3). Aronson.

Lorayne and Lucas. *The Memory Book.* Ballantine Books.

Lundsteen, Sara W. *Listening: Its Impact on Reading and The Other Language Arts.* 1971. NCTE-ERIC—Urbana, Ill.

Mills, Ernest P. *Listening: Key to Communication* (Vardamann Management & Communication Ser.). (Illus). 1974. pap. (ISBN 0–442–80021–5). Van Nos Reinhold.

Moray, Neville. *Listening and Attention.* lib. bdg. (ISBN 0–88307–409–5). Gannon; pap. (ISBN 0–14–080066–2). Penguin.

Morley, Joan. *Improving Aural Comprehension.* Student's Workbook, Teacher's Book of Readings. LC 70–185904. 1972. tchr's bk. of readings. (ISBN 0–472–08666–9); student's wkbk (ISBN 0–472–08665–0). U of Mich Pr.

National Education Association & Stanford E. Taylor. *Listening (What Research Says to the Teacher Ser.).* 1973. pap. (ISBN 0–8106–1012–4); filmstrip (ISBN 0–8106–1118–X). NEA.

Nichols, R. and L. A. Stevens. *Are You Listening?* 1957. (ISBN 0–07–046475–8). McGraw-Hill.

Plaister, T. *Developing Listening Comprehension for ESL Students: The Kingdom of Kochen.* 1976. (ISBN 0–13–204479–X); tapes (ISBN 0–13–204495–1). Prentice-Hall.

Russell, David H. and Elizabeth F. Russell. *Listening Aids Through the Grades.* LC 59–8373. 1959. pap. text ed. (ISBN 0–8077–2080–1). Tchrs Coll.

Spearritt, Donald. *Listening Comprehension, a Factoral Analysis.* (Australian Council for Educational Research). 1962. Verry.

Steil, Lyman K., Larry Barker. *Effective Listening: Developing Your Ear-Q.* 1980. Gorsuch Scarisbrick, Pub.

Stocker, Clausell S. *Listening for the Visually Impaired: A Teaching Manual.* 1974. pap. (ISBN 0–398–02936–9). C. C. Thomas.

Templer, J. C. *Further Listening Comprehension Texts.* (gr. 9–12). 1972. pap. text ed. (ISBN 0–435–28728–1); tchr's ed. (ISBN 0–435–28729–X). Heinemann Ed.

———. *Listening Comprehension Tests.* (gr. 9–12). 1974. pap. text ed. (ISBN 0–435–28736–2); tchr's ed. (ISBN 0–435–28737–0). Heinemann Ed.

Weaver, Carl H. *Human Listening: Process and Behavior.* 1972. Bobbs-Merrill.

Wolvin, Andrew D., Carolyn Gwynn Coakley. *Listening Instruction.* (No. 334). SCA/ERIC. 1979.

Yates, Virginia. *Listening and Note-taking. 2nd ed.* 1970. McGraw-Hill.

Feedback Processes in Task Groups

Beth Haslett and John R. Ogilvie

Human communication involves dialogue between at least two people. An essential part of this dialogue is FEEDBACK, the response listeners give to others about their behavior. Both communicators give feedback—they respond to each others' behavior. Feedback from others enables us to understand how our behavior affects them, and allows us to modify our behavior to achieve desired goals. Finally, feedback is essential for personal growth and development since others' responses to our behavior help us define who we are.

The setting in which feedback occurs is also important. Task groups, like any work context, are rich in information (Hanser & Muchinsky, 1978). Considerable research suggests that individuals actively seek information about themselves and their role in the group (Ashford & Cummings, 1983; Larson, 1984). A key motivator for this search is uncertainty. It is this uncertainty that gives feedback its value (Ashford & Cummings, 1983). When uncertain, individuals feel a tension or uneasiness and seek to reduce those feelings through feedback from others. Early stages of group development are fraught with uncertainty; members are tentative and reluctant to take action. Thus, in task-oriented groups, feedback is a primary means of reducing uncertainty and moving the group along to productive ends.

The function of feedback in systems and cybernetics has long been recognized. Negative feedback acts to correct deviations in the performance of a system, which serves to stabilize and maintain it. An example will help to clarify this point. A thermostat in a house controls the furnace by giving the furnace feedback. When the temperature in the house falls below a certain point, say 60 degrees for the brave and energy conscious, the thermostat signals this drop to the furnace which then starts up. When the temperature rises to a certain level, the thermostat signals a shutdown and the furnace no longer runs. This is an example of a closed loop system, using negative feedback. The thermostat uses only one type of information, which serves to maintain a relatively steady state of room temperature.

Positive feedback in systems terminology is not "good news." It is the amplification of deviations which act to de-stabilize a system. A manager may at times amplify a disagreement for constructive ends. The disagreement serves as a basis for making changes, which are temporarily de-stabilizing but beneficial in the long run. Humans, however, do not function as *closed systems* restricted to only limited forms of information. Interpersonal feedback occurs in an open system setting, using negative and positive feedback features. As such, it is varied, flexible and gathered from a variety of sources.

This article will focus on feedback processes in small task groups. Task groups are a collection of individuals who work interdependently on a task to accomplish a goal. They are different from informal or friendship groups in that they have a specific purpose to achieve or accomplish. Task groups could include a group of four students required to make a presentation on the dangers of acid rain or a task force in a corporation deciding on which configuration of computer technology to acquire. We all belong to task groups, whether they are in work organizations or social clubs. Groups interact over time to reach goals and satisfy needs (Palazzolo, 1981). They also evolve a structure for individual roles and norms to guide behavior. For the group, feedback provides important information on group interaction and group performance. Feedback can improve the effectiveness of group performance since it provides information about how successful the group has been and gives specific suggestions for improvement.

Our research has tried to understand what makes some feedback work more effectively than others. In this paper we will draw on the results of a recently completed study (Ogilvie & Haslett, 1985), in which we videotaped a group of students who had to complete several tasks. They were also required to meet and exchange feedback with one another. We then played the videotape of the feedback session to other students several semesters later and asked them to evaluate the way in which feedback was exchanged. Thus, our conclusions are based on our research of task groups, and our suggestions for giving feedback effectively are based on our own personal experiences with groups. In what follows, we will present a discussion of the nature of the feedback process; the factors influencing the feedback process and offer suggestions for giving feedback effectively.

The Nature of Feedback

Given the important functions of feedback for group performance, it seems crucial that a clear understanding of feedback be developed. However, feedback as a concept and as a process is poorly understood. Scholars analyzing feedback have attempted to conceptualize the underlying dimensions of feedback in order to better understand how feedback works.

Table 1.
Composite Dimensions of Feedback

Dimensions
Message:
Sign (+ or −)
Clarity / Accuracy / Relevance
Source:
Multiple locations
Forceful
Trustworthy
Responsive

Dimensions of Feedback

Dimensions reflect the distinct underlying features of feedback that are evaluated by people. A number of studies have detailed different aspects of feedback. Falcione (1974) had workers fill out a questionnaire on the feedback which they received from their supervisors. He found that workers were sensitive to the reciprocity, perceptiveness, responsiveness and permissiveness of the feedback. O'Reilley and Anderson (1980) found that managers rated three dimensions of feedback as important: its perceived accuracy and relevance, its developmental nature, and the quantity of feedback. They judged the relevance and accuracy of the feedback as more important than the amount of feedback. Herold and Greller (1977) asked people in a variety of settings how often they received feedback on many different topics. From analysis of these responses, they identified five dimensions of feedback: negative feedback, positive feedback from persons higher in authority, positive feedback from peers, internal (or self-determined) criteria, and work flow feedback. Since each study asked people to evaluate different aspects of feedback in different contexts, these underlying dimensions appear quite diverse.

To address this diversity, we (Ogilvie & Haslett, 1985) had students observe and assess feedback with a set of descriptive adjectives compiled from other studies. In our study, the critical dimensions in the feedback process were its dynamism, its trustworthiness, its clarity, its mood or general tone, and its critical nature. This study identified some of the same feedback features as previous studies, establishing the critical nature of feedback.

Several conclusions can be drawn from these studies. (See Table 1 for a set of general underlying dimensions.) The positiveness or critical nature of the feedback appears to be very important. This feature reflects the valence (positive or negative) of the feedback. Another important feature is the clarity, accuracy or relevance of the message. Other important dimensions of feedback involve the *source* of the feedback. Feedback comes from multiple sources, and those sources are judged on the basis of their trustworthiness, forcefulness and responsiveness.

Feedback and Group Performance

Since we have defined task groups in terms of accomplishing goals, we will present a model which discusses group productivity and performance. Hackman and Morris (1975) developed a model of group performance, emphasizing the interaction processes among group members. Across groups, performance can vary widely; some groups perform well with little apparent difficulty. Others struggle constantly and still barely reach mediocrity. According to Hackman and Morris

> "The challenge is to identify, measure and change those aspects of group interaction process that contribute to such obvious differences in group effectiveness." (1975, p. 46)

To this end, they identified three determinants of performance. First, group members need relevant skills and knowledge. If those skills are absent, group performance will be hurt, and goals cannot be attained. Second, sufficient motivation must be present to coordinate activities with fellow group members and complete tasks. The third determinant is the selection of appropriate task performance strategies. Groups can have the necessary knowledge and effort, but may not be effective because of inappropriate approaches to completing the task. (See Figure 1 for a model of this process.)

This model can also be used to understand the functions of feedback, its influence on performance, and its influence on the attitudes of group members (Nadler, 1979). One important function of feedback is to correct inappropriate behavior of members. This corrective effect is often called *cueing*. It signals that the task behavior is not desired, and has the effect of correcting inappropriate strategies. Feedback can also function to set goals and *motivate* members; this addresses the effort determinant. Individuals may receive feedback judging their effort to be below the group's standard (i.e., norms) or that more cooperation is needed to accomplish goals. Supervisory appraisals often establish specific goals to motivate future performance. These appraisals may also suggest areas for skill improvement or enhancement. Similarly, other group members may suggest specific areas of knowledge or skill development through feedback which can improve performance. This type of feedback functions to develop members' *potential* for future activities. By developing new skills and acquiring knowledge, feedback functions to help individuals to acquire some degree of mastery over their environment (Ashford & Cummings, 1983). Thus, feedback appears relevant for all aspects of group performance. To be effective, performance must be measured or assessed and feedback sought from multiple sources. In short, groups cannot be effective without feedback.

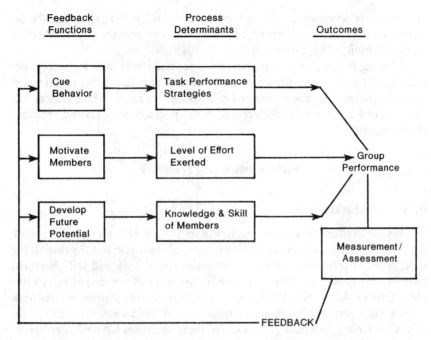

Figure 1. Feedback and group performance. (Adapted from Nadler, 1979.)

Feedback as a Communicative Process

While the underlying dimensions of feedback are useful in revealing the complexity of feedback, additional insight into feedback can be gained when feedback is viewed as a communicative process (Ilgen, Fisher & Taylor, 1979). That is, while feedback is an essential component of any communication model, feedback itself can be studied as communication. As suggested by dimensional studies and other research, we can assess feedback by examining the *source* of the feedback, the feedback *message* itself (e.g., is the feedback positive or negative, is it task-oriented or process-oriented, etc.?) and the *receiver* of the feedback (e.g., an individual, group, or organization).

Ilgen, Fisher and Taylor (1979) attempted to understand how and why individuals respond to feedback. They identified four important processes in feedback. First, individuals must *perceive* the feedback. Second, they must *accept* it. Third, they must then develop the *intentions to respond* and finally must set specific, moderately difficult *goals for improvement.*

They concluded that the perception of feedback is a function of the source, message and recipient. In addition, they suggest that the perception and acceptance of feedback are critical elements in determining the receiver's response to feedback. Generally, the source of the feedback has the greatest impact on its acceptance, although other research has indicated that the influence of the source and message interact with one another (Ilgen, Mitchell & Fredrickson, 1981; Ogilvie & Haslett, 1985).

Viewing feedback as a communicative process allows us to look more specifically at the different aspects of feedback. We now turn to an examination of factors influencing the giving and receiving of feedback. These factors will be examined as source characteristics, message characteristics and recipient characteristics.

Factors Influencing Feedback

A. Source Characteristics

We receive feedback from a variety of sources. In task groups and in work organizations, there are generally five sources of feedback: self (intrinsic), the task, peers, supervisors, and the organization itself. Task and self-generated sources are psychologically closer to the individual and are seen as more valuable (Greller & Herold, 1975). More external, distant sources of feedback require more scrutiny because they cannot be trusted as automatically as intrinsic sources. If feedback from some of these sources is blocked, other problems arise. Obstruction of task and supervisory sources of feedback results in higher levels of anxiety among workers. Blockage of supervisory sources is also strongly related to job satisfaction and intention to leave the company (Walsh, Ashford & Hill, 1985).

A number of other characteristics of these sources have been found to influence the feedback process. Among the influential variables are the trustworthiness of the source, the power and status of the source, the relationship between the source and recipient, and communicative style of the source.

1. *Trustworthiness.* A source's trustworthiness and credibility (believability) are major influences on the acceptance of feedback (O'Reilly & Anderson, 1980). These two issues—trustworthiness and credibility—cannot be discussed separately since we tend to believe those we trust, and trust those whom we believe. Feedback from credible, trustworthy sources receives more attention as well as acceptance from recipients. Those giving positive feedback to others are also perceived as being more trustworthy and credible. Leaders' feedback is also perceived as being more accurate, trustworthy and credible than that of peers, although peers and leaders show high agreement on their feedback of others.

In our study, trust was an important dimension of giving feedback. Trusted feedback was also viewed as being credible and fair. When comparing the trustworthiness of feedback to other variables, we found that it was associated with perceptions of how effectively the feedback was given. Feedback that was communicated in a responsive and relaxed manner was also more trusted. Trust seems linked to reciprocity. If the person believes that you are fair in giving feedback, you should be relaxed and responsive to them. If you are defensive and nervous, then the feedback will not be trusted. Clearly, trust is an important feature; it may be the "golden rule" of feedback. If you trust the feedback, you assume that the motives and intentions of the source are fair.

2. *Power and Status of the Source.* In general, the more powerful the source, the more attention and acceptance the recipients give the feedback. Power can be measured in a number of ways. A supervisor who has direct control over his/her employees will exert a powerful influence over the people s/he supervises. This influence may also explain the strong effect that the obstruction of supervisory feedback has on employees. The absence of information causes anxiety and uncertainty. Thus, leaders generally are perceived as giving more accurate, credible feedback.

Power could also be measured in terms of expertise. We are not likely to accept feedback from a source we consider inexperienced or unknowledgeable about a particular area. Generally, it appears that, for feedback to be readily accepted, the source of the feedback must have some competency with respect to the type of feedback being given.

Our research suggests that in many groups where there is no formally designated leader, the manner in which feedback is given can also have much influence on the receiver. In our research dynamism (a combination of activity and strength) accounted for much of the variation in perceptions of feedback. Dynamism was most strongly related to the overall impression group members leave and accounted for most of the individual differences in the way that feedback was given. Similarly, a communication style that was verbally assertive was strongly related to dynamism and to perceptions of the effectiveness with which the feedback was given.

3. *Communicator Style.* Communicator style refers to the *manner* in which feedback is given. The more consideration and influence a leader has, the greater perceived relevance for that leader's

feedback. Ogilvie and Haslett (1985) found significant
communicative differences across group members in their style of
giving feedback. Group members varied in the dynamism, clarity,
mood and criticalness of their feedback. Effectiveness of feedback
was significantly related to the source's verbally assertive style,
dynamism, responsiveness and being relaxed. Dynamism and
clarity of feedback were also positively related to the impression
group members made. Feedback style has also been positively
related to a recipient's job satisfaction and acceptance of feedback.

B. Message Characteristics

1. *Content*. A message can contain several types of information. One
   type of information refers to behaviors which help to attain a
   desired goal. This type of information is referred to as *referent*
   information and is similar to the cueing function described above.
   Thus, a feedback message containing referent information should
   improve group productivity. Another type of information is more
   subjective—it tells a person how their behavior is perceived and
   evaluated. This type of message contains *appraisal* information and
   is actually more useful to the individual in reducing their
   uncertainty about their role in the group.
2. *Timing*. A number of studies have demonstrated that effective
   feedback is more effective when closer in time to the occurrence.
   That is, feedback should be given relatively close to the behaviors
   or job being done. Delays may reduce the impact and relevance of
   the feedback.
3. *Channel*. Feedback can be given across a number of different
   modes or channels: feedback can be written or oral, verbal or
   nonverbal. Zajonc (1980) found that important affective/evaluative
   information is given nonverbally, while cognitive information is
   presented verbally. The evaluative content delivered through
   nonverbal channels is similar to the appraisal content mentioned
   above. Thus, some channels may be used more for some types of
   content than others. Both effect and cognitions are important
   aspects of giving feedback (Larson, 1984).

   Furnham (1982) investigated the effect of message content and
   channel on giving messages. He found that people preferred to give
   messages face-to-face, rather than by writing or the telephone. In
   general, "the nature of the communication to be made determines
   the choice of situation in which to communicate." Subjects

preferred to communicate most messages in a one-on-one situation, especially for messages that were situation-specific (e.g., giving bad news or disclosing some personal information).

Daft and Lengel (1984) have noted that the channels or media used to communicate vary in terms of their information richness. Face-to-face communication is the most rich while data on a computer printout are relatively low in richness. Very rich media, like oral communication, allow for more rapid, timely feedback and are more useful in solving complex problems where more feedback is needed.

4. *Message Valence.* Perhaps the most important message characteristic influencing feedback is whether it is positive or negative (i.e., its sign or valence). In general, positive messages are more accepted than negative while negative messages seem to be rejected unless it is from a high status source. Positive messages produce higher trust among individuals as well as enhance group cohesion. Generally, individuals also find positive messages more believable and acceptable. Gordon (1985) also found a significant correlation between individuals' giving positive information and their receiving positive comments. The more a group member was perceived as giving conducive feedback, the more s/he received in turn.

In contrast, negative messages are often not transmitted to the intended recipient. People are reluctant to give negative information to others, even while they acknowledge that the intended recipients have a right to know, and a greater desire and interest to know than others. This generalization has been documented in a wide variety of situations, across different communicators and recipients, and across different channels. Tesser and Rosen (1976) found that pleasantness of a message was significantly correlated with the likelihood of its being transmitted ($r = .73$). If there is a negative message to be transmitted, frequently a subordinate is asked to do it. They suggest that people are reluctant to transmit negative messages because they fear being negatively evaluated themselves; they are concerned about the mood created for the intended recipient, and they experience guilt and anxiety over transmitting the message. Tesser and Rosen also suggest that negative messages are threatening to the self-image of the intended recipient, and thus would negatively influence the relationship between the source and intended recipient. However, negative messages have the greatest potential for improving performance. The manner in which these messages are delivered is most critical so that one avoids eliciting defensive reactions and/or damaging the relationship. (See the last section of this for more suggestions on giving feedback.)

C. Recipient Characteristics

The characteristics of the intended recipient also influence the feedback process. People send messages to accomplish specific goals, and that are designed for a specific target audience. It seems reasonable to assume that individuals design their feedback with specific purposes and specific recipients in mind. Since feedback is designed to give an individual information about his/her behavior, obviously those messages will vary as a function of the particular intended recipient. While some studies have explored the recipient's characteristics and their impact on the feedback process, more research needs to be done in this area.

1. *Recipient's Mind Set*. One of the most influential factors in determining the recipient's response to feedback is his/her mind set or frame-of-reference when feedback is received. This temporary frame-of-reference influences their perception, acceptance, and response to feedback. If an employee has just had a difficult time with a customer, they will not be receptive to a co-worker providing critical feedback about her/his work habits. Expectations can also influence a recipient's mind set and be a major factor in his/her perception of feedback (Ilgen, et. al., 1979). We tend to see and hear what we expect, distorting the feedback received.

2. *Personal Qualities*. Several more stable enduring characteristics of the recipient also influence the feedback process. Self-esteem and social anxiety were two personality variables which have been studied in this context (Ilgen, et. al., 1979). People who have varying degrees of self-esteem interpret feedback differently. Individuals with high *self-esteem* interpret negative feedback in an ambiguous way, and thus do not respond as strongly to it. In contrast, people with high *social anxiety* anticipate receiving more negative feedback than those having less social anxiousness, and consequently tend to interpret feedback as being more negative.

   Varca and Levy (1984) examined several related variables in the way that people respond to feedback. They noted that critical feedback represents a threat to an individual's self-esteem. However, people may cope differently with these threats. Some choose to ignore or deny the threat posed by critical feedback.

These people are *repressors*. Repressors tend to have high self-esteem since the feedback is not seen as relevant. An alternative means of coping is to amplify the threat and its consequences by an excessive expression of anxious feelings. These individuals are *sensitizers*. The exaggeration by sensitizers helps to cope by reducing the possibility of consequences from negative events. Such exaggerated expectations of consequences are rarely met, and the sensitizer is much relieved. Again, like the previous paragraph sensitizers are similar to those with high social anxiety in that they interpret the feedback more negatively.

Source, message and recipient characteristics are summarized in Table 2.

Table 2.
Summary of Communication Features in Feedback

Source Characteristics	Message Characteristics	Recipient Characteristics
Trustworthiness	Content	Mind-Set
	Referent	
Power & Status	Appraisal	Expectations
Communication Style	Timing	Personality
Assertive		Repressors /
Dynamic	Channel	Self-Esteem
Relaxed		Sensitizers /
Responsive	Sign or Valence	Social Anxiety

How to Give Feedback

Giving and receiving feedback is an integral part of interpersonal communication. Many interactions will occur in a small group setting, whether it be a sorority or a task force recommending changes in organization structure. Within organizations, feedback is critical because employees need to perform their tasks adequately so the organization continues to survive. For every organizational member, then, understanding feedback is important. However, we also need to know how to give feedback effectively in order to maximize our performance and the performance of others. Giving feedback effectively is, of course, particularly important for those in managerial positions. In what follows, we suggest some general strategies for giving feedback effectively and deal particularly with the problems of giving negative feedback.

General Communicative Strategies

The best general suggestions for effective communication in small groups has been succinctly expressed by Gouran and Fisher (1984).

> In general, those communicative behaviors that are task-oriented, that serve to keep energy focused on the group's goals, and that show a concern with maintaining workable interpersonal relations have correspondingly positive effects on the quality of interaction, the ease with which a task is completed, members' aceptance of group positions, and the satisfaction of the participants. (p. 630)

Generally, then, maintaining good working relationships with others requires that we communicate as constructively as possible.

Some communicative strategies for giving feedback (and receiving it as well) that facilitate a constructive working environment are outlined below. First, in order for feedback to be effective, it needs to be fairly *direct* and *specific*. A general remark such as "That's the wrong way to do that" is so vague and general as to be of no value in changing how the task is done. In contrast, a specific, direct message such as "The water pressure must always be maintained at 100 pounds by adjusting this valve" details the necessary activities for successful task completion. An example from the small group which was videotaped in our study makes this point quite succinctly:

> C: I put __ as a dominator because he—asserts authority and espe- cially I think over __ umm—I think that the group impact I think— you know, I also put you as task and socially oriented but—I think it's a little annoying sometimes how—I don't know—it seems—like you ummmmmmm/
>
> D: /Say it.

In this situation, C is struggling for words, and D, who is receiving this feedback, quite clearly wants C to spit it out! Contrast this with the following example of specific, direct feedback:

> A: I put __ as a harmonizer, um, when we have a lot of tension in the group she tends to try and break it down . . .

Second, effective feedback needs to be *supported by evidence*. Generally people are much more responsive and accepting of comments when some rationale has been given. This can be seen in the following comment made in the small group feedback session.

> B: I see you in a very dominant role because of your personality. You're aggressive, you're assertive and you have your own ideas and you display them. Impact on the group as far as that's concerned I find very good for one thing because you provide direction and you also push the group to achieve . . .

In this example, a judgment was made, but B gave reasons for his judgment and the effect of these behaviors. In addition, providing reasons for actions may forestall or defuse critical reactions, as well as giving the appearance of thoughtful deliberation behind the recommendations.

Finally, feedback should clearly *separate the issue under discussion from the personalities* involved. That is, as Gouran and Fisher suggest, messages should be focused on the task to be accomplished. Both sources and targets of feedback messages should maintain a careful distinction between task and personality.

While these general strategies are useful in giving feedback to others, negative messages represent a situation that deserves special consideration. It deserves separate discussion because of people's general tendency to avoid sending negative messages, and the guilt and anxiety produced by giving negative messages. However, there are situations in which negative assessments must be given and our concern here is how they might be conveyed most effectively. (See Table 3 for a summary of suggestions on giving feedback.)

Table 3.
Summary of Suggestions for Giving Feedback

1. Be Specific and Direct.
2. Support comments with Evidence.
3. Separate the Issue from the Person.
4. "Sandwich" Negative Messages between Positive ones.
5. Pose the Situation as a Mutual Problem.
6. Mitigate or Soften Negative Messages to avoid overload.
7. Timing: Deliver Feedback Close to Occurrence.
8. Manner of Delivery:
   a. Assertive, Dynamic;
   b. Trustworthy, Fair & Credible;
   c. Relaxed and Responsive;
   d. Preserve public image of recipient.

Giving Feedback Containing Negative Messages

While a voluminous literature on feedback has noted the reluctance to transmit negative messages, very little research has addressed the issue of how such negative information can be transmitted. One study (Davies & Jacobs, 1985) looked at the effect of combining negative (N) and positive (P) messages and assessing the effectiveness of various combinations. Specifically, chains of feedback (PNP, PPN, NPN and NNP) were examined. It was found that the PNP chain (positive message, negative message and a final positive comment) was the most effective format for giving feedback. PNP sequences were rated as significantly more accurate, credible, desirable and had the most positive emotional response to it. In addition, PNP sequences contributed most to group cohesiveness and a positive group experience. Interestingly, NPN sequences were viewed most negatively and PPN sequences were not superior to NNP sequences except in desirability. This study suggests that when it is necessary to give negative information, it is most effective to "sandwich" the negative message between two positive comments. For example, "Our engineering division has been doing exceptionally well. Although your group has had the lowest performance, the latest figures show some improvement." The negative comment about low performance has been surrounded by positive comments.

Beyond "sandwiching" the negative feedback, another communicative strategy is to approach the problem area from a collective or collaborative perspective. That is, rather than saying what the problem with the target's group or behavior is, it is more effective to approach the situation as a *problem* which affects both of us. For example, instead of saying "Your group is really performing poorly," a supervisor might say "We seem to have a problem with the group's decreasing productivity. What do you think might be done about it?" The latter comments invite the subordinate to think constructively about an issue which admittedly affects both of them, rather than blaming the subordinate and creating resentment and hostility.

Another strategy might be to *mitigate* or *soften* the force of the negative message through the use of disclaimers or qualifications. Phrases of uncertainty, such as "I'm really not sure about this but I think that . . . ," or the use of tag questions such as "don't you think so too?," soften the force of a negative comment. In the videotape data collected by Ogilvie and Haslett (1985), group members frequently used disclaimers or tag questions to soften the force of their remarks and thus preserve all participants' positive public image. Below are some examples of this from our data.

> A: I also put, um, gatekeeper down for myself because I feel that I encourage others and facilitate participation and I'm always interested in what other people have to say within the group.
> *And I guess that's, I don't know,* a positive impact. I'm sure there are negative things about what I do *but I'm not quite sure* what they are.

In this example, the underlined portion reflects A's qualifications about what the effect of her actions are and thus weakens her self-criticism. Another member of the group, a male, uses the same qualifying strategy in giving feedback to other group members on their performance.

> B: *I think, I find that I don't know,* I see us struggling to be dominating, a dominant role, we seem like we're trying to compete with one another at times for either attention or even impact and input into the group.

The uncertainty projected through these comments softens the impact of the negative comment, and lessens the likelihood of a negative response to the initial negative comments. Such qualifiers help preserve good working relationships when difficult evaluative comments must be made. And all groups will experience moments when negative comments must be made.

Finally, the *language* used in giving feedback is important. Generally, group members should be descriptive in their language, rather than being evaluative. The American Management Association, in its pamphlet on supervisory management, suggests that supervisors focus on describing the problem, rather than blaming employees for the problem. For example, instead of stating "Bill, you are arrogant and domineering," rephrase that and say, "Bill, many colleagues perceive your attitude as being arrogant and domineering." With that rephrasing, attention is focused on the behavior rather than the person: this lessens the likelihood of a negative, defensive response on the part of Bill.

Generally, then, although negative messages are difficult to give and receive, it can be done when attention is given to *how* such feedback can be constructively given. We suggest that the most important consideration is to maintain everyone's positive public image. By maintaining all participants' public image, the group, as a whole, preserves good working relationships among its members. This, in turn, enables the group to be productive, efficient and cohesive. When negative feedback must be given, members can: (1) sandwich the negative comment with positive comments; (2) frame the problem or issue as one which involves both of you; (3) use qualifiers to soften the force of the negative feedback; (4) give reasons for the negative feedback, and (5) use descriptive rather than evaluative language.

Conclusions and Implications

Throughout this article, we have suggested that feedback is a central component of human communication. Feedback is a complex, multifaceted process which is critical to interpersonal and group effectiveness since it enables communicators to understand the effects of their behavior.

Feedback, itself, as a process, may also be analyzed as a separate communicative activity. We have analyzed feedback as a communicative process, and assessed the impact of source, message and recipient on the feedback process. The most influential source characteristics are the source's power and status, trustworthiness, credibility, forcefulness and responsiveness. It is also important to keep in mind that feedback comes from many different sources, and that each source may be valued for a different type of feedback. The feedback message, to be effective, should be clear, accurate, relevant and positive.

Negative feedback is generally avoided by both source and recipient, and anxiety and guilt are associated with negative feedback. Finally, recipients of feedback perceive feedback differently as a function of self-esteem and other personal characteristics. While these general findings provide insight into the feedback process, feedback processes are still in need of further study. We have little understanding, for example, of the complex interactions among the various dimensions of feedback. For example, what occurs when a trusted source gives very negative feedback? What are the effects of that negative feedback on the source's perceived trustworthiness and his/her subsequent relationship with the recipient?

Given the complexity of feedback, and its importance, we have suggested some strategies to follow in order to enhance the effectiveness of feedback given to others. Generally, sources need to be constructive, clear, direct and specific. In addition, a source's remarks should clearly separate the issue from the recipient's personality: critique the behavior at issue rather than the person.

Negative feedback, as already pointed out, creates special difficulties because of the general avoidance of negative messages. However, at times, negative feedback must be given and we suggested a number of strategies by which this could be done to maximize the feedback's effectiveness. In particular, we suggest trying to "sandwich" the negative comments among positive comments; to use descriptive rather than evaluative language; and to maintain all participants' positive public image.

To effectively communicate, we believe it is particularly important to communicate in such a way that all participants have positive attitudes about themselves and others in that group. Even very difficult, negative comments can be given *if sufficient attention has been paid to how to express those comments as constructively as possible.* This, we submit, is especially important in giving feedback to others and the most challenging part of the communicative process. With the information provided in this article, hopefully both sources and recipients will have a better understanding of the feedback process and how to give/receive feedback with maximum effectiveness.

References

Ashford, S. J. & Cummings, L. L. (1983). Feedback as an individual resource: Personal strategies of creating information. *Organizational Behavior and Human Performance, 32,* 370–398.

Daft, R. L. & Lengel, R. H. (1984). Information richness: A new approach managing information processing and organizational design. In B. Staw & L. L. Cummings (Eds.) *Research in Organizational Behavior,* volume 6, 118–133.

Davies, D. and Jacobs, A. (1985). "Sandwiching" complex interpersonal feedback. *Small Group Behavior, 16,* 387–396.

Falcione, R. (1974). Communication climate and satisfaction with immediate supervision. *Journal of Applied Communication Research, 2,* 13–20.

Furnham, A. (1982). The message, the context and the medium. *Language and Communication,* *2,* 33–47.

Gordon R. (1985). Self-disclosure of interpersonal feedback. *Small Group Behavior, 16,* 411–413.

Gouran, D. and Fisher, B. A. (1984). The function of human communication in the formation, maintenance, and performance of small groups. In G. Miller & M. Knapp, Eds., *The handbook of interpersonal communication.* Sage: Beverly Hills, CA.

Greller, M. M. & Herold. D. M. (1975). Sources of feedback: A preliminary investigation. *Organizational Behavior and Human Performance, 13,* 244–256.

Hackman, J. R. & Morris, C. G. (1975). Group tasks, group interaction process and group performance effectiveness: A review and proposed integration. In L. Berkowitz (Ed.) *Advances in Experimental Social Psychology, 8,* New York: Academic Press.

Hanser & Muchinsky (1978). Work as an Information Environment. *Organizational Behavior and Human Performance, 21,* 47–60.

Herold, D. M. & Greller, M. M. (1977). Feedback: The definition of a construct. *Academy of Management, 20*(1), 142–147.

Ilgen, D. R., Fischer, C. D. & Taylor, M. S. (1979). Consequences of individual feedback on behavior in organizations. *Journal of Applied Psychology, 64*(4), 349–371.

Ilgen, D. R., Mitchell, T. R. & Frederickson, J. W. (1981). Poor performers: Supervisors and subordinates responses. *Organizational Behavior and Human Performance, 27,* 386–410.

Larson, J. M., Jr. (1984). Performance feedback processes: A preliminary model. *Organizational Behavior and Human Performance, 34,* 42–76.

Larson, J. R. (1986). Supervisors' performance feedback to subordinates: The impact of subordinate performance valence and outcome dependence. *Organizational Behavior and Human Decision Processes, 37,* 391–408.

Nadler, D. A. (1979). The effects of feedback on task group behavior: A review of experimental research. *Organizational Behavior and Human Performance, 23,* 309–338.

Ogilvie, J. R. & Haslett, B. (1985). Communicating Peer Feedback in a Task Group. *Human Communication Research, 12*(1), 79–98.

O'Reilly, C. & Anderson, J. (1980). Trust and communication of performance appraisal information: The effect of feedback on performance and job satisfaction. *Human Communication Research, 6,* 290–298.

Palazzolo, C. S. (1981). *Small groups, an introduction.* Belmont, CA: Wadsworth Publishing.

Tesser, A. & Rosen, S. (1975). Reluctance to transmit bad news. In L. Berkowitz (Ed.) *Advances in Experimental Social Psychology, 8,* 193–232, New York: Academic Press.

Varca, P. E. & Levy, J. C. (1984). Individual differences in response to unfavorable group feedback. *Organizational Behavior and Human Performance, 33,* 100–111.

Wallace, L. (1978). Nonevaluative approaches to performance appraisals. *Supervisory Management,* 2–9.

Walsh, J. P., Ashford, S. J. & Hill, T. E. (1985). Feedback obstruction: The influence of the information environment on employee turnover intentions. *Human Relations, 38*(1), 23–46.

Zajonc, R. (1980). Feeling and thinking: Preferences need no inferences. *American Psychologist, 35*(2), 151–175.

6

Group Communication: Performance and Practice

Chapter 4 offered essays concentrating on the theory of communication, and chapter 5 focused attention on the individual participant and the messages at the core of group interaction. It is still communication that ties together the articles in chapter 6. However, our attention is now directed to essays concerned with ways communication can be improved.

It is our contention that communication is an ongoing activity. It involves performing actions that produce reactions in other people. Inherent in this notion is the idea that much of one's communication behavior can be controlled, and therefore, can be improved. We now set forth five essays that ask you to examine your communication behavior, and where appropriate, to make necessary adjustments. These adjustments might range from manifesting empathy to helping resolve conflict within the group, as explained in these essays.

Communication apprehension (the fear or anxiety associated with either real or anticipated communication with another person) is a potential problem facing anyone who engages in communication. Nearly all of us suffer from some degree of anxiety as we attempt to share our ideas and feelings with other people. James C. McCroskey and Virginia P. Richmond examine this issue as it relates to small group communication. To help us understand and control communication apprehension they look at some reasons why people engage in or avoid communication encounters. They also talk about both the internal and external effects of communication apprehension. They place these feelings of anxiety in the small group context, and discuss how apprehension relates to such things as the amount of talk in a group, the choice of seats, message content, and perception. McCroskey and Richmond conclude their essay by offering some practical advice on how to control communication apprehension.

Whether in a small group or in a face-to-face situation, it is crucial to know all you can about your communication partner(s). Knowing who you are interacting with not only helps you formulate your messages, but it also enables you to more accurately judge the responses those messages are producing. Empathy is one of the most effective ways to accomplish those two objectives, for it allows you an opportunity to both understand and predict the behavior of others. For when we experience empathy, Gerald R. Miller and Mark Steinberg suggest that "we feel as if we were experiencing someone else's feelings as our own." As a means of further understanding the importance and workings of empathy, they discuss empathy from a variety of perspectives. They talk about what it is, how it operates, and how it can be improved.

The title of our next selection, "Conflict and Its Resolution", by Bobby R. Patton and Kim Giffin is a summary of the steps in conflict resolution. The major premise behind this piece is that conflict does exist in the small group setting, and that this conflict must be treated in a rational manner. As a means of resolving the conflicts that arise within and between groups, the authors discuss the levels of conflict, the differences between competitive and cooperative orientations, and the methods of handling conflict.

Just as an overabundance of conflict can impede a group's progress, so can a lack of critical testing, analyzing, and evaluating ideas impede progress. The tendency to minimize conflict and reach consensus at any expense is called "groupthink". As a participant in a group, you must work as hard at overcoming groupthink as you do at curing the ills of conflict. How to master groupthink is the subject of the next essay, by Steven A. Beebe and John T. Masterson. They begin by identifying six symptoms of groupthink. They then offer concrete proposals that can reduce the chances of groupthink occurring. All of their suggestions demand individual members take a role in seeing that this problem does not interfere with the group accomplishing its goal.

Being a competent communicator is an asset to anyone who takes part in small group activity. But what is a competent communicator? What characteristics does he or she possess? These and other questions are examined by Janis Andersen in an essay entitled "Communication Competency in the Small Group". In addition to looking at these issues, Andersen discusses specific strategies that you might pursue when you are a participant in a small group.

Communication Apprehension and Small Group Communication

James C. McCroskey and Virginia P. Richmond

Before signing up for a course in communication, students typically ask if they will have to give a speech. Why? Because most students, as well as other adults, experience some apprehension when confronted with presenting a speech to an audience. In fact, a national survey of Americans found that fear of public speaking is the number one fear in American society (Death is a poor third!). Of course, most communication situations, hence most communication courses, do not involve public speaking. Unfortunately, many people experience apprehension about communication in settings other than public speaking, such as communicating in a small group. In this chapter we will explore communication apprehension and its impact on small group communication.

Before you read beyond this paragraph, complete the questionnaire on page 418. Answer each question honestly; no one but you will see your score.

The questionnaire that you just completed is known as the Personal Report of Communication Apprehension, or more commonly PRCA. It has been completed by several thousand people, so that we know quite a bit about what a given score on the instrument may mean. Instructions for scoring the PRCA are on page 419. Follow those instructions so that you can obtain your four sub-scores as well as your overall PRCA score. After we have considered some other very important matters, we will return to a discussion of these scores and help you interpret the scores you obtained.

Communication Motivations

Life for a human being in American society is an almost continuous series of communication encounters. While many of these encounters are mediated (e.g., reading, watching television, listening to the radio), most involve live contact with other people in either a dyadic (two person) or small group settings. To be human is to communicate with one's fellow humans.

Even though communication is such a pervasive part of our everyday lives, the amount of communication in which one person engages may differ enormously from the amount in which another person engages. In general (although we will note important exceptions later), people engage in

James C. McCroskey and Virginia P. Richmond are affiliated with the Department of Speech Communication, University of West Virginia.

communication to the extent which they are motivated to communicate. There are many considerations which motivate us to communicate. Among these are the desire to establish a relationship with another person, the need to obtain information or understanding, the desire to influence another person, the need for decision-making, and recreation.

Establishing Relationships

Most of us want to be liked by others, to develop friendships. Communication is central to the development of such relationships. The way we communicate with others will determine, in large part, the degree to which they like us, and vice versa.

Obtaining Information and Understanding

Although we may obtain much information from the various media, to clarify this information and obtain more complete understanding we frequently need to interact with others, particularly those with more background or experience in the given area. Much small group communication is specifically devoted to this end.

Influence

In modern society we are all dependent on each other not only to prosper but also simply to survive. We cannot function as completely autonomous individuals. Thus, we must influence the behavior of others, and they must influence us as well. Such influence inherently requires communication.

Decision-Making

Both individuals and organizations constantly need to make decisions. While individuals *can* make decisions without communicating with others, it is comparatively rare that they actually do so. More commonly, we talk to others about tentative decisions to get their advice before we commit ourselves to the decisions. In an organizational environment it is even more rare for an individual to make an autonomous decision without communicating with others, (except on the most routine and mundane matters such as how many paper clips to buy). Virtually all decisions in organizations are made during or after extensive communication, typically in a small group context.

Recreation

For most people the simple act of communicating is just plain fun. It need not have any other purpose. Hence we go out for coffee with others, we join a bridge club or bowling team, we join a "bull session", we hold a cocktail party. Communication in these settings often is referred to as "phatic" communication, or communication for its own sake. The next hour we may not remember what was said, much less the next day; but we can remember that we enjoyed it.

Communication, then, is central to our success and happiness. It is the means by which we grow and thrive in our environment. In our modern society, it is not only normal to have a high motivation to communicate, it is almost an absolute necessity.

Communication Avoidance

While it is normal to be highly motivated to communicate in many situations, it is also normal to avoid communication in some. Two conditions are particularly likely to cause us to avoid communication. The first is when communicating will probably lead us to an unpleasant outcome. If our friend appears in a new shirt or blouse which we consider very unattractive, we are likely to say nothing to avoid offending the person. Similarly, if we strongly dislike a person, we are very likely to try to avoid communicating with that individual, in order to avoid conflict.

The second circumstance which is likely to cause us to avoid communication is the simple desire to be left alone. Most of us have experienced this feeling at times. We may take the phone off the hook for a while, or retreat to our study or bedroom. We may even take a vacation to a strange area where no one knows us and there will be minimal demands placed on us to communicate.

While such temporary withdrawal from and avoidance of communication is normal behavior for most of us, some people engage in such avoidance as a consistent pattern of behavior. They talk much less than other people. We commonly refer to these people as "shy". Although it is fairly easy to identify the shy person, we observe that they are much more quiet in most settings than are other people, it is much more difficult to determine why they are shy. The reason for this is that there are at least five different kinds of shy people. Let us consider each type.

The Skill Deficient

People tend to do what they do well and avoid doing what they do poorly. Many people in our society have low communication skills. As a result, these people are shy in situations where they believe (either correctly or incorrectly) that their skills are insufficient to communicate effectively. If these people are able to receive training which they perceive increases their skills, their shyness is likely to disappear.

The Social Introvert

Some people have a very high need and desire to be with other people (social extroverts), while others prefer to be alone most of the time (social introverts). Introverts behave in a shy manner because they have little motivation to interact with other people. Unlike individuals who are skill deficient, introverts are likely to show considerable variance in the degree of shy behavior they exhibit. In circumstances where they have little motivation to communicate, they will appear shy. In other circumstances, when more motivation to communicate is present, it will appear they are not shy at all.

The Alienated

Most people in any environment attempt to conform to the norms and values of the people in that environment. Each individual has needs and desires similar to the other individuals in that environment. The individual communicates in order to meet those needs and desires. Some people, however, do not share the norms and values of the other people in their environment. They do not have the same needs and desires. We refer to these people as "alienated" from the other people. Alienated individuals typically behave in a shy manner. In another environment they might not behave this way, but in the given environment they see little need to communicate because they perceive no benefits that they would obtain by communicating.

The Ethnically/Culturally Divergent

Each ethnic and cultural group has its own ways of behaving. Similarly, ethnic and cultural groups communicate in very different ways, sometimes even in different languages or dialects. In some groups, such as the general white North American culture, talk is highly valued. In others, much less value is placed on talking to others. Most people within any ethnic or cultural group quickly learn the communication norms of their group. The problem arises when one moves into an ethnically or culturally different group. The person, while possibly being a very effective communicator in her or his own group, is divergent from the other group members. Not only does the outsider have difficulty understanding what he or she should do to communicate effectively, the group members may have considerable difficulty figuring out how to adapt to the divergent person. Under such circumstances the ethnically or culturally divergent person is very likely to behave in a shy manner, but such shyness is restricted to circumstances in which the individual is with persons of a different ethnic or cultural background.

The Communication Apprehensive

Communication apprehension (CA) is the fear or anxiety associated with either real or anticipated communication with another person or persons. Communication apprehensives are normal people who are afraid to communicate. Such individuals typically are not skill deficient (although some are), are not necessarily introverted (although quite a few are), are not alienated, and are in an environment in which the ethnic and cultural backgrounds of others are not greatly different than their own. People who are fearful or anxious about communicating tend to behave in a shy manner.

Communication avoidance, or more simply, shyness, has various causes as we have just noted. The effects of such avoidance in most societies are quite negative. We will address some of these effects later. However, before turning our attention to such effects, we need to examine in more detail the number one cause of shyness—CA.

The Nature of CA

We asked you to complete the PRCA at the beginning of this chapter in order to provide you with information about yourself: what kinds of communication may cause you to be apprehensive and what kinds are not likely to do so. In general, high CA is a negative element in a person's life. It not only causes internal discomfort but it also can lead to shyness and ineffective or even counterproductive communication. It is essential, therefore, to be able to put your level of CA into perspective.

Such a sense of perspective is not common to people at either end of the CA continuum. People with high CA commonly report thinking that they are the only ones who feel that way. People with low CA often have a hard time understanding how anyone could be anxious about communication. People with moderate CA recognize that some situations bother them but not other situations, and assume that most people are bothered by fewer situations than they are.

In order to see your own level of CA in perspective you need to have an understanding of the four major types of CA. Let us examine each type.

CA as a Trait. Trait, or personality-type CA is an individual's general orientation toward communication, regardless of the context or situation. While for the majority of people this trait plays an unimportant part in everyday life, for those who are very low (about 20% of the population) or very high (also about 20% of the population) in trait CA it can play a dominating role in life. The PRCA is the best available measure of this trait. As with most personality-type measures, your PRCA score can predict your behavior only if your score is very high or very low. Such extreme scores suggest that your behavior is influenced as much by your general feelings about communication as by any specific communication situation in which you find yourself. People with very high PRCA scores are anxious in virtually all communication situations; people with very low PRCA scores are anxious in extremely few communication situations. If your score on the PRCA is 80 or above, that is a very high score. If your score is 50 or below, that is a very low score.

CA in a Generalized Situation. This type of CA related to generalized types of communication situations. The PRCA provides subscores for the four most common types of generalized situations—group discussions, meetings, interpersonal conventions, and public speaking. It is quite possible for a person to have very high (or low) CA about one type of situation but to have a very different level of CA about another type of situation. A subscore on the PRCA of 24 or above indicates high CA about that generalized situation. A subscore of 12 or below indicates a low CA level about that situation.

Although there is no necessary relationship between trait CA level and level of CA concerning any particular generalized situation, it is much more likely that a person who is high in trait CA will have high CA in more generalized situations. The reverse is true for the person with low trait CA.

It is very important to recognize the proportion of people who experience high CA in a given generalized situation. While about 20 percent of the population experience high trait CA, over 70 percent experience high CA in the public speaking context alone. In the meeting context about 50 percent experience high CA, while in the group context only about 25 percent do, and only about 10 percent report high CA in the interpersonal context. Thus, if you were exactly like the typical person who has completed the PRCA in the past, your highest subscore would be for public speaking with meetings, groups and interpersonal scores falling in that order. You should recognize, however, that many people's scores do not fall in that order. In fact, for some the order is exactly reversed. It all depends on what kind of situation is the most troublesome for the individual person.

CA with a Given Individual or Group Across Situations. Almost 95 percent of the population report having a CA about communicating with some person or group in their lives. The target that may produce this CA may be the boss, dad, teacher, a peer, or virtually anyone else in the person's environment. This type of CA is person (or group) specific. Another person or group in the same context would not produce the CA. Although it is not possible to predict which people or groups will make a person with moderate trait CA most comfortable or uncomfortable, we do know that people with high trait CA will find more people and groups who arouse apprehension in them and people with low trait CA will find fewer people and groups who arouse apprehension. The trait of high CA is reflected in an increased probability of fear or anxiety in any given situation, but does not indicate apprehension in all situations.

CA with a Given Individual or Group in a Given Situation. Virtually all of us experience CA from time to time with some person or group in some situation. Consider some examples: the teacher calls you into the office and informs you that he or she suspects you of cheating; with only five minutes notice you are expected to give a twenty-minute presentation to a group on a topic you know little about; you know you have offended someone and you need to talk to the person to apologize. In each of these examples the situation is unique in our experience with the other person. Thus, even though you would not usually experience CA when communicating with that individual, in the given situation apprehension is aroused.

In summary, then, what is communication apprehension? It is the fear or anxiety associated with either real or anticipated communication with another person or persons. The apprehension may stem from our basic personality, be a function of the type of communication expected, be attributed to the person or group with whom we are to communicate, or be unique to the specific circumstances of the interaction. From whatever source it comes, it causes us discomfort, may result in our behaving in a shy manner, and is likely to result in our being ineffective in our communication. The only fact that is certain is that at some point in our communicative lives we will experience it. For some people, the experience is much more common than it is for others.

Effects of CA

The effects of CA have been extensively researched and the results of this research have been summarized elsewhere.[1] We will not direct our attention to the results of the specific effects studies but rather will focus our attention or more global effect patterns. These patterns relate to internal effects and external effects.

Internal Effects. Although CA has behavioral implications, as we will note later, the primary experience of CA is internal to the individual. In fact, the only effect of CA that is universal is an internally experienced feeling of discomfort. The higher the CA, the greater the discomfort.

Since CA is experienced internally, it is impossible for any other person to be absolutely certain when another person is experiencing it. Some people fall apart when experiencing high CA, while others maintain a very cool and composed exterior. Similarly, the physiological response to CA, which is a heightened activation, is not meaningfully different from the physiological response to excitement. As an example, a person who is highly afraid to give a speech and one who is highly excited and looking forward to the speech will react physiologically in very similar ways. Thus, the only way to know if someone is experiencing high CA is to ask that person. If the individual chooses to tell you the truth, then you will know. If not, then you won't know.

External Effects. There is no externally observable behavior that is a universally predictable effect of CA. Nevertheless, there are some behaviors that are more likely and some which are less likely to occur as a function of varying levels of CA. Three patterns of behavioral response of high CA may be expected to be generally characteristic, and one pattern can be described as sometimes present, but atypical. We will consider each.

When people are confronted with a circumstance which they anticipate will make them uncomfortable, and they have a choice of whether or not to confront it, they may either decide to confront it and make the best of it or avoid it and thus elude the discomfort. Some refer to this as the choice between "fight" and "flight". Research in the area of CA indicates the latter choice should be expected in most instances. In order to avoid having to experience high CA, people may select occupations which involve low communication responsibilities, may choose housing units that reduce incidental contact with other people, may choose seats in classrooms or meetings that are less conspicuous, and may avoid social settings. At the interpersonal level, if a person makes us uncomfortable, we may simply avoid being around that person. Avoidance, then, is a common behavioral response to high CA.

Avoidance of communication is not always possible. A person can find her or himself in a situation which generates a high level of CA, with no advance warning, or in a situation in which communication is forced upon her or him by others. In such circumstances, withdrawal from communication is the behavioral pattern to be expected. This withdrawal may be complete, i.e., absolute silence, or partial, i.e., talking only as much as absolutely required. In a public speaking meeting, the response may be represented by a very short speech. In a meeting, class or small group discussion, it may be represented by talking only when called upon by others. In a conversation, it may be expressed by only answering questions or supplying agreeing responses, with no initiation of interaction.

Communication disruption is the third typical behavioral pattern associated with high CA. When the "flight" response is rejected or not available, the individual may attempt to "fight" on through. The person may lack fluency in verbal presentation, or have unnatural nonverbal behaviors. Equally probable are poor choices of communicative strategies, sometimes reflected in the after-the-fact "I wish I had (had not) said . . ." phenomenon. It is important to note, however, that such behaviors may be produced by inadequate communication skills as well as by high CA. Thus, inferring CA from observations of such behavior often is not appropriate.

Over-communication is an uncommon response to high CA, but it is the pattern exhibited by a small minority. This behavior represents over-compensation for high CA. It may reflect an extreme "fight" reaction: the attempt to succeed in spite of the felt discomfort. The person who elects to take a public speaking course in spite of extreme stage fright is a classic example. Less easily recognizable is the individual with high CA who attempts to dominate social situations. Most of the time people who employ this behavioral option are seen as poor communicators but are not recognized as having high CA; others may actually consider them people with very low CA.

The above discussions are addressed to behavioral patterns of people with high CA levels. One might assume that the behaviors of people with low CA would be the exact reverse. Although this assumption frequently is correct, it is not always correct. While people with low CA tend to seek opportunities to communicate rather than avoid them, to dominate interactions in which they are a member rather than withdraw from them; people with low CA may also have disrupted communication and over-communicate. The disruptions may stem from pushing too hard rather than from tension, but the behaviors may not always appear distinctly different to the observer. The person who over-communicates engages in very similar behavior, whether this stems from high or low CA.

CA in the Small Group Setting

As we have seen, CA has a very important impact on an individual's communication behavior, although that impact may be quite different for one person than for another. In no communication situation is CA more important than in the small group context. It is not an exaggeration to suggest that CA may be the single most important factor in predicting communication behavior in a small group. In numerous studies CA has been the most significant predictor of behavior, and in several it has been the only significant predictor. Let us look at some of the effects of CA observed in this context.

Amount of Talk. Numerous studies have replicated a very consistent finding: people with high CA talk much less in the small group setting than do people with low CA. This is a classic example of withdrawal. In each study people were unable to avoid being in the small group setting, and in each case those with high CA were found to be infrequent participants, while those with low CA were found to participate extensively. To state the point simply, people who are apprehensive about talking in a small group setting tend not to speak, even when forced into such a situation.

Choice of Seats. Avoidance of communication in the small group setting is evidenced by individuals' choices in seating within the group. In most seating arrangements there are positions which are the focus of attention and positions which are relatively obscure. Research indicates that the individuals with low CA regularly choose the positions which are the focus of attention while those with high CA regularly choose positions which are more obscure.

To illustrate this point, let us visualize a typical conference table with eight seats. The table is rectangular with a seat at each end and three along each side. The most focal seats are the two at opposite ends. The next most focal are the two in the middle along the sides. The other four seats permit more obscurity. The research indicates that people with high CA will carefully avoid sitting in either of the end seats or the middle seats while people with low CA will strive to obtain those seats. Sitting in obscure seats permits people with high CA to withdraw from communication more easily and be less likely to be addressed directly by others.

Communication Content. Several research studies have indicated that CA has an impact on the content of communication in the small group setting, most particularly on the content generated by people with high CA. Disruption of communication is a common impact. People with high CA have an abnormally high level of verbalized pauses and rhetorical interrogatives (such as "you know") in the small group setting. In addition, when they talk, people with high CA tend to say things that are not relevant to the ongoing discussion. Probably most important, people with high CA tend to avoid expressing disagreement in the small group setting. When asked their opinion they tend overwhelmingly to express agreement with the group, whether they actually are in agreement or not.

The small group setting seems not only to disrupt the communication of the person with high CA but also to disrupt the thought processes of these individuals. When asked to develop ideas privately, people with high CA generate as many ideas as other people. However, when placed in a small group setting these individuals generate far fewer ideas. In all likelihood these individuals are thinking more about how to cope with the communication demands of the setting than they are about the problem being discussed.

In sum, the person with high CA tends not to be a particularly effective member of a discussion group. They will avoid or withdraw from communication to the extent possible. If communication is thrust upon them, their communication probably will be disrupted, they will have less ideas to contribute, they may make comments that others will see as irrelevant, and they will tend to be very submissive to the ideas of the group majority. On the other side of the coin, people with low CA typically will dominate the interaction of the group, generate numerous ideas, make very relevant comments, and be quite willing to disagree with other group members.

Results of CA and Shy Behavior

As we have noted previously, CA is but one of several causes of shy behavior. Several research studies have examined the impact of either CA or shy behavior, or both, on the perceptions of other members of a group. The results have been very consistent, whether the focus of study was CA or shy behavior. Thus, we will consider these results together.

Perceived Behavior. People with high CA consistently are seen by other group members as being more nervous and less dominant than others by the other members of the group. Similar perceptions have been observed in simulation studies which did not involve actual communication but only informed research subjects about the amount of time a person talked in a hypothetical group.

Perceived Attractiveness. There are two types of attraction that are important in the small group setting, social and task. Social attraction relates to the degree to which a person likes to be with and interact with another person. Task attraction relates to the degree to which a person desires to work with another person. For a group to work well together, at least a moderate level of both task and social attraction among the group members is needed.

Both social and task attraction are related to the amount of talk in which a person engages in a small group. Except in the most extreme cases, the more a person talks in a group the more likely he or she will be perceived as attractive by the other group members. Of course, this presumes that the content of the talk is not averse to the other group members. As a result of this bias in favor of high verbalization, people with high CA tend to be considered less attractive, whereas people with low CA tend to be regarded as more attractive.

Perceived Leadership. In large measure leadership is a function of amount of talk. Numerous studies have all reached the same conclusion: the more a person talks in a group the more likely he or she will be perceived as the leader of the group by the other members as well as by outside observers. Consequently, it is not surprising that people with high CA seldom are seen as leaders in groups while people with low CA frequently are seen in this way.

Perceived Content Quality. Although there is no necessary relationship between quality of participation and quantity of participation, when we examine the perceptions of group members we observe that there is a strong relationship. People who participate more are seen as contributing more to the progress of the group. Even in controlled studies where people who were low talkers were the only ones to have the information needed by the group, the higher talkers were credited with making the more valuable contributions. Consequently, people with high CA typically are perceived as making contributions of less value than are people with low CA.

In sum, the amount a person talks in a group has a major impact on the perceptions of the other persons in that group. Low talkers are seen as less attractive, as exerting less leadership, and as providing contributions of lower quality. In some cases these perceptions are consistent with what actually goes on in the group, though in others they are not. In both cases, however, the perception is there and determines to a major extent how the various group members relate to each other. Low talkers, whether the reduced talk is a function of high CA or something else, are seen as less useful members of groups and tend to be rejected by other group members.

Controlling Your CA

As the previous sections have indicated, the results of experiencing high CA generally are negative. Few people wish their CA were higher, but many wish it were lower. As a result of this need to reduce CA, several methods to help overcome CA have been developed and tested. Formal treatment procedures are available in many places, and are generally highly beneficial. If you experience very high CA and would like to reduce your CA, you should explore the possibilities of obtaining help in this area.

If you find that no treatment or training program is available to you, you can employ methods on your own which will be of some help. There are three steps that we recommend, which others have found useful.

Step 1. Develop a thorough understanding of the process of human communication. If a course in communication theory is available, preferably one focusing on interpersonal communication, it can be very helpful to you. Research has indicated that studying about the human communication process can contribute to reduced CA. Many people develop high CA as a result of not understanding how the human communication process works and by making incorrect assumptions both about their own level of communication skill and that of other people. Such assumptions can be corrected by a good communication course.

Step 2. Learn to recognize when there is tension in your body and how to relax that tension. This may be learned by listening to specially prepared cassette tape recordings designed for this purpose. Such tapes are the core of the most successful formal treatment program for CA, known as systematic desensitization. Once you have learned to recognize tension and to relax that tension, you can use this method in actual communication situations to become more relaxed.

Relaxation tapes are available from a number of commercial organizations and may be available in your local bookstore. If you cannot locate one, check with a member of the faculty of your speech or communication department for the address of the Speech Communication Association. They will provide you a copy of such a tape at very low cost.

Step 3. Learn to identify the negative statements you make to yourself when you are communicating. When confronting a communication situation, people with high CA tend to say things like "I can't do this" and "Everyone thinks I am dumb". These statements usually are not made out loud, but only silently to oneself. Such thinking makes CA much worse.

Prepare a list of these negative statements. Write down whenever you are aware you are making such a remark. Develop a list of positive statements such as "I can do this," and "This is not so difficult." Practice repeating these positive statements to yourself when you feel tension during communication. Repeat one several times if you catch yourself using a negative statement.

If you follow these three steps, you should find your apprehension about communication reduced. However, do not expect miracles. Your CA will not disappear. Rather you should see a gradual reduction over a period of time. Remember, you took a long time to acquire your CA. It will not disappear quickly.

Personal Report of Communication Apprehension (PRCA–24)*

Directions: This instrument is composed of 24 statements concerning your feelings about communication with other people. Please indicate in the space provided the degree to which each statement applies to you by marking whether you (1) Strongly Agree, (2) Agree, (3) Are Undecided, (4) Disagree, or (5) Strongly Disagree with each statement. There are no right or wrong answers. Many of the statements are similar to other statements. Do not be concerned about this. Work quickly, just record your first impression.

_____ 1. I dislike participating in group discussions.

_____ 2. Generally, I am comfortable while participating in a group discussion.

_____ 3. I am tense and nervous while participating in group discussions.

_____ 4. I like to get involved in group discussions.

_____ 5. Engaging in a group discussion with new people makes me tense and nervous.

_____ 6. I am calm and relaxed while participating in group discussions.

_____ 7. Generally, I am nervous when I have to participate in a meeting.

_____ 8. Usually I am calm and relaxed while participating in meetings.

_____ 9. I am very calm and relaxed when I am called upon to express an opinion at a meeting.

_____ 10. I am afraid to express myself at meetings.

_____ 11. Communicating at meetings usually makes me uncomfortable.

_____ 12. I am very relaxed when answering questions at a meeting.

_____ 13. While participating in a conversation with a new acquaintance, I feel very nervous.

_____ 14. I have no fear of speaking up in conversations.

_____ 15. Ordinarily I am very tense and nervous in conversations.

_____ 16. Ordinarily I am very calm and relaxed in conversations.

_____ 17. While conversing with a new acquaintance, I feel very relaxed.

_____ 18. I'm afraid to speak up in conversations.

_____ 19. I have no fear of giving a speech.

_____ 20. Certain parts of my body feel very tense and rigid while giving a speech.

_____ 21. I feel relaxed while give a speech.

_____ 22. My thoughts become confused and jumbled when I am giving a speech.

_____ 23. I face the prospect of giving a speech with confidence.

_____ 24. While giving a speech I get so nervous, I forget facts I really know.

SCORING

Group = $18 - (1) + (2) - (3) + (4) - (5) + (6)$
Meeting = $18 - (7) + (8) + (9) - (10) - (11) + (12)$
Interpersonal = $18 - (13) + (14) - (15) + (16) + (17) - (18)$
Public = $18 + (19) - (20) + (21) -- (22) + (23) - (24)$
Overall CA = Group + Meeting + Dyadic + Public

Note

1. For a review of this research see McCroskey, James C. "Oral Communication Apprehension: A Summary of Recent Theory and Research," *Human Communication Research*, 4, 1977, 78–96.

References

Behnke, R. R. & Beatty, M. J. "A cognitive-physiological model of speech anxiety." *Communication Monographs*, 1981, 48, 158–163.

Daly, J. A., McCroskey, J. C., and Richmond, V. P. "The relationships between vocal activity and perceptions of communicators in small group interaction." *Western Speech Communication Journal*, 1977, 41, 175–187.

Ellis, D. G. "Trait predictors of relational control." *Communication Yearbook II* Ed. by Ruben, B. D. New Brunswick, NJ: *Transaction Books*, 1978.

Fenton, R. J. and Hopf, T. S. "Some effects of communication inhibition on small groups: Participation, member satisfaction, perceived effectiveness, credibility, and leadership." Paper presented at the Speech Communication Association convention, San Francisco, 1976.

Hurt, H. T. & Preiss, R. "Silence isn't necessarily golden: Communication apprehension, desired social choice, and academic success among middle-school students." *Human Communication Research*, 1978, 4, 315–328.

Jablin, F. M. and Sussman, L. "An exploration of communication and productivity in real brainstorming groups." *Human Communication Research*, 1978, 4, 329–337.

McCroskey, J. C. "Measures of communication-bound anxiety." *Speech Monographs*, 1970, 37, 269–277.

McCroskey, J. C. "Oral communication apprehension: A summary of recent theory and research." *Human Communication Research*, 1977, 4, 78–96.

McCroskey, J. C. *An introduction to rhetorical communication*. 4th Ed. Englewood Cliffs, NJ: Prentice Hall, 1982.

McCroskey, J. C., Hamilton, P. R., and Weiner, A. N. "The effect of interaction behavior on source credibility, homophily, and interpersonal attraction." *Human Communication Research,* 1974, 1, 42–52.

McCroskey, J. C., Daly, J. A. and Richmond, V. P. "The effects of communication apprehension on interpersonal attraction." *Human Communication Research,* 1975, 2, 51–65.

McCroskey, J. C., Daly, J. A., and Sorensen, G. "Personality correlates of communication apprehension." *Human Communication Research,* 1976, 2, 376–380.

McCroskey, J. C. and Richmond, V. P. *The quiet ones: Communication apprehension and shyness.* 2nd Ed. Dubuque, Iowa: Gorsuch Scarisbrick, 1982.

McCroskey, J. C. and Wheeless, L. R. *Introduction to human communication.* Boston: Allyn and Bacon, 1976.

Millar, D. P. and Yerby, J. "Regression analysis of selected personal characteristics as predictors of small group leadership." Paper presented at the Communication Apprehension Conference at the Speech Communication Association Convention, Louisville, Kentucky, 1982.

Phillips, G. M. *Help for shy people.* Englewood Cliffs, NJ: Prentice Hall, 1981.

Porter, D. T. "Communicator style perceptions as a function of communication apprehension." *Communication Quarterly,* 1982, 30, 237–244.

Powers, W. G. "The rhetorical interrogative: Anxiety or control?" *Human Communication Research,* 1977, 4, 44–47.

Quiggins, J. G. "The effects of high and low communication apprehension on small group member credibility, interpersonal attraction and interaction." Paper presented at the Speech Communication Association Convention, Chicago, 1972.

Sorensen, G. A. and McCroskey, J. C. "The prediction of interaction behavior in small groups: Zero history vs. intact groups." *Communication Monographs,* 1977, 44, 73–80.

Wells, J. A. and Lashbrook, W. B. "A study of the effects of systematic desensitization on the communicative anxiety of individuals in small groups." Paper presented at the Speech Communication Association convention, New Orleans, 1970.

Wenzlaff, V. J. "The prediction of leadership: A consideration of selected communication variables," M.S. Thesis, Illinois State University, 1972.

Wissmiller, A. P. and Merker, G. E. "Communication apprehension, social distance, and interpersonal judgments in small groups." Paper presented at the Speech Communication Association convention, San Francisco, 1976.

Zimbardo, P. G. *Shyness: What it is, what to do about it.* Reading, Mass.: Addison-Wesley, 1977.

Empathic Skills and the Development of Interpersonal Communication Effectiveness

Gerald R. Miller and Mark Steinberg

To communicate interpersonally, one must be able to leave the cultural and sociological levels of prediction and psychically travel to the psychological level. We have already examined some ways in which a communicator's patterns of control, as well as his cognitive style, influence his attempts to reach the interpersonal level. Certainly, the communicator's journey is more likely to be successful if he develops his ability to empathize. In this chapter we will discuss the importance of empathy in interpersonal communication. More specifically, we will develop a definition for empathy, suggest a model for viewing an important dimension of the empathic process, and survey some strategies for improving empathic skills. As the chapter proceeds, it will become apparent that acquiring these skills is crucial to becoming effective in interpersonal communication. In fact, empathic skills and interpersonal communication effectiveness may come to seem almost synonymous.

Toward a Definition for Empathy

Although the term *empathy* is relatively common, it means many things to many people. After surveying some of the literature in aesthetics and theatre, Gunkle pessimistically concluded that "the term, stretched to mean almost anything, has come to mean nothing" (1963, 15). Katz (1963) devotes a substantial part of his book to examining meanings for *empathy,* as well as distinguishing it from sympathy, projection, and insight. This rich background of meanings can be grouped into two broad categories: psychophysiological response and social perception skill.

Empathy As a Psychophysiological Response

All of us can probably remember watching someone suck a lemon and feeling the sour taste permeate our mouths. This response is not limited to citrus fruits. When asked her meaning for empathy, a student in one of Gerry's

From *Between People* by Gerald R. Miller and Mark Steinberg, 1975, Science Research Associates. Gerald R. Miller is Professor and Chair, Department of Communication, Michigan State University. Mark Steinberg is employed by the office of Substance Abuse Services, State of Michigan, Lansing, MI.

classes replied tersely, "Empathy is when you throw up, I throw up, too!" In a similar vein, we speak of the contagion of laughter, tears, or yawns. Indeed, it is a rare person who has never experienced this sort of psychophysiological identity with another, both in real life and vicariously through the entertainment media.

In its psychophysiological sense, empathy probably occurs most frequently when the empathizer uses multiple sensory channels. While the lemon effect can be produced by mere mention of sucking a lemon, observation of the lemon-sucker heightens it. Still, the auditory channel alone is often sufficient—as it was for listeners to radio soap operas, a vivid childhood remembrance of Gerry's. On weekday visits to his grandparents' home he invariably found people listening to "Valiant Lady," "Lorenzo Jones," "Ma Perkins," "Backstage Wife," ad nauseam. Tears flowed between commercials; joy was eagerly shared, and angry words ("You'll get yours, you _____ !") were voiced. The demise of radio in America as a source of entertainment resulted in more than unemployment for many organists. Today television and films have supplanted this mode of vicarious identification, combining auditory and visual sensations.

So intense is the psychophysiological response and so strong the sense of identity with another that some writers have resorted to rather mystical ways of describing the empathic process.

> When we experience empathy, we feel as if we were experiencing someone else's feelings as our own. We see, we feel, we respond, and we understand as if we were, in fact, the other person. *We stand in his shoes. We get under his skin. . . . When we take the position of another person, our imagination projects us out of ourselves and into the other person.* (Katz, 1963, p. 3) [italics ours]

Katz's words are by no means atypical. Empathy is most often defined using phrases akin to "putting yourself in someone else's shoes." Since all of us are forever trapped inside our own skins, however, any judgments we make about the emotional or cognitive states of others must be inferential. The raw materials for our inferences are the actual behaviors of other individuals and our own experiences with similar kinds of behaviors. Thus, when we say we can identify, or empathize, with someone sucking a lemon, we are saying that we have observed his lemon-sucking behavior and that our own experiences with lemons call forth biochemical changes similar to those occurring in his mouth.

We shall avoid bestowing an aura of mysticism on empathy, preferring to treat it primarily as a behavioral process. Although our approach may lack the imaginative or emotional appeal of the mysterious, we believe it has considerable communicative utility. To tell a prospective empathizer to put himself in another person's shoes, or to get inside someone else's skin, is not so helpful as giving him pointers on how to spot behavioral cues presented by others.

A psychophysiological response to someone can express support and understanding, but certainly empathy occurs more often than just when people share the same sensory-emotional reactions. The recipient of such an expression of empathy may or may not consider it to be a desirable response. If, for example, he becomes sick to his stomach, he may well get little relief from an empathic friend who does likewise. The friend is more likely to be perceived as empathically admirable if he tries to help alleviate the sick person's distress. We will have more to say about this later in this chapter when we set forth our transactional definition of empathy.

Empathy As a Social Perception Skill

In the social perception arena, empathy refers to *the accuracy with which an individual predicts the verbal responses of another.* More specifically, empathic ability is concerned primarily with responses reporting the person's emotional states or the way he feels about himself. High accuracy is equated with high empathic skill; low accuracy is taken as evidence of empathic limitations.

Self-Other Ratings To illustrate how empathic ability is assessed, we will briefly describe one of the most popular procedures, the self-other rating developed by Dymond (1949). This approach requires two persons (A and B) to provide the following ratings:

For person A:
  1. A rates himself (A).
  2. A rates B as he (A) sees him.
  3. A rates B as he thinks B would rate himself.
  4. A rates himself (A) as he thinks B would rate him.
For person B:
  1. B rates himself (B).
  2. B rates A as he (B) sees him.
  3. B rates A as he thinks A would rate himself.
  4. B rates himself (B) as he thinks A would rate him.

Typically, the raters use a five-point scale of intensity for rating such personality traits as self-confidence, superiority, unselfishness, friendliness, leadership, and sense of humor. The measure of A's empathic ability, for example, is determined by calculating how closely A's predictions of B's ratings correspond with B's actual ratings.

Suppose two friends, Mary and Ruth, wished to assess their mutual degree of empathy, using the sense of humor trait. On a five-point scale ranging from high to low, Mary would (1) rate her own sense of humor, (2) rate Ruth's sense of humor, (3) provide a rating that *predicts* how Ruth sees her own sense of humor, and (4) provide a rating that *predicts* Ruth's perception of Mary's sense of humor. Ruth would carry out the identical rating procedures. If both predicted the other's responses quite accurately, we would probably conclude that they have established an interpersonal relationship; if one was relatively successful but the other was not, we would say that the relationship reflects a mixed, interpersonal/noninterpersonal level; and if neither was very accurate, we would call the relationship noninterpersonal.

Degree of Empathy and Levels of Relationship We see empathy, when viewed as a social perception skill, as closely akin to the predictive process that characterizes interpersonal communication. To some extent, accurate prediction of another's self-perceptions requires the predictor to spot relevant individual differences. Still, we are not willing to view the processes of empathizing and communicating interpersonally as totally synonymous, particularly when research procedures such as the self-other approach are used as measures of empathy. Examination of some of the characteristics of this research method will reveal why we are reluctant to equate the two processes.

Typically, self-other ratings of empathic ability focus on personality traits. While the ability to make accurate discriminations about others' perceptions of their personalities may frequently aid the interpersonal communicator, his range of concern is naturally much broader. Consider once again our salesman seeking to move to the interpersonal level with a reluctant customer. He is not primarily concerned with predicting the customer's level of self-confidence accurately, but with selling his product. On many occasions, the salesman will achieve greater success by avoiding unnecessary speculation about unobservables, such as personality traits, and by focusing on the ways in which the customer is responding to his messages. In particular, he must ask himself how a customer's response differs from the responses of other customers with whom he has communicated successfully and, given these differences, how he might alter his communicative strategy to increase the likelihood of a sale. Successful discrimination is based on the salesman's skill in spotting subtle behavioral cues and then predicting appropriate message changes. In some instances, prediction may be improved by concern with personality traits, but in many others, the inclusion of personality inferences as part of the predictive equation only confuses and complicates the issue.

Predicting Personality Traits from Cultural or Sociological Data It is often possible to make accurate predictions about other's perceptions of their personality traits solely on the basis of cultural or sociological data, since people do not vary much in their self-ratings on certain personality characteristics. To demonstrate this consistency to yourself, ask several of your friends whether they have a good sense of humor. If more than one or two reply negatively, it will be surprising. By the same token, how many people are likely to see themselves as relatively unfriendly? Since our society assigns a positive value to traits such as having a good sense of humor or being friendly, most people like to believe they possess these personal characteristics.

Graphologists and fortune tellers have long been aware of such invariant areas of self-perception. If you wish to amaze your friends with your psychic powers, try this experiment. Ask several of them for handwriting samples, and tell them you will use the samples to provide them with descriptions of themselves. (If you think friends will feel you based your descriptions on other data, get the samples from relative strangers.) Then for every person, write the same description, including comments such as the following:

> Generally, you are friendly with other people and accept them for what they are. While you trust people most of the time, there are times when you feel others are taking advantage of you and when you believe you have not been given enough credit for things you have done. Occasionally you suffer from feelings of inadequacy. You have a good sense of humor and you are able to laugh at yourself when the occasion warrants.

Return the description to each of your friends and ask them whether it is accurate. Having performed the experiment several times in our classes, we are certain that most of your friends will marvel at the accuracy of your evaluation.

Empathy and Stimulus Discrimination This tendency for persons to perceive themselves similarly on certain personality dimensions poses an interesting dilemma for the prospective interpersonal communicator. If such perceptions are accurate—e.g., if almost everyone does have a good sense of humor—these traits are worthless predictive vehicles because variation is a necessary condition for discrimination. If, as is more likely, considerable variability is associated with these traits, many people are victims of their own self-delusions; they do not see themselves as others see them. Since empathic accuracy is defined as the correspondence between the ratings of the empathizer and those of the person with whom he is empathizing, a "good" empathizer accepts self-delusion as a given. By contrast, stimulus discrimination, as we have defined it, deals primarily with the ability to differentiate one person's behavior from another's. Thus, an important distinction can be drawn between the two processes: *when viewed as a social perception skill, empathy involves the ability to predict accurately others' self-perceptions; when conceived of as a crucial determinant of interpersonal communication effectiveness, stimulus discrimination involves the ability to identify ways that the actual behaviors and attitudes of an individual differ from the behaviors and attitudes of others.*

Given this distinction, a social perception skill view of empathy may sometimes actually prevent a communicator from moving to the interpersonal level. How could this apparently contradictory result occur? Assume you are a salesman for a company engaged in manufacturing a new multiple lock system for apartment doors—a flourishing business in this era of high crime rates. During your training period, the sales manager describes some customer problems you are likely to encounter. In particular, he points out that since most people see themselves as friendly and accessible, they are likely to resist the prison-like, inaccessible atmosphere created by an intricate lock system. Consequently, he stresses that your sales pitch should specifically minimize the infringement upon movement and the hostile atmosphere imposed by the adoption of such a system, in fact, he arms you with a particular sales pitch designed to overcome customer resistance on this point.

You successfully use this sales routine with your first three customers. Not only do you accept the manager's dictum concerning people's perceptions of their own friendliness, you detect behaviorial cues that these three customers are genuinely reluctant to further isolate themselves from their fellow men. But now you are face-to-face with customer four. Like the preceding three customers, he probably perceives himself as friendly and outgoing. Still, he is not behaving the same way they behaved. His words, his tone of voice, his reluctance to open the door fully are all cues that he is hostile, suspicious, and prefers to be left alone. Spontaneously, you decide to emphasize, rather than downplay, the increased privacy and inaccessibility offered by the lock system, and you are rewarded with a quick sale.

It is possible, though not probable, that the standard sales pitch would have yielded the same outcome. What is important is that a commitment to basing communicative predictions on empathic grounds, rather than stimulus discrimination, would have resulted in a different message strategy, one less likely to clinch the sale. Had an empathic framework been adopted, you would have been forced to reason as follows: "I know this customer perceives himself as friendly and outgoing, even though his behavior belies this perception. Hence, my messages should minimize the extent to which the new lock system will create a more inaccessible, remote environment." By contrast, a prediction based on stimulus discrimination stems from this line of reasoning: "Even though this customer thinks of himself as friendly and outgoing, his behavior indicates suspicion and hostility. Consequently, I should emphasize the greater privacy and inaccessibility to be gained from the lock system, rather than playing those factors down."

A Final Deficiency From a communication standpoint, there is yet another crucial deficiency in the typical definition of empathy as a social perception skill: it is *undirectional, rather than transactional.* The social perception viewpoint holds that a good empathizer is one who can accurately predict others' responses, particularly in regard to the ways they perceive themselves. From a transactional communication perspective, this definition is inadequate, for when we say that someone is a good empathizer, we mean not only that he can predict how we feel, but also that he communicates with us in ways we find rewarding. We believe a transactional definition of empathy best suits the dynamics of human communication in general and interpersonal communication in particular.

A Transactional Definition for Empathy

Assume you have an acquaintance who is remarkably adept at sensing your current emotional state, even though you may try to conceal it from him. When you are upset or unhappy, he detects your mood unerringly; when you are joyous and happy, this fact never escapes his attention. But despite his sensitivity to your every emotion, you avoid contact with him because he is unable or unwilling to communicate in ways you find satisfying. Rather than reducing your sadness, he heightens or ignores it; rather than rejoicing with you, he discovers a communicative means of transforming your happiness to gloom. In short, you view him as a "bad news" communicator.

Most of you probably know the kind of person we have just described. We doubt that you would characterize him as a good empathizer, even though he is extremely talented at reading your emotional states. Transactionally, empathy embraces two major steps:

1. *The prospective empathizer must be able to discriminate accurately the ways that the individual's motivational and attitudinal posture differs from others.*
2. *Accurate discriminations must be followed by behaviors that are viewed as desirable, or rewarding, by the persons who are the objects of prediction.*

While our hypothetical acquaintance has no trouble accomplishing the first step, he falls short on the second.

Step 1 closely parallels the previously discussed definitions of empathy as a social perception skill. Even here it differs in one important respect, placing emphasis on accurate behavioral prediction based on subtle verbal and nonverbal cues, rather than on predictive agreement with the self-perceived attitudes and motives of the other. In drawing this distinction, we are not arguing that there is one correct, preferred way to gauge motives and attitudes. Sometimes, the best evidence we have is the other person's verbal descriptions of his feelings. At times, however, as we have already indicated, these verbal responses may conflict with other behaviors, e.g., an individual may say that he is friendly and outgoing, and yet he may behave just the opposite. Given such conflicting evidence, predictive accuracy is usually enhanced by relying on behavioral cues other than the individual's verbal report about his usual attitudes toward others.

Step 2 places the definition within the transactional view of communication discussed in chapter 2 [Miller-Steinberg text]. Like beauty, empathy is in the eye (or perhaps more descriptively, the perceptions) of the beholder. No matter how accurately someone reads us, we do not bestow the title "good empathizer" upon him unless he also communicates with us in rewarding ways. This fact suggests that the most effective interpersonal communicators not only read cues well, but also select the appropriate communication behaviors implied by the cues.

This transactional definition should not be interpreted as an attempt to impose our values on the communication process. We do not think it necessary to equate "good empathizers" with "nice guys." Still, from a transactional perspective, communicators reserve the accolade "good empathizer" for those who respond to them in rewarding ways. For that matter, an unscrupulous communicator, skilled in exercising effective environmental control, may meet both of our conditions for empathic response and still use his empathic skills to manipulate the other person in devious ways.

Conflict and Its Resolution

Bobby R. Patton and Kim Giffin

What does the word *conflict* mean to you? To many people it means quarreling, arguing, and fighting. We would suggest, however, that there is a positive dimension to conflict. Just as we know that conflict is inevitable because of the differences in people, we know that without conflict there would be no innovations, creativity, or challenging of existing norms and practices. The key to whether or not conflict should be viewed positively is in the method of its resolution.

In this chapter we shall discuss the levels of conflict within the individual, within the group, and among groups, the differences in competitive and cooperative orientations, and the methods of handling conflict.

The Levels of Conflict

Conflict typically involves some obstacle to achieving a desired goal; it often arises when someone has a chance to win at the expense of someone else. Competition in a game or a particular job exemplifies this type of conflict. Yet it doesn't take two to quarrel; sometimes we are in conflict with ourselves.

Conflict within the Individual

If our desires are denied, we become frustrated. If there are alternative routes to satisfying our desires, we feel internal conflict. Social psychologist H. J. Leavitt defines conflict as "a pulling in two directions at the same time. The obstacles one meets are not brick walls but drags that pull back as one goes forward . . . frying-pan-and-fire situations, or donkey-between-the-bales-of-hay situations."[1]

Conflict forces the individual to choose, to make a decision among available alternatives. An individual may respond to conflict with disruptive or with constructive effects.

Among the disruptive approaches are the following.

1. *Aggression.* A direct attack may be made on one or another alternative. Wright studied the behavior of children three to six years of age in conflict situations. In a free-play period the children were allowed to play freely

Source: Chapter 7 from *Decision-Making and Group Interaction,* 2nd Edition, by Bobby R. Patton and Kim Giffin. Reprinted by permission of Harper and Row, Publishers, Inc.

with toys for fifteen minutes. Frustration was then induced by placing the best toys behind a wire screen. The experimenter became the target of direct aggression by 37 percent of the children during the frustrative session: with name calling, to hitting with blocks, and tearing the aggressor's records.[2]

2. *Withdrawal.* Some persons have little tolerance for conflict situations and withdraw into themselves rather than be forced to make a decision. In a group situation such a person will change the subject, joke, mediate, or become silent, when areas of conflict become exposed.

3. *Ego-defensive reactions.* The purpose of this approach is not to solve the problem but to protect the ego and maintain a possibly inaccurate feeling of self-esteem. Haney cites as examples of such reactions:[3]

> . . . *fantasy* (wish-fulfilling dreams, day-dreaming, etc.); *projecting* (imputing one's thoughts and desires to others); *rationalization* (finding "justifiable" reasons for our behavior or convincing ourselves that the goal is really undesirable—assuming the "sour grapes" attitude); *repressing* (attempting to ignore, deny, or forget troublesome things); *regressing* (reverting to childish ways); *identifying* (becoming ego-involved with others); *blaming others* (excusing ourselves by finding others responsible for our failures—"scape-goating"); *overcompensating* (trying to overcome one's deficiencies to "make up" for one's feelings—but in an excessive manner); *sublimating* (getting indirect but socially acceptable satisfaction).

These "defense mechanisms" protect the individual from anxiety, though at the price of a certain degree of reality denial, or distortion.

A possible constructive effect of internal conflict for the individual may be that he is impelled to make a greater effort to reach the goal in the best way. If the conflict is still unresolved, he may redefine the problem or change the goal, as suggested by Krech and his associates:[4]

> One obvious way of removing conflict, its consequent frustration, and increased tension is to make choices among the alternatives . . . sometimes the choice is an absolute one; in other cases the person decides to attain this goal first, and later that one. In either case the increased tension helps to force a choice—and choice in conflict situations is adaptive behavior. The tension has brought about a redefining of the situation, so that the conflict is eliminated.

Conflict may thus make a person reexamine himself, his goal, and the means of attaining that goal.

Another way of considering internal conflict is in terms of cognitive dissonance. In Chapter 2 (of Patton and Giffin) we referred to Festinger's theory, which postulates that, when a person engages in behavior inconsistent with his attitudes or beliefs, he will feel the discomfort of cognitive dissonance, which serves to motivate him to resolve it. This dissonance, or inconsistency, forces a person to make an attitudinal adjustment.

One source of internal conflict is an individual's affiliations with divergent reference groups in which different needs are fulfilled. A teenager, for example, may feel conflict between peer pressures and family expectations on such issues as dating behavior, drinking, and the use of drugs. Speaking of another level, Kiesler and Kiesler cite research on the conflicting role demands of school superintendents.[5]

> They found that the school superintendent has three roles to play: the role of school superintendent from the point of view of the school board; the role of school superintendent as regarded by the parents; and his role *vis-a-vis* the teachers within the school system. The school board wants the school to run smoothly and as inexpensively as possible. The parents would like to see their children in smaller classes, but not at the expense of a tax increase. The teachers want higher salaries. At particular times of the year these three roles become especially divergent, and the conflict thus produced for the school superintendent becomes torturous indeed.

These internal conflicts are often the result of group influences and may, conversely, affect the progress of the group.

Conflict within the Group

There are numerous other reasons for internal group conflict. Any perceived changes, ranging from leadership roles to group structure to activities to new membership, may provoke conflict. The conflicts are inevitable; the nature of the group will determine if they are handled openly or reduced to the level of the hidden agenda (discussed in Chapter 3 of Patton and Giffin). Even the changing nature of a group's membership may introduce conflict. In a teenage gang the member's interests and maturity levels may change at different rates of time.

Kemp calls for a "creative handling of conflict" and proposes a "fresh, incisive look at conflict" by consideration of the following points:[6]

1. Productive conflict arises because group members are so bound together that their actions affect one another; that is, they have accepted the fact that they have become interdependent.
2. Conflict occurs because people care. Often group members who have great creative differences share a very deep relationship. Because they care about one another and the group as a whole, they are willing to make, if necessary, a costly emotional response to help improve a situation.

3. Each member has different needs and values. These differences become evident and produce conflict unless the members repress their individual differences and assign the direction of the group to an authority figure. Sometimes, rather than accept the fact of their creative differences, members allow themselves to be taken over by such a leader.

Conflict situations in groups may be classed as two types, *distributive* and *integrative*.[7] A distributive situation is one in which a person can win only at someone else's expense, such as in a poker game. An integrative situation is one in which the members of the group integrate their resources toward a common task, as in working together on a jigsaw puzzle. Research teams work in an integrative manner, whereas a buying and selling transaction involves distributive bargaining.

The National Training Laboratories have identified two opposite modes of behavior, Approach A and Approach B. Approach A is associated with behavior in distributive social situations; Approach B, with behavior in integrative.[8]

Approach A	*Approach B*
1. Behavior is purposeful in that one's own goals are pursued.	1. Behavior is purposeful in that goals held in common are pursued.
2. Secrecy.	2. Openness.
3. Accurate personal understanding of own needs, but these are publicly disguised or misrepresented: Don't let them know what you really want most, so that they won't know how much you are really willing to give up to get it.	3. Accurate personal understanding of own needs and accurate representation of them.
4. Unpredictable, mixed strategies, utilizing the element of surprise.	4. Predictable; while flexible behavior is appropriate, it is not designed to take the other party by surprise.
5. Threats and bluffs.	5. Threats or bluffs are not used.
6. Search behavior is devoted to finding ways of appearing to become committed to a position; logical, nonrational, and irrational arguments alike may serve this purpose.	6. Search behavior is devoted to finding solutions to problems and utilizing logical and innovative processes.

Approach A	*Approach B*
7. Success is often enhanced (where teams, committees, or organizations are involved on each side) by forming a bad stereotype of the other, by ignoring the other's logic, by increasing the level of hostility. These tend to strengthen ingroup loyalty and convince others that you mean business.	7. Success demands that stereotypes be dropped, that ideas be given consideration on their merit regardless of sources, and that hostility not be induced deliberately. In fact, positive feelings about others are both a cause and an effect of other aspects of Approach B.
8. A pathological extreme occurs when one assumes that everything that prevents the other from reaching *his* goal also must facilitate one's own movement toward *his* goal; thus, one would state his own goals as being the negation of others' achievement.	8. A pathological extreme occurs when one will assume that whatever is good for others and the group is necessarily good for oneself. Cannot distinguish own identity from group or other person's identity. Will not take responsibility for own self.
9. Etc.	9. Etc.

Engaging in the distributive approach causes problems for the task-oriented group. Among the problems are:[9]

1. Development of we-they and superiority-inferiority complexes within the group. The group may splinter if the distributive behavior is sustained.
2. In groups with internal competitive pressure individuals tend to overestimate their contributions and unrealistically downgrade the work of others.
3. Under competitive pressures group members think they understand one another when in fact they do not. These distortions in perception cause areas of agreement to go unrecognized.

Labor-management negotiations characteristically utilize this distributive approach in a between-groups pattern of interaction. Labor wins at management's expense. An integrative approach would attempt to discover ways that both parties might gain. We shall discuss this alternative in greater detail when we suggest alternative modes of handling conflict.

Conflict of the integrative type can have positive benefits for the group. Only when members feel comfortable in the group can conflict safely emerge. Basic problems cannot usually be resolved without some conflict due to the different values, feelings, and perceptions of the members. For the conflict to center on issues rather than on personalities and exaggerations requires an acceptance of individual differences and some degree of mutual trust.

Group conflict may either bring out the best in a group or literally tear the group apart. The over-all social structure of the group may determine which occurs. As sociologist Lewis Coser states:[10]

> In loosely structured groups and open societies, conflict, which aims at a resolution of tension between antagonists, is likely to have stabilizing and integrative functions for the relationship. By permitting immediate and direct expression of rival claims, such social systems are able to readjust their structures by eliminating the sources of dissatisfaction. The multiple conflicts which they experience may serve to eliminate the causes for dissociation and to re-establish unity. These systems avail themselves, through the toleration and institutionalization of conflict, of an important stabilizing mechanism.
>
> In addition, conflict within a group frequently helps to revitalize existent norms; or it contributes to the emergence of new norms. In this sense, social conflict is a mechanism for adjustment of norms adequate to new conditions.

Although conflict is inevitable in groups, it may be either functional or disruptive.

Conflict Among Groups

Whether we are aware of it, our future goals and fortunes are greatly affected by the states of harmony or conflict between groups. Problems of intergroup relations include conflict between political groups, religious groups, economic groups, labor and management, and young and old, and across international boundaries.

The classic study of conflicts between groups was made by Sherif and Sherif. They studied groups of young boys 11 and 12 years old at camp sites under experimentally manipulated conditions. The boys were all selected from stable, white, Protestant families from the middle socio-economic level; they were well adjusted and had no past records of behavioral problems. No cultural, physical or economic differences were present in the sample. In a 1954 "robbers' cave" experiment two groups were formed separately and kept unaware of the presence of the other until competitive tournament games in various sports between the two groups were arranged. A series of mutually frustrating events arose naturally in the course of the tournament events. Stealing and burning of the opponent's flag, scuffling cabin raids, and name calling resulted. The experimenters tested and validated the following hypotheses:[11]

> 1. *When members of two groups come into contact with one another in a series of activities that embody goals which each group urgently desires but which can be attained by one group only at the expense*

of the other competitive activity toward the goal changes with time into hostility between the groups and among their members. Prizes were offered in the sports contests, and cumulative scores were kept for the various events, which included baseball, football, a tug of war, a treasure hunt and tent pitching. Good sportsmanship deteriorated as the events progressed, and the cheer "2–4–6–8, who do we appreciate?" changed to "2–4–6–8, who do we appreci-hate?" Accusations of "dirty players" and "cheaters" abounded and led to the overt physical attacks.

2. *In the course of such competitive interaction toward a goal available only to one group, unfavorable attitudes and images (stereotypes) of the out-group come into use and are standardized, placing the out-group at a definite social distance from the in-group.* Members of each group were asked to rate their fellow members and the opponents in the other group during the height of friction. Adjectives applied to the in-group were: "brave, tough, and friendly," while the out-group were "sneaky, smart alecks, stinkers." The ratings were assigned on the basis of "all of them are . . ." to "none of them are . . ."

3. *Conflict between two groups tends to produce an increase in solidarity within the groups.* Pride and group solidarity increased as the conflict and hostility grew. After the tournament the sociometric choices became exclusively restricted to one's group, and members of other groups were rejected. At a beach outing, each group stuck together despite many distractions.

4. *The heightened solidarity and pride in the group will be reflected in an overestimation of the achievements of fellow members and in a lower estimation of the achievements of members of the out-group.* A game of bean toss was introduced, in which the goal was to collect as many of the beans scattered on the ground as possible within a limited time. A judgment was called for by exposing, with an opaque projector, the supposed collection of each individual. Actually, thirty-five beans were exposed each time. The members of each group overestimated the number of beans collected by his fellow group members and made significant lower estimates of the performance of the out-group members.

5. *Relations between groups that are of consequence to the groups in question, including conflict, tend to produce changes in the organization and practices within the groups.* In one group the leadership changed hands when the leader who had emerged prior to the conflict was reluctant to take aggressive actions. In the other group a boy perceived as a low-status bully during group formation emerged as a hero during the inter-group encounters.

In the study it became unmistakably clear that overt differences are unnecessary for the rise of intergroup hostility, social distances, stereotyped images, and negative attitudes in a group of "normal" youngsters. Although physical appearance, language, and culture may serve to intensify differences, conflict itself becomes a major contributing variable.

Cooperation and Competition

Implicit in our discussion of the levels of conflict has been the contrast between cooperative and competitive orientations. Within the individual we find these conflicting pressures; within the group we find the distributive and the integrative approaches to problem situations; in conflicts between groups we find the role that competition plays in creating and intensifying intergroup hostility.

Deutsch has contributed a number of productive findings in his studies of cooperation and competition. Several of his studies have been based uon a matrix called the "prisoner's dilemma." It derives its name from a situation in which two suspects in a crime are questioned separately by the police and are told that, if they will give evidence that will convict the other, they will receive a lighter sentence than otherwise. The matrix appears as follows:

Person II

		Choice X: trust	Choice Y: mistrust
Choice A: trust		(I)+ (II)+	(I)− (II)+
Person I			
Choice B: mistrust		(I)+ (II)−	(I)− (II)−

In terms of this matrix, if the two suspects trust each other, they will respond with A and X (not giving evidence); and both will gain. If they do not trust each other, they will respond with B and Y; and both will lose. If one trusts and the other does not, A-Y and B-X, the trusting person loses and the other gains.

Using this model, Deutsch conducted a study in which each person in a pair of subjects had to decide whether to push a red or a green button. If both pushed red, they each lost a dollar; if both pushed green, they each won a dollar; if one pushed red and one green, the subject pressing green had to pay the other two dollars. Deutsch observed:[12]

> A superficial rational calculation of self-interest would lead each player to press his red button since he either wins as much as he can or loses as little as he can this way. But if both players consider only their self-interest and press their red buttons, each of them will lose. Players oriented toward defeating the other player or to their self-interest only, when matched with similarly oriented players, do in fact choose the red button and do end up losing consistently. I believe our current international situation is in some aspects similar to the game I have described . . . any attempt on the part of any individual or nation to increase its own welfare or security (without regard to the security or welfare of the others) is self-defeating. In such situations the only way an individual or nation can avoid being trapped in a mutually reinforcing, self-defeating cycle is to attempt to change the situation so that a basis of mutual trust can develop.

In another experiment Deutsch developed a conceptual scheme for predicting the consequences of cooperative interdependence and competitive interdependence in groups.[13] The cooperative interdependent situation is one in which a member performs a self-beneficial act and thereby benefits all members of the group. In the competitively interdependent situation a member acts for self benefit and thereby reduces the payoff that the other will receive. To establish the two conditions, different methods were used for determining the grades in a basic psychology course. To create cooperative interdependence one group of students was told that they would be compared with other groups on total performance and that each member of the group would receive the grade awarded the total group. To create competitive interdependence another group was told that their individual grades would be based on a ranking within the group.

Deutsch found, as he had hypothesized, that in the cooperative situation there was greater coordination of effort, less homogeneity with respect to amount of participation, more specialization, decisions more rapidly made, more achievement pressure, more effective communication, greater productivity, and better interpersonal relations. He concluded:[14]

> To the extent that the results have any generality, greater group or organizational productivity may be expected when the members or subunits are cooperative rather than competitive in their interrelationships. The communication of ideas, coordination of efforts, friendliness, and pride in one's group which are basic to group harmony and effectiveness appear to be disrupted when members see themselves to be competing for mutually exclusive goals. Further, there is some indication that competitiveness produces greater personal insecurity through expectations of hostility

from others than does cooperation. The implications for committees, conferences, and small groups in general appear fairly obvious.

In Deutsch's experiments and in similar ones made by Loomis[15] communication was a significant variable. The amount of communication has a direct relationship with perceived trust. This facet of group interaction will be examined more fully in Chapter 8 (of Patton and Giffin).

When we consider the comparative results of cooperative and competitive orientations, the conclusion is inescapable that groups should work to achieve cooperative, integrative behavior.

Methods of Handling Conflict

We have repeatedly suggested that conflict, whether at the individual, the group, or the intergroup level, has a potential for both functional and disruptive consequences.

We shall now note some of the specific means of channeling conflicts into productive results.

At the individual level internal conflicts may be viewed as dissonance problems. One way of minimizing the discomfort that a person experiences when he finds himself doing something inconsistent with his attitudes is to modify those attitudes. A group of college students was tested to determine their attitudes on the three controversial issues of universal military training, dorm hours for women students, and de-emphasis of collegiate athletics.[16] Students with definite opinions were asked to debate the topic on the side opposite to their true beliefs. Half the subjects were reinforced by being told that they had won the debate, according to the votes of members of the class; the other half were told they had lost the debate. The winners underwent a significant attitude change, in the direction of the argument they had publicly supported, while the losers went in the opposite direction, intensifying their original beliefs.

Another way of minimizing discomfort is by reconciling discrepant judgments. In a group situation this approach forces an individual to look for good reasons that rationally account for the disagreement in such fashion as to allow him to accommodate both his judgment and that of the group. Thus he may decide that the question asked actually could be interpreted in quite different ways, leading to different and equally correct answers. This form of cognitive reconciliation obviously makes it easier for a person to stick to his own judgment.

Within a group conflict can best be handled through open communication based upon mutual trust. The conflict should be kept to the issue instead of becoming a personalized, polarized argument. Feelings have a place and should be communicated, but they should not become confused with the central issue. As Zaleznik and Moment state:[17]

> The optimum norm would allow free expression of feelings but would require that the expressions be treated as data and processed as is the other data related to the group task. Thus the individual may express himself, but he is forced to think twice. If he does not concern himself with how his feeling relates to what is going on in the group, he can be sure that others will do so. This does not imply prosecution or justification; it means that the group and its individual members accept responsibility for understanding and processing all the relevant data at their disposal. It also implies a model for responsible individual behavior.

Conflict may move to the hidden-agenda level and persist long after an issue has apparently been settled.

Hopefully, if group members utilize a cooperative integrative approach, a genuine integration of ideas will be found to meet the full demands of all parties in disagreement, or else a compromise may be identified, in which each receives part of what he wants. The significant variable of communication, needed for the prerequisite stage of mutual trust, will be discussed in the next chapter.

At the *intergroup* level Sherif and Sherif utilized what they called *superordinate goals* to bring the boys in the "robber's cave" experiment out of the state of conflict. The operating principle was the "if conflict develops from mutually incompatible goals, common goals should promote cooperation."[18] Camp activities were planned in such a way that desirable goals could not be achieved by the efforts of only one in-group; both groups were forced to cooperate toward the common goal. One such goal involved repairing a sabotaged water-supply system. Others included cooperatively raising money to obtain a movie that both groups wanted to see and moving a stalled food truck. All the tasks were accomplished by the cooperative efforts of the two groups.

After the boys had participated in these cooperative activities, sociometric tests were again administered. The results revealed that attitudes toward members of the out-group had clearly changed. While the friendship choices remained primarily within each in-group, the choices of out-group members as friends had increased, and there was less total rejection of out-group members. As Sherif says[19]:

> Our findings demonstrate the effectiveness of a series of superordinate goals in the reduction of intergroup conflict hostility, and their by-products. They also have implications for other measures proposed for reducing intergroup tensions.
> It is true that lines of communication between groups must be opened before prevailing hostility can be reduced. But, if contact between hostile

groups takes place without superordinate goals, the communication channels serve as media for further accusations and recriminations. When contact situations involve superordinate goals, communication is utilized in the direction of reducing conflict in order to attain the common goals.

The identification and utilization of superordinate goals seem to have genuine effectiveness in reducing intergroup conflict.

Summary

Although conflict is inevitable, it may be positive in some instances negative in others, and irrelevant in still others.

Individuals can resolve their internal conflicts by resorting to aggression, withdrawal, and ego-defense mechanisms or by changing their attitudes so as to bring about internal consistency or by accepting differences as they exist.

Within a group a distributive approach to conflict problems leads to distrust and competition, whereas an integrative approach promotes openness and cooperation.

Between groups sustained conflict over mutually desired goals attainable to only one group provokes hostile and aggressive acts, social distance, negative stereotypes, and also internal group solidarity and changed relationships. Establishing superordinate goals provides a framework of cooperation among the rival groups and effectively reduces the negative conflict.

Cooperativeness leads to coordination of effort, productivity, good human relations, and other positive benefits. Competitiveness leads to distrust and insecurity. The implications for all groups are readily apparent.

Notes

1. H. J. Leavitt, *Managerial Psychology,* Chicago, University of Chicago, 1964, p. 53. Cited and abstracted in W. V. Haney, *Communication and Organizational Behavior Text and Cases,* Homewood, Ill., Irwin, 1967, p. 124.
2. M. E. Wright, "The influence of frustration upon the social relations of young children," *Character and Personality,* 12 (1943–1944), 111–122.
3. Haney, *op. cit.,* pp. 124–125.
4. D. Krech, R. S. Crutchfield, and N. Livson, *Elements of Psychology,* New York, Knopf, 1969, p. 757.
5. C. A. Kiesler and S. B. Kiesler, *Conformity,* Reading, Mass., Addison-Wesley, 1970, pp. 37–38. From research reported in N. Gross, A. W. McEachern, and W. S. Mason, "Role conflict and its resolution," in *Readings in Social Psychology* (E. E. Maccoby, T. M. Newcomb, and E. L. Hartley, eds.), New York, Holt, Rinehart & Winston, 1958, pp. 447–458.
6. C. G. Kemp, "The creative handling of conflict," *Perspectives on the Group Process,* Boston, Houghton Mifflin, 1970, p. 262.
7. This analysis was made in the *1968 Reading Book* of the National Training Laboratories Institute of Applied Behavioral Sciences.
8. Ibid.

9. These consequences and others are reported in R. R. Blake and J. S. Mouton, "Reactions to intergroup competition under win-lose conditions," *Management Science,* July, 1961.

10. L. Coser, *The Functions of Social Conflict,* New York, Free Press, 1964, p. 154.

11. M. Sherif and C. W. Sherif, *Social Psychology,* New York, Harper & Row, 1969, pp. 239, 221–266.

12. M. Deutsch, "A psychological basis for peace," in *Preventing World War III: Some Proposals* (Q. Wright, W. M. Evan, and M. Deutsch, eds.), New York, Simon & Schuster, 1962, p. 380.

13. M. Deutsch, "The effects of cooperation and competition upon group process," in *Group Dynamics* (D. Cartwright and A. Zander, eds.), New York, Harper & Row, 1968, pp. 461–482.

14. Ibid.

15. J. L. Loomis, "Communication, the development of trust and cooperative behavior," *Human Relations,* 12 (1959), 305–315.

16. W. A. Scott, "Attitude change through reward of verbal behavior," *J. Abnormal Soc. Psychol.,* 55 (1957), 72–75.

17. A. Zaleznik and D. Moment, *The Dynamics of Interpersonal Behavior,* New York, Wiley, 1964, p. 178.

18. Sherif and Sherif, *op. cit.* p. 266.

19. M. Sherif, "Superordinate goals in the reduction of intergroup conflicts," *Am. J. of Sociol.,* 63 (1958), 356.

Groupthink

Steven A. Beebe and John T. Masterson

Frank Baxter, chairperson of the board of Eastern Oil Company, was meeting with other members of the board of directors. The agenda was to decide whether Eastern Oil would merge with Southern Oil Company. Baxter called the meeting to order. After the preliminary reading and approval of the minutes from the last meeting, Baxter stated that he thought the merger between Eastern and Southern Oil Companies would benefit both companies. As soon as Baxter finished presenting his opinion, other board members quickly chimed in, offering their support of the merger. None of the board members stated any objections to the deal; they supported Baxter's decision 100 percent. One member, however, felt that the merger might violate antitrust legislation by creating a monopoly in the southeastern United States. He also noted that the government would probably oppose the merger. But other board members quickly tried to gloss over the potential problem. One member confidently stated, "The government should not have any power to affect how we run our corporation. After all, it's *our* company."

After a few additional supportive comments from other board members, the group voted to approve the merger between Eastern and Southern Oil Companies. After the meeting, one member commented, "I wish all the group meetings I participated in would go as smoothly as our board meetings. We always seem to get along so well together. Baxter does a great job as chairperson."

"Yes," observed another member, "he certainly has our respect. We always support what he has to say."

Upon first analysis of this board of directors meeting, you might think it is a good example of an effective group meeting. There is little uncertainty and the chairperson appears to have the support of his group. All seems well. But by analyzing the meeting more closely, we see that the group is not functioning as well as it should; it is not taking advantage of the benefits of working together. This board of directors is a victim of **groupthink.**

Groupthink occurs when a group strives to minimize conflict and reach a consensus at the expense of critically testing, analyzing, and evaluating ideas. A lack of critical thinking results when a group reaches decisions too quickly, without properly considering the implications of their decisions. Sociologist

Irving Janis feels that many poor governmental decisions and policies formulated in recent years are the result of groupthink. After studying minutes of meetings and transcripts of conversations, he concluded that a lack of healthy disagreement contributed to inept decisions such as the Bay of Pigs invasion in 1962. The Kennedy administration's decision to attack Cuba was the product of a group of presidential advisors who were reluctant to voice their private doubts about invading Cuba. Janis has also noted that the Watergate break-in was ultimately the result of a group plagued by groupthink. Members of the Committee to Reelect the President believed that they needed information that was kept at the Democratic headquarters in the Watergate office complex. Again, even though some members privately felt that breaking into the Democratic headquarters to take the information was wrong, they did not raise their objections and the burglary took place. *The pressure for consensus resulted in groupthink.*

Groups most prone to experiencing groupthink have leaders who are held in high esteem. Since these leaders' ideas are often viewed as sacrosanct, few people disagree. A group may also exerience groupthink if its members consider themselves highly cohesive. They take pride in getting along so well with one another and try to provide support and encouragement to other members' ideas.

Symptoms of Groupthink

Can you identify groupthink when it occurs in groups to which you belong? Do you know how to guard against an overly dependent attitude toward consensus? Can you help reduce the likelihood that groupthink will occur in your group? Here are some of the common symptoms of groupthink. See if you think of some group communication experiences that exemplify groupthink.

Critical Thinking Is Not Encouraged or Rewarded.

If you are working in a group and disagreement or controversy is openly labeled as counterproductive, the chances are that groupthink is alive and well. One of the prime advantages of working in groups is having the opportunity to evaluate ideas so that the best possible solution can be obtained. If group members seem overly proud of the fact that peace and harmony prevail at their meetings, groupthink is likely to occur.

Group Members Feel that Their Group Can Do No Wrong.

Members of the Committee to Reelect the President did not consider the possibility of failing to obtain information from the Democratic headquarters. They felt their group was invulnerable. This sense of invulnerability is a classic symptom of groupthink. Another symptom is when members dismiss a potential threat to the group goal as a minor problem. In our opening example with the Eastern Oil Company merger, the potential problem of government intervention was quickly dismissed. The group had the feeling that their decision was a good one and that no outside threat could interfere with their plans. If your group feels a consistent spirit of overconfidence in dealing with problems that may interfere with the stated goals, conditions are ripe for groupthink.

Group Members Are Overly Concerned About Justifying Their Actions.

Groups who experience a high degree of cohesiveness like to feel that they are acting in the best interest of their group. Therefore, a group that experiences groupthink likes to rationalize its position on the issues. Group members are particularly susceptible to feelings of tension and dissonance. If the group's position is attacked, the group may respond in several ways to deal with the resulting tension and conflict. First, a group may try to destroy the credibility of the one who makes the attack. For example, a group of students working on a group project for a small group communication class received some negative feedback about their progress from their instructor. The group responded by saying that the instructor was not a good teacher and would not know a good group if he saw one. The group tried to rationalize its poor performance by attacking the credentials of the person who stated the criticism. A group may also avoid information that is contrary to the opinion of the group. The star of a Broadway production received poor reviews from one of the local papers. She responded by refusing to read the rest of the review and vowed never to read that particular paper again. Similarly, if a group receives criticism from someone, it may not seek advice from that person again. Finally, a group may listen only selectively to less-than-positive information about a decision it has reached. If a group is criticized, it may rationalize the criticism to diminish the impact of the comments. Groups susceptible to groupthink are overly concerned about convincing themselves that they have made proper decisions in the past and that they will make good decisions in the future.

Group Members Apply Pressure to Those Who Do Not Support the Group

Have you ever voiced an opinion contrary to the majority opinion and quickly realized that other group members were trying to pressure you into going along with the rest of the group? Groups prone to groupthink have a low tolerance for members who do not go along with the group. Controversy and conflict injected by a dissenting member threaten the *esprit de corps*. Therefore, a person voicing an idea different from the group's position is often punished. Sometimes the pressure is subtle, taking the form of a frown or grimace. Group members may not socialize with the dissenting member. Or group members may not listen attentively to the dissident. Usually their first response is trying to convince this member to reconsider his or her position. Members may try to persuade the dissident to conform; but, if the member still does not agree with the others, he or she may be expelled from the group. Of course, if a group member is just being stubborn or unfairly obstinate, the others should try to reason with the dissenter. But don't be too quick to label someone as a troublemaker simply because he or she maintains an opinion different from that of most other group members.

Group Members Often Believe that They Have Reached a True Consensus

A significant problem in groups whose members experience groupthink is that members are not aware that groupthink is occurring. They feel that they have reached a genuine consensus—that a spirit of unity prevails. For example, suppose you and a group of your friends are trying to decide which movie to see on Friday night. Someone suggests, "Why don't we see *Gone with the Wind*"? Even though you have seen the movie on television, you don't want to inject a note of contention so you agree with the suggestion. Other group members also agree.

After your group has seen the movie and you're coming out of the theatre, you overhear another one of your friends say, "I enjoyed the movie better when I saw it on television." After a quick poll of the group, you discover that most of your friends have already seen the movie! They agreed to see it only because they did not want to hurt anyone's feelings. They *thought* everyone else was in agreement. While it appeared that the group had reached consensus, there were actually only a few people who agreed with the decision. Therefore, even if you feel that the rest of the group agrees and that you are the only person who feels that a different solution would be best, your group could still be experiencing groupthink. Just because your group seems to have reached a consensus does not necessarily mean that all of the members truly agree.

Group Members Are Overly Concerned about Reinforcing the Leader's Beliefs

Leaders of small groups often emerge because they suggest some of the best ideas, motivate group members, or devote themselves to the goals of the group more than anyone else. But if group members place too much emphasis on the credibility or infallibility of their leader, there's a good chance that groupthink will occur. Leaders who like to be surrounded by people who will always agree with their ideas lose the advantage of working in small groups. Most of us do not like criticism. We do not like to be told that our ideas are inept or inappropriate. Therefore, it is easy to see why group leaders would be attracted to those who agree with their positions. But testing the quality of solutions requires different opinions. A leader who is sensitive to the problem of groupthink will try to solicit and tolerate all points of view from the group.

Suggestions to Reduce Groupthink

While we have identified six symptoms of groupthink, you still may be asking yourself, "So what?" You may agree that groupthink, which is characterized by a lack of conflict or controversy, should not occur in an effective task-oriented group, but what you really want to know is, "How can I reduce the chances of groupthink occurring in my group?" We expect theory to do more than just describe what happens; it should also suggest ways of *improving* communication. To help prevent groupthink, consider the following specific suggestions which are based on the initial observation made by Janis, as well as on the theory and research of other small group communication researchers.

The Group Leader Should Encourage Critical, Independent Thinking

We noted that one characteristic of groupthink is that the group members generally agree with the group leader. The leader of a small group can help alleviate the groupthink problem by encouraging members to think independently. The leader should make it clear that he or she does not want the group to reach an agreement until each member has critically evaluated the issues. Most group leaders want to command the respect of their groups. But, insisting that the group always agree with the leader does not constitute respect; instead, it may demonstrate a fear of disagreement. Thus, if you find yourself in a leadership role in a small group, you should encourage disagreement not just for the sake of argument, but for the purpose of eliminating groupthink. Even if you are not in a leadership position, you can encourage a healthy discussion by voicing any objections that you have to the ideas being discussed. Don't permit instant, uncritical agreement in your group.

Group Members Should Be Sensitive to Status Differences that May Affect Decision Making

Imagine that you are a young architect assigned to help design a new dinner theater for a large futuristic shopping center. When you first meet with the other architects assigned to the project, the senior member of your firm presents to the group a rough sketch of a theater patterned after a mid-1800s American opera house. While the design is both practical and attractive, you feel that it is incongruous with the ultramodern design of the rest of the center. Because of the status difference between the younger architects and the senior architect, you and your contemporaries are tempted to laud the design and keep your reservations to yourselves. Doing so would result in groupthink. Groups should not yield to status differences when evaluating ideas, issues, and solutions to problems. Instead, they should consider the merits of the suggestions, weigh the evidence, and make a decision about the validity of the idea without becoming overly concerned about the status of the person making the suggestion. Of course, we realize that this is easier to suggest than it is to implement. Numerous studies suggest that a person with more credibility is going to be more persuasive. Cereal companies utilize this principle when they hire famous athletes to sell breakfast food. The message is, "Don't worry about the quality of the product. If this Olympic gold medal winner eats this stuff, you'll like it, too." When analyzing the impact of the famous athlete, we realize that the athlete's fame and status do not necessarily make the cereal good. Yet we still might buy the cereal. We make a decision based on emotion rather than on fact. Group members sometimes make decisions this way too. Be on your guard to avoid agreeing with a decision just because of the status or credibility of the person making the suggestion. Evaluate the quality of the solution on its *own* merits.

Invite Someone from Outside the Group to Evaluate the Group's Decision-making Process

Sometimes an objective point of view from outside the group can help avoid groupthink. Many large companies hire consultants to evaluate the decision making that occurs within the organization. But you don't have to be part of a multinational corporation to ask someone to analyze the process of your group's decisions. If you are working on a group project or on a committee, ask someone from outside the group to sit in on one of your group meetings. At the end of the meeting, ask the guest observer to summarize the observations and evaluations he or she has made about the group. Inviting someone from outside your group may make some members uncomfortable, but, if you explain why the visitor is present (or, better yet, if the group can reach an agreement that an outside observer would help improve the decision-making process), the group will probably accept the visitor and eagerly await the objective observations. Sometimes an outsider can identify unproductive group norms more readily than a group member can. Chapter Eleven identifies additional criteria for observing and evaluating small group communication.

Assign a Group Member the Role of the Devil's Advocate

If a pattern of no disagreement develops in a group, members may enjoy the satisfaction of "always getting along" with each other and may never realize that their group suffers from groupthink. If you find yourself in a group of pacifists, it may be useful to play the role of the devil's advocate by trying to raise objections and potential problems. Or, you might ask someone else to play the role. If someone periodically assumes the role of "disagreer," the group is more likely to consider the available alternatives.

The Peterson Plastics Company has been steadily losing employees to its competitor, Wilson Plastics, Inc. A group of management executives met to discuss how to ensure greater employee retention. The vice president for personnel strongly advocated offering a substantial pay bonus to employees after six months, one year, and five years, arguing that employees about to receive such a bonus will probably not change jobs. Several of the junior executives in the group know, however, that money is not really an issue in this case. Peterson is losing employees because its plant is neither air conditioned nor well ventilated, while Wilson offers employees an air-conditioned working environment. But the junior executives hesitated to introduce contention by countering the vice president's proposal. Because of groupthink, they reached a less than satisfactory decision to offer pay bonuses. If the management group had considered the negative consequences of its decision by having someone play the devil's advocate, it might have opted for a better way to retain employees. Again, the myth that conflict and disagreement have a negative influence on a group's productivity results in a poor quality solution. Assign someone to consider the negative aspects of a suggestion *before* it is implemented. It could save the group from groupthink and enhance the quality of the group's decision.

Ask Group Members to Subdivide into Small Groups (or to Work Privately) and to Consider Potential Problems with the Suggested Solutions

The larger the group the less likely that all group members will be able to voice their objections and reservations. Most of the work conducted by the Congress of the United States is done in small committees. The members of Congress realize that in order to hear and thoroughly evaluate bills and resolutions, small groups of representatives must work together in committees.

If you are working in a group too large for everyone to discuss the issues, suggest breaking up into groups of two or three people, each to compose a list of objections to the proposals. The lists could be forwarded to the secretary of the group who could then weed out the duplicate objections and identify the common points of contention. Even in a group of seven or eight members, it may be useful to form two subcommittees to evaluate the recommendations of the group. The principles here are to permit group members to participate frequently and to encourage them to evaluate the issues carefully. Individuals could also be asked to write down their personal objections to the proposed recommendations and then present the list to the group.

The previous clues for identifying and correcting groupthink should help improve the quality of your group's decisions by capitalizing on opposing points of view. But a textbook summary of a few suggestions for dealing with groupthink may lead you to the false assumption that the groupthink problem can easily be corrected. It cannot. It may seem like we have overemphasized how to avoid groupthink. But, because of the prevalent attitude that conflict should be avoided, we feel it necessary to provide some specific guidelines for identifying and avoiding groupthink. In essence, *be critical of ideas, not people.* Some controversy is useful. Ideally, groups should strive for an optimum amount of controversy so that they will not be lulled into groupthink. But the group should not make extra efforts to create conflict. An important goal of a decision-making group is to obtain the best unanimous decision possible— to reach consensus.

Communication Competency in the Small Group

Janis Andersen

What is a competent communicator? What qualities do we attribute to a competent communicator? What must one do in order to be thought of as a competent communicator? These questions are not new. They have been of interest to people for thousands of years. Despite this interest, a *definitive* answer still eludes us.

However, there is now an emerging body of literature that provides us with some insights and suggests strategies we might pursue in order to be competent communicators. This essay will explore the factors of communication competence in the small group setting. Specifically, I will discuss what competent communication is and isn't. I will examine some of the contributors to competent communication, and suggest strategies that you can pursue that will make you a more competent communicator when you are a participant in a small group.

Defining Competence

Defining competent communication is a difficult task. In a critique of competence literature that I presented to a communication conference several years ago, I suggested that communication competence and pornography shared a common problem: they are both easy to recognize but difficult to define. As the story goes, when the Supreme Court was wrestling with the definition of pornography several years ago one of the justices is reported to have stated, "I'll be darned if I can define pornography, but I sure do know it when I see it."

We are all able to identify easily those of our friends and group members who are competent in their communication. We know that a competent communicator is one who recognizes "Hi" as a greeting and not as a comment about one's state of consciousness, or that a competent communicator recognizes "How are you?" as a ritual dictating a "Fine, thank you" response rather than a detailed health report. Competent communicators are able to negotiate communication exchanges smoothly while satisfying a variety of human needs. But what is it that one does or possesses to accomplish competent communication?

Janis Andersen is affiliated with the Department of Speech Communication, San Diego State University.

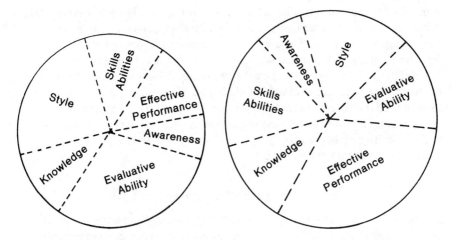

Figure 1. Circles of competence.

Communication competence is many different things. Some think of communication competence as an ability one has or uses in communication exchanges. Others treat it as a phenomenon that occurs when one possesses a body of knowledge about effective communication. Some argue that communication competence, by definition, insures effective communication performance, whereas others take the position that competence and performance are two different concepts. The latter believe that one can know (competence) something without being able to effectively utilize that knowledge in interactions (performance), that one can perform effectively without always knowing or understanding what one is doing. Competence is, to some, a style or a systematic way of communicating, but to others competence is an awareness of the communication event combined with the ability accurately to evaluate the communication exchange.

All these approaches can be useful if we view competence as an additive construct with equifinality. An additive construct is one whereby each of the components additionally contribute to the final end product. The more of each component and the more components overall one masters, the more competent one becomes. Equifinality means that there are many routes that lead equally well to the final destination. There is no magic formula that has to be followed in a communication exchange in order to be competent; instead, there are many combinations of skills and knowledge which lead to competent interaction.

Figure 1 shows this visually.

The complete circle represents competence. The lines are dotted between the components to emphasize that the size of each segment of the circle varies.

A circle of competence can be achieved by piecing together a few large components or many smaller components (equifinality principle). Furthermore, since competence is additive, all circles of competence are not the same size. Greater mastery of components leads to larger circles of competence.

Small group participants can achieve greater communication competence by enhancing their communication skills and abilities, improving their performance effectiveness, increasing their knowledge of the communication process, heightening their awareness of the communication exchange, improving their evaluative ability, and/or simply increasing or mastering any other component of competent communication.

Competence Components

In a well-documented summary of the research on communication competence, Spitzberg (1982) categorizes six distinct types of communication competence. The first kind of competence is *fundamental competence.* This construct is broader than the rest and refers in general to a person's ability to adapt appropriately to the surrounding world. Adaptability or flexibility is viewed as a characteristic of survival and is thus fundamental to overall competent behavior. *Linguistic competence* is the most narrow skill, referring only to a person's ability to use linguistic or language codes, rules, and norms correctly and appropriately. When people use acceptable grammar and sentence structure, they are linguistically competent.

Communication competence, as Spitzberg uses this term, refers to a person's ability to engage in appropriate social behavior. Communication competent individuals do and say socially appropriate things at socially apppropriate times. They are aware of social expectations regarding communication exchanges and they adhere to these rituals. They adapt their behavior both to the context and to their listeners. *Social competence* refers to the display of behaviors that form the basis of effective and appropriate interaction. Three essential skill constellations are role taking, empathy, and interaction management. Competent communicators take account of and adapt to the roles of the other interactants. They express their concern, caring, and feeling in appropriate ways and they handle the procedural components of the interaction (e.g., conversation initiation, conversation termination, and proper allocation of speaking turns) effectively.

Strategic or *interpersonal competence* emphasizes a person's ability to control the communication environment, solve interpersonal or relational problems, and achieve goals. Interpersonally competent individuals possess a variety of strategies for dealing with individuals or with relational problems,

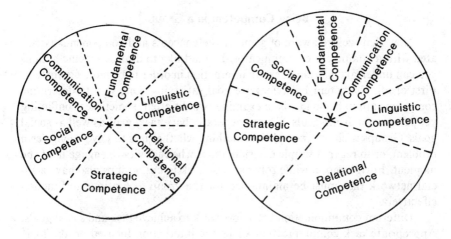

Figure 2. Kinds of competence: More circles of competence.

and they select effective strategies from their repertoire. The sixth kind, *relational competence,* stresses the relationship between competent communication and desirable outcomes. Relationally competent individuals achieve their communication goals, utilizing appropriate communication and social skills, and they are sensitive to the needs of the other interactants. Relationally competent individuals achieve their own goals while at the same time satisfying the other interactants' goals. By definition, relational competence is satisfying and rewarding to all participants in the interaction.

These six kinds of competence provide us with a different way to view the circle of competence. Remembering that competence is an additive attribute that can be achieved in many ways (equifinality principle), these components provide us with insights into where to focus attention to improve our competence. Figure 2 depicts circles of competence from this perspective.

Competent communicators are flexible; they can adapt to a changing environment and a changing communication context. They use language correctly and they formulate messages according to proper linguistic codes and norms. Competent communicators do and say socially appropriate things at socially appropriate times. They possess adequate skills so that they are able effectively to engage in role taking, empathetic expression, and interaction management. They talk at appropriate times; they don't say too much or too little. They control the communication environment, solve any problems which they confront in appropriate ways, and attain the goals they set out to achieve. In addition to all these accomplishments, they are sensitive to the other interactants, and they are sure to make the other people feel good about them, the communication exchange, and the outcomes.

Being Competent in a Group

Now that we are aware of some of the concepts and components associated with a competent communicator, I would like to discuss specific actions you can undertake in a small group interaction in order to be more competent. First of all, competent behaviors are goal satisfying. One way to determine competent group behaviors is to examine two different, sometimes conflicting yet paramount group goals. Groups generally have task goals as well as social goals. Groups wish to accomplish something whether it is to solve a long-term problem, or to reach a simple decision about what activity to engage in at the moment. Furthermore, while solving these task issues, groups also have a social network that must be maintained for the group to continue to function effectively.

Different communication behaviors work to achieve task and social goals. Appropriate task communication keeps the interaction focused on the topic and flowing smoothly. Expressing your opinion, seeking or giving clarification, providing information, or aiding others to recall information, are examples of appropriate task behaviors. Keeping conversations focused on the topic and resisting premature topic shifts also aid task accomplishment. Nonverbally, it is important to indicate attentiveness through direct eye contact, direct body orientation, forward body leaning, head nods, and other positive nonverbal signs of encouragement. In many ways it is as important to *look* interested as it is to *be* interested. When people sense that another group member is interested, they will continue their task orientation, but it is difficult to keep conversations focused when no one seems to be paying any attention.

Social networks are enhanced by verbal and nonverbal cohesion behaviors. Communicating agreement or approval, sharing compliments, indicating shared interests and opinions, and remarking on things that show personal interest produce closer social networks. When appropriate, self disclosure builds tighter social relationships, particularly if the disclosure is positive. Nonverbally, smiling, sitting or standing closer to group members, or moving the overall group closer together physically, leaning forward, engaging in direct eye contact, touching warmly, and actively listening enhance social goals.

Most of us generally tend to be more effective and more comfortable with either task or social roles. Employing our skills and predispositions we habitually provide either task or social reinforcers to other group members and engage in behaviors more likely to foster one of the two group goals. Competent communicators have the communication skills to enhance task and social goals; they move from one to the other depending on the individual situation and the most important group goal at the moment.

One way to improve your competence is to identify which of these two goals is more difficult or uncomfortable for you to achieve. If a group is working seriously, do you try to distract members, introduce levity, and generally bring the group to a more social level? If so, you may need to work on improving your task related communication skills. On the other hand, if a group is enjoying itself, conversing about disjointed topics, and acting spontaneously and not very purposefully, do you feel the urge to introduce a structure and move the group on to more task oriented topics? This may indicate a general discomfort in the pursuit of social goals and an area for improvement for you. Groups tend to shift back and forth between task and social activity, and competent communicators sense which activity is more necessary to the group at the moment, actively participating in the appropriate or needed activity. Obviously, group leaders may change a group's focus from a social to a task goal, or vice versa, but they orchestrate this change at an appropriate time.

Competent communication behaviors evidence flexibility and adaptability. This is a second general area to explore in discussing competent group interaction. Groups generally move through stages and each of these phases of group development calls for appropriate kinds of communication. Tuckman and Jensen (1977) identified five typical phases that groups go through in their development: forming, storming, norming, performing, and adjourning. During the forming stage group members are becoming acquainted with each other and they are testing out the situation. In this phase competent interaction focuses on the expression of positive attitudes and feelings. Disagreement or any expression of deviance should be avoided if possible. It is important to appear friendly, open, interested and interesting during this phase of group development. Participants can communicate openness to each other by engaging others in interaction, responding warmly to invitations by others to interact, and by assuming open body positions. People appear more approachable when their eyes are open (eye contact), when their mouth is wider (smiles), and when their body signals are open (open arm gestures and body positioning such that you can orient yourself face-to-face with other group members).

The second phase of development, storming, calls for different communication behaviors. During this phase group members respond in emotional ways to task demands. Disagreements on how best to accomplish the task are common and appropriate; deviance is tolerated. Competent communicators in this phase are assertive but not aggressive. They share their differing opinions without offending other group members. They keep the disagreement task-focused and they avoid personal attacks. They listen openly and supportively to other group participants, allowing others to express their opinions fully. They do not interrupt when interruptions are likely to be taken personally by group members. They are certain, however, to insure that their opinion receives a fair hearing. They avoid defensive statements and they try to structure the proceedings so as not to create a win-lose situation.

Norming is the phase where groups develop greater cohesion. Group tensions are generally resolved during the storming phase; and this third phase is characterized by more supportive, positive communication exhanges. If a group were past the storming phase and into the norming phase, a competent communicator would alter his or her communication to be more agreeable, even if he or she was not in full agreement about the outcome.

Performing is the stage during which the group task is completed. Although group members are highly supportive and may occasionally focus on social goals during this phase, the major emphasis is placed on task goals. Competent communicators focus their attention on task accomplishing behaviors.

The final group phase is the adjourning phase. This is the time for group members to separate; once again a totally positive attitude is the competent behavior. Conflict and disagreements are avoided so that members leave with positive feelings which make them feel good about group members and group accomplishments.

Competent communicators are skilled in all phases of group development, and they are adaptable enough to implement effective communication behavior at the appropriate phase of group development. You can improve your overall group competence by becoming sensitive to group phases and the appropriateness of your communication skills. Are you generally a pleasant person who likes to avoid conflict and disagreement? Then you are probably effective at forming and adjourning but very ineffective in storming. Socially oriented individuals tend to be better at norming, while task oriented individuals are better at performing. Communicators who are less competent fail to alter their communication style throughout group development, whereas competent communicators adapt, implementing the appropriate communication behavior at the appropriate group phase.

Competent communicators are sensitive to the needs of others. Without neglecting their own goal accomplishment, they help other interactants achieve goals. They engage in communication behaviors that confirm other participants. Confirming behaviors recognize the presence and importance of others; they positively reinforce another's self concept and signal acceptance of that individual.

We recognize another's presence in many different ways. Obviously, it is essential to recognize another's presence nonverbally. You know how difficult it is to interact with someone who is looking all around the room rather than at you when you are interacting. Moreover, we recognize the existence of others in more subtle ways. Using another's name, incorporating another's idea into a statement mentioning his or her contribution, or following up on someone else's comment are ways to recognize and confirm others. Interruptions and topic shifts are examples of behaviors which do not confirm, since they ignore the presence and the message of another.

Accepting others is also confirming. We accept others when we smile at them, nod our head in approval, move closer to them physically, touch them appropriately and warmly, spend time with them, or in other ways reduce overall psychological distance. Verbal expressions of approval and agreement are confirming. When disagreeing with a statement it is preferable to express the disagreement in a way that does not express lack of confirmation of the person. Killer statements like "That's a stupid idea. Let's. . . ," "How dumb! Why don't we. . . ," or "What a ridiculous idea. Why don't we . . ." are "disconfirming".

A final area to examine in searching for competent group behaviors is that of interaction management. Competent communicators manage the interaction, engaging in talk that is appropriate in time and in amount. As a general rule, people perceive others more positively when they interact more. Group leaders are often selected because of their relatively large amounts of talk time. However, it is quite possible to talk too much and be perceived as impolite, inconsiderate, inattentive, and domineering. However, in our society we value "talkativeness"; it is more likely that members will be thought of as submissive, disinterested, or unwilling to contribute to the overall group effort if they talk less than their fair share. A fair share of talk time is generally slightly more than what would be yours if the talk time were equally distributed among all group members. Appropriate amounts of verbal participation in group encounters is characteristic of competent communicators.

These are a few of the many ways in which small group participants can improve their communication competence. Now that you know what communication competence is, and you are learning what is normative and appropriate in small group settings, you will be able to think of many additional areas of application. One final word of caution, however, reminds us that competence as a measure of effectiveness is associated with appropriateness.

Final Caution

The research studies of communication competence are based on a performance model of communication developed by Goffman (1959, 1967). According to this perspective, communication is a game of proper "face work" (image management) being performed by "actors" (senders and receivers who play roles) whom Goffman (1967, p. 3) views as being "wind-up robots" who are stuck in among fellow actors, with the major goal being to create an "orderly traffic of behavior" (organized flow of interaction). Interactants are competent when they present appropriate "faces and lines" (1959). Faces are the overall images people present and lines are the messages they send. Appropriate faces and lines are those which are supported by other interactants, without jeopardizing their own face and line.

Our society currently values appropriateness, conformity, and smoothness. If you intend to be effective within groups that operate in the mainstream of our society, it would be foolish to ignore these norms even if you don't fully agree with them. But it is also wise to be aware of some of the costs involved in always being appropriate.

A danger to one's sense of self and to our society appears when the role of competent communicator becomes a substitute for the self and an excuse for moral failing. Competent communication is an amoral behavior, but it becomes immoral when it serves as a substitute for doing the right thing. Competent communication is a means to an end; it is simply a tool. Your own sense of ethics and morality must determine when this tool should be used, i.e., when the end is just, fair, and right.

References

Goffman, E. *The presentation of self in everyday life*. Garden City, NY: Doubleday Anchor Books, 1959.

Goffman, E. *Interaction ritual*. Garden City, NY: Doubleday Anchor Books, 1967.

Spitzberg, B. H. "Competence in communicating: A model of relational competence." Unpublished manuscript, University of Wisconsin, 1982.

Tuckman, B. N. & Jensen, M. A. C. "Stages of small-group development revisited." *Group and Organization Studies*, 2, 1977, 419–427.

7

Group Leadership: Approaches and Styles

One of the most intriguing expressions of human behavior is the leadership-followership phenomenon. Who are leaders and what makes them so are fascinating questions people have been seeking to answer since the beginning of civilization. We are, as yet, uncertain why and under what circumstances some become leaders and others remain followers. Despite the extensive literature on leaders and leadership produced by philosophers, political scientists, and psychologists, we have no universal theory of leadership and no formula for producing leaders.

Plato believed that only a select few with superior wisdom should be leaders. St. Paul said only those deemed worthy through divine blessing could truly lead. Machiavelli felt that those princes who had the cunning and the ability to organize power and knowledge in the defense of the state should be followed. Thomas Carlyle held that certain men were born with superior courage and insight, which caused them to rise to leadership positions. Hegel and Marx doubted that any individuals had superior strength and influence, but rather, they maintained that some men understood history and the power of events, and were able to lead by making people aware of the direction and force of socio-economic changes. John Stuart Mill perceived leaders as naturally endowed great men who used their powers of persuasion to enlighten groups and their political skill to bring followers to greater achievement. William James held that leaders arose out of moments or events that brought their genius to the fore, a genius not based on personal power, but on the ability to help resolve the problems of the moment. Elton Mayo exemplifies the contemporary "impersonal leadership" school, holding that power and wisdom reside within groups, and it is the leader's function to provide effective conditions for group interaction, rather than impose authority on the group. This brief, obviously oversimplified, description of various theories of leadership serves to show why it has been so difficult to agree upon a concept of leadership or upon the qualifications for leadership.

Not only have we been unable to agree upon a theory of leadership, there are those who question the very notion of leadership. They believe our present emphasis on individualism and freedom of choice is at odds with the traditional reliance on strong, effective leaders. Some people would purposefully avoid leadership positions because they believe it requires the manipulation of other persons and limits people's freedom of choice. These individuals tend to associate leadership with elitism and the kind of power-seeking which sometimes leads to corruption of group goals and unnecessary intergroup conflict. Some would go so far as to say that modern education and mass communication make leaders unnecessary. As yet, however, there has been no noticeable change in leaders or leadership, and apparently there are no successful groups without leadership. Even when some members of a group consciously avoid leader roles, others arise to fill the void. The question, then, is not whether there should or should not be leaders, but what constitutes the most effective and desirable leadership for a given group.

Some of the confusions and disagreements concerning this topic can be traced to a failure to distinguish between "the leader" and "leadership." If nothing else, twentieth century social science research has established that leadership is a function of group process, rather than a series of traits residing in an individual. It is clear that there is no such thing as "a leader" apart from some particular group or organization. We know that individuals form groups to satisfy needs that cannot otherwise be satisfied, and they accept direction for the same reason. A leader or leadership roles represent a means of fulfilling the group's needs better than could be done without them. Leaders lead because groups demand it and rely on leaders to satisfy needs. In this frame of reference, it is impossible to describe the "universal" leader or the "ideal" leader. We can, however, describe leadership *functions* and *roles,* and then discover which members perform accordingly. In this way, it is possible to distinguish between "leadership" as the function, and "the leader," the person who is performing this function in a particular context.

Insight into leadership functions and styles as part of the dynamics of small groups is the basis for the selections that appear in this chapter. Each essay has been chosen because it throws some light on the various leadership approaches available to fulfill the leadership needs of small groups.

We begin with an essay by Martin M. Chemers. Chemers reviews over seventy years of scientific study on leadership. He perceives the study of leadership being divided into three interrelated periods: the trait period, approximately 1910 till World War II; the behavior period, from the onset of World

War II through the late 1960s; and the contingency period, the late 1960s to the present. After a discussion of these three periods and an analysis of what they revealed about leadership, Chemers advances some specific conclusions that may help us to predict the directions leadership studies might take in the future.

The next selection is from the book *Leadership and Organization,* by Robert Tannenbaum, Irving R. Wechsler, and Fred Massarik. These authors are concerned with building a basic, systematic theory of leadership (which they believe is still a long way in the future), and they start by presenting a frame of reference according to which we can identify the variables constituting leadership effectiveness. Their frame of reference approach includes a brief history of leadership concepts, a communication-oriented definition of leadership, and a discussion of the components of leadership.

"Leading in Organizational Groups" by Robert L. Husband is predicated on the assumption that leadership has been a powerful force in the history of humankind. Husband also believes many of the components of this phenomenon still remain a mystery hundreds of years later. He poses three important questions to help answer some of the unresolved issues. First, what is leadership and how do people attempt to lead? Second, do different people tend to lead differently? Third, what does the group or situation have to say about how leaders lead? While seeking answers, Husband looks at various styles and types of leadership. He is interested in how leadership is reflected in the organizational setting and he examines four of the prominent organizational leadership types (positional, political, administrative, and relational).

A differing approach to leadership styles can be found in the article that follows, 'Styles of Leadership," by James F. Kinder. He examines the behavior of leaders as described by followers. He states that there are four "styles" when viewed from this perspective: "dominant-hostile," "dominant-warm," "submissive-hostile," and "submissive-warm." He then considers the effects of each style on the group.

It is generally agreed (and there is research to support it) that "leaders who are considerate to the members of their group generally will be more effective than leaders who are inconsiderate." It is also recognized that consideration and goodwill are usually manifested in nonverbal ways as well. Therefore, group leaders need become more effective in face-to-face encounters by adapting their nonverbal communication to the individual group members with whom they interact. To help facilitate that adaptation, Martin L. Remland presents an essay entitled "Adaptive Leadership and Nonverbal Displays of Status in Small Groups". More specifically, he offers a taxonomy for classifying various ways in which superior status is communicated nonverbally in an organization. Remland concludes his analysis by offering some suggestions for reducing negative nonverbal messages.

"The Skills of Leading Small Groups in American Business and Industry" by H. Lloyd Goodall, Jr. brings another dimension to the study of leadership and organizational communication. He points out that leading requires the ability to ask and answer a variety of questions about group members, the task, the situation, and the history of the group. He gives examples of the choices available to leaders and explains the effects on the communicative process.

Philosophers from Buddha to Bob Dylan have tried to call our attention to the simple truth that change is inevitable. Whether we like it or not, nothing remains the same—including groups and organizations. Our final essay is concerned with the kinds of changes that take place in these two contexts. How leaders must prepare for, cope with, and utilize change to their advantage are some of the issues examined by Steven C. Schoonover and Murray M. Dalziel in their article "Developing Leadership for Change". The basic premise is one that all leaders must learn to accept—"a leader's choice is not whether to change, but how."

The Social, Organizational, and Cultural Context of Effective Leadership

Martin M. Chemers

The Nature of Leadership

Organizational Functions

A first principle in the study of group effectiveness is that a group is relatively inefficient. A group, as opposed to an individual working alone, must coordinate the knowledge, abilities, and actions of its members.[1] The time, effort, and resources devoted to coordination represent potential decrements in performance. However, there are many tasks which cannot be accomplished by a single individual. Such tasks necessitate the creation of groups. Many tasks further require the coordination of several groups into larger organizations. The dictionary defines the word *organize* as "to make into a whole with unified and coherent relationships." Thus, a primary function of any organization is to create this unified set of groups in coherent relationships. All organizations must attend to two major functions in accomplishing this goal.

One function, which can be called *internal maintenance,* refers to the efforts of the organization to maintain the integrity of its various subsystems. An apt analogy is to the internal maintenance activities of the human body. Any living organism must coordinate its various parts to maintain a steady state or equilibrium which permist life to proceed. A human being must maintain a relatively constant body temperature, blood saline level, neuronal activity level, and so forth. The organism accomplishes this function through the activities of preprogrammed systems which respond to stimulation from sensing devices within the system. Task-directed organizations have a similar function. Day-to-day activities within the organization must be reliable and predictable. Job descriptions, standard operating procedures, and chains of command are examples of preprogrammed organizational systems designed to maintain equilibrium. Payroll forms, monthly reports, and inventory statements are sensing devices which establish and maintain the accountability of subsystems. Thus, the modern organization is built around a pervasive set of rules, regulations, and functions which ease the performance of standard duties and routine activities. The maintenance of these internal regularities is so

From M. M. Chemers, "The Social, Organizational, and Cultural Context of Effective Leadership," in *Leadership: Multidisciplinary Perspectives,* by B. Kellerman (Ed.), © 1984, pp. 95–112. Reprinted by permission of Prentice-Hall, Inc., Englewood Cliffs, New Jersey.

essential to organizational functioning that it is possible to lose sight of another essential responsibility of organizations, *external adaptability.* An organization which overemphasizes internal maintenance turns inward, losing touch with the demands of its environment.

External adaptability requires that an organization be sensitive to its environment and internally flexible enough to respond to change. An effective organization is one which balances the functions of internal maintenance and external adaptability. Control and order coexist with responsiveness and change. The requisite amount of emphasis on each function is influenced by the larger environment of which the organization is a part. An adaptive human being changes his or her wardrobe as the seasons change. Likewise, an effective organization attends and responds to changes in the supply of resources, the demand for a product, the availability of capital, or other critical aspects of its environment.

Small-Group Functions

Organizational functions have their analogues at the level of the small group or unit. Here the function of internal maintenance is translated into the *motivation* and *control* of group members. The leader must direct the activities of subordinates and motivate them to carry out those activities efficiently. The rules, regulations, and systems of the larger organization, or general context, guide the leader in the direction of subordinates. A well-defined and structured task specifies the group's goal and procedures for reaching the goal. However, just as an organization's environment presents new challenges requiring response, so also a work unit or small group will be confronted with tasks for which no standard operating procedures exist. The leader and the group must then engage in the functions of *information processing* and *decision making.* Goals are defined, problems are solved, and procedures for attaining objectives are developed.

An extensive body of leadership research has demonstrated that the styles, behaviors, and activities of leadership which can accomplish these disparate organizational and small-group functions are quite different. Current organizational and leadership theory adopts the notion of "contingency." This notion argues that the organizational structure or leadership style which will be most effective depends or is contingent upon the nature of the task environment. Contemporary research attempts to identify and categorize the most critical features of the leadership situation and relate them to the most important aspects of leadership style and behavior.

Contemporary Leadership Theory

A Brief History

The scientific study of leadership can be roughly divided into three periods: the trait period, from around 1910 to World War II, the behavior period, from the onset of World War II to the late 1960s, and the contingency period, from the late 1960s to the present.

Traits. The early research on leadership emergence and leadership effectiveness proceeded from the premise that, somehow, those who became leaders were different from those who remained followers. The objective of the research was to identify specifically what unique feature of the individual was associated with leadership. The success of the mental testing movement in the early part of the century encouraged researchers to employ the recently developed "personality tests" in their search for the leadership trait. A large number of studies were done in which leaders and followers were compared on various measures hypothesized to be related to leadership status or effectiveness. Measures of dominance, social sensitivity, moodiness, masculinity, physical appearance, and many others were used. The typical research design involved the administration of one or more individual difference measures to members of an organization that had leaders and followers (for example, a military unit, industrial organization, or university student bodies). The scores of leaders and followers on the measures were compared for significant differences.

In 1948, Ralph Stogdill[2] reviewed over 120 such trait studies in an attempt to discern a reliable and coherent pattern. His conclusion was that no such pattern existed. The mass of inconsistent and contradictory results of the trait studies led Stogdill to conclude that traits alone do not identify leadership. He pointed out that leadership situations vary dramatically in the demands which they place upon the leader. For example, compare the desirable traits and abilities for a combat military officer with those for a senior scientist on a research team. Stogdill predicted that leadership theorizing would be inadequate until personal and situational characteristics were integrated.

Behaviors. The failure of the trait approach and the growing emphasis on behaviorism in psychology moved leadership researchers in the direction of the study of leadership behavior. A classic study of leadership styles was conducted by Kurt Lewin and his associates.[3] These researchers trained graduate research assistants in behaviors indicative of three leadership styles: autocratic, democratic, and laissez-faire. The autocratic style was characterized by the tight control of group activities and decisions made by the leader. The democratic style emphasized group participation and majority rule, while the laissez-faire leadership pattern involved very low levels of any kind of activity by the leader. Groups of preadolescent boys were exposed to each leadership style and the effects measured. Results indicated that the democratic style had somewhat more beneficial results on group process than the other styles. The importance of this study is not so much in its results but in its definition of leadership in terms of behavioral style. Also the emphasis on autocratic, directive styles versus democratic and participative styles had a profound impact on later research and theory.

In the 1950s, the research focus turned even more basic and behavioral. A number of independent researchers using rating scales,[4] interviews,[5] and observations[6] attempted to identify the specific, concrete behaviors in which leaders engaged. Here the emphasis was to move away from the focus on the internal states of leaders (that is, their values or personalities, as well as any preconceived leadership styles) to the more basic question of what it is that leaders actually do.

The most comprehensive study of leader behavior employed a rating scale labeled the Leader Behavior Description Questionnaire (LBDQ).[7] After extensive observation and rating of large numbers of military and industrial leaders, it was found that most of the variation in leader behavior could be described by two major clusters or factors of behavior. One factor which included items relating to interpersonal warmth, concern for the feelings of subordinates, and the use of participative two-way communication was labeled *Consideration* behavior. A second factor whose items stressed directiveness, goal facilitation, and task-related feedback was labeled *Initiation of Structure*. A number of other research projects confirmed the existence of these two general behavioral configurations, although they might be labeled *employee oriented* versus *production oriented*[8] or *task* versus *socioemotional*.[9]

The identification of two reliable dimensions of leader behavior was a major step forward for the field of leadership. Optimism was high that research had finally cracked open the complexity of leadership effects. Unfortunately, attempts to relate the behavioral factors to group and organizational outcomes proved quite difficult. Although the leader's consideration behavior was generally associated with subordinate satisfaction, this was not always the case. Furthermore, the relationship between leader-structuring behavior and group productivity revealed very few consistent patterns.[10]

During both the trait and behavior eras, researchers were seeking to identify the "best" style of leadership. They had not yet recognized that no single style of leadership is universally best across all situations and environments. For this reason, leadership theorists were quite disappointed when the behavior patterns which they had identified were not consistently related to important organizational outcomes such as group productivity and follower satisfaction.

Current Theory

Contingency Approaches. The reliable prediction of the effects of leadership style on organizational outcomes awaited the development of the modern contingency theories. The first of these was developed by Fred Fiedler.[11,12] Fiedler's approach centered on a personality measure called the "esteem for the least-preferred co-worker" or LPC scale which he found to be related to group performance. The person who fills out the scale is asked to rate an individual with whom the rater had difficulty accomplishing an assigned task. The most widely accepted interpretation of the meaning of this measure is that a person who gives a *very negative* rating to a poor co-worker is the kind of person for whom task success is very important. Such a person might be labeled "task motivated." A leader who gives a least-preferred co-worker a relatively positive rating would appear to be more concerned with the interpersonal than the task aspects of the situation, and is called "relationship motivated."[13,14,15]

A considerable body of research[16] indicates that the task-motivated leader is more attentive to task-related aspects of the leadership situation, more concerned with task success, and under most circumstances, more inclined to behave in a structuring, directive, and somewhat autocratic style. The relationship-motivated leader, on the other hand, is more attentive and responsive to interpersonal dynamics, more concerned with avoiding conflict and maintaining high morale, and more likely to behave in a participative and considerate leadership style.

After a very extensive series of studies covering some fifteen years, Fiedler[17] determined that leadership style alone was not sufficient to explain leader effectiveness. He set about to develop a model which integrated situational parameters into the leadership equation. He saw the most important dimension of the situation to be the degree of certainty, predictability, and control which the leader possessed. Fiedler developed a scale of *situational control* based on three features of the situation. These were: 1) leader-member relations, that is, the degree of trust and support which followers give the leader; 2) task structure, that is, the degree to which the goals and procedures for accomplishing the group's task are clearly specified; and 3) position power, that is, the degree to which the leader has formal authority to reward and punish followers. The research results indicate that neither style is effective in all situations. In *high control* situations, where predictability is assured by a clear task and a cooperative group, the task-motivated leader is calm and relaxed but maintains a strong emphasis on successful task accomplishment, which is very effective. However, under conditions of *moderate control,* caused by an ambiguous task or an uncooperative group, the task-motivated leader becomes anxious, over-concerned with a quick solution, and sometimes overly critical and punitive. The more open, considerate, and participative style of the relationship-motivated leader can address the problems of low morale or can create an environment conducive to successful problem solving and decision making, making the relationship-motivated leader more effective under these conditions. The crisis nature of the *low control* situation calls for a firm and directive leadership style which is supplied by the task-motivated leader. Such a situation is too far gone to be quickly solved via a participative or considerate style, although such styles may be effective in the long run.

The Contingency Model, as Fiedler's theory is called, has been the subject of considerable controversy.[18,19,20] Arguments have raged over the meaning of the LPC scale, the appropriateness of situational variables, and the general predictive validity of the theory. However, a recent extensive review[21] indicated that the predictions of the theory are strongly supported by data from both laboratory and organizational studies.

Research on the Contingency Model has been quite extensive and broad. The person/situation perspective has provided insights into leadership phenomena which were obscured by "one best way" approaches. One example is in the area of leadership training. Reviews of research on leadership training[22] had concluded that such training had few consistent effects on group performance or subordinate satisfaction. However, Contingency Model research on the effects of leadership training[23,24] has shown that training has its most powerful effects on the leader's situational control. Training provides the leader with knowledge, procedures, and techniques which increase his or her sense of control over the group's task activities. Since the relationship of leadership style to group performance varies across different levels of situational control, the increased control provided by training can either improve or lower a particular leader's performance. For example, if a situation was of moderate control for untrained leaders, the relationship-motivated leaders would perform most effectively. Leadership training which clarified and structured the task would change the situation into one of high control. Under these conditions, the task-motivated leaders would perform better than the relationship-motivated leaders. With the task-motivated leaders getting better and the relationship-motivated leaders getting worse, the net effect of training would appear to be null. However, when both leadership style and situational control are analyzed, the effects of training become clear. These findings helped to explain why leadership training has not been found to be a consistent positive factor in leadership effectiveness. More importantly, the utility of the situational-control dimension as a mediator of leadership effectiveness gained further support, suggesting that aspects of certainty, predictability, and control could well be the most critical factors in the leadership equation.

A number of other contingency-oriented leadership theories have also addressed the relationship of leadership decision-making style to group performance and morale. The best known of these approaches is the Normative

Decision Theory presented by Vroom and Yetton.[25] These authors have identified a range of decision-making styles. These include *autocratic* styles, in which the leader makes a decision alone without consulting subordinates; *consultative* styles, in which the leader makes the decision, but after consulting with subordinates; and a *group* style, in which the leader allows subordinates to share in the decision-making responsibility. The dimension which underlies the range of decision styles is the degree to which the leader allows the followers to participate in the process of decision making. As the word *normative* in the name of the theory implies, the model specifies which of the styles is most likely to yield effective decisions under varying situations. Like Fiedler's Contingency Model, and other contingency theories, it is assumed that there is no one best way to make decisions, and that the most effective style will depend on the characteristics of the situation.

The situational characteristics which are considered most important in this model are 1) the expected support, acceptance, and commitment to the decision by subordinates and 2) the amount of structured, clear, decision-relevant information available to the leader. Three general rules determine which styles or sets of styles will be most effective. The first rule is that, other things being equal, autocratic decisions are less time-consuming and, therefore, more efficient. However, the second rule specifies that if the leader does not have sufficient structure and information to make a high-quality decision, he or she must consult with subordinates to gain the necessary information and enlist their aid and advice. The third general rule specifies that if the leader does not have sufficient support from subordinates to be assured that they will accept the decision, the leader must gain subordinate acceptance and commitment through participation in decision making.

Research support for the Normative Decision Theory is somewhat sparse.[26,27] Managers who are asked to recall and describe the characteristics of good and poor decisions that they have made in the past have been shown to usually describe situations and styles that would be predicted by the theory. Such recollective analyses are clearly open to distortion and bias. However, a comparison of Normative Decision Theory with the Contingency Model, described earlier, helps to strengthen and clarify both theories.

The two most important features of Fiedler's situational-control dimension are leader-member relations and task structure, which are extremely similar to Vroom and Yetton's characteristics of follower acceptance and structured information availability. Thus, the various situations presented in Vroom and Yetton's analysis would fit closely into Fiedler and situational-control dimension. Further, Fiedler's task-motivated and relationship-motivated leaders are typically described as using decision styles which fall toward the two poles of Vroom and Yetton's dimension of style. Task-motivated leaders are more likely to tend toward autocratic or minimally consultative styles while relationship-motivated leaders more often use group-oriented and participative styles.[28,29,30] The two theories make very similar predictions. Autocratic decisions are likely to be efficient and effective when the leader has a clear task and the support of followers. Relatively more participative decisions will fare better when either support or clarity are absent.

Despite the similarity of the two theories, they diverge sharply on the question of the ability of people to modify and change their decision styles. The normative model assumes that leaders can quickly and easily change their behavior to fit the demands of the situation, while Fiedler sees leadership style arising out of stable, enduring, well-learned personality attributes which are quite difficult to change. Some research by Bass and his associates[31] on decision styles is relevant to this question. Bass and others identified five decision styles which are quite close to those already discussed. These are called directive, negotiative, consultative, participative, and delegative. In a large survey conducted in several organizations, Bass asked managers to rate a number of features of the leadership situation which affect or are affected by these decision styles. The results do indicate that the effects of decision style on group performance and subordinate satisfaction depend on the situation, although the pattern of results in these studies is not yet clear and consistent. However, of great interest was Bass's finding that the various leadership styles were not independent of one another. The directive and negotiative styles seem to form one related set, while consultative, participative, and delegative form another. This suggests that some leaders across many situations tend to use more directive, task-oriented, autocratic styles while another type of leader is more likely to employ the participative, open, relationship-oriented styles. The possibility, then, that leadership decision and behavioral style are stable and enduring aspects of the individual leaders seems reasonable.

Another prominent contingency theory of leadership is the Path Goal Theory.[32,33] This is a more restricted theory which deals primarily with the effects of specific leader behavior on subordinate motivation and satisfaction, rather than the more general issues of decision making and performance. The Path-Goal research has studied the effects of the Leader Behavior Description Questionnaire categories of considerate and structuring behavior. The theory predicts that leader-structuring behavior will have the most positive effects on subordinate psychological states when the subordinate's task is unclear and/ or difficult, that is, unstructured. The structure provided by the leader helps to clarify the *path* to the *goal* for the subordinates. On the other hand, consideration behavior will have its most positive effects when subordinates have a boring or distasteful job to perform. Subordinates then appreciate the "strokes" provided by their boss, more than they would if their job were intrinsically satisfying.

It is difficult to integrate Path Goal Theory with the more general theories of leadership discussed earlier. It is not concerned with participative decision styles. In fact, it is not concerned with decisions at all, and might more properly be thought of as a theory of supervision under conditions where the supervisor has high clarity and follower support. However, even with this model, the dimension of clarity, predictability, and certainty of the situation is a variable of critical importance. Research support for the Path-Goal Theory is variable. The most clear and consistent results show up on studies of follower satisfaction rather than group performance. However, a most interesting recent finding by Griffin[34] indicates that in addition to job characteristics, the needs, attitudes, and expectations of the follower have an important effect on the follower's reaction to leader behavior. Griffin found that managers who scored high on a measure of the need for personal growth preferred not to receive structuring supervision, even under conditions of ambiguity. These subordinates would rather work the problem out for themselves. Conversely, subordinates low in growth need were not upset by a boring, routine job. The supervisor's considerate behavior had little effect since the subordinates were not really suffering. This result is especially important because the theoretical orientations of the three theories described so far tend to largely ignore the characteristics of subordinates.

Transactional Approaches. The theories discussed above might all be regarded as "leader oriented" approaches. They tend to focus most of their attention on the leader's actions and attitudes. Although followers make their appearance in features related to leader-subordinate relationships, the leader is clearly the central figure and prime actor. However, some transactional or exchange theories of leadership addressing the relationship between leader and followers have had considerable impact.

One of the most important bodies of research in leadership are the studies of leader legitimation by Hollander.[35,36] Hollander developed the notion of "idiosyncrasy credit" to refer to the freedom which valued group members are given to deviate somewhat from group norms, that is, to act idiosyncratically. Idiosyncrasy credits are earned through the demonstration of competence and shared values which serve to make the group member more indispensable to the group. The individual's achieved value, which is the same as status, allows him or her to introduce new ideas and new ways of doing things into the group or society, thus creating adaptability and change. Hollander's work shows us that the legitimation of leadership is a process of social exchange. Members of groups exchange their competence and loyalty for group-mediated rewards which range from physical rewards such as income or protection to the less tangible rewards of honor, status, and influence.

The work of George Graen and his associates[37,38,39] has shown that the nature of exchange processes between leaders and subordinates can have far-reaching effects on group performance and morale. Research with the Vertical Dyad Linkage model has shown that a leader or manager develops a specific and unique exchange with each of his or her subordinates. These exchanges might range from a true partnership in which the subordinate is given considerable freedom and autonomy in defining and developing a work-related role to exchanges in which the subordinate is restrained, controlled, and little more than a "hired hand." As might be expected, the more positive exchanges are associated with higher subordinate satisfaction, reduced turnover, and greater identification with the organization.[40]

On the one hand, these findings are not surprising. Good interpersonal relationships in dyads make people feel better about each other, themselves, and their work. The importance of this research is that it redirects our attention to the relationship between leader, follower, and situation, and encourages a broader and more dynamic approach to the study of the leadership phenomenon. However, the Vertical Dyad Linkage Model does not elucidate the causes of good and poor exchanges.

Over the years, a number of studies have examined follower effects on the leadership process. Although not organized into a comprehensive theory, the research makes some interesting and important points. For example, a number of studies[41,42,43] have shown that leader activity, specifically the leader's willingness to engage in attempts to move the group toward its goals, is dramatically affected by followers' responses to the influence attempts. Leaders lead more with follower acceptance.

Individual differences in follower attitude or personality traits have long been associated with leadership effects. Early studies by Haythorn[44] and Sanford[45] showed that differences in authoritarian versus egalitarian attitudes of followers determined reactions to leader's style. A recent study by Weed and others[46] updates the same effect. They found that followers who are high in dogmatism respond better to leaders who engage in high levels of structuring behavior. Low-dogmatism followers perform better with considerate leader behavior.

A number of other characteristics, including need for achievement,[47] work values,[48,49] and locus of control[50,51] have been shown to impact on leader behavior and follower attitudes. At this point, the literature on follower characteristics is not well integrated. However, the results occur frequently enough to suggest that leadership theorizing will benefit from attention to leader *and* follower characteristics and to the resultant relationship.

Cognitive Approaches. Perception and cognition have played a major role in leadership research. Many dependent measures such as leader-behavior ratings, satisfaction, and role ambiguity, are judgmental or memory processes.

Social psychology has been strongly influenced by attribution theory[52,53,54] which is concerned with the cognitive processes which underlie interpersonal judgments. Recently, leadership theorists have begun to apply attribution-theory-based propositions to judgments involved in the process of leadership.

One of the key features of interpersonal judgments is the strong tendency for an observer to develop causal explanations for another person's behavior. Explanations of a person's behavior often center on the question of whether the behavior was determined by factors internal to the actor, such as ability or motivation, or factors external to the actor, such as situational forces, role demands, or luck. Reliable findings indicate that observers have a strong bias to attribute an actor's behavior to internal causes.[55] This tendency may result from the observer's desire for a sense of certainty and predictability about the actor's future behavior. Further, if the observer might be considered responsible for the actor's behavior, internal attributions to the actor remove that responsibility. For example, a teacher might be inclined to attribute a student's poor academic performance to a lack of ability, thereby relieving the teacher of responsibility for that performance.

Recent work by Green and Mitchell[56] has adapted some of the propositions of attribution theory to the processes which leaders use to make judgments about subordinate performance. They have shown that these processes are affected by factors which are not directly related to the subordinate's actual behavior. Studies[57,58] indicate that supervisors make more negative and more internal attributions when the negative outcomes of a subordinate's behavior are more severe. This happens even when the behavior in the two situations is identical. For example, nursing supervisors asked to judge a hypothetical subordinate's performance made more negative judgments of a nurse who left a railing down on a patient's bed if the patient fell out of bed than if the patient did not. These judgments have important implications for later actions the supervisor might take with respect to promotion, termination, or salary. The role-making processes which are discussed in the Vertical Dyad Linkage model might benefit from an analysis of the ways in which supervisory judgments affect leader-follower exchanges.

Calder's[59] attribution theory of leadership argues that leadership processes and effects exist primarily as perceptual processes in the minds of followers and observers. In fact, most of the measuring instruments used in leadership research ask the respondent for perceptions of the leadership process. These perceptions, judgments, and attributions are distorted by the biases which the perceiver brings to the situation. Each individual holds an implicit personal theory of leadership which serves as a cognitive filter to determine what the observer will notice, remember, and report about the leadership process.

A number of recent studies[60,61,62] indicate that such implicit theories are especially problematic in ratings of leader behavior. Raters who are led to believe that a group has performed well or poorly will modify their ratings of leader behavior to conform to the performance feedback. In other words, if I think that good leaders are very considerate of their followers, I am more likely to notice and report the consideration behavior of leaders whom I believe have performed well.

Ayman and Chemers[63] have found that the structure of leader-behavior ratings depends more on the culture of the raters than on the behavior of the leader. These researchers factor analyzed leader-behavior ratings made by Iranian subjects. They found that the structure of the behavior ratings was very different from the structure normally found in studies in the United States and Europe. In most leadership studies done in Western Europe and the United States, analyses of leader-behavior ratings yield two distinct and independent behavior clusters. These are the familiar structuring, task-directed behaviors and the considerate, relationship-directed behaviors. However, the Ayman and Chemers analysis of ratings made by Iranian followers resulted in a single category of behavior which included both structuring and considerate items. This global factor depicting a directive but warm supervisor was labeled "benevolent paternalism." Furthermore, the factor was found to be strongly related to group performance as assessed by superiors and to satisfaction with supervision expressed by subordinates. Interestingly, this unique pattern of behavior ratings was found when the leaders being rated were Iranian or American. This led Ayman and Chemers to conclude that leader-behavior ratings are more a function of the implicit theories which guide the "eye of the beholder" than they are of what the leader actually does.

On the one hand, these distortions in the observation of leadership effects are very problematic. This is especially true for research with certain theories (for example, Path-Goal Theory, the Normative Decision Theory, and the Vertical Dyad Linkage Model) because in many tests of these theories subjects are asked to rate several aspects of the leadership situation, for example, their leader's behavior and their own satisfaction. The relationships observed among these measures may reflect the implicit theories held by the subjects rather than accurate reflections of the constructs studied. However, it is also true that perception, judgments, and expectations form the core of interpersonal relationships. The desire and expectations of a subordinate for some type of leader behavior (for example, consideration) may elicit or compel that behavior. This represents an interesting and necessary area for future research.

Cross-Cultural Approaches. Berry[64] has argued that American psychology is "culture bound" and "culture blind." The generalizability of our findings are bounded by the fact that most of our research is done with European or American samples. Furthermore, because we rarely compare cultures, we are blind to the potential effects of cultural differences. Chemers[65] points out that this problem becomes more salient when we attempt to export our theories and training programs to cultures which are different from those in which the theories were developed. Cross-cultural research can benefit leadership theory in two ways. Comparative studies can show us the generalizability of Euro-American theories, helping us to recognize the inherent limitations in their transfer to other cultures. More importantly, comparative research gives us a much broader range of variables which may highlight relationships previously ignored. For example, since most studies done in the developed countries are done on subjects who are relatively well educated and technologically sophisticated, educational level becomes a background variable to which we pay little attention. However, in a broader context, the socialization or educational background of workers may be an important determinant of work-related attitudes and responses.

Leadership researchers have not totally ignored culture, but the results of the research leave much to be desired. Reviews by Roberts,[66] Nath,[67] Barrett and Bass,[68] and Tannenbaum[69] all concluded that the cross-cultural research on leadership has been characterized by weak methodologies and by a paucity of theory, both of which make the interpretation of the scattered findings very difficult. However, a few cross-cultural models do exist. Neghandhi[70] presented a model of cultural effects on organizational structure in which cultural or national differences act indirectly on management practices by affecting the organizational environment. He argues that organizational structure and managerial policy are more important than cultural factors in determining behavior. This view contrasts with earlier views[71] which saw culture as directly determining managerial values, attitudes, and behavior.

The actual role of culture probably lies somewhere between these two views. Neither culture nor organizational structure are static forces. Rather, they interact in dynamic process influencing one another, and both contribute to managerial attitudes and behavior. For example, studies which have compared the attitudes or behaviors of managers have found national differences somewhat moderated by organizational policy.[72] Unfortunately, after we have dealt with the broad question of whether culture is important, we are still left with few theories which make any specific predictions about the role of culture in shaping leadership process.

A potentially useful theoretical framework relating values to managerial and organizational process has been offered by Hofstede.[73,74,75] Comparing responses to a value survey of managers from forty countries, Hofstede found that the pattern of results could be described by four factors. These are 1) power distance, that is, the relative importance of status; 2) tolerance for uncertainty; 3) individualism versus collectivism; and 4) masculinity. Hofstede[76] argues that a culture's standing on these four value dimensions determines the kind of organizational structure and managerial policies that will be most likely to develop. For example, he argues that cultures which have a low tolerance for uncertainty combined with a low emphasis on status are likely to develop highly bureaucratic organizational structures to reduce ambiguity. Cultures which are also low in tolerance for uncertainty but high in power distance will develop autocratic organizational structures, in which the high-status persons resolve ambiguity by fiat.

The validity of much of the cross-cultural research has been questioned by Ayman and Chemers.[77] In a study of the leadership behavior of Iranian managers, these researchers found that traditional measures of leadership behavior and subordinate satisfaction resulted in very different factor structures in their Iranian sample than did those measures when used with European or American samples. Ayman and Chemers[78] and Chemers[79] argue that the imposition of Euro-American theories, measures, and research designs on other cultures may lead to very inaccurate conclusions.

Summary and Conclusions

We can now look back on over seventy years of scientific research on leadership in small groups. For much of that time, the literature has been characterized by false starts, dead ends, and bitter controversies. Even today, the student of leadership is consistently confronted with acrimonious debates among theorists, giving the field an appearance of chaotic disarray. In fact, much of the controversy resembles a "tempest in a teapot." Various theories say much the same thing in slightly different ways, and advocates engage in quibbling over relatively minor differences. The current crop of theories has more which unites than separates them. The last twenty years of research has reinforced and clarified certain common threads, and the study of leadership stands poised for a thrust into a new era of growth. Let us examine these commonalities and the directions toward which they point.

At the broadest level, most contemporary theories adopt a contingency perspective. One would be hard put to find an empirical theory of leadership which holds that one style of leadership is appropriate for all situations. At a somewhat deeper level, the similarities continue. The most frequent dimensions on which leader behavior, style, or decision processes are differentiated are 1) the relative focus of the leader on goal-directed task functions versus morale-oriented interpersonal functions, and 2) the relative use of autocratic, directive styles versus democratic, participative styles. These related dichotomies have been part and parcel of the leadership equation since the first behavioral studies of the late 1940s and early 1950s.

Turning to the situational parameters embodied in most current theories, another area of commonality is revealed. Almost all of the contemporary approaches are concerned with the degree of predictability, certainty, and control which the environment affords to the leader. At an even more specific level most approaches integrate interpersonal and task features into the specification of the situation. Indeed, in retrospect, it is hard to imagine how it could be otherwise. Leadership involves a job to do and people to do it with. The likelihood of successful goal accomplishment must, then, depend upon the degree to which the support of the people and the control of the task are facilitative.

Finally, a careful examination of these leadership theories results in a common set of predictions as well. Autocratic decisions and directive styles in which the leader tells followers what to do are most likely to work when the leader knows exactly what to tell the subordinates (that is, a structured task) and when the subordinates are inclined to do what they are told (that is, good follower acceptance and loyalty). When the leader is not so sure what to do or not so sure that followers will go along, considerate and participative styles have the double benefit of encouraging follower acceptance and increasing follower input into the problem-solving process.

The presence of common themes in the research literature does not mean that we have answered all the questions and solved all the problems in leadership. The contingency approaches do provide us with a stable platform from which to step into the next set of issues. However, these issues are quite complex and will require a more integrated, multifaceted, and systemic view of leadership process.

A major gap in most current leadership theories is the lack of attention to the leaders and followers, as people. We focus on behavior or decision style with very little understanding of the values, needs, and motives which give rise to the observed behaviors. It is assumed that any leader can engage in any behavior, and that leaders and followers can easily identify the correct or ideal set of behaviors in a situation. When the possibility arises, as it has recently, that our observation of behavior may be flawed, we are left with nowhere to turn.

The differences in the factor structure of leader behavior across cultures highlights the role of personal values in the social process of leadership. In the research done in the Western industrialized nations, for example, leader behaviors which are directive and task oriented are usually differentiated from those that are more considerate and interpersonally oriented. The two sets of behaviors load on separate and distinct factors. However, Ayman and Chemers's[80] research in developing nations such as Iran and Mexico reveals a different pattern. The leaders who have the highest group performance and the most satisfied subordinates are those who combine directive task styles with interpersonal warmth and consideration. The factor structure of leader-behavior ratings in these cultures indicates that both structuring and considerate behavior correlate within a single global cluster.

In order to understand why leader-behavior factors differ across cultures, it is necessary to have some theory about the manner in which culture affects behavior. The culture, through the processes of socialization, helps to shape the needs, values, and personality of leaders and followers. The personality of the leader will affect the kinds of behaviors most often used. Further, cultural norms create expectations and judgments about the appropriate behavior of leaders and their group members. The cultural expectations of the society's members then influence the patterns of leadership exhibited.

Thus, one interpretation of the differences in leader-behavior patterns across cultures relates to the very strong emphasis on individualism in the Western democracies and on collective, group-oriented values in much of the rest of the world. When individual responsibility and individual autonomy are stressed, considerate supervisory behavior is that which reinforces the autonomy of subordinates; in other words, egalitarian, participative leadership. Thus considerate behavior is generally likely to be somewhat incompatible with high levels of directive and structuring behavior. However, in more collective and authoritarian cultures, in which group members subordinate individuals' goals to group needs, a leader can maintain control over subordinates *and* satisfy them, by being directive and structuring in a warm, supportive, "fatherly" manner. Cultural values are reinforced by social norms which prescribe elaborate codes of politeness and make the exercise of a "benevolent paternalism" the most acceptable mode of behavior.

The role of culture in leadership is much broader and more complex than the abbreviated explanation given here. But this analysis does turn our attention to the role of the leader's and the follower's personalities as an influence on behavior and the perception of behavior. The research on follower characteristics makes it very plain that the way in which one individual reacts to the behavior of another is dependent upon individual differences in styles and needs as well as variations in situational characteristics.

The transactional and exchange theories have shown that the relationship between leaders and followers is a dynamic one extending longitudinally in time. Roles are defined, negotiated, and redefined. People move toward or away from one another with effects on motivation, satisfaction, and individual and group performance. Observations and judgments are made which facilitate and enhance positive or negative relationships. Admittedly, such dynamic relationships are difficult to study. It is also true, however, that leadership theory will make major strides forward when we can begin to tie together the ways in which personal characteristics influence judgments which, in turn, influence role perception and performance which, subsequently, determine group behavior and effectiveness.

This simplistic trait approaches were superseded by the behavioral studies which were replaced by the contingency theories. The next major era of leadership research will begin with the recognition that group and organizational performance are dependent upon the interplay of social systems. A social-systems approach will recognize that the leadership process is a complex, multifaceted network of forces. Personal characteristics of leaders and followers interact in the perception of and reaction to task demands and to each other. The small group is further embedded in an organizational and societal context which influences personal characteristics, social roles, and situational contingencies. If general leadership theory can begin to span the gaps between the various levels of analysis (that is, individual, group, organization, society), the resultant theories will provide us with a much stronger base, not only for understanding leadership but also for improving its quality.

Notes

1. Ivan D. Steiner, *Group Process and Productivity.* (New York: Academic Press, 1972).
2. Ralph M. Stogdill, "Personal Factors Associated with Leadership: A Survey of the Literature," *Journal of Psychology,* 25 (1948), pp. 35–71.
3. Kurt Lewin, Ronald Lippitt, and Ralph K. White, "Patterns of Aggressive Behavior in Experimentally Created Social Climates," *Journal of Social Psychology,* 10 (1939), pp. 271–99.
4. Ralph M. Stogdill, Carroll L. Shartle, Willis L. Scott, Alvin E. Coons, and William E. Jaynes, *A Predictive Study of Administrative Work Patterns* (Columbus: Ohio State University, Bureau of Business Research, 1956).
5. Robert L. Kahn and Daniel Katz, "Leadership Practices in Relation to Productivity and Morale," in Dorwin Cartwright and Alvin Zander, eds., *Group Dynamics* (New York: Harper & Row, 1953).
6. Robert F. Bales and Paul E. Slater, "Role Differentiation in Small Decision Making Groups," in Talcott Parsons and Robert F. Bales, eds., *Family, Localization, and Interaction Processes* (New York: Free Press, 1945).
7. Ralph M. Stogdill and Alvin E. Coons, eds., *Leader Behavior: Its Description and Measurement* (Columbus: Ohio State University, Bureau of Business Research, 1957).
8. Kahn and Katz, *Group Dynamics.*
9. Bales and Slater, *Family, Localization, and Interaction Processes.*
10. Abraham Korman, "Consideration, Initiating Structure, and Organizational Criteria—A Review," *Personnel Psychology,* 19 (1966), pp. 349–62.
11. Fred E. Fiedler, "A Contingency Model of Leadership Effectiveness," in Leonard Berkowitz, ed., *Advances in Experimental Social Psychology,* vol. 1 (New York: Academic Press, 1964).
12. ———, *A Theory of Leadership Effectiveness* (New York: McGraw-Hill, 1967).
13. ———, "The Contingency Model and the Dynamics of the Leadership Process," in Leonard Berkowitz, ed., *Advances in Experimental Social Psychology.*
14. Fred E. Fiedler and Martin M. Chemers, *Leadership and Effective Management,* (New York: Scott, Foresman, 1974).
15. Robert W. Rice, "Construct Validity of the Least Preferred Co-worker Score," *Psychological Bulletin,* 85 (1978), pp. 1199–1237.
16. Ibid.
17. Fiedler, *A Theory of Leadership Effectiveness.*
18. Ahmed S. Ashour, "Further Discussion of Fiedler's Contingency Model of Leadership Effectiveness: An Evaluation," *Organizational Behavior and Human Performance,* 9 (1973), pp. 339–55.

19. George Graen, Kenneth M. Alveres, James B. Orris, and John A. Martella, "Contingency Model of Leadership Effectiveness: Antecedent and Evidential Results," *Psychological Bulletin,* 74 (1970), pp. 285–96.

20. Terrence R. Mitchell, Anthony Biglan, Gerald R. Oncken, and Fred E. Fiedler, "The Contingency Model: Criticism and Suggestions," *Academy of Management Journal,* 13 (1970), pp. 253–67.

21. Michael J. Strube and Joseph E. Garcia, "A Meta-analytical Investigation of Fiedler's Contingency Model of Leadership Effectiveness," *Psychological Bulletin,* 90 (1981), pp. 307–21.

22. Robert J. House, "T-Group Education and Leadership Effectiveness: A Review of the Empirical Literature and a Critical Evaluation," *Personnel Psychology,* 20 (1967), pp. 1–32.

23. Martin M. Chemers, Robert W. Rice, Eric Sundstrom, and William M. Butler, "Leader LPC, Training and Effectiveness: An Experimental Examination," *Journal of Personality and Social Psychology,* 31 (1975), pp. 401–9.

24. Fred E. Fiedler, "The Effects of Leadership Training and Experience: A Contingency Model Interpretation," *Administrative Science Quarterly,* 17 (1972), pp. 453–70.

25. Victor H. Vroom and Paul. W. Yetton, *Leadership and Decision-Making* (Pittsburgh: University of Pittsburgh Press, 1973).

26. Arthur G. Jago and Victor H. Vroom, "An Evaluation of Two Alternatives to the Vroom/Yetton Normative Model," *Academy of Management Journal,* 23 (1980), pp. 347–55.

27. Victor H. Vroom and Arthur G. Jago, "On the Validity of the Vroom-Yetton Model," *Journal of Applied Psychology,* 63 (1978), pp. 151–62.

28. Martin M. Chemers, Barbara K. Goza, and Sheldon I. Plumer, "Leadership Style and Communication Process: An Experiment Using the Psychological Isotope Technique," *Resources in Education* (September 1979).

29. Martin M. Chemers and George J. Skrzypek, "An Experimental Test of the Contingency Model of Leadership Effectiveness," *Journal of Personality and Social Psychology,* 24 (1972), pp. 172–77.

30. Rice, "Construct Validity of the Least Preferred Co-worker Score."

31. Bernard M. Bass, Enzo R. Valenzi, Dana L. Farrow, and Robert J. Solomon, "Management Styles Associated With Organizational, Task, Personal, and Interpersonal Contingencies," *Journal of Applied Psychology,* 60 (1975), pp. 720–29.

32. Robert J. House, "A Path-Goal Theory of Leadership," *Administrative Science Quarterly,* 16 (1971), pp. 321–38.

33. Robert J. House and Gary Dessler, "The Path-Goal Theory of Leadership: Some Post Hoc and A Priori Tests," in James G. Junt and Lars L. Larsen, eds., *Contingency Approaches to Leadership* (Carbondale, Il: Southern Illinois University Press, 1974).

34. Ricky N. Griffin, "Relationships Among Individual, Task Design, and Leader Behavior Variables," *Academy of Management Journal,* 23, (1980), pp. 665–83.

35. Edwin P. Hollander, "Conformity, Status, and Idiosyncrasy Credit," *Psychological Review,* 65, pp. 117–27.

36. Edwin P. Hollander and James W. Julian, "Studies in Leader Legitimacy, Influence, and Innovation," in Leonard Berkowitz, ed., *Advances in Experimental Social Psychology,* vol. 5 (New York: Academic Press, 1970).

37. Fred Dansereau, Jr., George Graen, and William J. Haga, "Vertical Dyad Linkage Approach to Leadership Within Formal Organizations: A Longitudinal Investigation of the Role Making Process," *Organizational Behavior and Human Performance,* 13 (1975), pp. 46–78.

38. George Graen and James F. Cashman, "A Role-Making Model of Leadership in Formal Organizations: A Developmental Approach," in J. G. Hunt and L. L. Larsen, eds., *Leadership Frontiers* (Kent, Ohio: Kent State University Press, 1975).

39. George Graen, James F. Cashman, Steven Ginsburgh, and William Schiemann, "Effects of Linking-Pin Quality of Work Life of Lower Participants," *Administrative Science Quarterly,* 22 (1977), pp. 491–504.

40. George Graen and Steven Ginsburgh, "Job Resignation as a Function of Role Orientation and Leader Acceptance: A Longitudinal Investigation of Organizational Assimilation," *Organizational Behavior and Human Performance,* 19 (1977), pp. 1–17.

41. Alex Bavelas, Albert H. Hastorf, Alan E. Gross, and W. Richard Kite, "Experiments on the Alteration of Group Structure," *Journal of Experimental Social Psychology,* 1 (1965), pp. 55–70.

42. Lawrence Beckhouse, Judith Tanur, John Weiler, and Eugene Weinstein, "And Some Men Have Leadership Thrust Upon Them," *Journal of Personality and Social Psychology,* 31 (1975), pp. 557–66.

43. Leopold W. Gruenfeld, David E. Rance, and Peter Weissenbert, "The Behavior of Task Oriented (Low LPC) and Socially Oriented (High LPC) Leaders Under Several Conditions of Social Support," *Journal of Social Psychology,* 79 (1969), pp. 99–107.

44. William Haythorn, Arthur Couch, Don Haefner, Peter Langham, and Launor F. Carter, "The Effects of Varying Combinations of Authoritarian and Egalitarian Leader and Follower," *Journal of Abnormal and Social Psychology,* 53 (1956), pp. 210–19.

45. Frederick Sanford, "Research on Military Leadership," in John Flanagan, ed., *Psychology in the World Emergency* (Pittsburgh: University of Pittsburgh Press, 1952).

46. Stanley E. Weed, Terrence R. Mitchell, and William Moffitt, "Leadership Style, Subordinate Personality, and Task Type as Predictors of Performance and Satisfaction With Supervision," *Journal of Applied Psychology,* 61 (1976), pp. 58–66.

47. Richard M. Steers, "Task-goal Attributes, N Achievement, and Supervisory Performance," *Organizational Behavior and Human Performance,* 13 (1975), pp. 392–403.

48. Milton R. Blood, "Work Values and Job Satisfaction," *Journal of Applied Psychology,* 53 (1969), pp. 456–59.

49. Ramon J. Aldage and Arthur P. Brief, "Some Correlates of Work Values," *Journal of Applied Psychology,* 60 (1975), pp. 757–60.

50. Thomas L. Ruble, "Effects of One's Locus of Control and the Opportunity to Participate in Planning," *Organizational Behavior and Human Performance,* 16 (1976), pp. 63–73.

51. Douglas E. Durand and Walter R. Nord, "Perceived Leader Behavior as a Function of Personality Characteristics of Supervisors and Subordinates," *Academy of Management Journal,* 19 (1976), pp. 427–31.

52. Fritz Heider, *The Psychology of Interpersonal Relations* (New York: John Wiley, 1958).

53. Edward E. Jones and Keith E. Davis, "From Acts to Dispositions," in Leonard Berkowitz, ed., *Advances in Experimental Social Psychology,* vol 2. (New York: Academic Press, 1965).

54. Harold H. Kelley, "The Processes of Causal Attribution," *American Psychologists,* 28 (1973), pp. 107–28.

55. Jones and Davies, "From Acts to Dispositions."

56. Stephen G. Green and Terrence R. Mitchell, "Attributional Processes of Leaders in Leader-Member Interactions," *Organizational Behavior and Human Performance,* 23 (1979), pp. 429–58.

57. Terrence R. Mitchell and Laura S. Kalb, "Effects of Outcome Knowledge and Outcome Valence in Supervisors' Evaluations," *Journal of Applied Psychology,* 66 (1981), pp. 604–12.

58. Terrence R. Mitchell and Robert E. Wood, "Supervisors' Responses to Subordinate Poor Performance: A Test of an Attributional Model," *Organizational Behavior and Human Performance,* 25 (1980), pp. 123–38.

59. Billy J. Calder, "An Attribution Theory of Leadership," in Barry M. Staw and Gerald R. Slancik, eds., *New Directions in Organizational Behavior* (Chicago: St. Clair, 1977).

60. Dov Eden and Uri Leviatan, "Implicit Leadership Theory as a Determinant of the Factor Structure Underlying Supervisory Behavior Scales," *Journal of Applied Psychology,* 60 (1975), pp. 736–41.

61. Robert G. Lord, John F. Binning, Michael C. Rush, and Jay C. Thomas, "The Effect of Performance Cues and Leader Behavior in Questionnaire Rating of Leadership Behavior," *Organizational Behavior and Human Performance,* 21 (1978), pp. 27–39.

62. H. Kirk Downey, Thomas I. Chacko, and James C. McElroy, "Attribution of the 'Causes' of Performance: A Constructive, Quasi-Longitudinal Replication of the Staw (1975) Study," *Organizational Behavior and Human Performance,* 24 (1979), pp. 287–89.

63. Roya Ayman and Martin M. Chemers, "The Relationship of Leader Behavior of Managerial Effectiveness and Satisfaction in Iran," *Journal of Applied Psychology,* 68 (1983), pp. 338–341.

64. John W. Berry, "On Cross-Cultural Comparability," *International Journal of Psychology,* 4 (1969), pp. 119–28.

65. Martin M. Chemers, "Leadership and Social Organization in Cross-Cultural Psychology," paper presented to the Meetings of the American Psychological Association, Los Angeles, 1981.

66. Karlene H. Roberts, "On Looking at an Elephant: An Evaluation of Cross-Cultural Research Related to Organizations," *Psychological Bulletin,* 74 (1970), pp. 327–50.

67. Robert A. Nath, "A Methodological Review of Cross-Cultural Management Research," in Jean Boddewyn, ed., *Comparative Management and Marketing* (Glenview, IL.: Scott, Foresman, 1969).

68. Gerald V. Barrett and Bernard M. Bass, "Cross-Cultural Issues in Industrial and Organizational Psychology," in M. D. Dunnette, ed., *Handbook of Industrial and Organizational Psychology* (Chicago: Rand McNally, 1975).

69. Arnold S. Tannenbaum, "Organizational Psychology," in Harry C. Triandis and Richard W. Brislin, eds., *Handbook of Cross-Cultural Psychology, Social Psychology,* vol. 5 (Boston: Allyn & Bacon, 1980).

70. Anant R. Negandhi, "Comparative Management and Organizational Theory: A Marriage Needed," *Academy of Management Journal,* 18 (1975), pp. 334–44.

71. Richard N. Farmer and Barry M. Richman, *Comparative Management and Economic Progress* (Homewood, Il.: Richard D. Irwin, 1965).

72. Tannenbaum, "Organizational Psychology."

73. Geert Hofstede, "Nationality and Espoused Values of Managers," *Journal of Applied Psychology,* 61 (1976), pp. 148–55.

74. ———, "Motivation, Leadership, and Organization: Do American Theories Apply Abroad?" *Organizational Dynamics* (Summer 1980).

75. ———, Culture's Consequences: *International Differences in Work-Related Values* (London: Sage, 1981).

76. Ibid.

77. Ayman and Chemers, "The Relationship of Leader Behavior to Managerial Effectiveness and Satisfaction in Iran."

78. Ibid.

79. Chemers, "Leadership and Social Organization in Cross-Cultural Psychology."

80. Ayman and Chemers, "The Relationship of Leader Behavior to Managerial Effectiveness and Satisfaction in Iran."

Leadership: A Frame of Reference*

Robert Tannenbaum, Irving R. Wechsler and Fred Massarik

Introduction

The word *leadership* has been widely used. Political orators, business executives, social workers, and scholars employ it in speech and writing. Yet, there is widespread disagreement as to its meaning. Among social scientists, the theoretical formulations of the leadership concept have continued to shift, focusing first upon one aspect and then upon another. Much still needs to be done to develop a basic, systematic theory. The time seems ripe for attempting a careful statement of a frame of reference which may serve to make available research more meaningful, and which may guide future research and practice.[1] Specifically, such a frame of reference can perform the useful function of pointing to the variables which need to be measured. It can help us to state hypotheses concerning the key variables underlying leadership effectiveness. It can also provide meaningful objectives for the development of more adequate leaders.

A Brief Historical View

The history of the "leadership" concept highlights the shifting focus in theoretical orientation. Early leadership research focused on the *leader* himself, to the virtual exclusion of other variables. It was assumed that leadership effectiveness could be explained by isolating psychological and physical characteristics, or traits, which were presumed to differentiate the leader from other members of his group. Studies guided by this assumption generally proved none too fruitful. Almost without exception universal traits proved elusive, and there was little agreement as to the most useful traits. Gouldner reviews some of the empirical and conservatively interpreted evidence relating to "universal traits," such as intelligence and psychosexual appeal. However, he concludes: "At this time there is no reliable evidence concerning the existence of

*This chapter is a slightly modified version of an article under the same title by Robert Tannenbaum and Fred Massarik, *Management Science*, vol. 4, no. 1, pp. 1–19, October, 1957. Robert Tannenbaum is affiliated with the Department of Psychology at The Medical College of Pennsylvania. Irving R. Wechsler is affiliated with the Department of Business Management at Manhattan Community College in New York. Fred Massarik is affiliated with the Department of Management at the University of California in Los Angeles.

universal leadership traits."[2] It does not now seem surprising that this approach proved rather sterile. Leaders do not function in isolation. They must deal with followers within a cultural, social, and physical context.

With the fall from grace of the trait approach, the emphasis swung away from the leader as an entity complete unto himself. Instead, the *situationist* approach came to the fore. The situationists do not necessarily abandon the search for significant leader characteristics, but they attempt to look for them in situations containing common elements. Stogdill, after examining a large number of leadership studies aimed at isolating the traits of effective leaders, comes to the following conclusion: "The qualities, characteristics and skills required in a leader are determined to a large extent by the demands of the situation in which he is to function as a leader."[3]

More recently the *follower* has been systematically considered as a major variable in leadership research. This approach focuses on personal needs, assuming that the most effective leader is the one who most nearly satisfies the needs of his followers.[4]

There have been many attempts to assess recent developments in leadership theory. The trait approach, the situationist approach, and the follower-oriented approach have variously been discussed and evaluated by a number of authors including Stogdill, Jenkins, Gouldner, and Sanford.[5] On the basis of their work, it has become increasingly clear that, in the words of Sanford,[6]

It now looks as if any comprehensive theory of leadership will have to find a way of dealing, in terms of one consistent set of rubrics, with the three delineable facets of the leadership phenomenon:

1. the leader and his psychological attributes
2. the follower with his problems, attitudes and needs, and
3. the group situation in which followers and leaders relate with one another.

To concentrate on any one of these facets of the problem represents oversimplification of an intricate phenomenon.

Consequently, the frame of reference which we present is an attempt to take into account these three facets.

A Basic Definition of Leadership

We define leadership as *interpersonal influence, exercised in a situation and directed, through the communication process, toward the attainment of a specified goal or goals.*[7] Leadership always involves attempts on the part of a *leader* (influencer) to affect (influence) the behavior of a *follower* (influencee) or followers in *situation*.

This definition has the virtue of generality. It does not limit the leadership concept to formally appointed functionaries, or to individuals whose influence potential rests upon the voluntary consent of others. Rather, it is applicable to *all* interpersonal relationships in which influence attempts are involved. Relationships as apparently diverse as the superior-subordinate, the staff-line, the consultant-client, the salesman-customer, the teacher-student, the counselor-counselee, the husband-wife, or the parent-child are all seen as involving leadership. Thus, our proposed frame of reference, based on the definition and given continuing substance through a flow of relevant research findings from many disciplines, can be useful in understanding a wide range of social phenomena.

One way of characterizing our definition of leadership is to say that it treats leadership as a *process* or *function* rather than as an exclusive attribute of a *prescribed role*. The subordinate often influences the superior; the customer, the salesman; and the group member, the chairman. In any given relationship, the roles of the influencer and the influencee often shift from one person to the other. Conceptually, the influence process or function is present even though the specific individuals taking the roles of influencer and influencee may vary. Thus, the leader role is one which is rarely taken continuously by one individual, even under specific conditions with the same persons. Instead, it is one that is taken at one time or another by each individual.

One criticism of our definition is that it unrealistically focuses on what appears to be a two-person relationship to the exclusion of group phenomena. For a number of reasons, we find this criticism unconvincing. First, the influencee at any given time may be more than one individual; an entire group may be considered to be the "follower." Second, since the leader role is not restricted to a formally prescribed person, the notion of shared leadership is consistent with our view. Finally, the presence of other persons—with their values, beliefs, and customary modes of behavior—in the context of any given (and often momentary) interpersonal relationship represents a complex of variables which we take into account as part of the situation. Our focus is on a relationship which is often transitory and always affected by situational contexts.

The Components of Leadership

Having made these general observations about the definition, we will now discuss in greater detail some considerations that arise in connection with its major components.

Interpersonal Influence

The essence of leadership is interpersonal influence, involving the influencer in an attempt to affect the behavior of the influencee through communication. We use the word *attempt* advisedly, in order to draw a distinction between influence efforts and influence effects.

To many, an act of leadership has occurred only if specified goals have been achieved. Under this interpretation, whether or not an individual may be called a leader in a given influence instance depends upon whether or not he is successful. If he is not, no leadership has occurred. Were we to accept this notion of leadership, we would be faced with the necessity of finding a satisfactory term for labeling unsuccessful influence efforts. It is our preference to let leadership refer to influence attempts and to treat the assessment of leadership effectiveness as a separate matter. Thus a person who attempts to influence others but is unsuccessful is still a leader in our view, although a highly ineffective one.

It is useful to draw a distinction between power and leadership. Power is potential for influence. However, even though an individual may possess considerable power in relationship to another, he may for a number of reasons (his personal values, apparent lack of necessity to do so, misjudgment) not use all of the power available to him. A leadership act reflects that portion of the power available to an individual which he chooses to employ at the time.[8]

It should be noted, in contrast to the above view, that the concept *power* frequently connotes a potential for coercion, based, for example, upon physical force, informal social pressure, law, and authority. In actuality, a given leader typically has available not only these external sources providing him with power, but also power derived from such inner resources as understanding and flexibility.

Exercised in Situation

The concept *situation* is to be found in much of the recent writing on leadership. An analysis of this literature indicates that the term has been variously used to denote an activity or a particular set of activities engaged in by a group; group characteristics, including interpersonal relationships; group goals or needs; and the cultural context.[9]

It seems appropriate to us to define *situation* as including only those aspects of the objective context which, at any given moment, have an attitudinal or behavioral impact (whether consciously or unconsciously) on the individuals in the influence relationship, and to recognize that the situation of the leader and that of the follower may differ from each other in many respects. Both the phenomenological field and unconscious modes of response to external stimuli are relevant here. Stimuli having independent empirical reality, but having no impact on one or the other of the individuals, cannot be viewed as components of their respective situations. It is thus important to know, though not always easy operationally to ascertain, which stimuli external to the leader and the follower affect each as they interact in the influence relationship.

The objective context of any influence relationship might include any or all of the following:

1. Physical phenomena (noise, light, table and chair arrangement, etc.)
2. Other individuals, including the members of the specific group of which the leader and follower are a part
3. The organization
4. The broader culture, including social norms, role prescriptions, stereotypes, etc.
5. Goals, including personal goals, group goals, and organizational goals

In reality, goals are an essential part of the concepts of group, organization, and culture. However, because of their special importance to the study of leadership, we here treat them separately.

An individual may influence the behavior of others by manipulating elements of their environment (situation). Thus, placing physical facilities in close proximity so that people can work near each other rather than in isolation may promote higher levels of productivity and/or job satisfaction. Since our definition limits leadership to interpersonal influence exercised through the communication process, we would not associate manipulation of situational components with leadership except in a special case—that in which such manipulation is intended by the leader as a communication symbol per se, carrying with it such implications as "this is a good place to work," "they always have our interests at heart," and the like.

The Communication Process

Our definition of leadership concerns only that interpersonal influence which is exercised throughout the communication process. We thus exclude, for example, the direct physical manipulation of another person, since such coercion, in its pure form, does not utilize symbolic means. One the other hand, we include threats and other coercive devices which can be imparted only by means of communication.

There are many problems involved in differentiating conceptually between the communication[10] and the leadership processes. We view communication as the sole process through which a leader, as leader, can function. The objective of a communicator, as communicator, is to transmit a message from himself to a communicatee which the latter will interpret as the former desires. The communicator's goal is to convey meanings, or ideas, without distortion.

The leader is interested in more than simply conveying his ideas for their own sake. With rare exceptions, the leader's final objective is not solely to bring about attitude change. Rather, the leader makes use of communication as the medium through which he tries to affect the follower's attitudes so that the follower will be ready to move or will actually move in the direction of the specified goal. Of course, there is often a time lag between a change in the follower's attitude and the actual or potential goal movement.

An individual may communicate effectively without being an effective leader. He may desire, for example, that another individual leave the room, and he tells him so. The other individual may say, "I understand you want me to leave the room," and yet remain seated. The leader has been understood, the meaning he has transmitted presumably has been received without distortion, and effective communication has taken place. However, the leader has not succeeded in changing the follower's attitudes in such a way that this follower has been motivated to behave in accordance with the specified goal (overt behavior involving leaving the room). Thus, the leadership attempt has been ineffective.

As our later discussion will suggest, a leader, in order to be effective, needs to select those communication behaviors from his repertory which are likely to "strike the right chord" in the follower's personality make-up, resulting in changed attitudes and behavior in line with the desired goal.

Directed toward the Attainment of a Specified Goal or Goals

All leadership acts are goal-oriented. The leader uses his influence to achieve some desired (although often unconscious) goal or goals. These goals toward which individuals exert their influence fall into four categories, whose differences have considerable relevance for leadership theory. The following classification should not suggest that any given influence effort is necessarily aimed exclusively at one single goal. Often a complex of goals is involved, as when a leader brings about the attainment of organizational goals and at the same time satisfies some of his own needs.

Organizational Goals In formal organizations, managers (as leaders) are those who are held responsible by their superiors for influencing others (subordinates) toward the attainment of organizational goals. These goals are the rationally contrived purposes of the organizational entity. Since these goals often have little or no direct motivational import to the followers, the manager's task of leadership often requires him to use other inducements which do have relevance to the need systems of the followers.

Group Goals In small, informal, face-to-face groups the relevant goals are those which evolve through the interaction of the members of the group. They reflect (although not necessarily unanimously) "what the group wants to do." In such a situation, the leader is anyone who uses his influence to facilitate the group's attainment of its own goals. The achievement of a position of effective influence in such groups depends upon an individual's sensitivity to the group's objectives and upon his skill in bringing about their realization.

Personal Goals of the Follower In such activities as teaching, training, counseling, therapy, and consulting, the leader often uses his influence to assist the follower in attaining his own (the follower's) personal goals.[11] For example, through the establishment of an atmosphere of warmth, security, and acceptance, and through the use of facilitative methods, the leader aids another person to reach ends he has not been able to reach by himself.

Personal Goals of the Leader Leaders also use their influence primarily to meet their own needs. At times such personal motives are at the level of consciousness and can be made explicit, but often they lie at the unconscious level where they are hidden from the leader. A teacher may think that he lectures to a class because "this is the best way to teach," without realizing that in so doing he feels more secure because the students never have a chance to "show him up." Likewise, a supervisor may harshly discipline a subordinate because "it is important to keep people in line," although a deep-felt need to express hostility receives some satisfaction through his behavior.

The issue of conscious and unconscious intent poses some knotty problems for both leadership theory and research. Should we be concerned only with objectives that can be made explicit by the leader, or should we admit unconscious motives? If we attempt the latter, by what operational methods do we define the hidden purposes? Unconscious purposes frequently do motivate the leader even though, with the exception of projective techniques, we have few methods available for operationalizing such hidden motives.

Leadership Effectiveness

Our definition of leadership focuses on influence efforts rather than upon influence effects. However, once leadership has been exercised, it becomes appropriate to raise questions about the effectiveness of such leadership.

The effectiveness of any influence attempt must always be assessed with reference to the leader's intended goal or goals. This again points up the crucial nature of the conscious-unconscious intent issue discussed above. No leadership act is inherently effective or ineffective; it might be either, depending upon the goals with reference to which it is assessed. Further, regardless of the leader's intended purpose, a given act of a leader might be seen as effective when viewed by his superior in terms of organizational goals, and at the same time be seen as ineffective when viewed by his subordinates in terms of informal-group goals.

Many operational problems are involved in assessing leadership effectiveness. The very multiplicity of coexisting goals encountered in most real-life situations makes clear-cut measurement difficult. Further, the usual goal clusters contain elements that have differential weight in the attainment of still "higher" goals in a hierarchy. An industrial organization, for example, may have many goals: high employee morale, labor peace, high productivity, contribution to community welfare, etc. These several goals may all contribute to a more inclusive goal, as culturally or organizationally espoused: increased profits. High productivity and labor peace may be viewed as "more important" subgoals for the attainment of profits than employee morale or community welfare. Or, indeed, the opposite may be the case.

Specific leadership acts may also assist the attainment of certain goals while retarding the attainment of others. Finally, all leadership acts are in fact intertwined with numerous nonleadership acts (involving perhaps such factors as accounting procedures, production control, and technological progress), all of which may contribute to organizational success. Therefore, one often encounters real difficulty in the assessment of leadership effectiveness per se.

Our concept of leadership effectiveness is nonmoral in that it implies nothing about the goodness or badness of the goals of influence, nor for that matter, about the influence methods used to achieve these goals. The ethical evaluation involves factors different from those involved in effectiveness evaluation. For example, a gangster's effort—involving lies and coercion—to lead a teen-ager into a life of crime may prove to be a highly effective, although repugnant, leadership act.

Perhaps the most challenging question relating to leadership effectiveness is the one which focuses upon the variables most closely associated with such effectiveness. What can be said about the leadership process which may help us better to understand that which makes for leadership effectiveness?

Consistent with our definition of leadership, we feel that effectiveness in leadership is a function of the dynamic interrelationship of the personality characteristics of the leader, the personality characteristics of the follower, and the characteristics of the situation within the field of each individual.

We have already pointed out that the *situation* has a differential impact on both the leader and the follower as they interact. The *personality of the follower* (as it manifests itself in a given situation) becomes a key variable with which the leader must deal. The needs, attitudes, values, and feelings of the follower determine the kinds of stimuli produced by the leader to which the follower will respond. The *personality of the leader* (also manifesting itself in a situation) influences his range of perception of follower and situation, his judgment of what is relevant among these perceptions, and thence his sensitivity to the personality of the follower and to the situation. The leader's personality also has impact on his behavioral repertory (action flexibility) and on his skill in selecting appropriate communication behaviors.

Notes

1. The evolution of the frame of reference proposed in this chapter cannot be attributed to any one individual; rather, most persons who have been members of the Human Relations Research Group, Institute of Industrial Relations and School of Business Administration, UCLA, during the past few years have played a significant role in its development. These persons, in addition to the present authors, are Paula Brown, Raymond Ezekiel, Arnold Gebel, Murray Kahane, Verne Kallejian, Gertrude Peterson, Clovis and Pat Shepherd, Eugene Talbot, and Irving R. Wechsler.
2. Alvin W. Gouldner (ed.), *Studies in Leadership* (New York: Harper & Brothers, 1950), pp. 31–35, especially p. 34.
3. See Ralph M. Stogdill, "Personal Factors Associated with Leadership: A Survey of the Literature," *Journal of Psychology*, vol. 25, p. 63, January, 1948.
4. For example, see Fillmore H. Sanford, *Authoritarianism and Leadership* (Philadelphia: Institute for Research in Human Relations, 1950), chap. 1.
5. See Stogdill, *Leadership;* Gouldner, *Leadership* (Introduction); William D. Jenkins, "A Review of Leadership Studies with Particular Reference to Military Problems," *Psychological Bulletin*, vol. 44, pp. 54–79, January, 1947; Fillmore H. Sanford, "Research in Military Leadership," in his *Current Trends: Psychology in the World Emergency* (Pittsburgh: University of Pittsburgh Press, 1952), pp. 45–59.
6. Sanford, "Research in Military Leadership," p. 60.
7. Essentially, our definition subsumes definitions 1B, 1C, and 1E in the Ohio State "Paradigm for the Study of Leadership," all of which have to do with influence. The Ohio State definitions follow:

    "1B. (The leader is the) individual who exercises positive influence acts upon others.

    "1C. (The leader is the) individual who exercises more, or more important, positive influence acts than any other member in the group.

    "1E. (The leader is the) individual who exercises most influence in goal-setting and goal-achievement."

    See Richard T. Morris and Melvin Seeman, "The Problem of Leadership: An Interdisciplinary Approach," *American Journal of Sociology*, vol. 56, no. 2, p. 151, September, 1950. Reasons for our use of *situation* rather than *a situation* are presented on page 26.
8. For a relevant discussion of power, see D. Cartwright, *Toward a Social Psychology of Groups: The Concept of Power*, presidential address delivered before the Society for the Psychological Study of Social Issues, Cleveland, Ohio, Sept. 5, 1953, p. 19. Mimeographed.
9. For varying views of "situation," see Daniel Bell, " 'Screening' Leaders in a Democracy," *Commentary*, vol. 5, no. 4, pp. 368–375, April, 1948; Gouldner, *Leadership;* J. K. Hemphill, *Situational Factors in Leadership*, The Ohio State University Studies, Bureau of Educational Research Monograph no. 32 (Columbus: The Ohio State University, 1949); Jenkins, *Leadership;* Paul Pigors, *Leadership or Domination* (Boston: Houghton Mifflin Company, 1935); Sanford, *Authoritarianism and Leadership;* Melvin Seeman, "Role Conflict and Ambivalence in Leadership," *American Sociological Review*, vol. 18, pp. 373–380, August, 1953; Stogdill, *Leadership*.

10. For two excellent discussions of the communication process, see Franklin Fearing, "Toward a Psychological Theory of Human Communication," *Journal of Personality,* vol. 22, pp. 71–88, September, 1953; Wendell Johnson, "The Fateful Process of Mr. A. Talking to Mr. B.," *Harvard Business Review,* vol. 31, pp. 49–56, January-February, 1953.

11. See, for example, Carl R. Rogers, *Client-centered Therapy* (Boston: Houghton Mifflin Company, 1951); and Thomas Gordon, *Group-centered Leadership* (Boston: Houghton Mifflin Company, 1955). No selflessness on the part of the leader is implied. His need satisfaction comes through remuneration for his services and/or gratification from serving others.

Leading in Organizational Groups

Robert L. Husband

People lead. They lead in corporations, small informal groups, community committees, church programs, educational activities, and international affairs. Their role of leader may involve nothing more than calling a meeting to order, or it could entail high-level decisions which affect the lives of millions. Regardless of the level, leadership and its outcomes have been socially and emotionally powerful issues for hundreds of years.

But what is leadership and how do people attempt to lead? Do different people tend to lead differently? And, what does the group or situation have to say about how leaders lead? These questions serve as a central focus of this essay. Hopefully, as we attempt to answer them we will gain both a better understanding of organizational leadership, in general, and, more specifically, how people attempt to lead organizational groups.

Within the first section of the essay some general ideas about the concept of leadership will be developed. In addition, the major dimensions which have traditionally been used to make distinctions about how people lead differently will be discussed. The second part of the essay will be devoted to developing a typology of organizational leadership behavior which integrates these underlying dimensions of leadership. Finally, the personal and organizational implications of these different types or styles of organizational leadership will be discussed.

Leadership: What It Is and What It Isn't

Determining exactly what leadership *is* has been no small task. In fact, one of the major problems in studying leadership has been trying to define the terms "leader" and "leadership". As early as 1949 there were at least 130 different definitions of these two terms cited in the social sciences.[1] Although many attempts have been made to create common definitions or at least classify the various definitions into broad categories, such efforts have usually been unsuccessful.

Perhaps the closest thing to a consensus on the definition of leadership is that it is a social influence process. Such a definition suggests at least two things. First, leadership is a process. It is not a set of personality characteristics (traits) or a collection of prescribed behaviors (roles) that somehow operate independent of the responses of the follower or the situation. Leadership

This original essay appears here in print for the first time. All rights reserved. Permission to reprint must be obtained from the publisher and the author. Robert L. Husband is affiliated with the Department of Speech Communication, University of Illinois at Urbana-Champaign.

occurs in the interpersonal interaction between a leader and the led. It is a transaction negotiated by the leader and follower rather than a preestablished set of actions by the leader.

Moreover, leadership is a process that occurs over time. It is not a series of one-time acts or events. Any particular act or effort to influence others becomes a part of the cummulative influence efforts made by a leader over time. Although any given act or action may serve as a good indication of a person's leadership approach, it really becomes a part of the myriad of activities which take place over weeks, months and years. This is particularly true within organizational groups that have considerable histories and longevity. Hence, within leader-follower interactions, actions should never be viewed as isolated unrelated acts; but rather they must be seen as a part of a tapestry or pattern of behaviors.

Second, to define leadership as influence is to implicitly suggest the inherent nature of change as an aspect of leadership. To lead is to induce change. In general, we all want to believe that somehow leadership, in a group or organization, makes a difference. How often have we heard someone say, "Things will be different around here when we get some leadership". People expect leaders to bring about change, to get things done, to make things happen, to inspire, to motivate. To influence someone is to change them—their behavior, their attitude, their beliefs or their values. So central is this notion of change to our understanding of influence and leadership, that it is this idea of creating change that helps us most to distinguish "leading" from such allied concepts as "managing", "supervising", "directing" and "coordinating". One of the critical questions regarding leadership, then, is how do people try to institute change? Do they use brute force and demand change or do they attempt to persuade and cajole people into change?

Leadership Styles and Types

Recognizing leadership as a social influence process still leaves unanswered the question of how people go about trying to lead or influence others. Of the little we know about leadership, the idea that people tend to prefer and rely upon relatively consistent patterns of behavior, or styles, in leading is fairly well established.[2] By styles, we mean the consistent and stable patterns of actions individuals use over time when they are leading a group or organizational unit. When these styles are observed to be used by a variety of leaders across many different situations they are called types.

Being human, we are creatures of habit and training. Even though we can be very spontaneous and creative in relating to others, all of us fall back upon regular patterns of behavior. These patterns reflect our values and beliefs about others and the way the world operates. They also reveal our need to assert control and maintain some degree of predictability within our lives. However, even though we fall back on these styles or behavioral patterns, which help them to become relatively consistent and stable, they are by no means invariant or unalterable.

Leadership styles, like all patterns of behavior, tend to vary in their degree of rigidity and flexibility. We can all think of leaders who have been very rigid (i.e., used one set of behaviors regardless of the situation) and others who have been very flexible (i.e., used a variety of behaviors) in their leadership activities. Leadership styles also change over time. Leaders may realize that particular patterns of behaviors are not working and decide to change to others, either temporarily or permanently. Or, they may decide to broaden their repertoire of leadership behaviors, in general, and use a variety of styles adapted to the situation.

The point is, to talk about leadership styles or types is not to suggest that we are talking about some fixed set of behaviors or actions that are predetermined and unchangeable. In fact, most recent research on leadership argues that leadership effectiveness is based on the flexible use of different styles in different situations and contexts.[3]

Some Underlying Dimensions of Leadership Styles

With rare exception, when leadership styles have been studied and identified, they have been rooted within one of three conceptual distinctions: 1) task/relationship, 2) directive/participative, and 3) power/influence. Over time, these distinctions have become the major underlying dimensions of various leadership styles and typologies.[4]

The dimension of "task-oriented" vs. "relationship-oriented" leadership is the most prominent and popular way of thinking about leadership styles, today. Based on early research on small groups, this distinction reflects the belief that there are two distinct sets of functions to be performed within small groups; namely, "task" functions and "social or group maintenance" functions.[5] From this small group perspective, leaders have been viewed as having psychological propensities toward one or the other of these two functions. That is, they have been seen as preferring to engage in activities which either attend to the tasks of a small group or activities which attend to maintaining harmonious relationships within the group.

By and large the "task" orientation of small group research is translated into a "positional or structural role" orientation in leadership studies at an organizational level. For example, the Ohio State Leadership Studies program, one of the most extensive research programs ever initiated on leadership in organizational settings, identified two main leadership dimensions: "initiating structure" and "consideration".[6] The latter is very similar to the social or relationship function in small group research. However, the former dimension makes a significant shift away from a "task" orientation to a "structural" orientation. Within this perspective, leaders are said to work more at clarifying and defining the structure in which followers work than they do at actually accomplishing the task. They create or "initiate" this structure for the follower by establishing well-defined patterns of organization, detailing channels of communication and determining policies and procedures for getting the job done.

One explanation for such a move may be the distinctly different character of leadership in large, complex, often bureaucratic organizations. In these organizations, individuals who are designated to provide leadership frequently do not work on specific tasks themselves. They manage or supervise those that do. Hence, their role is to facilitate the process of getting the task accomplished. For them, the task becomes the process and the process becomes the task. Hence, task and process become fused; inseparably linked. Often, this results in an emphasis, not necessarily upon doing the right job, but upon doing the job "right". That is, according to the proper policy and procedures.

Another major dimension which has served as a basis for determining different leadership styles has been the degree to which leaders permit followers to participate in decision-making and other group processes. Having its genesis in the early autocratic, democratic, and laisse-faire concepts of leadership;[7] those who follow this tradition tend to distinguish leadership styles based on the relative degree of leader and follower influence over group processes, in particular, decision-making. At one end, are the autocratic leaders who have a style that is very directive in which they control all the decisions for a group. While at the other end, are the laisse-faire leaders who are very nondirective and give over all the decision-making responsibility to the followers. Obviously, somewhere in the middle are the democratic leaders who maintain a balance of leader control and follower participation in group processes.

In recent years this notion has resurfaced within the concept of decision-centralization.[8] When leaders exert complete control over decision-making and permit little participation among followers they are said to centralize their decision-making and have a very controlling style. On the other hand, if they encourage significant participation and afford followers great latitude in decision-making, their style is said to be participative with highly decentralized decision-making.

A final dimension underlying leadership styles is that of social power. The concepts of power and social influence have been closely linked. So have the concepts of social influence and leadership. Yet, interestingly enough, the specific relationship between power and leadership has been ambiguously established at best. Many have acknowledged power to be a central concept in discussing leadership, but few have attempted to clarify the exact relationship between power and leader behavior.

One of the problems appears to be with the power concept itself. Power has most often been defined as the potential to influence others. People are said to have power over others if they are able to exert influence over them. The natural corollary of this position is that people who exert influence over others are said to have power over them. This perspective treats power and influence as two parts of the same process. One is a potential (power), the other is an outcome (influence).

Another way of thinking about power and influence, however, is to see them as two different and separate means or vehicles for inducing change. Leaders have a variety of means available to them to induce change in followers. We can really divide all of these different means into two categories. The first is composed of those means which are made available to leaders by the organization or system in which they operate. Such means are usually embedded in the role or position a leader occupies in the system. They include the leader's legitimate right to coerce, require, reprimand, withhold, reward and punish by virtue of his or her status, or position within the organization. In short, leaders in organizations are given the privilege or opportunity to control external or situational variables which are important to followers. This is said to be power.

It is important to reiterate that power is embedded in the social fabric of organizational life. It is inherently tied to the social system in which individuals act, *not* the individuals themselves. People have power because of their position in a social system. Think of your earlier school years. Were not fourth graders more "powerful" than third graders, and who dared challenge the "power" of seniors? Clearly, it was their "position" in relation to those lower in the social system that gave them their power. For leaders and members of organizations, the focal point of this power is the formal position they hold in organizational groups. Certain positions (frequently referred to as leadership positions) simply offer individuals greater resources and control over rewards and sanctions.

The other set of means available to leaders when they attempt to induce change are those based on the personal characteristics of the leader and the interpersonal relationships he or she establishes with others, person-to-person. Most people implicitly conceive of these means constellating around the term influence. Influence distinguishes itself from power in that it is not embedded in the social system. On the contrary, it is exclusively and directly tied to the personal relationships which develop between leaders and followers. It is built upon the leader's ability to understand and respond to the social psychological character of others; their needs, motivations, and goals. In the end, influence does not rely on the roles, rules, or structure of the social system, but upon

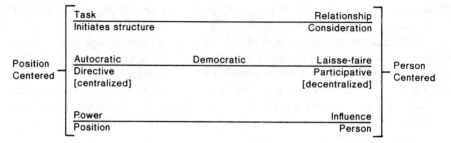

Figure 1. Underlying dimensions of leadership styles.

the personal and relational characteristics of the leader. People are said to have influence when others have consciously or unconsciously chosen to permit them to affect their lives.

Figure 1 depicts, on separate continua, the three different distinctions discussed above.

Why spend so much time on these different distinctions? One reason is that these dimensions serve, so widely, as the basis for most discussions on leadership styles and types. Therefore, it is simply important to know them. Another reason is that most typologies of leadership styles rely upon just one of the underlying dimensions rather than examining all three simultaneously. For example, a currently popular typology is Paul Hersey and Kenneth H. Blanchard's model of four leadership styles: Telling, Selling, Participating, Delegating.[9] These leadership styles are based on the "task/relationship" distinction outlined above. As a result of relying upon just one dimension, we often blur or confuse the different distinctions, treat them as synonymous, or even worse, simply ignore that there may be important differences between them when developing our models of leadership styles.

Four Organizational Leadership Types

If we try not to ignore any of these prominent dimensions underlying different patterns of leadership behavior, what kind of typology of leadership styles might be developed? And, how might the different dimensions fit together to form different types of leadership behavior. These are the questions that were asked when a set of organizational leaders were observed for over 300 hours.[10] The findings proved very interesting. They generated a typology of four distinct types of organizational leadership styles.

As you read through the following typology see if you can determine how each type reflects the different dimensions outlined in the previous section. In addition, it may be helpful in more fully understanding the typology to think of leaders in your own past who fit these different types. One last thing. You might want to ask yourself the question, "Which type am I?" Or at least, "Do any of these come close to how I see myself as a leader?"

The Positional Leader

There is a type of organizational leader who relies almost exclusively upon his or her position within the organization to provide leadership. These leaders, which we refer to here as *positional leaders,* spend most of their time and attention while interacting with others on the tasks and roles which must be performed both by themselves and by other group members. Tasks and, even more importantly, roles become the major avenue through which the leader relates to group members. These leaders, particularly in formal organizational groups, like to be identified by title and prefer to maintain a relationship with their subordinates that is highly professional and primarily impersonal. It is not uncommon to hear this type of leader say, "I never get too close to my staff, it's not a good idea" or "There's no reason to get too close to others in this group, they've got a job to do and so do I."

Positional leaders like to exert direct control over subordinates, and do so by relying upon rules, procedures and organizational structure. For example, these leaders in maintaining very centralized operations (a common feature of positional leadership) often set up elaborate committee structures and create an inordinate number of policies and procedures for getting things done. In small organizational work groups this same orientation is more readily visible through the positional leader's tendency to organize tasks, set deadlines and give out assignments without much consultation with group members.

Most often, positional leaders, are very directive and even autocratic in their communication behavior. For instance, they tend to be very directive in leading meetings. When positional leaders are running meetings there is very little toleration for chit-chat or casual conversation. Positional leaders, in general, display limited patience for nonbusiness communication during meetings. Indeed, one way of identifying positional leaders in formal organizational groups is that they are "all business".

Moreover, regarding communication, positional leaders use communication to get the job done. They have an explicit purpose in communicating which is primarily to get the task accomplished. Positional leaders, as a result, maintain a very limited view of the role of communication in leading. For them, it is primarily a highly utilitarian and unidirectional activity. It also should occur within a rule-governed and role-bound context. That is, positional leaders tend to set and follow rules and expect others to do likewise. It would not be uncommon to hear a positional leader state, "You need to use the proper channels if you want to communicate with me." They also expect others to understand and stay within their proper roles when they communicate. In short, positional leaders expect others to "know their place" and stay in it.

The power residing in the managerial position is the major source of control and the achievement of organizational goals for positional leaders. These leaders rarely attempt to establish strong interpersonal relationships with followers. As a result, there is usually not a sufficiently developed relationship to afford them any direct nonrole related influence over the follower. This becomes compounded by the frequent use of role or position-oriented communication with subordinates which maintains strong role identities.

"I am the boss, you are the subordinate. Let's not forget that, okay?".

The Political Leader

The most striking characteristic of political leaders, a second type of organizational leader, is their combined concern for exerting direct control over group activities while at the same time maintaining strong interpersonal relationships with group members. At first this may seem like the ideal form of leadership. Here is a person who wants to get the job done, but is also interested in the interpersonal harmony. The potential problem with this type of leadership is that the leader so strongly wants to control the outcomes of work group activities that he or she is not beyond using or manipulating interpersonal relationships to achieve such control. When taken to the extremes this type of leadership can be very devious, devisive and harmful to the organizational work group.

In their desire to exert high control political leaders are very much like positional leaders. But whereas the positional leader exerts control through well-defined procedures, structures, rules and regulations, the political leader's efforts to control are primarily directed through the manipulation of interpersonal relationships. Political leaders see themselves as highly relationship oriented. They take considerable pains to establish, develop and nurture strong interpersonal relationships with others. They, unlike the positional leader who tends to relate to subordinates in more formal, impersonal and role-bound patterns, usually foster highly personal relationships with subordinates; sometimes almost possessive relationships. Things are treated and taken as personal by the political leader.

In small organizational work groups, political leaders operate in very personable, informal and interpersonally sensitive ways. At the same time, it is clearly evident that they want to have some direct hand in controlling or directing the group's activities. Most often they will attempt to exert this control not by encouraging the development of formal procedures, rules or structures, but more by informally convincing and persuading others toward their point of view.

Political leaders tend to view communication as an interpersonal exchange. Its primary purposes are to establish strong interpersonal work relationships and to exert control in interpersonal situations. Political leaders tend to talk longer, louder, more often and in more declarative-assertive ways in groups. They also use communication to create a highly personal context in which to operate. In this regard, it is not uncommon for political leaders to use highly possessive and even familial terminology. The ultimate and classic example of a political style of leadership is portrayed in the movie, *The Godfather*. A depiction of the Mafia, a multimillion dollar organization, the Godfather, or the "Don", is the head of the "family" and those who work for the organization are members of the "family".

This orientation toward both high control and highly personal relationship-centered communication often creates conflicting images of the political leader. Direct subordinates frequently view these leaders as warm, caring, and considerate. In many situations, political leaders commonly have the most loyal and dedicated followers among any of the leadership types. Peers and colleagues, on the other hand, regularly see them to be manipulative, devious, demanding, overbearing and not to be trusted. It is not uncommon to hear said about a political leader, "There he goes again, working the crowd!". Political leaders do spend considerable energy and effort managing the impressions others have of them within the organization.

In general, political leaders' use of power or influence to gain or maintain control is difficult to ascertain. Although they are not at all opposed to using the power available to them through their position, and indeed in most cases do, their highly personal style tends to cloud or disguise both references to their position and even more blatant power strategies.

The Administrative Leader

Administrative leaders are best identified by their commitment to activities which "get the job done" while at the same time encouraging participation by subordinates in a variety of organizational group processes. Much like positional leaders, administrative leaders work at the organizational demands of their role. They develop well defined operations, are organized, efficient, and tend to focus on work related tasks and responsibilities. In essence, they attend to the details of the job along with trying to maintain a positive relationship with group members.

However, administrative leaders are usually not seen by others as highly relationship-oriented people. It is not that they dislike or engender negative feelings among others, they merely are not viewed as extremely personal or intensely interpersonal in work relationships, like the political leader might be for example. Yet, they are not "all business" like the positional leader, either. Their interpersonal communication with others tends to center mainly on work related issues and responsibilities.

Much of what places administrative leaders somewhere between positional and political leaders regarding their interpersonal relationships with others is the manner in which they communicate. Administrative leaders tend to encourage discussion of work related issues among subordinates. During group meetings, they ask questions and invite extensive participation. They seem to genuinely care about what others think on issues and communicate that care by soliciting opinions and listening. On the other hand, they spend little time drawing out others' feelings about issues, or discussing how given decisions and activities might affect others personally. In small organizational work groups, the administrative leader comes across as very efficient, interested in others' opinions, but highly task-oriented.

The key to understanding administrative leaders is that, although they are concerned about seeing the task accomplished, they are equally concerned about maintaining a high level of group participation in decision-making and other group processes. These leaders tend to be quite decentralized in their office operations and evidence little need to directly control group members or their activities as long as people "stay on task". Their concern for high participation by other group members should not be confused, though, with a more generalized relationship orientation. Administrative leaders do not necessarily foster strong interpersonal relationships with subordinates, particularly in the work setting. However, their lessened need for direct control over the decisions and activities of others causes them to be viewed as at least concerned about people. To the degree that they give group members increased autonomy and encourage them to participate they are perceived as person-centered.

In general, administrative leaders rely upon personal influence as a means of inducing change and exerting control in a work situation. As a result of giving subordinates significant latitude in decision-making and other group processes, these leaders establish fairly solid interpersonal relationships which in turn serve as a basis or vehicle for inducing change. Moreover, because administrative leaders demonstrate a commitment to independent thinking and egalitarianism they are much more inclined to try to persuade and convince followers toward a new direction than simply force them toward it. However, administrative leaders are not opposed to openly using the power of their position, and frequently do so if it is necessary to get the job done.

The Relational Leader

Relational leaders are characterized by behavior patterns which emphasize both strong personal relationships with group members and encourage a high degree of participation by others in group processes. By far and away, the most noticeable characteristic of relational leaders is the intense person-centeredness of their activities. These leaders, more than any other, express openly and consistently their concern for the happiness and well-being of their subordinates. Group member satisfaction and group cohesion are central issues for the relational leader.

A considerable amount of relational leaders' communication is devoted to reducing "distance" between themselves and other group members. They view communication as highly interpersonal and attend primarily to its relational aspects. They seek wherever possible to create a warm affective environment. They are highly person-centered in how they communicate with others. To a degree, they are very similar to the political leader in their commitment to personal relationships. The one major difference is that their person-centeredness lacks the utilitarian quality of the political leader. Relational leaders simply do not appear to have a need to direct and control the activities of the work group like the political leader.

In small organizational work groups the relational leader will attend primarily to group maintenance or social emotional functions of the group. For example, they are less concerned with specific task accomplishment than they are with group member satisfaction. One relational leader offered a reason for his best staff meeting of the year by commenting, "My staff really opened up and talked. For three hours. We never even got around to the items we needed to discuss." Meetings led by relational leaders will usually be quite informal, almost casual, with considerable discussion about the feelings and concerns of group members. This stands in stark contrast to the positional leader whose meetings are much more formal and devoted to information dissemination.

Relational leaders are seen as warm, supportive and considerate toward group members. They also tend to be viewed by colleagues and peers as supportive and interpersonally sensitive to others. They do not, by and large, attend to activities which initiate structure in the work environment. For example, relational leaders do not place much of a priority on deadlines, reports, and organizational details; or as one leader graphically described it, "I'm not very good at moving the trash". This is not to say that they are disorganized or fail to accomplish tasks. It is just that accomplishing organizational tasks tends not to be their highest priority in leading.

Personal influence, with rare exception, is the major means relational leaders use to exert control. In fact, relational leaders often reject the power inherent in their position as either bad or unavailable. Indeed, they often find

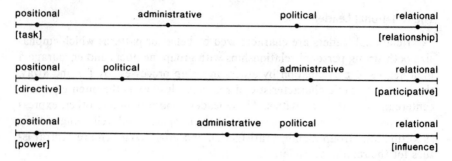

Figure 2. The four leadership types across the three different underlying dimensions.

their formal position as interfering with their ability to establish desired relationships with subordinates. For example, it would not be uncommon to hear a relational leader declare, "You know my position as supervisor simply gets in the way of me being effective with my subordinates." Or, "We just don't have any power, not *real* power!" It would seem important to point out here, that frequently these types of leaders, because of their rejection of the position they hold, become the most frustrated, disillusioned and alienated of the four different types, when confronted with the concrete, impersonal, and political nature of large bureaucratic organizations.

In summary, we have explored four types of leaders that can be found in organizational work groups. They vary according to: 1) their commitment to people or tasks; 2) the amount of direct control they seek to exert over others which is evidenced in the amount of participation they afford subordinates in group processes; and 3) their preference for power or influence as a means of exerting control. Figure 2 is designed to help more clearly differentiate the different leadership types along these different dimensions.

Implications

What is to be gained from the above typology? At the very least, it provides a way of thinking about the different patterns of leadership behavior that people use in organizational groups. The patterns are painted in sufficiently large brush strokes to make them relatively easy to identify. They also do not degenerate into a massive laundry list of leadership behaviors. Yet, at the same time, the four different types maintain the distinctiveness of some very important dimensions underlying organizational leadership behavior that often get treated as either synonymous or mutually exclusive. Resultingly, the typology should be both manageable and meaningful.

It also offers some rather simple, but different ideas about the concepts of power and influence. Power is inherent in the position the leader occupies in the organization. Influence is tied to the leader's personal ability to develop and nurture interpersonal relationships. The four different types of leadership suggest that people prefer, and are able to use more skillfully, one or the other in trying to exert control in group activities. Interestingly enough, however, because of the other dimensions underlying leadership styles the differential use of power or influence is not always readily visible.

On a more personal note, the typology should help us to understand how others attempt to lead and why they lead differently. It may also give us an insight into understanding our own leadership activities. To know where others are "coming from," or for that matter, where we ourselves are "coming from", is no small feat. It is an advantage in organizational life, of some significance, to be able to recognize and anticipate how and why others act the way they do. Such recognition and anticipation clearly gives us an edge in our work relationships.

Beyond these possible personal benefits of understanding the four different types or patterns of organizational leadership, it may be helpful to conclude with some general speculations about how this typology might be manifest in different organizational settings and at different organizational levels. This kind of speculating rests on the assumption that organizations—their structures, cultures, roles, and processes—shape and condition in some manner the character of leadership enacted within them. Such an assumption seems not only safe, but reasonable.

In essence, different types of organizations can be expected to encourage different leadership behaviors, if not in type at least in degree. To illustrate, could we not easily envision that a certain type of leadership, such as positional leadership, might be more strongly encouraged and reinforced in the Armed Forces than, let's say, a human service organization? Similarly, would we not expect human service organizations to generally foster more relational types of leadership?

Such alignments are not only possible, but highly plausible and can serve in some situations as a good "rule of thumb." However, we must be duly cautious in too quickly making these kinds of inferences. For example, to assume that because I tend to be a relational leader, I would be well suited for a leadership role in a human services organization may lead to frustration, disappointment and disillusionment. In fact, this is exactly what happened to several of the organizational leaders we studied.

What we discover is that organizations, in general, tend to pull leaders away from the extremes of positional and relational leadership. These extreme patterns of behavior tend to be modified to achieve greater effectiveness within specific organizational contexts. For instance, extreme forms of relational behavior are likely to be modified by organizational supervisors who want the job to get done. On the other hand, highly positional behaviors are likely to be modified in the direction of increased relational sensitivity through pressure from subordinates. The latter, generally, tends to happen less frequently and to less of a degree than the former.

Regarding organizational level, it appears that political leaders tend to rise more frequently up the organizational hierarchy and tend to occupy more positions at or near the top. To some degree this may be the result of their successful efforts at managing others' impressions of them. More likely, it is the outcome of a combination of things. First, political leaders tend to be much more aware of the "internal politics" of the organization. Accordingly, they recognize the connections which need to be made and the activities to avoid in moving toward the top. Second, they spend considerably more time and energy establishing both their power and influence bases within the organization. Hence, not only do they recognize the important "connections", but they have become strongly connected. Finally, political leaders that do move up the organization seem to be able to accomplish the tasks that are required, while at the same time engendering support through strong interpersonal relationships from above and below them.

Whether it is more important to understand the implications of the different types of leadership at a personal level or at an organizational level remains up to the reader to decide. Certainly, being more informed as to the general patterns people use in attempting to lead and the implications of these patterns for organizational success is valuable at both levels. Possibly, the most important conclusion to be drawn is captured best in the age old adage, "To be forewarned, is to be forearmed."

Notes

1. See Bernard M. Bass, *Leadership, Psychology and Organizational Behavior* (West Port, Conn: Greenwood Press, 1960).
2. Bernard M. Bass's updated review, *Stogdill's Handbook of Leadership* (New York: Free Press, 1981) and Gary Yukl's *Leadership in Organizations* (Englewood Cliffs, NJ: Prentice-Hall, 1981) most clearly summarize the work which has been done on leadership styles.
3. Paul Hersey and Kenneth Blanchard make this argument most cogently in their text, *Management of Organizational Behavior, 4th ed.,* (Englewood Cliffs, NJ: Prentice-Hall, 1982) which has now become highly popularized in Blanchard's, *The One-Minute Manager* (New York: Berkley Books, 1982).
4. The best single source for a discussion of all the different typologies of leadership styles is Bernard Bass, *Stogdill's Handbook of Leadership,* (New York: Free Press, 1981).
5. Early research programs by Robert F. Bales, R. F. Bales, *Interaction process analysis* (Reading, MA: Addison-Wesley, 1950), "Task roles and social roles in problem-solving groups". In E. E. MacCoby, T. M. Newcomb, & E. L. Hartley (eds.), *Readings in social psychology* (New York: Holt, Rhinehart & Winston, 1958); and L. F. Carter and his associates, L. F. Carter, W. Haythorn, B. Shriver, & J. T. Lanzetta, "The behavior of leaders and other group members". *Journal of Abnormal Social Psychology, 46,* (1951), 589–595, and L. F. Carter, "Leadership and small group behavior". In M. Sherif & M. O. Wilson (eds.), *Group relations at the crossroads* (New York: Harper, 1953) initiated this distinction.

6. The two best reviews and summaries of research employing these dimensions, besides *Stogdill's Handbook on Leadership,* are Andrew Korman, "Consideration, initiating structure, and organizational criteria—A review," *Personnel Psychology, 19,* (1966), 349–61; and Edwin A. Fleishman, "Twenty years of consideration and structure". In *Current Developments in the Study of Leadership,* Edwin A. Fleishman & James G. Hunt (eds.), (Carbondale, IL: Southern Illinois Press, 1973).

7. This distinction was first made for research purposes by Kurt Lewin, Ronald Lippitt and Ralph White, "Patterns of Aggressive Behavior in Experimentally Created Social Climates," *Journal of Social Psychology, 10,* (1939), 114–33.

8. See, for examples, Frank Heller and Gary Yukl, "Participation, Managerial Decision-making, and Situation Variables," *Organizational Behavior and Human Performance, 4,* (1969), 114–33; Gary Yukl, "Toward a Behavioral Theory of Leadership," *Organizational Behavior and Human Performance 6,* (1971), 414–40; and Gary Yukl, *Leadership in Organizations* (Englewood Cliffs, NJ: Prentice-Hall, 1981).

9. For a detailed discussion of this model see Paul Hersey and Kenneth H. Blanchard, *Management of Organizational Behavior: Utilizing Human Resources, 4th ed.,* (Englewood Cliffs, NJ: Prentice-Hall, 1982).

10. See Robert L. Husband, "Toward a Grounded Typology or Organizational Leadership Behavior," *Quarterly Journal of Speech, 71,* (1985), 103–118.

Styles of Leadership

James F. Kinder

Many of us take leadership for granted and yet it is essential to business, government and the voluntary organizations that shape the way we live, work and play.

Each one of us is some way involved in leading others whether we happen to be the Prime Minister, president of our own company, chairman of a voluntary committee, or head of a family. The problems of leadership are important whether we have many subordinates, one subordinate or whether we are trying to influence members of our peer group.

Leadership is more than an appointed position—it's more than the personal qualities of the leader—it's more than just having authority over someone. Leadership is the process of influencing others so that they, along with you, reach a mutually acceptable goal in a way that is satisfying to all.

Implied in the discussion of leadership are motives of the leader. Presumably a leader is interested in influencing others, in striving for effective results and in providing achievement satisfaction for himself and others.

The concept of leadership is usually analyzed in terms of the leader, those whom he is leading, and the situation in which leadership takes place. Our discussion focuses on the behavior of the leader and the reaction of the followers to his behavior.

Our focus then is on behavior: the behavior of the leader as it is *seen* by the persons he is leading. The key word here is *seen*. All of us tend to react to others in terms of the behavior which we observe. We do not usually make allowances for behavior which is unacceptable to us unless we have known an individual over many years, and most of our work associations are of relatively short duration. We interact with others in terms of observable behavior. As a subordinate I am concerned with *what* you do to me, not in what you *intended* to do.

In the study of leadership it is important then that we analyze various types of behavior initiated by the leader or to put it another way—the analysis of leadership styles.

A helpful way of identifying leadership styles is through the use of a behavioral model. For example, one of the earliest models portrays the implications of the use of democratic as opposed to autocratic leadership. Other

Reprinted by permission of James F. Kinder and the *Canadian Personnel Journal*, May 1971, pp. 35–41. James F. Kinder is a business management consultant.

models combine a leader's concern for production and his concern for people and describe four or five leadership styles.

There are many behavioral analysis models but all have one thing in common—they are concerned with how a leader gets the job done and how he handles people in getting that job done.

Lawrence Appley, retired President of the American Management Association once said that the world is composed of four kinds of people:

☐ those who make things happen
☐ those to whom things happen
☐ those who watch things happen
☐ those who do not even know that things are happening

This is one way of indicating that various "styles" of behavior exist.

The model to be used in our discussion combines four basic behavioral traits—Dominance, Submission, Warmth and Hostility. It may be shown visually this way:

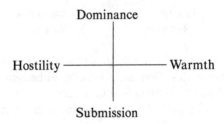

The evidence of dominance is shown by a person who leads, advises, directs, initiates, takes over situations, organizes, believes in structure, volunteers, and generally takes responsibility.

A person who is submissive is willing to accept others' leadership and guidance. In fact, he enjoys following others and tends to be a low risk-taker. In situations that require leadership he tends to nominate others for the task.

Individuals who show warmth have a genuine concern for others. They tend to be confident, friendly, approachable, cheerful, have a sense of humor and, on occasion, can be self-sacrificing.

Hostile individuals tend to be cold, indifferent, competitive and intolerant of other people's ideas. A hostile person is self-centered, does not listen to others and has very little sense of humor.

Using the four basic behavioral traits we can identify four leadership styles in our model.

An individual who combines the traits of dominance and hostility we call Dominant-Hostile and identify with the symbol L1.

The other three styles may be identified as follows:

Submissive-Hostile	—L2
Submissive-Warm	—L4
Dominant-Warm	—L3

The symbols L1, L2, L3 and L4 are useful to us in discussing the implications of the model. They are useful in the sense that we can establish almost instant understanding of the type of behavior we are seeking to understand.

Our model can now be shown as follows:

Dominant- Hostile		Dominant- Warm
L1		L3
L2		L4
Submissive- Hostile		Submissive- Warm

The style model we are using implies that all behavior may be analyzed in four separate categories: Dominant-Hostile, Submissive-Hostile, Submissive-Warm, and Dominant-Warm and that each of us fits neatly into one of the categories. Unfortunately human behavior is much more complex than this.

For example—a person who is usually Dominant-Warm will at times show evidence of submissiveness and/or hostility. Sometimes the submissive worm turns and shows flashes of leadership. On occasion the hostile person will show warmth toward certain people.

The point is that behavior should be analyzed in terms of what is happening in the current situation, not that a certain style once identified will always be used.

The purpose of behavior analysis through a style model is not to categorize but to be able to recognize here-and-now behavior in understandable terms.

With this purpose in mind, it might be helpful to illustrate briefly how the four styles may be recognized.

L1. Dominant-Hostile

The Dominant-Hostile leader is usually perceived as one who puts the immediate task above all other considerations. He is ineffective in that he makes it obvious that he has no concern for others' feelings and has little confidence in the efforts of other people. While this attitude promotes fear it also produces dislike and thus people are motivated to work only when the Dominant-Hostile is present. The Dominant-Hostile cannot understand why so many people are uncooperative; he does not fully realize that cooperation to him means doing it his way.

Further understanding may be achieved by considering the leader's action in handling certain managerial situations.

For example:

Control of Work Assignments
"Do it this way and do not change it unless you check with me."

Mistakes Made by Others
"Who is responsible for this?"

Decision Making
"My mind is already made up; do not confuse me with facts."

Attitude to Meetings
"Committees are a waste of time, the fastest way to get things done is to do it yourself."

Attitude to Suggestions Made by Others
"We tried that before and it does not work."

L2. Submissive-Hostile

The Submissive-Hostile leader is seen as one who often shows his lack of interest in both task and relationships. He is less effective not only because of his lack of interest but also because of his effect on others' morale. He may be seen not only as shirking his own duties but also as hindering the performance of others through intervention or by withholding information.

Likely to be resistant to change or accepts change and then sabotages it—withholds information, aims at minimum output, impedes others, lowers morale.

Control of Work Assignments
"I don't care how you do it, as long as it's done."

Mistakes Made by Others
"Forget it—we all make mistakes."

Decision Making
"It's entirely up to you."

Attitude to Meetings
"Another meeting!—let's get it over with as soon as possible."

Attitude to Suggestions Made by Others
"Good idea. I'll pass it on to Bill."

L4. Submissive-Warm

The Submissive-Warm leader is basically a kindly soul who puts happy relationships above all other considerations. He is ineffective because his desire to see himself and be seen as a "good guy" prevents him from risking even mild disagreement in order to improve production.

He believes that happy people produce more and that production is less important than good fellowship. He strives to create a warm, pleasant, social atmosphere where an easygoing work tempo may be maintained.

He spends much of his time trying to find ways to make things easier for his people.

Control of Work Assignments
"How are things going, Charlie?"

Mistakes Made by Others
"Ah! forget it, we all make mistakes; better luck next time."

Decision Making
"I had nothing to do with the decision but it seems fair so I think we should go along with it."

Attitude to Meetings
"Yeh, the meeting may not accomplish much but it gives all of us an opportunity to get to know each other better."

Attitude to Suggestions Made by Others
"Wonderful idea, Joe, never thought of doing it that way. I'll discuss it with the others."

L3. Dominant-Warm

The Dominant-Warm leader is perceived as one who seeks his main task as maximizing the effort of others toward both short and long term goals. He sets high standards for production and performance but recognizes that because of individual differences he will have to treat everyone a little differently. He is effective, in that his commitment to both task and people is evident to all and acts as a powerful motivating force.

He welcomes disagreement and comment as they relate to the task. He sees such behavior as necessary, normal and appropriate.

He believes that differences can be worked through, that conflict can be resolved, and that commitment will result.

Control of Work Assignments
"Go ahead, Bill, I'll keep in touch to see if I can be helpful if you run into difficulty."

Mistakes Made by Others
"Let's see if we can determine *what* went wrong so it isn't likely to happen again."

Decision Making
"Let's discuss it before we proceed: I'd like your opinion."

Attitude to Meetings
"Tomorrow?—*great*, it will give us all an opportunity to express our views and decide on action."

Attitude to Suggestions Made by Others
"Sounds like a good idea; let's talk it over and see if it can be implemented."

A leader might ask himself—
What are some of the practical applications of behavior at work?
What does a study of behavior mean to me?
Is my leadership behavior consistent?
Is there a "best style" of leadership?
What are my assumptions about people and how they work?
Can I really change my behavior?

The answers to some or all of these questions may be found in studying the model.

Research seems to indicate that we are basically consistent in our behavior and therefore we show a predominant style over a period of time. Our actions are a result of our value system about people and how work gets done. For example, if we believe that people are lazy, indifferent and irresponsible and therefore they will have to be pushed, coerced or ordered to do a job we will use a Dominant-Hostile style (L1).

There also seems to be some evidence that in most situations a style which involves others in planning and goal setting, that is, Dominant-Warm (L4), is the best style to use for effective results.

An understanding of behavior in style terms enables the leader to better understand the actions of others. For example, if a leader operates in a Dominant-Hostile fashion he should not be surprised if he gets either a Dominant-Hostile reaction or, worse still, a Submissive-Hostile attitude.

No behavior change in either the leader or the subordinate can take place until there is some understanding of what behavior choice is available; until there is some understanding of the results of a behavior choice; until there is some belief that by changing behavior a more effective result will be achieved.

In our society we tend to over-complicate issues and leadership is no exception. There have been guidelines in the past on good leadership practice. One of the best was stated by Lao-Tzu, a Chinese philosopher in the 6th Century, B.C. It is entitled "The Way of Life According to Lao-Tzu" and goes like this:

"A leader is best
When people barely know that he ex-
*   ists,*
Not so good when people obey and
*   acclaim him,*
Worst when they despise him.
Fail to honor people,
They fail to honor you;
But of a good leader, who talks little,
When his work is done, his aim ful-
*   filled,*
They will all say, "We did this our-
*   selves."*

A leadership style well worth adopting.

Adaptive Leadership and Nonverbal Displays of Status in Small Groups

Martin Remland

Is it possible to save our big companies? Sure, it's the easiest thing in the world. All we've got to have is a little leadership. Absolutely, there is a vacuum in corporate America now, a horrible leadership vacuum. We're turning out very bright, very able people who could have been incredible leaders, but they are manipulators, numbers guys. They destroy tens of thousands of jobs. Now we've got to change the emphasis, which we can do, and put it on leadership and building and making our companies competitive (H. Ross Perot, 1986, p. 62).

Before the 1950s, the study of leadership was limited to the simple notion that leaders are born and not made. Put simply, a good leader was thought to be someone who possessed certain traits such as intelligence, confidence, energy, initiative, and insight. But a more fruitful approach soon emerged which focused on what leaders do rather than on the kind of people they are. This approach, which allowed for the possibility that persons could be educated and trained to become leaders, involved an effort to isolate certain categories of behavior associated with the exercise of leadership. Most of this behavioral research found that leaders do some things that are task-oriented and other things that are people-oriented. Based on the early findings of the Ohio State Leadership Studies, group leaders would do the former in order to "initiate structure" in their work groups (i.e., assign duties, schedule meetings, set agendas, establish performance standards, impose decision making procedures, etc.) and they would do the latter in order to show "consideration" toward group members (i.e., actions that communicate friendship, respect, concern, and mutual trust).

In his call for more leadership, the noted entrepreneur, H. Ross Perot laments the consequences of failing to treat individuals in organizations with the respect to which they are entitled:

In many of our huge corporations we treat people like commodities. And people cannot be managed. Inventories can be managed, but people must be led. And when people are reacting to being treated improperly, they are not doing their best work. And when they're not doing their best work, our international competitors can beat us. That is the core of our problem. It's not robots, it's not technology, it's how we treat our people (Perot, p. 62).

There is little doubt that leaders who are considerate to the members of their group generally will be more effective than leaders who are inconsiderate (Stogdill, 1974). As a result, leaders often make some attempt to involve members of their work group in the decision making process. Indeed, encouraging individuals to participate in decision making and problem solving is an important way to demonstrate an interest in the unique contributions that can be made by persons at all levels within an organization. The use of "quality circles" in many organizations certainly attests to the concern of top management that individuals be treated with dignity and respect and that their input be taken seriously. Yet such efforts may fall far short, if they are not consistent with the leader's behavior in face-to-face contacts. In the final analysis, the people-oriented skills of any leader are sure to be tested in each of these encounters, where impressions are continually shaped and reshaped.

An important component of face-to-face interaction, and a topic that has gained a great deal of attention in recent years, is nonverbal communication. Much of what is expressed in face-to-face encounters is simply not conveyed by the spoken word. One well known researcher estimates that more than 90 percent of our attitudes and feelings probably are communicated through various nonverbal channels (Mehrabian, 1972). Moreover, when our words appear to contradict the messages we convey with our faces, voices, and body movements, what we say is likely to be much less convincing than how we say it.

In a well known essay, Robert Tannenbaum (1961) defines leadership as, "interpersonal influence, exercised in situation and directed through the communication process, toward the attainment of a specific goal or goals (p. 24)." This view of leadership is important for two reasons. First, it highlights the importance of understanding how one's ability to influence may be dependent upon the situation. Recent "contingency" approaches to the study of leadership have, in fact, been aimed at isolating the various situational variables that determine leadership effectiveness. The essential principle underlying what has been called "adaptive leadership" can be stated as follows: "the more managers adapt their style of leader behavior to meet the particular situation and the needs of their followers, the more effective they will tend to be in reaching personal and organizational goals (Hersey and Blanchard, 1977, p. 101)." The second reason that Tannenbaum's definition of leadership is important is because it correctly identifies the communication process as the means through which leaders exert influence over their followers. This brings us to the central question I will attempt to answer in this essay: How can group leaders become more effective in face-to-face encounters by adapting their nonverbal communication to the individual group members with whom they interact? To begin this analysis, I will discuss the process of group leadership within the general framework of social exchange theory.

Leadership and Social Exchange in Small Groups

A social exchange view of leadership is an attempt to explain how the influence of a leader is negotiated within a group. According to this view, a superior gains influence over subordinates by exchanging behavior in a trade that is considered "equitable" by the parties involved. In short, a group leader contributes knowledge and guidance to the group in exchange for status and esteem satisfaction. The behaviors exchanged are both rewarding and costly to the interactants. The group leader is expected to guide the group toward the attainment of their goals (cost) and in return is rewarded with increased status over others in the group (benefit). Group members give up a measure of self-esteem in their deference to the leader (cost) and are rewarded with knowledge and supervision (benefit). The influence of the group's leader depends on his or her ability to keep the exchange in a reasonable state of balance or equilibrium (the relative state in which group members regard the exchange as fair). As social exchange theorists T. O. Jacobs (1971) explains:

> Thus the group provides status and esteem satisfaction in exchange for unique contributions to goal attainment. Where these two benefits are in balance, a state of equity exists, and the superordinate is secure in his acceptance by the group. But when they are not in balance, as when the superordinate receives esteem satisfactions or demands status perquisites which the group views as excessive in terms of the contribution he makes to the group in return, a state of disequilibrium may exist and the superordinate may lose influence potential within the group—perhaps even his superordinate status if the group is free to depose him (p. 339).

At this point, it seems reasonable to ask about the relevance of communication. Briefly, effective communication allows the leader to keep the exchange in a state of equilibrium. One way is for the leader to monitor the messages conveyed in face-to-face meetings with group members. Each time a subordinate interacts with a superior face-to-face, the cost to the subordinate (esteem lost) and the benefit to the superior (esteem gained) are evident in the myriad behaviors used by both to display status. I use the term "displays of status" to refer to the whole range of culture bound actions that symbolize one person's power to dominate another; in other words, behaviors that function as status symbols. Clearly, some behaviors are signs of more status than are other behaviors. For example, ordering someone to complete an assignment would seem to imply more authority and hence greater status than would a pat on the back, a firm handshake, a loud tone of voice, or a derogatory remark. Nevertheless, as we will see shortly, all such actions can serve as status symbols in face-to-face interactions.

Based on social exchange theory, one way to conceptualize considerate leadership behavior in the context of face-to-face interactions can be stated as: *Behavior that communicates high esteem or regard for individual group members by reducing the status differential they perceive between themselves and their superior.* Of course, since the leader occupies a more powerful position in the organization's hierarchy than other members of the group, we would expect his or her behavior naturally to exhibit more status than others in the group. In a face-to-face interaction, the differential in behavioral displays of status between the group leader and a member of the group is a measure of how costly the interaction is to the group member (esteem lost) and consequently, how rewarding it is to the leader (esteem gained). This claim is based on at least two important propositions:

1. Behavioral displays of status in face-to-face interactions genuinely reflect feelings of self-esteem.
2. Feeling of self-esteem are relative; they are affected by discrepancies between the status displays of two or more persons.

The first proposition implies that you are likely to feel better about yourself if you behave in a high status manner than in a low status manner. The second proposition assumes that you may feel better about yourself while interacting with someone who behaves in a low status manner than with someone who behaves in a high status manner.

Some research appears to support the general position taken here. Several studies in organizations have found that when "status differentials" (supervisory actions which call attention to the unequal status of the interactants) are imposed in a superior-subordinate relationship, the superior tends to be viewed as relatively inconsiderate (Jacobs, 1971, p. 217). The implication is that in relationships where a subordinate's esteem cost seems to be "excessive" (as reflected in status differentials) a considerate leader can communicate respect for the subordinate by taking actions that minimize the differential in status that exists between them. This is merely another way of saying that a considerate group leader will make some attempt to treat group members as though they were his or her equal.

From a social exchange perspective, the group leader would be seen as more considerate to the extent that he or she is given "credit" for reducing the esteem cost of the group members with whom interactions take place. To briefly illustrate, suppose Ms. Jones routinely consults with each member of her work group before making any final decisions. These consultations will tend to make group members feel important. The members of Ms. Jones' group will feel important because they are being encouraged to act in a way that is indicative of high status in an organization. Ms. Jones will be seen as considerate to the extent that she is given credit for promoting such behavior among the members of her group and, consequently, for decreasing the psychological cost that characterizes their role as subordinates in the group.

The behavioral displays of status found in face-to-face interactions are no less important than are the actions that determine the role of subordinates in decision making. We are just much less aware of them. In the section that follows, considerate leadership behavior is discussed as an exchange in which nonverbal displays of status are traded for interpersonal influence within a small group.

Leadership and Nonverbal Communication in Small Groups

Much of the nonverbal behavior found in face-to-face meetings represents conscious or unconscious displays of status. Not surprisingly, our feelings about self and others will be noticeably affected by these status symbols, whether we are aware of them or not. Consider the following episode:

> Once I scheduled an appointment at 2:00 P.M. with an attorney to discuss a civil case. At 2:10 P.M., when he hadn't arrived, I asked his secretary if he was out to lunch. She smiled cunningly and said, "He'll probably be a *few* minutes late, as usual." I immediately became resentful and was convinced that he was having a few drinks while I was kept waiting. Finally, at 2:25 P.M. he entered the office, walked over to me, and introduced himself. Just as I expected to be taken into his office, he promptly excused himself to visit "briefly" with one of his partners. I remained standing, even though I felt rather awkward. After five more minutes, he returned and led me into his office. As I sat down, I noticed that he left the door open. I began to discuss the details of the case, during which time he both listened to me *and* signed about eight to ten papers on his desk. About ten minutes later the phone rang; he answered and said, "I'm sorry, I can't talk to you now; I'm with a client." No sooner had he hung up the phone than it rang again. This time he turned his swivel chair around so that his back was facing me. He spoke with his caller, a female friend, for about ten more minutes. When he resumed eye contact with me, I gave him a dirty look! He promptly buzzed his secretary and asked her to "hold all calls." He then got up and shut the door. Just as I thought he was settling down to finally give me the attention I was paying for (at $40 per hour), he placed both feet upon his desk, removed a brush from his desk drawer, and began to shine his shoes! (Goldhaber, 1986, p. 187)

How would you react to this kind of treatment? While there isn't much doubt that the attorney's behavior toward his client was inconsiderate, we don't know whether or not his lack of consideration was intentional. In fact, many of the actions described in the incident above are performed with little or no awareness of how they might be interpreted by others. Upon learning that his client was upset, the attorney might actually wonder what he did that could have caused such a problem.

Rules Governing Nonverbal Displays of Status in Small Groups

When viewed from a "rules of conduct" perspective, much of the behavior witnessed in an organization can be explained as a product of contextual rules. Actions become both predictable and understandable when they are guided by the norms and rules of a group. Such rules define the way an individual is obliged to behave in the presence of others and the way others are expected to act in return.

Even the most trivial of actions observed in a face-to-face interaction can say something about the nature of that relationship when such actions are governed by the rules of a group. This is readily apparent in the military where an enlisted person will salute an officer out of deference to his or her higher rank, in a corporate office where an executive vice president freely interrupts the plant manager to tell her a joke, or in a university library where the college dean approaches a faculty member and pats him on the back. In each case, an image of one's self in relation to another is symbolized by particular nonverbal behaviors; behaviors that communicate the relative status of the interactants in the organization's hierarchy.

According to the sociologist Erving Goffman (1967), when the norms of a group lead individuals to act similarly toward each other, the relationships formed are said to be "symmetrical." In contrast, "asymmetrical" relationships are created when group norms lead members to behave differently toward one another. In most formal organizations, persons of unequal status (due to their rank in the hierarchy) will develop asymmetrical relationships. At this point, we can begin to consider the subtle nonverbal cues that characterize most superior-subordinate interactions.

A rather sizeable body of scientific research has accumulated over the years in support of the belief that when superiors communicate with subordinates face-to-face, the unequal nature of the relationship is acted out by the way the interactants use their bodies, the distance between them, and the time available. In an earlier essay (Remland, 1981), I proposed a taxonomy for classifying the various ways in which superior status is communicated nonverbally in an organization. A similar but somewhat modified version is presented here:

I. PHYSICAL NORMS
    A. Relaxation
    B. Attentiveness
    C. Adornment
II. SPATIAL NORMS
    A. Protection
    B. Expansion
    C. Invasion
III. TEMPORAL NORMS
    A. Frequency
    B. Punctuality
    C. Content
    D. Duration

Physical Norms

These are the norms that refer to patterns of behavior regarding the bodily movement and attire of superiors and subordinates. In terms of bodily movement (often referred to as kinesics), higher status appears to allow individuals to act in a more relaxed and inattentive manner. In the attorney-client episode described earlier, the attorney displayed status by putting his feet up on his desk and by continuing to ignore the presence of his client (i.e., he signed papers while supposedly listening, he excused himself to visit with someone else, he answered the telephone and turned his back on the client).

Specific relaxation cues that have been correlated with status in research studies on nonverbal communication include body lean and asymmetrical positioning of arms and legs. Generally, higher status is associated with what might be called an "easy going" demeanor. Following this principle, we might add to our list other behaviors that also communicate physical relaxation such as facial and vocal expressions that are free of tension. In addition, the norms of organizational life seem to allow superiors to dress in a more casual manner than their subordinates, if they wish to do so.

Inattention is ordinarily signalled by not facing or looking at the subordinate, especially when the subordinate is talking. Unresponsive facial expressions (i.e., not laughing at a joke) and gestures (i.e., not nodding in agreement) also reflect a subtle lack of involvement; a prerogative of status.

Perhaps the most common status symbols evident in superior-subordinate interactions, which are influenced by group norms, are the clothing and accessories of the participants. Typically, higher status persons in an organization wear more expensive clothes than do their lower status counterparts. In fact, it might be possible in some organizations to identify the superior and the subordinate in a conversation simply by looking at the quality of their respective suits, shoes, or jewelry. It seems clear that various nonverbal displays of status in the form of relaxation, inattention, and physical appearance allow superiors to send the implicit message: "My body is more important than your body."

Spatial Norms

Spatial behavior also differentiates superiors from subordinates. The territory of higher status individuals is generally less accessible than is the territory of lower status persons. In our culture, superiors are afforded greater protection than their subordinates; they are harder to get to. The environment tends to be structured in a way that insulates "important" people against unwanted intrusions. In universities, like most organizations, the inaccessibility of an individual is directly related to his or her position in the pecking order. Would it be easier for you to meet with a faculty member in your department or with the Dean of the college?

In addition, higher status persons tend to use more space than those of lower status. Often, what they own is larger and thus occupies more space. Big homes, cars, swimming pools, and even televisions, for example. When interacting with subordinates face-to-face, superiors take more liberties with the space around them than their subordinates do; they appear to feel more mobile and might be observed walking around while the group members they are addressing remain fixed in the same place. In addition, their gestures are more expansive. And, they often use up more "acoustic" space by talking in a louder tone of voice than their subordinates do.

Invading the territory and personal space of others is also a sign of status in an organization. Entering a superior's office without permission would certainly be foolish since it would violate the unspoken rules of most organizations. Yet, while it is inappropriate for a subordinate to invade the territory of his or her superior, a similar invasion of the subordinate by the superior might very well go unnoticed. When communicating face-to-face, the interpersonal distance maintained during the interaction seems to depend on who approaches whom. If the subordinate approaches the superior, they will probably end up standing farther apart than if the superior had approached the subordinate. The reason this tends to happen is that the subordinate is likely to feel more apprehensive about "getting too close" than his or her superior would feel. The fact that higher status persons are less reluctant to invade the personal space of those lower in status also applies to touching and gazing behavior. Superiors usually touch subordinates in social encounters more than subordinates touch them. And, subordinates are less likely to "stare" at their superiors since staring represents the kind of intrusive eye contact that is reserved for intimates or high status individuals.

If we think back for a moment to our attorney-client interaction we may recall some of these nonverbal displays of status. For example, they met to discuss business on the attorney's "ground" which immediately gave the territorial edge to the attorney (we can only speculate about the various status symbols that might have been in the attorney's office). Second, after introducing himself, the attorney walked away and left his client standing in one place. Third, he generally moved around a lot more than his client did throughout the entire episode. Furthermore, it might not be difficult to imagine the attorney initiating a handshake with his client or leading the client into his office by placing his hand on the client's back. These actions, and many more, allow high status persons to say: "My territory is more important than your territory," or "I have access to more space than you do."

Temporal Norms

High status persons often control the time of low status persons in very subtle ways. First, superiors tend to decide when they will meet with their subordinates. Thus, conversational frequency is determined by the individual in a relationship with the higher rank. Second, the subordinate is usually more punctual than is the superior. Being late for an appointment is much less offensive if you happen to be the boss. Third, the superior sets the agenda for even the most casual conversations. More than likely, the topic of discussion will be controlled by the high status person. The superior may simply "hold the floor" longer, interrupt more, or change the topic more than the subordinate will. In all of these unobtrusive ways, a superior is able to control the content of a given interaction without much resistance. Finally, the amount of time communicating is likely to be controlled by the superior. This happens because the decision to terminate or prolong a conversation usually is made by the higher status individual.

In group meetings, the leader is expected to control time in many of these ways so that decisions can be made and problems solved as expeditiously as possible. Therefore, we expect the leader to schedule meetings, set agendas, monitor group discussion, and adjourn meetings. Many of these status symbols, however, seem far less important in the context of interpersonal encounters. Instead, they often serve only to remind the subordinate of the unequal nature of the relationship.

For example, how many things did the attorney do in his brief meeting with the client to control the client's time? He was late for the appointment, he kept the client waiting even after he arrived, and he interrupted the client.

Ultimately, temporal norms work to satisfy the needs of the high status person in a relationship at the expense of the lower status person. Our culture places a great deal of value on time; in an organization, time is money. Superiors and subordinates tend to interact in ways that reflect the former's monopoloy on time. Without speaking a word, the message is clear: "My time is more important than your time."

Implicit Rules

While the norms of a group are represented by patterns of behavior that typically differentiate superiors from subordinates, rules indicate what behaviors a group considers appropriate or inappropriate. As Shimanoff (1980) explains, "A rule is a followable prescription that indicates what behavior is obligated, preferred, or prohibited in certain contexts (p. 57)." In the small group context, for instance, rules let group members know "who says what to whom when with what duration and frequency through what medium and by what decision procedure (Shimanoff, 1984, p. 42)."

By and large, nonverbal displays of status are governed by "implicit" rather than "explicit" rules. The essential difference is that explicit rules are formally stated—they can be seen and/or heard frequently by the members of a group, whereas implicit rules are unstated but still known by group members. "Implicit rules are neither written nor openly discussed," says Shimanoff (1980), "and yet, even without this explicit acknowledgement, group members conform to these rules (p. 31)." Following the implicit rules that govern nonverbal displays of status between superiors and subordinates effectively reinforces the basic dictum of organizational life: "The superior is more important than the subordinate." Although the rules are rarely codified, they are routinely obeyed.

But rule-generated behavior doesn't explain many of the subtle actions that differentiate superiors from subordinates. As important are the allowances given to persons of high status which encourage them to deviate from the implicit rules constraining persons of lower status. These deviations have been called "rule allowance" behaviors and result from consistently allowing particular people or groups to violate certain rules. For example, although normally it is considered rude to stare or yell at someone, we are much more likely to tolerate such behaviors from a superior than we are from a subordinate.

Thus, some implicit rules are intended to prescribe status-differentials; others are intended to prohibit inappropriate behaviors. When individuals in an organization follow the first set of rules and allow violations of the second set based on status, the result is a climate in which status differentials are the norm. To illustrate, consider the following implicit rules belonging to the first set (they prescribe status differentials):

R1: Superiors should have more office space than their subordinates.

R2: Individuals should dress in a way that is commensurate with their rank in the organization.

R3: Group leaders should not allow a single member of the group to monopolize a discussion.

R4: High status persons should be more insulated from distractions in their working environment than low status persons should be.

These rules clearly punctuate the unequal nature of superior-subordinate relationships. They are intended to foster expectations within an organization that lead directly to the emergence of legitimate status symbols. And, they are justified by organizations on the grounds that compliance should enhance leadership effectiveness.

In contrast, the second set of rules (those that prohibit inappropriate behaviors) must be violated by persons who will not be punished for the violation (i.e., the superior in a relationship) if they are to serve as legitimate displays of status. Some examples of these implicit rules are:

R5: You should not be late for any scheduled appointment.

R6: You should pay close attention to the person you are listening to.

R7: You should avoid wearing strange and unconventional attire to a business meeting.

R8: You should not enter someone's office without first knocking and getting permission to enter.

R9: You shouldn't interrupt the person you are listening to.

Although they are intended to govern the actions of all, it is quite clear that they restrict the actions of low status persons substantially more than they restrict the actions of high status individuals. As I noted earlier in the sections on physical, spatial, and temporal norms, superiors deviate from these implicit rules more than their subordinates do. As a result, non-compliance with these rules becomes an effective way of communicating status.

Nonverbal displays of status symbolize one individual's power to dominate another. The common denominator is the *implicit communication of disregard;* disregard for the physical presence, space, and time of another person. Though guided by the unspoken rules of an organization and operating largely out of awareness, they nevertheless call attention to the unequal nature of superior-subordinate interactions. By minimizing "excessive" differentials in status between themselves and their subordinates, group leaders may be better able to attain group goals.

Adaptive Leadership and Nonverbal Displays of Status

From a social exchange perspective, it is easy to see how leadership performance can suffer when nonverbal displays of status are needlessly employed (i.e., when they serve no other purpose except to make the leader feel more important than the members of his or her group), and where excessive differentials in status between a superior and a subordinate are created and maintained. In such cases, interaction can become very costly to the subordinate (esteem is lost when one feels inferior to another) and might be too costly when compared to the benefits received (amount of knowledge and guidance obtained from the leader). If face-to-face encounters with a superior are perceived as aversive and threatening, the subordinate may simply avoid such encounters. The result is an organizational climate in which management inadvertently discourages the open and free-flowing exchange of ideas so necessary for success.

Many of today's most successful companies apparently realize this. They have adopted various measures to reduce status differentials between superiors and subordinates, in the belief that such actions motivate their employees and improve communication throughout the company. And, there is evidence that they might be correct. In their book, *In Search of Excellence,* Peters and Waterman (1982) detail what they found to be the most common characteristics of America's best run companies. One important lesson is summarized as follows:

> Treat people as adults. Treat them as partners; treat them with dignity; treat them with respect. Treat *them*—not capital spending and automation—as the primary source of productivity gains. These are the fundamental lessons from the excellent companies research. In other words, if you want productivity and the financial reward that goes with it, you must treat your workers as your most important asset. In *A Business and Its Beliefs,* Thomas J. Watson, Jr. puts it well: "IBM's philosophy is largely contained in three simple beliefs. I want to begin with what I think is the most important: our *respect for the individual.* This is a simple concept, but in IBM it occupies a major portion of management time. We devote more effort to it than anything else (p. 238)."

While a lot of companies paid "lip service" to this people-orientation, the successful companies adopted very specific policies and programs that challenged many of the customs and implicit rules about how superiors and subordinates are supposed to be treated. For example:

> Another of the more striking characteristics of the excellent companies is the *apparent absence of a rigidly followed chain of command.* Of course, the chain of command does exist for big decisions, but it is not used much for day-to-day communication. For information exchange, informality is

the norm. People really do wander around, top management is in regular contact with employees at the lowest level (and with customers), everyone *is* typically on a first name basis (Peters and Waterman, 1982, p. 262).

The successful companies emphasized the accessibility of top management and the importance of listening actively to everyone in the organization. In addition to these substantive efforts, the authors also found that many companies worked hard to invent euphemisms for labeling their employees in a way that would break down traditional stereotypes based on rank and status.

> Most impressive of all the language characteristics in the excellent companies are the phrases that upgrade the status of the individual employee. Again, we know it sounds corny, but words like Associate (Wal-Mart), Crew Member (McDonald's) and Cast Member (Disney) describe the very special importance of individuals in the excellent companies (Peters and Waterman, 1982, p. 261).

Although these efforts to reduce status differentials are notable and effective, they cannot supplant the kind of mutual respect that comes from regular face-to-face interactions in which excessive displays of status are avoided. As we observed earlier, whenever a subordinate interacts with a superior face-to-face, behavior is exchanged (often unknowingly) in a way that symbolizes the superior's authority over the subordinate. Some loss of esteem to the subordinate is, of course, inevitable. But the cost to the subordinate may be excessive in relationships where the nonverbal behavior of the superior severely degrades the time, territory, or presence of his/her subordinate. This fact brings up the need for adaptive leadership—treating some members of the group differently than other members.

Group leaders need to be aware of the behaviors displayed with each member of the group. Since subordinates display some status nonverbally, the "punitive" nature of the relationship will depend on the extent to which the leader displays more status than an individual member of the group. The *differential* reflects the unequal nature of the relationship (of course, this premise does not, but should take into account the myriad ways status is expressed verbally as well). The greater the differential (as perceived by the group member), the more degrading the relationship. Interaction becomes more aversive and costly to the subordinate as the differential increases (suggesting the subordinate's relative inferiority). The leader's nonverbal message becomes: "I am more important than you are."

By adapting nonverbally to certain group members in face-to-face meetings it becomes possible for a leader to communicate respect for the time, space, and physical presence of those individuals. This kind of "behavioral flexibility" can decrease the esteem cost incurred by group members which would probably result in the following outcomes:

1. The group leader would be judged as considerate.
2. Interaction with the group leader would be seen as less damaging to the group member's self-esteem.
3. Upward communication within the group would increase.

I found some support for the first outcome in a laboratory experiment I conducted a few years ago (Remland, 1984). In that experiment, four videotapes of a superior-subordinate role play were prepared in which the actors' nonverbal displays of status were manipulated as either high or low in status. High status behaviors included a relaxed posture, indirect body orientation, loud tone of voice, inattention, and spatial invasion. Low status behaviors included a tense posture, direct body orientation, soft and hesitating speech, and attentive eye contact. This resulted in four videotaped scenarios using the same two actors and the same script: tape 1—superior and subordinate displaying high status; tape 2—superior displaying low status with subordinate displaying high status; tape 3—superior displaying high status with subordinate displaying low status; and tape 4—superior and subordinate displaying low status. Subjects in the experiment were asked how considerate they thought the superior was toward the subordinate. The results of the experiment confirmed the importance of status differentials; the behavior of *both* the superior and the subordinate determined subjects' ratings of the superior. He was seen as most inconsiderate when his behavior was high in status and the subordinate's behavior was low in status; in contrast, he was seen as most considerate when his behavior was low in status and the subordinate's behavior was high in status. In the two tapes that showed the superior and the subordinate acting similarly toward each other (either both high status or both low status), the superior was seen as equally considerate. Thus, evaluations of the superior were influenced by the differential between the superior's nonverbal behavior and the subordinate's nonverbal behavior rather than the behavior of the superior alone.

We now return to the question raised at the start of this essay: How can group leaders become more effective in face-to-face encounters by adapting their nonverbal communication to the individual group members with whom they interact? By monitoring the status differentials expressed in face-to-face encounters with individual group members, leaders can make an effort to behave in a considerate manner. This, of course, requires some basic skill in both the decoding and encoding of nonverbal messages.

Leaders need to become aware of the nonverbal messages conveyed by the members of their group in face-to-face situations. To illustrate, consider the behavior of two group members as described by a hypothetical group leader:

Person A—Very attentive; always looks at me either for approval or to show that he/she is listening. Nods in agreement frequently. Facial expressions are pleasant and very responsive. Overall posture and movement is somewhat tense. Gestures are inhibited and body position takes up little space. Often looks down and speaks in a soft and nervous manner. Very careful not to stare and never touches or gets close to me. Lets me hold the floor and never interrupts. Always talks about what I want to talk about; never changes the subject. Spends little time talking. Very punctual.

Person B—Very inattentive; seems indifferent to what I'm saying. Frequently looks around the room while I'm talking. Facial expressions are unpleasant and not responsive. Rarely nods to indicate agreement or to show support. Overall postures and movements are very relaxed; speech pattern is slow and relaxed. Gestures are expansive. Moves around freely while speaking and listening. Often raises voice and occasionally stares at me in a threatening manner. Touches me occasionally and is not reluctant to stand or sit very close to the leader. Holds the floor in conversation for long periods of time; interrupts often. Frequently late for appointments.

Obviously, person A's nonverbal behavior is quite low in status. In contrast, person B acts in a way that is very high in status. Interaction with the leader for person A is likely to be more costly (esteem lost) than it would be for person B, if the leader behaves similarly toward both. Assuming that the leader has correctly interpreted each individual's nonverbal communication as low and high in status respectively (decoding skill), some attempt could be made by the leader to act in a way that would minimize the status differential perceived by person A (encoding skill). This would have the effect of making interaction less costly for person A and, ultimately, might encourage further interactions. This objective could be accomplished by the group leader in any number of ways (deviating from some of the rules that prescribe status differentials or increasing compliance with some of the rules that prohibit inappropriate behavior; see the section on implicit rules).

But the group member who displays high status poses a different sort of problem. There is little need for the leader to make interaction less costly for person B. In fact, in some cases interaction with group members who act like person B may be more costly to the leader than to the group member. Insubordination is a potential outcome that could result when group members begin to disregard the presence, time, and space of their leader; the leader surely needs to command the respect of his or her followers in order to lead effectively. Consequently, in some cases a group leader may need to select behaviors that say, "I am more important than you are."

While a considerable amount of behavioral flexibility is needed for a leader to change the way he or she communicates nonverbally, it seems feasible for group leaders to make the few adjustments needed to avoid relationships where *excessive* differentials in status exist. Nevertheless, some cautions are in order:

1. Some group leaders may need the esteem satisfaction that comes from acting in a high status fashion. These status symbols may be very rewarding.
2. Sudden and dramatic changes in behavior might be viewed by group members as insincere and manipulative, particularly when such behaviors seem contrived rather than spontaneous.
3. Status differentials might not be viewed as "excessive" if the group leader contributes a great deal of knowledge and guidance to the group; status differentials are undesirable primarily when the cost (esteem lost) to the members of the group outweigh the benefits they receive (successful supervision).
4. It seems possible that group members with certain personality traits or values might expect or even demand that leaders act in ways that reinforce status differentials.

Clearly, the difficulties involved in recommending that leaders try to change their nonverbal behaviors cannot be overstated. Some resistance, for example, is likely to be based on the belief that much of our social behavior represents our "real selves" and thus should not be tampered with. Furthermore, the long-term and frequent use of nonverbal behaviors that we are not fully aware of suggests a conditioning process that would be difficult to affect.

Conclusion

Much of a group leader's time is spent in face-to-face communication with the members of the group. Although efforts to involve group members in the decision-making process help to foster a working environment in which people are respected as individuals, the people-oriented skills of a leader ultimately will be tested in face-to-face interactions.

The implicit rules in an organization lead superiors to act in subtle ways that show little respect for the physical presence, space, and time of their subordinates. When excessive differentials in status between superiors and subordinates make interaction costly to subordinates, interpersonal communication is discouraged. Even leaders with the best of intentions may be seen by members of their group as inconsiderate when they consistently abuse their "right" to act in a high status manner.

References

Goffman, E. *Interaction Ritual.* Garden City, NY: Anchor Press, 1967.

Goldhaber, G. *Organizational Communication.* Dubuque, Iowa: Wm. C. Brown, 1986.

Hersey, P. and Blanchard, K. *Management of Organizational Behavior.* Englewood Cliffs, NJ: Prentice-Hall, 1977.

Jacobs, T. O. *Leadership and Exchange in Formal Organizations.* Human Resources Organization, 1971.

Mehrabian, A. *Nonverbal Communication.* Chicago, ILL: Aldine-Atherton, 1972.

Perot, H. R. Perot to Smith: GM must change. *Newsweek.* December 15, 1986, 58–62.

Peters, T. and Waterman R. H. *In Search of Excellence.* NY: Harper and Row, 1982.

Remland, M. Developing leadership skills in nonverbal communication: A situational perspective. *Journal of Business of Communication.* Summer, 1981, 18, 17–29.

Remland, M. Leadership impressions and nonverbal communication in a superior-subordinate interaction. *Communication Quarterly* Winter, 1984, 32, 41–48.

Shimanoff, S. *Communication Rules: Theory and Research.* Beverly Hills, CA: Sage, 1980.

Shimanoff, S. Coordinating group interaction via communication rules. In *Small Group Communication.* Cathcart, R. and Samovar, L., eds. Dubuque, Iowa: Wm. C. Brown, 1984, 31–44.

Stogdill, R. *Handbook of Leadership.* NY: The Free Press, 1974.

Tannenbaum, R. et al. *Leadership and Organization.* NY: McGraw-Hill, 1961.

The Skills of Leading Small Groups in American Business and Industry

H. Lloyd Goodall, Jr.

Introduction to the Roles of Leaders in Business and Industry

Leadership is at least partially a set of behaviors you know when you see. Leadership does *not* always consist of the same set of behaviors, however, which makes the study of leadership and the development of leading skills difficult. For example, you know there are times when you want a strong leader to direct the activities of the group. Under these circumstances you may respond favorably to an individual who tells you what to do, who does not encourage much discussion, and who operates in an autocratic style.

If you change circumstances you may also need to change the style of leadership. When small groups are exploring alternative solutions to a problem the autocratic style of leadership may impede progress. Instead, you may want a leader who encourages diverse discussions on a variety of issues, who joins group members in exchanging ideas and opinions rather than directing them, and who operates in a more democratic style.

Between these two ends of the leadership style continuum are other choices about behaviors affecting group interaction. You may want a leader who possesses a keen sensitivity to the needs of group members, who responds not only to what they say and do, but also to how they feel. You may want a leader with special skills in conflict resolution. You may want a person leading the group who acts more like "one of the gang" instead of a "leader." Your demands on leadership are as diverse as the situations and contingencies leaders must be able to respond to.

Leadership is not simply one set of definable behaviors. We respond to other characteristics of leaders beyond their verbal and nonverbal communication. We often feel more comfortable working in a group directed by a proven leader, someone with expertise and experience in group interaction. We may also be affected by the sex of the leader. Women have long regarded attaining leadership positions in organizations as a desirable goal. As women began acquiring leadership roles in American businesses and industries, men had to learn how to adapt their behavior to the presence and leadership style of women. It was not that women led groups differently, but rather that an unprecedented change was occurring, and the sex of the leader was the most

H. Lloyd Goodall, Jr. is affiliated with the Department of Speech at the University of Alabama.

obvious characteristic of the change. We also respond to the attractiveness, both physical and psychological, of a leader. These are some of the traits affecting our perceptions of, and responses to, leaders.

This essay addresses the question of leadership of small groups in American business and industry. I call it a "question of leadership" because making effective choices about leading requires the ability to ask and answer a variety of important questions about the group members, the task to be accomplished, the situation, and the history of the group interaction. The question of leadership also directs us to a variety of interpersonal and group skills, ranging from selecting group members to calling meetings to order, from planning agendas to resolving disputes between and among group members. Finally, the question of leadership requires us to implement our answers to these issues effectively, efficiently, and consistently.

First, I will examine the essence of leading: the skill of adapting communication behavior to the needs and expectations of group members and group situations. Second, I will investigate some common problems associated with leading small groups, and ways of overcoming them. One result of reading this essay should be an improved understanding of leadership in organization. Another benefit may well be the ability to develop skills capable of meeting the challenge of leadership. However, before we begin, examine the following statement concerning aspects of leading. It should be made part of your general awareness of what leadership means.

William McA., 55 years old, CEO of an industrial concern.

Leadership ability is very important to any organization. We tell our recruiters how to spot leadership potential in candidates for entry-level positions and on up the corporate ladder. Once someone is hired, we train him, often spending as much as a quarter of a million dollars over ten or fifteen or twenty years developing leadership skills. So we expect a great deal from our leaders. We know a leader has to be able to take heat from both sides—from superiors who constantly demand more and better results, and from subordinates who blame the leader for anything and everything that can go wrong. That is simply part of the job. I guess the bottom line is this: can a person handle the responsibilities of being a leader without showing signs of cracking up? We've lost some of our best managers to drugs—especially alcohol. We've lost others to bad marriages, bad love affairs, bad relations with other managers, and so forth. You know what's sad? These kids come here looking for a good job after college. They're smart, they're trainable. They all say the same thing—"I want to be a leader." If they only knew what that really meant I bet most of them wouldn't want to be leaders at all.

Leadership is not a responsibility or a personal commitment to be taken lightly. If developing leadership skills is important to you in your professional career, this essay can only suggest what you will actually need to know. Learning leadership skills may mark you as a desirable recruit for any organization, and knowing how to make productive use of leading skills may help you rise on the organizational ladder. But these skills alone will not help you cope with the stress of leadership. However, unless these basic skills are learned it is doubtful that you will have the opportunity to see whether or not you can meet the demands and challenges of leadership.

The Essence of Leading

For many people fresh to the study of leadership the phrase "being a leader" attains an almost mystical quality. It is as if suddenly, inexplicably, out of the great somewhere beyond, someone or something endowed some of us with "it." This "it" of leading, like a "real-me" or "perfect self" or other ineffable inventions of the imagination, is never quite spelled out, never parsed for content and meaning. "It" just simply happens. Either you have "it" or you don't. If you do have "it," you somehow have powers over others who respect you, and who respond to your commands.

If the essence of leadership were some mystical, magical, unnamable gift, some great wonderful "it" which a person possessed then the study of leadership would resemble worship. We worship that which we cannot rationally understand. However, leadership can be understood, and should not be an object of worship, but rather a systematic unveiling of the knowledge, skills, and practices of those ordinary people who may seem to be blessed with "it," but who actually have learned *how to do* "it."

Let's begin with what a potential group leader should be aware of when she or he thinks about the nature of small groups. I suggest that such a person should consider the small group as an organism capable of modification and change over time. The parts of the small group are human and fallible, they consist of individual persons who want to be happy and productive, who need the comfort, kindness, and support of others, and who will make mistakes, feel anxious about participating in the group and who worry about things, events, and people who have nothing whatsoever to do with the group's task. Participants will be motivated by both hope of reward and fear of failure. In any small group at any particular time and place in history, what was said and done during group meetings and outside of them by the group's members was neither predestined, preconditioned, or predicted by fate. In any small group the process of carrying out the assignment, and the results attained by whatever happened within the group setting, depended solely upon the *choices made about what was said and done by the leader and group members.* Expressed in another way, a group may be defined by the choices made about communication.

I suggest this way of thinking about a small group because it can facilitate two appropriate attitudes necessary for productive group leadership:

(1) The need to see group members as *individuals* as well as members of the group.
(2) The need to see *choices about communication* as central to everything that will happen within the small group.

A leader who treats group members as individuals, and who is capable of monitoring the communication within the group as well as making appropriate choices about his or her own communication, will induce the group members to reciprocate. Such leaders will become aware of the importance of responding to each other as persons, and of making productive choices about words and behaviors displayed in the group. The best leaders are capable of inducing cooperative behavior within a group by setting a positive example. And it has been my experience that to set a positive example requires thinking about the group in the way just described.

If what I have written appears to you to be a circular argument, consider the implications of my advice. First, I advocate thinking about group members as individuals as well as members of the group. What possible advantage does this attitude engender? Listen to Deanna:

Deanna L., 29 years old, task leader of a high-tech computer software firm.

When I first became a group leader I thought it meant that I had to give orders. So I told everyone what to do. Eventually each one of them told me where to go. I learned the first principle of effective leadership: You must learn how to respond to individuals as well as employees. As individuals they have cares, worries, hopes, fears, and resentments just like you do. They need to see their self-respect mirrored back to them by others who count. They need to matter, to feel like they couldn't just be replaced by someone else or a machine. As employees they already know the rules. They understand the rights of command, and usually they will obey them if they are treated fairly. But as a group leader you have to know when you are responding to them as an individual or as an employee. You have to respond to each group member both ways, but perhaps more importantly, at least for me, is to be conscious of the difference and to be able to make productive use of the difference. One of my goals has been to get my groups to stop telling me where to go, and to begin asking me where they should be going. I reached that goal last year, and when it happened, I think I thought of myself as a leader for the very first time.

Deanna's experiences demonstrate the importance of treating group members as persons who are valuable because of the contribution they can make to the group. This is not something a group leader can say; it is an attitude reflected in her or his words and actions while leading the group.

Second, I advocate the need to see communication as central to everything that happens within the group. Inherent to this view is the notion that you can exercise *choice* over what you say and do. Effective group leaders choose ways and means of accomplishing specific goals. They do not just assemble a group, provide directives, and talley the results. They think about the nature of the group in light of what they plan to accomplish, about the various expertise, experience, and skills available among group members, and their individual characters and personalities. *Effective group leaders adapt their choices about communicating to the needs and expectations of group members and the group situation.* Let me explain the reasons for developing this attitude.

Perhaps the significance of this attitude can be best understood by answering this question: "Why don't you just say the first thing that comes to mind? After all, we live in a country in which the freedom of speech is a guaranteed right. You are free to say anything to anyone, so why don't you?" The answer is simply that you have learned not to. You have learned, probably very early in life, that you can accomplish more by being sensitive to the needs and expectations of others. By exerting control over what you say and do in any situation, you optimize the opportunities for success. By taking into account your past experiences with others, your storehouse of information about their skills, abilities, needs, and desires, you can find better ways of obtaining their cooperation.

A second reason for exercising conscious choice in your communication with others is essentially pragmatic. The better you adapt your communication to others, the more likely they will adapt their communication to you. A good group leader is able to persuade group members to adapt their choices of communication to the needs and expectations of each other and to you as their group leader. As a group leader you have the responsibility to encourage communication practices which can guide the group toward its goal. If your leadership of the group is seriously questioned by the group members, then it is probable that the results of the group work will also be questionable.

The essence of leading is the ability to adapt communication to the needs and expectations of the group members and the group situation. The question becomes more difficult once this attitude is accepted. The problem then is *how?* Julia T. Wood, a pioneering theorist and researcher in the area of group performance, advocates focusing on two interrelated aspects of leadership which affect any small group: (1) analysis of group members and situation, and (2) behavioral flexibility.[1]

Analyzing the Group Members and Situation

You cannot be a group leader unless the members of the group are willing to respond to your leadership. To establish a productive leadership role within the small group, you need to develop an appreciation for the unique needs and expectations of each member in the group. The adaptive approach to leading affirms that a leader must be able to: (a) analyze the goals and rewards of each group member, (b) demonstrate acceptance of this analysis by treating group members with consideration and respect, (c) structure group meetings by using agendas which clarify precise goals and outcomes and sanction behaviors capable of leading to the accomplishment of the group's objectives, (d) make rewards contingent on group members' performance during the meetings, and (e) consistently reassess the changing dynamics of the group in relation to its task to revise strategies as needed.

Analyzing the group and situation is a continuous task for any group leader. People change, and the effective leader must be responsive to these changes when they occur. Forcing group members to adhere to a pre-established notion of what ought to happen during group meetings, without taking into account their feelings and goals, may mean that no matter what rewards are offered, the group will not be able to attain its goals effectively and efficiently. The more the group rebels against the methods of the leader, the less effective the group will be. The more competent the group leader is in defining objectives for the group, and explaining how individual goals can be met while satisfying the objectives, the more effective the group should be. Consider Herb's experience:

Herb W., 40 years old, project director for an engineering firm.

I grew up in this organization. Mostly I worked for the same guy, a very autocratic group leader who told you what he wanted and that was it. Either you accomplished the task he gave you, or you didn't. No middle ground. I guess I learned how to be a leader from watching him operate. When I was promoted and became a project leader I adopted his ways—at least at first. I couldn't understand why everyone hated me. I just figured I was being a good manager—you know, weeding out the talent from the goof-offs. But then I lost Helen. Helen had been my most productive worker—always on time, always willing to go the extra mile to complete a project. She was swell. When I was told she resigned I couldn't believe it. I asked to see her. I thought she had been given a better offer by another company and I was willing to top it. But that wasn't it. She was leaving because she couldn't stand the way I "bullied" people—that is exactly what she said. She laid it on the line for me that afternoon and I've never forgotten it. I was hurt. I didn't know how to be a leader, I just knew I was in the position and had to be one. So I behaved like the only one I knew and made the same mistakes he did. Only I lost Helen. Since that afternoon I have made real changes in the way I treat people. I only wish I had known how sooner.

Like most of us, Herb learned by experience. Unfortunately in his case, he lost a valued worker before the experience made any sense to him. Unless you know how to examine experience for meaning, it is difficult to learn from it. All the experience in the world of business will not make you a better leader unless you perceive the need to *learn how to lead.*

The adaptive approach to leading advances the proposition that you can learn how to lead if you are taught what to look for when analyzing group members and situations. There are four areas for preparation by effective leaders:[2]

1. *The issues or agenda must be foreseen.* A group leader should prepare an agenda for each group meeting and circulate it among the group members. If group members want to modify the agenda, they should be able to do so by contacting the leader and explaining the need for the change. Thus, the group will have a *public* agenda to guide interactions.

   The group leader should also have a *private* agenda. Prior to each group meeting, the leader should prepare a list of questions to generate discussion of the agenda items and to promote feedback. After the meeting the leader can use this list to check on her or his effectiveness.

2. *The group and the individual members must be analyzed.* Any human group is composed of individuals with strengths and weaknesses, skills, experience, and personal goals. The effective leader develops the ability to figure out what each of these qualities or deficiencies are for each group member. The leader should prepare for group meetings by thinking through the agenda in relation to the needs and expectations of group members. By learning to ask questions about how the issues might affect each individual in the group, the leader can prepare for potential problems. Who may be most directly affected by this item on the agenda? Who has the most to gain (or to lose) by this decision? Who has experience we can use? How can I get this person more involved in the interaction—what motivates him or her? By "psyching out" the group members and situation before the meeting, the leader can better critique his or her own behavior after the meeting. How well did I accomplish my objectives with each individual in the group? This should be the guiding question for analysis of performance during the meeting.

3. *The physical situation in which the group will assemble must be anticipated.* The group leader is usually responsible for setting the time of the meeting and arranging for any and all group interaction aids, including the conference table, chairs, chalkboards, flipcharts, etc. The effective leader will ask for suggestions from group members about their special needs and will try to meet them. For example, some persons are seriously distressed by cigarette, cigar, or pipe smoke in a closed room. The leader should establish a smoking policy appropriate to members of the group. The size of the group must be considered when preparing tables and chairs. Using a long conference table capable of seating twelve when you have a small group of four or five members may make group members feel uncomfortable. The comfort of the group members should be the guiding consideration of leaders preparing for the physical situation of the group.

4. *The leader's personal style must be appropriately selected.* In addition to analyzing the needs and expectations of group members, leaders must also analyze themselves. What are my needs and expectations? What are my strengths and weaknesses? What does my past experience contribute to this problem or decision? By asking questions about your own ability to participate in the discussion, a leader prepares for the meeting through self-analysis. Leaders must be aware of their own prejudices and biases in leading behavior—am I generally autocratic or democratic or laissez-faire in my approach? Which of these styles is most appropriate for this group and this situation? What obstacles are there to overcome with this group? Are there members present who desire to be the group leader? How can what I know about past interactions shape my performance in this situation? Are there likely to be disputes between particular group members? How should I act if these disputes occur? What specific statements should be made to effectively guide the group through the agenda?

These four areas for leadership effectiveness should guide your preparation for discussions and your choices of leading strategies. However, there is a second vital component to learning leadership behavior in the adaptive approach: *behavioral flexibility.*

Behavioral Flexibility

Another condition for success in the adaptive approach is what happens *during* the group meeting. All the preparing accomplished by the leader must pay off in the actual performance of the group meeting. In order to attain the goal of an effective and efficient group meeting, a leader must learn how to *adapt the choice of behavior* to the needs and expectations of each group member during discussions. Successful adaptation of behavior to the demands of the given situation requires an appreciation of the value of behavioral flexibility, as well as considerable skill employing it.

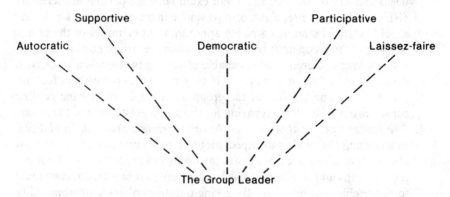

Figure 1. Styles of leading.

Behavioral flexibility means developing a wide repertoire of self-presentations which can be used in group situations. The key to using any one of the self-presentations is formulating an *appropriate goal* for the responses you make to group members. Consider your choices of behavior to comprise a *range of available styles* of leading. Then recall your goal for responses made to group members, regarding it as a specific strategy based on analysis of which style is likely to gain the desired response from the group member. Figure 1 displays how these styles of leading may be visualized as points in a leadership continuum.

The second step in developing behavioral flexibility is to use what management theorists refer to as a "contingency" approach to leading.[3] By "contingency," I mean taking into account all of the information you have about the group members, the situation, the nature of the discussion, your goals for the meeting, then making your choice of a behavioral strategy based on your analysis of this information.

Third, your style of leading may need to change during the course of the group meeting. If the group leader feels that the group is reaching premature consensus under a supportive style of leading, then the leader may need to adapt to this contingency by switching to a more participative style. The objective and test of effective choices of leadership behavior is the ability to get the group members *to follow your lead.* When your style of leading changes, it helps the group to change and adapt.

The fourth step in developing a flexible style of leading is to convince group members of the legitimacy and honesty of your self-presentations. This does not mean to change your basic personality. It does mean to persuade your group that you can temporarily modify behaviors so as to respond to urgent circumstances. This goal may be the most difficult to accomplish for most persons. We are seldom equally comfortable with different styles of behavior; we tend to prefer one or two patterns of conduct. Group members learn to expect these preferred patterns of behavior. If the leader changes styles too quickly, or is not convincing when moving from an autocratic to a democratic style, the members are likely to become suspicious of the leader's motive for the change. Consider the following statement:

Marcy M., 27 years old, team member of a defense system subcontractor.

. . . Then my boss went away on one of those "management training" weekends. When he came back he tried to act like a different person. Where he had been helpful and considerate, he became "Management by Results" oriented. He was pretty funny, to tell the truth. No one knew how to behave around him because we all knew what he was really like. The change just didn't fit. I guess he picked up on how we were responding to him because it didn't last more than a week. Then he was back to his old self and we got some work done.

Marcy's statement is important for two reasons. First, it points out how persons learn to expect certain behavioral patterns to define an individual's personality. When the person changes, the people around him or her tend to resist. Second, Marcy's case is a good example of how a change in behavior can be nullified by uncooperative group members. Her boss returned to "his old style" of leading because the new style was not allowed to pay off.

Effective changes in behavioral flexibility do not occur overnight, or even on a long weekend. It takes time for group members to accept changes, especially if they seem abrupt or insincere. Had Marcy's boss said "Look, I went to a really interesting training session last weekend and I want to try to implement some new ideas from it in our group," he might have been more successful. You need to *prepare* group members for style changes. Simply changing your style of leading and expecting others to accept the change runs counter to human nature. For changes to be accepted they must evolve slowly, with adequate preparation made along the way.

The adaptive approach to preparation for group meetings includes the ability to be flexible in choices made about communication behaviors. One of this approach's major strengths is its assumption that through effective management of one's own communication optimal group outcomes may be achieved. Another strength of this approach is its reliance on performance in the given case. No matter how well a leader prepares for leading, if the objectives of the meeting are not consistently met, if contingencies are not responded to, then the choices of leading behavior have not been effective. A third strength of the adaptive approach is simply that it emphasizes learning communication skills leadership emphasizes to influence group outcomes and goals. The adaptive approach assumes these skills can be learned by almost anyone, and that they can be improved by examining experiences in specific small group settings.

Now that you have examined the bases for the adaptive approach to leading, you are ready to explore a few of the problems which face most leaders.

Overcoming Leadership Problems in the Small Group

The theme of this essay has been the need for leaders to learn how to adapt their communication to the needs and expectations of group situations and group members. An effective leader is an individual who possesses a genuine desire to lead, an understanding of leadership roles and functions, and an ability to demonstrate competency in the skills of leading others while striving to accomplish objectives. Failure in any one of these essential areas may lead to problems of leadership which will adversely affect the group.

Self-analysis is essential to effective leadership; it is crucial in developing behavioral flexibility, and the ability to choose among available styles. Self-analysis is vital in learning how to monitor your actions and statements, as well as their effects on individual group members. For an effective group leader, the study of human behavior, and particularly of *how behavior attains meaning* within the group, is a continuous and challenging task. Each group, each group member, and each new group situation will produce its own norms for communicating and relating. The leader who is able to adapt to these new situations and norms will serve both the group's best interests and his or her own.

No matter how careful your preparation, no matter how flexible your style of leading, and how much information and persuasion you can muster at any one place and time, problems will occur in groups. The best way to learn how to overcome problems is to develop critical questions aimed at improving your analysis of self, situation, together with ways and means of overcoming difficulties when they arise. Here are some critical questions which can help you improve your ability to overcome leadership problems:

1. *What is the goal of my group?* A leader must always be mindful of the group's goal, and of his or her responsibility to help the group reach its goal. However, simply knowing how to state the group's goal does not provide insights into how to overcome leadership problems when they arise. Learn to also ask:
   —How does this goal fit into the organization's objectives?
   —How will we know whether or not we have reached our goal?
   —Have I provided adequate awareness of our goal and associated tasks for the group members to accomplish it?
   —Are there any extended obstacles which may prevent us from reaching our goal?
   —What can be done to overcome these obstacles?
2. *What are the goals of the individual group members?* A leader should be consciously aware of the personal goals of each group member. This information can often be used to motivate or persuade group members in reaching group goals. Learn to ask:
   —How do these goals enhance our ability to accomplish the objective?
   —How do these goals conflict with our ability to accomplish the objective?
   —How can I be instrumental in overcoming potential or real sources of conflict?
   —What factors outside of the group setting may influence the behavior of each group member?
   —Are there hierarchical or territorial problems which may affect our discussions?
   —Are there interpersonal problems which may affect our discussions?
   —What can I do to overcome these potential sources of difficulty?
3. *What are the patterns of influence generated within my group?* A group leader should be able to isolate and identify the opinion leaders on particular issues within the group. The leader should also be able to deal productively with the personal power of each group member in relation to other group members. Learn to ask:
   —Who says what to whom with what effect?
   —What are the sources of personal power for each group member?
   —How do these sources of power conflict? How might they be coordinated?
   —What is my authority within the group? Who disputes my authority and why?

——How do the individual group members respond to my authority and power?

4. *What are the equities and inequities within this group?* A group leader should strive to equitably apportion resources, rewards, assignments, and punishments among group members. Learn to ask:
   ——What rewards are sought by individuals in this group?
   ——What punishments are meted out by individual group members, and for what reasons are they meted out?
   ——What are my group's standards for apportioning resources among members?
   ——Who regularly expresses distress during group meetings? What is the source of his or her distress?
   ——How can I be instrumental in alleviating distress of group members?

5. *How effective are the agendas and procedures used by this group?* The group leader is responsible for setting agendas and initiating procedures for problem-solving and decision-making. Learn to ask:
   ——Are group members well prepared for group meetings? If not, why? Am I providing enough material concerning the agenda?
   ——Do group members take an active role in shaping the agenda/procedures? If so, does this indicate dissatisfaction with my agendas and procedures?
   ——Do I provide adequate understanding of the agenda and procedures?
   ——What can be done to improve the efficiency of the group's communication?
   ——How can I be instrumental in improving the efficiency of the group?

This is not an exhaustive list, but it should point the way for you to develop your own questions. Although I encourage you to develop an adaptive approach to leading a group, remember, no leader can be all things to all group members. There will undoubtedly be times when your rationality, your communicative skills, and your willingness to cooperate with the group will clash with their personal goals and professional aspirations. To discipline yourself as a leader also means to be aware of the possibility of error and human frailty.

Conclusion

Communication is both the means and the goal of effective leadership in small groups. You can learn how to be a more effective leader by learning how to improve the choices you make among the words you speak and the actions you perform. The adaptive approach to leading requires that you develop skill in responding to the needs and expectations of group members and group situations. This essay has provided a brief synopsis of the essential skills of leading groups in American business and industry. No essay, however, can make you a leader. The ideas and advisories provided here can only document some of the attitudes and practices of leadership. Your ability to discipline yourself, to apply these understandings to your own choices of behavior within the group, and to be continually alert to the challenges of leadership will be the true test of your skill in leading.

Notes

1. Julia T. Wood, "Leading in Purposive Discussions: A Study of Adaptive Behavior," COM-MUNICATION MONOGRAPHS, 44 (June 1977), 152–165. For an experiencial treatment of this material available for classroom use, see Julia T. Wood, "Leading as a Process of Persuasion and Adaptation," in J. W. Pfeiffer and J. E. Jones (Eds.), 1976 GROUP FA-CILITATORS' ANNUAL HANDBOOK. Lajolla, CA: University Associates, 1976, 132–135.
2. For an extended discussion of these areas, see Gerald M. Phillips, Douglas J. Pedersen, and Julia T. Wood, GROUP DISCUSSION: A PRACTICAL GUIDE TO PARTICIPATION AND LEADERSHIP. Boston: Houghton Mifflin Co., 1979.
3. See Fred E. Fiedler, "The Contingency Model—New Directions for Leadership Utilization," JOURNAL OF CONTEMPORARY BUSINESS, 3 (1974), 65–79. See also D. R. Hampton, C. E. Summer, and R. A. Webber, ORGANIZATIONAL BEHAVIOR AND THE PRAC-TICE OF MANAGEMENT, 3rd ed. Glenview, ILL: Scott, Foresman, and Co., 1978.

Developing Leadership
for Change

Stephen C. Schoonover and Murray M. Dalziel

"Change takes place no matter what deters it. . . . There must be measured, laborious preparation for change to avoid chaos."

—Plato

Ancient and modern pundits alike have been preoccupied with change. In all human endeavors change is inevitable. In its most raw and destructive form, change is truly "chaos"—a loss of control. When people in business initiate change or respond to it with adaptations that increase productivity, we call it innovation. But, how can change be harnessed to competitive advantage? And how can "chaos" be avoided?

In a drive to cut costs, a major old-line manufacturing company with a conservative workforce decided to institute a new manufacturing process based on the "just in time" principle. Inventories would be slashed; workers would be much more dependent on one another. Rumors about radical "Japanese-style" management spread rapidly. Japanese grafitti and sketches of top management in kimonos appeared in washrooms; unions held emergency meetings decrying the undermining of worker integrity and the "American Way."

Unfortunately, management had guaranteed a morale problem. They resisted making public knowledge the significant recent corporate losses and the vital savings on inventory. And they failed to publicize their sincere belief that corporate survival was at stake and that increased teamwork and tapping the energy and ingenuity of workers was a critical step in becoming competitive.

Many organizations have been victims of a poorly-planned, wrenching change experience that has caused unexpected problems. A conservative view is to "leave things as they are," but history reminds us that change is inevitable. The innovative leader *expects* it, *fosters* it, *plans* it, *directs* it, and *uses* it for competitive advantage.

Why Change?

Successful businesses must provide a stable environment for productive work. They also must adapt constantly to: new market pressures; the changing composition and values of consumers; new information and technologies; and shifting practices and processes within.

In a very real sense change often is a prerequisite for organizational survival. It also helps people grow: New ways of exercising and creating power are discovered; new skills are developed; new ways of sharing and teaming are made possible. In short, both individuals and organizations can profit from a spirit of exploration and growth.

Changes can rejuvenate organizations, but only when channeled to:
□ Improve productivity or quality of products and services;
□ Confront dissatisfaction; and
□ Create new opportunities.

The leadership of a large, heavy manufacturing corporation decided to introduce handheld microprocessors for inventory control. Anticipating significant resistance, the company publicized its plans up front and then debugged the new practice with a small, highly visible group of independent workers with little stake in the change process—"crane drivers" on the loading dock. Soon after introducing the new devices, the drivers became steadfast advocates of the change. Their group even developed a slogan—"The Best Is At Hand." As word spread about the ease-of-use and efficiency of the hand-held microprocessors, other workers actually requested them.

The Best Change Practices

Change leadership is a key role in any modern organization. It requires a range of skills that few possess naturally. Typically, simple over-sights, lack of persistence, and human barriers underlie failed change efforts.

To determine the best change practices, we conducted and analyzed a series of interviews with change leaders in a variety of leading-edge companies. We have found that three groups of factors decide success (See figures 1–4). They represent the critical assets or barriers in all change processes, and therefore should be the primary focus of any leader's efforts. Besides defining a framework for diagnosing vulnerabilities, we also specified effective strategies or "best practices" for overcoming barriers in each of the major dimensions of change (See figures 5–7).

Change leaders can take the chance out of change by focusing on the critical areas of modification and the best practices to guide the process. To be effective, leaders must ensure enough flexibility for creative problem-solving,

---

History of Change: The prior experience of the organization in accepting change.

Clarity of Expectations: The degree to which the expected results of change are shared across various levels of the organization.

Origin of the Problem: The degree to which those most affected by the change initiated the idea or problem the change solves.

Support of Top Management: The degree to which top management sponsors the change.

Compatibility with Organizational Goals: The degree to which the proposed change corresponds to past and present organizational practices and plans.

Figure 1. Five dimensions of organizational readiness.

Inventor: Integrates trends and data into concepts, models, and plans; envisions the "big picture" first; adapts plans.

Entrepreneur: Instinctively focuses on organizational efficiency and effectiveness; identifies critical issues and new possibilities; actively seeks advantages and opportunities.

Integrator: Forges alliances; gains acceptance of himself, his team, and their program; relates practical plans to strategic plans and organizational issues.

Expert: Takes responsibility for the technical knowledge and skills required for the change; uses information skillfully and explains it in a logical way.

Manager: Simplifies, delegates, assigns priorities; develops others; gets the job done at all costs.

Figure 2. Five change-team roles.

Clarifying Plans is the process in which implementors define, document, and specify the change.

Integrating New Practices is the process in which an organization incorporates change into its operations.

Providing Education refers to those programs in which end users learn about and use new processes and procedures.

Fostering Ownership is the process through which end users come to identify new processes and procedures as their own, rather than regarding them as changes imposed upon them.

Giving Feedback is the process in which a detailed objective is monitored and used to judge the effectiveness of the implementation plan.

Figure 3. Five dimensions of the implementation process.

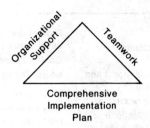

Comprehensive
Implementation
Plan

Figure 4. Effective planned change

---

1. History of Change

Inform end users fully; avoid surprises

Make a reasonable case for change in end users' terms

Spend more time talking

Involve end users in diagnosing vulnerabilities

Start implementation with receptive workers

Start implementation with a small part of the change for quick, visible payoff

Publicize successes

2. Clarity of Expectations

Emphasize the benefits of change—to the organization, the unit, and end users

Avoid surprises; specify possible impact, outcomes, and problems

Make change plans public

Solicit formal and informal feedback

3. Origin of the Problem

Specify who wants the change and why

Clarify end users' concerns about the change

Specify the effects of the change on day-to-day operations and work routines

Present potential problems clearly and completely

Set goals that confront end-user problems first

Use feedback as a barometer of how fast to proceed with implementation plans

4. Support of Top Management

Define top-management concerns

Develop an influence network—top management allies, informal coalitions

Implement a small part of the change for quick results and good publicity

Develop a formal management review from top management's perspective

5. Compatibility of the Change

Frame the change in terms of present organizational values and goals

Integrate the change into ongoing procedures when possible

Make change plans overt, common knowledge

Start the change in an accepting environment

Don't oversell the change

Figure 5. Organizational readiness problem solving strategies.

1. Inventor

Make a wide search for change suggestions

Review the common organizational and social sources of innovation

Talk about potential future problems

Discuss the "What if" implications of new technologies, market changes, etc.

Use your team to review products and services periodically

2. Entrepreneur

Work on tolerating partial answers, interim solutions, mistakes

Practice framing ideas so that they "sell"

Develop change resources and influence networks

Develop planning and goal-setting skills

3. Integrator

Develop interpersonal skills

Develop informal alliances and coalitions, as well as a formal team

Protect the change project from the usual organizational pressures

Confront conflicts and clarify distortions

Inform and update key personnel

4. Expert

Acquire knowledge and skills, or be responsible for finding experts

Develop skills of working with "outside" consultant(s)

Develop presentation skills

Update team members and end users

Monitor change plans

5. Manager

Develop coaching skills

Set goals skillfully

Specify, review, and revise change plans

Delegate responsibility freely

Take responsibility for outcomes

Keep morale high with frequent face-to-face feedback

Figure 6. Change-team roles: improvement strategies

enough protection to maintain work-group *esprit,* and enough control to complete specific critical tasks. In practice, four simple principles support the best change efforts:

1. Focusing on the proven critical barriers to change in organizations.
2. Choosing and enacting those selective "best practices" that fit the organizational setting.
3. Thinking about and completing any planned innovation in small, unintimidating steps.
4. Following a proven management framework that promotes understanding the change, refining appropriate implementation strategies, setting appropriate goals, formulating clear plans and completing critical action steps (See figure 8, page 000).

Change often is a reaction to pressures or a response to innovation. However, organizations sometimes make the wrong change for wrong reasons, or the wrong change for the right reasons, or the right change in an inefficient and stressful way. Therefore, the first organizing step in planned change is to *test and specify your ideas.* By specifying change plans, a leader not only maps an initial direction, but also increases commitment.

1. Clarifying Plans

Make one person responsible for implementation plans

Formulate clear, simple, time-bound goals

Make specific plans with milestones and outcomes

Make plans public

Give and solicit frequent face-to-face feedback

2. Integrating New Practices

Limit the amount of change introduced at any one time

Slow the change process

Introduce the change to receptive users first

Ensure that the rationale and procedure for change are well known

3. Providing Education

Involve the end users and incorporate their experience

Provide "hands-on" training whenever possible

Design training from end users' perspective

Train motivated or key end users first

Evaluate the effects of training or work practices and end-users attitudes

4. Fostering Ownership

Ensure that the change improves end users' ability to accomplish work

Provide incentives for end users applying the change

Specify milestones for getting end-user feedback

Incorporate end-user suggestions in the implementation plans

Publicize end-user suggestions

5. Giving Feedback

Document and communicate the expected outcomes of the change

Ensure frequent face-to-face feedback

Identify clear milestones

Make sure feedback includes the large organization

Acknowledge key successes

Figure 7. Implementation process problem-solving strategies

Figure 8. Effective leadership steps

Information Gathering

Information gathering is a process that operates from the beginning to the end of the change implementation.

Leaders direct the change process as much by example as by management skills. Therefore, the first prerequisite for discovering assets and barriers to change is open-mindedness and self-questioning that results in a personal inventory of organizational practices and available people and resources.

After self-inquiry, effective change agents form wider visions of organizational vulnerabilities by assessing employee and management attitudes and practices. They gather a variety of opinions from colleagues and end-users of the change, managers from other sections of the business, and even those outside the organization who use its products or services. Short, efficient, focused discussions can yield the vital information in the normal course of a few days without disrupting the work routine.

A spirit of inquiry also fosters effective group involvement and dialogue, both among system implementors and selected groups of end users. In fact, information-gathering is in itself an intervention—a method of comparing perceptions and confronting descrepancies among various organizational groups.

Defining Barriers to Change

Often skilled leaders instinctively focus on critical barriers to change, and then foster it by directing the attention of decision-makers and end-users to a selective group of factors. All too often, vital vulnerabilities are left unattended. The five attributes of *Organizational Readiness,* the five roles of the effective *Change Team* and the five aspects of an effective *Implementation Process* provide a focus for discovering and confronting the critical vulnerabilities that interfere with planned change (See figures 1–4, page 548).

Hidden issues and personality conflicts inevitably influence all planned change. Leaders must confront these aspects of their organizations, but in a very special way. By making step-by-step plans the priority, while respecting the feelings and contributions of individuals, leaders can map a creative course that avoids personal issues and individual and group regression.

Setting priorities, however, requires more than determining selected vulnerabilities and avoiding emotional pitfalls. All barriers to change are not equally important to confront. Moreover, barriers to change are often deeply imbedded in stubborn, long-standing attitudes and practices. Trying to resolve too many problems in the context of a planned change can prove impossible, if not destructive. Therefore, a leader must focus on problems that would have very significant costs to the organization if ignored, and on factors that have the most positive leverage on productivity, quality, or worker satisfaction. Most often, these priorities are clarified in discussions that try "what if" simulations for the various vulnerabilities defined as problems.

To fullfill these mandates:

☐ Focus on the most common barriers to change;
☐ Discuss behaviors, not personalities;
☐ Confront only a few problems that have the highest potential cost to the organization if not addressed.

In addition, remember that although the major goal may be planned change, organizational development is a frequent salutory by-product.

Confronting Barriers

Problem-solving is a process that requires openness, creativity, and flexibility. It starts when you decide which organizational barriers to confront, and is applied during each subsequent step in the change process. Goal-setting, planning, feedback, and plan revision, although defined as separate tasks, each rely on effective problem-solving techniques.

Vulnerabilities defined by the three major dimensions of change must be translated into workable problems that are *clearly defined, small and specific in scale,* and *easily understood and accepted by implementors and end-users alike.* This requires wisdom, effort, and collaboration—and prompt action.

Once the process of discovering obstacles has begun, timely interventions are a prerequisite for building or maintaining momentum. In part, the problem-solving strategies ("best practices") speed the process of confronting obstacles. By encouraging the consideration of a variety of solutions, particularly suggestions from end-users, leaders can tailor solutions to the workplace. This means visible plans, in clear terms, framed in a manner that makes sense to those who must live with them.

Beyond defining the problem in an acceptable manner, the skilled leader also provides appropriate, timely resources, such as information or education about new procedures and processes. In addition, the good leader must increase the support of employees by:

☐ Increasing interpersonal, group, and written communications;
☐ Increasing opportunities for management feedback;
☐ Reporting frequently on the status of the problem-solving process; and
☐ Rewarding each step in confronting barriers to change.

Use the following checklist to rate the quality of the goals you set.

___ Easy to understand.
___ Simply expressed.
___ Results-oriented, not activity-oriented.
___ Limited in number and scope.
___ Challenging.
___ Specific in their description of the following:
    ___ Qualities
    ___ Quantities
    ___ Responsible People
    ___ Constraints, and
    ___ Costs
___ Time-bound with specific deadlines and milestones.
___ Subject to measurement and feedback.

Figure 9. Have you set change goals that will work?

Planning and Implementing

How can a leader make and complete plans most effectively? Often projects fail because they lack focus, or because steps are ill-defined or too difficult to implement. The first key to avoiding these pitfalls is effective goal-setting. Goals, whether implicit or explicit, drive productive actions in a business setting. Moreover, evidence shows that just the act of setting goals increases the probability for goal completion and overall productivity.

In the initial planning phases of purposeful change, leaders must strike a careful balance. Specific goals are necessary for good work, but may produce opposition from anxious participants in the change process. Therefore, creative goal-setting is necessary. (See figure 9). Leaders must:

1. Set broad performance goals in early phases of change with a great deal of dialogue to involve participants.
2. Set specific goals with short timelines covering only the initial phase of the change. This also gives immediate and probably positive feedback about the process of change.
3. Set preliminary goals focused on outcomes that are immediate concerns of end users.

Most often, the best way to begin the goal-setting process is by asking, "What results do I want?" After defining a best outcome, then ask, "What objective measures or accomplishments represent an *excellent* result?" Make sure you allow adequate dialogue about these questions within your management team and with co-workers, and that you take the time to improve goals by simplifying, objectifying, and testing them.

Well-defined goals are a prerequisite for productive actions. However, they provide only one aspect of a plan—clear outcomes in the change process. They must be incorporated into a comprehensive framework—an action plan—to be truly effective. An *excellent* implementation plan:

☐ Assigns priorities to tasks;
☐ Simplifies and organizes the change process;
☐ Specifies responsibilities; and
☐ Outlines methods for measuring progress and making necessary revisions.

The plan represents a roadmap that expresses ideas and concerns in discrete, workable terms. It makes sure that you assess the critical factors that enhance or impede innovation and translate them into practical strategies and reachable goals.

Maintaining and Promoting Change

A leader's role in planned change extends well beyond the phase of implementation. By debriefing the experience, he or she refines plans and supports change as both a cultural value and a means of personal growth. In addition, the communication feedback and networking so vital for a specific project can become part of a leader's management repertoire through techniques such as:

☐ Periodic team meetings to discuss possible change plans;
☐ Larger organizational meetings with top management or other segments of the business to discuss vulnerabilities and opportunities;
☐ Organizational performance appraisals; or
☐ Consultant feedback about possible changes and barriers to change.

Change in any business system is inevitable. Competition, evolution, creativity, and even individual rebelliousness, inexorably alter the landscape of all organizations over time. Because of this inevitability *a leader's choice is not whether to change, but how.* Particularly in these turbulent times, when social, attitudinal, and technological changes are pervasive, managers must either embrace change as a normal, healthy process in the service of growth and adaptation, or perish because of their investment in the status quo. When values and knowledge undergo rapid change, people—their ideas, tolerances, skills, and idiosyncrasies—become the primary adaptive resource of organizations. In the new workplace, change must be acknowledged—even embraced—as a constant companion to be nurtured and exploited to competitive advantage.

8

Small Group Evaluation: Process and Participation

Although the expression might be a cliché, in truth "practice does make perfect." Not practice that repeats bad mistakes, but practice that is evaluated and turned into constructive advice. This approach to learning is, or should be, part of most group experiences. All groups can profit from careful observation and skillful evaluation. Our emphasis upon evaluation and criticism is predicated on the belief that small group communication is an activity that people engage in. It is something *they do,* and as such, it can be improved. But improvement demands more than mere participation. Simply being in a group, or reading about one, does not guarantee success. Specific group interactions must be analyzed.

Feedback regarding the group and its members may take a variety of forms. Evaluations may be oral or written. The members may judge their own performances and that of the group's. On many occasions outside observers can watch the group and supply critical comments. The data generated by personal or outside evaluations can be objective (e.g., counting the number of times each person talks) or subjective (e.g., preparing an essay on one's reaction to his or her role as leader). Evaluations may be offered during various stages of the group's progress or at the conclusion of the meeting. And if the members are fortunate enough, they can stop and start a video tape of the previous meeting and discuss their performance. What is important in all of these procedures is that the members of the group are receiving feedback about their strengths and weaknesses.

Regardless of what form the evaluation takes, most experts agree that improvement will not be forthcoming unless group processes and individual contributions are measured against some standards of good and bad, right and wrong. These criteria enable the group to isolate and measure *what* happened, *why* it happened, and *what can be done* about it. Having an established set of criteria also gives the participants goals to strive for as they systematically collect and interpret material regarding their deliberations. The four essays in this chapter offer a variety of instruments with which to observe and evaluate group performance and, subsequently, to improve that performance.

Our first selection, by John K. Brilhart, tells us what to look for when evaluating group procedures and individual behaviors. Brilhart stresses the importance of evaluation to improvement when he notes, "Unless practice is constantly evaluated, it may result in bad habits. The means to learning is practice with analysis and evaluation leading to change in future discussions." To this end, Brilhart examines the role of the observer and the tools for observing and evaluating.

Also subscribing to the main thesis of this chapter (i.e., that participation and practice in small groups *must* include constructive evaluation), Larry A. Samovar and Stephen W. King present five instruments that may provide group members with descriptive and evaluative feedback: (1) the "Who Talks to Whom and How Often" form, (2) the "Type of Contribution" form, (3) the "Group Evaluation" form, (4) the "Individual Participant Evaluation" form, and (5) the "Leader Evaluation" form. What is unique about the Samovar and King forms is that in order to illustrate the nature and value of these rating instruments, the authors demonstrate how each of them might appear as filled out for a hypothetical group discussion.

Albert C. Kowitz and Thomas J. Knutson approach the topic of process and participant evaluation by focusing on a number of problems often faced by members of task groups. They contend that most problems can be traced to content (what the group talks about), procedure (the "rules" and organization of the group), and personnel (how the members treat each other). They diagnose these areas by offering a practice study guide. This guide takes the form of a series of questions and a performance checklist. Each of these allows the participants to identify, deal with, and learn from their evaluation.

Our final essay is aimed toward you discovering something about *your* leadership style. Fred E. Fiedler and Martin M. Chemers offer a method by which you can identify that style (the Least Preferred Co-worker (LPC) Scale), and also find the conditions under which you would be most productive as a leader. It is their conclusion that "your effectiveness as a leader will depend on how well your style fits your leadershp situation."

Observing and Evaluating Discussions

John K. Brilhart

As many writers have pointed out, the old motto "practice makes perfect" should be revised to read "practice makes permanent." So it is in discussion. Unless practice is constantly evaluated, it may result in bad habits. The means to learning is practice with analysis and evaluation leading to change in future discussions.

Constructive evaluation depends on observation and feedback of information about how a discussion group is doing. Through reading this book, listening to your instructor, and classroom practice you are developing a participant-observer orientation. Even while you are participating in discussion, a part of your attention is given to observing how you and your group are proceeding. One cannot both observe and participate in the same instant, so attention must be shifted rapidly from the content of the discussion to the processes of the group. As skill is developed in being a participant-observer, a discussant becomes more and more able to supply both the functional roles needed by the group and feedback about what is going on. Evaluative feedback can be used by the group to change or correct any lack of information, attitudes, norms or procedures which keep the group from being as productive as it might be.

Skillful as one may become at maintaining a participant-observer orientation, he will sometimes become so involved in the interaction over an important issue that he will lose perspective. Then a nonparticipating observer will be helpful. Any group learning the skills and attitudes of discussion (such as in a speech class) will benefit from the feedback of a nonparticipating observer. The first part of this chapter describes the role of the observer, suggests how he or she can be most useful to a group and supplies him or her with some forms for guiding his or her observations. Some of these techniques and forms can be used by leaders and members, even when a nonparticipating observer is not present. The final part of the chapter considers interpersonal feedback and confrontation as a means to developing personal insight and proficiency in discussion.

As a result of studying this chapter and practice in applying its content, you should:

1. Be able to describe the role of a reminder-observer and a critic-observer;
2. Be able to prepare a specific set of questions which you would seek to answer as observer of any specific group to which you are assigned;

From John K. Brilhart, "Observing and Evaluating Discussions," *Effective Group Discussion* (Wm. C. Brown Company Publishers: Dubuque, Iowa, 1967, pp. 163–187: 2nd edition, 1974). John K. Brilhart is affiliated with the Department of Speech Communication, University of Nebraska.

3. Be able to explain how to reduce defensive reactions to your observations;
4. Distinguish between process and content observations;
5. Be able to devise postmeeting reaction forms appropriate to any group of which you are a member, chart the flow and frequency of verbal interaction, diagram role functions of members, and use group, member, and leader rating scales;
6. Give direct interpersonal feedback that will be honest and helpful to fellow group members;
7. Describe how you are perceived as a discussant by your classmates.

The Role of the Observer

Every student of discussion and group processes needs the experience of observing discussion groups at work. As students have remarked countless times, "It looks different when you are sitting outside the discussion." The observer can see clearly what he was only vaguely aware of while discussing. After observing other discussants, she may be motivated to change her own conduct as a discussant. It is therefore suggested that you observe as many discussions as possible. In the speech classroom, it is wise for you to change frequently from being a discussant in one group to being an observer of another.

A very useful technique is the "fishbowl" arrangement in which a discussion group is surrounded by a circle of nonparticipating observers. These observers may all be focusing on the same aspects of group process and/or content, or may be assigned to observe, evaluate, and report on different factors (e.g., leadership, patterns of group problem solving, use of information, roles of members, verbal and nonverbal communication). Observers can be assigned on a one-to-one basis to participants and "alter egos" who make whispered suggestions to the discussant behind whom they sit; or when asked to do so indicate how they think their discussant feels or what he or she means by some action or comment.

Do not try to observe everything at once. Limit your focus to a few aspects of the discussion, perhaps at first to only one. Later, with experience, confidence, and increased awareness of the dynamics of a group, you will be ready to observe without a definite focus. You will then be able to decide as you watch which characteristics of the group are most important to assess in detail. No observer can simultaneously chronicle the content and flow of interaction, take notice of various group and individual objectives, judge the information and logic of remarks, assess the atmosphere and note the organization of the discussion. If the observer tries to do so, the result is sure to be confusion which will reduce both his personal learning and his ability to give feedback to the group.

The nonparticipating observer can do three types of things, sometimes all during a single discussion: learn from the example of others; remind the group of techniques or principles of discussion they have overlooked; supply critical evaluations of the discussion. Responsibilities as reminder and critic to the group will be discussed in the following pages.

The Reminder-Observer

Often group members need to be reminded of what they already know. During interaction they may fail to notice what has been happening or to remember useful attitudes and techniques. To help them, a type of reminder-observer role has been developed. The reminder helps the group without offering any criticism. Many of your classroom discussions will be improved by having one member participate only as a reminder-observer. The reminder role should be changed from one discussion to another in order to give everyone a chance to remind without depriving anyone for a long time of the chance to practice discussion skills. Once you have developed skill in maintaining a participant-observer orientation, you will be able to act as a reminder to nonclassroom discussion groups in which you are a participant. If you serve as a model, gradually you will notice that all members of a continuing group begin to remind.

Before serving as a reminder, the following guidelines for reminder-observers should be studied carefully. They are designed to reduce defensive reactions to your observations.

DO:
1. Stress the positive, pointing out what a group is doing well.
2. Emphasize what is most important, rather than commenting on everything you may have observed.
3. Focus on the processes of the group rather than on the content and issues per se.
4. Put most of your remarks in the form of questions, keeping in mind that all authority for change rests with the group. You have no authority except to remind, report, and raise questions.
5. Remain completely neutral, out of any controversy about either content or procedure. You can do this by asking questions in a dead-pan manner, such as, "I wonder if the group realizes that we have discussed _____ , _____ and _____ in the space of five minutes?" "Are we ready for consideration of possible solutions?" "I wonder if John and Amy understand each other's points of view?" "I wonder if we all understand the purpose of our committee?" "Is everyone getting an equal chance to participate?" Such questions remind the group of principles of good discussion without leveling specific criticisms.

6. Show trends and group characteristics rather than singling out individual discussants for comment (unless absolutely necessary).
7. Interrupt the discussion only when you believe the group is unlikely to become aware of what is troubling it. First give the group enough time to correct itself.

DON'T:
1. Play the critic-umpire, telling anyone he or she is wrong.
2. Argue with a member of the group. If your question is ignored, drop it.
3. Tell the group what they should do. You are not playing expert or consultant: your only job is to remind the group members of what they know but have overlooked.

When serving as observer, there are many things you might look for. The content of this book can provide you with a sort of checklist for observing. Some specific things you might notice when serving as reminder are suggested by the following questions:

1. Are the group goals clear? What helped or hindered in clarifying them?
2. Are all members aware of their area of freedom?
3. Is the group gathering information to define the problem fully, or has it become solution-centered too soon?
4. Do members seem to be well prepared for discussing the topic?
5. Is information being accepted at face value or tested for dependability?
6. Has a plan for the discussion been worked out and accepted by the group?
7. Does the discussion seem to be orderly and organized?
8. Do discussants display attitudes of inquiry and objectivity toward information, issues, and the subject as a whole?
9. To what degree does the group climate seem to be one of mutual respect, trust, and cohesiveness?
10. Do all members have an equal opportunity to participate?
11. Is the pattern of interaction open, or unduly restricted?
12. How sound is the reasoning being done by the group?
13. How creative is the group in finding potential solutions?
14. Is judgment deferred until all possible solutions can be listed and understood?
15. Does the group have a list of specific and useful criteria, and is it applying them to possible solutions?
16. While evaluating ideas, is the group making use of information from earlier parts of the discussion?
17. Are periodic summaries being used to help members recall and move on to new issues without undue redundancy?
18. Are there any hidden agendas hampering the group?

19. Are any norms or procedures hampering the group?
20. Are there any breakdowns in communication due to poor listening, by-passing or stoppers?
21. Is the style of leadership appropriate to the group?
22. If a designated leader is present, is he or she encouraging the sharing of leadership by other members?
23. Is the discussion being recorded and charted accurately?
24. Is the degree of formality appropriate to the group size and task?
25. What else seems to be affecting the group's attempts to achieve a goal?

In addition to serving as reminder during the discussion, afterward a reminder-observer may be able to help the group by leading a discussion of the discussion or by making a detailed report of his observations. At this point she can take either of two approaches, depending on what the group wants from her and her degree of expertise:

1. a reporter, who describes the meeting without judgment, diagnosis or suggestions for future meetings;
2. an interpreter, who in addition to reporting also offers explanations for the behavior of the group as seen from an impartial vantage point.

The Critic-Observer

A critic-observer may do considerable reminding, but his or her primary function is as a critic. Such an observer belongs only in the classroom or training group. In some cases the critic-observer is primarily an advisor, either to the group as a whole or to a designated leader. For example, your instructor may interrupt a discussion to point out what she feels is going wrong and to suggest a different technique or procedure. After you have become a proficient observer, you might take the role of critic-advisor for a small discussion group in another speech class or perhaps even for a group in your own class.

The critic-observer usually makes a more detailed report after the discussion than does the reminder-observer. In addition to describing and interpreting important aspects of the discussion, the critic will express opinions about weak and strong points of it. He or she may compliment the group, point out where and how it got into trouble, and even place blame or take an individual member to task. This must be done cautiously and with tact. Many students hesitate to criticize the participation of others, and some balk at accepting criticism leveled at them. Discussants can be helped to give and accept criticism by reminding them of two points: (1) All criticism should be constructive, objective, sincere, and designed to help. (2) All critiques should include both positive and negative comments, with the good points being presented first.

The critic-observer, of course, will look for the same kinds of group behavior as will the reminder. In general, judgments should cover at least four
basic general aspects of the discussion: (1) the group product, including how
well it has been assessed, how appropriate it seems to be to the problem, and
how well group members support it; (2) the group process, including patterns
of interaction, decision making, problem solving, and communication; (3) the
contributions and functional roles of individual members; and (4) leadership,
especially if a designated leader is present. Different criteria will be needed
for public and private groups, learning and problem-solving groups, advisory
and action groups. Observation and rating forms can be developed by the student of small groups for various types of discussions and groups. The forms
included in this chapter are suggestive general models which should be modified or used as guides for the preparation of specific forms and rating scales
adapted to specific situations in your class or natural groups.

Tools for Observing and Evaluating

Any group can improve its efficiency and atmosphere by taking time out
for unstructured evaluation. The designated leader is in the best position to
initiate such a bootstrap operation by suggesting the group take some time to
study and discuss its activity. If this is not done on some periodic basis, there
is danger of its being neglected. For this reason, regular times for assessment
have been built into the operations of many business, government and military
groups. Also, a systematic review is likely to be more objective than one which
is undertaken during a crisis. However, if group evaluation is limited to regular periods following scheduled meetings, much of importance may be forgotten. Also, taking a break for an unplanned evaluation may correct a
damaging attitude or procedure before a serious breakdown can occur within
the group; therefore, it seems advisable for a continuing discussion group to
use both routine and spontaneous discussions of discussion (unstructured evaluation sessions).

Many tools for more formal observation and evaluation of both groups
and individual discussants have been developed and reported elsewhere. In this
book a few of the more important tools are reported, especially those likely to
be helpful for a class in discussion or fundamentals of speech. Instruments for
assessing a group are presented first, followed by those for evaluating individual participants and designated leaders.

Evaluating the Group

Postmeeting Reaction Sheets, or PMR's as they are called for short, are
frequently used to get objective reactions from discussants. Since PMR's are
anonymous, a participant can report personal evaluations without any threat

to self. A PMR may be planned by a chairperson or other designated leader, by an instructor, by a group or by the organizers of a large conference. The PMR's are distributed, completed and collected immediately following the discussion. Figures 1, 2 and 3.

A PMR sheet consists of a simple questionnaire designated to elicit frank comments about important aspects of the group and the discussion. Questions should be tailored to fit the purposes and needs of the person preparing the questionnaire. Sometimes the questions concern substantive items, sometimes interpersonal matters and sometimes matters of technique and procedure. Two or more types of questions may be mixed on a PMR.

The results of the questionnaires should be tallied and reported back to the group as soon as possible, either in printed form or by posting on a blackboard or chart. The results then become a guide for review of past practice and for planning new practices. The questions must be designed to produce data which can readily be tabulated, summarized and reported.

Interaction Diagrams

A diagram of interaction made by an observer will reveal a lot about the relationships among members of a group. The diagram can reveal who is talking to whom, how often each member participates orally, and any dominating persons. A model interaction diagram is shown in Figure 4. Notice the data at the top of the sheet; the names of all participants are located around the circle in the same order in which they sat during the discussion. Each time a person speaks an arrow is drawn from his or her position toward the person to whom the remark was addressed. If a member speaks to the entire group, a longer arrow points towards the center of the circle. Subsequent remarks in the same direction are indicated by short cross marks on the base of the arrow.

Rating Scales

Rating scales can be used by critic-observers to record their judgments about any aspect of the group and its discussion, including group climate, cohesiveness, efficiency, satisfaction, degree of mutual respect, organization of discussion, adequacy of information and the like. A five-point scale is adequate for most purposes. A discussion class can profitably prepare and use its own scales to evaluate a variety of group characteristics. Two or more observers working independently of each other can rate each group and then check the similarity of their ratings. Whenever ratings on the same scale are more than one point apart, the observers can learn by discussing the reasons for their different ratings. Sample scales are shown in Figure 5, illustrating how you can construct your own.

POSTMEETING REACTION SHEET

Instructions: Check the point on each scale that best represents your honest judgment. Add any comments you wish to make which are not covered by the questionnaires. Do *not* sign your name.

1. How satisfied are you with the *results* of the discussion?

very satisfied	moderately satisfied	very dissatisfied

2. How well *organized and systematic* was the discussion?

disorderly	just right	too rigid

3. How do you feel about the *style of leadership* supplied by the chairperson?

too autocratic	democratic	weak

4. *Preparation for this meeting* was

thorough	adequate	poor

5. Did you find yourself *wanting to speak* when you didn't get a chance?

almost never	occasionally	often

6. How do you feel about *working again* with this same group?

eager	I will	reluctant

Comments:

Figure 1. Postmeeting reaction sheet.

POSTMEETING REACTION SHEET

1. How do you feel about today's discussion?
   excellent _____ good _____ all right _____ so-so _____ bad _____

2. What were the strong points of the discussion?

3. What were the weaknesses?

4. What changes would you suggest for future meetings?

(you need not sign your name)

Figure 2. Postmeeting reaction sheet.

Evaluating Individual Participants

Almost any aspect of individual participation can be evaluated by preparing appropriate forms. An analysis of roles of members can be made by listing the names of all members in separate columns on a sheet on which the various functions described in Chapter 2 [Brilhart text] are listed in a vertical column at the left side of the sheet (Figure 6). Each time a participant speaks, a tally is made in the column after the role function just performed. If a member performs more than one function in a single speech, two or more tallies are made. The completed observation form will indicate what functions were supplied adequately, who took harmful roles, what was the degree of role flexibility of each participant in the discussion and so forth.

Figure 7 shows a simple rating form which can be completed by a critic-observer for each participant. The forms can be filled in near the end of the discussion and then handed to the participants. This form was prepared by a group of students and has been used extensively to rate students engaged in practice discussions. Although only illustrative of many types of scales and forms which could be used, it has the virtue of being simple and brief, yet focuses on some of the most important aspects of participation. A somewhat more detailed rating scale for individual participants is shown in Figure 8. Each form could be filled out by an observer, or each participant in a small group might prepare one for every other member of the group.

All of the previously described observation forms and rating scales can be used to analyze and appraise functional leadership.

REACTION QUESTIONNAIRE

Instruction: Circle the number which best indicates your reactions to the following questions about the discussion in which you participated:

1. *Adequacy of Communication:* To what extent do you feel members were understanding each others' statements and positions?

0	1	2	3	4	5	6	7	8	9	10

Much talking past each   Communicated directly with
other, misunderstanding   each other, understanding well

2. *Opportunity to Speak:* To what extent did you feel free to speak?

0	1	2	3	4	5	6	7	8	9	10

Never had a   All the opportunity to
chance to speak   talk I wanted

3. *Climate of Acceptance:* How well did members support each other, show acceptance of individuals?

0	1	2	3	4	5	6	7	8	9	10

Highly critical   Supportive and receptive
and punishing

4. *Interpersonal relations:* How pleasant and concerned were interpersonal relations?

0	1	2	3	4	5	6	7	8	9	10

Quarrelsome, status   Pleasant, empathic,
differences emphasized   concerned with persons

5. *Leadership:* How adequate was the leader (or leadership) of the group?

0	1	2	3	4	5	6	7	8	9	10

Too weak (   ) or   Shared, group-centered,
dominating (   )   and sufficient

6. *Satisfaction with role:* How satisfied are you with your personal participation in the discussion?

0	1	2	3	4	5	6	7	8	9	10

Very dissatisfied   Very satisfied

7. *Quality of product:* How satisfied are you with the decisions, solutions, or learnings that came out of this discussion?

0	1	2	3	4	5	6	7	8	9	10

Very displeased   Very satisfied

8. *Overall:* How do you rate the discussion as a whole apart from any specific aspect of it?

0	1	2	3	4	5	6	7	8	9	10

Awful, waste of time   Superb, time well spent

Figure 3. Reaction questionnaire.

INTERACTION DIAGRAM

frequency and direction of participation

Group _____

Time _____

Begin _____

End _____

Place _____

Observer _____

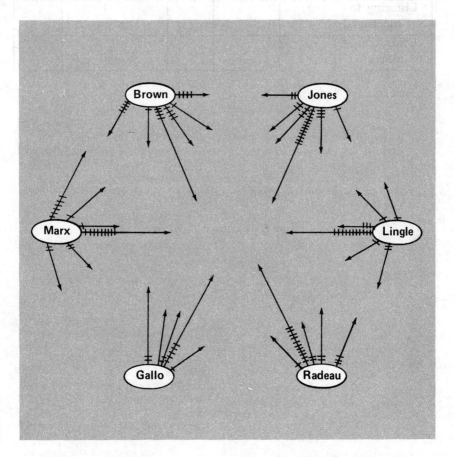

Figure 4. Interaction diagram (Frequency and direction of participation).

DISCUSSION EVALUATION

Date _____   Group _____

Time _____   Observer _____

Group Characteristic	5 excellent	4 good	3 average	2 fair	1 poor
Organization of discussion					
Equality of opportunity to speak					
Group orientation, mutual respect					
Listening to understand					
Evaluation of ideas					

Comments:

Figure 5. Discussion evaluation.

DISCUSSANT FUNCTIONS

Date _____   Group _____

Time _____   Observer _____

Participants' Names

Role Functions						
Group Task	1.	Idea initiating				
	2.	Information seeking				
	3.	Information giving				
	4.	Opinion seeking				
	5.	Opinion giving				
	6.	Elaborating				
	7.	Coordinating				
	8.	Orienting				
	9.	Energizing				
	10.	Recording				
Maintenance	11.	Supporting				
	12.	Harmonizing				
	13.	Tension relieving				
	14.	Gatekeeping				
	15.	Norming				
Self-Centered	16.	Blocking				
	17.	Attacking				
	18.	Recognition seeking				
	19.	Horseplaying				
	20.	Dominating				
	21.	Advocating				

Figure 6. Discussant functions.

PARTICIPANT RATING SCALE

for   Date _____

_____

(name)   Observer _____

1. Did she make useful *substantive contributions to the discussion?* (well prepared, supplied information, adequate reasoning, etc.)

5	4	3	2	1
Outstanding in quality and quantity		Fair Share		Few or none

2. Did she contribute to *efficient group procedures?* (agenda planning, relevant comments, summaries, self-discipline)

5	4	3	2	1
Always relevant, aided organization		Relevant, no aid in order		Sidetracked, confused group

3. How constructive and cooperative was her *attitude?* (listen to understand, responsible, agreeable, group centered, open-minded)

5	4	3	2	1
Very responsible and constructive				Self-centered, stigmas

4. Did she *speak* well? (clear, to group, one point at a time, consise)

5	4	3	2	1
Brief, clear, to group				Vague, indirect, wordy

5. How *valuable* was she to the group? (overall rating)

5	4	3	2	1
Most valuable				Least Valuable

Suggestions:

Figure 7. Participant rating scale.

DISCUSSION PARTICIPATION EVALUATION

For _____

Instructions: Circle the number which best reflects your evaluation of the discussant's participation on each scale.

Superior   Poor

1	2	3	4	5	1. Was prepared and informed.
1	2	3	4	5	2. Contributions were brief and clear.
1	2	3	4	5	3. Comments relevant and well timed.
1	2	3	4	5	4. Spoke distinctly and audibly to all.
1	2	3	4	5	5. Contributions made readily and voluntarily.
1	2	3	4	5	6. Frequency of participation (if poor, too low ( ) or high ( ).
1	2	3	4	5	7. Nonverbal responses were clear and constant.
1	2	3	4	5	8. Listened to understand and follow discussion.
1	2	3	4	5	9. Openminded.
1	2	3	4	5	10. Cooperative and constructive.
1	2	3	4	5	11. Helped keep discussion organized, following outline
1	2	3	4	5	12. Contributed to evaluation of information and ideas.
1	2	3	4	5	13. Respectful and tactful with others.
1	2	3	4	5	14. Encouraged others to participate.
1	2	3	4	5	15. Assisted in leadership functions.
1	2	3	4	5	16. Overall rating in relation to other discussants.

Comments:

Evaluator _____

Figure 8. Discussion participation evaluation.

Improvement: Evaluating People and Groups

Larry A. Samovar and
Stephen W. King

Traditionally instructors have suggested that the best way to improve, whether in tennis, bridge, or group discussion, is to *practice*. Practice *without feedback* is not likely to be of any instructional value and may even cause you to habituate bad habits. The only way you are likely to improve, either individually or as a group, is to compare your actual group discussion behavior to desired behavior and strive toward that ideal.

Unfortunately, there is not a set of five, ten, or thirty-six "rules" or "ideals" that, if followed, will guarantee an effective group discussion or make you a competent discussion participant. Rather, as Fisher has observed, there are "several general principles which may guide but do not guarantee effective communicative behavior in group decision making."[1] Fisher suggested that these guidelines are that you should "(1) be verbally active, (2) develop communicative skills, (3) be sensitive to the group process, (4) commit yourself to the group, (5) avoid despair over apparent slowness, (6) confront social problems, (7) avoid formula answers, (8) be critical, (9) be creative, and (10) be honest."[2] While these guidelines may not recommend behaviors sufficiently specific to direct your behavior in groups, one thing is clear: if you are going to make your actual discussion practices more like the behavior you desire, the first step is an accurate description of your discussion behavior. That is, you need concise information regarding how you and the group acted. In this chapter we will present several tools to help you describe and evaluate individual and group discussion behavior.

Two Approaches to Description and Evaluation

Description and evaluation of group discussion can come from two qualitatively different sources—observers of the group and participants in the group. For instance, as you participate in a group discussion your behavior can be recorded and evaluated by an observer who is not a member of the group or your behavior can be assessed by someone in the group, including yourself. For two important reasons there is considerable difference between these two

From *Communication and Discussion in Small Groups* by Larry A. Samovar and Stephen W. King. Copyright 1981 by Gorsuch Scarisbrick Publishers. Used with permission of the publisher. Larry A. Samovar is affiliated with the Department of Speech Communication, San Diego State University and Stephen W. King is Dean of the School of Communication, California State University at Chico.

sources of description and evaluation. First, the observer can devote his or her entire attention to assessment, while the participant can only devote partial attention to description and evaluation as he or she must participate in the ongoing discussion. As a result, the assessment by a participant may be based on incomplete or inaccurate information. Second, the participant is likely to be affected by the course of the discussion and his or her ratings will reflect biases created during the discussion. For example, if you were a minority of one dissenting from the decision of the group and you then had to assess the "open-mindedness" of the other group members, your judgments might be colored by what had happened during the discussion.

Despite and because of the potential differences, description and evaluation from both observers and group participants are needed for a full and accurate assessment of group behavior. Valuable information can be gained by comparing the ratings of members and observers. Furthermore, you can learn a great deal about group operation as an observer. Accordingly, we will provide you with both participant rating tools and observer rating instruments. We will divide our presentation of the various rating forms into those that *describe* group operation and those that *evaluate* aspects of the group or individual group members. To illustrate the nature and value of each of the rating instruments we will show you each form as it might be filled out on a hypothetical group discussion.

Descriptive Rating Instruments

Obviously, comprehensive description of some aspect of an ongoing group discussion is logically limited to being done by an observer. Furthermore, even very attentive observers cannot describe everything that happens during a group discussion; their observations must be focused on a particular part of the group discussion. Therefore, the two descriptive instruments we present here each focuses on a specific dimension of the group discussion. The first form focuses on *who talked to whom and how often.* (See Figure 1.) This form is completed by an observer keeping a tally of each time one person talks to another person during the course of the discussion. The line to the side of the name of a group member is for recording contributions made to the group as a whole. The example in Figure 1 is a completed "who talks to whom and how often" form for the hypothetical group discussion we mentioned earlier.

From the description of the discussion contained in Figure 1 it is apparent that (a) Steve and Sally talked the most, (b) Sam talked the least, (c) Susan never spoke to Sam and vice versa, (d) Susan and Sally spoke primarily to each other, and (e) most of Steve's comments were made to the group as a whole. This type of information is useful in that it enables you to see various communication patterns that were present in the group. Once these patterns

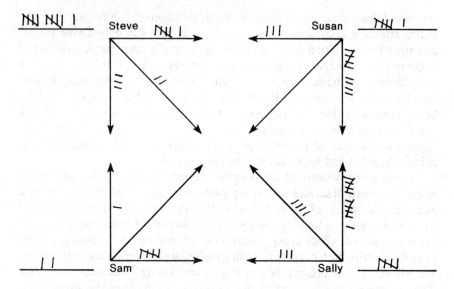

Figure 1. Completed "Who talks to whom and how often" form.

have been identified, you can decide if the amount and direction of interaction aided or hindered the group progress.

The second type of descriptive instrument focuses on the *kinds of contributions* that individual group members make during a discussion. (See Figure 2.) As with the previous form a tally mark is made that classifies each person's contribution into one of the eleven categories.[3] For example, when the observer hears Steve say, "I have some data on that; the Bureau of Labor Statistics said in 1980 that 4 out of 5 families have at least two sources of income," the rating task is to classify that remark as best fitting one of the eleven categories. In this case the remark would be a "substantiation." Figure 2 represents a completed "Type of Contribution" form for the same discussion as was described in Figure 1.

The data from Figure 2 provides much of the same information about our hypothetical group discussion as was contained in the first form we presented; for example, Sally and Steve talked the most and Sam talked the least. However, in addition, the data in Figure 2 reveals that (a) Steve appeared to have done his research and primarily introduced ideas and substantiation, (b) Susan helped the group deal with ideas and information by synthesizing, summarizing, and clarifying, (c) Sam mostly asked questions and accepted or rejected other people's ideas, and (d) Sally contributed to the group in diverse ways.

GROUP _____ II

OBSERVER _____ Clyde

DATE _____ 2-28-81

Type of Contribution	Member #1 Steve	Member #2 Susan	Member #3 Sam	Member #4 Sally
1. Initiates ideas	卌 ||	||		|||
2. Restates ideas	||				||
3. Clarifies ideas			|||			
4. Substantiates ideas	卌			||	
5. Extends ideas					|||
6. Simple request					|||	||
7. Simple response to request	||				|||
8. Modifies idea			||		|||
9. States acceptance or rejection	||			||	||
10. Synthesizes			|||		||
11. Summarizes			卌			
TOTAL	21	18	8	23

Figure 2. Completed "Type of contribution" form.

These two descriptive instruments are not the only ones available to characterize what occurs during a group discussion; however, they do provide a great deal of descriptive information. For example, from the data on these instruments we can learn who participated the most and least, who spoke to whom, who spoke most and least to the group as a whole, and what types of contributions each person made in the course of the discussion. Another whole group of instruments helps us evaluate the group discussion.

Evaluation

Evaluative rating tools help us assess *how well* a particular person accomplished certain tasks, the entire group operated, or a leader functioned. Evaluative rating instruments can be used by both observers and participants as they are completed at the conclusion of the discussion. All three rating forms we will present can be worded for use by either the participants or an observer. For example, when a rating form calls for an evaluation of "How effectively X listened," the X can be a group member being rated by an observer, a group member being rated by another group member, or a group member rating himself or herself. We will present one rating form each for *overall group evaluation, individual participant evaluation,* and *leader evaluation.* We will continue to use our hypothetical group discussion to illustrate the use of each form.

Group Evaluation. The "Group Evaluation" rating form assesses how well the group as a whole accomplished or handled several important group discussion tasks and responsibilities. When the discussion is concluded the rater simply puts an "X" at the position on the seven point scale that best reflects his or her judgment of how well the group did on each of the eight criteria and makes any comments about the group that might be helpful. Figure 3 illustrates a completed "Group Evaluation" form for our hypothetical group discussion.

The completed form in Figure 3 reveals that the rater, Clyde, felt that while the group introduced useful information and reached a valuable decision, they did not encourage Sam's participation or work effectively toward group cohesiveness. If the "Group Evaluation" forms completed by the group participants differ greatly from those completed by observers, you should consider possible reasons for the disparity in evaluation.

GROUP ___II___

RATER ___Clyde___

DATE ___2-28-81___

GROUP CHARACTERISTIC

RATING

EXCELLENT | POOR

1. Organization of discussion

2. Established and maintained cohesiveness

3. Respected and encouraged all group members

4. Spoke effectively

5. Listened effectively

6. Used information well

7. Quality of decision

8. Overall evaluation

COMMENTS: Sam didn't seem involved and wasn't encouraged to participate. A lot of good information introduced.

Figure 3. Completed "Group evaluation" form.

Individual Participant Evaluation

The "Individual Participant Evaluation" form assesses how well an individual member accomplished essential group and individual tasks and functions. When the discussion is concluded this form can be completed by an observer, other members of the group, or the participant himself or herself. Again, the rater circles the number on the scale reflecting his or her judgment of how well the individual met each criteria. Figure 4 shows an "Individual Participant Evaluation" form completed about Steve's participation in our hypothetical discussion.

The evaluation of Steve's participation shown in Figure 4 suggests that he had prepared well, had a great deal of information, and his thinking contributed significantly to the group decision-making. However, the rater felt that Steve did not listen well and was insensitive to the other group members. This kind of discussion profile information, especially if it is consistent from both observers and other group members, is extremely useful for individuals as they attempt to improve their discussion behavior.

Leader Evaluation Form

The final evaluation form we will present is the "Leader Evaluation" form. . . . Leadership functions can and, we suggested, should be shared by all group members. However, when a group discussion leader is appointed or emerges as leader by virtue of his or her position in an organization, the "Leader Evaluation" form is a useful tool for assessing how well the leader accomplished the essential leadership functions. As with the completion of the form previously described, the rater reflects his or her judgment of how well the leader did with the listed leadership functions by circling the appropriate rating on the "Leader Evaluation" form. The form illustrated in Figure 5 assumes that Steve was the assigned leader of the hypothetical discussion we have been assessing throughout this chapter.

The evaluation of Steve's leadership shown in Figure 5 suggests that he failed to perform several important leadership functions. If this information were given to Steve at the conclusion of the discussion, especially if combined with the information from the other forms discussed in this chapter, he would have a very clear idea of the specific areas he would need to work on to improve his leadership ability.

NAME OF GROUP MEMBER ___Steve___

NAME OF RATER ___Clyde___

GROUP ___II___

DATE ___2-28-81___

PARTICIPANT CHARACTERISTIC	EXCELLENT			RATING			POOR
	1	2	3	4	5	6	7
1. Preparation	①	2	3	4	5	6	7
2. Speaking	1	2	③	4	5	6	7
3. Listening	1	2	3	④	5	6	7
4. Open-mindedness	1	2	③	4	5	6	7
5. Sensitivity to others	1	2	3	4	⑤	6	7
6. Worth of information	①	2	3	4	5	6	7
7. Worth of thinking	1	②	3	4	5	6	7
8. Group orientation	1	2	3	④	5	6	7
9. Worth of procedural contributions	1	2	3	④	5	6	7
10. Assistance in leadership function	1	2	③	4	5	6	7
11. Overall evaluation	1	2	③	4	5	6	7

COMMENTS: Steve had a lot of good information but didn't really seem interested in other group members.

Figure 4. Completed "Individual participant evaluation" form.

NAME OF LEADER __Steve__

NAME OF RATER __Clyde__

GROUP __II__

DATE __2 - 28 - 81__

RATING

LEADERSHIP FUNCTIONS	EXCELLENT						POOR
1. Open discussion	1	②	3	4	5	6	7
2. Asked appropriate questions	1	2	3	4	⑤	6	7
3. Offered reviews	1	2	3	4	⑤	6	7
4. Clarified ideas	1	2	3	4	⑤	6	7
5. Encouraged critical evaluation	1	2	3	④	5	6	7
6. Limited irrelevancies	1	2	3	④	5	6	7
7. Protected minority viewpoints	1	2	③	4	5	6	7
8. Remained impartial	1	2	③	4	5	6	7
9. Kept accurate records	1	②	3	4	5	6	7
10. Concluded discussion	1	②	3	4	5	6	7
11. Overall leadership	1	2	3	④	5	6	7

COMMENTS: Steve seemed more concerned with own participation and not with leading the group.

Figure 5. Completed "Leader evaluation" form.

Summary

In this chapter we argued that improvement of individual and group performance in group discussion can only occur through *practice* combined with *feedback*. Accordingly, we presented and illustrated the use of five instruments for providing descriptive and evaluative feedback: (1) the "Who Talks to Whom and How Often" form, (2) the "Type of Contribution" form, (3) the "Group Evaluation" form, (4) the "Individual Participation Evaluation" form, and (5) the "Leader Evaluation" form. Finally, we illustrated how the information these forms provide groups, individual group members, and leaders can be the starting point for improvement in group discussion.

References

1. B. Aubrey Fisher. *Small Group Decision Making: Communication and Group Process.* (New York: McGraw-Hill Book Company, 1974), p. 193.
2. *Ibid.*
3. Adapted from Laura Crowell. *Discussion: Method of Democracy.* (Chicago: Scott, Foresman and Company, 1963), p. 180.

Process and Performance Evaluation:
Problems and Solutions

Albert C. Kowitz
and
Thomas J. Knutson

Introduction

We have presented information in the previous chapters about group process and performance. We suggested that a group must provide essential informational needs, procedural needs, and interpersonal needs to develop an effective and acceptable decision proposal. We also commented on external constraints that affect a group's decision-making process. If a group uses its resources effectively and external constraints are not prohibitive, it should make satisfactory progress toward reaching its goals. Nonetheless, task-oriented groups do encounter difficulties. Interaction among members and progress toward goals are often not as satisfactory as we would like. We may become disenchanted, discouraged, and disappointed with our group's activity. Our group experiences process loss, that is, our group does not utilize the potential of its membership.

If you have read carefully so far, you will undoubtedly experience fewer problems in your small group discussions. You now have appropriate information to assist you as your group makes progress toward its goals. In this chapter we focus on common problems experienced by those involved in small group communication. We suggest possible solutions to those problems and refer you to sections in this book where information about these problems is presented in more detail. In other words, this chapter helps you to identify and correct problems of small group communication. You will find it useful as a practical guide to which you can refer in your future small group experiences.

Diagnosing Problems of Small
Group Communication

We have emphasized that small group processes can be broken down into three dimensions: informational, procedural, and interpersonal. We have organized the remainder of this chapter in terms of these dimensions to further

From Albert C. Kowitz and Thomas J. Knutson, *Decision Making in Small Groups: The Search for Alternatives.* Copyright © 1980 by Allyn and Bacon, Inc. Reprinted with permission. Albert C. Kowitz is affiliated with the Department of Communication at California State University in Sacramento. Thomas J. Knutson is affiliated with the Department of Communication at California State University in Sacramento.

assist you in your analysis of process-oriented problems. The major problems encountered by task-oriented groups include poor information, attempting solutions before defining problems, inadequate progress toward achievement of goals, unsatisfactory coordination of member activity, and failure to maintain member interest. All of these problems may be the result of more specific problems. In the following sections we have presented specific problems and have tried to identify the general problem. In almost all instances, the general problem will be one of the five we mentioned above. Next, we examine the problem from different points of view. Is it a problem associated with the informational dimension? Is it a problem associated with the procedural dimension? Is it a problem associated with the interpersonal dimension? Possibly, the problem reflects issues associated with more than one dimension. Try to be as specific as you can in describing your group's difficulty. Once the problem has been identified, apply the recommendations we give below that seem most appropriate.

Diagnosing Problems Related to the Informational Dimension

Remember that the informational dimension pertains to the content of the task itself. Issues related to this dimension include task analysis, selection and presentation of information, and constraints.

Problem 1: Is the task suitable for group effort? Some common symptoms of this problem include one member doing most of the work, all members performing essentially the same subtasks and very little discussion of issues.

Recommendation: Examine whether the task is open-ended, permits division of labor or requires diversity of member backgrounds. If your present task does not entail these critical task demands, you should consider choosing a different topic. If this task was assigned to your group (e.g., your department head asked your group to solve a departmental problem), you should discuss with the person who made the assignment the possibility that the task might not be suitable for group effort. Finally, if your group decides to keep the topic, you should expand the scope of the task so that issues open to discussion are included.

Problem 2: Has your group correctly identified the primary requirements of its task? We discussed the primary requirements of descriptive, discussion, and problem-solving tasks. Often problem-solving groups discuss the merits of solutions before they have carefully described the problem. This behavior reflects a basic misunderstanding of primary requirements for problem-solving tasks.

Recommendation: Identify the type of task your group is working on (descriptive, discussion, or problem solving). Then list the primary requirements associated with your type of task. Focus on the group's problem before discussing actual solutions. Without a clearly understood problem, group efforts at solution result in little more than wasted time.

Problem 3: Is the task easy or too difficult for group assignment? The elements related to difficulty include range of required information, number of issues, and number of alternatives.

Recommendation: If your task entails discussion of too little information, too few issues, and too few alternatives, you should consider expanding the scope of the task, select a new task, or suggest that members can better complete the task by working independently. If your task entails discussion of too much information, too many issues, and too many alternatives, you should narrow the scope of your topic.

Problem 4: Are group members losing interest in the task because required informational and skill variety is too low or too high? Informational variety refers to diversity in methods of information search and diversity in sources of information. Skill variety includes such behaviors as organizing and coordinating group activity, resolving conflicts, and delegating and directing action.

Recommendation: If your task entails too little variety, you will want to expand the scope of your task to create a need for greater informational and skill variety. If you cannot expand the problem, you probably do not need a group to solve it. If your task requires too much variety, you will want to reduce the scope of your task in order to create and appropriate interest level. Groups cannot do everything: frustration and disinterest result from trying to do too much and, in the process, accomplish very little.

Problem 5: Is the group failing to make progress toward its goal because too little information is available? Successful completion of the group's task requires an adequate information base. If you find group members consistently report "I don't know" or "We ought to look into that," your group is not conducting sufficient informational research to complete its task.

Recommendation: Examine your group's strategy in terms of information search. List your information search objectives and determine which segments of your information needs are completed and which segments are incomplete. Once your informational needs are clear, make specific assignments to group members regarding information search.

Problem 6: Have your group members failed to agree on priorities and values regarding their task? The most common symptom of this problem is a sense of going in circles. Your group will meet, make superficial agreements, and then discuss the same issues again at the next meeting.

Recommendation: Have each member write a list of priorities and value statements. Members can then present their positions as lucidly and logically as possible. Treat differences of opinion as a sign of incomplete information sharing. Assign one member the task of writing the list of priorities as they are discussed and agreed upon.

Problem 7: Is the range of alternatives considered by your group too conventional or ordinary? Is the group discussing worn-out options and solutions? Your cue to this problem is a sense that this option has been tried before or that the particular option is usually recommended for this task or problem.

Recommendation: Your group might profitably examine assumptions or constraints associated with your discussions. Have members list their personal, social, and organizational assumptions (constraints) regarding the task and alternatives associated with the task. Discuss these constraints and try to identify the constraints that are preventing your group from creatively analyzing your task.

Problem 8: Has your group reached premature agreement on an alternative or solution? Often groups will agree on an alternative or solution very early in their discussion. You will notice that when the group has agreed on an alternative, that expression of differences of opinion will be discouraged, and that information search will be directed toward support of that alternative or solution.

Recommendation: At least two options are open to you and your fellow group members. One possibility is to obtain permission to play "devil's advocate." You might suggest to your group that a decision was reached very quickly and that it would be helpful to discuss the alternative or solution in more detail. When your group agrees to this action, you can begin to argue against the decision to test its strengths and weaknesses. A second option is to introduce other alternatives or solutions. If your group members are willing to listen to your suggestions, the introduction of new proposals will create uncertainty. This uncertainty will lead to a broader range of information search and a more comprehensive discussion of alternatives.

Diagnosing Problems Related
to the Procedural Dimension

The procedural dimension of small group communication relates to the coordination of group member activities. The leader of a group typically engages in considerable behavior on the procedural dimension, but all members should have the capability of performing procedural behaviors. Remember the analogy between the procedural comments and the guidance system on a space capsule headed for the moon. Just as the guidance system makes adjustments in the capsule's course, each group member should be able to summarize group activity, delegate and direct action, introduce and formulate goals, assist with role and norm development, and, in general, keep the group moving toward its goal.

Problem 1: Do members in your group express frustration by complaining, "We're not making progress," "We're just spinning our wheels," "We'll never finish this job"?

Recommendation: This problem frequently occurs in groups where the emphasis is placed on either the informational dimension or the interpersonal dimension. Attention to procedural details can manage this frustrating experience. If you are in a group in which members express this type of dissatisfaction, go to the procedural dimension in an effort to point out what the group has already accomplished. Summarize the group's progress and demonstrate the group's success in approaching its goal.

If the group in fact has not made sufficient headway, obviously a summary will not be very helpful. In this case, guide the discussion to deliberation over what needs to be done in order to complete the task. Many times group members have the necessary information but lack the ability to organize their information. In this case, provide the group with orientation statements that keep the group headed toward its goal.

Problem 2: Do members in your group continually return to discuss the same issues over and over again?

Recommendation: We suggested earlier that a task-oriented group develop a concrete strategy for accomplishing its task. A group has agreed on an inappropriate strategy when it goes in circles by returning to discuss the same issues. Probably the most appropriate action to take is to stop and agree on your group's goals and how your group hopes to achieve these goals. We recommend that a member of your group write down the strategy so the group may refer to it from time to time while working on its task.

Problem 3: Do members of your group express uncertainty regarding what information is relevant to your group's task? Sometimes a member will report the results of her or his information search only to find that other members think the information is irrelevant.

Recommendation: These symptoms suggest that your group has not sufficiently narrowed its task. Your group needs to discuss what issues are to be included in the task and what are to be excluded.

Problem 4: Do group members talk too much and waste time accomplishing simple tasks?

Recommendation: This problem typically occurs as a function of leadership and problems low in solution multiplicity. Someone in the group should provide more directive leadership. Someone should take the initiative and guide the group in quickly solving its task or simply point out that the group has solved its problem and recommend adjournment.

Problem 5: Do group members seem reluctant to participate and consequently, make little headway in solving complex problems?

Recommendation: This problem frequently is caused by inappropriate leadership. In a situation where a group's problem is high in solution multiplicity, the leader should avoid directive leadership. When a group faces a complex problem, members providing leadership functions should encourage toleration for a variety of points of view. The leader should operate on the procedural dimension to invite participation, which in turn allows the group to benefit from more information. The leader who facilitates this information distribution will find a greater willingness to participate as well as a higher quality decision.

Problem 6: Does the group spend considerable time joking around and engaging in social conversation when they should be processing information suitable for solving problems?

Recommendation: This problem could be caused by a failure to handle primary tension, a topic discussed in Chapter 5 (Kowitz and Knutson text). This tension results from an inability to stabilize the roles performed by individual members. Members should be made to understand their respective responsibilities. Once the members understand what is expected of them, primary tension decreases and the group can make progress on the task.

Problem 7: Does the group direct the majority of its remarks to one member or do some members fail to participate sufficiently?

Recommendation: The manner in which the group arranges itself can cause this problem. Chapter 3 (Kowitz and Knutson text) provides information relating to the group's seating arrangement. Members should arrange themselves so that each participant has an equal opportunity to communicate with every other participant. When seating arrangement facilitates equal participation, but unequal communication still occurs, try to encourage others to talk and then reinforce them for doing so. Group size also has an effect on participation. Large groups inhibit participation. You may wish to reduce the size of the group.

Problem 8: Do members continually express dissatisfaction with the quality of the group's decision-making practices?

Recommendation: Many times the roots of this problem rest in the group's norms. Your group may wish to list and examine your group's work-oriented norms (see Chapter 6 Kowitz and Knutson text). Perhaps your group's information search and presentation are too restricted. Perhaps your group spends too much of its time socializing. Perhaps your decision-making practices are inappropriate. Two common decision-making rules that usually result in inferior decisions are permitting one group member to make the decision and the majority vote. In most instances, the best decision-making rule is consensus. Consensus is a decision rule whereby all members must agree to a decision before it is accepted by the group.

Diagnosing Problems Related to the Interpersonal Dimension

The interpersonal dimension reflects the attitudes members hold toward one another and the perception of capabilities and personality traits of group members. A pleasant interpersonal atmosphere provides a base that facilitates member participation in the group's activities. Groups have considerable difficulty achieving their goals when experiencing an unpleasant interpersonal atmosphere. To complicate matters even further, interpersonal problems are usually the most difficult to solve.

Problem 1: Do group members experience considerable interpersonal conflict that threatens the continuance of the discussion?

Recommendation: When groups experience severe "personality" conflict, the value of group membership decreases. Members become dissatisfied and cohesiveness suffers. Of course, no magic formula can be applied to solve personality conflicts. If they can be managed, however, your best strategy involves discussion on the procedural dimension. Some communication experts recommend "sticking to the facts" under conditions of interpersonal conflict. We have not found this to be a useful strategy. If you experience interpersonal conflict, presenting additional information has little effect. On the other hand, a sincere acknowledgement of the difficulty and subsequent discussion about how to handle the conflict allows the group to continue achieving its goal. If your group is unable to solve its interpersonal conflicts, you may find it useful to ask a knowledgeable person outside the group to mediate the conflict.

Problem 2: Do members express dissatisfaction about their participation in the group's activities?

Recommendation: Our society does not encourage us to comment on positive aspects of one's performance. Usually we are quick to notice shortcomings and faults. Often our comments about the work of others reflect these negative features. Our behavior in task-oriented groups is often in keeping with this societal norm. Hence, we comment on the shortcomings of one's performance and fail to express our positive reactions to one's work for the group. We recommend that you make positive comments regarding the performance of your fellow group members. Obviously you must be discriminating regarding these comments. You do not want to commend someone for poor work. Nonetheless, when members adequately perform their responsibilities, you should feel free to commend them.

Problem 3: Do one or more of your group members express unwillingness to cooperate with the group?

Recommendation: The success of your group will depend on the willingness of its members to cooperate, accept responsibility, and freely participate. Of course, many other elements enter into the equation for success, but without member cooperation your group will not be able to begin work. We suggest that you confront this problem directly. Ask the uncooperative members why they are unwilling to engage in group activities. Perhaps you will find there are issues for uncooperativeness that can be addressed by the group. If you find that the member(s) are not willing to cooperate under any circumstances, we recommend that the member(s) withdraw from the group and that you seek new member(s).

Problem 4: Do you find that the interpersonal atmosphere seems negative and unpleasant?

Recommendation: An unpleasant group atmosphere usually results from a sequence of negative comments. These comments may reflect the nature of the task, progress toward goals, or the performance of group members. Sometimes individual members are blamed for group failures. Sometimes derogatory comments are made about the motives or personality of group members. We suggest that your group list the negative comments that are creating the unpleasant atmosphere. Then examine the basis for these statements. Finally look for ways to express positive comments about the task and member performance. If the situation has deteriorated too far, you may wish to disband the group and recommend that a new group be formed for the task.

Problem 5: Do you find that one member dominates the group and intimidates other members?

Recommendation: This problem usually results when a person with high status is a member of the group. Some professionals such as medical doctors, supervisors, vice-presidents, or parents may dominate the group and inadvertently create an atmosphere in which other members do not feel at ease in voicing their ideas or opinions. This situation should be addressed by the group. Why do members feel reluctant to participate? The successful resolution of this problem depends on the attitude of the high-status member. This member must be willing to listen to the other members, must be willing to modify her or his behavior, and must be willing to accept recommendations made by the other members. If this participatory attitude is not forthcoming, there is little reason for continuance of the group.

Forms for Assessing Group Process

We have listed throughout the book essential informational, procedural, and interpersonal functions required for effective group performance. From time to time, you may wish to check the performance of your group against the recommendations in this book. To assist you, we have developed a Group Function Form. On a separate sheet of paper, have each group member respond to each item on the Group Function Form. Then, on another sheet, compile a tally for each of the sixteen items. For example, the results for item 1, Creative Analysis of Task, might turn out as follows for a group of seven members:

1. Creative Analysis of Task $a = 3$
   $b = 3$
   $c = 1$
   $d = 0$

If most of the tallys are on the adequate side, your group is likely to be performing that function satisfactorily. When the tallys fall on the inadequate side, your group should discuss the issue and plan how to correct the deficiency. To help you with your diagnosis and treatment, we have indicated the location in the book where you can find material on the respective group functions.

Form For Assessing Performance of Group Functions

	Very adequate	Fairly adequate	Fairly inadequate	Very inadequate
Informational Functions (Chapter 3)				
1. Creative Analysis of Task	a	b	c	d
2. Information Giving	a	b	c	d
3. Opinion Giving	a	b	c	d
4. Evaluation and Criticism	a	b	c	d
5. Elaboration	a	b	c	d
6. Integration	a	b	c	d
Procedural Functions (Chapter 4)				
7. Eliciting Communication	a	b	c	d
8. Delegating and Directing Action	a	b	c	d
9. Summarizing Group Activity	a	b	c	d
10. Conflict Management	a	b	c	d
11. Process Evaluation	a	b	c	d
12. Tension Release	a	b	c	d
Interpersonal Functions (Chapter 4)				
13. Positive Reinforcement	a	b	c	d
14. Solidarity	a	b	c	d
15. Cooperativeness	a	b	c	d
16. Respect toward Others	a	b	c	d

Task Orientation Checklist

The task orientation checklist is an inventory of how effectively your group analyzes and discusses your task. The first issue is whether the task is appropriate for group effort (see Chapter 8, pp. 130–133 [Kowitz and Knutson text] for more detail). If your group can answer "yes" on task appropriateness, it is useful to proceed to step 2. If not, your group will find it useful to select a different task or redefine your present task. The second step pertains to the appropriateness of your group's strategy (see Chapter 9, pp. 155–159). When your group is satisfied with its strategy, you will be searching for information and presenting information to your group. At this point you will want to examine how effectively your group is processing information. . . . Your group can use this checklist to evaluate the effectiveness of your group effort. It is set up in a sequential manner. Your group may wish to use the form at various times as you work toward completion of your task.

Task Orientation Checklist

1. Appropriateness of Task			
a. Open-ended	yes	no	undecided
b. Permits division of labor	yes	no	undecided
c. Calls for varied member backgrounds	yes	no	undecided
2. Appropriateness of Strategy			
a. Task properly limited	yes	no	undecided
b. Goals are clear and concrete	yes	no	undecided
c. Means for achieving goals are clear	yes	no	undecided
3. Appropriateness of Information Processing			
a. An adequate range of information is available to the group	yes	no	undecided
b. Group members discuss issues from different points of view	yes	no	undecided
c. Decisions are made by consensus	yes	no	undecided
4. Appropriateness of Decision Proposal			
a. Decision proposal is logically sound	yes	no	undecided
b. Decision proposal is empirically sound	yes	no	undecided
c. Means for implementing decision proposal is clear	yes	no	undecided

Summary

We have tried to give you a systematic means for diagnosing group process problems and for finding solutions to these problems. We do, however, want to leave you with a disclaimer: do not feel that all of the problems associated with small group communication will be identified and cured based only on your reading and understanding of this book. The tremendous complexity of small group communication defies universal, simple answers to detailed problems. We are confident, however, that your future experiences in small group communication will be more effective and more exciting as you put your new ideas to the test. Even though we will probably never know as much as we should about small group communication, you now know more than most small group participants. Your job is to help them get the most out of every group to which you belong.

Identifying Your Leadership Style

Fred E. Fiedler and Martin M. Chemers

Your performance as a leader depends primarily on the proper match between your leadership style and the control you have over your work situation. This chapter will help you identify your leadership style and the conditions in which you will be most effective. *Carefully read the following instructions and complete the Least Preferred Co-worker (LPC) Scale.*

Instructions

Throughout your life you have worked in many groups with a wide variety of different people—on your job, in social groups, in church organizations, in volunteer groups, on athletic teams, and in many other situations. Some of your co-workers may have been very easy to work with. Working with others may have been all but impossible.

Of all the people with whom you have ever worked, think of the one person now or at any time in the past with whom you could work *least well*. This individual is not necessarily the person you *liked* least well. Rather, think of the one person with whom you had the most difficulty getting a job done, the *one* individual with whom you could work *least well*. This person is called your *Least Preferred Co-worker* (LPC).

On the scale below, describe this person by placing an "X" in the appropriate space. The scale consists of pairs of words which are opposite in meaning, such as *Very Neat* and *Very Untidy*. Between each pair of words are eight spaces which form the following scale:

Very Neat ____ ____ ____ ____ ____ ____ ____ ____ Very Untidy
                8   7   6   5   4   3   2   1

Think of those eight spaces as steps which range from one extreme to the other. Thus, if you ordinarily think this least preferred co-worker is *quite neat*, write an "X" in the space marked 7, like this:

Very								Very
Neat	8	7	6	5	4	3	2	1	Untidy
	Very Neat	Quite Neat	Somewhat Neat	Slightly Neat	Slightly Untidy	Somewhat Untidy	Quite Untidy	Very Untidy

Think of the person with whom you can work least well . . .

However, if you ordinarily think of this person as being only *slightly neat,* you would put your "X" in space 5. If you think of this person as being *very untidy* (not neat), you would put your "X" in space 1.

Sometimes the scale will run in the other direction, as shown below:

Frustrating ____ ____ ____ ____ ____ ____ ____ ____ Helpful
            1   2   3   4   5   6   7   8

Before you mark your "X," look at the words at both ends of the line. *There are no right or wrong answers.* Work rapidly; your first answer is likely to be the best. Do not omit any items, and mark each item only once. Ignore the scoring column for now.

Now describe the person with whom you can work least well. Then go on to page 599.

LEAST PREFERRED CO-WORKER (LPC) SCALE

										Scoring
Pleasant	8	7	6	5	4	3	2	1	Unpleasant	____
Friendly	8	7	6	5	4	3	2	1	Unfriendly	____
Rejecting	1	2	3	4	5	6	7	8	Accepting	____

Tense									Relaxed	____
	1	2	3	4	5	6	7	8		

Distant									Close	____
	1	2	3	4	5	6	7	8		

Cold									Warm	____
	1	2	3	4	5	6	7	8		

Supportive									Hostile	____
	8	7	6	5	4	3	2	1		

Boring									Interesting	____
	1	2	3	4	5	6	7	8		

Quarrelsome									Harmonious	____
	1	2	3	4	5	6	7	8		

Gloomy									Cheerful	____
	1	2	3	4	5	6	7	8		

Open									Guarded	____
	8	7	6	5	4	3	2	1		

Backbiting									Loyal	____
	1	2	3	4	5	6	7	8		

Untrustworthy									Trustworthy	____
	1	2	3	4	5	6	7	8		

Considerate									Inconsiderate	____
	8	7	6	5	4	3	2	1		

Nasty									Nice	
	1	2	3	4	5	6	7	8		

Agreeable									Disagreeable	____
	8	7	6	5	4	3	2	1		

Insincere									Sincere	____
	1	2	3	4	5	6	7	8		

Kind _____ _____ _____ _____ _____ _____ _____ Unkind _____
　　　　8　　7　　6　　5　　4　　3　　2　　1

Total _____

Did you answer all the questions? If not, do so before you read further. To determine your LPC score, look back at the scale. Under each "X" you marked is a number. For each line, write that number in the scoring column at the right of the page. Then add your scores and enter the total at the bottom of the page. *Be sure to check your addition!*
We use these scores to identify two main types of leadership styles.

- If your score is 64 or above, you are a *high* LPC person. We call high LPC people *relationship-motivated*.

- If your score is 57 or below, you are a *low* LPC person. We call low LPC people *task-motivated*.

Your score on the LPC scale is a measure of your leadership style. It tells something about your basic goals in a work setting—that is, what you feel you must accomplish to be satisfied with yourself and your performance. Although you may have been able to think of several people who are hard to work with, or almost none with whom you could not work, this scale should have described the *one* person with whom you *least* prefer working.

The person who has a low LPC score describes the least preferred co-worker in very negative, rejecting terms such as unfriendly, uncooperative, or cold. In effect, the low LPC person tells us, "Work is extremely important to me; therefore, if you are a poor co-worker who prevents me from getting the job done, I find it hard to accept you. If you frustrate me in my job, then I can see nothing else good about you." This is a strong emotional reaction to people with whom a low LPC person cannot work. For this reason, the low LPC leader is called a *task-motivated* person.

The high LPC leader says something quite different: "It is true that I can't work with you. But that doesn't mean that you might not be friendly, sincere, or pleasant." The task is important, but not so important that the high LPC person rejects the least preferred worker as an individual. The high LPC person says, "I may not want to work with you, but I would not mind being with you socially." This type of person is more interested in good relationships with other people. That is why we call the high LPC leader *relationship-motivated*.

The group with scores between about 58 and 63 is not clearly relationship- or task-motivated. Many people in this middle group have a mix of motivations and goals. Therefore they are harder to classify. If your score falls between 58 and 63, you will need to determine for yourself which LPC type fits you best. You will be able to do this from reading the descriptions on the following pages.

Whatever your score, note carefully that both the high and the low LPC leaders are very effective in situations which match their style. Neither type is outstanding in all situations. *We cannot stress this point too often.* Both leadership styles have good points and bad, and each will be effective in the right situation. And high and low LPC leaders are equally liked by their subordinates, again depending on the situation.

The rest of this chapter describes the typical behavior of people who score high and low on the LPC scale. You will, of course, want to see how well these descriptions seem to fit you. However, don't expect to find each and every characteristic of the high or the low LPC person in yourself or in others whose LPC score you happen to know. These sketches are *types*. They are designed to give you a feeling for how the average high or low LPC person tends to behave in various situations.

Some people find it hard to recognize themselves in these sketches. This is because people behave differently in various situations. Often you may not act as you think you do. Most of us are quite startled when we accidently hear how others describe us. Common reactions are, "Is this really me?" or "Is this really the way I behaved then?" It is similar to the way many people react when they hear themselves on a tape recorder, or see themselves on television.

Whatever your first impression might be, the LPC score tends to accurately reflect a leader's personality in various situations. Remember that nobody is perfect. The secret of effective leadership is to recognize your strengths and to make the most of them. You may not like everything about your leadership style and everything that describes your style may not fit you as a person. However, you should look at these descriptions as guidelines which will help you to improve your leadership performance.

Relationship-Motivated Leaders (LPC Score of 64 and Above)

High LPC leaders get their major satisfaction from good personal relations with others. In fact, they need good relations in order to feel at ease with themselves. Their self-esteem depends much on how other people regard them and relate to them. As a result, high LPC people are very concerned about what others think and sensitive to what their group members feel. In a work setting relationship-motivated leaders encourage group members to participate and to offer different ideas. They do not usually get upset when things are complicated and they like creative problem solving situations.

However, as you well know, we don't behave the same way in all situations. In particular, some people become withdrawn and shy when they are insecure, while others become bossy and noisy. Some people handle stressful situations by remaining calm and self-controlled while others tend to fall apart. Some people respond to stress on the job by throwing themselves into their work, while others seek encouragement and support from their co-workers. We must, then, learn to recognize how a person behaves when everything is under control, and how this same person will behave in an uncertain, uncontrolled situation. *This is of critical importance in understanding leadership*. Later we will discuss in detail how to tell whether a situation is high, moderate, or low in control. For the moment, let us see how the high LPC person reacts under these different conditions.

In *low control situations* (situations which are stressful for some people and challenging for others), high LPC leaders look for support from their group members. They will be considerate of subordinates' feelings, nonpunitive, and concerned with the welfare of the group. The high LPC leaders thus may pay less attention to the task. They can become so concerned with seeking the support of the group that they fail to get the job done. In extremely stressful situations, high LPC leaders may withdraw from the leadership role altogether and not give the direction which the group needs.

In *moderate control situations,* relationship-motivated leaders are really in their element. The situation has just enough uncertainty to challenge them, yet not enough to make them lose sight of the job. The high LPC's concern with their group members' feelings enable them to get the group's support in performing the task. If group conflict exists, or if the group's support of the leader is lukewarm, the relationship-motivated person is able to work around it by being tactful and sensitive to problems before they become damaging to task performance.

In *high control situations,* the leader does not have to worry about the group's support and about how to do the job. Under these conditions, relationship-motivated leaders are likely to feel bored and unchallenged. Some high LPC leaders react to this situation by becoming involved with details and reorganizing their work. They try to control the group members too much. They tend to become stricter, more concerned with discipline, and more heavy handed in their management, and thus are often seen by subordinates as bossy. Some high LPC leaders may seek to impress their superiors by giving a lot of orders and highly structuring the task. As a result, their performance tends to suffer.

Summary of High LPC Leaders

Relationship-motivated, or high LPC leaders (score of 64 or above), tend to rely on good personal relations and group participation to complete their primary task. When everything is going well and the situation is under control, they often become bored and look for other challenges in the job. Many high LPC leaders then become inconsiderate of their group members, using too much control and punishment.

In low control situations, their need for group support is very high and often interferes with getting the job done. In moderate control situations, the challenge of the job and the need for good relations with group members provides a balance which results in good leadership performance.

Task-Motivated Leaders (LPC score of 57 and below)

Task-motivated (low LPC) people find their main satisfaction in getting things done. They gain more self-esteem from concrete achievement than from the opinions of others. They feel most comfortable working from clear guidelines and standard operating procedures. If these guidelines are missing, the low LPC leader will try to create them.

In *low control situations,* task-motivated leaders concentrate on the job. They are not too dependent on the good opinions of others, and they are able to work well even if they have little support from their group members. Under these conditions, their main concern is to control their group. As a result, low LPC leaders may seem harsh and punishing in their need to complete the task.

Low LPC leaders are no-nonsense people who are likely to take charge early and start organizing things. In committee meetings, they tend to move right in, and get down to business. They quickly assign tasks, provide schedules, and check on progress. Group members may not always like the low LPC leaders' way of going about the job. But the group often respects them for getting results under difficult conditions.

In *high control situations,* when they know that the job will get done, task-motivated leaders relax and take time to consider the feelings of their group members. They are pleasant and considerate. Unlike relationship-motivated leaders, low LPC people are not bored when everything is going well. In high control situations, they take the opportunity to learn more about their group and about how to do the job even better. They also resent interference from their superiors.

In *moderate control situations,* especially situations involving personal conflict, task-motivated leaders tend to be less effective. They find these situations difficult and stressful. They may bury themselves in their work rather than dealing with the needs of their group members. They are unable to handle personality clashes and usually find that the group resents their lack of concern.

Summary of Low LPC Leaders

Task-motivated, or low LPC leaders (score of 57 and below), are strongly motivated to complete successfully any task they have accepted. They do this through clear and standardized work procedures and a no-nonsense attitude about getting down to work. As long as everything is under control, they are pleasant and considerate; they care about the opinions and feelings of their subordinates. But in low control situations, they tend to neglect group members' feelings "—business before pleasure." Low LPC leaders gain esteem primarily from successfully completing their tasks. Unlike high LPC leaders, low LPC leaders perform well under stressful conditions and are not bored by highly controlled situations. In moderate control situations, the low LPC leader focuses on the task, ignoring group members' needs. As a result, group conflict may damage task performance.

Remember, low LPC people are as well liked as are the high LPC leaders. They do not necessarily have poor personal relations with their group members. After all, many people like bosses who do not get personally involved with them and who run a "tight ship."

Summary of LPC Scale

In summary, the Least Preferred Co-worker scale measures an individual's primary goal or motivation in a work setting. All leaders have concern for both task and relationships. However, in any one situation, different types of leaders will emphasize these concerns differently. For example, in a low control situation, the task-motivated leader's main concern is to get the job done while the relationship-motivated leader will first seek the support of the group. In a high control situation, the task-motivated leader will have time to be involved with the group because he knows the job is getting done while the relationship-motivated leader will show more concern for the task.

The descriptions of relationship- and task-motivated leaders are useful in understanding the two different approaches to leadership. However, whether you are a "true type" or a combination of leadership styles, remember that *your effectiveness as a leader will depend on how well your style fits your leadership situation,* not on whether you score high or low on the LPC scale.

Index